THE PHENOMENOLOGY READER

"This well-designed reader is as close as one can get to capturing the whole of phenomenology in a single volume. The introduction gives lucid guidance to the beginner while its tracking of the historical background to phenomenology has rich material for scholars as well. This collection would make an excellent textbook for courses and seminars."

Donn Welton, *SUNY, USA*

"A judiciously selected and carefully edited series of readings in phenomenology. It will make an ideal sourcebook for students and an excellent textbook for teachers."

Simon Critchley, *University of Essex*

"In addition to such central figures as Brentano, Husserl, Heidegger, Sartre, Merleau-Ponty, and Gadamer, this book also contains clear introductions to, and useful excerpts from, Reinach, Scheler, Stein, de Beauvoir, Arendt, Derrida, and Ricoeur. The result is a rich, informative, reliable, and highly readable guide to phenomenology from its inception to the present day."

David Bell, *Sheffield University*

The Phenomenology Reader constitutes the most comprehensive collection of primary texts from this philosophical tradition that has been published to date. In presenting many of the major ideas expounded by the great phenomenologists themselves, it provides the English speaker with a first-hand account of the birth, consolidation and evolution of this central movement in recent European Philosophy. The carefully selected readings chart the most famous thinkers of this movement, such as Husserl, Heidegger, Sartre, and Derrida, as well as lesser known figures such as Stein and Scheler. *The Phenomenology Reader* includes readings from: Brentano, Husserl, Reinach, Scheler, Stein, Heidegger, Gadamer, Arendt, Sartre, Merleau-Ponty, de Beauvoir, Levinas, Derrida, and Ricoeur.

The editors have provided clear and accessible introductions to all the thinkers and selections, together with up-to-date bibliographies of primary and secondary literature in English. Dermot Moran's comprehensive introduction to the whole volume provides an excellent step into this major philosophical movement. This book should prove a valuable starting-point for all those who wish to learn about and engage with phenomenology and twentieth century philosophy.

Dermot Moran is Professor of Philosophy at University College Dublin and Editor of the *International Journal of Philosophical Studies*. He is author of *Introduction to Phenomenology* (Routledge, 2000) and editor of Edmund Husserl, *Logical Investigations* and E. Husserl, *The Shorter Logical Investigations* (Routledge, 2001), trans. J. N. Findlay.

Timothy Mooney is Lecturer in Philosophy at University College Dublin.

Reviews of Dermot Moran's *Introduction to Phenomenology*:

"[*Introduction to Phenomenology*] is an outstanding success."

Times Literary Supplement

"*Introduction to Phenomenology* is comprehensive in its wider-ranging coverage of many key figures; it explores numerous specific issues in some depth, often with attention to fine details, and, most distinctively, it can be read cover to cover without any prior knowledge of phenomenology or the history of twentieth-century European philosophy."

Inquiry

THE PHENOMENOLOGY READER

Edited by
Dermot Moran and Timothy Mooney

London and New York

First published 2002
by Routledge
11 New Fetter Lane, London EC4P 4EE

Simultaneously published in the USA and Canada
by Routledge
29 West 35th Street, New York, NY 10001

Routledge is an imprint of the Taylor & Francis Group

Editorial matter © 2002 Dermot Moran and Timothy Mooney

Typeset in Times and Franklin Gothic by
RefineCatch Limited, Bungay, Suffolk
Printed and bound in Great Britain by
MPG Books Ltd, Bodmin

British Library Cataloguing in Publication Data
A catalogue record for this book is available from the British Library

Library of Congress Cataloging in Publication Data
Routledge phenomenology reader / ed[ited by] Dermot Moran and Timothy Mooney.
p.   cm
Includes bibliographical references and index.
1. Phenomenology.   I. Title: Phenomenology reader.   II. Moran, Dermot.
III. Mooney, Timothy, 1962–
B829.5 .R68   2002
142′.7–dc21   2001048693

ISBN 0–415–22421–7 (hbk)
ISBN 0–415–22422–5 (pbk)

CONTENTS

CONTENTS

CONTENTS

PREFACE

The Phenomenology Reader aims to make accessible to the English-speaking reader a representative selection of translations of primary readings of the phenomenological tradition, perhaps the most broadly influential movement of European philosophy in the twentieth century. Phenomenology was inspired by the descriptive psychology practised by Franz von Brentano and was inaugurated by Edmund Husserl in his *Logical Investigations* (1900/1901, trans. J. N. Findlay, with a Preface by Michael Dummett and edited with a new Introduction by Dermot Moran, 2 volumes, Routledge, 2001). This radical method of approaching problems attracted some of the best minds of the twentieth century (e.g. Scheler, Heidegger, Gadamer, Sartre, de Beauvoir, Merleau-Ponty, Arendt, Derrida, Levinas, Ricoeur), and, in one form or another, engaged with most of the competing philosophical currents of the era. The readings selected here offer a representative selection of these thinkers. The choice of readings is intended to lead the reader through the main stages in the development of phenomenology, as already outlined in Dermot Moran, *Introduction to Phenomenology* (Routledge, 2000). The selections are taken from the key works of philosophers from Franz von Brentano, one of the founders of empirical psychology, to Jacques Derrida, the leading advocate of deconstruction.

We would like to thank Lester Embree, Brian Elliott, Brian O'Connor, Simon Critchley, Richard Kearney, Tony Bruce, Siobhan Pattinson, Mary Buckley and Thom Brooks for their assistance.

Dermot Moran and Timothy Mooney
University College Dublin

ACKNOWLEDGEMENTS

Many of the extracts in this collection have been edited for reasons of space and to make them stand as independent readings. We are grateful to the following copyright holders for granting permission to reproduce these texts:

Franz von Brentano, *Psychology from an Empirical Standpoint*, trans. A. C. Rancurello, D. B. Terrell and L. L. McAlister (London and New York: Routledge, 1995), pp. xxvii–xxix; and pp. 77–100.

Franz von Brentano, *Descriptive Psychology*, trans. and ed. Benito Müller (London and New York: Routledge, 1995), pp. 137–42.

Franz von Brentano, *The True and the Evident*, ed. Oskar Kraus, trans. Roderick M. Chisholm, Ilse Politzer and Kurt R. Fischer (London and New York: Routledge & Kegan Paul/Humanities Press, 1966), pp. 77–9.

Edmund Husserl, *Logical Investigations*, trans. John N. Findlay (London and New York: Routledge & Kegan Paul/Humanities Press, 1970), Vol. 1, pp. 248–66; and Vol. 2, pp. 552–96.

Edmund Husserl, *The Phenomenology of Internal Time Consciousness*, trans. James Churchill (Bloomington: Indiana University Press, 1964), pp. 50–80.

Edmund Husserl, "Pure Phenomenology, its Method and its Field of Investigation", in *Husserl. Shorter Works*, trans. Robert Welsh Jordan, ed. Peter McCormick and Frederick Elliston (Notre Dame, IN/Brighton: University of Notre Dame Press/ Harvester Press, 1981), pp. 10–17.

Edmund Husserl, *Ideas Pertaining to a Pure Phenomenology and to a Phenomeno-logical Philosophy, First Book*, trans. F. Kersten (The Hague: Nijhoff, 1983), §§87–96, pp. 211–35.

Edmund Husserl, *The Crisis of European Sciences and Transcendental Phenomen-ology. An Introduction to Phenomenological Philosophy*, trans. David Carr (Evanston: Northwestern University Press, 1970), pp. 103–37.

Adolf Reinach, "Concerning Phenomenology", trans. Dallas Willard, *The Personalist*, Vol. 50 (1969), pp. 194–221.

Max Scheler, *Formalism in Ethics and Non-Formal Ethics of Values*, trans. Manfred Frings and Roger L. Funk (Evanston: Northwestern University Press, 1973), pp. 382–415.

Edith Stein, *On the Problem of Empathy*, trans. Waltraut Stein (Washington, DC: ICS Publications, 1989), pp. 41–56.

Martin Heidegger, *On Time and Being*, trans. John Macquarrie and Edward Robinson (SCM Press Ltd, 1962). Reprinted by permission of HarperCollins Publishers, Inc.

ACKNOWLEDGEMENTS

Martin Heidegger, *History of the Concept of Time. Prolegomena*, trans. Theodore Kisiel (Bloomington: Indiana University Press, 1992), pp. 27–53.

Martin Heidegger, *Being and Time*, trans. John Macquarrie and Edward Robinson (Oxford/New York: Blackwell/Harper & Row, 1962), pp. 49–63; and pp. 91–119.

Hans-Georg Gadamer, *Truth and Method*, 2nd Revised Edition, trans. Joel Weinsheimer and Donald G. Marshall (London: Sheed & Ward, 1989), pp. 265–307.

Hannah Arendt, "What is Existenz Philosophy?", *Partisan Review*, Vol. XIII (1946), pp. 34–56.

Hannah Arendt, "Labor, Work, Action", in James W. Bernauer (ed.), *Amor Mundi. Explorations in the Faith and Thought of Hannah Arendt* (Dordrecht: Nijhoff, 1987), pp. 29–42.

Jean-Paul Sartre, "Intentionality: A Fundamental Idea of Husserl's Philosophy", trans. Joseph P. Fell, *Journal of the British Society for Phenomenology*, Vol. 1, No. 2 (1970), pp. 4–5.

Jean-Paul Sartre, *The Transcendence of the Ego*, trans. Forrest Williams and Robert Kirkpatrick (New York: Farrar, Straus & Giroux, 1972), pp. 31–106.

Jean-Paul Sartre, *Being and Nothingness*, trans. Hazel T. Barnes (London: Routledge, 1995), pp. 47–69.

Maurice Merleau-Ponty, *Phenomenology of Perception*, trans. Colin Smith (London: Routledge, 1962), pp. 73–89.

Maurice Merleau-Ponty, *The Primacy of Perception and Other Essays*, ed. and trans. James M. Edie (Evanston, IL: Northwestern University Press, 1964), pp. 12–27.

Simone de Beauvoir, *The Second Sex*, trans. and ed. H. M. Parshley (London: Picador, 1988), pp. 65–91; and pp. 608–39.

Emmanuel Levinas, *Totality and Infinity*, trans. Alfonso Lingis (Pittsburgh: Duquesne University Press, 1969), pp. 194–219.

Emmanuel Levinas, "Beyond Intentionality", in Alan Montefiori (ed.) *Philosophy in France Today*, trans. Kathleen McLaughlin (Cambridge: Cambridge University Press, 1983), pp. 100–15.

Jacques Derrida, *Speech and Phenomena and Other Essays on Husserl's Theory of Signs*, trans. David B. Allison (Evanston, IL: Northwestern University Press, 1973), pp. 58–69; and pp. 129–60.

Paul Ricoeur, *Hermeneutics and the Human Sciences*, ed. and trans. John B. Thompson (Cambridge: Cambridge University Press, 1981), pp. 101–28.

Every effort has been made to obtain permission to reproduce copyright material. If any proper acknowledgement has not been made, or permission not received, we invite copyright holders to inform us of the oversight.

EDITOR'S INTRODUCTION

Dermot Moran

Phenomenology as a way of seeing and as a movement

Phenomenology may be characterised initially in a broad sense as the unprejudiced, descriptive study of whatever appears to consciousness, precisely in the manner in which it so appears. Phenomenology as thus understood emerged as an original philosophical approach at the end of the nineteenth century in the school of Franz Brentano, and was developed by Edmund Husserl and his successors to become a major tradition of philosophising throughout the world during the twentieth century. At the dawn of the twenty-first century, it continues to offer a vibrant and challenging alternative to contemporary naturalistic accounts of consciousness and meaning.

Phenomenology is usually characterised as a *way of seeing* rather than a set of doctrines. In a typical formulation, the founder of phenomenology Edmund Husserl (1859–1938), in his late work *Crisis of European Sciences and Transcendental Phenomenology* (1936 – hereafter *Crisis*), presents *phenomenology* as approaching 'whatever appears as such', including everything meant or thought, in the *manner* of its appearing, in the 'how' (*Wie*) of its manifestation.[1] Similarly, Husserl's colleague and protégé Martin Heidegger (1889–1976) could proclaim in his methodological discussion of phenomenology at the beginning of his *Being and Time* (1927), section 7: "The expression 'phenomenology' signifies primarily a *methodological conception*. This expression does not characterize the what of the objects of philosophical research as subject-matter, but rather the *how* of that research" (SZ § 7, 27; 50).[2] This approach involves the practice of taking a fresh *unprejudiced* look – i.e. untainted by scientific, metaphysical, religious or cultural presuppositions or attitudes – at the fundamental and essential features of human experience in and of the world.

According to Husserl's own slogan, phenomenology aimed to return to 'the things themselves', avoiding constructivist system-building so prevalent in traditional philosophy, or reasoning on the basis of some preconceived and uninterrogated starting-point (as traditional rationalisms and empiricisms were wont to do). Instead, fundamental philosophical issues are examined through attention to the manner in which things and meanings show themselves, come to self-evidence, or come to be 'constituted' for us, as Husserl put it, invoking a concept from the Kantian tradition. The phenomenological approach is primarily *descriptive*, seeking to *illuminate* issues in a radical, unprejudiced manner, paying close attention to the evidence that presents itself to our grasp or intuition. Husserl frequently speaks of phenomenological *description* (*Beschreibung, Deskription*) as *clarification* (*Klärung*), illumination

1

(*Erhellung*), *enlightenment* (*Aufklärung*), even as *conceptual analysis* (*Begriffsana-lyse*), whatever assists in elucidating the meaning of the phenomenon in question without resorting to purely causal or 'genetic' explanation (*Erklären*). Due to its con-cern to treat the phenomenon concretely in all its fullness, phenomenology stands opposed to naturalism, scientism and reductionism, and to all forms of explanation that draw attention away from the manner of the appearance of the phenomena in question. Or, as the French phenomenologist Maurice Merleau-Ponty (1908–1961) put it, phenomenology seeks to restore the richness of the world as experienced; it wants to be present at the birth of the world for us.

It is important to grasp the difference between the phenomenological approach and other kinds of scientific approach, for example, the psychological, physiological or causal-explanatory approaches prevalent in the natural sciences. Husserl insisted on this point, but it still gives rise to endless confusion. First of all, Husserl is emphatically not challenging the importance, necessity or validity of explanatory scientific accounts. Investigations into the physical and chemical nature of the brain and its processing are a necessary part of science. But that is not the function of a phenomenological description, which is a mode of approach that can be used in all areas of science, but which specifically focuses on the manner objects are consti-tuted in and for subjects. It focuses on the structure and qualities of objects and situations as they are experienced *by the subject*. What Husserl calls the *paradox* or *mystery of subjectivity* – as the *site of appearance of objectivity* – is its theme.

Phenomenology aims to describe in all its complexity the manifold layers of the experience of objectivity as it emerges at the heart of *subjectivity*. It is critical of all forms of *objectivism* that attend only to what appears and not to the relation of the appearing to the subject. Put in another and perhaps less satisfactory way, phenom-enology describes, in its own terms, the essential and irreducible nature of the experience of *consciousness* in the world – less satisfactory, because the appeal to consciousness can hardly avoid invoking the spectre of Cartesianism, with its ghostly isolated subject and its problematic dualism (and for this reason Heidegger tended to avoid the term 'consciousness' altogether). In fact, however, in their attempt to do justice to the essential and irreducible relations between human comportment and the world, phenomenologists seek to overcome the traditional dichotomies of modern philosophy, especially the subject–object distinction of trad-itional epistemology, with its attendant account of knowledge as a representation of the object immanent in the subject.

Husserl insisted that phenomenology as the fundamental science of all sciences had to be *presuppositionlessness*, i.e. its descriptions had to avoid the presumptions both of the modern philosophical and the scientific traditions. Of course, this claim to a presuppositionless starting-point is itself highly problematic and soon came under scrutiny within the phenomenological movement. Given the historically rooted nature of human knowledge, the total absence of all presupposition would be impossible in a science, and thus what is aimed at is, at best, as Gadamer has suggested, freedom from *undisclosed* prejudices. In fact, the manner in which phe-nomenological description had to come to terms with the recognition that some presuppositions are necessary for any form of understanding led to the fusion of phenomenology with the older discipline of hermeneutics, the art or practice of interpretation, beginning with Heidegger, who, as we shall discuss below, drew on the hermeneutical tradition of Friedrich Schleiermacher (1768–1834) and Wilhelm

Dilthey (1833–1911), and continuing with the explicitly hermeneutical orientations of, for instance, the contemporary German thinker Hans-Georg Gadamer (b. 1900) and the contemporary French philosopher Paul Ricoeur (b. 1913).

Husserl cherished his own role as founder of a new science, even characterising himself as a Moses leading his people to new land of what he came to call – invoking the language of German Idealism – *transcendental subjectivity*, i.e. the a priori structure and content of object-constituting subjectivity. Husserl also liked to see himself as a radical follower of the French philosopher René Descartes (1596–1650), who sought to provide the sciences with a secure epistemological foundation, immune from all sceptical doubt, by starting with the unshakable truth of one's self-presence in each act of one's own thinking, expressed in his *cogito ergo sum*. Husserl sometimes portrayed his own efforts as a revival of the Cartesian project of founding the sciences on strict certainty, an attempt to explore the essence of the *cogito* without falling prey to naïve metaphysical assumptions involving substance, as he believed Descartes had. Thus he characterised phenomenology as "the secret nostalgia of all modern philosophy" in his programmatic 1913 work *Ideen zu einer reinen Phänomenologie und phänomenologischen Philosophie* (*Ideas pertaining to a Pure Phenomenology and to a Phenomenological Philosophy, First Book* – hereafter *Ideas* I).[3] In other words, phenomenology actually provided the secure science sought by Descartes and by Kant (whom Husserl also criticised for getting lost in a purely speculative faculty psychology). Husserl's best-known formulation of his transcendental idealist analysis of the structures of consciousness came in his *Cartesian Meditations*. First published in French translation in 1931, it remains the most popular introduction to his work.[4] But, over the course of his long career, and in various universities in which he worked, Husserl characterised the essence of phenomenology in many different ways. While his official theoretical allegiance was to a radicalised form of transcendental idealism, his research manuscripts suggest other ways of developing phenomenological themes, often with more attention to corporeality, intersubjectivity and the experience of otherness or alterity. Thus, in *Crisis*, Husserl was drawn to analyse the 'life-world' (*Lebenswelt*), which is indissolubly linked with and grounds human experience, the analysis of which offered a corrective to the reductive scientism which Husserl felt had become enmeshed in the modern scientific outlook and practice. As more of Husserl's unpublished manuscripts finally see the light of day, new dimensions of phenomenology are being uncovered, which are attracting renewed attentions from philosophers worldwide.

For Husserl, phenomenology unfolded as a living, endlessly expanding field of 'infinite tasks', which could be carried forward only by inquirers philosophising together (*symphilosophein*), co-workers concerned about the future of humanity itself, a humanity conceived of as a rational community of knowledge, where science fulfils rather than dehumanises the human world. In laying out these 'infinite tasks', he assigned regions to be explored by the many gifted disciples gathered around him. Thus, his Göttingen assistant Adolf Reinach (1883–1917) would undertake the phenomenology of law, and his Freiburg assistant Martin Heidegger would develop the phenomenology of religion.[5] But Husserl was rarely satisfied with their efforts, which he tended to see as misinterpretations or distortions of his own work, leading him to feel unappreciated and even betrayed. Husserl, too, was rather unfortunate in his choice of would-be successors. His most controversial choice of successor was Martin Heidegger, whom he had warmly embraced since their first meeting in

Freiburg in 1916 and whom he supported for appointment to his own Chair in Freiburg on his retirement in 1928. Heidegger, however, went on to promote a rather different vision of phenomenology in *Sein und Zeit* (*Being and Time*, 1927), as we shall see, which inspired many philosophers to abandon Husserl and his transcendental idealism for an existential analysis of Dasein.

Late in his career, and also due to his official exclusion from university activities by the Nazi anti-Semitic laws, Husserl felt particularly isolated, characterising himself as a 'leader without followers'. In 1935, he bitterly acknowledged the impossibility of achieving the ideal of philosophy as a science, when he proclaimed: "Philosophy as science, as serious, rigorous, indeed apodictically rigorous science – *the dream is over*" (*der Traum ist ausgeträumt*, *Crisis*, p. 389; Hua VI 508). But even here, in this poignant farewell, Husserl is not renouncing the ideal as an ideal; he is simply acknowledging the bitter truth that philosophers have not understood this ideal and have been tempted away into irrational substitutes for scientific philosophy. It is not Husserl who has ended the dream but those supposed followers who have been seduced by historicism and an irrational philosophy of life (*Lebensphilosophie*), and indeed have been drawn into anthropology of the life-world, as he understood Heidegger's account of human existence (*Dasein*) to be. As he himself put it, 'the phenomenological movement! I now count myself as its greatest enemy.' Nevertheless, post-Husserlian phenomenology tended to lead off from various starting-points, most of which were – at least tentatively – first explored by Husserl. Thus, the first fifty years of phenomenology can be seen correctly, as Paul Ricoeur has put it, as a series of *heresies* devolving from Husserl. For this reason, we have included selections from different phases of Husserl's career.

Over the course of the twentieth century, the originally German phenomenological movement spread through Europe, North and South America, and to Asia, especially Japan and Korea but increasingly in China. It broadened into a loosely defined collection of original thinkers committed to a certain orientation in thinking. In understanding the development of phenomenology, it is useful to invoke the categories of the American phenomenologist Lester Embree who has identified four "successively dominant and sometimes overlapping tendencies": *realistic phenomenology* (early Husserl, Adolf Reinach, Scheler); *constitutive phenomenology* (the mature Husserl, Gurwitsch, Becker); *existential phenomenology* (Heidegger, Arendt, Sartre, Merleau-Ponty, Michel Henry); and *hermeneutic phenomenology* (Gadamer, Ricoeur, *et al*).[6] In this introduction, we shall have something to say about these four tendencies within phenomenology, although we shall not attempt to keep them distinct. Heidegger, for example, had both an existential and a hermeneutic orientation, whereas Scheler is both a realistic and a constitutive phenomenologist. We should also note that phenomenology in the contemporary setting has incorporated postmodern, gender and even environmental elements in its efforts to understand the nature of living in the age of global technology and interculturalism. We can offer merely an outline sketch of some of these developments here.

The 'phenomena' of phenomenology and the science of essences

As we have seen, *phenomenology* means literally the *science of phenomena*, the science which studies appearances, and specifically the *structure* of appearing – the *how* of appearing – giving the *phenomena* or manifest appearances their due, remaining loyal to the modes of appearance of things in the world, whether they belong to the physical, mathematical, cultural, aesthetic, religious, or other domains. The *phenomena* of phenomenology are to be understood in a deliberately broad sense as including all forms of appearing, showing, manifesting, making evident or 'evidencing', bearing witness, truth-claiming, checking and verifying, including all forms of seeming, dissembling, occluding, obscuring, denying and falsifying. In short, phenomenology studies, in the words of the contemporary French phenomenologist Michel Henry (b. 1922), *the essence of manifestation*,[7] or, as the American phenomenologist Lester Embree puts it, the varieties of *evidencing*.

In examining the nature of manifestation and disclosure, phenomenology also comes to recognise that many things are not disclosed or can only be approached through a detour, specifically the conditions which enable disclosure, which allow manifestation to take place, for example, the background of the 'world' itself. In its focus on meaning, phenomenology paid particular attention to *the living experience of meaning*, or intending to mean (Ricoeur's *vouloir-dire*), and hence to the peculiar nature of the human encounter with the 'surrounding world' (*Umwelt*) and the kind of objectivities normally encountered there. Indeed, phenomenology was the first movement to focus on the specific conditions of human embeddedness in an environment, and to make visible the phenomenon of the environment itself. In his mature work Husserl focused on the structure of our everyday manner of human being in the world, the structure of what Husserl termed 'the natural attitude' (*die näturliche Einstellung*), first publicly discussed in *Ideas* I, which at once both revealed the world in a certain way while itself remaining concealed. In other words, the very 'naturalness' of the natural world acts to conceal the manner in which this 'normal' world is constituted by the activities of the conscious subjects who inhabit that world. The phenomenological attitude, then, is not the normal engaged or absorbed attitude, but requires, as we shall see, a change of orientation, a detachment or disengagement – what Husserl called *epoché* and *reduction* – to bring the nature of the experience more to light.

It is crucial to emphasise at this point that phenomenology does not subscribe to the assumption that the phenomena are somehow to be distinguished from *things in themselves*. To say that phenomenology is interested in appearings does not mean that it is committed to *phenomenalism*, the doctrine that claims that all that exists is the appearances to the senses, or, on the other hand, to a Kantian bifurcation between *phenomena* and *things in themselves* or *noumena*. Phenomenology neither wishes to claim that all that exists can simply be reduced to appearings, nor to affirm an unknown and unknowable reality behind appearances. Both claims distort the essence of the phenomenological point of view, which begins from the experience of things appearing to the subject, to consciousness. Since all showing or manifesting or evidencing is precisely *of* something *to* someone, it is fundamental to phenomenology to attempt to think through the nature of the essential *correlation* between mind and world, rather than beginning with one or other as given, as traditional idealisms and realisms have done. Phenomenology begins with the *essential correlation* between objectivity and subjectivity, between the thing that appears and the conscious subject to which it appears, what Husserl calls in *Ideas* I the *noetic-noematic correlation* uncovered by reflection on the nature of intentional acts and their objects.

The phenomena, then, are *the things themselves*, as they show themselves to be, in other words, what is self-given, and not something that is a representation of an outer world. Thus, for example, in the phenomenology of religion, the focus is on the manner in which the sacred is experienced by the religious practitioner – or indeed as denied by the atheist – rather than on the attempt to ascertain if there really is or is not a domain of the sacred as it were 'behind' the belief. Phenomenology seeks a direct intuition of the essence of the object or situation. According to the phenomenologist Max Scheler, it attempts to achieve full self-givenness in realms currently approached only through the mediation through symbols. Thus Scheler writes:

> Phenomenology has reached its goal when every symbol and half-symbol is completely fulfilled through the "self-given," including everything which functions in the natural world-view and in science as a *form* of understanding (everything "categorial"); when everything transcendent and only "meant" has become *immanent* to a lived experience and intuition. It has reached its goal at the point where there is no longer any transcendence or symbol. Everything which elsewhere is still formal becomes, for phenomenology, a material for intuition. And the attitude phenomenological philosophy has toward a religious object or an ethical value is exactly the same as the one it has toward the color *red*.
>
> That which constitutes the unity of phenomenology is not a particular region of facts, such as, for example, mental or ideal objects, nature, etc., but only *self-givenness* in *all* possible regions.[8]

Phenomenology then does not stop with the appearance but seeks the essence of the appearance. It aims to be a *science of essences*, a science that makes the essences of things that appear visible to the enquirer, similar to the manner in which geometry, another eidetic science, studies the essential relations that hold in space. The claim of phenomenology is that the facts of the matter as disclosed to consciousness may be described in such a way that the *essences* of those facts and their intertwined laws can be exhibited, as well as the modes of our access thereto. As Husserl puts it in the 1913 Second Edition of the *Logical Investigations*:

> This phenomenology, like the more inclusive *pure phenomenology of experiences in general*, has, as its exclusive concern, experiences intuitively seizable and analysable in the pure generality of their essence, not experiences empirically perceived and treated as real facts, as experiences of human or animal experients in the phenomenal world that we posit as an empirical fact. This phenomenology must bring to pure expression, must *describe* in terms of their essential concepts and their governing formulae of essence, the essences which directly make themselves known in intuition, and the connections which have their roots purely in such essences. Each such statement of essence is an *a priori* statement in the highest sense of the word.[9]

Phenomenology then is to be an a priori science of the essences of all possible objects and experiences. It aims to arrive at a pure essential intuition of 'pure experiences' (*reine Erlebnisse*) in their essential natures as perceptions, willings, acts of imagining, and so on. Phenomenology is a kind of specialised reflection on the nature of consciousness, not as a factually occurring set of psychical acts, but understood in its object-constituting role, as that which makes cognition in the widest sense possible at all. Thus Husserl inserts a clear definition of phenomenology (echoing *Ideas* I § 75) in the revised Appendix to the Sixth Investigation (note the repeated stress on the word 'pure'):

> *Phenomenology* is accordingly the theory of experiences in general, inclusive of all matters, whether real (*reellen*) or intentional, given in experiences, and evidently discoverable in them. Pure phenomenology is accordingly the theory of the essences of 'pure phenomena', the phenomena of 'pure consciousness' or of a 'pure ego': it does not build on the ground, given by transcendent apperception, of physical and animal, and so of psychophysical nature, it makes no empirical assertions, it propounds no judgements which relate to objects transcending consciousness: it establishes no truths concerning natural realities, whether physical or psychic – no psychological truths, therefore, in the historical sense – and borrows no such truths as assumed premises. It rather takes all apperceptions and judgemental assertions which point beyond what is given in adequate, purely immanent intuition, which point beyond the pure stream of consciousness, and treats them purely as the experiences they are in themselves: it subjects them to a purely immanent, purely descriptive examination into essence.
>
> (LI VI Appendix, II, p. 343; Hua XIX/2 765)

Phenomenology must study and bring to clarification the nature of the essence of subjective acts of cognition in their most general, ideal sense, *Erkenntnis überhaupt*. This is to be an investigation of the pure possibility of cognition in its non-natural essence, disregarding all empirical instantiation in humans, animals, angels or extraterrestrial beings.

Intuition and givenness

The chief characteristic of Husserlian and indeed all phenomenology, then, is that it is oriented entirely towards what is given immediately in *intuition* (*Anschauung*). Intuition, immediacy, givenness, are Husserl's key interlinked terms; or, as Heidegger put it in one of his lecture courses, 'givenness' (*Gegebenheit*) is the 'magic word' (*Zauberwort*) of phenomenologists and a stumbling-block to others. Givenness and intuition are correlative terms; the character of the intuiting corresponds to the character of the givenness or manifestation. *Givenness* is to provide the measure of all comprehension. Phenomenology does not speculate about essences or make inferences, it is supposed to grasp them directly in immediate 'intuition'. As Husserl wrote in 1930 in his Author's Preface to the English Edition of *Ideas* I:

> But in the transcendental sphere we have an infinitude of knowledge previous to all deduction, knowledge whose mediated connexions (those of intentional implication) have nothing to do with deduction, and being entirely

intuitive prove refractory to every methodically devised scheme of constructive symbolism.[10]

Intuition has played a major role in philosophy from Plato onwards, but especially in
modern philosophy, for example, in both Descartes and Kant. For Descartes, deductions must be grounded in intuitions that are immediately and self-evidently given.
For Kant, intuition (*Anschauung*) is one of the two key components of knowledge –
the other being the concept (*Begriff*). Kant distinguished sharply between two separate faculties – the faculty of intuition or *sensibility* (*Sinnlichkeit*) and the faculty of
concepts or rules, *understanding* (*Verstand*).[11] These two faculties provide two distinct 'sources of knowledge' (*Erkenntnisquellen*), as he says in the *Critique of Pure
Reason* (A260/B316). Kant, however, understood intuition rather narrowly as the
purely passive, sensuous material for knowledge, whereas Husserl wanted to attend
to the kind of self-evidence manifest in various kinds of intuition and thus required a
much broader notion of intuition. In the *Logical Investigations* Husserl presents his
own phenomenological breakthrough in terms of a clarification of the precise ways
that intuition and perception – understood in a broadened sense – could play a role
in philosophy. In the Sixth Logical Investigation he broadened his key concepts of
intuition (*Anschauung*) and *perception* (*Wahrnehmung*), beyond the purely sensuous,
so that one can speak of intuiting a conflict or a synthesis (LI VI §37, II p. 262;
Hua XIX/2 649).

Husserl's phenomenological descriptions began with acts of simple sensuous
perception and he used the kind of fulfilment achieved in these acts as his exemplar
of acts of meaning fulfilment in general. But he did not want to give the impression
that all our intuitive knowledge consisted of such sensuous acts. In the Sixth Logical
Investigation he introduced a new notion of *categorial intuition* to rectify what he
thought of as a falsification of the experience of consciousness being purveyed by
empiricism, positivism and indeed neo-Kantianism. Husserl maintains that we must
be allowed to speak of the possibility of intuition of complex situations or states of
affairs such as the intuition of unity, or of synthesis, or the intuition of other categorial situations. These were a genuine and non-sensuous form of intuiting, hitherto
neglected by the empiricist tradition.

Emphasising his commitment to a philosophy which based itself solely on what is
validly given in intuition, Husserl – in his next major work after the *Investigations* –
Ideas I (1913), § 24, lays down his fundamental principle, which he calls his *principle
of all principles* (*das Prinzip aller Prinzipien*):

> that every originary presentive intuition is a legitimizing source (*Rechts-
> quelle*) of cognition, that everything originarily (so to speak in its "personal"
> actuality) offered to us in "intuition" is to be accepted simply as what it is
> presented as being, but also only within the limits in which it is presented
> there.
>
> (*Ideas* I, §24, p. 44; Hua III/1 44)

Every act of knowledge is to be legitimised by 'originary presentive intuition' (*originär
gebende Anschauung*). This conception of originary presentive intuition is at the core
of all Husserl's philosophy. Indeed, he criticises traditional empiricism for naïvely
dictating that all judgements be legitimised by experience, instead of realising that

many different forms of intuition underlie our judgements and our reasoning processes (*Ideas* I, §19, p. 36; Hua III/I 36).

Intuitions, for Husserl, or what the American phenomenologist Robert Sokolowski calls 'registerings' or 'registrations',[12] occur in all experiences of understanding; but in cases of genuine certain knowledge, we have intuition with the highest form of fulfilment (*Erfüllung*) or evidence (*Evidenz*), or 'self-evidence'. When I *see with insight* that 2 + 2 = 4 in the sense of grasping the state of affairs itself rather than simply manipulating the symbols, I have as clear an intuition as I can have. Husserl believed that similar intuitive fulfilments occurred in many types of experience, and were not just restricted to the truths of mathematics. When I see a blackbird in the tree outside my window, I also have an intuition fulfilled with all the certainty of the sensuously given 'bodily presence' (*Leibhaftigkeit*) of the blackbird presenting itself to me. Husserl distinguished between these kinds of experience and other experiences where the object is not immediately present, for instance, in acts of memory or expectation. In general Husserl was fascinated by the contrast between intuitive self-givenness and various forms of symbolic representation. He was led by reflection on these kinds of experience to want to develop in the Sixth Investigation a classification of all conscious experiences, with an eye to considering their essential natures and the kinds of intuitive fulfilment proper to them.

The origins and forerunners of phenomenology in the philosophical tradition

Although Martin Heidegger maintained in *Being and Time* (1927) that a genuinely phenomenological approach to being and truth, untainted by the subjectivism of modern philosophy, could be found in its most authentic form in ancient Greek philosophy, in fact, as a distinctive philosophical method, phenomenology emerged gradually only in the context of post-Cartesian modern philosophy, and specifically in post-Kantian German philosophy which focused mainly on psychological and epistemological problems, often confusing these domains in a manner which inhibited the successful progress of scientific knowledge. Heidegger himself, in *Being and Time*, acknowledged that the term 'phenomenology' could be traced back to the late Scholastic tradition, and specifically to the school of Wolff (SZ § 7, 28; 51). In fact, the first specific reference to 'phenomenology' may be traced to Johann Heinrich Lambert (1728–1777); the fourth section of whose *Novus Organon* bears the title 'Phenomenology of transcendental Optics' (*Phaenomenologia oder optica transcendentalis*).[13] By this Lambert meant a 'science of appearance' that would proceed from the appearances to truth in itself, just as optics studies perspective in order to deduce true features of the object seen. Immanuel Kant (1724–1804), who greatly admired Lambert, employs the term 'phenomenology' in several places in his writings, ranging from his early letters to his mature treatises. Thus, in a letter to Lambert of 2 September 1770, Kant states, 'metaphysics must be preceded by a quite distinct, but merely negative science (*Phaenomenologica generalis*)'.[14] Kant's *Metaphysical Foundations of Natural Science* (*Metaphysische Anfangsgründe der Naturwissenschaft*, 1786) has an entire section entitled 'Phenomenology', dealing with the area of motion or rest in relation to its appearances to our external senses. Phenomenology, on this account, is that branch of science which deals with things in their manner of appearing to us, for example, relative motion, or properties – such as

9

colour – are dependent on the human observer. Indeed, Kant's whole enquiry into the conditions for the possibility of objectivity – as seen from the subjective side – may also be understood as phenomenology, and was so understood by Hegel and later by Heidegger, but it is unlikely to have influenced Husserl at least in terms of his terminological decisions.[15]

Johann Gottlieb Fichte (1762–1814) also made use of the term 'phenomenology' in his *Wissenschaftslehre* lectures of 1804 to refer to the manner of deriving the world of appearance, which illusorily appears to be independent of consciousness from consciousness itself.[16] Although Fichte was a philosopher to whom Husserl turned in his later Freiburg years – indeed he lectured on him in 1917 – it is unlikely that Fichte influenced Husserl's early choice of the term. Similarly, Husserl, at least when he was formulating his conception of phenomenology, knew next to nothing about G. W. F. Hegel's *Phenomenology of Spirit* (1807), where the term 'phenomenology' is used in a sense closer to the twentieth-century meaning, as that discipline which describes the unfolding or coming to consciousness of truth. Hegel himself seems to have borrowed the term from Karl Reinhold who employed it in the title of his *Elementen der Phänomenologie oder Erläuterung des rationalen Realismus durch seine Anwendung auf die Erscheingungen* (1802). Hegel envisaged phenomenology as only a certain preparatory part of systematic philosophy, and indeed he proclaimed: "The Kantian philosophy may be most accurately described as having viewed the mind as consciousness, and as containing the propositions only of a *phenomenology* (not of a *philosophy*) of mind."[17]

Although it has become usual to trace the origins of phenomenology back to Hegel, in fact the Hegelian version of phenomenology only came to be recognised by Husserl's followers after the important lectures of Alexandre Kojève on Hegel's *Phenomenology of Spirit* given in Paris in the 1930s.[18]

After Hegel, the term 'phenomenology' continued to have some isolated occurrences during the latter half of the nineteenth century. Sir William Hamilton (1791–1856), the Scottish philosopher who influenced Brentano, refers, in his *Lectures on Metaphysics*,[19] to the 'Phenomenology of Mind' or 'Philosophy of Mind'. In 1894, the physicist and philosopher Ernst Mach (1838–1916) proposed a 'general physical phenomenology' describing all our experiences of physics as a basis for general physical theories. Evidently, Husserl was familiar with Mach's use of the term and acknowledged Mach as a forerunner of phenomenology in his Amsterdam lectures, where he characterises himself as involved in "a certain radicalizing of an already existing phenomenological method".[20] But the true origins of phenomenology in the sense it is discussed by the authors in the *Reader* may be located in the descriptive psychology practised by Franz Brentano (1838–1917), and by his students, notably Carl Stumpf (1848–1936).

Franz Brentano attempted to found a descriptive science of consciousness. He was an admirer of the scientific empiricism of Aristotle and indeed of David Hume, of the exact descriptive psychological projects of George Berkeley, John Stuart Mill and William Hamilton, of the positivism of Comte and Mach, and of German psychologists such as Friedrich Lange. He aimed to establish philosophy on a strictly scientific basis, in deliberate opposition to what he regarded as the obscurantism and mystification of the traditions that dominated German philosophy at the time, namely neo-Kantianism and Hegelianism.

In *Psychology from an Empirical Standpoint* (1874),[21] now recognised as one of the foundational texts of modern experimental psychology, Brentano proposed to specify the subject matter of the science of psychology, in the course of which he sought the defining characteristics of the domain of mental phenomena. He proposed the intentional relatedness of the mental act to its object as an essential positive characteristic of the mental. Brentano's 1889 lectures on "Descriptive Psychology",[22] of which Husserl possessed a transcript, significantly, are subtitled "Descriptive Phenomenology", and here he laid down the basis for his descriptive science of the a priori laws of consciousness. Brentano's *descriptive psychology*, or *phenomenology*, then, is an a priori science of the acts, contents and objects of consciousness, described in the manner in which they appear to consciousness.

In 1900, the term 'phenomenology' featured in the title of Alexander Pfänder's (1870–1941) *Phänomenologie des Wollens* (*Phenomenology of Willing. A Psychological Analysis*, 1900), his prize-winning *Habilitation* thesis, written under Theodor Lipps at Munich.[23] Pfänder's work related indirectly to Brentano. Pfänder wants to examine the nature of willing itself, exhibiting what he calls a 'piety' (*Pietät*) towards the phenomena.[24] The observation of conscious experiences of willing must proceed using what he calls "the subjective method" by examining *retrospectively* what goes on when we orient ourselves towards something in willing it. Furthermore, the essence of willing has to be cleared up before we can correlate bodily processes with it.[25] The procedure involves identifying the proper parts of a psychic act by bringing them to intuition. As Pfänder writes: "To analyze a fact of consciousness means to divide it into its parts or elements and specifically both into its separable parts and those which are distinguishable only in abstracto."[26]

The aim of this close description of the facts of consciousness is to find essential laws of consciousness, to achieve essential insights. This is indeed a good description of phenomenological practice, but the precise moment of inauguration of phenomenology as a distinct method, however, must be credited to Edmund Husserl in his breakthrough work *Logische Untersuchungen* (*Logical Investigations*, 1900–1901).

Edmund Husserl, a mathematician who had studied in Berlin with world-famous mathematicians such as Carl Weierstrass and Leopold Kronecker, and completed a doctorate in mathematics in Vienna with a student of Weierstrass, studied philosophy in Vienna from 1884 to 1886 with Franz Brentano from whom he absorbed a deep suspicion of what he regarded as an unscientific, mythical, speculative philosophy (Hegelianism), and a deep appreciation for the tradition of empiricism, especially David Hume. Indeed, Hume's attempt to explain all the sciences in terms of the 'science of man' and, specifically, psychology, or the study of human understanding, struck a chord with both Brentano and Husserl. Thus, much later, in his 1930 Foreword to the first English translation of *Ideas* I made by Boyce-Gibson, Husserl claimed that Hume's *Treatise* was "the first systematic sketch of a pure, although not yet eidetic phenomenology".[27] Husserl – in line with the analysis of his student Adolf Reinach – read Hume as a *transcendental phenomenologist*, since Hume realised that causation is not something occurring externally in the world so much as a set of connections imposed on the world, constituted in consciousness out of our experience of temporal relations (succession, contiguity and so on), that is, that objectivity had a subjective genesis.[28] Hume, for Husserl, had the essentially phenomenological insight that the life of consciousness is 'a life of achievement' or 'performance' (*leistendes Leben*, *Crisis* § 26, p. 90; Hua VI 93), that is, the result of

11

an act of sense-giving constitution. As Husserl says, Hume was the first to take Descartes seriously and focus on the inside of consciousness as a clue to the constitution of the outside world. Similarly, much earlier in his *Logical Investigations* Husserl explicitly praises Berkeley for carrying out a 'phenomenology of inner experience' (LI III § 2, II, p. 5; Hua XIX/1 232). In other words, the empiricist tradition was in effect a proto-phenomenology.

The *Logical Investigations* focused specifically on the clarification of logical and formal knowledge and the rejection of psychologism; nevertheless, the work suggested promising ways of investigating consciousness in all its forms. Here Husserl announced his plan for a phenomenology of the acts of logical cognition, acts of thinking and knowing generally. In the Introduction to Volume II of that work, in discussing the need for a wide-ranging theory of knowledge, Husserl speaks of "the phenomenology of the experiences of thinking and knowing" (LI, Intro. § 1, I, p. 166; Hua XIX/1 6). Brentano's discussion of *intentionality* inspired Husserl, who saw in it the possibility of a *science of pure consciousness*, removed from naturalistic and causal misconstruals. Husserl initially characterised phenomenology as a *method* for approaching epistemological problems, ancillary to psychology, but he soon came to believe that phenomenology provided a unique approach to meaning, and hence could provide both the foundation for philosophy itself and also for the other sciences. Phenomenology could be an overall 'science of science'. Specifically, as Husserl would later put it, it could discover "the ABC of consciousness".[29]

The *Logical Investigations* was quickly adopted as the foundational text for the phenomenological movement as it developed in Germany. Gradually, however, especially in his lectures at Göttingen, Husserl himself extended the reach of phenomenology until it took on for him the role of *first philosophy*, borrowing from Aristotle's conception of *prote philosophia*. He came to conceive of phenomenology as co-extensive with philosophy itself, and with the specifically philosophical attitude (a point on which Scheler too would insist). After 1905, he began to conceive of phenomenology as a kind of *transcendental idealism*, a radicalisation of Kant's project, which recognised that all meaning had its source in the transcendental ego. In later years, he also began to recognise two aspects to transcendental phenomenology – a static and a genetic side. Husserl's own radical reflections and corrections of his earlier work, his changes of direction and intensification of efforts in particular problematic, set the pace for the evolution of phenomenology, as Husserl gradually distanced himself from the form descriptive phenomenology had taken among the first set of admirers of the *Logical Investigations*. But let us first look more closely at the emergence and development of the conception of phenomenology in Husserl's own work.

Husserl's *Logical Investigations* as a breakthrough work

Husserl's *Logical Investigations* does not purport to offer a 'systematic presentation' (*eine systematische Darstellung*) of formal logic, but rather an 'epistemological clarification' (*eine erkenntniskritische Klärung*, LI III, II, p. 3; Hua XIX/1 228) of the fundamental concepts required in the elucidation of the nature of thought and knowledge. Husserl was actually trying to address the foundational problems affecting formal mathematics, logic and the formal sciences, leading him to raise "questions of the essence of the form of knowledge itself" (LI, Foreword to First Edition, I, p. 2;

Hua XVIII 6), and specifically to seek to clarify the key concepts such as consciousness, mental act, content, meaning intention, meaning fulfilment, judgement and so on.

This conception of phenomenology, as a way of approaching and clarifying concepts, emerges only tentatively in the course of the Investigations themselves, especially in the First, Fifth and Sixth, though it is clear Husserl was formulating his approach gradually through the 1890s especially in his critical studies of the existing logical literature. The Fifth Investigation focuses specifically on the elucidation of the intentional structure of consciousness, in order to give a deeper characterisation of the different features involved in any expressive act of meaning. The Sixth Investigation looked at the manner in which acts of meaning intention are correlated to acts of fulfilment, leading to a discussion of the experience of truth in judgement.

In his Introduction to the First Edition of the *Logical Investigations*, phenomenology was presented as essentially descriptive psychology of the Brentanian kind: "Phenomenology is descriptive psychology. Epistemological criticism is therefore in essence psychology, or at least capable of being built on a psychological foundation" (LI, Introduction, I, p. 176; Hua XIX/1 24).

While phenomenology was to support psychology, it was opposed to psychologism. In the First Edition, he does not clearly differentiate phenomenology from what he himself refers to as *Erkenntnistheorie*, 'epistemology' or 'theory of knowledge' (LI, Introduction, I, p. 166; Hua XIX/1 7), understood in the neo-Kantian manner as the investigation of the conditions, especially the concepts and laws, which make objective knowledge possible, rather than as an attempt to refute scepticism concerning the possibility of genuine knowledge.

Husserl also initially characterised phenomenology as a kind of radical 'conceptual analysis' (*Begriffsanalyse*), offering a clarification of *concepts*. The Introduction even speaks of 'analytical phenomenology' (LI, Introduction, § 4, I, p. 172; Hua XIX/1 17). Husserl speaks of 'fixing' – he uses the term '*fixieren*' – concepts by defining their boundaries and stabilising their shifting senses by differentiating and disambiguating them into their specific essential meanings. Husserl, in this sense, proceeds in the manner of Aristotle, defining terms, then noting new uses and analogous expressions and so on. In the *Investigations*, however, Husserl does not offer an explicit theoretical characterisation of the nature of this clarification; instead he exhibits it in practice in the actual analyses he carried out there. However, in a draft of a later work known as *Ideas* III, he understands it in terms of connecting concepts back to the intuitions that found them and also to the running through in intuition of the various stages or layers of the concept itself.[30]

In the Second Logical Investigation Husserl also speaks of 'meaning analysis' (*Bedeutungsanalyse*, LI II, § 31, I, p. 287; Hua XIX/1 115), but he did not mean to focus exclusively on linguistic analysis in the manner of his contemporaries G. E. Moore and Bertrand Russell. Thus, in his 1913 draft Preface to the Second Edition of the *Investigations*, Husserl explicitly repudiated the interpretation of phenomenology as a kind of 'meaning analysis' or 'semantic analysis' (*Bedeutungsanalyse*), which relied exclusively on the interpretation of language.[31] For Husserl, phenomenology was not simply the clarification of our linguistic expressions, but a more deep-seated attempt to analyse the very senses or meanings which we constitute through our acts and which receive expression in language. He was suspicious of the stranglehold of grammar on our thinking (a suspicion he passed on to the young

Heidegger), but equally suspicious of purely grammatical analyses that did not focus on the essential acts involved. As Husserl says in the Sixth Investigation (LI VI § 40), grammatical distinctions offer a clue to meaning distinctions, but they are not the whole of the meaning distinction and do not simply mirror it. For Husserl, meanings are clarified through phenomenological reflection secured in intuition.

Husserl's development of transcendental phenomenology

Gradually, Husserl realised that the true import of phenomenology could not be accommodated within psychology or even epistemology. The focus on the essential structures of acts and objects of consciousness needed to be articulated in a manner that removed all assumptions driven by scientific or indeed everyday *naturalism*. After his discovery of the reduction in 1905, he gradually distanced himself from his initial characterisation of phenomenology as a direct eidetic seeing driven by realist sympathies. He came to see the phenomenological reduction as the very essence of phenomenology, involving a liberation of the essence of thought acts and contents from their psychological consideration as facts of nature, and the similar exclusion of the ordinary psychological ego as the locus of these acts (see Husserl's Foreword to the Second Edition). Husserl referred to this orientation towards the eidetic in terms of a breakthrough to 'pure' consciousness understood in terms of transcendental subjectivity. Thus, in the Foreword to Second Edition of the *Logical Investigations*, he speaks of his book as a 'breakthrough work' (*ein Werk des Durchbruchs*, LI I, p. 3; Hua XVIII 8),[32] that is, his breakthrough into phenomenology as an eidetic science.

Husserl himself portrays phenomenology as slowly dawning on him between the *Logical Investigations* and *Ideas* I (1913) and tended to emphasise the importance of carrying out systematic removal of the natural attitude in order to gain a new orientation on the phenomena of consciousness, thought not as bits of the world, psychic occurrences, but as essential structures which have meanings entirely independent of the world. Phenomenology is now portrayed as a parallel science to psychology, and not necessarily exclusively as a clarification of logical terms and concepts. The phenomenological domain comes into view as that set of a priori conditions (not just formal conditions but material conditions, conditions which belong to the essence of consciousness itself) which determine the relation between what occurs as natural psychical acts in the world, and the purely ideal senses or thoughts which these psychical acts grasp and instantiate.

The exclusion of the natural attitude and the reduction

Husserl came to see phenomenology as facing down misleading conceptions of science, specifically the distortions latent in *naturalism* and *psychologism*, at least in the guise that these tendencies presented themselves at the end of the nineteenth century, and especially to oppose 'the naturalisation of consciousness' (*die Naturalisierung des Bewusstseins* – a phrase Husserl himself employs in his 1910–1911 essay, "Philosophie als Strenge Wissenschaft" ("Philosophy as a rigorous science")) being carried out by various versions of psychology and positivism.[33] As late as his Amsterdam lectures of 1929, Husserl was opposing this 'prevailing naturalization of the mental' as an enduring prejudice, originating in Descartes, Hobbes and

Locke, and which continued to haunt even Brentano's attempts at descriptive psychology.[34] Husserl saw phenomenology as a corrective to naturalism and continued to uphold the aim of scientific philosophy, which he acknowledged was present in distorted fashion in positivism.

Husserl announced his change of direction in *Ideas* I, published in his newly founded *Jahrbuch* in 1913. He now maintained that phenomenology excludes all psychical acts understood as natural performances in a natural world (i.e. as events in time captured within the nomological net of the natural world), and must be the science of *pure* or even *absolute* consciousness. At the basis of all acts of meaning lay the domain of transcendental subjectivity, which could not be accessed in normal reflection because all consciousness has an inbuilt world-affirming, 'positing' or 'thetic' character. This 'position taking' (*Stellungnahme*) is so deep-rooted that it distorts any attempt to study the structures which might be involved in the constitution of the world itself. Therefore Husserl proposed a kind of detour, or reduction, a series of methodological attempts to neutralise or suspend or put out of court the thetic character of our intentional acts to focus attention on the modes of consciousness in which objects appear. Since they cannot actually or literally be 'unplugged', they can be neutralised only by a kind of 'bracketing' or 'suspension' of the thesis of the natural attitude. This stepping back is different from the normal critical or reflective standpoint, which belongs to the natural attitude and is coloured with its prejudices, and remains, as Husserl says, within the *horiz*on of the world (*Crisis* § 40). The proposed reduction is to uncover the structures involved in the original constitution.

Ideas I offered Husserl's first published account of one of his greatest achievements, namely his identification of *the natural attitude* (*die natürliche Einstellung*) in which we live first of all and most of the time: in a world spread out in space and located at a moment in the flow of time which also spreads out before us, surrounded by objects, both natural and cultural, and by other living organisms, plants, animals and people. All other attitudes, including the scientific attitude, take their origin from the natural attitude and usually refer back to it. The *natural attitude* is actually a complex constellation of attitudes, attitudes which underlie our sense of a world itself with its aspects of familiarity and strangeness. Thus the notion of the natural attitude has as its correlative the notion of world, 'surrounding world' or 'environment' (*Umwelt*). In fact, it was Husserl who first developed the concept of *world* that became so central to Heidegger's analysis of Dasein in *Being and Time*. Our sense of the world is actually conveyed through a certain orientation or mood; traditional ontology, as Heidegger declares, was done in the mood of everydayness.

In order to gain access to the constituting nature of consciousness, Husserl proposes a radical disruption or suspension of the natural attitude, a transcendental turn, according to which the whole of nature is to be treated as nothing but a correlate of consciousness, a point missed by naturalism. The essence of the correlation between consciousness and its object is masked and systematically distorted unless we make efforts to separate out the normal, world-positing or 'thetic' character of the acts. The phenomenologist must operate the bracketing and reduction in order to focus only on the meaning-constituting character of the act, its act character, its nature as a noetic act embedded in a network of such acts which have essential interconnections with each other. Intrinsically correlated to the noetic act is the *noema* or the 'meant' now taken not as an ideal entity free of the world nor as a piece of the world but as pure condition for meaning, that which makes meaning possible. The same perceptual noema can 'found' or 'motivate' different judgements. Husserl's account of the noema has been compared favourably with Frege's notion of *Sinn*, however, the noema is the correlate of an act and hence is the act plus the manner in which the act objectivates its content. The 'logical sense', as Husserl calls it, is only one abstracted part of the more complex noema. We cannot discuss this complex issue further here, but we have included a reading from *Ideas* I which discusses the noema in some detail.

Husserl's late work all takes place within the reduction, although the reduction is construed in different ways beginning with Cartesian scepticism or with a consideration of the life-world. In whatever form, the reduction is essentially a transcendental reflection on the manner in which objectivity is constituted. Increasingly in his late writings Husserl paid more attention to the role of time in this transcendental genesis, and his work develops both static and genetic approaches. On the 'genetic' side, Husserl's late work shows a marked affinity with that of Hegel. In the *Crisis*, for example, Husserl engages in an intellectual reconstruction of some of the moments of primary founding (*Urstiftung*) in Western culture, for example, the discovery of the Pythagorean theorem, which, once discovered, becomes an enduring possession of humankind.

Phenomenology after Husserl

Husserl's *Logical Investigations* was first given serious notice by philosophers and psychologists gathered around Theodor Lipps at the University of Munich. This so-called 'old phenomenology' (*Altphänomenologie*) of the Munich School, which included Johannes Daubert, Alexander Pfänder, Moritz Geiger, Hedwig Conrad-Martius, Adolf Reinach and Max Scheler, understood phenomenology as eidetic description, the attempt to accurately distinguish the essential natures of the acts of consciousness and so on. Johannes Daubert is credited with being the first of the Munich students to travel to Göttingen to study with Husserl, and returned to set up a circle for the study of Husserl's philosophy. Soon afterwards, Adolf Reinach, a trained lawyer, became Husserl's assistant and was considered the great hope for the future of phenomenology until he was killed in action in the First World War in 1917. Max Scheler (1874–1928) was an inspirational philosopher who had an extraordinary influence in Germany during the second decade of the twentieth century. He taught in Munich with Lipps, and was deeply impressed by the *Logical Investigations* and especially its account of categorial intuition in the Sixth Investigation, but he was not drawn to Husserl's complex theorising about the nature of the phenomenological method. Scheler drew on the strong tradition of German sociological thinking (Max Weber) as well as on the philosophy of life of Eucken, Simmel and others, to develop a realistic philosophy of the experience of embodied emotions in Munich, Göttingen and later in Berlin. He was enthusiastic in his defence of the necessity of essential viewing, and was particularly drawn to the phenomenology of value and of the emotions. Scheler also argued for the experience of being as central to all experience, and on this issue, Heidegger was a huge admirer of Scheler. Scheler was especially critical of Kant's account of ethical value. His *Der Formalismus in der Ethik und die materiale Werkethik* (1913–1916) opposed Kantian ethical formalism on the basis of his phenomenology of the experience of value.

Edith Stein (1891–1942) and Roman Ingarden (1893–1970), who joined Husserl in Göttingen, developed Husserl's realist phenomenology in exciting and original directions. Stein in particular was assigned the task of putting shape and order on Husserl's extensive and disconnected research manuscripts, and she worked in particular on his draft of *Ideas* II, his attempted revision of the Sixth Logical Investigation, and his *Lectures on the Internal Consciousness of Time*, the published versions of which show evidence of Stein's extensive editorial intervention. Stein followed Husserl to Freiburg where she continued to assist Husserl, but her own work developed in the directions she herself was interested in – for example, the experience of *empathy* and the nature of *embodiment* – before her conversion to Catholicism in 1922 led her in quite another direction. After her conversion she tried to graft Thomism on to phenomenology in a metaphysical way, somewhat at odds with her mentor's approach, although she and Husserl remained firm friends. Born a Jew, she became a Carmelite nun and died in a Nazi concentration camp in 1942. Ingarden was active in developing phenomenological analyses of the literary object and of the work of art, and played a role in the development of phenomenology in Poland.

Although Husserl had already been attracting international students in small numbers at Göttingen, it was only after he moved to Freiburg in 1916, and especially during the 1920s, that he became the leading figure in German philosophy. He also developed a considerable international reputation, as is evidenced by his invitations to lecture in London (in 1922), Paris (in 1929) and Amsterdam (in 1929). But Husserl was soon overshadowed by the publication of Heidegger's *Sein und Zeit* in 1927, which continued to invoke phenomenology but now linked to the project of hermeneutics and fundamental ontology. Heidegger had been developing his own conception of phenomenology in his lectures at Freiburg (1919–1923) and Marburg (1923–1928). Whereas Husserl emphasised the centrality of consciousness approached in terms of the intentional correlation between subject and object, and sought to peel back the distorting layers of the natural attitude to grasp the nature of transcendental constituting consciousness, Heidegger in *Being and Time* offered what at first sight appeared to be a new, non-Husserlian vision of phenomenology which dropped reference to both consciousness and intentionality and introduced a new way of approaching human 'being-in-the-world' through its special inquiry into the nature of human existence (*Dasein*).

Being and Time claimed to be an exercise in fundamental ontology, seeking an understanding of the meaning of the age-old 'question of Being' (*die Seinsfrage*). Although ostensibly a treatise in phenomenology, it contained few references to Husserl and moved phenomenology away from description into hermeneutics, and away from the science of consciousness towards the study of existence and ontology. In his etymological analysis of the term 'phenomenology' into its component parts *phainomenon* and *logos*, Heidegger even claimed that phenomenology had been understood more originally by the ancient Greeks, although at the same time he acknowledged (SZ § 7, 38; 62) that this book could not have been written had not Husserl made the 'breakthrough' to phenomenology in his *Logical Investigations*.

In *Being and Time* Heidegger specifically linked phenomenology with the hermeneutical tradition stemming from Schleiermacher and Dilthey, to the point of claiming that phenomenology must be understood as hermeneutical:

Our investigation itself will show that the meaning of phenomenological description as a method lies in *interpretation* (*Auslegung*). The *logos* of the phenomenology of Dasein has the character of a *hermeneuein*, through which the authentic meaning of Being, and also those basic structures of Being which Dasein possesses, are made known to Dasein's understanding of Being. The phenomenology of Dasein is a *hermeneutic* in the primordial signification of that word, where it designates this business of interpreting. (SZ § 7, 37; 61–62).

Heidegger is emphasising the importance of *tradition* (also taken up by Gadamer) and the manner in which all thought has to be approached in terms of presuppositions. Contrary to Husserl, there cannot be presuppositionless philosophising; rather, Heidegger endorses the view that understanding develops through a circling back and forth between presumption and surprise, the so-called 'hermeneutic circle'. *Being and Time* also downplayed the analysis of human beings in terms of consciousness and intellectual cognition and gave more attention to human 'being-in-the-world' (*In-der-Welt-sein*), and the importance of *linguisticality* (*Sprachlichkeit*) in any attempt to understand meaning. Most of all, Heidegger's leading concern was to use phenomenology to revitalise the age-old metaphysical *question concerning the meaning of Being* (*die Seinsfrage*), a question which had been forgotten in modern philosophy. Thus Heidegger wanted to put phenomenology in the service of fundamental ontology.

Relations between Husserl and Heidegger became strained after Husserl read *Being and Time* and realised how much Heidegger had departed from his vision of transcendental phenomenology. Husserl immediately embarked on a series of lectures and publications meant as a corrective to Heidegger's distorted version of phenomenology. For Husserl, Heidegger's *Being and Time* was a kind of anthropology undertaken in the natural attitude that failed to understand the true meaning of the transcendental reduction. Furthermore, much to the horror of the elderly Husserl, in the early 1930s Heidegger became an enthusiastic advocate of National Socialism, and in 1933 was elected Rector of Freiburg University, where his inaugural address pledged the university to the service of Hitler. During the 1930s, also, inspired by his reading of Nietzsche and of German poets such as Hölderlin, Heidegger's thought underwent a turning away from transcendental philosophy and towards a kind of poetic, meditative thinking, directed against what he characterised as the technological framing of the age, a framing which had been enabled by but had deformed the ancient Greek approach to the 'event' or 'happening' (*Ereignis*) of being.

Even during his so-called 'phenomenological decade' (1919–1929), Heidegger was never a slavish follower of Husserl. Indeed, he rejected and even ridiculed Husserl's conception of the transcendental ego and other central aspects of Husserl's thought right from the beginning of his lecturing career (after 1919), and intended *Being and Time* to kill off the 'old man'. As he caustically remarks in a letter: "Founder of Phenomenology – no one knows what that means anymore."[35] For example, in his lecture course for the Summer Semester 1923, Heidegger asserts that:

> Phenomenology can only be appropriated phenomenologically, i.e., only through *demonstration* and not in such a way that one repeats propositions, takes over fundamental principles, or subscribes to academic dogmas. A

large measure of critique is initially required for this, and nothing is more dangerous than the naïve *trust in evidence* exhibited by followers and fellow travellers. If it is the case that our relation to the things themselves in seeing is the decisive factor, it is equally the case that we are frequently deceived about them and that the possibility of such deception stubbornly persists. Perhaps called once to be the conscience of philosophy, it has wound up as a pimp for public whoring of the mind, *fornicatio spiritus* (Luther).[36]

With Heidegger's personal falling out with Husserl, it was left to Husserl's later assistants, Eugen Fink, Ludwig Landgrebe and Stephan Strasser, to carry on the legacy of Husserlian philosophy. Indeed, it was due to the efforts of a hitherto unknown graduate from Louvain, Fr. Herman Van Breda, who had never met Husserl, that Husserl's papers and manuscripts were rescued from the Nazis and brought to safety in the Husserl Archive of the Catholic University of Louvain in Belgium.

Heidegger's anti-subjectivist characterisation of human being-in-the-world and his emphasis on the 'linguisticality' of human experience were taken up by Hans-Georg Gadamer (b. 1900). Gadamer, who trained as a classicist with Paul Natorp and later Heidegger, accepted Heidegger's claim that phenomenology must proceed in hermeneutic fashion, sensitive to the manner in which tradition shapes and constrains the meanings we encounter in the world. Initially, he developed his hermeneutics through the interpretation of Plato in particular, but he was also interested in the nature of the work of art and attended Heidegger's 1935 lectures on "The Origin of the Work of Art". However, his real impact came with the publication of *Wahrheit und Methode* (*Truth and Method*, 1960).[37] In this work, Gadamer argues that humans are essentially involved in the historically situated and finite task of understanding the world, a world encountered and inhabited in and through language. As Gadamer puts it, 'language is the medium of the hermeneutic experience' (TM 384; 361); that is, language is the medium in which understanding is realised. Furthermore, for Gadamer, language has its true being in 'speech' (*Sprache*), the kind of speech which occurs in the context of a 'conversation' (*ein Gespräch*, TM 446; 422). Philosophy, then, is a conversation leading towards mutual understanding, towards the overlapping of horizons which Gadamer calls 'fusion of horizons' (*Horizontsverschmelzung*, TM 306; 290). Furthermore, against the Enlightenment aim of eliminating prejudice, Gadamer paradoxically wants to rehabilitate prejudice, in the sense of recognising the presuppositions we bring to any situation or encounter with others.

Hannah Arendt (1906–1975) first encountered Heidegger when she became a student at Marburg, and was particularly impressed by his lectures on Aristotle's *Nicomachean Ethics* and on Plato's *Sophist*. Forced to leave Germany because of the Nazis, Arendt emigrated to the USA where she developed her own independent way of analysing human life or dwelling 'in the midst of the world', but drew deeply on her contact with Heidegger, including his interpretations of Plato and Aristotle. Arendt's own phenomenological account of human freedom and sociality and the conditions which make political action possible are set out in *The Human Condition* (1958). Arendt was never a subscriber to a particular practice of the phenomenological method but her approach may be understood as phenomenological in broader terms.

DERMOT MORAN

Phenomenology outside Germany

Husserl's *Logical Investigations* had an early and considerable influence on philosophy elsewhere in Europe, with followers in Russia (Gustav Shpet and later Roman Jakobson) and in Poland, due to the efforts of Husserl's student, Roman Ingarden, who returned there. Husserl was well received in Czechoslovakia, due to his old friend Thomas Masaryk and Jan Patočka (1907–1977), and, most notably, in France, originally through Jean Héring (1890–1966), but principally due to Emmanuel Levinas (1906–1995), who had studied with both Husserl and Heidegger in Freiburg in 1928, and had translated Husserl's Paris lectures of 1929 into French. Levinas introduced phenomenology to French readers through his pioneering study, *Theory of Intuition in Husserl's Phenomenology* (1930),[38] which explicitly compared Husserl with Henri Bergson, the most prominent French philosopher of the time. Although Levinas published many articles on Husserl and Heidegger, he did not really achieve recognition for his own ethical approach until the publication of *Totalité et infini* (*Totality and Infinity*) in 1961.[39]

Phenomenology went on to have a considerable following in France through the writings of Jean-Paul Sartre, Maurice Merleau-Ponty, Mikel Dufrenne and Gilles Deleuze, although it also gradually metamorphosed into structuralism (Michel Foucault) and subsequently into deconstruction (Jacques Derrida). Husserl even had some influence on French anthropology through Lucien Lévy-Bruhl (1857–1939), who had been present at Husserl's Paris lectures in 1929 and engaged in correspondence with him. In France, phenomenology was given a radical existential interpretation, especially in the writings of Sartre, Merleau-Ponty and Simone de Beauvoir.

Jean-Paul Sartre (1905–1980) was a brilliant *littérateur*, an accomplished novelist and playwright, as well as a bohemian intellectual and left-wing political activist who popularised existentialism in post-war Europe. His first published work, *Transcendence of the Ego*,[40] sought to repudiate the traditional view that the ego is an inhabitant of consciousness, whether as an element to be found 'materially' in consciousness (as some psychologists maintain), or, as in the Kantian account, as a formal organisational aspect of consciousness. Rather, for Sartre, the ego is outside consciousness altogether, "a being of the world, like the ego of the other" (*un être du monde, comme l'égo d'autrui*, TE 31). Sartre argues that if consciousness were not self-consciousness it would not be consciousness at all: "Indeed the existence of consciousness is an absolute because consciousness is consciousness of self" (TE 40). Consciousness is aware of itself because it is aware of objects.

Sartre followed up his essay on Husserl with two books devoted to a psychological and phenomenological study of imagination. The earlier 1936 study, *L'imagination*, contained more of Sartre's criticisms of previous theories, including those of Berkeley, Hume and Bergson, as well as the psychologists Bühler, Titchener, Köhler, Wertheimer, Koffka and others. His next study, *L'Imaginaire*, in 1940, offered his own positive, *descriptive* phenomenological study of the nature and role of imaginative consciousness. Sartre is best known for his massive study *L'Être et le néant* (*Being and Nothingness*, 1943),[41] subtitled "Essay on Phenomenological Ontology", which suggests the influence of Heidegger's *Being and Time*, and which Sartre had begun studying in the early 1940s. *Being and Nothingness* contrasts objects and consciousness in terms of the distinction between 'being in itself' (*être en soi*) and 'being for itself' (*être pour soi*). Consciousness is pure for itself and hence has no internal content or being but is always in a process of becoming, of aiming to be something in itself. Sartre's account of the fluctuations of consciousness is meant to underscore the fact that human existence is radically free. There are many different structural ways in which humans either face up to or occlude their freedom, the main manner of occlusion being 'self-deception' or 'bad faith' (*mauvaise foi*), the analysis of which is a *tour de force* in the book.

Maurice Merleau-Ponty (1908–1961), who became a close colleague of Sartre's until they fell out over political matters, offers a radical description of the primary experiences of embodied human existence and a critique of various forms of objectivism and scientism (both rationalistic and empiricist) in his major work, *Phenomenology of Perception* (1945).[42] He sought to avoid Husserl's idealism by returning to our pre-predicative experiences. As he puts it in a late essay, "La métaphysique dans l'homme" ("The Metaphysical in Man"), the aim of his philosophy is "to rediscover, along with structure and the understanding of structure, a dimension of being and a type of knowledge which man forgets in his natural attitude".[43]

Jacques Derrida (b. 1930) began his philosophical career rather conventionally as a student of Husserlian phenomenology, writing a number of close, critical studies of both the *Logical Investigations* and Husserl's late essay, "On the Origin of Geometry". Derrida sought to expose the hidden metaphysical presuppositions of traditional Husserlian phenomenology, which, in his view, far from being a presuppositionless science, actually belonged to the history of metaphysics. Phenomenology, far from being a radical presuppositionless pure science of consciousness, was in fact the apotheosis of the old metaphysics. Indeed, Husserlian phenomenology, with its commitment to self-identical ideal truths, remains, for Derrida, trapped in "the metaphysics of presence in the form of ideality".[44] Although Derrida seeks to go beyond phenomenology and indeed philosophy, nevertheless his work takes off from the ambiguities and tensions in Husserl's enterprise and Derrida likes to see himself as operating within the context of the Husserlian *epoché*.

Phenomenology in America and Britain

Due to the *Logical Investigations*, Husserl had attracted American students including William Ernest Hocking and later Marvin Farber, Dorion Cairns and Fritz Kaufmann. Through the 1920s phenomenology spread to Japan, and after the Second World War it enjoyed a major renaissance in the USA up through the 1960s. Sartre would recall that his life was broken in two by the Second World War, and phenomenology suffered a similar fate, with Husserl's own work being threatened by the rise of the Nazis, and by the enforced emigration of so many phenomenologists – Aron Gurwitsch, Alfred Schütz, Hannah Arendt. All had to flee, first to France and then to the USA, some assisted by Husserl's American students Marvin Farber and Dorion Cairns. A new phenomenological tradition began to take root in America, specifically at the New School for Social Research in New York, during the 1940s and 1950s.

By contrast with America, Husserl never became particularly influential in England, although he was read by philosophers such as Gilbert Ryle. More recently, however, especially through the writings of Michael Dummett, David Bell, and scholarly work on the origins of analytic philosophy, Husserl has been recognised alongside Gottlob

Frege as a major philosopher with interesting insights into the nature of logic, and issues connected with meaning and reference. Some contemporary analytic philosophers of mind in both the UK and the USA have been attracted to Husserlian phenomenology because of its rigorous attempt to provide an anti-naturalistic approach to the essence of consciousness and of cognitive acts in the broadest sense, and because of its accounts of intentionality, a concept which plays an important role in the work of Daniel Dennett and John R. Searle, among others.

The current situation: what is living and what is dead?

Having been in vogue in France in the 1950s and in the USA in the 1960s, during the latter half of the twentieth century phenomenology gradually became eclipsed as a programme and as a unique method, giving way to broader and less scientific conceptions of continental philosophy, which include critical theory, post-structuralism, hermeneutics, postmodernism and multiculturalism. However, recent developments, including the interest in the history of analytic philosophy, discussions concerning consciousness arising out of the recent revival of the programme of the naturalisation of consciousness, the critique of naturalism, and questions concerning the relation between philosophy and the sciences, have generated new interest in the contribution of phenomenology to these themes.[45] There is undoubtedly a certain sense in which phenomenology has now receded into history as a movement and is no longer championed as the *exclusive* method of philosophy. It is certainly no longer viable in the form of a rigorous foundational science as originally conceived by Husserl, just as the project of producing an ideal clarified language has disappeared from contemporary philosophy of language.

Phenomenology's enduring contribution is its patient descriptive analyses of the phenomena of consciousness with its emphasis on the ineliminable role of consciousness in knowledge and its rejection of the modern tradition of representationalism and naturalism. Phenomenology has a richer understanding of the subjective and the relation between subjectivity and objectivity, whereby objectivity is an achievement or production of subjectivity. In this world, there is no objectivity without subjectivity. Furthermore, Husserl has shown how complex even basic perceptual acts are, a complexity which will be appreciated by those trying to replicate these achievements in machines. Phenomenology's emphasis on world-constituting consciousness is a powerful antidote to naturalism in all its forms, and it is probably the only philosophy which has attempted to concretely describe the manner of the self-relation of the ego or self, and its experience of others in empathy. In terms of its complex analysis of the nature of human being-in-the-world, phenomenology still has much to offer contemporary philosophy.

University College Dublin

Notes

1 Edmund Husserl, *Die Krisis der europäischen Wissenschaften und die transzendentale Phänomenologie. Eine Einleitung in die phänomenologische Philosophie*, hrsg. W. Biemel, Husserliana (hereafter 'Hua') VI (The Hague: Nijhoff, 1962, reprinted 1976), trans. David Carr as *The Crisis of European Sciences and Transcendental Phenomenology. An Introduction to Phenomenological Philosophy* (Evanston: Northwestern University Press, 1970),

§ 38, p. 144. Hereafter '*Crisis*' and page number of the Carr translation, followed by Husserlian volume and page number.

2 M. Heidegger, *Sein und Zeit*, Seventeenth Edition (Tübingen: Max Niemeyer, 1993), p. 27; Seventh Edition ed. trans. John Macquarrie and Edward Robinson as *Being and Time* (Oxford: Blackwell, 1967), p. 50. Hereafter 'SZ' and section number, German pagination, followed by pagination of English translation (e.g. the reference here is: SZ § 7, 27; 50).

3 The critical edition is published in Hua Vol. III/1 as *Ideen zu einer reinen Phänomenologie und phänomenologischen Philosophie. Erstes Buch: Allgemeine Einführung in die reine Phänomenologie* 1. Halbband: *Text der 1.–3. Auflage*, hrsg. Karl Schuhmann (The Hague: Nijhoff, 1977), trans. F. Kersten as *Ideas Pertaining to a Pure Phenomenology and to a Phenomenological Philosophy, First Book* (Dordrecht: Kluwer, 1983). Hereafter '*Ideas* I' followed by paragraph number and page number of English translation and Husserliana volume number and pagination of German. The reference here is *Ideas* I, § 62, p. 142; Hua III/1 118.

4 E. Husserl, *Méditations cartésiennes: introduction à la phénoménologie*, trans. G. Peiffer and E. Levinas (Paris: Armand Colin, 1931). The German text was not published until 1950 as *Cartesianische Meditationen und Pariser Vorträge*, hrsg. Stephan Strasser, Hua I (The Hague: Nijhoff, 1950), trans. D. Cairns as *Cartesian Meditations. An Introduction to Phenomenology* (The Hague: Nijhoff, 1960).

5 As Hans-Georg Gadamer has confirmed in his communication to Burt Hopkins, recorded in *Research in Phenomenology*, Vol. XXIX (1999), p. 213.

6 See Lester Embree *et al.*, eds, *Encyclopedia of Phenomenology* (Dordrecht: Kluwer, 1997), pp. 2–6.

7 Michel Henry, *The Essence of Manifestation* (The Hague: Nijhoff, 1973).

8 Max Scheler, "Phenomenology and the Theory of Cognition", in *Selected Philosophical Essays*, trans. David R. Lachterman (Evanston: Northwestern University Press, 1973), p. 145.

9 Edmund Husserl, *Logische Untersuchungen*, erster Band, *Prolegomena zur reinen Logik*, text der 1. und der 2. Auflage, hrsg. E. Holenstein, Hua XVIII (The Hague: Nijhoff, 1975), and *Logische Untersuchungen*, zweiter Band, *Untersuchungen zur Phänomenologie und Theorie der Erkenntnis*, in zwei Bänden, hrsg. Ursula Panzer, Hua XIX (Dordrecht: Kluwer, 1984), trans. J. N. Findlay, ed. Dermot Moran *Logical Investigations*, 2 vols (London: Routledge, 2001). Hereafter 'LI' followed by Investigation number, paragraph number, volume and page number of English translation, followed by German pagination of Husserlian edition. The reference here is LI, Intro. § 1, I, p. 166; Hua XIX/1 6.

10 E. Husserl, "Author's Preface to the English Edition," *Ideas. General Introduction to Pure Phenomenology*, trans. W. R. Boyce-Gibson (London: Collier-Macmillan, 1962), p. 6.

11 See I. Kant, *Logic*, Introduction §1, trans. Robert S. Hartman and Wolfgang Schwarz (New York: Dover Press, 1988), p. 13: "just as sensibility is the faculty of intuitions, so the understanding is the faculty of thinking, that is, of bringing the presentations of the senses under rules."

12 Robert Sokolowski, *Husserlian Meditations* (Evanston: Northwestern University Press, 1974), p. 32.

13 See Karl Schuhmann, " 'Phänomenologie': Eine begriffsgeschichtliche Reflexion," *Husserl Studies* I (1984), pp. 31–68, esp. p. 35.

14 H. Spiegelberg, *The Phenomenological Movement. A Historical Introduction*, Third Edition (Dordrecht: Kluwer, 1994), p. 11. See also M. Inwood, 'Phenomenology', in *A Hegel Dictionary* (Oxford: Blackwell, 1992), pp. 214–216.

15 See E. W. Orth, "Can 'Phenomenology' in Kant and Lambert be Connected with Husserlian Phenomenology?," in T. Seebohm and J. Kockelmans, eds, *Kant and Phenomenology* (Washington, DC: Center for Advanced Research in Phenomenology, 1984).

16 See J. Hoffmeister's Introduction to the Meiner edition of G. W. F. Hegel, *Phänomenologie des Geistes* (Hamburg: Meiner, 1952), pp. vii–xvii.

17 G. W. F. Hegel, *Enzyklopädie des philosophischen Wissenschaften* III (Hamburg: Meiner, 1991), §415, p. 345; trans. as *Hegel's Philosophy of Mind: Part Three of the Encyclopaedia of the Philosophical Sciences (1830)* by William Wallace and A. V. Miller (Oxford: Clarendon Press, 1971), p. 156.

18 See A. Kojève, *Introduction to the Reading of Hegel. Lectures on the Phenomenology of Spirit*, assembled by Raymond Queneau, ed. Allan Bloom, trans. James H. Nichols (Ithaca, NY: Cornell University Press, 1980).
19 Sir William Hamilton, *Lectures on Metaphysics and Logic*, ed. H. L. Mansel and John Veitch, 4 vols (Edinburgh: William Blackwood & Sons, 1869), Volume 1, p. 129 and p. 153.
20 On Ernst Mach, see Spiegelberg, *The Phenomenological Movement*, p. 8 and p. 23n. 11. For Husserl's reference to Mach in his Amsterdam lectures, see "The Amsterdam Lectures on Phenomenological Psychology", trans. Richard Palmer, in T. Sheehan and R. Palmer, eds, *Edmund Husserl, Psychological and Transcendental Phenomenology and the Confrontation with Heidegger (1927–31)*, Collected Works VI (Dordrecht: Kluwer, 1997), p. 213.
21 F. Brentano, *Psychologie vom empirischen Standpunkt*, 3 vols (Hamburg: Felix Meiner Verlag, 1973), trans. A. C. Rancurello, D. B. Terrell, and L. L. McAlister as *Psychology from an Empirical Standpoint*, Second Edition, with new Introduction by Peter Simons (London: Routledge, 1995).
22 F. Brentano, *Deskriptive Psychologie*, ed. R. Chisholm and W. Baumgartner (Hamburg: Meiner, 1982), trans. B. Müller as *Descriptive Psychology* (London: Routledge, 1995).
23 Alexander Pfänder, *Phänomenologie des Wollens. Eine psychologische Analyse* (Leipzig: Johan Ambrosius Barth Verlagsbuchhandlung, 1900), Third Edition reprinted in *Alexander Pfänders Gesammelte Schriften*, Vol. 1 (Munich, 1963); the Introduction to this work is translated in A. Pfänder, *Phenomenology of Willing and Motivation and Other Phaenomenologica*, trans. Herbert Spiegelberg (Evanston: Northwestern University Press, 1967). Hereafter reference is to the English translation.
24 Pfänder, *Phenomenology of Willing*, p. 7.
25 Ibid., p. 9.
26 Ibid., p. 10.
27 E. Husserl, *Nachwort zu meinen Ideen*, in *Ideen zu einer reinen Phänomenologie und phänomenologischen Philosophie. Drittes Buch, Die Phänomenologie und die Fundamente der Wissenschaften*, hrsg. Marly Biemel, Hua V (The Hague: Nijhoff, 1952, reprinted 1971), p. 155; trans. W. R. Boyce-Gibson, in *Ideas. A General Introduction to Pure Phenomenology*, p. 23, trans. altered.
28 See also Husserl, *Crisis* §§ 24–26 and his *Formale und transzendentale Logik. Versuch einer Kritik der logischen Vernunft. Mit ergänzenden Texten*, hrsg. Paul Janssen (The Hague: Nijhoff, 1974), trans. D. Cairns, *Formal and Transcendental Logic* (The Hague: Nijhoff, 1969), § 100, p. 256: "Hume's greatness . . . lies in the fact that . . . he was the first to grasp the universal *concrete problem* of transcendental philosophy. In the concreteness of purely egological internality, as he saw, everything objective becomes intended to (and, in favorable cases, perceived), thanks to a subjective genesis."
29 Edmund Husserl wrote this in the Guest Book of Ludwig Binswanger; see L. Binswanger, "Dank an Edmund Husserl", *Edmund Husserl 1859–1959 Recueil commémorative publié à l'occasion du centenaire de la naissance du philosophe*, ed. Van Breda and J. Taminiaux (The Hague: Nijhoff, 1959), p. 65. The phrase also appears in his *Erste Philosophie* lectures of the early 1920s.
30 See E. Husserl, *Ideen zu einer reinen Phänomenologie und phänomenologischen Philosophie. Drittes Buch, Die Phänomenologie und die Fundamente der Wissenschaften*, hrsg. Marly Biemel, Hua V, pp. 93–105, trans. Ted E. Klein and W.E. Pohl as *Ideas Pertaining to a Pure Phenomenology and to a Phenomenological Philosophy, Third Book*. Collected Works I (The Hague: Nijhoff, 1980), pp. 80–90.
31 E. Husserl, *Introduction to the Logical Investigations. Draft of a Preface to the Logical Investigations*, ed. E. Fink, trans. P. J. Bossert and C. H. Peters (The Hague: Nijhoff, 1975), p. 49. Hereafter 'Draft of a Preface'.
32 See also *Ideas I*, Introduction, p. xviii; Hua III/1 2, and Husserl, *Draft of a Preface*, p. 32.
33 See E. Husserl, *Philosophie als Strenge Wissenschaft*, Logos 1910/1911, reprinted in *Aufsätze und Vorträge 1911–1921*, hrsg. H.R. Sepp and Thomas Nenon, Hua XXV (Dordrecht: Kluwer, 1986), p. 9; trans. as "Philosophy as a Rigorous Science", in Q. Lauer, *Edmund Husserl, Phenomenology and the Crisis of Philosophy* (New York: Harper Books, 1965), p. 80.
34 Husserl, *Psychological and Transcendental Phenomenology and the Confrontation with Heidegger (1927–31)*, p. 219; Hua IX 309–10.

35 Quoted in Sheehan and Palmer, eds, *Edmund Husserl, Psychological and Transcendental Phenomenology and the Confrontation with Heidegger (1927–31)*, p. 17.
36 Martin Heidegger, *Ontologie (Hermeneutik der Faktizität)*, ed. Käte Bröcker-Oltmanns, Gesamtausgabe 63 (Frankfurt: Klostermann, 1988), § 10, trans. John van Buren, *Ontology – The Hermeneutics of Facticity* (Bloomington: Indiana University Press, 1999), p. 37.
37 H.-G. Gadamer, *Wahrheit und Methode. Grundzüge einer philosophischen Hermeneutik* (Tübingen: Lohr, 1960, Second Edition, 1965). The Fourth German Edition is translated by Joel Weinsheimer and Donald G. Marshall as *Truth and Method*, Second Revised Edition (London: Sheed & Ward, 1989). Hereafter 'TM' followed by page number of English translation; followed by the pagination of the German Second Edition.
38 E. Levinas, *La Théorie de l'intuition dans la phénoménologie de Husserl* (Paris: Félix Alcan, 1930, reprinted Paris: Vrin, 1963), trans. A. Orianne as *The Theory of Intuition in Husserl's Phenomenology*. (Evanston: Northwestern University Press, 1973).
39 E. Levinas, *Totalité et infini: Essai sur l'extériorité* (The Hague: Martinus Nijhoff, 1961), trans. A. Lingis as *Totality and Infinity. An Essay on Exteriority* (Pittsburgh: Duquesne University Press, 1969).
40 J.-P. Sartre, "La Transcendance de l'égo. Esquisse d'une déscription phénoménologique", *Recherches philosophiques*, 6 (1936/7), pp. 85–123, reprinted as a separate book, *La Transcendance de l'égo* (Paris: Vrin, 1966), trans. Forrest Williams and Robert Kirkpatrick as *The Transcendence of the Ego* (New York: Farrar, Straus & Giroux, 1957, reprinted 1972). Hereafter 'TE' followed by page number of the English translation.
41 J.-P. Sartre, *L'Être et le néant. Essai d'ontologie phénoménologique* (Paris: Gallimard, 1943), trans. Hazel E. Barnes as *Being and Nothingness. An Essay on Phenomenological Ontology* (London: Routledge, 1995).
42 M. Merleau-Ponty, *Phénoménologie de la perception* (Paris: Gallimard, 1945), trans. C. Smith as *Phenomenology of Perception* (London: Routledge & Kegan Paul, 1962).
43 M. Merleau-Ponty, "La métaphysique dans l'homme", *Sens et non-sens* (Paris: Nagel, 1966), trans. as "The Metaphysical in Man", by Hubert Dreyfus and Patricia Allen Dreyfus, in *Sense and Nonsense* (Evanston: Northwestern University Press, 1964), p. 92.
44 J. Derrida, *La Voix et le phénomène* (Paris: Presses Universitaires de France, 1967), p. 9, trans. David B. Allison, with additional essays, in *Speech and Phenomena and other Essays on Husserl's Theory of Signs* (Evanston: Northwestern University Press, 1973), p. 10.
45 For further discussion, see Dermot Moran, "Analytic Philosophy and Phenomenology", in Lester Embree, Samuel J. Julian and Steve Crowell, eds, *The Reach of Reflection: Issues for Phenomenology's Second Century*, Proceedings of Center for Advanced Research in Phenomenology Symposium, Florida Atlantic University, 2001 (West Harford: Electron Press, 2001).

Further reading

Critchley, Simon. Ed. *The Blackwell Companion to Continental Philosophy*. Oxford: Blackwell, 1998.
Embree, Lester. Ed. *The Encyclopedia of Phenomenology*. Dordrecht: Kluwer, 1997.
Hammond, Michael, Jane Howarth and Russell Keat. *Understanding Phenomenology*. Oxford: Blackwell, 1991.
Kearney, Richard. *Dialogues with Contemporary Continental Thinkers*. Manchester: Manchester University Press, 1984.
Kearney, Richard. *Modern Movements in European Philosophy*. Manchester: Manchester University Press, 1986.
Kearney, Richard. Ed. *Continental Philosophy in the Twentieth Century*. London: Routledge, 1994.
Moran, Dermot. *Introduction to Phenomenology*. London and New York: Routledge, 2000.
Pfänder, A. *Phenomenology of Willing and Other Phaenomenologica*. Trans. Herbert Spiegelberg. Evanston: Northwestern University Press, 1967.

Sajama, Seppo and Matti Kamppinen. *A Historical Introduction to Phenomenology*. London and New York: Croom Helm, 1987.

Sokolowski, Robert. *Introduction to Phenomenology*. Cambridge: Cambridge University Press, 2000.

Solomon, Robert. Ed. *Phenomenology and Existentialism*. New York: Harper and Row, 1972.

Spiegelberg, Herbert. *The Context of the Phenomenological Movement*. The Hague: Nijhoff, 1981.

Spiegelberg, Herbert. *The Phenomenological Movement. A Historical Introduction*. Third Revised and Enlarged Edition with the Assistance of Karl Schuhmann. Dordrecht: Kluwer, 1994.

Straus, Erwin W. Ed. *Phenomenology: Pure and Applied*. Pittsburgh: Duquesne University Press, 1964.

Zaner, Richard. M. *The Way of Phenomenology: Criticism as a Philosophical Discipline*. New York: Pegasus, 1970.

Zaner, Richard M. and Don Ihde. Eds. *Phenomenology and Existentialism*. New York: Putnam's Sons, 1973.

Part I

FRANZ VON BRENTANO
Intentionality and the Project of
Descriptive Psychology

FRANZ CLEMENS VON BRENTANO
(1838–1917)

Introduction

Born into an aristocratic family in Germany in 1838, Franz Clemens von Brentano studied philosophy and theology at the universities of Munich, Würzburg, Berlin, Münster and Tübingen. He focused in particular on Aristotle and Thomas Aquinas and wrote both his doctoral thesis, *On the Several Senses of Being in Aristotle* (1862) and his *Habilitation* thesis, *The Psychology of Aristotle. In Particular His Doctrine of the Active Intellect* (1866) on Aristotle. He became a Catholic priest in 1864 and began lecturing at the university of Würzburg, where he was quickly recognised as a charismatic teacher. However, in 1873, he resigned his position for theological reasons connected with his opposition to the doctrine of Papal Infallibility, and soon after left the priesthood.

Brentano was appointed Professor at the University of Vienna in 1874 and in the same year published *Psychology from an Empirical Standpoint*, the first part of a larger planned work, in which he laid the foundations for a new scientific psychology based on the classification and description of mental acts. This work is one of the foundational texts of empirical psychology, and its section entitled *The Classification of Mental Phenomena* was so popular that it was reprinted separately in 1911. At Vienna, Brentano attracted brilliant students, including Freud, Meinong, Husserl, Höfler, Twardowski, Ehrenfels, Masaryk and Kraus, but, in 1880, due to his marriage, he had to resign his Chair, although he was allowed continue as *Privatdozent*. Between 1887 and 1891, he developed his programmatic lectures on "descriptive psychology" (also termed "psychognosy" or "phenomenology"), which sharpened the contrast between this descriptive and apodictic science and all "genetic psychology". Having failed to regain his Chair, in 1895 he retired from teaching and moved first to Italy and later to Switzerland, where he died in 1917. Throughout his life he maintained his interest in Aristotle, but in later years he wrote on metaphysics, ethics, and on scientific and mathematical questions. Our readings aim to show Brentano as a forerunner of phenomenology.

Brentano demanded strictness or *exactitude* in philosophy, as in science. His models of exact philosophy were Aristotle, Aquinas, Descartes, the British Empiricists and Comte. He opposed Kant and Hegel and speculative philosophy generally, which he regarded as vacuous. In establishing empirical psychology as a science, Brentano emphasised accurate *description* of mental states over causal *explanation*. Brentano maintained that we have direct and indubitable knowledge of our mental acts but only indirect knowledge of the external world. We know only phenomena and not things in themselves; however, mental phenomena, he believed, are given to us directly as they really are. Inner perception (*innere Wahrnehmung*), then, is *the* psychological method, since all mental acts, besides being directed at objects, carry an additional or secondary awareness of the act itself.

According to Brentano, mental acts are divided into three fundamental kinds: *ideas* or *presentations* (*Vorstellungen*), *judgements*, and what he called "the phenomena of love and hate", which included feelings, emotions and volitions. Ideas are simply presentations of some content, namely entertaining the idea of a triangle, or a colour and so on; judgements assert or deny something, whereas phenomena of love and hate are experiences of attraction or repulsion. Brentano maintained that there was a strict law governing mental phenomena whereby every mental act is either a presentation or based on a presentation. Judgements then either assert or deny the underlying presentation. Thus to judge "gold is yellow" is, for Brentano, to *assert* "yellow gold" as existing.

Brentano further divided mental phenomena into two classes that he termed, somewhat misleadingly, "physical" and "psychical phenomena". For Brentano, the distinctive characteristic of each mental act is that it has an object or content, leading him to revive the Scholastic conception of intentionality or directedness to an object. Brentano sought to express the peculiar status of intentional objects in terms of their "inexistence", emphasising the in-dwelling of the object in the act, but later revised his views to argue that we can only conceive of existent or real objects. All other forms of reference are fictional, brought about by the nature of language.

Our first selection is taken from his major work *Psychology from an Empirical Standpoint* (1874). We have reprinted the Foreword where Brentano explains in what sense psychology is to be understood as empirical: "experience alone is my teacher". This reading is followed by the first chapter of Book Two, entitled "The Distinction between Mental and Physical Phenomena", where Brentano attempts to lay down a positive characterisation of the nature of mental acts. Brentano rejects all negative criteria, for example, the traditional Cartesian position which held that mental events differ from physical events in being non-extended. As a positive characterisation, Brentano suggests that all mental phenomena are intentional; that is, they relate to an object, whether or not that object actually exists. It was this identification of the intentionality of mental acts which inspired Husserl's phenomenology of consciousness.

The third short reading is drawn from Brentano's 1889 lectures on "Descriptive Psychology", in which the concept of "phenomenology" is introduced as a synonym for descriptive psychology as an a priori science which operates by intuition rather than induction, a view which would strongly influence Husserl's conception of phenomenological method.

Our fourth reading is a letter from 1905, showing Brentano rejecting and revising his earlier view of intentional objects to deny that he meant to give them some kind of peculiar ontological status. Brentano revised his views many times, and the dispute over the nature of intentional objects continued among his students, especially Alexius Meinong, Anton Marty, Kasimir Twardowski and, of course, Edmund Husserl.

Further reading

Brentano, Franz. *Descriptive Psychology*. Trans. B. Müller. London: Routledge, 1995.
Brentano, Franz. *On the Several Senses of Being in Aristotle*. Trans. R. George. Berkeley: University of California Press, 1975.

Brentano, Franz. *The Psychology of Aristotle*. Trans. R. George. London: University of California Press, 1977.

Brentano, Franz. *Psychology from an Empirical Standpoint*. Trans. A. C. Rancurello, D. B. Terrell and L. L. McAlister. Second Edition. New Introduction by Peter Simons. London: Routledge, 1995.

Brentano, Franz. *The True and the Evident*. Trans. R. Chisholm. London: Routledge & Kegan Paul, 1966.

Albertazzi, Liliana, Massimo Libardi and Roberto Poli. Eds. *The School of Franz Brentano*. Dordrecht: Kluwer, 1996.

Chisholm, Roderick M. and Peter Simons. "Brentano, Franz Clemens (1838–1917)", in E. Grant, ed., *Routledge Encyclopedia of Philosophy* (London: Routledge, 2000), Vol. 2, pp. 12–17.

McAlister, Linda L. Ed. *The Philosophy of Franz Brentano*. London: Duckworth, 1976.

Moran, Dermot. "The Inaugural Address: Brentano's Thesis", *Proceedings of the Aristotelian Society*. Supplementary Volume LXX, 1996, pp. 1–27.

Smith, Barry. *Austrian Philosophy. The Legacy of Franz Brentano*. Chicago, IL: Open Court, 1994.

Stegmüller, Wolfgang. "The Philosophy of Self-Evidence: Franz Brentano", in *Main Currents in Contemporary German, British and American Philosophy*. Dordrecht: Reidel, 1969.

1

PSYCHOLOGY FROM AN EMPIRICAL STANDPOINT

Foreword to the 1874 Edition

The title which I have given this work characterizes both its object and its method. My psychological standpoint is empirical; experience alone is my teacher. Yet I share with other thinkers the conviction that this is entirely compatible with a certain ideal point of view. The way in which I conceive of psychological method will be presented in more detail in the first of the six books into which this work is divided. The first book discusses psychology as a science, the second considers mental phenomena in general. A third book, to follow, will investigate the characteristics of, and the laws governing, presentations; the fourth will concern itself with the characteristics and laws of judgements; and the fifth with those of the emotions and, in particular, of acts of will. The final book will deal with the relationship between mind and body, and there we shall also pursue the question of whether it is conceivable that mental life continues after the disintegration of the body.

Thus the plan of this work embraces all the different and essential fields of psychology. It is not our purpose, however, to write a compendium of this science, although we shall nevertheless strive to make our presentation clear and comprehensible enough for anyone interested in philosophical investigations. We often dwell at great length upon certain specific problems, and we are more concerned that the foundations be firmly established than we are with comprehensiveness. Perhaps people will find this careful method exaggerated and tedious, but I would rather be criticized for this than be accused of not having tried to justify my assertions sufficiently. Our most urgent need in psychology is not the variety and universality of the tenets, but rather the unity of the doctrine. Within this framework we must strive to attain what first mathematics and then physics, chemistry, and physiology have already attained, i.e. a core of generally accepted truths capable of attracting to it contributions from all other fields of scientific endeavor. We must seek to establish a single unified science of psychology in place of the many psychologies we now have.

In addition, just as there is no specifically German truth, there is no specifically national psychology, not even a German one. It is for this reason that I am taking into account the outstanding scientific contributions of modern English philosophers no less than those of German philosophers.

F. von Brentano, *Psychology from an Empirical Standpoint*, 1995, trans. A. C. Rancurello, D. B. Terrell and L. L. McAlister, pp. xxvii–xxix. London and New York: Routledge.

There is no doubt that science is badly served by indiscriminate compromises, since they sacrifice the unity and coherence of the doctrine to the unity and agreement of the teachers. Indeed, nothing has led to a splintering of philosophical outlooks more than eclecticism.

In science, just as in politics, it is difficult to reach agreement without conflict, but in scientific disputes we should not proceed in such a way as to seek the triumph of this or that investigator, but only the triumph of truth. The driving force behind these battles ought not to be ambition, but the longing for a common subordination to truth, which is one and indivisible. For this reason, just as I have proceeded without restraint to refute and discard the opinions of others whenever they seemed to be erroneous, so I will readily and gratefully welcome any correction of my views which might be suggested to me. In these investigations and in those which will follow I assail quite frequently and with great tenacity even the most outstanding investigators such as Mill, Bain, Fechner, Lotze, Helmholtz and others, but this should not be interpreted as an attempt either to lessen their merit or weaken the power of their influence. On the contrary, it is a sign that I, like many others, have felt their influence in a special way and have profited from their doctrines, not only when I have accepted them, but also when I have had to challenge them. I hope, therefore, that following my example, others can benefit from a thoroughgoing evaluation of their theories.

I am also very well aware of the fact that frequently my arguments will be directed against opinions which I do not consider to be of great intrinsic interest. I was prompted to undertake a rather detailed study of these opinions because at the present time they enjoy an undue popularity and exert a lamentable influence upon a public which, in matters of psychology even less than in other fields, has not yet learned to demand scientific cogency.

Quite frequently the reader will find that I advance opinions which have not been expressed before. It will, I believe, be readily apparent that in no instance have I been concerned with novelty for its own sake. On the contrary, I have departed from traditional conceptions only reluctantly and only when I was compelled to do so by the dominating force of reasons which seemed, to me at least, to be overpowering. Moreover, a closer analysis will reveal that even when I seem to be expressing the most original ideas, to some extent these views have already been anticipated. I have not failed to call attention to such earlier anticipations, and even when my viewpoint has developed independently of previous analogous views, I have not neglected to mention them, since it has not been my concern to appear to be the inventor of a new doctrine, but rather the advocate of a true and established one.

If earlier theories sometimes turn out to be viewed only as anticipations of more accurate doctrines, my own work can be no more than a mere preparation for future, more perfect accomplishments. In our own time a certain philosophy, which succeeded for a while in presenting itself as the final embodiment of all science, was soon seen to be unimprovable rather than unsurpassable. A scientific doctrine which precludes further development toward a more perfect life is a stillborn child. Contemporary psychology, in particular, finds itself in a situation in which those who claim to be its experts betray a greater ignorance than those who confess with Socrates, "I know only one thing – that I know nothing."

The truth, however, lies in neither extreme. There exist at the present time the beginnings of a scientific psychology. Although inconspicuous in themselves, these beginnings are indisputable signs of the possibility of a fuller development which will some day bear abundant fruit, if only for future generations.

Aschaffenburg
March 7, 1874

2

THE DISTINCTION BETWEEN MENTAL AND PHYSICAL PHENOMENA

1. All the appearances of our consciousness are divided into two great classes – the class of physical and the class of mental phenomena. We spoke of this distinction earlier when we established the concept of psychology, and we returned to it again in our discussion of psychological method. But what we have said is still not sufficient. We must now establish more firmly and more exactly what was only mentioned in passing before.

This seems all the more necessary since neither agreement nor complete clarity has been achieved regarding the delimitation of the two classes. We have already seen how physical phenomena which appear in the imagination are sometimes taken for mental phenomena. There are many other such instances of confusion. And even important psychologists may be hard pressed to defend themselves against the charge of self-contradiction. For instance, we encounter statements like the following: sensation and imagination are distinguished by the fact that one occurs as the result of a physical phenomenon, while the other is evoked by a mental phenomenon according to the laws of association. But then the same psychologists admit that what appears in sensation does not correspond to its efficient cause. Thus it turns out that the so-called physical phenomenon does not actually appear to us, and, indeed, that we have no presentation of it whatsoever – certainly a curious misuse of the term "phenomenon"! Given such a state of affairs, we cannot avoid going into the question in somewhat greater detail.

2. The explanation we are seeking is not a definition according to the traditional rules of logic. These rules have recently been the object of impartial criticism, and much could be added to what has already been said. Our aim is to clarify the meaning of the two terms *physical phenomenon* and *mental phenomenon*," removing all misunderstanding and confusion concerning them. And it does not matter to us what means we use, as long as they really serve to clarify these terms.

To this end, it is not sufficient merely to specify more general, more inclusive definitions. Just as deduction is opposed to induction when we speak of kinds of proof, in this case explanation by means of subsumption under a general term is opposed to explanation by means of particulars, through examples. And the latter

F. von Brentano, *Psychology from an Empirical Standpoint*, 1995, trans. A. C. Rancurello, D. B. Terrell and L. L. McAlister, pp. 77–100. London and New York: Routledge.

kind of explanation is appropriate whenever the particular terms are clearer than the general ones. Thus it is probably a more effective procedure to explain the term "color" by saying that it designates the class which contains red, blue, green and yellow, than to do the opposite and attempt to explain "red" by saying it is a particular kind of color. Moreover, explanation through particular definitions will be of even greater use when we are dealing, as in our case, with terms which are not common in ordinary life, while those for the individual phenomena included under them are frequently used. So let us first of all try to clarify the concepts by means of examples.

Every idea or presentation (*Vorstellung*) which we acquire either through sense perception or imagination is an example of a mental phenomenon.[1] By presentation I do not mean that which is presented, but rather the act of presentation. Thus, hearing a sound, seeing a colored object, feeling warmth or cold, as well as similar states of imagination are examples of what I mean by this term. I also mean by it the thinking of a general concept, provided such a thing actually does occur. Furthermore, every judgement, every recollection, every expectation, every inference, every conviction or opinion, every doubt, is a mental phenomenon. Also to be included under this term is every emotion: joy, sorrow, fear, hope, courage, despair, anger, love, hate, desire, act of will, intention, astonishment, admiration, contempt, etc.

Examples of physical phenomena, on the other hand, are a color, a figure, a landscape which I see, a chord which I hear, warmth, cold, odor which I sense; as well as similar images which appear in the imagination.

These examples may suffice to illustrate the differences between the two classes of phenomena.

3. Yet we still want to try to find a different and a more unified way of explaining mental phenomena. For this purpose we make use of a definition we used earlier when we said that the term "mental phenomena" applies to presentations as well as to all the phenomena which are based upon presentations. It is hardly necessary to mention again that by "presentation" we do not mean that which is presented, but rather the presenting of it. This act of presentation forms the foundation not merely of the act of judging, but also of desiring and of every other mental act. Nothing can be judged, desired, hoped or feared, unless one has a presentation of that thing. Thus the definition given includes all the examples of mental phenomena which we listed above, and in general all the phenomena belonging to this domain.

It is a sign of the immature state of psychology that we can scarcely utter a single sentence about mental phenomena which will not be disputed by many people. Nevertheless, most psychologists agree with what we have just said, namely, that presentations are the foundation for the other mental phenomena. Thus Herbart asserts quite rightly, "Every time we have a feeling, there will be something or other presented in consciousness, even though it may be something very diversified, confused and varied, so that this particular presentation is included in this particular feeling. Likewise, whenever we desire something . . . we have before our minds that which we desire."[2]

Herbart then goes further, however. He sees all other phenomena as nothing but certain states of presentations which are derivable from the presentations themselves. This view has already been attacked repeatedly with decisive arguments, in particular by Lotze. Most recently, J. B. Meyer, among others, has set forth a long criticism of it in his account of Kant's psychology. But Meyer was not satisfied to deny that feelings and desires could be derived from presentations. He claims that phenomena of this kind can exist in the absence of presentations.[3] Indeed, Meyer believes that the lowest forms of animal life have feelings and desires, but no presentations and also that the lives of higher animals and men begin with mere feelings and desires, while presentations emerge only upon further development.[4] Thus Meyer, too, seems to come into conflict with our claim.

But, if I am not mistaken, the conflict is more apparent than real. Several of his expressions suggest that Meyer has a narrower concept of presentation than we have, while he correspondingly broadens the concept of feeling. "Presentation," he says, "begins when the modification which we experience in our own state can be understood as the result of an external stimulus, even if this at first expresses itself only in the unconscious looking around or feeling around for an external object which results from it." If Meyer means by "presentation" the same thing that we do, he could not possibly speak in this way. He would see that a condition such as the one he describes as the origin of presentation, already involves an abundance of presentations, for example, the idea of temporal succession, ideas of spatial proximity and ideas of cause and effect. If all of these ideas must already be present in the mind in order for there to be a presentation in Meyer's sense, it is absolutely clear that such a thing cannot be the basis of every other mental phenomenon. Even the "being present" of any single one of the things mentioned is "being presented" in our sense. And such things occur whenever something appears in consciousness, whether it is hated, loved, or regarded indifferently, whether it is affirmed or denied or there is a complete withholding of judgement and – I cannot express myself in any other way than to say – it is presented. As we use the verb "to present," "to be presented" means the same as "to appear."

Meyer himself admits that a presentation in this sense is presupposed by every feeling of pleasure and pain, even the lowliest, although, since his terminology differs from ours, he calls this a feeling and not a presentation. At least that is what seems to me to emerge from the following passage: "There is no intermediate state between sensation and non-sensation. . . . Now the simplest form of sensation need be nothing more than a mere *sensation of change* in one's own body or a part thereof, caused by some stimulus. Beings endowed with such sensations would only have a *feeling of their own states.* A sensibility of the soul for the changes which are favorable or harmful to it could very well be directly connected with this *vital feeling* for the events beneath one's own skin, even if this *new sensitivity* could not simply be derived from that feeling: such a soul could have *feelings* of pleasure and pain *along with the sensation.* . . . A soul so endowed still has no Presentations."[5] It is easy to see that what is, in our view, the only thing which deserves the name "feeling," also emerges according to J. B. Meyer as the second element. It is preceded by another element which falls under the concept of a presentation as we understand it, and which constitutes the indispensable precondition for this second phenomenon. So it would seem that if Meyer's view were translated into our terminology, the opposition would disappear automatically.

Perhaps a similar situation obtains, too, in the case of others who express themselves in a manner similar to Meyer's. Yet it may still be the case that with respect to some kinds of sensory pleasure and pain feelings, someone may really be of the opinion that there are no presentations involved, even in our sense. At least we cannot deny that there is a certain temptation to do this. This is true, for example, with regard to the feelings present when one is cut or burned. When someone is cut he has no perception of touch, and someone who is burned has no feeling of warmth, but in both cases there is only the feeling of pain.

Nevertheless there is no doubt that even here the feeling is based upon a presentation. In cases such as this we always have a presentation of a definite spatial location which we usually characterize in relation to some visible and touchable part of our body. We say that our foot or our hand hurts, that this or that part of the body is in pain. Those who consider such a spatial presentation something originally given by the neural stimulation itself cannot deny that a presentation is the basis of this feeling. But others cannot avoid this assumption either. For there is in us not only the idea of a definite spatial location but also that of a particular sensory quality analogous to color, sound and other so-called sensory qualities, which is a physical phenomenon and which must be clearly distinguished from the accompanying feeling. If we hear a pleasing and mild sound or a shrill one, harmonious chord or a dissonance, it would not occur to anyone to identify the sound with the accompanying feeling of pleasure or pain. But then in cases where a feeling of pain or pleasure is aroused in us by a cut, a burn or a tickle, we must distinguish in the same way between a physical phenomenon, which appears as the object of external perception, and the mental phenomenon of feeling, which accompanies its appearance, even though in this case the superficial observer is rather inclined to confuse them.

The principal basis for this misconception is probably the following. It is well known that our perceptions are mediated by the so-called afferent nerves. In the past people thought that certain nerves served as conductors of each kind of sensory qualities, such as color, sound, etc. Recently, however, physiologists have been more and more inclined to take the opposite point of view.[6] And they teach almost universally that the nerves for tactile sensations, if stimulated in a certain way, produce sensations of warmth and cold in us, and if stimulated in another way produce in us so-called pleasure and pain sensations. In reality, however, something similar is true for all the nerves, insofar as a sensory phenomenon of the kind just mentioned can be produced in us by every nerve. In the presence of very strong stimuli, all nerves produce painful phenomena, which cannot be distinguished from one another. When a nerve transmits different kinds of sensations, it often happens that it transmits several at the same time. Looking into an electric light, for example, produces simultaneously a "beautiful," i.e. pleasant, color phenomenon and a phenomenon of another sort which is painful. The nerves of the tactile sense often simultaneously transmit a so-called sensation of touch, a sensation of warmth or cold, and a so-called sensation of pleasure or pain. Now we notice that when several sensory phenomena appear at the same time, they are not infrequently regarded as *one*. This has been demonstrated in a striking manner in regard to the sensations of smell and taste. It is well established that almost all the differences usually considered differences in taste are really only differences in the concomitant olfactory phenomena. Something similar occurs when we eat food cold or warm; we often think that it tastes different while in reality only the temperature sensations differ. It is not surprising, then, if we do not always distinguish precisely between a phenomenon which is a temperature sensation and another which is a tactile sensation. Perhaps we would not even distinguish between them at all if they did not ordinarily appear independently of one another. If we now look at the sensations of feeling, we find, on the contrary, that their phenomena are usually linked with another sort of sensation, and when the excitation is very strong these other sensations sink into insignificance beside them. Thus the fact that a given individual has been mistaken about the appearance of a particular class of sensory qualities and has believed that he has had one single sensation instead of two is very easily explained. Since the intervening idea was accompanied by a relatively very strong feeling, incomparably stronger than that which followed upon the first kind of quality, the person considers this mental phenomenon as the only new thing he has experienced. In addition, if the first kind of quality disappeared completely, then he would believe that he possessed only a feeling without any underlying presentation of a physical phenomenon.

A further basis for this illusion is the fact that the quality which precedes the feeling and the feeling itself do not have two distinct names. The physical phenomenon which appears along with the feeling of pain is also called pain. Indeed, we do not say that we sense this or that phenomenon in the foot with pain; we say that we feel pain in the foot. This is an equivocation, such as, indeed, we often find when different things are closely related to one another. We call the body healthy, and in reference to it we say that the air, the food, the color of the face, etc., are healthy, but obviously in another sense. In our case, the physical phenomenon itself is called pleasure or pain after the feeling of pleasure or pain which accompanies the appearance of the physical phenomenon, and there, too, in a modified sense of the words. It is as if we would say of a harmonious chord that it is a pleasure because we experience pleasure when we hear it, or, too, that the loss of a friend is a great sorrow for us. Experience shows that equivocation is one of the main obstacles to recognizing distinctions. And it must necessarily be the largest obstacle here where there is an inherent danger of confusion and perhaps the extension of the term was itself the result of this confusion. Thus many psychologists were deceived by this equivocation and this error fostered further errors. Some came to the false conclusion that the sensing subject must be present at the spot in the injured limb in which a painful phenomenon is located in perception. Then, since they identified the phenomenon with the accompanying pain sensation, they regarded this phenomenon as a mental rather than a physical phenomenon. It is precisely for this reason that they thought that its perception in the limb was an inner, and consequently evident and infallible perception.[7] Their view is contradicted by the fact that the same phenomena often appear in the same way after the amputation of the limb. For this reason others argued, in a rather skeptical manner, against the self-evidence of inner perception. The difficulty disappears if we distinguish between pain in the sense in which the term describes the apparent condition of a part of our body, and the feeling of pain which is connected with the concomitant sensation. Keeping this in mind, we shall no longer be inclined to assert that there is no presentation at the basis of the feeling of sensory pain experienced when one is injured.

Accordingly, we may consider the following definition of mental phenomena as indubitably correct: they are either presentations or they are based upon presentations in the sense described above. Such a definition offers a second, more simple explanation of this concept. This explanation, of course, is not completely unified because it separates mental phenomena into two groups.

4. People have tried to formulate a completely unified definition which distinguishes all mental phenomena from physical phenomena by means of negation. All physical phenomena, it is said, have extension and spatial location, whether they are phenomena of vision or of some other sense, or products of the imagination, which presents similar objects to us. The opposite, however, is true of mental phenomena; thinking, willing and the like appear without extension and without spatial location.

According to this view, it would be possible for us to characterize physical phenomena easily and exactly in contrast to mental phenomena by saying that they are those phenomena which appear extended and localized in space. Mental phenomena would then be definable with equal exactness as those phenomena which do not have extension or spatial location. Descartes and Spinoza could be cited in support of such a distinction. The chief advocate of this view, however, is Kant, who explains space as the form of the intuition of the external sense.

Recently Bain has given the same definition:

> The department of the Object, or Object-World, is exactly circumscribed by one property, Extension. The world of Subject-experience is devoid of this property. A tree or a river is said to possess extended magnitude. A pleasure has no length, breadth, or thickness; it is in no respect an extended thing. A thought or idea may refer to extended magnitudes, but it cannot be said to have extension in itself. Neither can we say that an act of the will, a desire or a belief occupy dimensions in space. Hence all that comes within the sphere of the Subject is spoken of as the Unextended.
>
> Thus, if Mind, as commonly happens, is put for the sum-total of Subject-experiences, we may define it negatively by a single fact – the absence of Extension.[8]

Thus it seems that we have found, at least negatively, a unified definition for the totality of mental phenomena.

But even on this point there is no unanimity among psychologists, and we hear it denied for contradictory reasons that extension and lack of extension are characteristics which distinguish physical and mental phenomena.

Many declare that this definition is false because not only mental phenomena, but also many physical phenomena appear to be without extension. A large number of not unimportant psychologists, for example, teach that the phenomena of some, or even of all of our senses originally appear apart from all extension and spatial location. In particular, this view is quite generally held with respect to sounds and olfactory phenomena. It is true of colors according to Berkeley, of the phenomena of touch according to Platner, and of the phenomena of all the external senses according to Herbart and Lotze, as well as according to Hartley, Brown, the two Mills, H. Spencer and others. Indeed it seems that the phenomena revealed by the external senses, especially sight and the sense of touch, are all spatially extended. The reason for this, it is said, is that we connect them with spatial presentations that are gradually developed on the basis of earlier experiences. They are originally without spatial location, and we subsequently localize them. If this were really the only way in which physical phenomena attain spatial location we could obviously no longer separate the two areas by reference to this property. In fact, mental phenomena are also localized by us in this way, as, for example, when we locate a phenomenon of anger in the irritated lion, and our own thoughts in the space which we occupy.

This is one way in which the above definition has been criticized by a great number of eminent psychologists, including Bain. At first sight he seems to defend such a definition, but in reality he follows Hartley's lead on this issue. He has only been able to express himself as he does because he does not actually consider the phenomena of the external senses, in and for themselves, to be physical phenomena (although he is not always consistent in this).

Others, as we said, will reject this definition for the opposite reason. It is not so much the assertion that all physical phenomena appear extended that provokes them, but rather the assertion that all mental phenomena lack extension. According to them, certain mental phenomena also appear to be extended. Aristotle seems to have been of this opinion when, in the first chapter of this treatise on sense and sense objects he considers it immediately evident, without any prior proof, that sense perception is the act of a bodily organ.[9] Modern psychologists and physiologists sometimes express themselves in the same way regarding certain affects. They speak of feelings of pleasure or pain which appear in the external organs, sometimes even after the amputation of the limb and yet, feeling, like perception, is a mental phenomenon. Some authors even maintain that sensory appetites appear localized. This view is shared by the poet when he speaks, not, to be sure, of thought, but of rapture and longing which suffuse the heart and all parts of the body.

Thus we see that the distinction under discussion is disputed from the point of view of both physical and mental phenomena. Perhaps both of these objections are equally unjustified.[10] At any rate, another definition common to all mental phenomena is still desirable. Whether certain mental and physical phenomena appear extended or not, the controversy proves that the criterion given for a clear separation is not adequate. Furthermore, this criterion gives us only a negative definition of mental phenomena.

5. What positive criterion shall we now be able to provide? Or is there perhaps no positive definition which holds true of all mental phenomena generally? Bain thinks that in fact there is none.[11] Nevertheless, psychologists in earlier times have already pointed out that there is a special affinity and analogy which exists among all mental phenomena, and which physical phenomena do not share.

Every mental phenomenon is characterized by what the Scholastics of the Middle Ages called the intentional (or mental)[12] inexistence (*Inexistenz*) of an object, (*Gegenstand*) and what we might call, though not wholly unambiguously, reference to a content, direction toward an object (which is not to be understood here as meaning a thing), or immanent objectivity. Every mental phenomenon includes something as object within itself, although they do not all do so in the same way. In presentation something is presented, in judgement something is affirmed or denied, in love loved, in hate hated, in desire desired and so on.[13]

This intentional in-existence is characteristic exclusively of mental phenomena.

41

No physical phenomenon exhibits anything like it. We can, therefore, define mental phenomena by saying that they are those phenomena which contain an object intentionally within themselves.

But here, too, we come upon controversies and contradiction. Hamilton, in particular, denies this characteristic to a whole broad class of mental phenomena, namely, to all those which he characterizes as feelings, to pleasure and pain in all their most diverse shades and varieties. With respect to the phenomena of thought and desire he is in agreement with us. Obviously there is no act of thinking without an object that is thought, nor a desire without an object that is desired. "In the phenomena of Feelings – the phenomena of Pleasure and Pain – on the contrary, consciousness does not place the mental modification or state before itself; it does not contemplate it apart – as separate from itself – but is, as it were, fused into one. The peculiarity of Feeling, therefore, is that there is nothing but what is subjectively subjective; there is no object different from the self – no objectification of any mode of self."[14] In the first instance there would be something which, according to Hamilton's terminology, is "objective," in the second instance something which is "objectively subjective," as in self-awareness, the object of which Hamilton consequently calls the "subject-object." By denying both concerning feelings, Hamilton rejects unequivocably all intentional in-existence of these phenomena.

In reality, what Hamilton says is not entirely correct, since certain feelings undeniably refer to objects. Our language itself indicates this through the expressions it employs. We say that we are pleased with or about something, that we feel sorrow or grieve about something. Likewise, we say: that pleases me, that hurts me, that makes me feel sorry, etc. Joy and sorrow, like affirmation and negation, love and hate, desire and aversion, clearly follow upon a presentation and are related to that which is presented.

One is most inclined to agree with Hamilton in those cases in which, as we saw earlier, it is most easy to fall into the error that feeling is not based upon any presentation: the case of pain caused by a cut or a burn, for example. But the reason is simply the same temptation toward this, as we have seen, erroneous assumption. Even Hamilton recognizes with us the fact that presentations occur without exception and thus even here they form the basis of the feeling. Thus his denial that feelings have an object seems all the more striking.

One thing certainly has to be admitted; the object to which a feeling refers is not always an external object. Even in cases where I hear a harmonious sound, the pleasure which I feel is not actually pleasure in the sound but pleasure in the hearing. In fact you could say, not incorrectly, that in a certain sense it even refers to itself, and this introduces, more or less, what Hamilton was talking about, namely that the feeling and the object are "fused into one." But this is nothing that is not true in the same way of many phenomena of thought and knowledge, as we will see when we come to the investigation of inner consciousness. Still they retain a mental inexistence, a Subject-Object, to use Hamilton's mode of speech, and the same thing is true of these feelings. Hamilton is wrong when he says that with regard to feelings everything is "subjectively subjective" – an expression which is actually self-contradictory, for where you cannot speak of an object, you cannot speak of a subject either. Also, Hamilton spoke of a fusing into one of the feeling with the mental impression, but when carefully considered it can be seen that he is bearing witness against himself here. Every fusion is a unification of several things; and thus the pictorial expression which is intended to make us concretely aware of the distinctive character of feeling still points to a certain duality in the unity.

We may, therefore, consider the intentional in-existence of an object to be a general characteristic of mental phenomena which distinguishes this class of phenomena from the class of physical phenomena.

6. Another characteristic which all mental phenomena have in common is the fact that they are only perceived in inner consciousness, while in the case of physical phenomena only external perception is possible. This distinguishing characteristic is emphasized by Hamilton.[15]

It could be argued that such a definition is not very meaningful. In fact, it seems much more natural to define the act according to the object, and therefore to state that inner perception, in contrast to every other kind, is the perception of mental phenomena. However, besides the fact that it has a special object, inner perception possesses another distinguishing characteristic: its immediate, infallible self-evidence. Of all the types of knowledge of the objects of experience, inner perception alone possesses this characteristic. Consequently, when we say that mental phenomena are those which are apprehended by means of inner perception, we say that their perception is immediately evident.

Moreover, inner perception is not merely the only kind of perception which is immediately evident; it is really the only perception in the strict sense of the word. As we have seen, the phenomena of the so-called external perception cannot be proved true and real even by means of indirect demonstration. For this reason, anyone who in good faith has taken them for what they seem to be is being misled by the manner in which the phenomena are connected. Therefore, strictly speaking, so-called external perception is not perception. Mental phenomena, therefore, may be described as the only phenomena of which perception in the strict sense of the word is possible.

This definition, too, is an adequate characterization of mental phenomena. That is not to say that all mental phenomena are internally perceivable by all men, and so all those which someone cannot perceive are to be included by him among physical phenomena. On the contrary, as we have already expressly noted above, it is obvious that no mental phenomenon is perceived by more than one individual. At the same time, however, we also saw that every type of mental phenomenon is present in every fully developed human mental life. For this reason, the reference to the phenomena which constitute the realm of inner perception serves our purpose satisfactorily.

7. We said that mental phenomena are those phenomena which alone can be perceived in the strict sense of the word. We could just as well say that they are those phenomena which alone possess real existence as well as intentional existence. Knowledge, joy and desire really exist. Color, sound and warmth have only a phenomenal and intentional existence.

There are philosophers who go so far as to say that it is self-evident that phenomena such as those which we call physical phenomena *could not* correspond to any reality. According to them, the assertion that these phenomena have an existence different from mental existence is self-contradictory. Thus, for example, Bain says that attempts have been made to explain the phenomena of external perception by supposing a material world, "in the first instance; detached from perception, and, afterwards, coming into perception, by operating upon the mind." "This view," he says, "involves a contradiction. The prevailing doctrine is that a tree is something in itself apart from all perception; that, by its luminous emanations, it impresses our mind and is then perceived, the perception being an effect, and the unperceived tree [i.e. the one which exists outside of perception] the cause. But the tree is known only through perception; what it may be anterior to, or independent of, perception, we cannot tell; we can think of it as perceived but not as unperceived. There is a manifest contradiction in the supposition; we are required at the same moment to perceive the thing and not to perceive it. We know the touch of iron, but we cannot know the touch apart from the touch."[16]

I must confess that I am unable to convince myself of the soundness of this argument. It is undoubtedly true that a color appears to us only when we have a presentation of it. We cannot conclude from this, however, that a color cannot exist without being presented. Only if the state of being presented were contained in the color as one of its elements, as a certain quality and intensity is contained in it, would a color which is not presented imply a contradiction, since a whole without one of its parts is indeed a contradiction. But this is obviously not the case. Otherwise, it would also be absolutely inconceivable how the belief in the real existence of physical phenomena outside our presentation could have, not to say originated, but achieved the most general dissemination, been maintained with the utmost tenacity, and, indeed, even been shared for a long time by the most outstanding thinkers. Bain said: "We can think of a tree as perceived, but not as unperceived. There is a manifest contradiction in the supposition." If what he said were correct, his further conclusions could not be objected to. But it is precisely this which cannot be granted. Bain explains this statement by remarking, "We are required at the same moment to perceive the thing and not to perceive it." It is not correct, however, to say that such a demand is placed upon us, for, in the first place, not every act of thinking is a perception. Secondly, even if this were the case, it would only follow that we can think only of trees that have been perceived by us, but not that we can think only of trees *as perceived by us*. To taste a piece of white sugar does not mean to taste a piece of sugar *as white*. The fallacy reveals itself quite clearly in the case of mental phenomena. If someone said, "I cannot think about a mental phenomenon without thinking about it; therefore I can only think about mental phenomena as thought by me; therefore no mental phenomenon exists outside my thinking," his method of reasoning would be identical to that of Bain. Nevertheless, even Bain will not deny that his individual mental life is not the only one which has actual existence. When Bain adds: "we know the touch of iron, but it is not possible that we should know the touch apart from the touch," he obviously uses the word "touch" first to mean the object that is sensed and secondly to mean the act of sensing. These are different concepts, even though the word is the same. Consequently, only those who would let themselves be deceived by this equivocation could grant the existence of immediate evidence as postulated by Bain.

It is not correct, therefore, to say that the assumption that there exists a physical phenomenon outside the mind which is just as real as those which we find intentionally in us, implies a contradiction. It is only that, when we compare one with the other we discover conflicts which clearly show that no real existence corresponds to the intentional existence in this case. And even if this applies only to the realm of our own experience, we will nevertheless make no mistake if in general we deny to physical phenomena any existence other than intentional existence.[17]

8. There is still another circumstance which people have said distinguishes between physical and mental phenomena. They say that mental phenomena always manifest themselves serially, while many physical phenomena manifest themselves simultaneously. But people do not always mean the same thing by this assertion, and not all of the meanings which it has been given are in accord with the truth.

Recently Herbert Spencer expressed himself on this subject in the following vein: "The two great classes of vital actions called Physiology and Psychology are broadly distinguished in this, that while the one includes both simultaneous and successive changes the other includes successive changes only. The phenomena forming the subject matter of Physiology present themselves as an immense number of different series bound up together. Those forming the subject matter of psychology present themselves as but a single series. A glance at the many continuous actions constituting the life of the body at large shows that they are synchronous – that digestion, circulation, respiration, excretion, secretions, etc., in all their many sub-divisions are going on at one time in mutual dependence. And the briefest introspection makes it clear that the actions constituting thought occur, not together, but one after another."[18] Spencer restricts his comparison to physiological and physical phenomena found in one and the same organism endowed with mental life. If he had not done this, he would have been forced to admit that many series of mental phenomena occur simultaneously too, because there is more than one living being endowed with mental life in the world. However, even within the limits which he has assigned to it, the assertion he advances is not entirely true. Spencer himself is so far from failing to recognize this fact that he immediately calls attention to those species of lower animals, for example the *radiata*, in which a multiple mental life goes on simultaneously in *one* body. For this reason he thinks – but others will not readily admit it – that there is little difference between mental and physical life.[19] In addition he makes further concessions which reduce the difference between physiological and mental phenomena to a mere matter of degree. Furthermore, if we ask ourselves what it is that Spencer conceives as those physiological phenomena whose changes, in contrast to the changes of mental phenomena, are supposed to occur simultaneously, it appears that he uses this term not to describe specifically physical phenomena, but rather the causes, which are in themselves unknown, of these phenomena. In fact, with respect to the physical phenomena which manifest themselves in sensation, it seems undeniable that they cannot modify themselves simultaneously, if the sensations themselves do not undergo simultaneous changes. Hence, we can hardly attain a distinguishing characteristic for the two classes of phenomena in this way.

Others have wanted to find a characteristic of mental life in the fact that consciousness can grasp simultaneously only *one object*, never more than one, at a time. They point to the remarkable case of the error that occurs in the determination of time. This error regularly appears in astronomical observations in which the simultaneous swing of the pendulum does not enter into consciousness simultaneously with, but earlier or later than, the moment when the observed star touches the hairline in the telescope.[20] Thus, mental phenomena always merely follow each other, one at a time, in a simple series. However, it would certainly be a mistake to generalize without further reflection from a case which implies such an extreme concentration of attention. Spencer, at least, says: "I find that there may sometimes be detected as many as five simultaneous series of nervous changes, which in various degrees rise into consciousness so far that we cannot call any of them absolutely unconscious. When walking, there is the locomotive series; there may be, under certain circumstances, a tactual series; there is very often (in myself at least), an auditory series, constituting some melody or fragment of a melody which haunts me; and there is the visual series: all of which, subordinate to the dominant consciousness formed by some train of reflection, are continually crossing it and weaving themselves into it."[21] The same facts are reported by Hamilton, Cardaillac, and other psychologists on the basis of their experiences. Assuming, however, that it were true that all cases of perception are similar to that of the astronomer, should we not always at least have to acknowledge the fact that frequently we think of something and at the same time make a judgement about it or desire it? So there would still be several simultaneous mental phenomena. Indeed, we could, with more reason, make the opposite assertion, namely, that very often many mental phenomena are present in consciousness simultaneously, while there can never be more than one physical phenomenon at a time.

What is the only sense, then, in which we might say that a mental phenomenon always appears by itself, while many physical phenomena can appear at the same time? We can say this insofar as the whole multiplicity of mental phenomena which appear to us in our inner perception always appear as a unity, while the same is not true of the physical phenomena which we grasp simultaneously through the so-called external perception. As happens frequently in other cases, so here, too, unity is confused by many psychologists with simplicity; as a result they have maintained that they perceive themselves in inner consciousness as something simple. Others, in contesting with good reason the simplicity of this phenomenon, at the same time denied its unity. The former could not maintain a consistent position because, as soon as they described their inner life, they found that they were mentioning a large variety of different elements; and the latter could not avoid involuntarily testifying to the unity of mental phenomena. They speak, as do others, of an "I" and not of a "we" and sometimes describe this as a "bundle" of phenomena, and at the other times by other names which characterize a fusion into an inner unity. When we perceive color, sound, warmth, odor simultaneously nothing prevents us from assigning each one to a particular thing. On the other hand, we are forced to take the multiplicity of the various acts of sensing, such as seeing, hearing, experiencing warmth and smelling, and the simultaneous acts of willing and feeling and reflecting, as well as the inner perception which provides us with the knowledge of all those, as parts of one single phenomenon in which they are contained, as one single and unified thing. We shall discuss in detail later on what constitutes the basis for this necessity. At that time we shall also present several other points pertaining to the same subject. The topic under discussion, in fact, is nothing other than the so-called unity of consciousness, one of the most important, but still contested, facts of psychology.

9. Let us, in conclusion, summarize the results of the discussion about the difference between mental and physical phenomena. First of all, we illustrated the

specific nature of the two classes by means of *examples*. We then defined mental phenomena as *presentations* or as phenomena which are based *upon presentation*; all the other phenomena being physical phenomena. Next we spoke of *extension*, which psychologists have asserted to be the specific characteristic of all physical phenomena, while all mental phenomena are supposed to be unextended. This assertion, however, ran into contradictions which can only be clarified by later investigations. All that can be determined now is that all mental phenomena really appear to be unextended. Further we found that the *intentional in-existence*, the reference to something as an object, is a distinguishing characteristic of all mental phenomena. No physical phenomenon exhibits anything similar. We went on to define mental phenomena as the exclusive *object of inner perception*; they alone, therefore, are perceived with immediate evidence. Indeed, in the strict sense of the word, they alone are perceived. On this basis we proceeded to define them as the only phenomena which possess *actual existence* in addition to intentional existence. Finally, we emphasized as a distinguishing characteristic the fact that the mental phenomena which we perceive, in spite of all their multiplicity, *always* appear to us *as a unity*, while physical phenomena, which we perceive at the same time, do not all appear in the same way as parts of one single phenomenon.

That feature which best characterizes mental phenomena is undoubtedly their intentional in-existence. By means of this and the other characteristics listed above, we may now consider mental phenomena to have been clearly differentiated from physical phenomena.

Our explanations of mental and physical phenomena cannot fail to place our earlier definitions of psychology and natural science in a clearer light. In fact, we have stated that the one is the science of mental phenomena, and the other the science of physical phenomena. It is now easy to see that both definitions tacitly include certain limitations.

This is especially true of the definition of the natural sciences. These sciences do not deal with all physical phenomena, but only with those which appear in sensation, and as such do not take into account the phenomena of imagination. And even in regard to the former they only determine their laws insofar as they depend on the physical stimulation of the sense organs. We could express the scientific task of the natural sciences by saying something to the effect that they are those sciences which seek to explain the succession of physical phenomena connected with normal and pure sensations (that is, sensations which are not influenced by special mental conditions and processes) on the basis of the assumption of a world which resembles one which has three dimensional extension in space and flows in *one* direction in time, and which influences our sense organs.[22] Without explaining the absolute nature of this world, these sciences would limit themselves to ascribing to its forces capable of producing sensations and of exerting a reciprocal influence upon one another, and determining for these forces the laws of co-existence and succession. Through these laws they would then establish indirectly the laws of succession of the physical phenomena of sensations, if, through scientific abstraction from the concomitant mental conditions, we admit that they manifest themselves in a pure state and as occurring in relation to a constant sensory capacity. We must interpret the expression "science of physical phenomena" in this somewhat complicated way if we want to identify it with natural science.[23]

We have nevertheless seen how the expression "physical phenomenon" is sometimes erroneously applied to the above mentioned forces themselves. And, since normally the object of a science is characterized as that object whose laws such a science determines directly and explicitly, I believe I will not be mistaken if I assume that the definition of natural science as the science of physical phenomena is frequently connected with the concept of forces belonging to a world which is similar to one extended in space and flowing in time; forces which, through their influence on the sense organs, arouse sensation and mutually influence each other in their action, and of which natural science investigates the laws of co-existence and succession. If those forces are considered as the object of natural sciences, there is also the advantage that this science appears to have as its object something that really and truly exists. This could, of course, also be attained if natural science were defined as the science of sensation, tacitly adding the same restriction which we have just mentioned. Indeed, the reason why the expression "physical phenomenon" is preferred probably stems from the fact that certain psychologists have thought that the external causes of sensations correspond to the physical phenomena which occur in them, either in all respects, which was the original point of view, or at least in respect to three-dimensional extension, which is the opinion of certain people at the present time. It is clear that the otherwise improper expression "external perception" stems from this conception. It must be added, however, that the act of sensing manifests, in addition to the intentional in-existence of the physical phenomenon, other characteristics with which the natural scientist is not at all concerned, since through them sensation does not give us information in the same way about the distinctive relationships which govern the external world.

With respect to the definition of psychology, it might first seem as if the concept of mental phenomena would have to be broadened rather than narrowed, both because the physical phenomena of imagination fall within its scope at least as much as mental phenomena as previously defined, and because the phenomena which occur in sensation cannot be disregarded in the theory of sensation. It is obvious, however, that they are taken into account only as the content of mental phenomena when we describe the specific characteristics of the latter. The same is true of all mental phenomena which have a purely phenomenal existence. We must consider only mental phenomena in the sense of real states as the proper object of psychology. And it is in reference only to these phenomena that we say that psychology is the science of mental phenomena.

Notes

1 *Editor's Note*: "*Examples of mental phenomena.*" Brentano consequently understands "mental phenomenon" to mean the same as "mental activity," and what is characteristic of it, in his opinion, is the "reference to something as object," i.e. being concerned with something. With this the word φαινόμενον has become mere "internal linguistic form." The same thing holds true of the word "activity," since in Brentano's opinion every such activity, at least in men and animals, is a *passio*, an affection in the Aristotelian sense. So what we are concerned with is the sheer "having something as object" as the distinguishing feature of any act of consciousness, which Brentano also calls "state of consciousness."
2 *Psychologie als Wissenschaft*, Part II, Sect. 1, Chap. 1, No. 103. Cp. also Drobisch, *Empirische Psychologie*, p. 38, and others of Herbart's school.

3 *Kant's Psychologie* (Berlin, 1870), pp. 92 ff.

4 *Kant's Psychologie*, p. 94.

5 *Kant's Psychologie*, p. 92. J. B. Meyer seems to conceive of sensation in the same way as Überweg in his *Logik 1*, 2nd ed., p. 64. "Perception differs from mere sensation in that in sensation we are conscious only of the subjective state, while in perception there is another element which is perceived and which therefore stands apart from the act of perception as something different and objective." Even if Überweg's view of the difference between sensation and perception were correct, sensation would still involve a presentation in our sense. Why we consider it to be incorrect will be apparent later.

6 Cp. especially Wundt, *Principles of Physiological Psychology* (trans. Titchener), pp. 322 ff.

7 This is the opinion of the Jesuit, Tongiorgi, in his widely circulated philosophy textbook.

8 *Mental Science*, Introduction, Chap. 1.

9 *De Sensu et Sensibili*, 1, 436, b. 7. Cp. also what he says in *De Anima*, I, 1, 403 16, about affective states, in particular about fear.

10 The assertion that even mental phenomena appear to be extended rests obviously on a confusion of mental and physical phenomena similar to the confusion which we became convinced of above when we pointed out that a presentation is also the necessary foundation of sensory feelings.

11 *The Senses and the Intellect*, Introduction.

12 They also use the expression "to exist as an object (objectively) in something," which, if we wanted to use it at the present time, would be considered, on the contrary, as a designation of a real existence outside the mind. At least this is what is suggested by the expression "to exist immanently as an object," which is occasionally used in a similar sense, and in which the term "immanent" should obviously rule out the misunderstanding which is to be feared.

13 Aristotle himself spoke of this mental in-existence. In his books on the soul he says that the sensed object, as such, is in the sensing subject; that the sense contains the sensed object without its matter; that the object which is thought is in the thinking intellect. In Philo, likewise, we find the doctrine of mental existence and in-existence. However, since he confuses them with existence in the proper sense of the word, he reaches his contradictory doctrine of the *logos* and Ideas. The same is true of the Neoplatonists. St. Augustine in his doctrine of the *Verbum mentis* and of its inner origin touches upon the same fact. St. Anselm does the same in his famous ontological argument; many people have observed that his consideration of mental existence as a true existence is at the basis of his paralogism (cp. Überweg, *Geschichte der Philosophie*, II). St. Thomas Aquinas teaches that the object which is thought is intentionally in the thinking subject, the object which is loved in the person who loves, the object which is desired in the person desiring, and he uses this for theological purposes. When the Scriptures speak of an indwelling of the Holy Ghost, St. Thomas explains it as an intentional indwelling through love. In addition, he attempted to find, through the intentional in-existence in the acts of thinking and loving, a certain analogy for the mystery of the Trinity and the procession *ad intra* of the Word and the Spirit.

14 *Lecture on Metaphysics*, I, 432.

15 *Ibid.*

16 *Mental Science*, 3rd ed., p. 198.

17 *Editor's Note*: The attempt has been made to stamp Brentano as a phenomenalist on the basis of this sentence. That is completely mistaken. Brentano was always phenomenalism's most determined opponent. All he intends to say is that colored things, sounding extended things are intentionally given, i.e. we have them as objects, and that *such* qualitative extended things cannot be proved to exist, indeed that to affirm is in all probability a mistake. In this connection it is to be noted that the affirmation of colored extended things is false even when there *are* physical bodies. These bodies do not have qualities of color or sound, or the like; but every affirmation is an assertion of the entire content and our sensations are affirmative beliefs in what we sense. It is unconditionally certain that this belief, this impulse to grant their reality, is blind; i.e. it is not intrinsically logically justifiable, not experienced as being correct. This emerges from comparison with acts which are evident. At the same time it is extremely probable, according to all

the rules of induction and the calculation of probability, that the belief in the existence of qualitatively extended things is false. The demonstrative force of Locke's experiments and Aristotle's experiment with the round ball already reach that far. There are certain equivocations which may still work in favor of naive realism today (as when the physicist speaks of "pressure," but without thinking of the quality of pressure which we sense).

18 *Principles of Psychology*, 2nd edn. I, Sect. 177, 395.

19 *Principles of Psychology*, p. 397.

20 Cp. Bessel, *Astronomische Beobachtungen*, Sect. VIII Intro. (Königsberg, 1823), Intro. Struve, *Expedition Chronometrique*, etc. (Petersburg, 1844), p. 29.

21 *Principles of Psychology*, p. 398. Drobisch likewise says that it is a "fact that many series of ideas can pass simultaneously through consciousness, but, as it were, at different levels."

22 Cp. Überweg (*System der Logik*) in whose analysis not everything can be accepted. In particular, he is wrong when he asserts that the world of external causes is extended in space and time, instead of saying that it resembles one which is spatially and temporally extended.

23 This explanation does not coincide entirely with Kant's premises, but it approaches as far as possible his explanation. In a certain sense it comes nearer to J. S. Mill's views in his book against Hamilton (Chap. 11), without, however, agreeing with it in all the essential aspects. What Mill calls "the permanent possibilities of sensation," is closely related to what we have called forces. The relationship of our view with, as well as its essential departure from, Überweg's conception was already touched upon in the previous note.

3

DESCRIPTIVE PSYCHOLOGY OR DESCRIPTIVE PHENOMENOLOGY

From the Lectures of 1888–1889

The concept of descriptive psychology

1. By this I understand the analysing description of our phenomena.

2. By phenomena, however, [I understand] that which is perceived by us, in fact, what is perceived by us in the strict sense of the word.

3. This, for example, is not the case for the external world.

4. To be a phenomenon, something must exist in itself [*in sich sein*]. It is wrong to set phenomena in opposition to what exists in itself [*als sich Seienden*].

5. Something can be a phenomenon, however, without being a thing in itself, such as, for example, what is presented as such [*das Vorgestellte als solches*], or what is desired as such.

6. One is telling the truth if one says that phenomena are objects of inner perception, even though the term "inner" is actually superfluous. All phenomena are to be called inner because they all belong to one reality, be it as constituents or as correlates.

7. By calling the description of phenomena descriptive psychology one particularly emphasizes the contemplation of psychical realities. Genetic psychology is then added to it as the second part of psychology.

8. Physiology has to intervene forcefully in the latter, whereas descriptive psychology is relatively independent of it.

9. Descriptive psychology is the prior part [of psychology]. The relationship between it and genetic psychology is similar to the one between anatomy and physiology.

10. *The value of descriptive psychology.*

F. von Brentano, *Descriptive Psychology*, 1995, trans. and ed. Benito Müller, pp. 137–42. London and New York: Routledge.

(a) It is the foundation of genetic psychology.
(b) It has a value in itself because of the dignity of the psychical domain. [. . .]

The genesis of descriptive psychology

1. It would be a mistake to believe that, because our phenomena are partly real, partly non-real, it is possible to divide [the subject matter] such as to talk first of the ones and then of the others. The knowledge of the correlatives is one.

2. If we wish to describe the psychical domain, we must first show how the objects of our psychical activities and the differences in the modes of relation are to be understood.

3. The order according to the differences of the objects is sufficient. And for this we will only have to take into account the objects of presentations.

4. The order will be an affiliation [*Angliederung*]:

(a) Description of the objects of our experiences,
(b) of our original associations,
(c) of our superposed presentations,
(d) of the presentations of our inner perception.

Summary

1. I have briefly explained what I mean by descriptive psychology, and how it relates to genetic psychology and to psychology in general. This was followed by some remarks concerning the value of descriptive psychology and its difficulties. I have also explained my views on the way in which I wish to deal with the subject, and, in particular, on the way in which I wish to take into consideration last year's lectures.

2. Descriptive psychology, we said, sets itself the task of an analysing description of our phenomena, i.e. of our immediate experiential facts [*Erfahrungstatsachen*], or, what is the same, of the objects which we apprehend in our perception. In tackling this task today, we must above all provide a division [of the subject matter] which can be decisive for the order of the investigations. By perceptions we understand only those [features] which deserve that name truly and properly, and these are only those which, in contrast to the so-called outer perceptions, are usually called inner perceptions. The objects of inner perception exist truly and in themselves; for example, our thinking, our joy and our pain exist in themselves. It is thus an error to put phenomena in opposition to what exists in itself. What is required above all for something to be a phenomenon is rather that it exists in itself. Mind you, it is, however, not necessary that something which is a phenomenon be a thing in itself. Indeed this is not the case for much of what belongs to phenomena. The realities which fall into our perception are psychical, i.e. they display an intentional relation, a relation to an immanent object.

These realities are not possible without a correlate; and these correlates are not real.

3. The domain which we are to describe thus displays real and non-real phenomena.

Now, someone might possibly believe that from this we can infer grounds for dividing up [our] investigations. We could, say, first speak of the real and then of the non-real phenomena (or *vice versa*). But one will soon recognize that this is imprudent. The knowledge of correlatives is one [i.e. indivisible].

4. The matter must thus be approached completely differently. If we compare different psychical activities together with their correlates amongst one another, we will find that between them there is a difference either with respect to the object to which they refer, or with respect to the way in which they refer to it – in which case the difference can again be more or less profound and differentiated from various subordinate points of view. These two points of view are, in general, exhaustive; it can, however, also happen that differences occur simultaneously in both respects.

Examples:

imagine [*vorstellen*] a triangle,
wish for the luck of a friend.

5. If we want to describe a psychical activity, we will have to describe its particular object and the manner in which the activity refers to it. And if – according to the aims of descriptive psychology – we want to give a general description of the domain of our psychical activities, then we will have to show, in general, the nature of the objects of our psychical activities, and [the nature] of the differences of modes of relation in which we relate to them psychically.

It thus seems that we must take the difference of objects and the difference of modes of relation, one after the other, as decisive for the order of our investigation.

6. However, if we look more closely, we find that the order of the differences of objects is sufficient by itself.

This is so because the psychical relations and their differences themselves belong to the objects. Which is why an order according to objects can be fully sufficient for the whole.

7. In doing so we will only have to take the objects of presentations into consideration; for nothing can be an object of a psychical activity without at the same time being an object of a corresponding presentation.

8. Having said this, we shall order our description in the following manner: we give an analysing description

(a) of the objects of our experiences,
(b) of our original associations (or of our intuitive sensory mnemonic presentations [*sinnlich anschauliche Gedächtnisvorstellungen*]),

(c) of our superposed presentations (abstract presentations (concepts)),

(d) of the presentations of our inner perception.

The presentations of inner perception

Another question which can be raised is whether the presentations of one's own hearing [*Vorstellungen vom eigenen Hören*], seeing, etc., which we have when we experience sounds, colours, etc., belong likewise to the domain of experiences.

Aristotle spoke of a [perception (ἐν παρέργῳ)].

And today, many people might still be inclined to say that if one hears a tone, one's own hearing is concomitantly experienced.

However, this accompanying presentation of hearing itself turns out [(a)] to be a presentation of inner perception, and [(b)] to be more closely related to the other presentations of inner perception (such as, for example, the presentation of one's own judging, or wanting etc.) than to the experiential presentations [*Empfindungsvorstellungen*] of colours and sounds.

Admittedly, the other presentations of inner perception have also been called presentations of the inner sense. And if sense and experience are used correlatively and thus sensory presentation is taken to be the same as experiential presentation, then this would indicate that one wishes to count them all as experiential presentations.

Yet this would really be drawing somewhat bold conclusions, and moreover misinterpreting the intention in a majority of cases. The term "sense" has all too many equivocations (artistic sense, sense of justice). Why should it here not also be taken in a particular and, at most, analogous meaning?

At any rate, for the sake of clarity let me expressly say that we completely exclude from experiences the presentations which we have with the inner perception of our judging, our volition, etc. For them we have distinguished – as we may recall – a particular class [namely that of] (inner) perceptual presentations [*Wahrnehmungsvorstellungen*].

Experiences

[. . .]

Enough of the illustration of experiences by means of positive and negative examples.

If someone still desires a different analysis of the concept, then we can furthermore correctly say:

> experience is a *fundamental presentation with real psychical content* [of real physical phenomena (objects)]. [. . .]

4

LETTER TO ANTON MARTY

17 March, 1905

Dear Friend,

I have your kind letter. I see that the Roman Congress has also upset you a little. I wasn't disturbed myself, I must say, and I have tried to calm E. as well as K. in a letter sent today. Typographical errors are a nuisance, though, and because there were no offprints, I cannot even send a copy to you.

As for your account of Höfler's comments, I was baffled by the reference to the "content and immanent object" of thought (*"Inhalt" und "immanentes Objekt" der Vorstellung*).

When I spoke of "immanent object", I used the qualification "immanent" in order to avoid misunderstandings, since many use the unqualified term "object" to refer to that which is outside the mind. But by an *object* of a thought I meant what it is that the thought is about, whether or not there is anything outside the mind corresponding to the thought.

It has never been my view that the *immanent* object is identical with *"object of thought"* (*vorgestelltes Objekt*). What we think about is *the object* or *thing* and not the "object of thought". If, in our thought, we contemplate a horse, our thought has as its immanent object – not a "contemplated horse", but a *horse*. And strictly speaking only the horse – not the "contemplated horse" – can be called an object.

But the object need not exist. The person thinking may have something as the object of his thought even though that thing does not exist.

Of course it has long been customary to say that universals, *qua* universals, "exist in the mind" and not in reality, and such like. But this is incorrect if what is thus called "immanent" is taken to be the "contemplated horse" (*gedachtes Pferd*) or "the universal as object of thought" (*gedachtes Universale*). For "horse contemplated in general by me here and now" would then be the object of a general thought about a horse; it would be the correlate of me as an *individually* thinking person, as having this *individual* object of thought as object of thought. One could not say that universals *as universals* are in the mind, if one of the characteristics of the "things existing in the mind" is that they are "objects of my thought".

When Aristotle said the αἰσθητὸν ἐνεργείᾳ is in one's experience, he was also speaking of what you call simply "object". But because we do use the word "in" here, I allowed myself the term "immanent object", in order to say, not that the

F. von Brentano, *The True and the Evident*, 1966, ed. Oskar Kraus, trans. Roderick M. Chisolm, Ilse Politzer and Kurt R. Fischer, pp. 77–9. London and New York: Routledge & Kegan Paul/Humanities Press.

object exists, but that it *is* an object whether or not there is anything that corresponds to it. Its *being* an object, however, is merely the linguistic correlate of the person experiencing *having* it as object, i.e., his thinking of it in his experience.

Aristotle also says that the αἴσθησις receives the εἶδος without the ὕλη, just as the intellect, of course, takes up the εἶδος νοητόν in abstraction from the matter. Wasn't his thinking essentially the same as ours? The "contemplated horse" considered as object would be the object of inner perception, which the thinker perceives whenever he forms a correlative pair consisting of this "contemplated horse" along with his thinking about the horse; for correlatives are such that one cannot be perceived or apprehended without the other. But what are experienced as primary objects, or what are thought universally as primary objects of reason, are never themselves the objects of inner perception. Had I equated "object" with "object of thought", then I would have had to say that the primary thought relation has no object or content at all. So I protest against this foolishness that has been dreamed up and attributed to me. Just what statement of my views is it that Höfler is attacking? Certain passages in my *Psychologie*? – Or perhaps something I am supposed to have said in my lectures? But where? When? Before what audience? I would indeed like to know. I haven't looked at the *Psychologie* or my notebooks for a long time, but, as I remember, I put the matter in the way I have just described. I would like to have it made clear that, unless something incorrect was said, which I do not believe, I have always held (in agreement with Aristotle) that "horse" and not "contemplated horse" is the immanent object of those thoughts that pertain to horses. Naturally, however, I did say that "horse" is thought or contemplated by us, and that insofar as we do think of it (N.B., insofar as we think of the *horse* and not of the "contemplated horse") we have "horse" as (immanent) object.

But enough for now . . .

F.B.

Part II

EDMUND HUSSERL
Founder of Phenomenology

EDMUND HUSSERL (1859–1938)

Introduction

Edmund Husserl was born in Prossnitz, Moravia (now Prostejov, Czech Republic) in 1859. He studied mathematics and philosophy in the universities of Leipzig and Berlin (with the famous mathematician Carl Weierstrass), completing his doctorate in mathematics at the University of Vienna in 1882. Following a brief period as Weierstrass's assistant, Husserl moved to Vienna to study philosophy with Franz Brentano from 1884 to 1886. He then completed his *Habilitation* thesis, *On the Concept of Number, Psychological Analyses*, at Halle, with Brentano's former student, Carl Stumpf in 1887. His first book, *The Philosophy of Arithmetic* (1891), an expansion of his *Habilitation* thesis, applied descriptive psychology, as practised by Brentano and Stumpf, to account for the composition of numbers in consciousness, as a first step to providing a theoretical foundation for arithmetic. During the 1890s Husserl deepened his research into fundamental issues in mathematics and logic, and corresponded with leading mathematicians, including Georg Cantor and Gottlob Frege. The results of a decade's work were his 'ground-breaking' *Logical Investigations* (1900–1901), in two volumes, that promoted a new approach to analysing the experiences of thought and knowing through 'phenomenology'.

The first book, *Prolegomena to a Pure Logic* (1900), defended logic as an a priori science of pure truths – tautologies – and rejected the attempt (known as *psychologism*) to reduce logic to psychology as falsifying the true meaning of science, denying the ideality of the realm of logical and mathematical objects, and leading to relativist and sceptical consequences. Husserl thereby distanced himself from his own earlier psychological approach in *Philosophy of Arithmetic*. The second book of the *Investigations* (1901) contained six Investigations that analysed and clarified the component elements involved in logical acts and acts of knowing in the broadest sense. The First Investigation examined expressive acts that involve meanings, attempting to specify the conditions under which these acts are meaning intending and meaning fulfilling. The Second Investigation rejected traditional empiricist explanations of the formation of logical concepts through abstraction and argued for the direct seeing of abstract meanings. The Third Investigation offered a pure a priori theory of the relations between parts and wholes ('mereology') in the most general sense. The Fourth Investigation outlined a 'pure formal grammar' of the a priori rules governing meaningful utterance as opposed to nonsense, in any language whatsoever. The Fifth and Sixth Investigations focused on the essential features of acts of consciousness, their contents and objects, specifically the intentional structure of such acts and the manner in which they (in the form of judgements) become truth bearers. The Sixth Investigation, in particular, discussed Husserl's original concept of 'categorial intuition', that is, that we intuit not just sensuous particulars but also the categorial forms which appear in judgements, a discussion that would have a decisive influence on Martin Heidegger's formulation of the question of being.

Husserl had taught at Halle as *Privatdozent* since 1889, but in 1901 he moved to the University of Göttingen, famous for its school of formalist mathematicians around David Hilbert and Felix Klein. He was dissatisfied with the approach taken in the *Investigations*, and, influenced by his reading of Descartes and Kant, he began to re-conceive 'phenomenology' as a transcendental science of pure consciousness, access to which required a special orientation, involving a 'bracketing' of the natural attitude, and a *reduction* from the realm of fact to pure essentiality. This transcendental approach was first publicly articulated in his programmatic *Ideas Pertaining to a Pure Phenomenology and to a Phenomenological Philosophy*, Book I (1913). Thereafter Husserl developed the idea of phenomenology more systematically as the foundational science of all sciences, as a revival of 'first philosophy', and as a radical transcendental idealism. However, Husserl also carried out phenomenological studies of the experience of time, of material bodies in space, and the experience of corporeality and intersubjectivity, studies that prevent his thought from being understood as idealist in some world-denying sense.

In 1916, Husserl moved to the University of Freiburg im Breisgau, where he became a philosopher of world renown, attracting brilliant students (Hans-Georg Gadamer, Hannah Arendt, Herbert Marcuse, Rudolf Carnap, Alfred Schütz and Jan Patočka all visited) and distinguished assistants, including Martin Heidegger, Ludwig Landgrebe and Eugen Fink. However, Husserl published no book between 1913 and 1928, the year in which his lectures *On the Phenomenology of the Consciousness of Internal Time* appeared, edited by Martin Heidegger. After his retirement in 1928, Husserl became very active both in lecturing and writing. *Formal and Transcendental Logic*, a development of his lectures on logic from the early 1920s, appeared in 1929. He delivered lectures in Paris in 1929, introducing transcendental phenomenology as a radicalisation of Cartesian first philosophy, beginning with the single meditating self. These were first published in the French translation of Emmanuel Levinas and Gabrielle Peiffer as *Méditations Cartésiennes* (*Cartesian Meditations*) in 1931. The Fifth Cartesian Meditation offered Husserl's analysis of the problem of the constitution of others, i.e. the problem of intersubjectivity.

Husserl's ambitions to develop a Cartesian-style fundamental philosophy as a clarification of rational knowledge were challenged by the growing political turmoil and irrationality of the 1930s. Of Jewish origins, he was directly affected by the non-Aryan laws of 1933, leading eventually to his suspension from the university. Isolated and under official restrictions in Germany, nevertheless he continued his philosophical research with lectures abroad, in Prague and Vienna in 1935 and 1936, resulting in the publication in Belgrade of his brilliant *The Crisis of European Sciences and Transcendental Phenomenology* in 1936. A last work, *Experience and Judgement*, co-edited by Ludwig Landgrebe, appeared in 1938. Husserl was editing his huge collection of unpublished manuscripts when he died in 1938. These manuscripts now form the basis of the Husserlian edition of his works, now running at more than thirty volumes.

Husserl's conception of phenomenology developed through his life. Initially, he conceived of phenomenology as a science of description of a priori truths and laws connected primarily with epistemological acts, acts of cognition. 'Phenomenology' was equated with a radicalised 'theory of knowledge' in the *Logical Investigations*. Gradually, he came to recognise that the sphere of constitutive subjectivity uncovered by phenomenology represented a far greater, even infinite, field of researches. Overall, Husserl was concerned with the problem of how *objective truth* could be constituted in and through *subjective acts* of consciousness, what Husserl called "the enigma of subjectivity". In later years, Husserl shifted his attention to studying the process of the emergence and preservation of truths within historical human communities, the process of the achievement of intersubjective confirmation and validity. In other words, he supplemented his concern with the nature of *static* constitution of objectivity with a *genetic* account, which was concerned to study how the objective sciences have emerged from their cultural context, out of human practices embedded in the life-world. In his final years, his manuscripts suggest he had moved to a metaphysical position whereby all acts are related to the transcendental ego, whose core is a kind of 'standing living present'.

Our first reading is taken from the Introduction to Volume Two of the *Logical Investigations*, where Husserl lays out his initial understanding of phenomenology as a presuppositionless science which seeks to bring to intuition the essences of thought and knowledge in their most complete generality, through exploring the analytic connections between meaning intentions and meaning fulfilments in a way that rigorously avoids psychologism. In the First Edition of this Introduction Husserl (see §6 Note 3 of the reading) still equated phenomenology with Brentanian descriptive psychology, but in the Second Edition (1913) he revised his view to stress the eidetic nature of the science of pure phenomenology, removed from all contingent facts about the world, and all 'real states' of animal organisms in the natural order. Pure phenomonology, like pure mathematics, then operates with intuitions which are ideal and universal. Pure phenomenology will overcome all naiveté in the sciences.

Our second reading, "Consciousness as Intentional Experience", is drawn from the important Fifth Logical Investigation, where Husserl offers his critique of Brentano's conception of intentionality as too narrowly based within the latter's project of identifying the domain of psychic phenomena. At the beginning of this Investigation Husserl lays out his own understanding of consciousness (not in the present selection), and then moves in Chapter 2 to analyse critically Brentano's claim that psychic acts are characterised by intentionality as their distinguishing feature. Husserl offers a careful critique of Brentano's Cartesian assumptions but does recognise that intentionality is the key to unlock the whole domain of pure consciousness. Every conscious lived experience intends something. Husserl also insists that in normal experience, the intended object is not part of the experience (as Brentano seemed to suggest) but transcends it. No talk of the immanence of the intentional object should be accepted; instead, intentionality must be recognised as that movement outwards whereby intentional acts come into contact with objects. In the course of this discussion, Husserl denies the oft repeated empiricist claim that what we are in contact with primarily are our own sensations. Instead, Husserl emphasises that what is intended directly is the object (e.g. a box) and that we do not perceive our own sensations. Sensations are, instead, part of the *matter* of the act.

Our third reading is taken from Husserl's lectures on the nature of our inner consciousness of time. In the *Logical Investigations* Husserl had given a static and monadic analysis of the intentional act, concentrating on the structure of an individual act of perceiving or thinking. In these lectures, Husserl now turns his attention to the dynamic and fluid character of our psychic stream and the manner in which past and present play a role in our continuous perceptions of objects. When we hear a familiar melody being played, the currently sounding note is heard, but the note just sounded is also retained, and there is also a certain expectation (or 'protention') of a certain sequence of notes to follow. This led Husserl to analyse very closely the manner in which perception is a composite structure of retention, protention and primary impression. Derrida criticised Husserl for seeking to retain the originary present impression as the most important of these structures, but Husserl's position is rather complicated on this matter.

Our fourth reading is from Husserl's Inaugural Lecture given in Freiburg in 1917, "Pure Phenomenology, its Method, and its Field of Investigation", where he outlines his vision of pure phenomenology as the study of phenomena understood in its widest sense. He points to the complexity of our experiences of objects, such that, while we experience only one side or profile of the object at a time, nevertheless, our consciousness is of the same object given under different conditions, rather than of a changing series of profiles. Husserl wants us to reflect on our natural consciousness by passing over to a new attitude which he calls the transcendental or phenomenological attitude, which excludes all reference to nature, and concentrates on what is given in pure reflection. Using this method of reduction, all our theoretical assumptions are put out of action and we must look again at the object now as given purely in consciousness. But pure experiencing is still not scientific knowledge and Husserl emphasises that pure phenomenology is an a priori science of things understood as pure possibilities and obeying ideal laws, for example, the idea of a purely spatial entity must be analysed in terms of its a priori laws and constraints.

Our fifth reading, "Noesis and Noema", is drawn from Husserl's 1913 work, his first book since the *Logical Investigations*, namely *Ideas Pertaining to a Pure Phenomenology and to a Phenomenological Philosophy*, where Husserl revisits his earlier analyses of the structure of the intentional relation, this time employing new terminology, which he hopes will bring the true structure of the intentional correlation to light. The 'noetic moment' of the act is what makes it an act of thinking, remembering, wishing and so on, whereas the noematic correlate is the object as thought, as remembered, as wished for and so on. This is what Husserl also calls the 'sense' of the act. For Husserl, the noema is reached only through a change of regard from the natural to the transcendental attitude. In the natural attitude we simply see a tree in the garden. In reflection on the act of seeing a tree, we apprehend not only the act of seeing but also its correlate the tree as seen. Whereas the real tree ('the tree simpliciter') can burn up, be cut down and so on, the noematic correlate is in a different space entirely and is not subject to such natural events: it has no real properties and is not subject to the natural forces in the world. Similarities between Husserl's noema and the Fregean notion of 'sense' (*Sinn*) has led to much discussion of the nature of Husserl's conception, which we cannot discuss further here.

Our Sixth and final reading is a section from *The Crisis of European Sciences* where Husserl explains his deviation from Kant and introduces his conception of the 'lifeworld' (*Lebenswelt*). Kant, for Husserl, could not free himself from a certain naturalistic orientation, inspired by the psychology of his day, and was therefore unable to understand the nature of the a priori in a truly original way. The Kantian exploration of the subjective conditions for the possibility of knowledge entirely missed the taken-for-granted, 'anonymous' world of ordinary lived experience. This section also makes clear the contrast Husserl draws between physical body (*Körper*) and living organic body (*Leib*) which would become central to the discussions of Edith Stein and Merleau-Ponty.

Further reading

Husserl, Edmund. *Cartesian Meditations*, trans. Dorion Cairns. The Hague: Nijhoff, 1967.
Husserl, Edmund. *Early Writings in the Philosophy of Logic and Mathematics*, trans. Dallas Willard. Collected Works V. Dordrecht: Kluwer, 1994.
Husserl, Edmund. *Experience and Judgment: Investigations in a Genealogy of Logic*, trans. J. S. Churchill and Karl Ameriks. Evanston, IL: Northwestern University Press, 1973.
Husserl, Edmund. *Formal and Transcendental Logic*, trans. Dorion Cairns. The Hague: Martinus Nijhoff, 1969.
Husserl, Edmund. *Husserl. Shorter Works*, trans. and ed. Frederick Elliston and Peter McCormick. Notre Dame: University of Notre Dame Press, 1981.
Husserl, Edmund. *Ideas Pertaining to a Pure Phenomenology and to a Phenomenological Philosophy, First Book*, trans. F. Kersten. The Hague: Nijhoff, 1983.
Husserl, Edmund. *Ideas Pertaining to a Pure Phenomenology and to a Phenomenological Philosophy, Second Book*, trans. R. Rojcewicz and A. Schuwer. Dordrecht: Kluwer, 1989.
Husserl, Edmund. *Introduction to the Logical Investigations. Draft of a Preface to the Logical Investigations*, ed. E. Fink, trans. P. J. Bossert and C. H. Peters. The Hague: Nijhoff, 1975.
Husserl, Edmund. *On the Phenomenology of the Consciousness of Internal Time*, trans. J. B. Brough. Collected Works IV. Dordrecht: Kluwer, 1990.
Husserl, Edmund. *Phenomenological Psychology. Lectures, Summer Semester 1925*, trans. J. Scanlon. The Hague: Nijhoff, 1977.
Husserl, Edmund. *Philosophy as a Rigorous Science*, 1911, in Lauer, Quentin. *Edmund Husserl. Phenomenology and the Crisis of Philosophy*. New York: Harper and Row, 1964.
Husserl, Edmund. *The Crisis of European Sciences and Transcendental Phenomenology. An Introduction to Phenomenological Philosophy*, trans. David Carr. Evanston: Northwestern University Press, 1970.
Husserl, Edmund. *The Idea of Phenomenology*, trans. Lee Hardy. Dordrecht: Kluwer, 1999.
Husserl, Edmund. *Thing and Space: Lectures of 1907*, trans. R. Rojcewicz. Collected Works VII. Dordrecht: Kluwer, 1997.
Bell, David. *Husserl*. London: Routledge, 1990.
Bernet, Rudolf, Iso Kern and Eduard Marbach. *An Introduction to Husserlian Phenomenology*. Evanston, IL: Northwestern University Press, 1993.
Derrida, Jacques. *Speech and Phenomena and other Essays on Husserl's Theory of Signs*, ed. and trans. David Allison. Evanston, IL: Northwestern University Press, 1973.
Elveton, R. O. Ed. *The Phenomenology of Husserl. Selected Critical Readings*. Second Edition. Seattle: Noesis Press, 2000.
Farber, Marvin. *The Foundation of Phenomenology*. Albany: State University of New York Press, 1943.
Levinas, Emmanuel. *The Theory of Intuition in Husserl's Phenomenology*, trans. A. Orianne. Evanston, IL: Northwestern University Press, 1973.
Moran, Dermot. *Introduction to Phenomenology*. London and New York: Routledge, 2000.
Moran, Dermot. "Heidegger's Critique of Husserl's and Brentano's Accounts of Intentionality", *Inquiry* Vol. 43 (2000), pp. 39–66.
Natanson, Maurice. *Edmund Husserl. Philosopher of Infinite Tasks*. Evanston, IL: Northwestern University Press, 1973.
Ricoeur, Paul. *Husserl. An Analysis of his Philosophy*. Evanston, IL: Northwestern University Press, 1967.

Smith, Barry and David Woodruff Smith. Eds. *The Cambridge Companion to Husserl*. Cambridge: Cambridge University Press, 1995.

Ströker, Elizabeth. *Husserl's Transcendental Phenomenology*. Stanford, CA: Stanford University Press, 1993.

Welton, Donn. Ed. *The Essential Husserl*. Bloomington: Indiana University Press, 1999.

1

INTRODUCTION TO THE
LOGICAL INVESTIGATIONS

§1 The necessity of phenomenological investigations as a preliminary to the epistemological criticism and clarification of pure logic

The necessity that we should begin logic with linguistic discussions has often been acknowledged from the standpoint of a logical technology. "Language", we read in Mill, "is evidently one of the principal instruments or helps of thought; and any imperfection in the instrument, or in the mode of employing it, is confessedly liable, still more than in almost any other art, to confuse and impede the process, and destroy all ground of confidence in the result. For a mind not previously versed in the meaning and right use of the various kinds of words, to attempt the study of methods of philosophizing, would be as if some one should attempt to become an astronomical observer, having never learnt to adjust the focal distance of his optical instruments so as to see distinctly."[1] A deeper ground for this necessity of beginning logic with linguistic analysis is, however, seen by Mill in the fact that it would not otherwise be possible to investigate the meaning of propositions, a matter which stands "at the threshold" of logical science itself.

This last remark of our distinguished thinker indicates a point of view regulative for *pure* logic, and, be it noted, for *pure* logic treated as a *philosophical* discipline. I assume accordingly that no one will think it enough to develop pure logic merely in the manner of our mathematical disciplines, as a growing system of propositions having a naïvely factual validity, without also striving to be philosophically clear in regard to these same propositions, without, that is, gaining insight into the essence of the modes of cognition which come into play in their utterance and in the ideal possibility of applying such propositions, together with all such conferments of sense and objective validities as are essentially constituted therein. Linguistic discussions are certainly among the philosophically indispensable preparations for the building of pure logic: only by their aid can the true *objects* of logical research – and, following thereon, the essential species and differentiae of such objects – be refined to a clarity that excludes all misunderstanding. We are not here concerned with grammatical discussions, empirically conceived and related to some historically given language: we are concerned with discussions of a most general sort which cover the wider sphere of an objective

E. Husserl, *Logical Investigations*, 1970, trans. J. N. Findlay, vol. 1, pp. 248–66. London and New York: Routledge & Kegan Paul/Humanities Press.

theory of knowledge and, closely linked with this last, the *pure phenomenology of the experiences of thinking and knowing*. This phenomenology, like the more inclusive *pure phenomenology of experiences in general*, has, as its exclusive concern, experiences intuitively seizable and analysable in the pure generality of their essence, not experiences empirically perceived and treated as real facts, as experiences of human or animal experients in the phenomenal world that we posit as an empirical fact. This phenomenology must bring to pure expression, must *describe* in terms of their essential concepts and their governing formulae of essence, the essences which directly make themselves known in intuition, and the connections which have their roots purely in such essences. Each such statement of essence is an *a priori* statement in the highest sense of the word. This sphere we must explore in preparation for the epistemological criticism and clarification of pure logic: our investigations will therefore all move within it.

Pure phenomenology represents a field of neutral researches, in which several sciences have their roots. It is, on the one hand, an ancillary to *psychology* conceived as an *empirical science*. Proceeding in purely intuitive fashion, it analyses and describes in their essential generality – in the specific guise of a phenomenology of thought and knowledge – the experiences of presentation, judgement and knowledge, experiences which, treated as classes of real events in the natural context of zoological reality, receive a scientific probing at the hands of empirical psychology. Phenomenology, on the other hand, lays bare the "sources" from which the basic concepts and ideal laws of *pure* logic "flow", and back to which they must once more be traced, so as to give them all the "clearness and distinctness" needed for an understanding, and for an epistemological critique, of pure logic. The epistemological or phenomenological groundwork of pure logic involves very hard, but also surpassingly important researches. To revert to what we set forth as the tasks of pure logic in the first volume of these *Investigations*, we have taken it upon us to give firm clarity to notions and laws on which the objective meaning and theoretical unity of all knowledge is dependent.[2]

§2 Elucidation of the aims of such investigations

All theoretical research, though by no means solely conducted in acts of verbal expression or complete statement, none the less terminates in such statement. Only in this form can truth, and in particular the truth of theory, become an abiding possession of science, a documented, ever available treasure for knowledge and advancing research. Whatever the connection of thought with speech may be, whether or not the appearance of our final judgements in the form of verbal pronouncements has a necessary grounding in essence, it is at least plain that judgements stemming from higher intellectual regions, and in particular from the regions of science, could barely arise without verbal expression.

The objects which pure logic seeks to examine are, in the first instance, therefore given to it in grammatical clothing. Or, more precisely, they come before us embedded in concrete mental states which further function either as the *meaning-intention* or *meaning-fulfilment* of certain verbal expressions – in the latter case intuitively illustrating, or intuitively providing evidence for, our meaning – and forming a *phenomenological unity* with such expressions.

In these complex phenomenological unities the logician must pick out the components that interest him, the characters of the acts, first of all, in which logical presentation, judgement and knowledge are consummated: he must pursue the descriptive analysis of such act-types to the extent that this helps the progress of his properly logical tasks. We cannot straightway leap, from the fact that theory "realizes" itself in certain mental states, and has instances in them, to the seemingly obvious truth that such mental states must count as the primary object of our logical researches. The pure logician is not primarily or properly interested in the psychological judgement, the concrete mental phenomenon, but in the logical judgement, the identical asserted meaning, which is one over against manifold, descriptively quite different, judgement-experiences.[3] There is naturally, in the singular experiences which correspond to this ideal unity, a certain pervasive common feature, but since the concern of the pure logician is not with the concrete instance, but with its corresponding Idea, its abstractly apprehended universal, he has, it would seem, no reason to leave the field of abstraction, nor to make concrete experiences the theme of his probing interest, instead of Ideas.

Even if phenomenological analysis of concrete thought-experiences does not fall within the true home-ground of pure logic, it none the less is indispensable to the advance of purely logical research. For all that is logical must be given in fully concrete fashion, if, as an object of research, it is to be made our own, and if we are to be able to bring to self-evidence the *a priori* laws which have their roots in it. What is logical is first given us in imperfect shape: the concept as a more or less wavering meaning, the law, built out of concepts, as a more or less wavering assertion. We do not therefore lack logical insights, but grasp the pure law with self-evidence, and see how it has its base in the pure forms of thought. Such self-evidence depends, however, on the verbal meanings which come alive in the actual passing of the judgement regarding the law. Unnoticed equivocation may permit the subsequent substitution of other concepts beneath our words, and an appeal on behalf of an altered propositional meaning may quite readily, but wrongly, be made on the self-evidence previously experienced. It is also possible, conversely, that a misinterpretation based on equivocation may distort the sense of the propositions of pure logic (perhaps turning them into empirical, psychological propositions), and may tempt us to abandon previously experienced self-evidence and the unique significance of all that belongs to pure logic.

It is not therefore enough that the Ideas of logic, and the pure laws set up with them, should be given in such a manner. Our great task is now *to bring the Ideas of logic, the logical concepts and laws, to epistemological clarity and definiteness.*

Here *phenomenological analysis* must begin. Logical concepts, as valid thought-unities, must have their origin in intuition: they must arise out of an ideational intuition founded on certain experiences, and must admit of indefinite reconfirmation, and of recognition of their self-identity, on the reperformance of such abstraction. Otherwise put: we can absolutely not rest content with "mere words", i.e. with a merely symbolic understanding of "words", such as we first have when we reflect on the sense of the laws for "concepts", "judgements", "truths" etc. (together with their manifold specifications) which are set up in pure logic. Meanings inspired only by remote, confused, inauthentic intuitions – if by any intuitions at all – are not enough: we must go back to the "things themselves". We desire to render self-evident in fully-fledged intuitions that what is here given in actually performed abstractions is what the word-meanings in our expression of the law really and truly stand for. In the practice of cognition we strive to arouse dispositions in ourselves which will keep our meanings unshakably the same, which will measure them sufficiently often against the mark set by reproducible intuitions or by an intuitive carrying out of our abstraction. Intuitive illustration of the shifting meanings which attach to the same term in differing propositional contexts likewise convinces us of the fact of equivocation: it becomes evident to us that what a word means in this or that case has its fulfilment in essentially different intuitive "moments" or patterns, or in essentially different general notions. By distinguishing among concepts confounded by us, and by suitably modifying our terminology, we then likewise achieve a desired "clearness and distinctness" for our logical propositions.

The phenomenology of the logical experiences aims at giving us a sufficiently wide descriptive (though not empirically-psychological) understanding of these mental states and their indwelling sense, as will enable us to give fixed meanings to all the fundamental concepts of logic. Such meanings will be clarified both by going back to the analytically explored connections between meaning-intentions and meaning-fulfilments, and also by making their possible function in cognition intelligible and certain. They will be such meanings, in short, as the interest of pure logic itself requires, as well as the interest, above all, of epistemological insight into the essence of this discipline. Fundamental logical and noetic concepts have, up to this time, been quite imperfectly clarified: countless equivo-cations beset them, some so pernicious, so hard to track down, and to keep con-sistently separate, that they yield the main ground for the very backward state of pure logic and theory of knowledge.

We must of course admit that many conceptual differentiations and circum-scriptions of the sphere of pure logic can become evident to the natural attitude without phenomenological analysis. The relevant logical acts are carried out and adequately fitted to their fulfilling intuitions, though there is no reflection on the phenomenological situation itself. What is most completely evident can, however, be confused with something else, what it apprehends can be misconstrued, its assured directives can be rejected. Clarifying researches are especially needed to explain our by no means chance inclination to slip unwittingly from an objective to a psychological attitude, and to mix up two bodies of data distinguishable in principle however much they may be essentially related, and to be deceived by psychological misconstructions and misinterpretations of the objects of logic. Such clarifications can, by their nature, only be achieved within a phenomeno-logical theory of the essences of our thought- and knowledge-experiences, with continuous regard to the things essentially meant by, and so belonging to the latter (in the precise manners in which those things are *as such* "shown forth", "represented" etc.). Psychologism can only be radically overcome by a pure phenomenology, a science infinitely removed from psychology as the empirical science of the mental attributes and states of animal realities. In our sphere, too, the sphere of pure logic, such a phenomenology alone offers us all the necessary conditions for a finally satisfactory establishment of the totality of basic distinc-tions and insights. It alone frees us from the strong temptation, at first inevitable, since rooted in grounds of essence, to turn the logically objective into the psychological.

The above mentioned motives for phenomenological analysis have an obvious and essential connection with those which spring from *basic questions of epistemology*. For if these questions are taken in the *widest* generality, i.e. in the "formal" generality which abstracts from all matter of knowledge – they form part of a range of questions involved in the full clarification of the Idea of pure logic. We have, on the one hand, the fact that all thought and knowledge have as their aim *objects* or *states of affairs*, which they putatively "hit" in the sense that the "being-in-itself" of these objects and states is supposedly shown forth, and made an identifiable item, in a multitude of actual or possible meanings, or acts of thought. We have, further, the fact that all thought is ensouled by a thought-form which is subject to ideal laws, laws circumscribing the objectivity or ideality of knowledge in general. These facts, I maintain, eternally provoke questions like: How are we to understand the fact that the being-in-itself of objectivity becomes "presented", "apprehended" in knowledge, and so ends up by becoming subjective? What does it mean to say that the object has "being-in-itself", and is "given" in knowledge? How can the ideality of the universal *qua* concept or law enter the flux of real mental states and become an epistemic possession of the thinking person? What does the *adaequatio rei et intellectus* mean in various cases of knowledge, according as what we apprehend and know, is individual or universal, a fact or a law etc.? These and similar questions can, it is plain, not be separated from the above-mentioned questions regarding the clarification of pure logic, since the task of clarifying such logical Ideas as Concept and Object, Truth and Proposition, Fact and Law etc., inevitably leads on to these same questions. We should in any case have to tackle them so that the essence of the clarification aimed at in phenomenological analyses should not itself be left obscure.

§3 The difficulties of pure phenomenological analysis

The difficulties of clearing up the basic concepts of logic are a natural consequence of the extraordinary difficulties of strict phenomenological analysis. These are in the main the same whether our immanent analysis aims at the *pure* essence of experiences (all empirical facticity and individuation being excluded) or treats experiences from an empirical, psychological standpoint. Psychologists usually discuss such difficulties when they consider introspection as a source of our detailed psychological knowledge, not properly however, but in order to draw a false antithesis between introspection and "outer" perception. The source of all such difficulties lies in the unnatural direction of intuition and thought which phenomenological analysis requires. Instead of becoming lost in the performance of acts built intricately on one another, and instead of (as it were) naïvely positing the existence of the objects intended in their sense and then going on to characterize them, or of assuming such objects hypothetically, of drawing conclusions from all this etc., we must rather practise "reflection", i.e. make these acts themselves, and their immanent meaning-content, our objects. When objects are intuited, thought of, theoretically pondered on, and thereby given to us as actualities in certain ontic modalities, we must direct our theoretical interest away from such objects, not posit them as realities as they appear or hold in the intentions of our acts. These acts, contrariwise, though hitherto not objective, must now be made objects of apprehension and of theoretical assertion. We must deal with them in new acts of intuition and thinking, we must analyse and describe them in their essence, we must make them objects of empirical or ideational thought. Here we have a direction of thought running counter to deeply ingrained habits which have been steadily strengthened since the dawn of mental development. Hence the well-nigh ineradicable tendency to slip out of a phenomenological thought-stance into one that is straightforwardly objective, or to substitute for mental acts, or for the "appearances" or "meanings" immanent in them, characters which, in a naïve performance of such acts, were attributed to their objects. Hence, too, the tendency to treat whole classes of genuinely subsistent objects, e.g. Ideas – since these may be evidently given to us in ideating intuitions – as phenomenological constituents of presentations *of* them.

A much discussed difficulty – one which seems to threaten in principle all possible immanent description of mental acts or indeed all phenomenological treatment of essences – lies in the fact that when we pass over from naïvely performed acts to an attitude of reflection, or when we perform acts proper to such reflection, our former acts necessarily undergo change. How can we rightly assess the nature and extent of such change? How indeed can we know anything whatever about it, whether as a fact or as a necessity of essence?

In addition to this difficulty of reaching firm results, capable of being self-evidently reidentified on many occasions, we have the further difficulty of *stating such results*, of *communicating them to others*. "Completely" self-evident "truths of essence", established by the most exact analysis, must be expounded by way of expressions whose rich variety does not compensate for the fact that they only fit familiar natural objects, while the experiences in which such objects become constituted for consciousness, can be directly referred to only by way of a few highly ambiguous words such as "sensation", "perception", "presentation" etc. One has, further, to employ expressions which stand for what is intentional in such acts, for the object to which they are directed, since it is, in fact, impossible to describe referential acts without using expressions which recur to the things to which such acts refer. One then readily forgets that such subsidiarily described objectivity, which is necessarily introduced into almost all phenomenological description, has undergone a change of sense, in virtue of which it now belongs to the sphere of phenomenology.

If we ignore such difficulties, others emerge concerned with the persuasive communication of our resultant insights to others. These insights can be tested and confirmed only by persons well-trained in the ability to engage in pure description in the unnatural attitude of reflection, trained in short to allow phenomenological relations to work upon them *in full purity*. Such purity means that we must keep out the falsifying intrusion of all assertions based on the naïve acceptance and assessment of objects, whose existence has been posited in the acts now receiving phenomenological treatment. It likewise prohibits any other going beyond whatever is essential and proper to such acts, any application to them of naturalistic interpretations and assertions. It forbids us, i.e., to set them up as psychological realities (even in an indefinitely general or exemplary fashion), as the states of "mind-endowed beings" of any sort whatsoever. The capacity for such researches is not readily come by, nor can it be achieved or replaced by, e.g., the most elaborate of trainings in experimental psychology.

Serious as are the difficulties standing in the way of a pure phenomenology in general, and of the phenomenology of the logical experiences in particular, they are by no means such as to make the whole attempt to overcome them appear hopeless. Resolute cooperation among a generation of research-workers, conscious of their goal and dedicated to the main issue, would, I think, suffice to decide the most important questions in the field, those concerned with its basic constitution. Here we have a field of *attainable* discoveries, fundamentally involved in the possibility of a *scientific* philosophy. Such discoveries have indeed nothing dazzling about them: they lack any obviously useful relation to practice or to the fulfilment of higher emotional needs. They also lack any imposing apparatus of experimental methodology, through which experimental psychology has gained so much credit and has built up such a rich force of cooperative workers.

§4 It is essential to keep in mind the grammatical side of our logical experiences

Analytic phenomenology, needed by the logician in his preparatory laying of foundations, is concerned "among other things", with "presentations" "and with them primarily"; it is, more precisely, concerned with those presentations to which *expression* has been given. In the complex objects of its study, its primary interest attaches to the experiences lying behind "mere expressions", experiences which perform roles either of meaning-"intention" or of meaning-fulfilment. It cannot, however, quite ignore the sensuous-linguistic side of its complex objects (the element of "mere expression" in them) nor the way in which this element is associated with the meaning that "ensouls" it. Everyone knows how readily and how unnoticeably an analysis of meaning can be led astray by grammatical analysis. Since the direct analysis of meaning is, however, difficult, we may welcome each aid, however imperfect, that indirectly anticipates its "results", but grammatical analysis is even more important in virtue of the errors its use promotes when it replaces a *true analysis of meaning*, than for any positive aid. Rough reflection on our thoughts and their verbal expression, conducted by us without special schooling, and often needed for the practical ends of thinking, suffice to indicate a certain parallelism between thinking and speaking. We all know that words mean something, and that, generally speaking, different words express different meanings. If we could regard such a correspondence as perfect, and as given *a priori*, and as one particularly in which the essential categories of meaning had perfect mirror-images in the categories of grammar, a phenomenology of linguistic forms would include a phenomenology of the meaning-experiences (experiences of thinking, judging etc.) and meaning-analysis would, so to speak, coincide with grammatical analysis.

Deep reflection is not, however, needed to show that a parallelism satisfying such far-reaching demands has as little foundation in grounds of essence as it obtains in fact. *Grammatically relevant distinctions of meaning* are at times *essential*, at times *contingent*, according as the practical aims of speech dictate peculiar forms for essential or contingent differences of meaning. (The latter are merely such as have a frequent occurrence in human intercourse.)

It is well-known, however, that differentiation of expressions does not merely depend on differences of meaning. I need point only to "shades" of meaning, or to aesthetic tendencies which fight against any bare uniformity of expression, or against discord in speech-sound or rhythm and so demand an abundant store of available synonyms.

The rough concomitances among verbal and thought-differences, and particularly among *forms* of words and thoughts, makes us naturally tend to seek logical distinctions behind expressed grammatical distinctions. It is, therefore, *an important matter for logic that the relation between expression and meaning should be made analytically clear*. We should perceive clearly that, in order to decide whether a distinction should, in a given case, count as logical or merely grammatical, we must go back from *vague* acts of meaning to the correspondingly clear, articulate ones, acts saturated with the fulness of exemplary intuition in which their meaning is fulfilled.

It is not enough to have the common knowledge, easily garnered from suitable examples, that grammatical differences need not coincide with logical ones. The common knowledge that such distinctions do not always go hand in hand – that languages, in other words, express material differences of meaning, widely used in communication, in forms as pervasive as the fundamental logical differences having their *a priori* roots in the general essence of meanings – such common knowledge may open the way to a dangerous radicalism. The field of logical forms may be unduly restricted. A wide range of logically significant forms may be cast forth as merely grammatical: only a few may be kept, such as suffice to leave some content to traditional syllogizing. Brentano's attempted reform of formal logic, valuable as it no doubt still is, plainly suffered from this exaggeration. Only a complete clearing-up of the essential phenomenological relations between expression and meaning, or between meaning-intention and meaning-fulfilment, can give us a firm middle stance, and can enable us to give the requisite clearness to the relations between grammatical and meaning-analysis.

§5 Statement of the main aims of the following analytical investigations

We accordingly pass to a series of analytic "investigations which will clear up the constitutive Ideas of a pure or formal logic, investigations which relate in the first place to the pure theory of logical forms". Starting with the empirical connection between meaning-experiences and expressions, we must try to find out what our variously ambiguous talk about "expressing" or "meaning" really amounts to. We must try to see what essential phenomenological or logical distinctions apply *a priori* to expressions, and how we may in essence describe, and may place in pure categories, the experiences – to deal first with the phenomenological side of expressions – that have an *a priori* fitness for the meaning-function. We must find out how the "presenting" and "judging" achieved in such experiences stand to their corresponding "intuition", how they are "illustrated", or perhaps "confirmed" or "fulfilled", in the latter, or rendered "evident" by it etc. It is not hard to see that investigations of such matters must precede all clarifications of the basic concepts and categories of logic. Among our introductory investigations we shall have to raise fundamental questions as to the acts, or, alternatively, the ideal meanings, which in logic pass under the name of "presentations" (*Vorstellungen*). It is important to clarify and prise apart the many concepts that the word "presentation" has covered, concepts in which the psychological, the epistemological and the logical are utterly confused. Similar analyses deal with the concept of *judgement* in the sense in which logic is concerned with it. So-called "judgement-theory" neglects this task: it is in the main, in respect of its essential problems, a theory of presentation. We are naturally not interested in a psychological theory, but in a phenomenology of presentation- and judgement-experiences as delimited by our epistemological interests.

As we probe the essence of the expressive experiences, we must also dig more deeply into their *intentional subject-matter*, their objective intention's ideal sense, i.e. into the unity of its meaning and the unity of its object. We must, above all, dwell upon the enigmatic double sense or manner, the two-sided context, in which the same experience has a "content", and the manner in which in addition to its real (*reell*) and proper content, an ideal, intentional content must and can dwell in it.

Here also belong questions relating to the "object-directedness" or "objectlessness" of logical acts, to the sense of the distinction between intentional and true objects, to the clarification of the Idea of truth in relation to the Idea of judgemental self-evidence, to the clarification of the remaining, closely connected logical and noetic categories. These investigations in part cover the same ground as those dealing with the constitution of logical forms, to the extent, of course, that we settle questions as to the acceptance or rejection of putative logical forms, or doubts as to their logical or merely grammatical distinctness from forms already recognized, in the course of our clarification of form-giving, categorial concepts.

We have thus vaguely indicated the range of problems to which the ensuing investigations will be oriented. These investigations make no claim to be exhaustive. Their aim is not to provide a logical system, but to do the initial spadework "for a philosophical logic which will derive clearness from basic phenomenological sources". The paths taken by such an analytic investigation will also naturally differ from those suitable to a final, systematic, logically ordered statement of established truth.

§6 Additional notes

Note 1 Our investigations will often inevitably take us beyond the narrow phenomenological sphere whose study is really required for giving direct evidence to the Ideas of logic. This sphere is itself not given to us initially, but becomes delimited in the course of our investigation. We are, in particular, forced beyond this sphere of research when we prise apart the many confused concepts obscurely confounded in our understanding of logical terms, and when we find which of them are truly logical.

Note 2 The phenomenological founding of logic involves the difficulty that we must, in our exposition, make use of all the concepts we are trying to clarify. This coincides with a certain wholly irremoveable defect which affects the systematic course of our basic phenomenological and epistemological investigations. If a type of thought requires prior clarification, we should not make uncritical use of its terms or concepts in that clarification itself. But one should not expect that one should only be required to analyse such concepts critically, when the actual interconnection of one's logical materials has led up to them. Or, put differently, systematic clarification, whether in pure logic or any other discipline, would in itself seem to require a stepwise following out of the ordering of things, of the systematic interconnection in the science to be clarified. Our investigation can, however, only proceed securely, if it repeatedly breaks with such systematic sequence, if it removes conceptual obscurities which threaten the course of investigation *before* the natural sequence of subject-matters can lead up to such concepts. We search, as it were, in zig-zag fashion, a metaphor all the more apt since the close interdependence of our various epistemological concepts leads us back again and again to our original analyses, where the new confirms the old, and the old the new.

Note 3 If *our* sense of phenomenology has been grasped, and if it has not been given the current interpretation of an ordinary "descriptive psychology", a part of natural science, then an objection, otherwise justifiable, will fall to the ground, an objection to the effect that all theory of knowledge, conceived as a systematic phenomenological clarification of knowledge, is built upon psychology. On this interpretation pure logic, treated by us as an epistemologically clarified, *philosophical* discipline, must in the end likewise rest upon psychology, if only upon its preliminary descriptive researches into intentional experiences. Why then so much heated resistance to psychologism?

We naturally reply that if psychology is given its old meaning, phenomenology is not descriptive psychology: its peculiar "pure" description, its contemplation of pure essences on a basis of exemplary individual intuitions of experiences (often freely *imagined* ones), and its descriptive fixation of the contemplated essences into pure concepts, is no empirical, scientific description. It rather excludes the natural performance of all empirical (naturalistic) apperceptions and positings. Statements of descriptive psychology regarding "perceptions", "judgements", "feelings", "volitions" etc., use such names to refer to the real states of animal organisms in a real natural order, just as descriptive statements concerning physical states deal with happenings in a nature not imagined but real. All general statements have here a character of empirical generality: they hold for *this* nature. Phenomenology, however, does not discuss states of animal organisms (not even as belonging to a possible nature as such), but perceptions, judgements, feelings *as such*, and what pertains to them *a priori* with unlimited generality, as *pure* instances of *pure* species, of what may be seen through a purely intuitive apprehension of essence, whether generic or specific. Pure arithmetic likewise speaks of numbers, and pure geometry of spatial shapes, employing pure intuitions in their ideational universality. Not psychology, therefore, but phenomenology, underlies all clarifications in pure logic (and in all forms of rational criticism). Phenomenology has, however, a very different function as the necessary basis for every psychology that could with justification and in strictness be called scientific, just as pure mathematics, e.g. pure geometry and dynamics, is the necessary foundation for all exact natural science (any theory of empirical things in nature with their empirical forms, movements etc.). Our essential insights into perceptions, volitions and other forms of experience will naturally hold also of the corresponding empirical states of animal organisms, as geometrical insights hold of spatial figures in nature.

Note 3 (First Edition)

The above Note 3 is a typical account of what Husserl had come to mean by "phenomenology" by the time that the Second Edition of the Logical Investigations *was published in 1913. It replaces the following Note, which indicates what he meant by the term when the First Edition was published in 1901:*

Phenomenology is descriptive psychology. Epistemological criticism is therefore in essence psychology, or at least only capable of being built on a psychological basis. Pure logic therefore also rests on psychology – what then is the point of the whole battle against psychologism?

The necessity of *this* sort of psychological foundation of pure logic, i.e. a strictly descriptive one, cannot lead us into error regarding the mutual independence of the two sciences, logic and psychology. For pure description is merely a preparatory step towards theory, not theory itself. One and the same sphere of pure description can accordingly serve to prepare for very different theoretical sciences. It is *not the full science of psychology that serves as a foundation for pure logic*, but certain classes of descriptions which are the step preparatory to the theoretical researches of psychology. These in so far as they describe the empirical objects whose genetic connections the science wishes to pursue, also form the substrate for those fundamental abstractions in which logic seizes the essence of its ideal objects and connections with inward evidence. Since it is epistemologically of unique importance that we should separate the purely descriptive examination of the knowledge-experience, disembarrassed of all theoretical psychological interests, from the truly psychological researches directed to empirical explanation and origins, it will be good if we rather speak of "phenomenology" than of descriptive psychology. It also recommends itself for the further reason that the expression "descriptive psychology", as it occurs in the talk of many scientists, means the sphere of scientific psychological investigation, which is marked off by a methodological preference for inner experience and by an abstraction from all psychophysical explanation.

§7 "Freedom from presuppositions" as a principle in epistemological investigations

An epistemological investigation that can seriously claim to be scientific must, it has often been emphasized, satisfy the *principle of freedom from presuppositions*. This principle, we think, only seeks to express the strict exclusion of all statements not permitting of a comprehensive *phenomenological* realization. Every epistemological investigation that we carry out must have its pure foundation in phenomenology. The "theory" that it aspires to, is no more than a thinking over, a coming to an evident understanding of, thinking and knowing as such, in their pure generic essence, of the specifications and forms that they essentially have, of the immanent structures that their objective relations involve, of the meaning of "validity", "justification", "mediate" and "immediate evidence", and their opposites, as applied to such structures, of the parallel specifications of such Ideas in relation to varying regions of possible objects of knowledge, of the clarified sense and role of the formal and material "laws of thought" seen in their *a priori* structural connections with the knowing consciousness etc. If such a "thinking over" of the meaning of knowledge is itself to yield, not mere opinion, but the evident knowledge it strictly demands, it must be a pure intuition of essences, exemplarily performed on an actual *given* basis of experiences of thinking and knowing. That acts of thought at times refer to transcendent, even to non-existent and impossible objects, is not to the case. For such direction to objects, such presentation and meaning of what is not really (*reell*) part of the phenomenological make-up of our experiences, is a descriptive feature of the experiences in question, whose sense it should be possible to fix and clarify by considering the experiences themselves. In no other way would it be possible.

We must keep apart from the pure theory of knowledge questions concerning the justifiability of accepting "mental" and "physical" realities which transcend consciousness, questions whether the statements of scientists regarding them are to be given a serious or unserious sense, questions whether it is justifiable or sensible to oppose a second, even more emphatically "transcendent" world, to the phenomenal nature with which science is correlated, and other similar questions. The question as to the existence and nature of "the external world" is a metaphysical question. The theory of knowledge, in generally clearing up the ideal essence and valid sense of cognitive thought, will of course deal with general questions regarding the possibility and manner of a knowledge or rational surmise about "real" objective things, things in principle transcending the experiences which know them, and regarding the norms which the true sense of such a knowledge requires: it will not enter upon the empirically oriented question as to whether we as men really can arrive at such knowledge from the data we actually have, nor will it attempt to realize such knowledge. On our view, theory of knowledge, properly described, is no theory. It is not science in the pointed sense of an explanatorily unified theoretical whole. *Theoretical explanation* means an ever increased rendering intelligible of singular facts through general laws, and an ever increased rendering intelligible of general laws through some fundamental law. In the realm of facts, our task is to know that what happens under given groups of circumstances, happens *necessarily*, i.e. according to *natural laws*. In the realm of the *a priori* our task is to understand the *necessity* of specific, lower-level relationships in terms of comprehensive general necessities, and ultimately in terms of those most primitive, universal relational *laws* that we call axioms. The theory of knowledge has nothing to explain in this theoretical sense, it neither constructs deductive theories nor falls under any. This is clear enough if we consider the most general, the so-to-say formal theory of knowledge that came before us in our *Prolegomena* as the philosophical completion of pure mathematics conceived in absolute width as including all *a priori*, categorial knowledge in the form of systematic theories. This theory of theories goes together with, and is illuminated by, a formal theory of knowledge which precedes all empirical theory, which precedes, therefore, all empirical knowledge of the real, all physical science on the one hand, and all psychology on the other, and of course all metaphysics. Its aim is not to *explain* knowledge in the psychological or psychophysical sense as a *factual* occurrence in objective nature, but to *shed light* on the *Idea* of knowledge in its constitutive elements and laws. It does not try to follow up the real connections of coexistence and succession with which actual acts of knowledge are interwoven, but to understand the *ideal* sense of the *specific* connections in which the objectivity of knowledge may be documented. It endeavours to raise to clearness the pure forms and laws of knowledge by tracing knowledge back to an adequate fulfilment in intuition. This "clearing up" takes place in the framework of a phenomenology of knowledge, a phenomenology oriented, as we saw, to the essential structures of pure experiences and to the structures of sense (*Sinnbestände*) that belong to these. From the beginning, as at all later stages, its scientific statements involve not the slightest reference to real existence: no metaphysical, scientific and, above all, no psychological assertions can therefore occur among its premises.

A purely phenomenological "theory" of knowledge naturally has an application to all naturally developed, and (in a good sense) "naïve" sciences, which it transforms into "philosophical" sciences. It transforms them, in other words, into sciences which provide us with clarified, assured knowledge in every sense in which it is possible to desire the latter. As regards the sciences of "reality", such epistemological clarification can as much be regarded as a "scientific" as a "metaphysical" evaluation.

The investigations which follow aspire solely to such freedom from metaphysical, scientific and psychological presuppositions. No harm will of course be done by occasional side-references which remain without effect on the content and character of one's analyses, nor by the many expository devices addressed to one's public, whose existence (like one's own) is not therefore presupposed by the content of one's investigations. Nor does one exceed one's prescribed limits if one starts, e.g., from existent languages and discusses the merely communicative meaning of their many forms of expression, and so on. It is easily seen that the sense and the epistemological worth of the following analyses does not depend on the fact that there really are languages, and that men really make use of them in their mutual dealings, or that there really are such things as men and a nature, and that they do not merely exist in imagined, possible fashion.

The real premises of our putative results must lie in propositions satisfying the requirement that what they assert permits of an *adequate phenomenological justification*, a fulfilment through *evidence* in the strictest sense. Such propositions must not, further, ever be adduced in some other sense than that in which they have been intuitively established.

Notes

1 *Logic*, Book 1, ch. 1, §1.
2 See the final chapter of the *Prolegomena*, §§66–7 in particular.
3 Cf. §11 of Investigation 1.

2

CONSCIOUSNESS AS INTENTIONAL EXPERIENCE

§9 The meaning of Brentano's demarcation of "psychic phenomena"

Among the demarcations of classes in descriptive psychology, there is none more remarkable nor more important philosophically than the one offered by Brentano under his title of "psychical phenomena", and used by him in his well-known division of phenomena into psychical and physical. Not that I can approve of the great thinker's guiding conviction, plain from the very terms that he uses, that he had achieved an exhaustive classification of "phenomena" through which the field of psychological research could be kept apart from that of natural science, and through which the vexed question of the right delimitation of the fields of these disciplines could be very simply solved. Possibly a good sense can be given to defining psychology as the science of psychical phenomena, and to the coordinated definition of natural science as the science of physical phenomena, but there are good reasons for disputing the view that the concepts which occur in Brentano's division are those found under like names in the definitions in question. It can be shown that not all "psychical phenomena" in the sense of a possible definition of psychology, are psychical phenomena (i.e. mental acts) in Brentano's sense, and that, on the other hand, many genuine "psychical phenomena" fall under Brentano's ambiguous rubric of "physical phenomena".[1] The value of Brentano's conception of a "psychical phenomenon" is, however, quite independent of the aims that inspired it. A sharply defined class of experiences is here brought before us, comprising all that enjoys mental, conscious existence in a certain *pregnant* sense of these words. A real being deprived of such experiences, merely having[2] contents inside it such as the experiences of sensation, but unable to interpret these objectively, or otherwise use them to make objects present to itself, quite incapable, therefore, of referring to objects in further acts of judgement, joy, grief, love, hatred, desire and loathing – such a being would not be called "psychical" by anyone. If one doubts whether it is at all possible to conceive of such a being, a mere complex of sensations, one has but to point to external phenomenal things, present to consciousness through sensational complexes, but not appearing as such themselves, and called by us "bodies" or "inanimate things", since they lack all psychical experiences in the sense of our examples. Turning aside from

E. Husserl, *Logical Investigations*, 1970, trans. J. N. Findlay, vol. 2, pp. 552–96. London and New York: Routledge & Kegan Paul/Humanities Press.

psychology, and entering the field of the philosophical disciplines proper, we perceive the fundamental importance of our class of experiences, since only its members are relevant in the highest ranks of the normative sciences. They alone, seized in their phenomenological purity, furnish concrete bases for abstracting the fundamental notions that function systematically in logic, ethics and aesthetics, and that enter into the ideal laws of these sciences. Our mention of logic recalls the particular interest which has inspired our whole probing into such experiences.

§10 Descriptive characterization of acts as "intentional" experiences

We must now dig down to the essence of Brentano's demarcation of phenomenal classes, of his concept of consciousness in the sense of psychical act. Moved by the interest in classification just mentioned, Brentano conducts his enquiry in the form of a two-edged separation of the two main classes of "phenomena" that he recognizes, the psychical and the physical. He arrives at a sixfold differentiation in which only two heads are relevant for our purpose, since in all the others misleading ambiguities do their destructive work, rendering untenable his notion of "phenomenon" in general and of "physical phenomenon" in particular, as well as his concepts of internal and external perception.

Of his two principal differentiations, one directly reveals the *essence* of psychical phenomena or acts. This strikes us unmistakably in any illustration we choose. In perception something is perceived, in imagination, something imagined, in a statement something stated, in love something loved, in hate hated, in desire desired etc. Brentano looks to what is graspably common to such instances, and says that "every mental phenomenon is characterized by what the mediaeval schoolmen called the intentional (or mental) inexistence of an object, and by what we, not without ambiguity, call the relation to a content, the direction to an object (by which a reality is not to be understood) or an immanent objectivity. Each mental phenomenon contains something as object in itself, though not all in the same manner."[3] This "manner in which consciousness refers to an object" (an expression used by Brentano in other passages) is presentative in a presentation, judicial in a judgement etc. etc. Brentano's attempted classification of mental phenomena into presentations, judgements and emotions ("phenomena of love and hate") is plainly based upon this "manner of reference", of which three basically different kinds are distinguished (each admitting of many further specifications).

Whether we think Brentano's classification of "psychical" phenomena successful, and whether we think it basically significant for the whole treatment of psychology, as Brentano claims it is, does not matter here. Only one point has importance for us: that there are essential, specific differences of intentional relation or intention (the generic descriptive character of "acts"). The manner in which a "mere presentation" refers to its object, differs from the manner of a judgement, which treats the same state of affairs as true or false. Quite different again is the manner of a surmise or doubt, the manner of a hope or a fear, of approval or disapproval, of desire or aversion; of the resolution of a theoretical doubt (judgemental decision) or of a practical doubt (voluntary decision in the case of deliberate choice); of the confirmation of a theoretical opinion (fulfilment of a

judgemental intention), or of a voluntary intention (fulfilment of what we mean
to do). Most, if not all, acts are complex experiences, very often involving intentions which are themselves multiple. Emotional intentions are built upon presentative or judging intentions etc. We cannot, however, doubt that to resolve
such complexes is always to come down on primitive intentional characters whose
descriptive essence precludes reduction into other types of experience, and that
the unity of the descriptive genus "intention" ("act-character") displays specific
differences, flowing from its pure essence, which take *a priori* precedence over
empirical, psychological matters-of-fact. There are essentially different species
and subspecies of intention. We cannot, in particular, reduce all differences in acts
into differences in the presentations or judgements they involve, with help only
from elements not of an intentional kind. Aesthetic approval or disapproval, e.g.,
is evidently and essentially a peculiar mode of intentional relation as opposed to
the mere presentation or theoretical assessment of the aesthetic object. Aesthetic
approval and aesthetic predicates may be asserted, and their assertion is a judgement, and as such includes presentations. But the aesthetic intention and its
objects are then *objects* of presentations and judgements: it remains essentially
distinct from these theoretical acts. To evaluate a judgement as valid, an emotional experience as elevated etc., presupposes analogous, closely related, not
specifically identical intentions. Just so in comparisons of judgemental with
voluntary decisions etc.

We take intentional relation, understood in purely descriptive fashion as an
inward peculiarity of certain experiences, to be the essential feature of "psychical
phenomena" or "acts", seeing in Brentano's definition of them as "phenomena
intentionally containing objects in themselves" a circumscription of essence,
whose "reality" (in the traditional sense) is of course ensured by examples.[4] Differently put in terms of pure phenomenology: Ideation performed in exemplary
cases of such experiences – and so performed as to leave empirical-psychological
conception and existential affirmation of being out of account, and to deal only
with the real phenomenological content of these experiences – yields us the pure,
phenomenological generic Idea of *intentional experience* or *act*, and of its various
pure species.[5] That not all experiences are intentional is proved by sensations and
sensational complexes. Any piece of a sensed visual field, full as it is of visual
contents, is an experience containing many part-contents, which are neither
referred to, nor intentionally objective, in the whole.

The discussions which follow will give precision and clarity to the fundamentally different uses of the word "content". Everywhere it will appear that what
one grasped in the analysis and comparison of instances of the two sorts of
contents, can be ideationally seen as a pure distinction of essence. The phenomenological assertions we aim at, are all meant by us (even without special
pointing) as assertions of essence.

A second characterization of mental phenomena by Brentano that has value
for us is the formula "that they are either presentations or founded upon presentations".[6] "Nothing can be judged about, nothing can likewise be desired, nothing
can be hoped or feared, if it is not presented."[7] In this characterization the term
"presentation" does not of course mean the presented content or object, but the
act of presenting this.

This characterization does not seem a suitable starting-point for our researches, since it presupposes a concept of "presentation" that has yet to be worked out: it is hard to draw distinctions among the word's highly ambiguous uses. The discussion of the concept of "act" will lead us naturally on to this. But the characterization is an important utterance, whose content prompts further investigations: we shall have to come back to it later.

§11 Avoidance of verbally tempting misunderstandings. (a) The "mental" or "immanent" object

While we adhere to Brentano's essential characterization, our departures from his opinions force us to abandon his terminology. It will be as well to drop talk of "psychical phenomena", or of "phenomena" at all, where we are dealing with experiences of the class in question. "Psychical phenomena" is a justifiable phrase only on Brentano's view that it fairly circumscribes the psychological field of research: on our view all experiences are in this respect on a level. The term "phenomenon" is likewise fraught with most dangerous ambiguities, and insinuates a quite doubtful theoretical persuasion, expressly professed by Brentano, that each intentional experience is a phenomenon. As "phenomenon" in its dominant use (which is also Brentano's) means an appearing object as such, this implies that each intentional experience is not only directed upon objects, but is itself the object of certain intentional experiences. One thinks here, mainly, of the experiences in which things "appear" in the most special sense, i.e. perceptions: "every psychical phenomenon is an object of inner consciousness". We have already mentioned the grave misgivings that keep us from assenting to this.

Further objections surround the expressions used by Brentano as parallel with, or roughly circumscribing, his term "psychical phenomenon", and which are also in general use. It is always quite questionable, and frequently misleading, to say that perceived, imagined, asserted or desired objects etc., "enter consciousness" (or do so in perceptual, presentative fashion etc.), or to say conversely that "consciousness", "the ego" enters into this or that sort of relation to them, or to say that such objects "are taken up into consciousness" in this or that way, or to say, similarly, that intentional experiences "contain something as their object in themselves" etc. etc.[8] Such expressions promote *two misunderstandings*: first, that we are dealing with a real (*realen*) event or a real (*reales*) relationship, taking place between "consciousness" or "the ego", on the one hand, and the thing of which there is consciousness, on the other; secondly, that we are dealing with a relation between two things, both present in equally real fashion (*reell*) in consciousness, an act and an intentional object, or with a sort of box-within-box structure of mental contents. If talk of a *relation* is here inescapable, we must avoid expressions which tempt us to regard such a relation as having psychological reality (*Realität*), as belonging to the real (*reellen*) content of an experience.

Let us first discuss our *second* misunderstanding more closely. It is particularly suggested by the expression "immanent objectivity" used to name the essential peculiarity of intentional experiences, and likewise by the equivalent scholastic expressions "intentional" or "mental inexistence" of an object. Intentional experiences have the peculiarity of directing themselves in varying fashion to presented objects, but they do so in an *intentional* sense. An object is "referred to"[9] or "aimed at" in them, and in presentative or judging or other fashion. This means no more than that certain experiences are present, intentional in character and, more specifically, presentatively, judgingly, desiringly or otherwise intentional. There are (to ignore certain exceptions) not two things present in experience, we do not experience the object and beside it the intentional experience directed upon it, there are not even two things present in the sense of a part and a whole which contains it: only one thing is present, the intentional experience, whose essential descriptive character is the intention in question. According to its particular specification, it constitutes the full and sole presentation, judgement etc. etc., of this object. If this experience is present, then, *eo ipso* and through its own essence (we must insist), the intentional "relation" to an object is achieved, and an object is "intentionally present"; these two phrases mean precisely the same. And of course such an experience may be present in consciousness together with its intention, although its object does not exist at all, and is perhaps incapable of existence. The object is "meant", i.e. to "mean" it is an experience, but it is then merely entertained in thought, and is nothing in reality.

If I have an idea of the god Jupiter, this god is my presented object, he is "immanently present" in my act, he has "mental inexistence" in the latter, or whatever expression we may use to disguise our true meaning. I have an idea of the god Jupiter: this means that I have a certain presentative experience, the presentation-of-the-god-Jupiter is realized in my consciousness. This intentional experience may be dismembered as one chooses in descriptive analysis, but the god Jupiter naturally will not be found in it. The "immanent", "mental object" is not therefore part of the descriptive or real make-up (*deskriptiven reellen Bestand*) of the experience, it is in truth not really immanent or mental. But it also does not exist extramentally, it does not exist at all. This does not prevent our-idea-of-the-god-Jupiter from being actual, a particular sort of experience or particular mode of mindedness (*Zumutesein*), such that he who experiences it may rightly say that the mythical king of the gods is present to him, concerning whom there are such and such stories. If, however, the intended object exists, nothing becomes phenomenologically different. It makes no essential difference to an object presented and given to consciousness whether it exists, or is fictitious, or is perhaps completely absurd. I think of Jupiter as I think of Bismarck, of the tower of Babel as I think of Cologne Cathedral, of a regular thousand-sided polygon as of a regular thousand-faced solid.[10]

These so-called immanent contents are therefore merely intended or intentional, while truly *immanent contents*, which belong to the real make-up (*reellen Bestande*) of the intentional experiences, are *not intentional*: they constitute the act, provide necessary *points d'appui* which render possible an intention, but are not themselves intended, not the objects presented in the act. I do not see colour-sensations but coloured things, I do not hear tone-sensations but the singer's song etc. etc.[11]

What is true of presentations is true also of other intentional experiences that are built upon them. To represent an object, e.g. the Schloss at Berlin, to oneself, is, we said, to be minded in this or that descriptively determinate fashion. To *judge* about this Schloss, to delight in its architectural beauty, to cherish the wish that one could do so etc. etc., are new experiences, characterized in novel phenomenological terms. All have this in common, that they are modes of objective intention, which cannot be otherwise expressed than by saying that the Schloss is perceived, imagined, pictorially represented, judged about, delighted in, wished for etc. etc.

We shall need more elaborate investigation to determine the justification of talking figuratively about the object presented in a presentation, judged in a judgement etc., as well as the full sense of talk about the relation of acts to objects. It is clear, at least, as far as we now have penetrated, that it will be well to avoid all talk of immanent objectivity. It is readily dispensed with, since we have the expression "intentional object" which is not exposed to similar objections.

As regards misleading talk of the intentional "containment" of objects in acts, it is undeniable that the parallel, equivalent locutions – "the object is a conscious datum", "is in consciousness", "is immanent in consciousness" etc. – suffer from a most damaging ambiguity; "being conscious" (*bewusst*) here means something quite different from the possible senses given to it in the two previously discussed meanings of "consciousness". All modern psychology and epistemology have been confused by these and similar equivocations. With psychological thought and terminology as influential as they are now, it would be ill-advised to set up our own terms in opposition to those of contemporary psychology. Our first concept of consciousness, given an empirical-psychological slant, covers the whole stream of experience which makes up the individual mind's real unity, together with all aspects that enter into the constitution of this stream. This conception shows signs of spreading to psychology, and we therefore decided in our last chapter to give the preference to it, though we did so in phenomenological purity and not from a properly psychological angle. We must therefore exercise some necessary care in talking of consciousness as inner perception, or in talking of it as intentional relation, even if we do not altogether avoid such "uses", which would scarcely be practicable.

§12 (b) The act and the relation of consciousness or the ego to the object

The situation is similar as regards the first misunderstanding we mentioned, where it is imagined that consciousness, on the one hand, and the "matter in consciousness" on the other, become related to one another in a real sense. ("The ego" is here often put in the place of "consciousness".) In *natural reflection*, in fact, it is not the single act which appears, but the ego as one pole of the relation in question, while the other pole is the object. If one then studies an act-experience, which last tempts one to make of the ego an essential, selfsame point of unity in every act. This would, however, bring us back to the view of the ego as a relational centre which we repudiated before.

But if we simply "live" in the act in question, become absorbed, e.g., in the perceptual "taking in" of some event happening before us, in some play of fancy, in reading a story, in carrying out a mathematical proof etc., the ego as relational centre of our performances becomes quite elusive. The idea of the ego may be specially *ready* to come to the fore, or rather to be recreated anew, but only when it is really so recreated, and built into our act, do *we* refer to the object in a manner to which something descriptively ostensible corresponds. We have here, in the actual experience described, a correspondingly complex act which presents the ego, on the one hand, and the presentation, judgement, wish etc., of the moment, with its relevant subject-matter, on the other. From an *objective* standpoint (and so, too, from the standpoint of natural reflection) it is doubtless the case that in each act the ego is intentionally directed to some object. This is quite obvious since the ego is either no more than the "conscious unity", or contemporary "bundle", of experiences, or, in a more natural empirically-real (*realer*) perspective, the continuous thing-like unity, constituted in the unity of consciousness as the personal subject of our experiences, the ego whose mental states these experiences are, that performs the intention, percept, or judgement in question. If such and such an intentional experience is present, the ego *eo ipso* has the corresponding intention.

The sentences "The ego represents an object to itself", "The ego refers presentatively to an object", "The ego has something as an intentional object of its presentation" therefore mean the same as "In the phenomenological ego, a concrete complex of experiences, a certain experience said, in virtue of its specific nature, to be a presentation of object *X*, is really (*reell*) present". Just so the sentence "The ego judges about the object" means the same as "such and such an experience of judging is present in the ego" etc. etc. In our *description* relation to an experiencing ego is inescapable, but the experience described is not itself an experiential complex having the ego-presentation as its part. We perform the description after an objectifying act of reflection, in which reflection on the ego is combined with reflection on the experienced act to yield a relational act, in which the ego appears as itself related to its act's object through its act. Plainly an essential descriptive change has occurred. The original act is no longer simply there, we no longer live in it, but *we attend to it and pass judgement on it*.

We must therefore avoid the misunderstanding which our present discussion has just ruled out, that of treating relation to an ego as of the essence of an intentional experience itself.[12]

§13 The fixing of our terminology

After these critical prolegomena, we shall now fix our own terminology, excluding as far as we can, and in their light, all conflicting assumptions and confusing ambiguities. We shall avoid the term "psychical phenomenon" entirely, and shall talk of "intentional experiences" wherever accuracy requires it. "Experience" must be understood in the phenomenological sense fixed above. The qualifying adjective "intentional" names the essence common to the class of experiences we wish to mark off, the peculiarity of *intending*, of referring to what is objective, in a presentative or other analogous fashion. As a briefer expression, in harmony with our own and foreign verbal usage, we shall use the term "act".

These expressions certainly have their defects. We speak of "intending" [not, of course, in English: *Trans.*] in the sense of specially noticing, or attending to something. *An intentional object need not, however, always be noticed or attended to.* Several acts may be present and interwoven with one another, but attention is emphatically active in one of them. We experience them all together, but we "go all out" (as it were) in this particular one. But it is not unfitting, in view of the traditional use of the term "intentional object", to which Brentano has given renewed currency, to speak in a correlative sense of "intention", especially when we have the term "attending" to do the work of "intention" in the other sense; we shall find reason to hold that attention does not involve a peculiar act.[13] Another ambiguity, however, confronts us. The term "intention" hits off the peculiarity of acts by imagining them to *aim* at something, and so fits the numerous cases that are naturally and understandably ranked as cases of theoretical aiming. But the metaphor does not fit all acts equally, and if we study the examples enumerated in §10, we cannot avoid distinguishing a *narrower* and a *wider* concept of intention. In our metaphor an act of *hitting the mark* corresponds to that of aiming, and just so certain acts correspond as "achievements" or "fulfilments" to other acts as "intentions" (whether of the judging or the desiring sort). The image therefore fits these latter acts quite perfectly; fulfilments are, however, themselves acts, i.e. "intentions", though they are not intentions – at least not in general – in that narrower sense *which points to corresponding fulfilments*. This ambiguity, once recognized, becomes harmless. But of course, where the narrower concept is wanted, this must be expressly stated. The equivalent term "act-character" will also help to avoid misunderstandings.

In talking of "acts", on the other hand, we must steer clear of the word's original meaning: *all thought of activity must be rigidly excluded.*[14] The term "act" is so firmly fixed in the usage of many psychologists, and so wellworn and loosed from its original sense that, after these express reservations, we can go on using it without concern. If we do not wish to introduce artificial novelties, strange alike to our living speech-sense and to historical tradition, we can hardly avoid inconvenience of the just-mentioned sort.

§14 Difficulties which surround the assumption of acts as a descriptively founded class of experiences

In all these terminological discussions, we have gone deep into descriptive analyses of a sort required by our interests in logic and epistemology. Before we go deeper, however, we shall have to consider some objections which affect the bases of our descriptions.

There are a group of thinkers who absolutely reject any marking-off of a class of experiences which have been described by us as "acts" or "intentional experiences". In this connection Brentano's original introduction of the distinction, and his aims in introducing it, have, with some surreptitious misunderstandings, produced confusion: they have kept the distinction's extraordinarily valuable descriptive content from being rightly assessed. Natorp, e.g., rejects it decisively. But when this distinguished thinker objects by saying that[15] "I can deal with a tone by itself or in relation to other contents of consciousness, without also paying regard to its being for an ego, but I cannot deal with myself and my hearing by themselves, without thinking of the tone", we find nothing in this that could confuse. Hearing certainly cannot be torn out of the hearing of a tone, as if it were something apart from the tone it hears. But this does not mean that two things are not to be distinguished: the tone heard, the object of perception, and the hearing of the tone, the perceptual act. Natorp is quite right in saying of the former: "Its existence for me is my consciousness of it. If anyone can catch his consciousness in anything else than the existence of a content for him, I am unable to follow him." It seems to me, however, that the "existence of something for me", is a thing both permitting and requiring further phenomenological analysis. Consider, first, differences in the mode of attention. A content is differently present to me, according as I note it implicitly, not relieved in some whole, or see it in relief, according as I see it marginally, or have specially turned my focussing gaze upon it. More important still are differences between the existence of a content in consciousness in the sense in which a sensation so exists, without being itself made a perceptual object, and of a content which *is* made such an object. The choice of a tone as an instance slightly obscures the distinction without altogether removing it. "I hear" can mean in psychology "I am having sensations": in ordinary speech it means "I am perceiving"; I hear the adagio of the violin, the twittering of the birds etc. Different acts can perceive the same object and yet involve quite different sensations. The same tone is at one moment heard close at hand, at another far away. The same sensational contents are likewise "taken" now in this, and now in that manner. What is most emphasized in the doctrine of apperception is generally the fact that consistency of stimulus does not involve constancy of sensational content; what the stimulus really provokes is overlaid by features springing from actualized dispositions left behind them by previous experiences. Such notions are, however, inadequate, and, above all, phenomenologically irrelevant. Whatever the origin of the experienced contents now present in consciousness, we can think that the same sensational contents should be present with a differing interpretation, i.e. that the same contents should serve to ground perceptions of different objects. Interpretation itself can never be reduced to an influx of new sensations; it is an act-character, a mode of consciousness, of "mindedness" (*Zumuteseins*). We call the experiencing of sensations in this conscious manner the perception of the object in question. What has here been made plain, in a context of natural existence, and by methods appropriate to psychology and natural science, will yield up its phenomenological substance if we abstract from the empirically real (*Realen*). If we consider pure experiences and their own essential content, we form Ideas of pure species and specific situations, in this case the pure species of Sensation, Interpretation, Perception in relation to its *perceptum*, and the relations of essence among these. We then see it to be a fact of essence that the being of a sensational content differs from that of the perceived object presented by it, which is not a reality in consciousness (*reell bewusst*).[16]

All this becomes clear if we change our field of illustration for that of vision. Let us lay the following considerations before a sceptic. I see a thing, e.g. this box, but I do not see my sensations. I always see *one and the same box*, however *it* may be turned and tilted. I have always the *same* "content of consciousness" – if I care to call the perceived object a content of consciousness. But each turn yields a *new* "content of consciousness", if I call experienced contents "contents of consciousness", in a much more appropriate use of words. Very different contents are therefore experienced, though the same object is perceived. The experienced content, generally speaking, is not the perceived object. We must note, further, that the object's real being or non-being is irrelevant to the true essence of the perceptual experience, and to its essence as a perceiving of an object as thus and thus appearing, and as thus and thus thought of. In the flux of experienced content, we imagine ourselves to be in perceptual touch with one and the same object; this itself belongs to the sphere of what we experience. For we experience a "consciousness of identity", i.e. a claim to apprehend identity. On what does this consciousness depend? Must we not reply that different sensational contents are given, but that we apperceive or "take" them "in the same sense", and that *to take them in this sense is an experienced character through which the "being of the object for me" is first constituted*. Must we not say, further, that the consciousness of identity is framed on a basis of these two sorts of experienced characters, as the immediate consciousness that they *mean the same*? And is this consciousness not again an act in our defined sense, whose objective correlate lies in the identity it refers to? These questions, I think, call for an affirmative and evident answer. I find nothing more plain than the distinction here apparent between contents and acts, between perceptual contents in the sense of presentative sensations, and perceptual acts in the sense of interpretative intentions overlaid with various additional characters. Such intentions, united with the sensations they interpret, make up the full concrete act of perception. Intentional characters and complete intentional acts are, of course, contents of consciousness in the widest descriptive sense of experiences: all differences predicable at all, are in this sense *eo ipso* differences of content. But within this widest sphere of what can be experienced, we believe we have found an evident difference between intentional experiences, in whose case *objective intentions* arise through *immanent characters* of the experiences in question, and experiences in whose case this does not occur, contents that may serve as the building-stones of acts *without being acts themselves*.

Examples that will serve to elucidate this distinction, and also to show up various characters of acts, are provided by comparing perception with memory, or comparing either with presentations by means of physical images (paintings, statues etc.), or of signs. Verbal expressions yield the best examples of all. Let us imagine[17] that certain arabesques or figures have affected us aesthetically, and that we then suddenly see that we are dealing with symbols or verbal signs. In what does this difference consist? Or let us take the case of an attentive man hearing some totally strange word as a sound-complex without even dreaming it is a word, and compare this with the case of the same man afterwards hearing the word, in the course of conversation, and now acquainted with its meaning, but not illustrating it intuitively? What in general is the surplus element distinguishing the understanding of a symbolically functioning expression from the uncomprehended verbal sound? What is the difference between simply looking at a concrete object *A*, and treating it as representative of "any *A* whatsoever"? In this and countless similar cases it is act-characters that differ. All logical differences, and differences in categorial form, are constituted in logical acts in the sense of intentions.

In analysing such cases the inadequacies of the modern theory of apperception become plain: it overlooks points decisive from a logical or epistemological standpoint. It does not do justice to phenomenological fact; it does not even attempt to analyse or describe it. Differences of interpretation are above all *descriptive* differences, and these alone, rather than obscure, hypothetical events in the soul's unconscious depths, or in the sphere of physiological happenings, concern the epistemologist. These alone permit of a purely phenomenological treatment, excluding all transcendent affirmations, such as the critique of knowledge presupposes. Apperception is our surplus, which is found in experience itself, in its descriptive content as opposed to the raw existence of sense: it is the act-character which as it were ensouls sense, and is in essence such as to make us perceive this or that object, see this tree, e.g., hear this ringing, smell this scent of flowers etc. etc. *Sensations*, and the acts "interpreting" them or apperceiving them, are alike experienced, *but they do not appear as objects*: they are not seen, heard or *perceived* by any sense. *Objects* on the other hand, appear and are perceived, but they are not *experienced*. Naturally we exclude the case of adequate perception.

The same holds in other cases: it holds, e.g., in the case of the "sensations" (or however we choose to call contents serving as bases to interpretation) which are found in acts of simple or representative imagining. It is an imaging interpretation that sets an imagined rather than a perceptual appearance before us, where experienced sensations mediate the appearance of a pictorially presented object (e.g. a centaur in a painting).[18] One sees at once that the very same thing which, in relation to the intentional object, is called its *presentation*, i.e. the perceiving, remembering, picturing, symbolizing intention directed towards it, is also called an *interpretation, conception, apperception* in relation to the sensations really present in this act.

I also regard it as relevantly evident, in regard to the examples just cited, that there are different "manners of consciousness", different intentional relations to objects: the character of our intention is specifically different in the case of perceiving, of direct "reproductive" recall, of pictorial representation (in the ordinary sense of the interpretation of statues, pictures etc.), and again in the case of a presentation through signs. Each logically distinct way of entertaining an object in thought corresponds to a difference in intention. To me it seems irrefragable that we only know of such differences because we envisage them in particular cases (apprehend them adequately and immediately), can then compare them and range them under concepts, and can thus make them into objects of varying acts of intuition and thought. From such "seeing" we can, through abstract Ideation, progress toward an adequate grasp of the pure species they exemplify, and of the connections of essence among these latter. When Natorp remarks that "all richness, all multiplicity of consciousness pertains rather to contents alone. Consciousness of a simple sensation does not differ, *qua* consciousness, from consciousness of a world: the 'being in consciousness' is entirely the same in both; their difference lies solely in their content", he seems to me not to be keeping apart quite distinct notions of consciousness and content, and to be erecting his identification into an epistemological principle. We have explained the sense in which we too teach that all multiplicity of consciousness depends on content. Content must mean experience, a real part of consciousness: consciousness itself must be the complex formed by experiences. The world, however, never is a thinker's experience. To refer to the world may be an experience, but the world itself is the object intended. It is immaterial, from the point of view of our distinction, what attitude one takes up to the question of the make-up of objective being, of the true, real inner being of the world or of any other object, or of the relation of objective being, as a "unity", to our "manifold" thought-approaches, or of the sense in which one may metaphysically oppose immanent to transcendent being. The distinction in question is prior to all metaphysics, and lies at the very gates of the theory of knowledge: it presupposes no answers to the questions that this theory must be the first to provide.

§15 Whether experiences of one and the same phenomenological kind (of the genus Feeling in particular) can consist partly of acts and partly of non-acts

A new difficulty arises in regard to the generic unity of intentional experiences.

It might be thought that the standpoint from which we divide experiences into intentional and non-intentional, is a merely external one, that the same experiences, or experiences of the same phenomenological class, may at times have an intentional relation to some object, and at times have none. The examples used to attest either concept, and also, in part, the attempted solutions of the problem, have already been discussed in literary fashion in regard to the debated issue as to whether the "intentional relation" suffices to demarcate "psychical phenomena" (the domain of psychology) or not. The debate centred chiefly in phenomena from the sphere of *feeling*. Since the intentionality of other feelings seemed obvious, two doubts were possible: one wondered whether intentionality might not perhaps attach loosely to the *acts* of feeling in question, belonging really to the presentations fused with them, or whether intentionality could be essential to the class of feelings, since one allowed it to some feelings while denying it to others. The connection between this commonly debated question and our present question has thus been made clear.

We must first see whether any sorts of feeling-experience are essentially intentional, and then whether other sorts of feeling-experience lack this property.

(a) Are there any intentional feelings?

Many experiences commonly classed as "feelings" have an undeniable, real relation to something objective. This is the case, e.g., when we are pleased by a melody, displeased at a shrill blast etc. etc. It seems obvious, in general, that every joy or sorrow, that is joy or sorrow *about* something we think of, is a directed act. Instead of joy we can speak of pleased delight in something, instead of sorrow we can speak of displeased or painful dislike of it, aversion from it etc. etc.

Those who question the intentionality of feeling say: Feelings are mere states, not acts, intentions. Where they relate to objects, they owe their relation to a complication with presentations.

No intrinsic objection is involved in this last position. Brentano who defends the intentionality of feelings, also maintains without inconsistency that feelings, like all acts that are not themselves presentations, have presentations as their foundations.[19] We can only direct ourselves feelingly to objects that are presented to us by inwoven presentations. No difference emerges between the disputing parties until someone is really prepared to maintain that feeling, considered in itself, involves nothing intentional, that it does not point beyond itself to a felt object, that only its union with a presentation gives it a certain relation to an object, a relation only intentional by way of *this* connection and not intrinsically so. This is just what the other party disputes.

Brentano thinks we have here two intentions built on one another: the underlying, founding intention gives us the *presented* object, the founded intention the *felt* object. The former is separable from the latter, the latter inseparable from the former. His opponents think there is only *one* intention here, the presenting one.

89

If we subject the situation to a careful phenomenological review, Brentano's conception seems definitely to be preferred. Whether we turn with pleasure to something, or whether its unpleasantness repels us, an object is presented. But we do not merely have a presentation, with an added feeling *associatively* tacked on to it, and not intrinsically related to it, but pleasure or distaste *direct* themselves to the presented object, and could not exist without such a direction. If two psychical experiences, e.g. two presentations, are associated in an objective-psychological sense, there is a phenomenologically discernible type of associative unity among the reproduced experiences which corresponds to the objective dispositions which govern them. Side by side with the intentional elation which each has to its object, there is also a phenomenological mode of connection: one idea, e.g. that of Naples, carries with it the idea of Vesuvius, the one is peculiarly bound up with the other, so that we say in regard to the objects presented – the mode of their presentation here essentially requires further description – that the one reminds us of the other. (This sentence is being used to express a phenomenological situation.) It is easily seen, however, that though all this in a sense constitutes a new intentional relationship, it does not turn each associated member into an object of the other's intention. The intentional relationships remain unconfused in their association. How indeed could they furnish an object, borrowed from an associated intention, to something not itself intentional? It is clear, further, that such a phenomenologically associative relation is extrinsic, not at all to be put on a level with the relation of pleasure to the pleasant. The presentation which reproduces is quite possible without such a reproductive function. But pleasure without anything pleasant is unthinkable. And it is unthinkable, not because we are here dealing with correlative expressions, as when we say, e.g., that a cause without an effect, or a father without a child, is unthinkable, but because *the specific essence of pleasure demands a relation to something pleasing*. Just so the feature known as conviction is unthinkable apart from something of which we are convinced. There is, similarly, no desire whose specific character can do without something desired, no agreement or approval without something agreed on or approved etc. etc. These are all intentions, genuine acts in our sense. They all "owe" their intentional relation to certain underlying presentations. But it is part of what we mean by such "owing" that they themselves really now *have* what they owe to something else.

It is plain, too, that the relation between founding (underlying) presentation and founded act cannot be correctly described by saying that the former *produces* the latter. We say that the object arouses our pleasure, just as we say in other cases that some circumstance inspires doubt, compels agreement, provokes desire etc. But the result of such apparent causation, the pleasure, doubt or agreement provoked, is itself through and through intentional. We are not dealing with an external causal relation where the effect conceivably could be what it intrinsically is without the cause, or where the cause brings something forth that could have existed independently.

Closer consideration shows it to be absurd in principle, here or in like cases, to treat an intentional as a causal relation, to give it the sense of an empirical, substantial-causal case of necessary connection. For the intentional object, here thought of as "provocative", is only in question as an intentional, not as an external reality, which really and psycho-physically determines my mental life. A battle of centaurs, seen in a picture or framed in fancy, "provokes" my approval just like some beautiful, real landscape: if I look on the latter psycho-physically as the real cause of my mentally provoked state of pleasure, this "causation" is altogether different from the causation we have when we see the visible landscape – in virtue of such and such a mode of appearing and such and such pictured colours and forms – as the "source", "ground" or "cause" of my pleasure. Pleasant-ness or pleasure do not belong as effect to this landscape considered as a physical reality, but only to it *as appearing in this or that manner*, perhaps as thus and thus judged of or as reminding us of this or that, in the conscious act here in question: it is as such that the landscape "demands", "arouses" such feelings.[20]

(b) Are there non-intentional feelings? Distinction between feeling-sensations and feeling-acts.

We may now ask more generally whether, in addition to the intentional varieties of feeling, there are not other *non*-intentional species. It may seem at first that an obvious "Yes" is the right answer. In the wide field of so-called sensory feelings, no intentional characters can be found. The sensible pain of a burn can certainly not be classed beside a conviction, a surmise, a volition etc. etc., but beside sensory contents like rough or smooth, red or blue etc. If we recall such pains, or any sensory pleasures (the fragrance of a rose the relish of certain foods etc. etc.), we find that our sensory feelings are blended with the sensations from the various sense-fields, just as these latter are blended with one another.

Every sensory feeling, e.g. the pain of burning oneself or of being burnt, is no doubt after a fashion referred to an object: it is referred, on the one hand, to the ego and its burnt bodily member, on the other hand, to the object which inflicts the burn. In all these respects there is conformity with other sensations: tactual sensations, e.g., are referred in just this manner to the bodily member which touches, and to the external body which is touched. And though this reference is realized in intentional experiences, no one would think of calling the referred sensations intentional. It is rather the case that our sensations are here function-ing as presentative contents in perceptual acts, or (to use a possibly misleading phrase) that our sensations here receive an objective "interpretation" or "taking-up". They themselves are not acts, but acts are constituted through them, wher-ever, that is, intentional characters like a perceptual interpretation lay hold of them, and as it were animate them. In just this manner it seems that a burning, piercing, boring pain, fused as it is from the start with certain tactual sensations, must itself count as a sensation. It functions at least as other sensations do, in providing a foothold for empirical, objective interpretations.

All this seems unobjectionable, and the whole question disposed of. We seem to have shown that *some* feelings are to be reckoned among intentional experiences, while others are non-intentional.

But we are led to doubt, then, whether two such sorts of "feelings" really form a single class. We spoke previously of "feelings" of liking and dislike, of approval and disapproval, of valuation and disvaluation – experiences obviously akin to theoretical acts of assent and rejection, of taking something to be probable or improbable, or to deliberative acts of judgemental or voluntary decision etc. Here we have a *kind*, a plain unity of essence, which included nothing but acts, where such sensations of pain and pleasure have no place: descriptively the latter belong, in virtue of their specific essence, among tactual, gustatory, olfactory and other sensations. Being at best presentative contents of objects of intention, but not themselves intentions, they manifest descriptive differences so essential, that we cannot seriously believe in the unity of a genuine class. In both cases of course, we speak of "feelings", i.e. in the case of the above-mentioned acts of liking as in the case of the above-mentioned sensations. This fact need not perplex, any more than our ordinary talk of "feeling", in the sense of touching, need lead us astray in the case of tactile sensations.

Brentano has already pointed to the ambiguity here dealt with, in discussing the intentionality of feelings. He draws a distinction, in sense if not in words, between *sensations* of pain and pleasure (feeling-sensations) and pain and pleasure in the sense of *feelings*. The contents of the former – or, as I should simply say, the former[21] – are in this terminology "physical", while the latter are "psychical phenomena", and they belong therefore to essentially different genera. This notion I regard as quite correct, but only doubt, whether the meaning of the word "feeling" does not lean predominantly towards "feeling-sensation", and whether the many acts we call "feelings" do not owe their name to the feeling-sensations with which they are essentially interwoven. One must of course not mix up questions of suitable terminology with questions regarding the factual correctness of Brentano's distinction.

Our distinction should constantly be kept in mind and fruitfully applied in analysing all complexes of feeling-sensations and feeling-acts. Joy, e.g., concerning some happy event, is certainly an act. But this act, which is not merely an intentional character, but a concrete and therefore complex experience, does not merely hold in its unity an idea of the happy event and an act-character of liking which relates to it: a sensation of pleasure attaches to the idea, a sensation at once seen and located as an emotional excitement in the psycho-physical feeling-subject, and also as an objective property – the event seems as if bathed in a rosy gleam. The event thus pleasingly painted now serves as the first foundation for the joyful approach, the liking for, the being charmed, or however one's state may be described. A sad event, likewise, is not merely seen in its thing like content and context, in the respects which make it an event: it seems clothed and coloured with sadness. The same unpleasing sensations which the empirical ego refers to and locates in itself – the pang in the heart – are referred in one's emotional conception to the thing itself. *These* relations are purely presentational: we first have an essentially new type of intention in hostile repugnance, in active dislike etc. Sensations of pleasure and pain may continue, though the act-characters built upon them may lapse. When the facts which provoke pleasure sink into the background, are no longer apperceived as emotionally coloured, and perhaps cease to be intentional objects at all, the pleasurable excitement may linger on for a while: it may itself be felt as agreeable. Instead of representing a pleasant property of the object, it is referred merely to the feeling-subject, or is itself presented and pleases.

Much the same holds in the sphere of desire and volition.[22] If difficulty is felt in the fact that desire does not always seem to require conscious reference to what is desired, that we are often moved by obscure drives or pressures towards unrepresented goals, and if one points especially to the wide sphere of natural instinct, where goal-consciousness is at least absent at the start, one may say: This is a case of mere sensations – we may speak analogically of "desire-sensations" – without needing to affirm the existence of an essentially new class of sensations – i.e. of experiences really lacking intentional reference, and so also remote in kind from the essential character of intentional desire. Alternatively one may say: Here we are dealing with intentional experiences, but with such as are characterized by indeterminateness of objective direction, an "indeterminateness" which does not amount to a privation, but which stands for a descriptive character of one's presentation. The idea we have when "something" stirs, when there is a rustling, a ring at the door, etc., an idea had before we give it verbal expression, has indeterminateness of direction, and this indeterminateness is of the intention's essence, it is determined as presenting an indeterminate "something".

Our one concept of desire might fit many cases, and our other concept others, and we might have to allow, not a relation of generic community between intentional and non-intentional urges or desires, but one of mere equivocation.

We must observe, also, that our classification is oriented to the concretely complex, and that the total character of such unities may at one time seem to depend on sensational features (e.g. pleasure on urge-sensations), at another on act-intentions which rest on these. The formation and use of our expressions will at times therefore point to sensory contents, at times to actintentions, so giving rise to the equivocations in question.

Additional Note. The obvious tendency of our conception is to attribute primary, genuine differences in intensity to underlying sensations, and to concrete acts only in a secondary manner, in so far as their concrete total character involves differences of intensity in their sensational basis. *Act-intentions*, the inseparable aspects which give acts their essential distinctive peculiarities, or which characterize them severally as judgements, feelings etc., *must be without intrinsic intensity*. Deeper analyses are, however, required here.

§16 Distinction between descriptive and intentional content

We have buttressed our notion of the essence of acts against objection, and given them a generic unity of essence in their character as intentions, as consciousnesses in the unique descriptive sense. We now introduce an important phenomenological distinction, obvious after our previous discussions, between the *real* (*reellen*)[23] and the *intentional* content of an act.

By the real phenomenological content of an act we mean the sum total of its concrete or abstract parts, in other words, the sum total of the *partial experiences* that really constitute it. To point out and describe such parts is the task of pure descriptive psychological analysis operating from an empirical, natural-scientific point of view. Such analysis is in all cases concerned to dismember what we inwardly experience as it in itself is, and as it is really (*reell*) given in experience, without regard either to genetic connections, or to extrinsic meaning and valid application. Purely descriptive psychological analysis of an articulated sound-pattern finds only sounds and abstract parts or unifying forms of sounds, it finds no sound-vibrations or organs of hearing etc.; it also never finds anything that resembles the ideal sense that makes the sound-pattern to be a name, nor the person to whom the name may apply. Our example suffices to make our intention clear. The real (*reell*) contents of acts are of course only known through descriptive analyses of this kind. That obscurities of intuition or inadequacies of descriptive conception – faults, in short, of method – may lead to much "manufacture" of sensations (to use Volkelt's phrase) cannot be denied. This, however, only concerns the legitimacy of particular cases of descriptive analysis. It is clear, if anything is clear, that intentional experiences contain distinguishable parts and aspects, and this alone is of importance here.

Let us now shift from our natural-scientific, psychological standpoint to an ideal-scientific, phenomenological one. We must exclude all empirical interpretations and existential affirmations, we must take what is inwardly experienced or otherwise inwardly intuited (e.g. in pure fancy) as pure experiences, as our exemplary basis for acts of Ideation. We must ideate universal essences and essential connections in such experiences – ideal Species of experiencing of differing levels of generality, and ideally valid truths of essence which apply *a priori*, and with unlimited generality, to possible experiences of these species. We thus achieve insights in a pure phenomenology which is here oriented to *real* (*reellen*) constituents, whose descriptions are in every way "ideal" and free from "experience", i.e. from presupposition of real *existence*. When we speak simply of the real (*reellen*), and in general of the phenomenological analysis and description of experiences, the tie-up of our discussions to psychological material is (we must keep on stressing) merely transitional, since none of its empirically real (*reellen*) conceptions and assertions of existence (e.g. of experiences as states of animal beings having experiences in a real (*realen*), space-time world) are at all operative, that *pure* phenomenological validity of essence is aimed at and claimed.[24]

Content in the real (*reellen*) sense is the mere application of the most general notion of content, valid in all fields to intentional experiences. If we now oppose *intentional*[25] to real (*reell*) content, the word shows that the peculiarity of intentional experiences (or acts) is now in question. Here, however, there are several concepts, all grounded in the *specific* nature of acts, which may be equally covered by the rubric "intentional content", and are often so covered. We shall first have to distinguish *three* concepts of the intentional content: the *intentional object* of the act, its *intentional material* (as opposed to its *intentional quality*) and, lastly its *intentional essence*. These distinctions will become familiar in the course of the following very general analyses, which are also essential to the more restricted aim of clarifying the essence of knowledge.

§17 The intentional content in the sense of the intentional object

Our first concept of intentional content needs no elaborate preliminaries. It concerns the intentional object, e.g. a house when a house is presented. That the intentional object does not generally fall within the real (*reellen*) content of an act, but rather differs completely from this, has been already discussed. This is not only true of acts pointing intentionally to "outer" things; it is also true in part of acts that point to our own present experiences, as when I speak of, e.g., my actually present, but "background" conscious experiences. Partial coincidence is only found where an intuition actually points to something "lived through" in the intentional act itself, as, e.g., in acts of adequate perception.

We must distinguish, in relation to the intentional content taken as object of the act, between *the object as it is intended*, and the *object* (period) *which* is intended. In each act an object is presented as determined in this or that manner, and as such it may be the target of varying intentions, judgemental, emotional, desiderative etc. Known connections, actual or possible, entirely external to the reality of the act, may be so cemented with it in intentional unity as to be held to attribute objective properties to the same presented object, properties not in the scope of the intention in question. Many new presentations may arise, all claiming, in virtue of an objective unity of knowledge, to be presenting the same object. In all of them the object *which* we intend is the same, but in each our intention differs, each means the object in a different way. The idea, e.g., of the German Emperor, presents its object as an Emperor, and as the Emperor of Germany. The man himself is the son of the Emperor Frederick III, the grandson of Queen Victoria, and has many other properties neither named nor presented. One can therefore quite consistently speak of the intentional and extra-intentional content of the object of some presentation, and one can use many other suitable, non-technical expressions, e.g. what we intend in the object, that would not lead to misunderstandings.

Another, yet more important, distinction goes with the distinction just drawn, that between *the objective reference of the act, taken in its entirety*, and the *objects to which its various partial, constituent acts refer*. Each act has its own appropriate, intentional, objective reference: this is as true of complex as of simple acts. *Whatever the composition of an act out of partial acts may be, if it is an act at all, it must have a single objective correlate*, to which we say it is "directed", in the *full, primary* sense of the world. Its partial acts (if they really are acts entering the complex act as parts, and not mere parts *of* this act) likewise point to objects, which will, in general, not be the same as the object of the whole act, though they may occasionally be the same. In *a secondary* sense, no doubt, the whole act may be said to refer to these objects also, but its intention only terminates on them inasmuch as its constituent acts primarily intend them. Or, seen from the other side, they are only the act's objects in so far as they help to make up its true object, in the manner in which this is intended. They function as terms of relations in which the primary object is seen as the correlated term. The act, e.g., corresponding to the name "the knife on the table" is plainly complex: the object of the whole act is a knife, of one of its part-acts, a table. But, as the whole nominal act refers to the knife as on the table, presents it in this relative position to the latter, one can say that the table is in a secondary sense an intentional object of the whole act. Again, to illustrate another important class of cases, the knife is the object *about* which we judge or make a statement, when we say that the knife is on the table; the knife is not, however, the primary or full object of the judgement, but only the object of its subject. The full and entire object corresponding to the whole judgement is the *state of affairs* judged: the same state of affairs is presented in a mere presentation, wished in a wish, asked after in a question, doubted in a doubt etc. The wish that the knife were on the table, which coincides (in object) with the judgement, is concerned with the knife, but we don't in it wish the knife, but that the knife should be on the table, that this should be so. The state of affairs must obviously not be confused with the judging of it, nor with the presentation of this judgement: I plainly do not wish for a judgement, nor for any presentation. Just so there is a corresponding question regarding the knife, but the knife is not (non-sensically) what we ask; we ask regarding the knife's position on the table, whether this actually is the case. So much for the first sense in which we speak of intentional contents. Since such talk is so highly ambiguous, we shall do well never to speak of an intentional content where an intentional object is meant, but to call the latter the intentional object of the act in question.

§18 Simple and complex, founding and founded acts

We have so far only learnt to attach one meaning to the term "intentional contents". Further meanings will develop in our ensuing investigations, where we shall attempt to seize on certain important peculiarities of the phenomenological essence of acts, and to throw light on the ideal unities rooted in these.

We start with the difference, previously noted, between simple and compound acts. Not every unitary experience compounded out of acts is for that reason a *compound* act, just as every concatenation of machines is not a compound machine. Our comparison illuminates our further requirements. A compound machine is a machine compounded out of machines, but so compounded, that it has a total performance into which the performances of the partial machines flow, and the like is the case in regard to compounded acts. Each partial act has its particular intentional reference, each its unitary object, and its way of referring to it. These manifold part-acts are, however, summed up in one total act, whose total achievement lies in the unity of its intentional reference. To this the individual acts contribute their individual performances: the unity of what is objectively presented, and the whole manner of the intentional reference to it, are not set up *alongside* of the partial acts, but *in* them, in the way in which they are combined, a way which realizes a unity of *act*, and not merely a unity of experience. The object of this total act could not appear as it does, unless the partial acts presented their objects in their fashion: their general function is to present parts, or to present externally related terms, or to present relational forms of the object etc. The same is true of the non-presentative aspects of the act that make out of the unified qualities in the partial acts the quality of whole acts, and so determine the specifically different ways in which the objects concerned in either sort of act are "taken up into consciousness".

We may take as an example the unity of categorical or hypothetical predication, where the total acts are plainly put together out of partial acts. The subject-member of a categorical assertion is an underlying act, a positing of a subject, on which the positing of a predicate, its attribution or denial, reposes. Just so the antecedent of a hypothetical assertion is constituent in a clearly demarcated part-act, upon which the conditional assertion is built. The total experience is in each case plainly one act, one judgement, whose single, total object is a single state of affairs. As the judgement does not exist alongside of, or between, the subject-positing and the predicating acts, but exists in them as their dominant unity, so, on the correlative side, the objective unity is the state of affairs judged, an appearance emergent out of subject and predicate, or out of antecedent and consequent.

The situation may be yet more complex. On such a structured act (whose members may themselves be further structured) a new act may be built, e.g. a joy may be built on the assertion of a state of affairs, a joy *in* that state of affairs. The joy is not a concrete act in its own right, and the judgement an act set up beside it: the judgement rather underlies the joy, fixes its content, realizes its abstract possibility for, without some such foundation, there could be no joy at all.[26] Judgements may similarly serve as foundations for surmises, doubts, questions, wishes, acts of will etc., and the latter acts may likewise serve to found other acts in their turn. There are therefore manifold ways in which acts may be combined into total acts. The briefest consideration makes plain that there are deep differences in the ways in which acts are concretely woven into other acts, or based upon underlying acts, and made possible by such concretion: the systematic investigation of such ways, even in descriptive, psychological fashion, is as yet hardly in its beginnings.

§19 The function of attention in complex acts. Instance of the phenomenological relation of verbal sound to sense

How far differences go in this direction will be plain from an example previously considered: the whole which is formed by expression and sense.[27] This will be quite as interesting as the examples just analysed. Further considerations will also illustrate the obvious to anyone, the fact that there are great differences in the energy, so to speak, with which acts assert themselves in an act-complex. Generally the greatest energy will be displayed by the act-character which comprehends and subsumes all partial acts in its unity – whether it be a particular act-intention like joy, or a form of unity that pervades all parts of the whole act. In this act, we live, as it were, principally; in the subordinate acts only in proportion to the importance of their achievements for the whole act and its intention. But plainly to talk of such differences of importance, is just to use other words to cover the "preferential living" in question, which some acts enjoy and others not.

Let us now consider our example. It concerns a union of the acts in which an expression, treated "as a sensuous verbal sound", is constituted, with the quite different act constitutive of its meaning, an essentially different connection, we may note, to that of the last-mentioned acts with the acts in which they have an immediate or a more remote intuitive fulfilment. Not only is the mode of union here essentially different, but also the energy with which certain acts are performed. The expression is indeed perceived, but our interest does not live in this perception; we attend, when not distracted, to the signified rather than the signs. Dominant energy resides in the sense-giving acts. The intuitive acts which perhaps accompany, and are inwoven into the total act's unity, lending it evidence, or illustrating it, or otherwise functioning in it, absorb our dominant interest in varying degree. They may be prominent, as in the perceptual judgement, or the analogously constituted picture-judgement, where our one wish is to express the perception or imagination in which we live, and likewise in the completely evident judgement of necessary law. They may recede and come to seem quite subsidiary, as in cases of imperfect or wholly unsuitable illustration of some dominant thought. They may then be a vanishing phantasm, to which practically no interest attaches. (In extreme cases one may even doubt whether accompanying picture-ideas really enter the unity of the expressive act at all, whether they are not mere accompaniments; coexisting with the acts in question but not forming a single act with them.)

For us it is especially important to get as much clarity as we can on this situation of expressions: we shall therefore dwell on some points in more detail.

Expression and sense are two objective unities, laid before us by certain acts. An expression itself, e.g. a written word, is, as our *First Investigation* showed,[28] as much a physical object as any penscratch or ink-blot on paper. It is "given" to us in the same sense as a physical object, i.e. it appears, and that it appears merely means, as it means elsewhere, that a certain act is experienced, in which certain sensory experiences are "apperceived" in a certain manner. The acts in question are naturally perceptual or imaginative presentations: in these the expression (as physically meant) is constituted.

What make the expression an expression are, we know, the acts attaching to it. These are not outside of it or beside it, or merely simultaneous in consciousness; they are one with it, and so one, that we can scarce avoid regarding them all as making up a *unitary total act*. (By the word "expression" we mean, with natural and convenient looseness, the act-unity which presents it.) A statement, an assertion, e.g., we should at once say, is a strictly unitary experience, which belongs to the genus Judgement. We do not find in ourselves a mere sum of acts, but a single act in which, as it were, a bodily and spiritual side are distinct. Just so an expressed wish is no mere *ensemble* of expression and wish – with perhaps an additional, debatable judgement regarding the wish – but a whole, an act, which we unhesitatingly call a wish. The physical expression, the verbal sound, may seem unessential to this unity, and it is unessential inasmuch as any other verbal sound might have replaced it and done duty for it: it could even have been wholly dispensed with. But if it is there, and serves as a verbal sound, it will be fused with the accompanying acts in a single act. Plainly the connection is in a certain sense extrinsic, since the expression as such, i.e. the manifest verbal sound or written sign etc., is not seen as part of the object meant in the whole act, nor even as really determining it, nor as having really to do with it. The contribution made by the acts constituting the verbal sound of a statement, differs characteristically from the contribution of the underlying acts illustrated and discussed above, or of the partial acts which pertain to the predicative members of complete predications. We must not, however, despite all this, question the presence of a certain intentional linkage between word and thing. Inasmuch, e.g., as the word names the thing, it once more appears as in some sense one with it, as belonging to it, even if not as materially part of it, or one of its material properties. Its material unrelatedness does not exclude a certain intentional unity, correlated with the interconnection of the corresponding acts to form a single act. This is confirmed if we recall the deep-set tendency to exaggerate the bond between word and thing, to invest it with objectivity, perhaps even to insinuate something of mystic unity into it.[29]

In the compound act which includes both appearing-expression and sense-giving acts, it is plainly the latter, or the act-unity which dominates both, which essentially fixes the character of the whole act. It is for this reason that we call experiences, whether expressed or unexpressed, by the same names: i.e., "judgement", "wish", etc. Certain acts in the compound are therefore peculiarly prominent, a fact incidentally noted when we said that, when we normally express something, we do not, *qua* expressing it, live in the acts constituting the expression as a physical object – we are not interested in this object – but we live in the acts which give it sense: we are exclusively *turned* to the object that appears in such acts, we *aim* at it, we *mean* it in the special, *pregnant* sense. We pointed out, also, that, while a special orientation to the physical expression is possible, it essentially changes the character of our experience: this no longer is "expressive" in the ordinary sense of the word.

Plainly we are here concerned with a case of the general fact of *attention*, to which long effort has not yet brought sufficient clearness.[30] Nothing has so hindered right views in this field as the by-passing of the fact that *attention is an emphatic function which belongs among acts in the above defined sense of intentional experiences*, and which is not descriptively graspable as long as "being experienced", in the sense of the mere existence of a content in consciousness, is confused with intentional objectivity. *Acts* must be present, before we can *live* in them or be *absorbed* in performing them, and when we are so absorbed (in various manners requiring further description) we mind the *objects* of these acts, we are primarily or secondarily oriented towards them, perhaps thematically concerned with them. Absorption in acts and minding objects are the same thing expressed from different angles.

As opposed to this, men speak of attention as if it were a name for modes of special relief imparted to *experienced* contents. At the same time there is still talk of these contents (the contemporary experiences themselves) as if they were the things to which we ordinarily say we are attending. We do not of course dispute the possibility of attending to experienced contents, but when this happens, such contents become objects of *internal* perception: such perception is not the mere being of the content in a conscious setting, but an *act* in which the content is rendered *objective*. *Intentional* objects of acts, and only intentional objects, are the things to which we are at any time attentive, and to which we can be so attentive. This accords with ordinary usage, whose true sense should be plain on the briefest reflection. To ordinary usage the objects of attention are always objects of inward or outward perception, objects of memory, of expectation, perhaps states of affairs in a scientific discussion, etc. Certainly we can only speak of attention where what we attend to is "in consciousness". What is not a "content of consciousness" cannot attract or hold attention nor become a theme of consciousness. The danger of this obvious truth lies in the equivocal term "content of consciousness". For the obvious truth does not mean that attention is necessarily directed to conscious contents in the sense of *experiences*, as if no one could attend to things, and to other real (*reale*) or ideal objects, which are not experiences. It means, rather, that there must be a basic act in which what we attend to becomes objective, becomes presented in the widest sense of this word. Such *presentation* can be non-intuitive as well as intuitive, can be utterly inadequate as much as adequate. One might, however, consider, from another angle, whether the *preference* an act enjoys over its fellows when we "live" in it, when we are primarily or secondarily "turned" towards its objects, are perhaps "specially concerned" with them, *should itself be reckoned as an act*. Such a view would make all dominant facts *eo ipso* complex. Should we not rather regard the phenomena of attention as mere ways – requiring much more detailed description of their several varieties – in which acts may be carried out? This would seem to be undoubtedly right.

But we do not wish to work out a "theory" of attention here, but to discuss the important role played by it in complex acts, in putting certain act-characters into relief, and so essentially influencing the phenomenological pattern of these acts.

§20 The difference between the quality and the matter of an act

We now turn from the distinction between the acts in which we "live" and the acts which proceed "on the side", to another extremely important, seemingly plain distinction lying in a quite different direction. This is the distinction between the general act-character, which stamps an act as merely presentative, judgemental, emotional, desiderative etc., and its "content" which stamps it as presenting *this*, as judging *that* etc. etc. The two assertions "2 × 2 = 4" and "Ibsen is the principal founder of modern dramatic realism", are both, *qua* assertions, of one kind; each is qualified as an assertion, and their common feature is their *judgement-quality*. The one, however, judges one content and the other another content. To distinguish such "contents" from other notions of "content" we shall speak here of the *matter* (material) of judgements. We shall draw similar distinctions between *quality* and *matter* in the case of all acts.

Under the rubric of "matter" we shall not divide, and then reassemble in unity, constituents of an act such as the subject-act, the predicate-act etc.: this would make the unified total content the act itself. What we here have in mind is something totally different. Content in the sense of "matter" is a component of the concrete act-experience, which it may share with acts of quite different quality. It comes out most clearly if we set up a series of identical utterances, where the act-qualities change, while the matter remains identical. All this is not hard to provide. We recall familiar talk to the effect that *the same content* may now be the content of a mere presentation, now of a judgement, now of a question, now of a doubt, a wish etc. etc. A man who frames the presentation "There are intelligent beings on Mars" frames the same presentation as the man who asserts "There are intelligent beings on Mars", and the same as the man who asks "Are there intelligent beings on Mars?", or the man who wishes "If only there are intelligent beings on Mars!" etc. etc. We have deliberately written out the closely correspondent expressions in full. To be alike in "content", while differing in act-quality has its visible grammatical expression; the harmony of grammatical forms points the way to our analysis.

What do we mean by the "same content"? Plainly the intentional objectivity of the various acts is the same. One and the same state of affairs is presented in the presentation, put as valid in the judgement, wished for in the wish, asked about in the question. This observation does not, however, go far enough, as we shall now show. In "real" (*reell*) phenomenological treatment objectivity counts as nothing: in general, it transcends the act. *It makes no difference what sort of being we give our object, or with what sense or justification we do so, whether this being is real* (real) *or ideal, genuine, possible or impossible, the act remains "directed upon" its object.* If one now asks how something non-existent or transcendent can be the intentional object in an act in which it has no being, one can only give the answer we gave above, which is also a wholly sufficient one. The object is an intentional object: this means there is an act having a determinate intention, and determinate in a way which makes it an intention towards this object. This "reference to an object" belongs peculiarly and intrinsically to an act-experience, and the experiences manifesting it are by definition intentional experiences or acts. *All differences in mode of objective reference are descriptive differences in intentional experiences.*

We must note, however, that this peculiarity revealed in the phenomenological essence of acts, of directing themselves to a *certain* object and not another, will not exhaust the phenomenological essence in question. We spoke of differences in mode of objective reference, but this lumps together totally distinct, independently variable differences. Some are differences in *act-quality*, as when we speak of such different ways of being intentional as being presented, being judged, being asked etc. Such variation intersects with the *other*, wholly independent variation in objective reference: one act may point to this, another to that object, regardless as to whether the acts are alike or different in quality. *Every quality can be combined with every objective reference.* This second variation therefore points to a second *side in the phenomenological content of acts, differing from their quality.*

In the case of this latter variation, which concerns the changing direction to objects, one does not speak of different "manners of objective reference", though the differentia of this direction lies in the act itself.

Looking more closely, we see another possibility of variation independent of quality which certainly prompts talk of different ways of referring to objects. We see, too, that the twofold variation just distinguished is not quite in a position to effect a neat separation of what must be defined as "matter" from quality. Our distinction posited two sides in every act: its quality, which stamped it as, e.g., presentation or judgement, and its matter, that lent it direction to an object, which made a presentation, e.g., present *this* object and no other. This is quite right, and yet is to some extent misleading. For one is at first tempted to interpret the situation simply: matter is that part of an act which gives it direction to this object and no other. Acts are therefore unambiguously determined by their quality, on the one hand, and by the object they will intend, on the other. This seeming obviousness is, however, delusive. One can readily see, in fact, that *even if quality and objective direction are both fixed at the same time, certain variations remain possible.* Two identically qualified acts, e.g. two presentations, may appear directed, and evidently directed, to the same object, without full agreement in intentional essence. The ideas *equilateral triangle* and *equiangular triangle* differ in content, though both are directed, and evidently directed, to the same object: they present the same object, although "in a different fashion". The same is true of such presentations as *a length of a + b units* and *a length of b + a units*; it is also true of statements, in other respects synonymous, which differ only in "equivalent" concepts. The same holds if we compare other types of equivalent assertions, e.g. *We shall have rain* and *The weather is becoming rainy.* If we consider a series of acts like the judgement *It will rain today*, the surmise *It may well rain today*, the question *Will it rain today?* and the wish *Oh that it would rain today!*, we see that it exemplified identity not only as regards objective reference in general, but also *as regards a new sense of objective reference*, a sense not fixed by the quality of the act.

Quality only determines whether what is already presented *in definite fashion* is intentionally present as wished, asked, posited in judgement etc. The matter, therefore, must be *that element in an act which first gives it reference to an object, and reference so wholly definite that it not merely fixes the object meant in a general way, but also the precise way in which it is meant.*[31] The matter – to carry clearness a little further – is that peculiar side of an act's phenomenological content that not only determines *that* it grasps the object but also *as what* it grasps it, the properties, relations, categorial forms, that it itself attributes to it. It is the act's matter that makes its object count as this object and no other, it is *the objective, the interpretative sense (Sinn der gegenständlichen Auffassung, Auffassungssinn)* which serves as basis for the act's quality (while indifferent to such qualitative differences). Identical matters can never yield distinct objective references, as the above examples prove. Differences of equivalent, but not tautologically equivalent expressions, certainly affect matter. Such differences must not be thought to correspond to any fragmentation of matter: there is not one piece of matter corresponding to an identical object, another to the differing mode of presenting it. Reference to objects is possible *a priori* only as being a definite manner of reference: it arises only if the matter is fully determined.

To this we may add an observation: act-quality is undoubtedly *an abstract aspect of acts*, unthinkable apart from all matter. Could we hold an experience possible which was a judging without definite subject-matter? This would take from the judgement its character as intentional experience, which is evidently part of its essence.

The same holds of matter. A matter that was not matter for presentation, nor for judgement, nor for . . . etc. etc., would be held to be unthinkable.

Talk about the manner of objective reference is ambiguous: at times it points to differences of quality, at times to differences of matter. We shall henceforth counteract such ambiguity by suitable locutions involving the terms "quality" and "matter". That such talk has yet other important meanings will appear in due course.[32]

§21 The intentional and the semantic essence

We shall postpone investigation of the difficult problems here involved, to treat of a new distinction, in which a new concept of intentional content arises, which has to be separated off from the full descriptive content of the act.

In each act's descriptive content we have distinguished quality and matter as two mutually dependent aspects. If both are taken together, it would at first seem, the act in question will merely have been reconstituted. Looked at more closely, however, another conception distinguishes itself from whose point of view *the two aspects, brought to unity, do not make up the concrete, complete act.* Two acts may in fact agree in respect of their quality and their matter, and yet differ descriptively. In so far as quality and matter now count for us (as will be shown later) as the wholly essential, and so never to be dispensed with, constituents of an act, it would be suitable to call the union of both, forming one part of the complete act, the act's *intentional essence.* To pin down this term, and the conception of the matter it goes with, we simultaneously introduce a second term. To the extent that we deal with acts, functioning in expressions in sense-giving fashion, or capable of so functioning – whether all acts are so capable must be considered later – we shall speak more specifically of the *semantic essence* of the act. The ideational abstraction of this essence yields a "meaning" in our ideal sense.

In justification of our conceptual determining, we may point to the following new series of identifications. We may say generally, and with good sense, that a man may, at different times, and that several men may, at the same or different times, have the same presentation, memory, expectation, perception, utter the same assertion or wish, cherish the same hope etc. etc.[33]

To have the same presentation means, but does not mean as much as, having a presentation of the same object. The presentation I have of Greenland's icy wastes certainly differs from the presentation Nansen has of it, yet the object is the same. Just so the ideal objects *straight line* and *shortest line* are identical, but the presentations – "straight" being suitably defined – different.

Talk about the same presentation, judgement etc. points to no individual sameness of acts, as if my consciousness were in some way conjoined with someone else's. It also means no relation of perfect likeness, of indiscernibility as regards inner constituents, as if the one act merely duplicated the other. We have the same presentation of a thing, when we have presentations in which the thing is not merely presented, but presented as exactly the same: following our previous treatment we may add "presented with the same interpretative sense" or "based on the same matter". In our "essence" we really have the same presentation despite other phenomenological differences. Such essential identity comes out most clearly when we reflect how presentations function in forming higher acts. For essential identity can be equivalently defined if we say: Two presentations are in essence the same, if exactly the same statements, and no others, can be made on the basis of either regarding the presented thing (either presentation being taken alone, i.e. analytically). The same holds in regard to other species of acts. Two judgements are essentially the same judgement when (in virtue of their content alone) everything that the one judgement tells us of the state of affairs judged, would also be told us by the other, and nothing more is told us by either. Their truth-value is identical, and this is clear to us when "the" judgement, the intentional essence uniting judgement-quality and judgement-matter, is the same.

Let us now be quite clear that *the intentional essence does not exhaust the act phenomenologically*. An imaginative presentation, qualified *as* merely imaginative, is unessentially altered in manner, if the fulness and vividness of the sensuous contents helping to build it up is increased or decreased, or, objectively put, if the object now appears with greater clearness and definiteness, now becomes lost in a mist, now becomes paler in colour etc. Whether or not one here assumes intensive differences, whether one concedes or denies a basic likeness between the sensory phantasms here present and the sensational elements in perception, all this makes little difference to the absolute qualities, forms etc. of the act, in so far as the act's intention, its *meaning*, stays unchanged, identically determined (identity of matter). We attribute these changes, not to the object, but to its "appearance"; we "mean" the object as constant and persistent, and we "mean" this in merely "feigning" fashion (identity of quality). As opposed to this, the *matter* of a unitary presentation changes if its object is given as changing (despite any overreaching form of unity to which the intentional object's identity-in-variety corresponds). The same is true when new features enrich our conception of an object, which is constantly before consciousness, features not previously part of the object's intentional content, of the object of our presentation as such.

The case of perception is similar. If many persons share the "same" percept, or repeat a previous one, we have merely an identity of matter, of intentional essence, which does not at all exclude change in the descriptive content of the experience. The same holds of the variable part played, or that can be played, by imagination in perception, in the putting of a perceived object before us. Whether or not images of the back of the cigarette-box float in front of me, with this or that degree of fulness, steadiness and vividness, is quite irrelevant to the essential content, the interpretative sense of my percept, to that side of it, in short which, suitably understood, explains and justifies talk of the "same percept" in opposition to a multiplicity of phenomenologically distinct perceptual acts. In each of such cases the object is presupposed as identical, is seen clothed with the same array of properties: it is "meant" or "apprehended" and posited in perceptual fashion.

A percept may, further, have the same matter as a flight of fancy: the latter may present an object or state of affairs in imagination as being "just the same" as it is perceptually apprehended in the percept. Nothing may be objectively ascribed in the one case which is not likewise ascribed in the other. Since the *quality* of the presentation may be identical (e.g. in the case of memory), we see that the specific differences of intuitive acts do not depend on their intentional essence.

Much the same may be said of any sort of act. Many persons cherish the *same* wish, when their optative intention is the same. This wish may in one person be fully expressed, in another unexpressed, in one person it may bring to full intuitive clarity its basic presentative content, in another it may be more or less "notional" etc. In each case the identity of essence plainly lies in the two aspects distinguished above, in an identity of act-quality and of matter. The same may be claimed for expressive acts, for the acts in particular which *lend meaning* to expressions: as said above by anticipation, their *semantic essence*, i.e. the really present (*reell*) phenomenological correlate of their meaning, coincides with their intentional essence.

We may confirm our notion of semantic essence (the act of meaning *in concreto*) by recalling the series of identities used above in Investigation 1 (§12) in order to draw a distinction between a unity of meaning and a unity of object, and the numerous examples of expressive experience which there illustrated our general notion of intentional essence. The identity of "the" judgement or of "the" statement consists in an identity of meaning repeated *as* the same in the many individual acts, and represented in them by their semantic essence. This leaves room for important descriptive difference in regard to other constituents of these acts, as we have pointed out in detail.[34]

Appendix to §11 and §20

Critique of the "image-theory" and of the doctrine of the "immanent" objects of acts

There are two fundamental, well-nigh ineradicable errors that have to be guarded against in the phenomenological interpretation of the relationship between act and subject:

1. The erroneous *image-theory*, which thinks it has sufficiently explained the fact of presentation – fully present in each act – by saying that: "*Outside* the thing itself is there (or is at times there); in consciousness there is an image which does duty for it."

To this notion we must object that it entirely ignores a most weighty point: that in a representation by images the *represented* object (the original) is *meant*, and meant by way of its image as an apparent object. This representative character is, however, no "real predicate", no intrinsic character of the object which functions as image: an object is not representative as, e.g., it is red and spherical. What therefore enables us to go beyond the image which alone is present in conscious-ness, and to refer to the latter *as* an image to a certain extraconscious object? To point to the resemblance between image and thing will not help. It is doubtless present, as an objective matter-of-fact, when the thing actually exists. But for consciousness, which is assumed only to possess the image,[35] this fact means noth-ing: it can throw no light on the essence of the representative relation to the object, to the original, which is external to itself. Resemblance between two objects, however precise, does not make the one be an image of the other. Only a presenting ego's power to use a similar as an image-representative of a similar – the first similar had intuitively, while the second similar is nonetheless *meant* in its place – makes the image *be* an image. This can only mean that the constitution of the image as image takes place in a peculiar intentional consciousness, whose *inner* character, whose *specifically* peculiar mode of apperception, not only consti-tutes what we call image-representation as such, but also, through its particular inner determinateness, constitutes the image-representation of this or that *definite* object. The reflective, relational opposition of image to original does not, how-ever, point to two genuinely apparent objects in the imaginative act itself, but rather to possible cognitive consummations, which new acts must realize, both fulfilling the imaginal intention and achieving a synthesis between the image and the thing it represents. Inaccurate oppositions of inner likenesses to outer objects cannot be allowed in a descriptive psychology, and much less in a pure phenom-enology. A painting only is a likeness for a likeness-constituting consciousness, whose imaginative apperception, basing itself on a percept, first gives to its pri-mary, perceptually apparent object the status and meaning of an image. Since the interpretation of anything as an image presupposes an object intentionally given to consciousness, we should plainly have a *regressus in infinitum* were we again to let this latter object be itself constituted through an image, or to speak seriously of a "perceptual image" immanent in a simple percept, *by way of which* it refers to the "thing itself". We must come to see, moreover, the general need for a constitu-tion of presented objects *for* and *in* consciousness, in consciousness's own circle of essential being. We must realize that a transcendent object is not present to consciousness merely because a content rather similar to it simply somehow *is* in consciousness – a supposition which, fully thought out, reduces to utter nonsense – but that all relation to an object is part and parcel of the phenomenological essence of consciousness, and can in principle be found in nothing else, even when such a relation points to some "transcendent" matter. This pointing is "direct" in the case of a straightforward presentation: it is mediate in the case of a "founded" presentation, e.g. one by way of images.

One should not talk and think as if an image stood in the same relation to consciousness as a statue does to a room in which it is set up, or as if the least light could be shed on the matter by inventing a hotch-potch of two objects. One must rise to the fundamental insight that one can only achieve the understanding one wants through a phenomenological analysis of the essences of the acts con-cerned, which are acts of the "imagination" in the wide, traditional sense of Kant and Hume. The essential and *a priori* peculiarity of such acts consists in the fact that in them "an object appears", sometimes straightforwardly and directly, and sometimes as "counting" as a "representation by images" of an object that resembles it. Here we must not forget that the representative image, like any apparent object, is itself constituted in an act in which the prime source of its representative character is to be sought.

Our exposition extends, *mutatis mutandis*, to the theory of representation in the wider sense of a *theory of signs*. To be a sign, likewise, is no real (*real*) predicate; it requires a founded conscious act, a reference to certain novel characters of acts, which are all that is phenomenologically relevant, and, in consequence of this last predicate, all that is really (*reell*) phenomenological.

2. It is a serious error to draw a real (*reell*) distinction between "merely immanent" or "intentional" objects, on the one hand, and "transcendent", "actual" objects, which may correspond to them on the other. It is an error whether one makes the distinction one between a sign or image really (*reell*) present in consciousness and the thing it stands for or images, or whether one substitutes for the "immanent object" some other real (*reelles*) datum of consciousness, a content, e.g., as a sense-giving factor. Such errors have dragged on through the centuries – one has only to think of Anselm's ontological argument – they have their source in factual difficulties, but their support lies in equivocal talk concerning "immanence" and the like. It need only be said to be acknowledged *that the intentional object of a presentation is the same as its actual object, and on occasion as its external object, and that it is absurd to distinguish between them*. The transcendent object would not be the object of *this* presentation, if it was not *its* intentional object. This is plainly a merely analytic proposition. The object of the presentation, of the "intention", *is* and *means* what is presented, the intentional object. If I represent God to myself, or an angel, or an intelligible thing-in-itself, or a physical thing or a round square etc., I mean the transcendent object named in each case, in other words my intentional object: it makes no difference whether this object exists or is imaginary or absurd. "The object is merely intentional" does not, of course, mean that it exists, but only in an intention, of which it is a real (*reelles*) part, or that some shadow of it exists. It means rather that the intention, the reference[36] to an object so qualified, exists, but not that the object does. If the intentional object exists, the intention, the reference, does not exist alone, but the thing referred to exists also. But enough of these truisms, which so many philosophers still manage to obfuscate so completely.

What we have said above does not, of course, stop us from distinguishing, as we said previously, between the object *tout court* which is intended on a given occasion, and the object *as* it is then intended – what interpretative slant is put upon it and with what possible fulness of intuition – and in the latter case peculiar analyses and descriptions will be appropriate.

Notes

1 My deviations from Brentano are not on the same lines as the qualifications that he found necessary to add to the inadequate simplifications of which he was clearly conscious (See *Psychologie vom empirischen Standpunkt*, I, pp. 127 *ff.*).

2 We could not say "experiencing contents", since the concept of "experience" has its prime source in the field of "psychic acts". Even if this concept has been widened to include non-acts, these for us stand connected with, ranged beside and attached to acts, in a unity of consciousness so essential that, were it to fall away, talk of "experiencing" would lose its point.

3 *Psychologie*, I, 115.

4 We are not therefore troubled by such vexed questions as to whether all mental phenomena, e.g. the phenomena of feeling, have the peculiarity in question. We must ask instead whether the phenomena in question *are* mental phenomena. The oddness of the question springs from the unsuitability of its wording. More about this later.

5 Within the framework of psychological apperception, the purely phenomenological concept of experience fuses with that of mental reality, or rather, it turns into the concept of the mental state of an animal being (either in actual nature or in an ideally possible nature with ideally possible animals, i.e. without existential implications). Later on the pure *phenomenological* generic Idea *intentional experience* transforms itself into the parallel, nearly related *psychological* generic concept. According as psychological apperception is kept out or kept in, the same sort of analysis has phenomenological or psychological import.

6 *Psychologie*, p. 111 (end of §3).

7 *Psychologie*, p. 104.

8 Cf. Brentano, *Psychologie*, pp. 266–7, 295 and *passim*.

9 No reference to selective attention or notice is included in the sense of the "reference" involved in our "intention". See also §13.

10 We may here ignore the various possible assertive traits involved in the believed being of what is presented. One should again recall that it is possible to leave out all presupposing of natural reality, persons and other conscious animals included therein in our completed studies, so that they are understood as discussions of *ideal* possibilities. One finally sees them in the light of methodological exclusions, which cut out whatever is matter of transcendent apperception and assertion, so as to being out what is *really* part of an experience and of its essence. Experience has then become the pure experience of phenomenology, from which psychological apperception has likewise dropped away.

11 As regards the seemingly obvious distinction between immanent and transcendent objects, modelled on the traditional schema of inner conscious image *v.* extraconscious being-in-itself.

12 Cf. the additional note to Investigation V Chapter I and my *Ideen zu einer reinen Phänomenologie*, l.c.

13 Cf. §19.

14 We are in complete agreement with Natorp (*Einleitung in die Psychologie*, 1st edn, p. 21) when he objects to fully serious talk about "mental activities", or "activities of consciousness", or "activities of the ego", by saying that "consciousness only appears as a doing, and its subject as a doer, because it is often or always accompanied by conation". We too reject the "mythology of activities": we define "acts" as intentional experiences, not as mental activities.

15 P. Natorp, *Einleitung in die Psychologie*, 1st edn, p. 18.

16 Last three sentences added in 2nd edn.

17 Cf. my "Psychological Studies . . .," *Philos. Monatshefte* XXX (1894), p. 182.

18 The much discussed dispute as to the relation between perceptual and imaginative presentation can have no satisfactory outcome in default of a properly prepared phenomenological foundation and consequent clarity in concepts and questions. The like holds of enquiries as to the relation of simple perception to representational or sign-consciousness. It can be readily shown, I think, that act-characters differ in such cases in pictorial representation, e.g. an essentially new mode of intention, is experienced.

19 *Psychologie*, I, pp. 116 *ff.*

20 Paragraph added in 2nd edn.

21 Here as elsewhere I identify the pain-sensation with its "content", since I do not recognize peculiar sensing acts. Naturally I reject Brentano's doctrine that presentative acts, in the term of acts of feeling-sensation, underlie acts of feeling.

22 I point here, for purposes of comparison, and perhaps completion, to H. Schwarz's *Psychologie des Willens* (Leipzig, 1900) which in §12 deals with similar questions.

23 In the First Edition I wrote "real *or* phenomenological" for "real". The word "phenomenological" like the word "descriptive" was used in the First Edition only in connection with *real* (*reelle*) elements of experience, and in the present edition it has so far been used predominately in this sense. This corresponds to one's natural starting with the psychological point of view. It became plainer and plainer, however, as I reviewed the

completed Investigations and pondered on their themes more deeply – particularly from this point onwards – that the description of intentional objectivity as such, as we are conscious of it in the concrete act-experience, represents a distinct descriptive dimension where purely intuitive description may be adequately practised, a dimension opposed to that of real (*reellen*) act-constituents, but which also deserves to be called "phenomenological". These methodological extensions lead to important extensions of the field of problems now opening before us and considerable improvements due to a fully conscious separation of descriptive levels. Cf. my *Ideen zu einer reinen Phänomenologie*, Book 1, and particularly what is said of *Noesis* and *Noema* in Section III.

24 Paragraph added in the Second Edition.
25 *Real* would sound much better alongside "intentional" but it definitely keeps the notion of thinglike transcendence which the reduction to *real* (*reell*) immanence in experience is meant to exclude. It is well to maintain a conscious association of the *real* with the thinglike.
26 We have here a case of "foundation" in the strict sense of our Third Investigation. We only use the term in this strict sense.
27 Investigation I, §§9, 10.
28 Cf. §10.
29 Cf. the attempts at more thorough-going analysis of the act complexes mentioned here in Inv. VI §6 ff.
30 We encountered this fact in criticizing the prevailing theory of abstraction. See Inv. II, §22.
31 Confusion results from unavoidable ambiguities in talk of the definite and the indefinite. One speaks, e.g., of the indefiniteness of perceptual judgements, which consists in the fact that the rear side of a perceived object is subsidiarily meant, but indefinitely, whereas the clearly seen front side seems definite. Or one speaks of the indefiniteness of "particular" assertions, e.g. *An A is B, Some A's are B's*, as opposed to the definiteness of the singular assertion "This *A* is *B*". Such definitenesses and indefinitenesses differ in sense from those in the text: they belong among the particularities of possible "matters", as will be plainer in what follows.
32 Cf. the enumeration in Inv. VI §27.
33 One constantly notices that all the empirical psychological aspects of the examples fall out and become irrelevant with the ideational group of the phenomenological difference of essence.
34 Cf. §§17, 30.
35 For the moment we permit ourselves this improper mode of expression, which in its proper interpretation assorts ill with the image-theory.
36 Which does not mean, we must repeat, that the object is noticed, or that we are thematically occupied with it, though such things are included in our ordinary talk about "referring".

3

THE PHENOMENOLOGY OF
INTERNAL TIME CONSCIOUSNESS

§11 Primal impression and retentional modification

The "source-point" with which the "generation" of the enduring Object begins is a primal impression. This consciousness is engaged in continuous alteration. The actual [*leibhafte*] tonal now is constantly changed into something that has been; constantly, an ever fresh tonal now, which passes over into modification, peels off. However, when the tonal now, the primal impression, passes over into retention, this retention is itself again a now, an actual existent. While it itself is actual (but not an actual sound), it is the retention of a sound that has been. A ray of meaning [*Strahl der Meinung*] can be directed toward the now, toward the retention, but it can also be directed toward that of which we are conscious in retention, the past sound. Every actual now of consciousness, however, is subject to the law of modification. The now changes continuously from retention to retention. There results, therefore, a stable continuum which is such that every subsequent point is a retention for every earlier one. And every retention is already a continuum. The sound begins and steadily continues. The tonal now is changed into one that has been. Constantly flowing, the *impressional* consciousness passes over into an ever fresh *retentional* consciousness. Going along the flux or with it, we have a continuous series of retentions pertaining to the beginning point. Moreover, every earlier point of this series shades off [*sich abschattet*] again as a now in the sense of retention. Thus, in each of these retentions is included a continuity of retentional modifications, and this continuity is itself again a point of actuality which retentionally shades off. This does not lead to a simple infinite regress because each retention is in itself a continuous modification which, so to speak, bears in itself the heritage [*Erbe*] of the past in the form of a series of shadings. It is not true that lengthwise along the flux each earlier retention is merely replaced by a new one, even though it is a continuous process. Each subsequent retention, rather, is not merely a continuous modification arising from the primal impression but a continuous modification of the same beginning point.

Up to this point, we have been chiefly concerned with the perception of the originary constitution of temporal Objects and have sought analytically to understand the consciousness of time given in them. However, the consciousness of temporality does not take place merely in this form. When a temporal Object has

E. Husserl, *The Phenomenology of Internal Time Consciousness*, 1964, trans. James Churchill, pp. 50–80. Bloomington: Indiana University Press.

expired, when its actual duration is over, the consciousness of the Object, now past, by no means fades away, although it no longer functions as perceptual consciousness, or better, perhaps, as impressional consciousness. (As before, we have in mind immanent Objects, which are not really constituted in a "perception.") To the "impression," "primary remembrance" [*primäre Erinnerung*], or, as we say, retention, is joined. Basically, we have already analyzed this mode of consciousness in conjunction with the situation previously considered. For the continuity of phases joined to the actual "now" is indeed nothing other than such a retention or a continuity of retentions. In the case of the perception of a temporal Object (it makes no difference to the present observation whether we take an immanent or transcendent Object), the perception always terminates in a now-apprehension, in a perception in the sense of a positing-as-now. During the perception of motion there takes place, moment by moment, a "comprehension-as-now;" constituted therein is the now actual phase of the motion itself. But this now-apprehension is, as it were, the nucleus of a comet's tail of retentions referring to the earlier now-points of the motion. If perception no longer occurs, however, we no longer see motion, or – if it is a question of a melody – the melody is over and silence begins. Thus no new phase is joined to the last phase; rather, we have a mere phase of fresh memory, to this is again joined another such, and so on. There continually takes place, thereby, a shoving back into the past. The same complex continuously undergoes a modification until it disappears, for hand in hand with the modification goes a diminution which finally ends in imperceptibility. The originary temporal field is obviously circumscribed exactly like a perceptual one. Indeed, generally speaking, one might well venture the assertion that the temporal field always has the same extension. It is displaced, as it were, with regard to the perceived and freshly remembered motion and its Objective time in a manner similar to the way in which the visual field is displaced with regard to Objective space.[1]

§12 Retention as proper intentionality

We must still discuss in greater detail what sort of modification it is that we designate as retentional.

One speaks of the dying or fading away, etc., of the content of sensation when veritable perception passes over into retention. Now, according to the statements made hitherto, it is already clear that the retentional "content" is, in the primordial sense, no content at all. When a sound dies away, it is first sensed with particular fullness (intensity), and there-upon comes to an end in a sudden reduction of intensity. The sound is still there, is still sensed, but in mere reverberation. This real sensation of sound should be distinguished from the tonal moment in retention. The retentional sound is not actually present but "primarily remembered" precisely in the now. It is not really on hand in retentional consciousness. The tonal moment that belongs to this consciousness, however, cannot be another sound which is really on hand, not even a very weak one which is qualitatively similar (like an echo). A present sound can indeed remind us of a past sound, present it, symbolize it; this, however, already presupposes another representation of the past. The intuition of the past itself cannot be a symbolization [*Verbildlichung*]; it is an originary consciousness. Naturally, we cannot deny that echoes exist. But where we recognize and distinguish them we are soon able to establish that they do not belong to retention as such but to perception. The reverberation of a violin tone is a very weak violin tone and is completely different from the retention of loud sounds which have just been. The reverberation itself, as well as after-images in general, which remain behind after the stronger givens of sensation, has absolutely nothing to do with the nature of retention, to say nothing of the possibility that the reverberation must necessarily be ascribed to retention.

Truly, however, it pertains to the essence of the intuition of time that in every point of its duration (which, reflectively, we are able to make into an object) it is consciousness of *what has just been* and not mere consciousness of the now-point of the objective thing appearing as having duration. In this consciousness, we are aware of what has just been in the continuity pertaining to it and in every phase in a determinate "mode of appearance" differentiated as to "content" and "apprehension." One notices the steam whistle just sounding; in every point there is an extension and in the extension there is the "appearance" which, in every phase of this extension, has its moment of quality and its moment of apprehension. On the other hand, the moment of quality is no real quality, no sound which really is now, i.e., which exists as now, provided that one can speak of the immanent content of sound. The real content of the now-consciousness includes sounds which, if the occasion should arise, are sensed; in which case, they are then necessarily to be characterized in Objectifying apprehension as perceived, as present, but in no wise as past. Retentional consciousness includes real consciousness of the past of sound, primary remembrance of sound, and is not to be resolved into sensed sound and apprehension as memory. Just as a phantasied sound is not a sound but the phantasy of a sound, or just as tonal sensation and tonal phantasy are fundamentally different and are not to be considered as possibly the same, except for a difference in interpretation, likewise primary, intuitive remembered sound is intrinsically something other than a perceived sound, and the primary remembrance of sound is something other than the sensation of sound.

§13 The necessity for the precedence of impression over every retention – self-evidence of retention

Is there a law to the effect that primary remembrance is possible only if continuously joined to a preceding sensation or perception, that every retentional phase is thinkable only as a phase, i.e., is not to be expanded into an interval which would be identical in all phases? One might say without reservation that this is absolutely evident. An empirical psychologist, accustomed to treating everything psychical as a mere succession of events, would of course deny this. Such a person would say: Why should not an originative [*anfangendes*] consciousness be thinkable, one which begins with a fresh remembrance without previously having had a perception? It may in fact be the case that perception is necessary to produce a fresh remembrance. It may actually be true that human consciousness can have memories, primary ones included, only after it has had perceptions, but the opposite is also conceivable. In contrast to this, we teach the *a priori* necessity of the precedence of a perception or primal impression over the corresponding retention. We must above all insist that a phase is thinkable only as a phase and without the possibility of an extension. A now-phase is thinkable only as the boundary of a continuity of retentions, just as every retentional phase is itself thinkable only as a point of such a continuum, that is, for every now of the consciousness of time. If this is true, however, an entire completed series of retentions should not be thinkable without a corresponding perception preceding it. This implies that the series of retentions which pertains to a now is itself a limit and is necessarily modified. What is remembered "sinks ever further into the past;" moreover, what is remembered is necessarily something sunken, something that of necessity permits an evident recollection [*Wiedererinnerung*] which traces it back to a now reproduced.

One might ask, however: Can I not have a memory, even a primary one, of an A which in truth has never existed? Certainly. Something even stronger can be asserted. I can also have a perception of A although in reality A does not exist. Accordingly, we do not assert as a certainty that when we have a retention of A (assuming A is a transcendent Object), A must precede the retention, although we do assert that A must have been perceived.

Whether A is the object of primary attention or not, it really is present as something of which we are conscious even if unnoticed or noticed only incidentally. If it is a question of an immanent Object, however, the following holds true: a succession, an alternation, a variation of immanent data, if it "appears," is absolutely indubitable. And within a transcendent perception, the immanent succession belonging essentially to the composition of this perception is also absolutely indubitable. It is *basically absurd* to argue: How in the now can I know of a not-now, since I cannot compare the not-now which no longer is with the now (that is to say, the memory-image present in the now)? As if it pertained to the essence of memory that an image present in the now were presupposed for another thing similar to it, and as with graphic representation, I could and must compare the two. Memory or retention is not figurative consciousness, but something totally different. What is remembered *is*, of course, not now; otherwise it would not be something that has been but would be actually present. And in memory (retention) what is remembered is not given as now: otherwise, memory or retention would not be just memory but perception (or primal impression). A comparison of what we no longer perceive but are merely conscious of in retention with something outside it makes no sense at all. Just as in perception, I see what has being now, and in extended perceptions, no matter how constituted, what has enduring being, so in primary remembrance I see what is past. What is past is given therein, and givenness of the past is memory.

If we now again take up the question of whether a retentional consciousness that is not the continuation of an impressional consciousness is thinkable, we must say that it is impossible, for every retention in itself refers back to an impression. "Past" and "now" exclude each other. Something past and something now can indeed be identically the same but only because it has endured between the past and now.

§14 Reproduction of temporal objects [*Objekten*] – secondary remembrance

We characterized primary remembrance or retention as a comet's tail which is joined to actual perception. Secondary remembrance or recollection is completely different from this. After primary remembrance is past [*dahin*], a new memory of this motion or that melody can emerge. The difference between the two forms of memory, which we have already touched on, must now be explained in detail. If retention is joined to actual perception, whether during its perceptual flux or in continuous union following its running-off, then at first sight it is natural to say (as Brentano has) that the actual perception is constituted on the basis of phantasies as representation [*Repräsentation*], as presentification. Now, just as immediate presentifications are joined to perceptions, so also can autonomous presentifications appear without being joined to perceptions. Such are the secondary remembrances. But (as we have already brought out in the critique of Brentano's theory) serious doubts arise. Let us consider an example of secondary remembrance. We remember a melody, let us say, which in our youth we heard during a concert. Then it is obvious that the entire phenomenon of memory has, *mutatis mutandis*, exactly the same constitution as the perception of the melody. Like the perception, it has a favored point; to the now-point of the perception corresponds a now-point of the memory, and so on. We run through a melody in phantasy; we hear "as if" [*gleichsam*] first the first note, then the second, etc. At any given time, there is always a sound (or a tonal phase) in the now-point. The preceding sounds, however, are not erased from consciousness. With the apprehension of the sound appearing now, heard as if now, primary remembrance blends in the sounds heard as if just previously and the expectation (protention) of the sound to come. Again, the now-point has for consciousness a temporal halo [*Hof*] which is brought about through a continuity of memory. The complete memory of the melody consists of a continuum of such temporal continuities or of continuities of apprehension of the kind described. Finally, when the melody presentified has been run through, a retention is joined to this as-if hearing; the as-if heard still reverberates a while, a continuity of apprehension is still there but no longer as heard. Everything thus resembles perception and primary remembrance and yet is not itself perception and primary remembrance. We do not really hear and have not really heard when in memory or phantasy we let a melody run its course, note by note. In the former case, we really hear; the temporal Object itself is perceived; the melody itself is the object of perception. And, likewise, temporal periods, temporal determinations and relations are themselves given, perceived. And again, after the melody has sounded, we no longer perceive it as present although we still have it in consciousness. It is no longer a present melody but one just past. Its being just past is not mere opinion but a given fact, self-given and therefore perceived. In contrast to this, the temporal present [*Gegenwart*] in recollection is remembered, presentified. And the past is remembered in the same way, presentified but not perceived. It is not the primarily given and intuited past.

On the other hand, the recollection itself is present, originarily constituted recollection and subsequently that which has just been. It generates itself in a continuum of primal data and retentions and is constituted (better, re-constituted) jointly with an immanent or transcendent objectivity of duration (depending on whether it is immanently or transcendently oriented). On the other hand, retention generates no objectivities of duration (whether originary or reproductive), but merely retains what is produced in consciousness and impresses on it the character of the "just past."[2]

§15 The modes of accomplishment of reproduction

Recollection can make its appearance in different forms of accomplishment. We accomplish it either by simply laying hold of what is recollected, as when, for example, a recollection "emerges" and we look at what is remembered with a glancing ray [*Blickstrahl*] wherein what is remembered is indeterminate, perhaps a favored momentary phase intuitively brought forth, but not a recapitulative memory. Or we accomplish it in a real, re-productive, recapitulative memory in which the temporal object is again completely built up in a continuum of presentifications, so that we seem to perceive it again, but only seemingly, as-if. The whole process is a presentificational modification of the process of perception with all its phases and levels, including retentions. However, everything has the index of reproductive modification.

The simple act of looking at or apprehending we also discover immediately on the basis of retention, as, for example, when a melody which lies within the unity of a retention is run through and we look back (reflect) on a part of it without producing it again. This is an act which, developed in successive stages, also in stages of spontaneity, e.g., the spontaneity of thought, is possible for everyone. The objectivities of thought, indeed, are also successively constituted. It appears, therefore, we can say that objectivities which are built up originally in temporal processes, being constituted member by member or phase by phase (as correlates of continuous, multiformed, cohesive, and homogenous acts), may be apprehended in a backward glance as if they were objects complete in a temporal point. But then this givenness certainly refers back to another "primordial" one.

This looking toward or back to what is retentionally given – and the retention itself – is realized in true representification [*Wiedervergegenwärtigung*]. What is given as just having been turns out to be identical with what is recollected.

Further differences between primary and secondary remembrance will be evident when we relate them to perception.

§16 Perception as originary presentation [*Gegenwärtigung*] as distinguished from retention and recollection

Any reference to "perception" still requires some discussion here. In the "perception of a melody," we distinguish the tone *given now*, which we term the "perceived," from those which *have gone by*, which we say are "not perceived." On the other hand, we call the *whole melody* one that is *perceived*, although only the now-point actually is. We follow this procedure because not only is the extension of the melody given point for point in an extension of the act of perception but also the unity of retentional consciousness still "holds" the expired tones themselves in consciousness and continuously establishes the unity of consciousness with reference to the homogeneous temporal Object, i.e., the melody. An Objectivity such as a melody cannot itself be originarily given except as "perceived" in this form. The constituted act, constructed from now-consciousness and retentional consciousness, is *adequate perception of the temporal Object*. This Object will indeed include temporal differences, and temporal differences are constituted precisely in such phases, in primal consciousness, retention, and protention. If the purposive [*meinende*] intention is directed toward the melody, toward the whole Object, we have nothing but perception. If the intention is directed toward a particular tone or a particular measure for its own sake, we have perception so long as precisely the thing intended is perceived, and mere retention as soon as it is past. Object-ively [*objektiver*] considered, the measure no longer appears as "present" but as "past." The whole melody, however, appears as present so long as it still sounds, so long as the notes *belonging to it*, intended in the *one* nexus of apprehensions, still sound. The melody is past only after the last note has gone.

As we must assert in accordance with the preceding statements, *this relativation* carries over to the individual *tones*. Each is constituted in a continuity of tonal data, and only a punctual phase is actually present as now at any given moment, while the others are connected as a retentional train. We can say, however, that a temporal Object is perceived (or intentionally known) as long as it is still pro-duced in continuous, newly appearing primal impressions.

We have then characterized *the past* itself as perceived. If, in fact, we do not perceive *the passing* [*Vergehen*], are we not, in the cases described, directly con-scious of the *just-having-been* of the "just past" in its self-givenness, in the mode of *being self-given*? Obviously, the meaning of "perception" here obtaining does not coincide with the earlier one. Further analysis is required.

If, in the comprehension of a temporal Object, we distinguish between percep-tive and memorial [*erinnerendes*] (retentional) consciousness, then the contrast between the perception and the primary remembrance of an Object corresponds to that between "now present" and "past." *Temporal Objects*, and this belongs to their essence, spread their content over an *interval of time*, and such Objects can be constituted only in acts which likewise constitute temporal distinctions. Tem-porally constitutive acts, however, are essentially acts which also constitute the present and the past. They have that type of "temporal Object-perception" which, in conformity with their peculiar apprehension constitution, we have described in detail. Temporal Objects must be thus constituted. This implies that an act which claims to give a temporal Object itself must contain in itself "now-apprehensions," "past-apprehensions," and the like, and, in fact, in a primordially constitutive way.

If we now relate what has been said about perception to the *differences of the givenness* with which temporal Objects make their appearance, then the *antithesis of perception* is *primary remembrance*, which appears here, and *primary expect-ation* (retention and protection), whereby *perception and non-perception continu-ally* pass over into one another. In the consciousness of the direct, intuitive comprehension of a temporal Object, e.g., a melody, the passage, tone, or part now heard is perceived, and not perceived is what is momentarily intuited as past. Apprehensions here pass continually over into one another and terminate in an apprehension constituting the now; this apprehension, however, is only an ideal limit. We are concerned here with a *continuum of gradations in the direction of an ideal limit*, like the convergence of various shades of red toward an ideally pure red. However, in this case, we do not have individual apprehensions correspond-ing to the individual shades of red, which, indeed, *can be given for themselves*. Rather, we always have and, according to the nature of the matter, can only have continuities of apprehensions, or better, *a single continuum which is constantly modified*. If somehow we divide this continuum into two adjoining parts, that part which includes the now, or is capable of constituting it, designates and constitutes the "gross" now, which, as soon as we divide it further, immediately breaks down again into a finer now and a past, etc.

Perception, therefore, has here the character of an act which includes a continuity of such characters and is distinguished by the possession of that ideal limit mentioned above. Pure memory is a similar continuity, but one which does not possess this ideal limit. In an ideal sense, then, perception (impression) would be the phase of consciousness which constitutes the pure now, and memory every other phase of the continuity. But this is just an ideal limit, something abstract which can be nothing for itself. Moreover, it is also true that even this ideal now is not something *toto caelo* different from the not-now but continually accommodates itself thereto. The continual transition from perception to primary remembrance conforms to this accommodation.

§17 Perception as a self-giving [*selbstgebender*] act in contrast to reproduction

Perception, or the self-giving of the actual present, which has its correlate in the given of what is past, is now confronted by another contrast, that of recollection, secondary remembrance. In recollection, a now "appears" to us, but it "appears" in a sense wholly other than the appearance of the now in perception. This now *is not perceived, i.e., self-given, but presentified*. It places a now before us which is not given. In just the same way, the running-off of a melody in *recollection* places before us a "just past," but does not give it. In addition, every individual in mere phantasy is temporally extended in some way. It has its now, its before and after [*sein vorher und Nachher*], but like the whole Object, the now, before, and after are merely imagined. Here, therefore, it is a question of an *entirely different concept of perception*. Here, *perception* is an act which brings something *other than itself before us*, an act which *primordially constitutes* the Object. *Presentification*, re-presentation, as the act which does not place an Object itself before us, but just presentifies – places before us in images, as it were (if not precisely in the manner of true figurative consciousness) – , is just the opposite of this. There is no mention here of a continuous accommodation of perception to its opposite. Heretofore, consciousness of the past, i.e., the primary one, was not perception because perception was designated as the act originally constituting the now. Consciousness of the past, however, does not constitute a now but rather a "*just-having-been*" [*ein soeben gewesen*] that intuitively precedes the now. However, if we call perception *the act in which all "origination" lies*, which *constitutes originarily*, then *primary remembrance is perception*. For only in *primary remembrance do we see what is past*; only in it is the past constituted, i.e., *not in a representative but in a presentative way*. The just-having-been, the before in contrast to the now, can be seen directly only in primary remembrance. It is the essence of primary remembrance to bring this new and unique moment to primary, direct intuition, just as it is the essence of the perception of the now to bring the now directly to intuition. On the other hand, recollection, like phantasy, offers us mere presentification. It is "as-if" the same consciousness as the temporally creative acts of the now and the past, "as-if" the same but yet modified. The phantasied now represents a now, but does not give us a now itself; the phantasied before and after merely represents a before and after, etc.

§18 The significance of recollection for the constitution of the consciousness of duration and succession

The constitutive significance of primary and secondary remembrance is seen in a different light if, instead of the mode of givenness of *enduring objectivities*, we turn our attention to the mode of givenness of *duration* and *succession* themselves.

Let us suppose that A appears as a primal impression and endures for a while, and along with the retention of A in a certain level of development B appears and is constituted as enduring B. Therewith, during these "processes," consciousness is consciousness of the same A "moving back into the past," the same A in the flux of these modes of givenness, and the same according to the "duration" belonging to the form of being appropriate to its content according to all points of this duration. The same is true of B and of the difference of both durations or their temporal points. In addition to the above, however, something new enters here: *B follows A*. There is a succession of two continuing sets of data given with a determinate temporal form, a temporal interval which encompasses the succession. The *consciousness of succession* is an originary giving [*gebendes*] consciousness; it is the "perception" of this succession. We shall consider now the reproductive modification of this perception, that is, recollection. I "repeat" *the consciousness of this succession:* remembering, I presentify it to myself. This I "*can*" do, in fact, as "often as I like." The presentification of a lived experience lies *a priori* within the sphere of my "freedom." (The "I can" is a practical "I can" and not a "mere idea.") Now what does the presentification of a lived experience look like and what belongs to its essence? One can say to begin with: I presentify to myself first A and then B. If I originally have A – B, now I have A′ – B′ (the mark ['] indicates memory). But this is inadequate, for it implies that I now have a memory A′ and "afterward" a memory B′, namely, in the consciousness of a succession of these memories. But then I should have a "perception" of the succession of these memories and no consciousness of the memory of them. I must therefore exhibit this consciousness through (A – B)′. This consciousness, in fact, includes an A′, B′, and also a –. To be sure, the succession is not a third part, as if the manner of writing down the signs one after the other denoted the succession. Nevertheless, I can write down the law

$$(A - B)' = A' - B'$$

meaning: there is present a consciousness of the memory of A and of B but also a modified consciousness of "B follows A."

If, as regards the originary giving consciousness, we now ask for a succession of enduring Objectivities – and, indeed, for the duration itself – we find that retention and recollection necessarily belong thereto. Retention constitutes the living horizon of the now; I have in it a consciousness of the "just past." But what is originarily constituted thereby – perhaps in the retaining of the tone just heard – is only the shoving back of the now-phase or the completed constituted duration, which in this completeness is no longer being constituted and no longer perceived. In "coincidence" with this "result" which is being shoved back, I can, however, undertake a reproduction. Then the pastness [*Vergangenheit*] of the duration is given to me *simpliciter* as just is the "re-givenness" [*Wiedergegebenheit*] of the duration. And it should be noted that it is only past durations that I can, in repeatable acts, "originarily" intuit, identify, and have objectively as the identical Object of many acts. I can re-live [*nachleben*] the present but it can never be given again. If I come back to one and the same succession (as I can at any time) and identify it as the same temporal Object, I carry out a succession of recollective lived experiences in the unity of an overlapping consciousness of succession thus:

$$(A - B) - (A - B)' - (A - B)'' \ldots .$$

The question is: what is this act of identification like? To begin with, the succession is a succession of lived experiences – the first being the originary constitution of a succession A – B, the second a memory of this succession, then the same thing again, and so on. The entire succession is given originarily as presence [*Präsenz*]. I can again have a memory of this succession, another memory of such a recollection, and so on *ad infinitum*. Essentially, every memory is not only repeatable in the sense that higher levels are possible at will, but also it is repeated as a sphere of the "I can."

What is the first recollection of the succession like? It is:

$$[(A - B) - (A - B)']'$$

Then, according to the earlier law, I can deduce that therein is set $(A - B)'$ and $[(A - B)']'$, therefore, a memory of the second level, that is, in the sequence, and naturally also the memory of the succession – '. If I repeat once again, I have still higher modifications of memory and at the same time the consciousness that in sequence I have again and again carried out a repeatable presentification. Such a thing takes place very often. I knock twice on the table and presentify the sequence to myself. Then I note that I first gave the succession perceptively and then remembered it. Then I note that I have accomplished just this noting, that is, as the third member of a series that I can repeat, etc. This is all very commonplace, especially in the phenomenological method of procedure.

In the succession of like Objects (identical as to content) which are given only in succession and never as coexisting, we have a peculiar coincidence in the unity of one consciousness. Naturally, this is meant only figuratively, for the Objects are indeed separated, known as a succession, divided by a temporal interval.

And yet, we have in the sequence unlike Objects, with like contrasted moments. Thus "lines of likeness," as it were, run from one to the other, and in the case of similarity, lines of similarity. We have an interrelatedness which is not constituted in a relational mode of observation and which is prior to all "comparison" and all "thinking" as the necessary condition for all intuition of likeness and difference. Only the similar is really "comparable" and "difference" presupposes "coincidence," i.e., that real union of the like bound together in transition (or in coexistence).

§19 The difference between retention and reproduction (primary and secondary remembrance or phantasy)

By this time our position regarding Brentano's theory that the origin of the apprehension of time lies in the sphere of phantasy is definitely determined. Phantasy is the mode of consciousness characterized as presentification (reproduction). Now, there is indeed such a thing as presentified time but it necessarily refers back to a primordially given time which is not phantasied but presented. Presentification is the opposite of the primordially giving act; no representation can arise from it. That is, phantasy is not a form of consciousness that can bring forth some kind of Objectivity or other, or an essential and possible tendency [Zug] toward an Objectivity as self-given. Not to be self-giving is precisely the essence of phantasy. Even the concept of phantasy does not arise from phantasy. For if we claim originarily to have given what phantasy is, then we must, of course, form phantasies, but this itself still does not mean givenness. We must naturally observe the process of phantasy, i.e., perceive it. The perception of phantasy is the primordially giving consciousness for the formation of the concept of phantasy. In this perception, we see what phantasy is; we grasp it in the consciousness of self-givenness.

That a great phenomenological difference exists between representifying memory and primary remembrance which extends the now-consciousness is revealed by a careful comparison of the lived experiences involved in both. We hear, let us say, two or three sounds and have during the temporal extension of the now a consciousness of the sound just heard. Evidently this consciousness is essentially the same whether out of the tonal configuration which forms the unity of a temporal Object a member is still really perceived as now, or whether this member no longer occurs, although we are still retentionally aware of the image. Let us assume now that it perhaps happens that while the continuous intention directed toward the sound or flow of the sound is still vivid, this same sound is reproduced once more. The measure which I have just heard and toward which my attention is still directed I presentify to myself in that inwardly I carry it out once more. The difference is obvious. In the presentification we now once more have the sound or sound-form together with its entire temporal extension. The act of presentification has exactly the same temporal extension as the earlier act of perception. The former reproduces the latter; it allows the passage to run off, tonal phase for tonal phase and interval for interval. It also reproduces thereby the phase of primary remembrance which we have singled out for the comparison. Nevertheless, the act of presentification is not a mere repetition and the difference does not merely consist in that at the one time we have a simple reproduction and at the other a reproduction of a reproduction. We find, rather, radical differences in content. They become apparent when, for example, we inquire what constitutes the difference between the sounding of the tone in the presentification and in the residual consciousness of it which we still retain in phantasy. The tone reproduced during the "sounding" is a reproduction of the sounding. The residual consciousness after the sounding has been reproduced is no longer a reproduction of the sounding but of the re-sounding [Er-klingens] which has just been but is still heard. This re-sounding is exhibited in an entirely different manner from that of the sounding itself. The phantasms which exhibit the tones do not remain in consciousness as if, for example, in the presentification each tone were constituted as an identical persisting datum. Otherwise, in presentification we could not have an intuitive idea of time, the idea of a temporal Object. The tone reproduced passes away; its phantasm does not remain identically the same, but is modified in a characteristic way and establishes the presentificational consciousness of duration, alteration, succession, and the like.

The modification of consciousness which changes an originary now into one that is *reproduced* is something wholly other than that modification which changes the now – whether originary or reproduced – into the *past*. This last modification has the character of a continuous shading-off; just as the now continuously grades off into the ever more distant past, so the intuitive consciousness of time also continuously grades off. On the other hand, we are not speaking here of a continuous transition of perception to phantasy, of impression to reproduction. The latter distinction is a separate one. We must say, therefore, that what we term originary consciousness, impression, or perception is an act which is continuously gradated. Every concrete perception implies a whole continuum of such gradations. Reproduction, phantasy-consciousness, also requires exactly the same gradations, although only reproductively modified. On both sides, it belongs to the essence of lived experiences that they must be extended in this fashion, that a punctual phase can never be for itself.

Naturally, the gradation of what is given originarily as well as of what is given reproductively indeed concerns the content of apprehension, as we have already seen. Perception is built upon sensations. Sensation which functions presentatively for the object forms a stable continuum, and in just the same way the phantasm forms a continuum for the representation [*Repräsentation*] of an Object of phantasy. Whoever assumes an essential difference between sensations and phantasms naturally may not claim the content of apprehension of the temporal phases just past to be phantasms, for these, of course, pass continually over into the content of apprehension of the moment of the now . . .

§24 Protentions in recollection

In order now to understand the disposition of this constituted unity of lived experience, "memory," in the undivided stream of lived experience, the following must be taken into account: every act of memory contains intentions of expectation whose fulfillment leads to the present. Every primordially constitutive process is animated by protentions which voidly [*leer*] constitute and intercept [*auffangen*] what is coming, as such, in order to bring it to fulfillment. However, the recollective process not only renews these protentions in a manner appropriate to memory. These protentions were not only present as intercepting, they have also intercepted. They have been fulfilled, and we are aware of them in recollection. Fulfillment in recollective consciousness is re-fulfillment [*Wieder-Erfüllung*] (precisely in the modification of the positing of memory), and if the primordial protention of the perception of the event was undetermined and the question of being-other or not-being was left open, then in the recollection we have a pre-directed expectation which does not leave all that open. It is then in the form of an "incomplete" recollection whose structure is other than that of the undetermined, primordial protention. And yet this is also included in the recollection. There are difficulties here, therefore, with regard to the intentional analysis both for the event considered individually, and, in a different way, for the analysis of expectations which concern the succession of events up to the actual present. Recollection is not expectation; its horizon, which is a posited one, is, however, oriented on the future, that is, the future of the recollected. As the recollective process advances, this horizon is continually opened up anew and becomes richer and more vivid. In view of this, the horizon is filled with recollected events which are always new. Events which formerly were only foreshadowed are now quasi-present, seemingly in the mode of the embodied present.

§25 The double intentionality of recollection

If, in the case of a temporal Object, we distinguish the content together with its duration (which in connection with "the" time can have a different place) from its temporal position, we have in the reproduction of an enduring being, and in addition to the reproduction of the filled duration, the intentions which affect the position, in fact, necessarily affect it. A duration is not imaginable, or better, is not positable unless it is posited in a temporal nexus, unless the intentions of the temporal nexus are there. Hence it is necessary that these intentions take the form of either past or future intentions. To the duality of the intentions which are oriented on the fulfilled duration and on its temporal position corresponds a dual fulfillment. The entire complex of intuitions which makes up the appearance of past enduring Objects has its possible fulfillment in the system of appearances which belong to the same enduring thing. The intentions of the temporal nexus are fulfilled through the establishment of the fulfilled nexuses up to the actual present. In every presentification, therefore, we must distinguish between the reproduction of the consciousness in which the past enduring Object was given, i.e., perceived or in general primordially constituted, and that consciousness which attaches to this reproduction as constitutive for the consciousness of "past," "present" (coincident with the actual now), and "future."

Now is this last also reproduction? This is a question which can easily lead one astray. Naturally, the whole is reproduced, not only the then present of consciousness with its flux but "implicitly" the whole stream of consciousness up to the living present. This means that as an essential *a priori* phenomenological formation [*Genese*] memory is in a continuous flux because conscious life is in constant flux and is not merely fitted member by member into the chain. Rather, everything new reacts on the old; its forward-moving intention is fulfilled and determined thereby, and this gives the reproduction a definite coloring. An *a priori*, necessary retroaction is thus revealed here. The new points again to the new, which, entering, is determined and modifies the reproductive possibilities for the old, etc. Thereby the retroactive power of the chain goes back, for the past as reproduced bears the character of the past and an indeterminate intention toward a certain state of affairs in regard to the now. It is not true, therefore, that we have a mere chain of "associated" intentions, one after the other, this one suggesting the next (in the stream). Rather, we have an intention which in itself is an intention toward the series of possible fulfillments.

But this intention is a non-intuitive, an "empty" intention, and its objectivity is the Objective temporal series of events, this series being the dim surroundings of what is actually recollected. Can we not characterize the non-general "surroundings" as a unitary intention which is based on a multiplicity of interconnected objectivities and in which a discrete and manifold givenness comes gradually to fulfillment? Such is also the case with the spatial background. And so also, everything in perception has its reverse side as background (for it is not a question of the background of attention but of apprehension). The component "unauthentic perception" which belongs to every transcendent perception as an essential element is a "complex" intention which can be fulfilled in nexuses of a definite kind, in nexuses of data.

The foreground is nothing without the background; the appearing side is nothing without the non-appearing. It is the same with regard to the unity of time-consciousness – the duration reproduced is the foreground; the classifying intentions make us aware of a background, a temporal background. And in certain ways, this is continued in the constitution of the temporality of the enduring thing itself with its now, before, and after. We have the following analogies: for the spatial thing, the ordering into the surrounding space and the spatial world on the one side, and on the other, the spatial thing itself with its foreground and background. For the temporal thing, we have the ordering into the temporal form and the temporal world on the one side, and on the other the temporal thing itself and its changing orientation with regard to the living now.

§26 The difference between memory and expectation

We must further investigate whether memory and expectation equal each other. Intuitive remembrance offers me the vivid reproduction of the expiring duration of an event, and only the intentions which refer back to the before and forward to the living now remain unintuitive.

In the intuitive idea of a future event, I now have intuitively the productive "image" of a process which runs off reproductively. Joined thereto are indeterminate intentions of the future and of the past, i.e., intentions which from the beginning of the process affect the temporal surroundings which terminate in the living now. To that extent, expectational intuition is an inverted memorial intuition, for the now-intentions do not go "before" the process but follow after it. As empty environmental intentions, they lie "in the opposite direction." How do matters stand now with the mode of givenness of the process itself? Does it make any essential difference that in memory the content of the process is determinate? Moreover, the memory can be intuitive but still not very determinate, inasmuch as many intuitive components by no means have real memorial character. With "perfect" memory, to be sure, everything would be clear to the last particular and properly characterized as memory. But, ideally, this is also possible with expectation. In general, expectation lets much remain open, and this remaining-open is again a characteristic of the components concerned. But, in principle, a prophetic consciousness (a consciousness which gives itself out as prophetic) is conceivable, one in which each character of the expectation, of the coming into being, stands before our eyes, as, for example, when we have a precisely determined plan and, intuitively imagining what is planned, accept it lock, stock, and barrel, so to speak, as future reality. Still there will also be many unimportant things in the intuitive anticipation of the future which as makeshifts fill out the concrete image.

The latter, however, can in various ways be other than the likeness it offers. It is, from the first, characterized as being open.

The principal differences between memory and expectation, however, are to be found in the manner of fulfillment. Intentions of the past are necessarily fulfilled by the establishment of nexuses of intuitive reproductions. The reproduction of past events permits, with respect to their validity (in internal consciousness) only the confirmation of the uncertainties of memory and their improvement by being transformed in a reproduction in which each and everything in the components is characterized as reproductive. Here we are concerned with such questions as: Have I really seen or perceived this? Have I really had this appearance with exactly this content? All this must at the same time dovetail into a context of similar intuitions up to the now. Another question, to be sure, is the following: Was the appearing thing real? On the other hand, expectation finds its fulfillment in a perception. It pertains to the essence of the expected that it is an about-to-be-perceived. In view of this, it is evident that if what is expected makes its appearance, i.e., becomes something present, the expectational situation itself has gone by. If the future has become the present, then the present has changed to the relatively past. The situation is the same with regard to environmental intentions. They are also fulfilled through the actuality of an impressional living experience.

Notwithstanding these differences, expectational intuition is something primordial and unique exactly as is intuition of the past.

Notes

1 No notice is taken in the diagram of the limitation of the temporal field. No end to retention is provided for therein, and, ideally at least, a form of consciousness is possible in which everything is retentionally retained.
2 For a discussion of further differences between retention and reproduction, cf. §19, pp. 119–20.

4

PURE PHENOMENOLOGY, ITS METHOD, AND ITS FIELD OF INVESTIGATION

Ladies and gentlemen, honored colleagues, dear comrades!

In all the areas within which the spiritual life of humanity is at work, the historical epoch wherein fate has placed us is an epoch of stupendous happenings. Whatever previous generations cultivated by their toil and struggle into a harmonious whole, in every sphere of culture, whatever enduring style was deemed established as method and norm, is once more in flux and now seeks new forms whereby reason, as yet unsatisfied, may develop more freely: in politics, in economic life, in technics, in the fine arts, and – by no means least of all – in the sciences. In a few decades of reconstruction, even the mathematical natural sciences, the ancient archetypes of theoretical perfection, have changed habit completely!

Philosophy, too, fits into this picture. In philosophy, the forms whose energies were dissipated in the period following the overthrow of Hegelian philosophy were essentially those of a renaissance. They were forms that reclaimed past philosophies, and their methods as well as some of their essential content originated with great thinkers of the past.

Most recently, the need for an utterly original philosophy has re-emerged, the need of a philosophy that – in contrast to the secondary productivity of renaissance philosophies – seeks by radically clarifying the sense and the motifs of philosophical problems to penetrate to that primal ground on whose basis those problems must find whatever solution is genuinely scientific.

A new fundamental science, pure phenomenology, has developed within philosophy. This is a science of a thoroughly new type and endless scope. It is inferior in methodological rigor to none of the modern sciences. All philosophical disciplines are rooted in pure phenomenology, through whose development, and through it alone, they obtain their proper force. Philosophy is possible as a rigorous science at all only through pure phenomenology. It is of pure phenomenology I wish to speak: the intrinsic nature of its method and its subject matter, a subject matter that is invisible to naturally oriented points of view.

Pure phenomenology claims to be the science of pure phenomena. This concept of the phenomenon, which was developed under various names as early as the

E. Husserl, *Husserl. Shorter Works*, 1981, ed. Peter McCormick and Frederick Elliston, trans. Robert Welsh Jordan, pp. 10–17. Notre Dame, IN/Brighton: University of Notre Dame/Harvester Press.

eighteenth century without being clarified, is what we shall have to deal with first of all.

We shall begin with the necessary correlation between object, truth, and cognition – using these words in their very broadest senses. To every object there correspond an ideally closed system of truths that are true of it and, on the other hand, an ideal system of possible cognitive processes by virtue of which the object and the truths about it would be given to any cognitive subject. Let us consider these processes. At the lowest cognitive level, they are processes of experiencing, or, to speak more generally, processes of intuiting that grasp the object in the original.

Something similar is obviously true of all types of intuitions and of all other processes of meaning an object even when they have the character of mere re-presentations that (like rememberings or pictorial intuitions or processes of meaning something symbolic) do not have the intrinsic character of being conscious of the intuited's being there "in person" but are conscious of it instead as recalled, as re-presented in the picture or by means of symbolic indications and the like, and even when the actuality valuation of the intuited varies in some, no matter what, manner. Even intuitions in phantasy, therefore, are intrinsically intuitions of objects and carry "object phenomena" with them intrinsically, phenomena that are obviously not characterized as actualities. If higher, theoretical cognition is to begin at all, objects belonging to the sphere in question must be intuited. Natural objects, for example, must be experienced before any theorizing about them can occur. Experiencing is consciousness that intuits something and values it to be actual; experiencing is intrinsically characterized as consciousness of the natural object in question and of it as the original: there is consciousness of the original as being there "in person." The same thing can be expressed by saying that objects would be nothing at all for the cognizing subject if they did not "appear" to him, if he had of them no "phenomenon." Here, therefore, "phenomenon" signifies a certain content that intrinsically inhabits the intuitive consciousness in question and is the substrate for its actuality valuation.

Something similar is still true of the courses followed by manifold intuitions which together make up the unity of one *continuous consciousness* of one and the same object. The manner in which the object is given within each of the single intuitions belonging to this continuous consciousness may vary constantly; for example, the object's sensuous "looks" – the way in which the object always "looks" different at each approach or remove and at every turning, from above or below, from left or right – may be forever new in the transition from one perception to continuously new perceptions. In spite of that, we have, in the way in which such series of perceptions with their changing sensuous images take their courses, intuitive consciousness not of a changing multiplicity but rather of one and the same object that is variously presented. To put it differently, within the pure immanence of such consciousness one unitary "phenomenon" permeates all the manifolds of phenomenal presentation. It is the peculiar characteristic of such states of affairs which makes for the shift in the concept "phenomenon." Rather than just the thoroughgoing *unity* of intuition, the variously changing modes in which the unity is presented, *e.g.*, the continuously changing perspectival looks of a real object, are also called "phenomena."

The extent of this concept is further broadened when we consider the higher cognitive functions: the multiform acts and coherency of referential, combinative, conceiving, theorizing cognition. Every single process of any of these sorts is, again, intrinsically consciousness of the object that is peculiar to it as a thought process of some particular sort or sorts; hence, the object is characterized as member of a combination, as either subject or *relatum* of a relation, etc. The single cognitive processes, on the other hand, combine into the unity of *one* consciousness that constitutes intrinsically a single synthetic objectivity, a single predicative state-of-affairs, for example, or a single theoretical context, an object such as is expressed in sentences like: "The object is related in this or that way," "It is a whole composed of these and those parts," "The relationship B derives from the relationship A," etc.

Consciousness of all synthetically objective formations of these kinds occurs through such multimembered acts that unite to form higher unities of consciousness, and it occurs by means of immanently constituted phenomena that function at the same time as substrates for differing valuations, such as certain truth, probability, possibility, etc.

The concept "phenomenon" carries over, furthermore, to the changing modes of being conscious of something – for example, the clear and the obscure, evident and blind modes – in which one and the same relation or connection, one and the same state-of-affairs, one and the same logical coherency, etc., can be given to consciousness.

In summary, the first and most primitive concept of the phenomenon referred to the limited sphere of those sensuously given realities [*der sinnendinglichen Gegebenheiten*] through which Nature is evinced in perceiving.

The concept was extended, without comment, to include every kind of sensuously meant or objectivated thing. It was then extended to include also the sphere of those synthetic objectivities that are given to consciousness through referential and connective conscious syntheses and to include these objects just the way they are given to consciousness within these syntheses. It thus includes all modes in which things are given to consciousness. And it was seen finally to include the whole realm of consciousness with *all* of the ways of being conscious of something and all the constituents that can be shown immanently to belong to them. That the concept includes *all* ways of being conscious of something means that it includes, as well, every sort of feeling, desiring, and willing with its immanent "comportment" [*Verhalten*].

To understand this broadening of the concept is very easy if one considers that emotional and volitional processes also have intrinsically the character of being conscious of something and that enormous categories of objects, including all cultural objects, all values, all goods, all works, can be experienced, understood, and made objective *as such* only through the participation of emotional and volitional consciousness. No object of the category "work of art" could occur in the objectivational world of any being who was devoid of all aesthetic sensibility, who was, so to speak, aesthetically blind.

Through this exposition of the concept "phenomenon" we obtain a preliminary conception of a general phenomenology, viz., a science of objective phenomena of every kind, the science of every kind of object, an "object" being taken purely as something having just those determinations with which it presents itself in consciousness and in just those changing modes through which it so presents itself. It would be the task of phenomenology, therefore, to investigate how something perceived, something remembered, something phantasied, something pictorially represented, something symbolized looks as such, *i.e.*, to investigate how it looks by virtue of that bestowal of sense and of characteristics which is carried out intrinsically by the perceiving, the remembering, the phantasying, the pictorial representing, etc., itself. Obviously, phenomenology would investigate in the same way how what is collected looks in the collecting of it; what is disjoined, in the disjoining; what is produced, in the producing; and, similarly, for *every* act of thinking, how it intrinsically "has" phenomenally in it what it thinks; how, in aesthetic valuing, the valued looks as such; in actively shaping something, the shaped as such; etc. What phenomenology wants, in all these investigations, is to establish what admits of being stated with the universal validity of theory. In doing so, however, its investigations will, understandably, have to refer to the intrinsic nature [*das eigene Wesen*] of the perceiving itself, of remembering (or any other way of re-presenting) itself, and of thinking, valuing, willing, and doing themselves – these acts being taken just as they present themselves to immanently intuitive reflection. In Cartesian terms, the investigation will be concerned with the *cogito* in its own right as well as with the *cogitatum qua cogitatum*. As the two are inseparably involved with each other in being, so, understandably, are they in the investigation as well.

If these are the themes of phenomenology, then it can also be called "science of consciousness," if consciousness be taken purely as such.

To characterize this science more exactly we shall introduce a simple distinction between phenomena and Objects [*Objekte*][1] in the pregnant sense of the word. In general logical parlance, any subject whatever of true predications is an object. In this sense, therefore, every phenomenon is also an object. Within this widest concept of object, and specifically within the concept of individual object, *Objects* and *phenomena* stand in contrast with each other. Objects [*Objekte*], all natural Objects, for example, are objects foreign to consciousness. Consciousness does, indeed, objectivate them and posit them as actual, yet the consciousness that experiences them and takes cognizance of them is so singularly astonishing that it bestows upon its own phenomena the sense of being appearances of Objects foreign to consciousness and knows these "extrinsic" Objects through processes that take cognizance of their sense. Those objects that are neither conscious processes nor immanent constituents of conscious processes we therefore call Objects in the pregnant sense of the word.

This places two separate sciences in the sharpest of contrasts: on the one hand, phenomenology, the science of consciousness as it is in itself; on the other, the "Objective" sciences as a totality.

To the objects, which are obviously correlated to each other, of these contrasted sciences there correspond two fundamentally different types of experience and of intuition generally: *immanent* experience and *Objective* experience, also called "external" or transcendent experience. Immanent experience consists in the mere viewing that takes place in reflection by which consciousness and that of which there is consciousness are grasped. For example, a liking or a desiring that I am just now executing enters into my experience by way of a merely retrospective look and, by means of this look, is given absolutely. What "absolutely" means here we can learn by contrast: we can experience any external thing only insofar as it presents itself to us sensuously through this or that adumbration [*Abschattung*]. A liking has no changing presentations; there are no changing perspectives on or views of it as if it might be seen from above or below, from near or far. It just is nothing foreign to consciousness at all that could present itself to consciousness through the mediation of phenomena different from the liking itself; to like is intrinsically to be conscious.

This is involved with the fact that the existence of what is given to immanent reflection is indubitable while what is experienced through external experience always allows the possibility that it may prove to be an illusory Object in the course of further experiences.

Immanent and transcendent experience are nevertheless connected in a remarkable way: by a change in attitude, we can pass from the one to the other.

In the natural attitude, we experience, among other things, processes in Nature [*Natur*]; we are adverted to them, observe them, describe them, subsume them under concepts [*bestimmen sie*]. While we do so, there occur in our experiencing and theorizing consciousness multiform conscious processes which have constantly changing immanent constituents. The things involved present themselves through continuously flowing aspects; their shapes are perspectivally silhouetted [*schatten sich ab*] in definite ways; the data of the different senses are construed in definite ways, *e.g.*, as unitary colorings of the experienced shapes or as warmth radiating from them; the sensuous qualities construed are referred, by being construed referentially and causally, to real circumstances; etc. The bestowing of each of these senses is carried out in consciousness and by virtue of definite series of flowing conscious processes. A person in the natural attitude, however, knows nothing of this. He executes the acts of experiencing, referring, combining; but, while he is executing them, he is looking not toward them but rather in the direction of the objects he is conscious of.

On the other hand, he can convert his natural attentional focus into the phenomenologically reflective one; he can make the currently flowing consciousness and, thus, the infinitely multiform world of phenomena at large the theme of his fixating observations, descriptions, theoretical investigations – the investigations which, for short, we call "phenomenological."

At this point, however, there arises what, in the present situation of philosophy, can be called the most decisive of questions. Is not what was just described as immanent reflection simply identical with internal, psychological experience? Is not psychology the proper place for the investigation of consciousness and all its phenomena? However much psychology may previously have omitted any systematic investigation of consciousness, however blindly it may have passed over all radical problems concerning the bestowal, carried out in the immanence of consciousness, of objective sense, it still seems clear that such investigations should belong to psychology and should even be fundamental to it.

The ideal of a *pure* phenomenology will be perfected only by answering this question; pure phenomenology is to be separated sharply from psychology at large and, specifically, from the descriptive psychology of the phenomena of consciousness. Only with this separation does the centuries-old conflict over "psychologism" reach its final conclusion. The conflict is over nothing less than the true philosophical method and the foundation of any philosophy as pure and strict science.

To begin with, we put the proposition: pure phenomenology is the science of *pure* consciousness. This means that pure phenomenology draws upon pure reflection exclusively, and pure reflection excludes, as such, every type of external experience and therefore precludes any copositing of objects alien to consciousness. Psychology, on the other hand, is science of psychic Nature and, therefore, of consciousness as Nature or as real event in the spatiotemporal world. Psychology draws upon *psychological* experiencing, which is an apperceiving that links immanent reflection to experience of the external, the extrinsic [*äusserer Erfahrung*]. In psychological experience, moreover, the psychic is given as event within the cohesion of Nature. Specifically, psychology, as the natural science of psychic life, regards conscious processes as the conscious processes of animate beings, *i.e.*, as real causal adjuncts to animate bodies. The psychologist must resort to reflection in order to have conscious processes experientially given. Nevertheless, this reflection does not keep to pure reflection; for, in being taken as belonging really to the animate body in question, reflection is linked to experience of the extrinsic. Psychologically experienced consciousness is therefore no longer pure consciousness; construed Objectively in this way, consciousness itself becomes something transcendent, becomes an event in that spatial world which appears, by virtue of consciousness, to be transcendent.

The fundamental fact is that there is a kind of intuiting which – in contrast to psychological experiencing – remains within pure reflection: pure reflection excludes everything that is given in the natural attitude and excludes therefore all of Nature.

Consciousness is taken purely as it intrinsically is with its own intrinsic constituents, and no being that transcends consciousness is coposited.

What is thematically posited is only what is given, by pure reflection, with all its immanent essential moments absolutely as it is given to pure reflection.

Descartes long ago came close to discovering the purely phenomenological sphere. He did so in his famous and fundamental meditation – that has nevertheless been basically fruitless – which culminates in the much quoted *"ego cogito, ego sum."* The so-called *phenomenological reduction* can be effected by modifying Descartes's method, by carrying it through purely and consequentially while disregarding all Cartesian aims; phenomenological reduction is the method for effecting radical purification of the phenomenological field of consciousness from all obtrusions from Objective actualities and for keeping it pure of them. Consider the following: Nature, the universe of spatiotemporal Objectivity, is given to us constantly; in the natural attitude, it already is the field for our investigations in the natural sciences and for our practical purposes. Yet, nothing prevents us from putting out of action, so to speak, any believing in the actuality of it, even though that believing continues to occur all the while in our mental processes. After all, speaking quite universally, no believing, no conviction, however evident, excludes by its essence the possibility of its being put in a certain way out of action or deprived of its force. What this means we can learn from any case in which we examine one of our convictions, perhaps to defend it against objections or to re-establish it on a new basis. It may be that we have no doubts at all about it. Yet, we obviously alter during the whole course of the examination the way we act in relation to this conviction. Without surrendering our conviction in the least, we still do not take part in it; we deny to ourselves acceptance, as truth, of what the conviction posits simply to be true. While the examination is being carried out, this truth is in question; it remains to be seen; it is to remain undecided.

In our instance, in the case of phenomenologically pure reflection, the aim is not to place in question and to test our believing in actualities foreign to consciousness. Nevertheless, we can carry out a similar putting-out-of-action for that consciousness of actuality by virtue of which the whole of Nature is existence which, for us, is given [*für uns gegebenes Dasein ist*]; and we can do so utterly *ad libitum*. For the sole purposes of attaining to the domain of pure consciousness and keeping it pure, we therefore undertake to accept no beliefs involving Objective experience and, therefore, also undertake to make not the slightest use of any conclusion derived from Objective experience.

The actuality of all of material Nature is therefore kept out of action and that of all corporeality along with it, including the actuality of my body, the body of the cognizing subject.

This makes it clear that, as a consequence, all psychological experience is also put out of action. If we have absolutely forbidden ourselves to treat Nature and the corporeal at all as given actualities, then the possibility of positing any conscious process whatsoever as having a corporeal link or as being an event occurring in Nature lapses of itself.

What is left over, once this radical methodological exclusion of all Objective actualities has been effected? The answer is clear. If we put every experienced actuality out of action, we still have indubitably given every phenomenon of experience. This is true for the whole Objective world as well. We are forbidden to make use of the *actuality* of the Objective world: for us, the Objective world is as if it were placed in brackets. What remains to us is the totality of the phenomena of the world, phenomena which are grasped by reflection as they are absolutely in themselves [*in ihrer absoluten Selbstheit*]. For, all of these constituents of conscious life remain intrinsically what they were; it is through them that the world is constituted.

So far as their own phenomenal content is concerned, they do not suffer in any way when believing in Objective actuality is put out of play. Nor does reflection, insofar as it grasps and views the phenomena in their own being, suffer in any way. Only now, in fact, does reflection become pure and exclusive. Moreover, even the belief in the Objective, the belief characteristic of simple experience and of empirical theory, is not lost to us. Instead, it becomes our theme just as it intrinsically is and in accord with what is implicit in it as its sense and as the substrate for what it posits; we view the belief; we analyze its immanent character; we follow its possible coherencies, especially those of grounding; we study in pure reflection what takes place in transitions to fulfilling insight, what is preserved of the meant sense in such transitions, what the fullness of intuition brings to this sense, what alteration and enrichment so-called evidence contributes, and whatever advances are made by what, in this connection, is called "attaining Objective truth through insight." Following this method of phenomenological reduction (*i.e.*, keeping out of action all believing in the transcendent), every kind of theoretical, valuational, practical consciousness can be made in the same manner a theme of inquiry; and all the Objectivities constituted in it can be investigated.

The investigation will take these Objectivities simply as correlates of consciousness and will inquire solely into the What and the How of the phenomena that
can be drawn from the conscious processes and coherencies in question. Things in
Nature, persons and personal communities, social forms and formations, poetic
and plastic formations, every kind of cultural work – all become in this way
headings for phenomenological investigations, not as actualities, the way they are
treated in the corresponding Objective sciences, but rather with regard to the
consciousness that constitutes – through the intermediary of an initially bewildering wealth of structures of consciousness – these objectivities for the conscious
subject in question. Consciousness and what it is conscious of is therefore what is
left over as field for pure reflection once phenomenological reduction has been
effected: the endless multiplicity of manners of being conscious, on the one hand,
and, on the other, the infinity of intentional correlates. What keeps us from trans-
gressing this field is the index that, thanks to the method of phenomenological
reduction, every Objective belief obtains as soon as it arises for consciousness.
The index demands of us: Take no part in this belief; do not fall into the attitude
of Objective science; keep to the pure phenomenon! Obviously, the index is universal in the scope in which it suspends acceptance of the Objective sciences
themselves, of which psychology is one. The index changes all sciences to science
phenomena; and, in this status, they are among its larger themes.

However, as soon as any proposition about things Objective, any one at all,
including even the most indubitable truth, is claimed to be a valid truth, the soil
of pure phenomenology is abandoned. For then we take our stance upon some
Objective soil and carry on psychology or some other Objective science instead of
phenomenology.

This radical suspension of Nature stands in conflict, to be sure, with our most
deeply rooted habits of experience and thinking. Yet it is precisely for this reason
that fully self-conscious phenomenological reduction is needed if consciousness is
to be systematically investigated in its pure immanence at all.

But still other reservations come to mind. Is pure phenomenology genuinely
possible as a science, and, if so, then how? Once the suspension is in effect, we are
left with pure consciousness. In pure consciousness, however, what we find is an
unresting flow of never recurring phenomena, even though they may be indubitably given in reflective experience. Experience by itself is not science. Since the
reflecting and cognizing subject has only his flowing phenomena genuinely and
since every other cognizing subject – his corporeality and consequently his consciousness [*seinem Erleben*] as well – falls within the scope of the exclusion, how
can an empirical science still be possible? Science cannot be solipsistic. It must be
valid for every experiencing subject.

We would be in a nasty position indeed if empirical science were the only kind
of science possible. Answering the question we have posed thus leads to most
profound and as yet unsolved philosophical problems. Be that as it may, pure
phenomenology was not established to be an empirical science, and what it calls
its 'purity' is not just that of pure reflection but is at the same time the entirely
different sort of purity we meet in the names of other sciences.

We often speak in a general, and intelligible, way of pure mathematics, pure
arithmetic, pure geometry, pure kinematics, etc. These we contrast, as a priori

131

sciences, to sciences, such as the natural sciences, based on experience and induction. Sciences that are pure in this sense, a priori sciences, are pure of any assertion about empirical actuality. Intrinsically, they purport to be concerned with the ideally possible and the pure laws thereof rather than with actualities. In contrast to them, empirical sciences are sciences of the de facto actual, which is given as such through experience.

Now, just as pure analysis does not treat of actual things and their de facto magnitudes but investigates instead the essential laws pertaining to the essence of any possible quantity, or just as pure geometry is not bound to shapes observed in actual experience but instead inquires into possible shapes and their possible transformations, constructing *ad libitum* in pure geometric phantasy, and establishes their essential laws, in *precisely* the same way pure phenomenology proposes to investigate *the realm of pure consciousness and its phenomena* not as de facto existents but as pure possibilities with their pure laws. And, indeed, when one becomes familiar with the soil of pure reflection, one is compelled to the view that possibilities are subject to ideal laws in the realm of pure consciousness as well. For example, the pure phenomena through which a possible spatial Object presents itself to consciousness have their a priori definite system of necessary formations which is unconditionally binding upon every cognizing consciousness if that consciousness is to be able to intuit spatial reality [*Raumdinglichkeit*]. Thus, the ideal of a spatial thing prescribes a priori to possible consciousness of such a thing a set rule, a rule that can be followed intuitively and that admits of being conceived, in accord with the typicality of phenomenal forms, in pure concepts. And the same is true of every principal category of objectivities. The expression 'a priori' is therefore not a cloak to cover some ideological extravagance but, is just as significant as is the 'purity' of mathematical analysis or geometry.

Obviously, I can here offer no more than this helpful analogy. Without troublesome work, no one can have any concrete, full idea of what pure mathematical research is like or of the profusion of insights that can be obtained from it. The same sort of penetrating work, for which no general characterization can adequately substitute, is required if one is to understand phenomenological science concretely. That the work is worthwhile can readily be seen from the unique position of phenomenology with regard to philosophy on the one hand and psychology on the other. Pure phenomenology's tremendous significance for any concrete grounding of *psychology* is clear from the very beginning. If all consciousness is subject to essential laws in a manner similar to that in which spatial reality is subject to mathematical laws, then these essential laws will be of most fertile significance in investigating facts of the conscious life of human and brute animals.

So far as philosophy is concerned, it is enough to point out that all ratio-theoretical [*vernunft-theoretische*] problems, the problems involved in the so-called *critique* of theoretical, valuational, and practical reason, are concerned *entirely* with *essential coherencies* prevailing between theoretical, axiological, or practical Objectivity and the consciousness in which it is immanently constituted. It is easy to demonstrate that ratio-theoretical problems can be formulated with scientific rigor and can then be solved in their systematic coherence only on the soil of phenomenologically pure consciousness and within the framework of a pure phenomenology. The critique of reason and all philosophical problems along with it can be put on the course of strict science by a kind of research that draws intuitively upon what is given phenomenologically but not by thinking of the kind that plays out value concepts, a game played with constructions far removed from intuition.

Philosophers, as things now stand, are all too fond of offering criticism from on high instead of studying and understanding things from within. They often behave toward phenomenology as Berkeley – otherwise a brilliant philosopher and psychologist – behaved two centuries ago toward the then newly established infinitesimal calculus. He thought that he could prove, by his logically sharp but superficial criticism, this sort of mathematical analysis to be a completely groundless extravagance, a vacuous game played with empty abstractions. It is utterly beyond doubt that phenomenology, new and most fertile, will overcome all resistance and stupidity and will enjoy enormous development, just as the infinitesimal mathematics that was so alien to its contemporaries did, and just as exact physics, in opposition to the brilliantly obscure natural philosophy of the Renaissance, has done since the time of Galileo.

Note

1 Following the practice of Dorion Cairns in his translation of Husserl's *Cartesian Meditations*, the word 'object', spelled with a small letter, has been and will be used throughout to translate *Gegenstand*; spelled with a capital letter, it translates *Objekt*. In the same way, words derived from *Gegenstand* or from *Objekt* will be translated with words derived from 'object', spelled with a small or with a capital letter, respectively. Where 'object' or one of its derivatives is the initial word in a sentence, the German word will be given in brackets. The practice appears to be justified perfectly by the manner in which the text proceeds to differentiate between the senses of *Gegenstand* and *Objekt*.

5

NOESIS AND NOEMA

§87 Preliminary remarks

The peculiarity of the intentive mental process is easily designated in its universality; we all understand the expression "consciousness of something," especially in *ad libitum* exemplifications. It is so much more difficult to purely and correctly seize upon the phenomenological essence-peculiarities corresponding to it. That this heading circumscribes a large field of painfully achieved findings and, more particularly, of eidetic findings, would seem even today alien to the majority of philosophers and psychologists (if we can judge by the literature). This is because nothing is accomplished by saying and discerning that every objectivating relates to something objectivated, that every judging relates to something judged, etc. Or that, in addition, one refers to logic, theory of knowledge, ethics, with their many evidences, and now *designates* these as belonging to the essence of intentionality. This is, at the same time, a very simple way of taking the phenomenological doctrine of essences as something very old, as a new name for the old logic and those disciplines which must be ranked with it. For without having seized upon the peculiar ownness of the transcendental attitude and having actually appropriated the pure phenomenological basis, one may of course use the word, phenomenology; but one does not have the matter itself. In addition, it does not suffice, let us say, to merely change the attitude, or to merely carry out the phenomenological reduction in order to make something like phenomenology out of pure logic. For how far logical and, in a like way, pure ontological, pure ethical, and whatever other apriori propositions one may cite, actually express something phenomenological, and to which phenomenological strata the respective ‹propositions› may belong, is not obvious. On the contrary, the most difficult problems of all are hidden, ‹problems› the sense of which is naturally concealed from all those who still have no inkling of the determinative fundamental distinctions. In fact, it is (if I may be allowed a judgment from my own experience) a long and thorny way starting from purely logical insights, from insights pertaining to the theory of signification, from ontological and noetical insights, likewise from the customary normative and psychological theory of knowledge, to arrive at seizing upon, in a genuine sense, the immanent-psychological and then phenomenological data, and finally to arrive at all at the concatenations of essence which make the

E. Husserl, *Ideas Pertaining to a Pure Phenomenology and to a Phenomenological Philosophy*, *First Book*, 1983, trans. F. Kersten, pp. 211–35. The Hague: Nijhoff.

transcendental relations intelligible apriori. Something similar is the case no matter from where we might set out on the way from objective insights to acquire phenomenological insights which essentially belong to them.

"Consciousness of something" is therefore something obviously understandable of itself and, at the same time, highly enigmatic. The labyrinthically false paths into which the first reflections lead, easily generate a skepticism which negates the whole troublesome sphere of problems. Not a few already bar access by the fact that they cannot bring themselves to seize upon the intentive mental process, e.g., the perceptual process, with the essence proper to it as perceptual process. Rather than living in the perception, adverted to the perceived in considering and theorizing they do not manage to direct the regard instead to the perceiving, or to the own peculiarities of the *mode* of givenness of the perceived, and to take what is offered in analysis of something immanent with respect to its essence, just as it is given. If the right attitude has been won, and made secure by practice, above all, however, if one has acquired the courage to obey the clear eidetic data with a radical lack of prejudice so as to be unencumbered by all current and learned theories, then firm results are directly produced, and the same thing occurs for everyone having the same attitude; there accrue firm possibilities of communicating to others what one has himself seen, of testing descriptions, of making salient the unnoticed intrusions of empty verbal meanings, of making known and weeding out errors by measuring them again against intuition – errors which are also possible here just as in any sphere of validity. But now to the matters at hand.

§88 Really inherent and intentive components of mental processes. The noema

If, as in the present deliberations generally, we begin with the most universal distinctions which, so to speak, can be seized upon at the very threshold of phenomenology, and which are determinative for all further methodic proceedings, then with respect to intentionality we immediately confront a wholly fundamental distinction, namely the distinction between the *components proper* of intentive mental processes and their *intentional correlates* and their components. We already touched upon this distinction in the preliminary eidetical deliberations of Part II. In that connection, in making the transition from the natural to the phenomenological attitude, the distinction served us to make clear the own peculiar being of the phenomenological sphere. But that it acquired a radical signification within this sphere itself, thus in the frame of the transcendental reduction, conditioning the entire set of problems pertaining to phenomenology: of that we could not speak there. On the one side therefore, we have to discriminate the parts and moments which we find by an *analysis of the really inherent* pertaining to mental processes, whereby we deal with the mental process as an object like any other, inquiring about its pieces or non-selfsufficient moments really inherent in it which make it up. But, on the other side, the intentive mental process is consciousness of something, and it is so according to its essence, e.g., as memory, as judgment, as will, etc.; and we can therefore inquire into what is to be declared as a matter of essential necessity about the side of this "of something."

Owing to its noetic moments, every intentive mental process is precisely noetic;[1]

it is of its essence to include in itself something such as a "sense" and possibly a manifold sense on the basis of this sense-bestowal and, in unity with that, to effect further productions [*Leistungen*] which become "senseful" precisely by ‹this sense-bestowal›. Such noetic moments are, e.g., directions of the regard of the pure Ego to the objects "meant" by it owing to sense-bestowal, to ‹the object› which is "inherent in the sense" for the Ego; furthermore, seizing upon this object, holding it fast while the regard adverts to other objects which appear in the "meaning" ["*Vermeinen*"]; likewise, producings pertaining to explicatings, relatings, comprisings, multiple position-takings of believings, deemings likely, valuings; and so forth. All of these are to be found in the mental processes in question, no matter how differently structured and varied they are. Now, no matter to what extent this series of exemplary moments refer to really inherent components of mental processes, they nevertheless also refer to what is *not really inherent*, namely by means of the heading of sense.

Corresponding in every case to the multiplicity of data pertaining to the really inherent noetic content, there is a multiplicity of data, demonstrable in actual pure intuition, in a correlative "*noematic content*" or, in short, in the "*noema*" – terms which we shall continue to use form now on.

Perception, for example, has its noema, most basically its perceptual sense,[2] i.e., the *perceived as perceived*. Similarly, the current case of remembering has its *remembered as remembered*, just as its ‹remembered›, precisely as it is "meant," "intended to" in ‹the remembering›; again, the judging has the *judged as judged*, liking has the liked as liked, and so forth. In every case the noematic correlate, which is called "sense" here (in a very extended signification) is to be taken *precisely* as it inheres "immanentally" in the mental process of perceiving, of judging, of liking; and so forth; that is, just as it is offered to us when we *inquire purely into this mental process itself*.

How we understand all of this will become clear by carrying out an exemplary analysis (which we will effect in pure intuition).

Let us suppose that in a garden we regard with pleasure a blossoming apple tree, the freshly green grass of the lawn, etc. It is obvious that the perception and the accompanying liking are not, at the same time, what is perceived and liked. In the natural attitude, the apple tree is for us something existing in the transcendent realm of spatial actuality, and the perception, as well as the liking, is for us a psychical state belonging to real people. Between the one and the other real things, between the real person or the real perception, and the real apple tree, there exist real relations. In such situations characterizing mental processes, it may be in certain cases that perception is "mere hallucination," the perceived, this apple tree before us, does not exist in "actual" reality. Now the real relation, previously meant as actually existing, is destroyed. Only the perception remains, but there is nothing actual there to which it is related.

Let us now go to the ‹transcendental› phenomenological attitude. The transcendent world receives its "parenthesis," we exercise the ἐποχή in relation to ‹positing› its actual being. We now ask what, of essential necessity, is to be discovered in the complex of noetic processes pertaining to perception and in the valuation of liking. With the whole physical and psychical world, the actual existence of the real relation between perceiving and perceived is excluded; and, nonetheless, a relation between perceiving and perceived (as well as between liking and liked) remains left over, a relation which becomes given essentially in "pure immanence," namely purely on the ground of the phenemenologically reduced mental processes of perceiving and liking precisely as they fit into the transcendental stream of mental processes. Precisely this situation, the purely phenomenological one, will occupy us now. Concerning hallucinations, illusions and perceptual deception of whatever sort, it may be that phenomenology has something to say, and perhaps even a great deal: but it is evident that here, in the role which they played in the natural attitude, they undergo exclusion. Here, in the case of perception and also in the case of any progressive concatencation of perceptions whatever (as when we consider the blossoming tree ambulando), there is no question to be raised of the sort whether or not something corresponds to it in "the" actuality. This posited actuality is indeed not there for us in consequence of judging. And yet, so to speak, everything remains as of old. Even the phenomenologically reduced perceptual mental process is a perceiving *of* "this blossoming apple tree, in this garden," etc., and, likewise, the reduced liking is a liking of this same thing. The tree has not lost the least nuance of all these moments, qualities, characteristics *with which it was appearing in this perception*, ‹with which› it ‹was appearing as› "*lovely*," "*attractive*," and so forth "in" *this liking*.

In our ‹transcendental› phenomenological attitude we can and must raise the eidetic question: *what the "perceived as perceived" is, which eidetic moments it includes in itself as this perception-noema.* We receive the answer in the pure directedness to *something given* in its essence, and we can faithfully describe the "appearing as appearing" in complete evidence. It is only another expression for this to say that we "describe perception in its noematic respect."

§89 Noematic statements and statements about actuality. The noema in the psychological sphere

It is clear that all these descriptive statements, even though they may sound like statements about actuality, have undergone a *radical* modification of sense; similarly, the described itself, even though it is given as "precisely the same," is yet something radically different by virtue of, so to speak, an inverse change of signs. "In" the reduced perception (in the phenomenologically pure mental process), we find, as indefeasibly belonging to its essence, the perceived as perceived, to be expressed as "material thing," "plant," "tree," "blossoming;" and so forth. Obviously, the *inverted commas* are significant in that they express that change in sign, the correspondingly radical significational modification of the words. The *tree simpliciter*, the physical thing belonging to Nature, is nothing less than this *perceived tree as perceived* which, as perceptual sense, inseparably belongs to the perception. The tree simpliciter can burn up, be resolved into its chemical elements, etc. But the sense – the sense *of this* perception, something belonging necessarily to its essence – cannot burn up; it has no chemical elements, no forces, no real properties.

Everything which is purely immanent and reduced in the way peculiar to the mental process, everything which cannot be conceived apart from it just as it is in itself, and which eo ipso passes over into the Eidos in the eidetic attitude, is separated by an abyss from all of Nature and physics and no less from all psychology – and even this image, as naturalistic, is not strong enough to indicate the difference.

Obviously the perceptual sense also belongs to the phenomenologically unreduced perception (perception in the sense of psychology). Thus one can make clear here at the same time how the phenomenological reduction can acquire for psychologists the useful methodic function of fixing the noematic sense by sharply distinguishing it from the object simpliciter, and recognizing it as something belonging inseparably to the psychological essence of the intentive mental process.

On both sides, in the psychological as well as in the phenomenological attitude, one must therefore not lose sight of the fact that the "perceived" as sense includes nothing in itself (thus nothing should be imputed to it on the ground of "indirect cognizances") other than what "actually appears" in the given case in something perceptually appearing and, more precisely, in the mode of givenness in which it is precisely something intended to in the perception. At any time a *specifically peculiar reflection* can be directed to this sense as it is immanent in the perception, and the phenomenological judgment has to conform in faithful expression to what is seized upon in it.

§90 The "noematic sense" and the distinction between "immanental" and "actual objects."

Like perception, *every* intentive mental process – just this makes up the fundamental part of intentionality – has its "intentional Object," i.e., its objective sense. Or, in other words: to have sense or "to intend to" something [*etwas "im Sinne zu haben"*], is the fundamental characteristic of all consciousness which, therefore, is not just any mental living [*Erlebnis*] whatever, but is rather a ‹mental living› having sense, which is "noetic."

Certainly what has become prominent as "sense" in the analysis of our examples does not exhaust the full noema; correspondingly, the noetic side of the intentive mental process does not merely consist of the moment of "sense-bestowal" proper specifically belonging to the "sense" as correlate. It will be shown directly that the full noema consists of a complex of noematic moments, that in ‹that complex› the specific sense-moment only fashions one kind of necessary *core-stratum* in which further moments are essentially founded which, therefore, should likewise be designated as sense-moments, but in an extended meaning.

Nevertheless, let us remain at first with what alone has clearly emerged. Without doubt we have shown that the intentive mental process is of such a character that in a suitable focusing of regard a "sense" is to be drawn from it. The situation defining the sense for us cannot remain concealed: the circumstance, namely, that the non-existence (or the conviction of non-existence) of the objectivated or thought of Object pure and simple pertaining to the objectivation in question (and therefore to any particular intentive mental process whatever) cannot steal its something objectivated as objectivated, that therefore the distinction between both must be made. Such a striking distinction has required expression in the literature. As a matter of fact, the Scholastic distinction between the "*mental*," "*intentional*" or "*immanental*" Object on the one hand, and the "*actual*" Object on the other hand, refers back to it. Nevertheless, it is an immense step to go from seizing upon a distinction pertaining to consciousness for the first time to its right, phenomenologically pure, fixing and correct valuation – and precisely this step, which is decisive for a harmonious, fruitful phenomenology, has not been effected. Above all, what is decisive consists of the absolutely faithful description of what is actually present in phenomenological purity and in keeping at a distance all the interpretations transcending the given. Here denominations already evince interpretations, and often quite false ones. These interpretations betray themselves here in expressions such as "mental," "immanental" Object, and the expression "intentional Object" requires them the least of all.

It would even be tempting to say: In the mental process the intention is given with its intentional Object which, as intentional Object, inseparably belongs to it, therefore itself *inherently* dwells within ‹the intention›. Indeed, it is and remains its ‹Object› meant, objectivated, and the like, no matter if the corresponding "actual Object" precisely is or is not in actuality, if it has been annihilated in the meantime, etc.

But if, in *this* way, we try to separate the actual Object (in the case of perception of something external, the perceived physical thing pertaining to Nature) and the intentional Object, including the latter ‹as› really inherently in the mental process as "immanent" to the perception, we fall into the difficulty that now *two* realities ought to stand over against one another while only *one* ‹reality› is found to be present and even possible. I perceive the physical thing, the Object belonging to Nature, the tree there in the garden; that and nothing else is the actual Object of the perceptual "intention." A second immanental tree, or even an "internal image" of the actual tree standing out there before me, is in no way given, and to suppose that hypothetically leads to an absurdity. The image as a really inherent component in the psychologically real perception would be again something real – something real which would *function* as a depicturing of another something real. But that can only be by virtue of a depicturing consciousness in which something first appears – with with which we would have a first intentionality – and this would function again in consciousness as a "picture Object" representing another "picture Object" – for which a second intentionality founded in the first intentionality would be necessary. It is no less evident that each particular one of these modes of consciousness already requires the distinction between the immanental and actual object, thus comprising the same problem which should have been resolved by the construction. Over and above this, in the case of perception, the construction is subject to the objection which we have discussed earlier[3] to include depictive functions in the perception of something physical signifies ascribing to it a picture-consciousness which, descriptively considered, is something of an essentially different kind of constitution. Nevertheless, the main point here is that perception and, then consequently, every mental process, requires a depictive function, unavoidably (as can be seen at once from our critique) leads to an infinite regress.

In contradistinction to such errors we have to abide by what is given in the pure mental process and to take it within the frame of clarity precisely as it is given. The "actual" Object is then to be "parenthesized." Let us reflect on what that signifies: if we begin as people in the natural attitude, then the actual Object is the physical thing there, outside ‹us›. We see it, we stand before it, we have directed

EDMUND HUSSERL

our eyes fixingly to it, and then we describe it and make our statements about it just as we find it there in space as what confronts us. Likewise we take a position toward it in valuing; what confronts us, what we see in space, pleases us, or determines us to act; we seize upon or manipulate what is given there, etc. If we now effect the phenomenological reduction, then every positing of something transcendent, thus above all what is inherent to perception itself, receives its excluding parentheses, and this is passed on to all of the founded acts, to every judgment of perception, to the positing of value, and possibly to the value judgment grounded in it. Implicit in this is that we only allow all these perceivings, judgings, etc., to be considered, to be described, as the essentialities which they are in themselves, to pin down what is evidently given with or in them. But we do not tolerate any judgment which makes use of the positing of the "actual" physical thing, nor of the whole "transcendent" Nature, or which "joins in" ‹that positing›. As *phenomenologists* we abstain from all such positings. But on that account we do not reject them by not "taking them as our basis," by not "joining in" them. They are indeed there, they also essentially belong to the phenomenon. Rather we contemplate them; instead of joining in them, we make them Objects, take them as component parts of the phenomenon – the positing pertaining to perception as well as its components.

And, keeping these excludings in their clear sense, we therefore ask quite universally, then, about what is evidentially "inherent" in the whole "reduced" phenomenon. Now, inherent too precisely in perception is this: that it has its noematic sense, its "perceived as perceived," "this blossoming tree there, in space" – understood with inverted commas – precisely the *correlate* belonging to the essence of phenomenologically reduced perception. Figuratively stated: the "parenthesis" undergone by perception prevents any judgment about perceived actuality (i.e., any ‹judgment› having its basis in unmodified perception, thus taking up into itself its positing). But it does not prevent the judgment about the fact that perception is consciousness *of* an actuality (the positing of which, however, should not be "effected"); and it does not prevent any description of this perceptually appearing "actuality" as appearing with the particular ways in which it is here intended to, appearing only "one-sidedly," in this or that orientation; and so forth. With minute care we must now take heed against attributing to the mental process anything which is not actually included in its essence, and ‹we must› "attribute" ‹what is included› exactly and just as it precisely is "inherent" in it.

§91 Extension to the widest sphere of intentionality

What was carried out in detail primarily in the case of perception actually holds now for *all kinds of intentive mental processes*. After the reduction we find the remembered as remembered in remembering, the expected as expected in expecting, the phantasied as phantasied in inventive phantasy.

"Inhering" in each of these mental processes in a noematic sense, and however this ‹noematic sense› may be akin in different mental processes, indeed perchance essentially quite alike with respect to a core-component, in any case the ‹noematic sense› is different in kind in various sorts of mental processes; what is common in a given case is at least differently characterized and is so of necessity. In every case

140

it may be a matter of the blossoming tree, and in every case this tree may appear in a certain way such that the faithful description of what appears as it appears necessarily results in the same expression. But for that reason the noematic correlates are still essentially different for perception, phantasy, presentiating something depicted, remembering, etc. At one time what appears is characterized as "actuality in person," at another time as fiction, then again as something presentiated in a remembering, etc.

These are characteristics which we *find present in* the perceived, phantasied, remembered, and so forth, as perceived, phantasied, remembered – *in the sense of the perception, in the sense of phantasy, in the sense of memory* – as something inseparable and as *something necessarily belonging in correlation to the respective kinds of noetic processes.*

Where it is a matter of describing the intentional correlates faithfully and completely, there we must also apprehend all such characteristics which are never accidental but are instead governed by eidetic law and fixed into rigorous concepts.

In this connection, we note what within the *full* noema (in fact, as we have previously indicated) we must separate *essentially different strata* which which are grouped around a *central "core,"* around a pure *"objective sense"* – around that which, in our examples, was describable with purely identical objective expressions because there can be something identical in the parallel mental processes which are different in sort. When, again, we set aside the parentheses effected on the positing, we see that, in a parallel way, corresponding to the different concepts of sense we must distinguish different concepts of *unmodified objectivities*, of which the "object simpliciter," namely the something identical which is perceived at one time, another time directly presentiated, a third time presented pictorially in a painting, and the like, only indicates *one* central concept. This indication is sufficient for us in a preliminary way for the moment.

Let us scrutinize the sphere of consciousness still further and try to get acquainted with the noetic-noematic structures in the principal modes of consciousness. In the actual demonstration we shall, at the same time, step by step, assure ourselves of the *complete* validity of the fundamental correlation between noesis and noema.

§92 The noetic and noematic aspects of attentional changes

In our preparatory chapters we spoke repeatedly of a species of remarkable changes in consciousness which cut across all other species of intentional events and thus make up a quite universal structure of consciousness having its own peculiar dimension: We spoke metaphorically of the pure Ego's "mental regard" or the "ray of its regard," of its advertings toward and turning away from. The relevant phenomena stood out unitarily for us with perfect clarity and distinctness. Wherever "attention" is spoken of originarily, they play a major role without being separated phenomenologically from certain other phenomena; and, mixed with these others, they are usually designated as modes of attention. For our part, we mean to retain the word and, moreover, to speak of *attentional changes*, but with exclusive reference to the events *we* have separated distinctly and the groups of phenomenal changes still to be described more precisely in what follows.

In this context it is a question of a series of ideally possible changes which already presuppose a noetic core and the characterizing moments of various genera which necessarily belong to it; of themselves, ‹these possible changes› do not alter the correlative noematic productions but, nevertheless, exhibit alterations of the *whole* mental process with respect to both its noetic and noematic sides. The ray of the pure Ego's regard sometimes goes through one noetic stratum and sometimes through another, or (as, e.g., in the case of rememberings within rememberings) through one encasement-level or another, sometimes straightforwardly, sometimes reflectively. Within the given total field of potential noeses and correlative objects of noeses we sometimes look at a whole, the tree, perhaps, which is perceptually present, sometimes at these or those parts and moments of it; then, again, we look at a nearby physical thing or at a complex context and process. Suddenly we turn our regard to an object of memory which "comes to mind:" Instead of going through the perceptual noesis, which, in a continuously unitary though highly articulated manner, constitutes for us the continually appearing world of physical things, the regard goes through a remembering noesis into a world of memory; it wanders about in this world, passes over into memories of other degrees or into worlds of phantasy, and so forth.

For the sake of simplicity, let us remain in *one* intentive stratum in the world of perception which stands there in simple certainty. Let us take a physical thing or a physical process of which there is a perceptual consciousness, and fix it, in idea, with respect to its noematic contents, while we take the whole concrete consciousness of physical thing or the physical process throughout the corresponding section of phenomenological duration, and fix *it* with respect to its full immanental essence. For the idea in question involves fixing of the attentional ray as wandering in a *determinate* manner ‹throughout that section of phenomenological duration,› since ‹the attentional ray› too is a moment of the mental process. It is then evident that modes of alteration of the fixed mental process are possible which we designate by the name, "alterations merely in the distribution of attention and its modes." It is clear that, throughout such alterations, the *noematic* composition of the mental process remains the same in so far as one can always say that the same objectivity is continuously characterized as being there in person, presenting itself in the same modes of appearance, in the same orientations, with the same appearing traits; that in the modes of indeterminate indication, of making non-intuitively copresent, and so forth, there is a consciousness of such and such a stock of content belonging to it. Selecting out and comparing parallel noematic components, we say that the alteration consists *merely* of the fact that, in one of the compared cases, one moment of the object is "favored" and, in another case, another; or of the fact that one and the same moment is "paid attention to primarily" at one time and only secondarily at another time, or "just barely noticed still," if not indeed "completely unnoticed" though still appearing. Those are indeed different modes belonging specifically to attention as such. Among them the group of *actionality modes* are separated from the *non-actionality mode*, from what we call complete inattention, the mode which is, so to speak, dead consciousness of something.

On the other hand, it is clear not only that these are modifications of the mental process itself with respect to its noetic composition, but also that they affect its *noema*, that, on the noematic side – without touching the identical noematic core – they present a separate genus of characterizations. Attention is usually compared to a spot light. The object of attention, in the specific sense, lies in the cone of more or less bright light; but it can also move into the penumbra and into the completely dark region. Though the metaphor is far from adequate to differentiate all the modes which can be fixed phenomenologically, it is still designative in so far as it indicates alterations in what appears, as what appears. These changes in its illumination do not alter what appears with respect to its own *sense*-composition; but brightness and obscurity modify its mode of appearance: they are to be found and described when we direct out regard to the noematic Object.

Obviously the modifications in the noema are not of such a kind that mere outward adjuncts are added to something which remains unvaryingly identical; on the contrary, the concrete noemas change through and through, it being a question of necessary modes belonging to the mode in which the identical is given.

Yet, on closer inspection, it is not the case that the *entire* noematic content (the *attentional core*, so to speak) characterized by this or that mode can be kept constant in contrast to any attentional modifications whatever. On the contrary, looked at from the noetic side it becomes apparent that certain noeses, either necessarily or with respect to their determined possibility, are conditioned by modes of attention and in particular, by positive attention in the distinctive sense ⟨of this word⟩. All "effecting of acts," the "actional takings of positions," e.g., "effecting" the settlement of a doubt, the "making" ["*Vollzug*"] of a refusal, the "effecting" of a subject-positing and a predicative positing-thereupon, the making [*Vollzug*] of a valuation or of a valuation for the sake of something else, the making of a choice, and so forth – all these presuppose positive attention to that toward which the Ego takes a position. But this in no way alters the fact that this functioning of the regard, which moves about and broadens or narrows its span, signifies a *dimension sui generis of correlative, noetic and noematic*, modifications, the systematic inquiry into the essence of which is among the fundamental tasks of general phenomenology.

It is in their actionality-modes that attentional formations have, in a preeminent manner, the *characteristic of subjectiveness*; and this characteristic is consequently acquired by all the functionings which become modalized by these modes or which, according to their specific sort, presuppose them. The ray of attention presents itself as emanating from the pure Ego and terminating in that which is objective, as directed to it or being diverted from it. The ray does not become detached from the Ego; on the contrary, it is itself an Ego-ray, and remains an Ego-ray. The "Object" is struck; it is the target, it is put into a relation to the Ego (and by the Ego itself) but is not "subjective." A position-taking which bears the Ego-ray is, because of it, an act of the Ego itself; the Ego does or undergoes, is free or conditioned. The Ego, as we also said, "lives" in such acts. Its living in them signifies, not the being of some "contents" or other in a stream of contents, but rather a multiplicity of describable manners in which the pure Ego, as the "free being" which it is, lives in certain intentive mental processes, those which have the universal modus cogito. But the expression, "as a free being," indicates nothing else than such modes of living pertaining to freely going out of itself or freely withdrawing into itself, spontaneous doing, being somehow affected by the Objects, suffering, etc. What goes on in the stream of mental processes outside the Ego-ray or the cogito is essentially characterized otherwise; it lies outside the Ego's actionality and yet, as we indicated earlier, it is appertinent to the Ego in so far as it is the field of potentiality for the Ego's free acts.

So much by way of a general characterization of the noetic–noematic themes which must be treated with systematic thoroughness in the phenomenology of attention.[4]

§93 Transition to the noetic–noematic structures of the higher spheres of consciousness

In the next series of considerations we wish to examine the structures which belong to the "higher" spheres of consciousness in which *a number of noeses are built up on one another in the unity of a concrete mental process* and in which, accordingly, the *noematic correlates* are likewise *founded*. Thus the eidetic law, confirmed in every case, states that there can be *no noetic moment without a noematic moment specifically belonging to it*.

Even in the case of noeses of a higher level – taken in concrete completeness – there at first emerges in the noematic composition a central core thrusting itself to the fore in a predominate way, the "meant Objectivity as Objectivity," the Objectivity in inverted commas as required by the phenomenological reduction. There this central noema must also be taken precisely in the modified Objective composition in which it is just that noema, something intended to as intended to. Because the Objective something taken in a modified way itself becomes, to be sure, under the heading of sense, as, e.g., in our scientific investigation of it, again an Objective something although of a dignity peculiar to it, one will subsequently see here that this *novel Objectivity* has its modes of givenness, its "characteristics," its manifold modes with which it is intended to in the full noema pertaining to the noetic mental process or to the species of mental process in question. Of course, here again all the distinctions in the noema must also correspond to parallel distinctions in the unmodified Objectivity.

It is then a further undertaking of more precise phenomenological study to discover what is prescribed according to eidetic law precisely by the species, and what is so prescribed by the differentiating particularities, for noemata of changing particularities of a fixed species (e.g., perception). But the restriction holds throughout: in the sphere of essences there is nothing accidental; everything is connected by eidetic relations, thus especially noesis and noema.

§94 Noesis and noema in the realm of judgment

As an example from this sphere of founded essences let us consider the *predicative judgment*. The noema of the judging, i.e., of the concrete judgmental process, is the "judged as judged;" that, however, is nothing else, or at least with respect to its main core, it is nothing else than what we usually call simply *the judgment*.

If the full noema is to be seized upon, the judgment must be taken here in the full noematic concreteness intended to in the concrete judging. What is judged must not be confused with what is judged about. If the judging is based on perceiving or on some other simply "positing" objectivating, the noema of the objectivating goes into the full concretion of the judgment (just as the objectivating noesis becomes an essential component of the concrete judgmental noesis) and takes on certain forms in the judging. That which is objectivated (as objectivated) receives the form of the apophantic subject, or that of the apophantic predicate, or some other such form. Here, for the sake of simplicity, let us disregard the higher stratum pertaining to verbal "expression." These "objects about which," especially the ones which take on ⟨apophantic⟩ subject⟨-forms⟩ [*Subjektgegenstand*] are the objects judged *about*. The whole which is formed out of them, *the total What which is judged* – and, moreover, taken precisely in the fashion (with the *characterization*, in the *mode of giveness*) in which it is "intended to" in the mental process – makes up the *full noematic correlate*, the "*sense*" (in the *broadest* signification of the word) of the judgmental process. Stated more pregnantly, it is the "sense in the How of its mode of givenness" in so far as this mode of givenness is to be found as a characteristic belonging to it.

In this connection, we must not overlook the phenomenological reduction which requires us to "parenthesize" the making of the judgment if we wish to acquire the *pure* noema of our judgmental process. If we do so, then we have in its phenomenological purity the full concrete essence of the judgmental process or, as we now express it, the *judgment-noesis, taken concretely as an essence*, and the *judgment-noema* belonging to and necessarily united with that noesis, the "*made judgment*" as an Eidos, and it also in its phenomenological purity.

Psychologistic readers will object to all these statements; they are not inclined to distinguish between judging [*Urteilen*] as an empirical mental process and judging [*Urteil*] as an "idea," an essence. For us this distinction has already been thoroughly established. But the reader who accepts it will also be perplexed. For he is required to recognize that this one distinction is by no means sufficient and that it is necessary to fix a number of ideas which lie on two different sides within the essence of judgmental intentionality. It must above all be recognized that here, as in the case of any other intentive mental process, the two sides, noesis and noema, must by essential necessity be distinguished.

Critically it may be remarked here that the concepts of the "*intentive*" and the "*cognitional essence*" which were established in the *Logical Investigations*[5] are indeed correct but are capable of a second interpretation since they can be essentially understood as expressions not only of noetic but also of noematic essences, and that the noematic interpretation, as carried through there one-sidedly in framing the concept of the judgment in pure logic is precisely not the one to be used in framing the judgment-concept of pure logic (i.e., the concept demanded by pure logic as pure mathesis in contrast to the concept of noetic judging demanded by normative logical noetics). The difference between the *making of a judgment* and the *judgment made*, a difference already recognized in ordinary speech, can serve to point out the correct view, namely that to the judgmental mental process there belongs *correlatively* as noema *the* judgment simpliciter.

The latter, then, should be understood as the "judgment" or *proposition in the sense of the word in pure logic* – except that pure logic is interested in the noema, not with respect to its components, but only in so far as it is conceived as exclusively determined by a *narrower* essence, to the more precise definition of which the above-mentioned attempt at a distinction in the *Logical Investigations* pointed the way. If we wish to obtain the full noema of a determinate judgmental process we must, as has already been said, take "the" judgment precisely as it is intended to in just that process; whereas, for formal logic, the identity of "the" judgment extends much further. An evident judgment, *S is p*, and "the same" judgment as a "blind" judgment are noematically different but identical with respect to a core of sense which alone is decisive from the standpoint of formal logic. The difference here is similar to that already mentioned between the noema of a perception and that of a parallel presentation which intends to the same object, with precisely the same set of determinations and with the same characterization (as "certainly existing," "doubtfully existing," or the like). The act-species are different, and there is wide room for phenomenological differences in other respects – but the noematic What is identical. Let us add that the idea of the judgment which has just been characterized and which functions as the fundamental concept in formal logic (that discipline within mathesis universalis pertaining to predicative significations) has as its correlate the noetic idea: "the judgment" in a second sense understood, namely, as any judging whatever, with an eidetic universality determined purely by the form. It is the fundamental concept in the formal noetic theory of correct judging.[6]

Everything just said is also true for other noetic mental processes; for example, it obviously holds good for all those which are essentially akin to judgings as predicative certainties: for the corresponding deemings possible, deemings likely, doubting, also rejectings. Among these the agreement can go so far that, in the noema, a sense-content occurs which is identical throughout and is merely furnished with different "characterizations." *The same* "S is p," as a *noematic core*, can be the "*content*" of a certainty, a deeming possible, a deeming likely, etc. In the noema the "S is p" does not stand alone; rather, as singled out of the noema by thinking, it is something non-selfsufficient; it is intended to with changing characterizations indispensable to the full noema: it is intended to with the characteristic of something "certain," "possible," "probable," "null," or the like – characteristics, to which the modifying inverted commas collectively belong and which, as correlates, are specifically coordinated with the noetic moments of considering-possible, considering-probable, considering-null, and the like.

With this, as we see at the same time, two fundamental concepts of "*judgment-content*" and likewise of likelihood-content, question-content, etc., are separated from one another. Not infrequently logicians use the term judgment-content in such a way that obviously (even though without the so necessary distinction) the noetic or the noematic-logical concept of judgment is meant, the two concepts which we previously characterized. The corresponding pairs of concepts pertaining to likelihoods, questions, doubts, etc., run parallel with them, naturally without ever coinciding with them or with one another. *Here*, however, a second sense of judgment-content results – as a "content" which the judgment «(or the judging)» can have identically *in common* with a likelihood (or a deeming likely), with a question (or an asking), and with other act-noemas or noeses.

§95 The analogous distinctions in the emotional and
volitional spheres

Analogous statements hold, then, as one can easily see, for the emotional and volitional spheres, for mental processes of liking or disliking, of valuing in any sense, of wishing, deciding, acting. All these are mental processes which contain many and often heterogeneous intentive strata, the noetic and, correspondingly, also the noematic ones.

In that connection, the stratifications, generally speaking, are such that the uppermost strata of the total phenomenon can be removed without the remainder ceasing to be a concretely complete intentive mental process, and, conversely, a concrete mental process can also take on a new noetic total stratum: as when a non-selfsufficient moment of "valuing" is stratified on a concrete process of simply objectivating or, on the other hand, is removed again.

If, in this manner, a perceiving, phantasying, judging, or the like, founds a stratum of valuing which overlays it completely, we have *different noemata or senses* in the *stratified whole* which is called a concrete mental process of valuing by being designated according to the highest level within it. The perceived as perceived specifically belongs as sense to the perceiving, but it is also included in the sense of the concrete valuing, founding the *latter's* sense. We must distinguish accordingly: the objects, the physical things, the qualities, the predicatively formed affair-complexes, which are present as valued in the valuing, or else the corresponding noemata of the objectivatings, the judgings, or the like, which found the value-consciousness; on the other hand, the value-objects themselves and the predicatively formed value-complexes themselves, or else the noematic modifications corresponding to them; and then, universally, the complete noemata belonging to the concrete value-consciousness.

By way of explanation let us say first of all that, for the sake of greater distinctness, we do well (here and in all analogous cases) to introduce distinctive relative terms in order to keep sharply separate valuable object and value-object, valuable predicatively formed affair-complex and predicatively formed value-complexes, valuable property and value-property (a term having itself two senses). We shall speak of the mere "thing" which is valuable, which has a value-characteristic, which has *value-quality*; in contradistinction, we speak of *concrete value* itself or the *value-Objectiveness* [*Wertobjektität*]. Likewise we shall speak of the *mere predicatively formed affair-complex* or the *mere lay of things* [*Sachlage*] and the *predicatively formed value-complex* or the *lay of values* [*Wertlage*], namely where the valuing has a consciousness of a predicatively formed affair-complex as its founding substratum. The value-Objectiveness involves its mere materially determinate thing [*Sache*]; it introduces, as a new Objective stratum, the *value-quality*. The predicatively formed value-complex contains the mere predicatively formed affair-complex belonging to it; in like manner the value-property contains the materially determinate thing-property and, in addition the value-quality.

Here too one must distinguish between the value-Objectiveness simpliciter and the *value-Objectiveness in inverted commas* which is included in the *noema*. Just as the perceived as perceived stands over against the perceiving in a way excluding the question of whether the perceived truly exists, so the valued as valued stands over against the valuing, and likewise in a way excluding the question of the being of the value (the being of the valued thing *and* the latter's being truly a value). One must exclude all actional positings in order to seize upon the noema. Moreover, careful attention must be paid to the fact that the *full* "sense" of the valuing includes its What in which it is intended to in the mental process of valuing in question, and that the value-Objectiveness in inverted commas is not, by itself, the full noema.

In like manner the distinctions made here can be made in the *volitional sphere*.

On one side we have the *deciding* which we effect together with the mental processes which it demands as a substratum, and which, when it is taken in its concreteness, it includes. To it belong many different noetic moments. Volitional positings are based on valuing positings, physical-thing positings, and the like. On the other side we find the *decision* as a peculiar kind of Objectiveness specifically belonging to the province of volition; and it is an Objectiveness obviously founded on other such noematic Objectivenesses. If, as phenomenologists, we exclude all our positings, the volitional phenomenon, as a phenomenologically pure intentive mental process, still retains its *"willed as willed,"* as a *noema belonging peculiarly to the willing: the "volition-meaning,"* precisely as it is a "meaning" in this willing (in the full essence ‹of the willing›) and with everything being willed and "aimed at."

We said, "the meaning." This word suggests itself in all these contexts, just as do the words "sense" and "signification." To the *meaning* [*Meinen*] or intending to [*Vermeinen*], then, corresponds the meant [*Meinung*]; to *signifying*, the *signification*. But the greatest precaution is called for with respect to these words because they all have been infected with so many equivocations by transference, not least of all by equivocations which arise from slipping from one to another of the correlative strata which we are trying to separate with scientific rigor. The scope of our present observations is the broadest extension of the essential genus, "intentive mental process." "Meaning," on the other hand, is normally spoken of in referring to narrower spheres which, however, function as substrata for other phenomena in the wider sphere. As technical terms, therefore, this word and cognate expressions should be used only with reference to those narrower spheres. In referring to the universalities involved, we are undoubtedly better served by our new terms and the attached analyses of examples.

§96 Transition to further chapters. Concluding remarks

We have bestowed such great care on working out universally the difference between noesis (i.e., the concretely complete intentive mental process, designated by a name emphasizing its noetic components) and noema because the seizing upon and mastering it are of the greatest importance for phenomenology, are indeed decisive for the legitimate grounding of phenomenology. At first glance it would seem to be something obvious: Any consciousness is a consciousness of something, and the modes of consciousness are highly diversified. On approaching more closely, however, we became sensible of the great difficulties involved. They concern our understanding of the mode of being of the noema, the way in which it is "implicit" in the mental process, in which it is "intended to" in the mental process. Quite particularly they concern the clean separation of those things which, as its really inherent components, belong to the mental process itself and those which belong to the noema, which must be assigned to the noema as its own ‹components›. Subsequently the correct analysis of the parallel structures of noesis and noema involves considerable difficulties. Even when we have succeeded in making some of the major relevant distinctions in examining the objectivatings and judgings, where they are first presented and for which logic has done valuable though far from adequate preliminary work, some effort and self-control is needed in order to actually make the parallel distinctions clearly given in the case of emotional acts, instead of only postulating and asserting them.

Here, in the context of our merely introductory meditations, we cannot undertake to develop parts of phenomenology systematically. Nevertheless, our aims require that we go into things more deeply than we have up to now and project the beginnings of such investigations. That is necessary in order to make noetic-noematic structures clear enough so that their significance for the problems and methods of phenomenology may become understandable. A detailed idea of the fruitfulness of phenomenology, the magnitude of its problems and the nature of its procedure is only achieved by actually entering province after province and seeing the extent of the relevant problems. But any such province is actually entered and becomes sensible as a field for solid work only when one makes the phenomenological distinctions and clarifications by which alone the sense of the problems to be solved in it can become understandable. Our further analyses and exhibitions of problems will be strictly confined to this style, as our previous efforts have been in part. However complicated the matters treated may seem to the novice, still we shall consider only restricted spheres. Naturally we shall give preference to what is relatively close to the gates of phenomenology and to what is unconditionally necessary in order to trace main systematic lines extending throughout the realm. *All of it* is hard and requires laborious concentration on the data of specifically phenomenological eidetic intuition. There is no "royal road" into phenomenology and therefore none into philosophy. There is only the *one* road prescribed by phenomenology's own essence.

Finally, the following remark would seem to be in order. Phenomenology is presented in our exposition as a *beginning* science. How many of the results of the analyses undertaken here are definitive, only the future can tell. Certainly much of what we have described will have to be described otherwise *sub specie aeterni*. But one thing we may and must strive for: that at each step we faithfully describe what we, from our point of view and after the most serious study, actually see. Our procedure is that of an explorer journeying through an unknown part of the world, and carefully describing what is presented along his unbeaten paths, which will not always be the shortest. Such an explorer can rightfully be filled with the sure confidence that he gives utterance to what, at the time and under the circumstances, *must* be said – something which, because it is the faithful expression of something seen, will always retain its value – even though new explorations will require new descriptions with manifold improvements. With a like conviction, in the sequel we propose to be faithful describers of phenomenological structures and, moreover, to preserve the habit of inner freedom even with respect to our own descriptions.

Notes

1 Cf. *Ideas* I §41.
2 Cf. *Logical Investigations* I §14 on the fulfilling sense (in that connection see Sixth Inv. §55 on "perceptual sense"); furthermore, for what follows, 5TH Inv. §20, on "matter" pertaining to the act; likewise 6TH Inv. §§25–29.
3 Cf. *Ideas* I, §43.
4 Attention is one of the chief themes of modern psychology. Nowhere does the predominantly sensualistic character of modern psychology show itself more strikingly than in the treatment of this theme, for not even the essential connection between attention and intentionality – this fundamental fact: that attention of every sort is nothing else than a fundamental species of *intentive* modifications – has ever, to my knowledge, been emphasized before. Since the appearance of the *Logische Untersuchungen* (see the statements in Second Investigation, §§22f., and Fifth Investigation §19, a few words are, to be sure, said occasionally about a connection between attention and "consciousness of objects" but, with few exceptions (I refer to the writings of Theodor Lipps and Alexander Pfander), in a manner showing a lack of understanding for the fact that what is in question here concerns the radically first *beginning* of the theory of attention and that the further investigation must be conducted within the limits of intentionality and, moreover, not forthwith as an empirical, but *first of all* as an eidetical investigation.
5 Cf. *op. cit.*, Fifth Investigation, §21.
6 As for Bolzano's concept of the "judgment in itself" or "the proposition in itself," the exposition in the *Wissenschaftslehre* (Sulzbach, 1837) shows that Bolzano had not made clear to himself the proper sense of his pioneer conception. He never saw that we have here *two* essentially possible interpretations, each of which yields something which might be called "the judgment in itself:" the specific essence of the judging process (the *noetic* idea) and the *noematic* idea correlative to the noetic idea. His descriptions and explanations are ambiguous. Given a mathematician's objective interest, he undoubtedly had the noematic concept in mind – though an occasional phrase seems to indicate the contrary (cf. *op. cit.*, Vol. 1, p. 95, the approving quotation from Mehmel's *Denklehre* ‹scl. *Versuch einer vollständigen analytische Denklehre als Vorphilosophie und im Geiste der Philosophie* (Erlangen, 1803)›). He had it in mind, precisely as the arithmetician has number in mind – being interested in operations with numbers but not in the phenomenological problem of the relationship between number and consciousness of number. Here in the sphere of logic, as well as every where else, phenomenology was something *quite alien* to the great logician. That cannot fail to be clear to anyone who has actually studied Bolzano's *Wissenschaftslehre* (which has unfortunately become so scarce) and who, in addition to that, is not inclined to confuse every working out of fundamental eidetic concepts – the phenomenologically naive production – with a phenomenological production. If one did this, then, in the interest of consistency one would have to say that every mathematician who creates concepts, e.g., Georg Cantor, as the genius who framed the fundamental concepts of the theory of sets, is a phenomenologist, including the unknown creator of the fundamental geometrical concepts in hoary antiquity.

6

THE WAY INTO PHENOMENOLOGICAL TRANSCENDENTAL PHILOSOPHY BY INQUIRING BACK FROM THE PREGIVEN LIFE-WORLD

§28 Kant's unexpressed "presupposition": the surrounding world of life, taken for granted as valid

Kant is certain that his philosophy will bring the dominant rationalism to its downfall by exhibiting the inadequacy of its foundations. He rightly reproaches rationalism for neglecting questions which should have been its fundamental questions; that is, it had never penetrated to the subjective structure of our world-consciousness prior to and within scientific knowledge and thus had never asked how the world, which appears straightforwardly to us men, and to us as scientists, comes to be knowable a priori – how, that is, the exact science of nature is possible, the science for which, after all, pure mathematics, together with a further pure a priori, is the instrument of all knowledge which is objective, [i.e.,] unconditionally valid for everyone who is rational (who thinks logically).

But Kant, for his part, has no idea that in his philosophizing he stands on unquestioned presuppositions and that the undoubtedly great discoveries in his theories are there only in concealment; that is, they are not there as finished results, just as the theories themselves are not finished theories, i.e., do not have a definitive scientific form. What he offers demands new work and, above all, critical analysis. An example of a great discovery – a merely preliminary discovery – is the "understanding" which has, in respect to nature, two functions:[1] understanding interpreting itself, in explicit self-reflection, as normative laws, and, on the other hand, understanding ruling in concealment, i.e., ruling as constitutive of the always already developed and always further developing meaning-configuration "intuitively given surrounding world." This discovery could never be actually grounded or even be fully comprehensible in the manner of the Kantian theory, i.e., as a result of his merely regressive method. In the "transcendental deduction" of the first edition of the *Critique of Pure Reason* Kant makes an

E. Husserl, *The Crisis of European Sciences and Transcendental Phenomenology. An Introduction to Phenomenological Philosophy*, 1970, trans. David Carr, pp. 103–37. Evanston: Northwestern University Press.

approach to a direct grounding, one which descends to the original sources, only to break off again almost at once without arriving at the genuine problems of foundation which are to be opened up from this supposedly psychological side.

We shall begin our considerations by showing that Kant's inquiries in the critique of reason have an unquestioned ground of presuppositions which codetermine the meaning of his questions. Sciences to whose truths and methods Kant attributes actual validity become a problem, and with them the spheres of being [*Seinssphären*] themselves to which these sciences refer. They become a problem in virtue of certain questions which take knowing subjectivity, too, into account, questions which find their answer in theories about transcendentally forming subjectivity, about the transcendental achievements of sensibility, of the understanding, etc., and, on the highest level, theories about functions of the "I" of "transcendental apperception." What had become an enigma, the achievement of mathematical natural science and of pure mathematics (in our broadened sense) as its logical method, was supposed to have been made comprehensible through these theories; but the theories also led to a revolutionary reinterpretation of the actual ontic meaning of nature as the world of possible experience and possible knowledge and thus correlatively to the reinterpretation of the actual truth-meaning of the sciences concerned.

Naturally, from the very start in the Kantian manner of posing questions, the everyday surrounding world of life is presupposed as existing – the surrounding world in which all of us (even I who am now philosophizing) consciously have our existence; here are also the sciences, as cultural facts in this world, with their scientists and theories. In this world we are objects among objects in the sense of the life-world, namely, as being here and there, in the plain certainty of experience, before anything that is established scientifically, whether in physiology, psychology, or sociology. On the other hand, we are subjects for this world, namely, as the ego-subjects experiencing it, contemplating it, valuing it, related to it purposefully; for us this surrounding world has only the ontic meaning given to it by our experiencings, our thoughts, our valuations, etc.; and it has the modes of validity (certainty of being, possibility, perhaps illusion, etc.) which we, as the subjects of validity, at the same time bring about or else possess from earlier on as habitual acquisitions and bear within us as validities of such and such a content which we can reactualize at will. To be sure, all this undergoes manifold alterations, whereas "the" world, as existing in a unified way, persists throughout, being corrected only in its content.

Clearly the content-alteration of the perceived object, being change or motion perceived as belonging to the object itself, is distinguished with self-evidence from the alteration of its manners of appearing (e.g., the perspectives, the near and far appearances) through which something objective of this type exhibits itself as being itself present. We see this in the change of [our] attitude. [If we are] directed straightforwardly toward the object and what belongs to it, [our] gaze passes through the appearances toward what continuously appears through their continuous unification: the object, with the ontic validity of the mode "itself present." In the reflective attitude, [by contrast,] we have not a one but a manifold. Now the sequence of the appearances themselves is thematic, rather than what appears in them. Perception is the primal mode of intuition [*Anschauung*]; it exhibits with primal originality, that is, in the mode of self-presence. In addition, there are other modes of intuition which in themselves consciously have the character of [giving us] modifications of this "itself there" as themselves present. These are presentifications, modifications of presentations;[2] they make us conscious of the modalities of time, e.g., not that which *is*-itself-there but that which *was*-itself-there or that which is in the future, that which *will-be*-itself-there. Presentifying intuitions "recapitulate" – in certain modifications belonging to them – all the manifolds of appearance through which what is objective exhibits itself perceptively. Recollecting intuition, for example, shows the object as having-been-itself-there, recapitulating the perspectivization and other manners of appearing, though in recollective modifications. I am now conscious of this perspectivization as one which has been, a sequence of subjective "exhibitions of," having-been in my earlier ontic validities.

Here we can now clarify the very limited justification for speaking of a sense-world, a world of sense-intuition, a sensible world of appearances. In all the verifications of the life of our natural interests, which remain purely in the life-world, the return to "sensibly" experiencing intuition plays a prominent role. For everything that exhibits itself in the life-world as a concrete thing obviously has a bodily character, even if it is not a mere body, as, for example, an animal or a cultural object, i.e., even if it also has psychic or otherwise spiritual properties. If we pay attention now purely to the bodily aspect of the things, this obviously exhibits itself perceptively only in seeing, in touching, in hearing, etc., i.e., in visual, tactual, acoustical, and other such aspects. Obviously and inevitably participating in this is our living body, which is never absent from the perceptual field, and specifically its corresponding "organs of perception" (eyes, hands, ears, etc.). In consciousness they play a constant role here; specifically they function in seeing, hearing, etc., together with the ego's motility belonging to them, i.e., what is called kinesthesis. All kinestheses, each being an "I move," "I do," [etc.] are bound together in a comprehensive unity – in which kinesthetic holding-still is [also] a mode of the "I do." Clearly the aspect-exhibitions of whatever body is appearing in perception, and the kinestheses, are not processes [simply running] alongside each other; rather, they work together in such a way that the aspects have the ontic meaning of, or the validity of, aspects of the body only through the fact that they are those aspects continually required by the kinestheses – by the kinesthetic-sensual total situation in each of its working variations of the total kinesthesis by setting in motion this or that particular kinesthesis – and that they correspondingly fulfill the requirement.

Thus sensibility, the ego's active functioning of the living body or the bodily organs, belongs in a fundamental, essential way to all experience of bodies. It proceeds in consciousness not as a mere series of body-appearances, as if these in themselves, through themselves alone and their coalescences, were appearance of bodies; rather, they are such in consciousness only in combination with the kinesthetically functioning living body [*Leiblichkeit*], the ego functioning here in a peculiar sort of activity and habituality. In a quite unique way the living body is constantly in the perceptual field quite immediately, with a completely unique ontic meaning, precisely the meaning indicated by the word "organ" (here used in its most primitive sense), [namely, as] that through which I exist in a completely unique way and quite immediately as the ego of affection and actions, [as that] in which I hold sway[3] quite immediately, kinesthetically – articulated into particular

153

organs through which I hold sway, or potentially hold sway, in particular kinestheses corresponding to them. And this "holding-sway," here exhibited as functioning in all perception of bodies – the familiar, total system of kinestheses available to consciousness – is actualized in the particular kinesthetic situation [and] is perpetually bound to a [general] situation in which bodies appear, i.e., that of the field of perception. To the variety of appearances through which a body is perceivable as this one-and-the-same body correspond, in their own way, the kinestheses which belong to this body; as these kinestheses are allowed to run their course, the corresponding required appearances must show up in order to be appearances of this body at all, i.e., in order to be appearances which exhibit in themselves this body with its properties.

Thus, purely in terms of perception, physical body and living body [*Körper und Leib*][4] are essentially different; living body, that is, [understood] as the only one which is actually given [to me as such] in perception; my own living body. How the consciousness originates through which my living body nevertheless acquires the ontic validity of one physical body among others, and how, on the other hand, certain physical bodies in my perceptual field come to count as living bodies, living bodies of "alien" ego-subjects – these are now necessary questions.

In our reflections we confined ourselves to the perceiving consciousness of things, to one's own perceiving of them, to my perceptual field. Here my own living body alone, and never an alien living body, can be perceived *as* living; the latter is perceived only as a physical body. In my perceptual field I find myself holding sway as ego through my organs and generally through everything belonging to me as an ego in my ego-acts and faculties. However, though the objects of the life-world, if they are to show their very own being, necessarily show themselves as physical bodies, this does not mean that they show themselves only in this way; and [similarly] we, though we are related through the living body to all objects which exist for us, are not related to them solely as a living body. Thus if it is a question of objects in the perceptual field, we are perceptually also in the field;[5] and the same is true, in modification, of every intuitive field, and even of every nonintuitive one, since we are obviously capable of "representing" to ourselves everything which is nonintuitively before us (though we are sometimes temporally limited in this). [Being related] "through the living body" clearly does not mean merely [being related] "as a physical body"; rather, the expression refers to the kinesthetic, to functioning as an ego in this peculiar way, primarily through seeing, hearing, etc.; and of course other modes of the ego belong to this (for example, lifting, carrying, pushing, and the like).

But being an ego through the living body [*die leibliche Ichlichkeit*] is of course not the only way of being an ego, and none of its ways can be severed from the others; throughout all their transformations they form a unity. Thus we are concretely in the field of perception, etc., and in the field of consciousness, however broadly we may conceive this, through our living body, but not only in this way, as full ego-subjects, each of us as the full-fledged "I-the-man." Thus in whatever way we may be conscious of the world as universal horizon, as coherent universe of existing objects, we, each "I-the-man" and all of us together, belong to the world as living with one another in the world; and the world is our world, valid for our consciousness as existing precisely through this "living together." We, as living in wakeful world-consciousness, are constantly active on the basis of our passive having of the world; it is from there, by objects pregiven in consciousness, that we are affected; it is to this or that object that we pay attention, according to our interests; with them we deal actively in different ways; through our acts they are "thematic" objects. As an example I give the observant explication of the properties of something which appears perceptively, or our activity of combining, relating, actively identifying and distinguishing, or our active evaluation, our projection of plans, our active realization of the planned means and ends.

As subjects of acts (ego-subjects) we are directed toward thematic objects in modes of primary and secondary, and perhaps also peripheral, directedness. In this preoccupation with the objects the acts themselves are not thematic. But we are capable of coming back and reflecting on ourselves and our current activity: it now becomes thematic and objective through a new act, the vitally functioning one, which itself is now unthematic.

The consciousness of the world, then, is in constant motion; we are conscious of the world always in terms of some object-content or other, in the alteration of the different ways of being conscious (intuitive, nonintuitive, determined, undetermined, etc.) and also in the alteration of affection and action, in such a way that there is always a total sphere of affection and such that the affecting objects are now thematic, now unthematic; here we also find ourselves, we who always and inevitably belong to the affective sphere, always functioning as subjects of acts but only occasionally being thematically objective as the object of preoccupation with ourselves.

Obviously this is true not only for me, the individual ego; rather we, in living together, have the world pregiven in this "together," as the world valid as existing for us and to which we, together, belong, the world as world for all, pregiven with this ontic meaning. Constantly functioning in wakeful life, we also function together, in the manifold ways of considering, together, objects pregiven to us in common, thinking together, valuing, planning, acting together. Here we find also that particular thematic alteration in which the we-subjectivity, somehow constantly functioning, becomes a thematic object, whereby the acts through which it functions also become thematic, though always with a residuum which remains unthematic – remains, so to speak, anonymous – namely, the reflections which are functioning in connection with this theme.[6]

Considering ourselves in particular as the scientists that we here factually find ourselves to be, what corresponds to our particular manner of being as scientists is our present functioning in the manner of scientific thinking, putting questions and answering them theoretically in relation to nature or the world of the spirit; and [the latter are] at first nothing other than the one or the other aspect of the life-world which, in advance, is already valid, which we experience or are otherwise conscious of either prescientifically or scientifically. Cofunctioning here are the other scientists who, united with us in a community of theory, acquire and have the same truths or, in the communalization of accomplishing acts, are united with us in a critical transaction aimed at critical agreement. On the other hand, we can be for others, and they for us, mere objects; rather than being together in the unity of immediate, driving, common theoretical interest, we can get to know one another observingly, taking note of others' acts of thought, acts of experiencing, and possibly other acts as objective facts, but "disinterestedly," without joining in performing these acts, without critically assenting to them or taking exception to them.

Naturally, all these things are the most obvious of the obvious. Must one speak about them, and with so much ado? In life certainly not. But not as a philosopher either? Is this not the opening-up of a realm, indeed an infinite realm, of always ready and available but never questioned ontic validities? Are they not *constant presuppositions* of scientific and, at the highest level, philosophical thinking? Not, however, that it would or could ever be a matter of utilizing these ontic validities in their objective truth.

It belongs to what is taken for granted, prior to all scientific thought and all philosophical questioning, that the world is – always is in advance – and that every correction of an opinion, whether an experiential or other opinion, presupposes the already existing world, namely, as a horizon of what in the given case is indubitably valid as existing, and presupposes within this horizon something familiar and doubtlessly certain with which that which is perhaps canceled out as invalid came into conflict. Objective science, too, asks questions only on the ground of this world's existing in advance through prescientific life. Like all praxis, objective science presupposes the being of this world, but it sets itself the task of transposing knowledge which is imperfect and prescientific in respect of scope and constancy into perfect knowledge – in accord with an idea of a correlative which is, to be sure, infinitely distant, i.e., of a world which in itself is fixed and determined and of truths which are *idealiter* scientific ("truths-in-themselves") and which predicatively interpret this world. To realize this in a systematic process, in stages of perfection, through a method which makes possible a constant advance: this is the task.

For the human being in his surrounding world there are many types of praxis, and among them is this peculiar and historically late one, theoretical praxis. It has its own professional methods; it is the art of theories, of discovering and securing truths with a certain new ideal sense which is foreign to prescientific life, the sense of a certain "final validity," "universal validity."

Here we have again offered an example of exhibiting what is "obvious," but this time in order to make clear that in respect to all these manifold validities-in-advance, i.e., "presuppositions" of the philosopher, there arise questions of being in a new and immediately highly enigmatic dimension. These questions, too, concern the obviously existing, ever intuitively pregiven world; but they are not questions belonging to that professional praxis and τέχνη which is called objective science, not questions belonging to that art of grounding and broadening the realm of objectively scientific truths about this surrounding world; rather, they are questions of how the object, the prescientifically and then the scientifically true object, stands in relation to all the subjective elements which everywhere have a voice in what is taken for granted in advance.

§29 The life-world can be disclosed as a realm of subjective phenomena which have remained "anonymous"

When we proceed, philosophizing with Kant, not by starting from his beginning and moving forward in his paths but by inquiring back into what was thus taken for granted (that of which Kantian thinking, like everyone's thinking, makes use as unquestioned and available), when we become conscious of it as "presuppositions" and accord these their own universal and theoretical interest, there opens up to us, to our growing astonishment, an infinity of ever new phenomena belonging to a new dimension, coming to light only through consistent penetration into the meaning and validity-implications of what was thus taken for granted—an infinity, because continued penetration shows that every phenomenon attained through this unfolding of meaning, given at first in the life-world as obviously existing, itself contains meaning- and validity-implications whose exposition leads again to new phenomena, and so on. These are purely subjective phenomena throughout, but not merely facts involving psychological processes of sense-data; rather, they are mental [*geistige*] processes which, as such, exercise with essential necessity the function of constituting forms of meaning [*Sinnesgestalten*]. But they constitute them in each case out of mental "material" which [itself] proves in turn, with essential necessity, to be mental form, i.e., to be constituted; just as any newly developed from [of meaning] is destined to become material, namely, to function in the constitution of [some new] form.

No objective science, no psychology – which, after all, sought to become the universal science of the subjective – and no philosophy has ever made thematic and thereby actually discovered this realm of the subjective – not even the Kantian philosophy, which sought, after all, to go back to the subjective conditions of the possibility of an objectively experienceable and knowable world. It is a realm of something subjective which is completely closed off within itself, existing in its own way, functioning in all experiencing, all thinking, all life, thus everywhere inseparably involved; yet it has never been held in view, never been grasped and understood.

Does philosophy fulfill the sense of its primal establishment as the universal and ultimately grounding science if it leaves this realm to its "anonymity"? Can it do this, can any science do this which seeks to be a branch of philosophy, i.e., which would tolerate no presuppositions, no basic sphere of beings beneath itself of which no one knows, which no one interrogates scientifically, which no one has mastered in a knowing way? I called the sciences in general branches of philosophy, whereas it is such a common conviction that the objective, the positive, sciences stand on their own, are self-sufficient in virtue of their supposedly fully grounding and thus exemplary method. But in the end is not the teleogical unifying meaning running through all attempted systems in the whole history of philosophy that of achieving a breakthrough for the insight that science is only possible at all as universal philosophy, the latter being, in all the sciences, yet a single science, possible only as the totality of all knowledge? And did this not imply that they all repose upon *one* single ground [*Grund*], one to be investigated scientifically in advance of all the others? And can this ground be, I may add, any other than precisely that of the anonymous subjectivity we mentioned? But one could and can realize this only when one finally and quite seriously inquires into that which is *taken for granted*, which is presupposed by all thinking, all activity of life with all its ends and accomplishments, and when one, by consistently interrogating the ontic and validity-meaning of these ends and accomplishments, becomes aware of the inviolable unity of the complex of meaning and validity running through all mental accomplishments. This applies first of all to all the mental accomplishments which we human beings carry out in the world, as

157

individual, personal, or cultural accomplishments. Before all such accomplishments there has always already been a universal accomplishment, presupposed by all human praxis and all prescientific and scientific life. The latter have the spiritual acquisitions of this universal accomplishment as their constant substratum, and all their own acquisitions are destined to flow into it. We shall come to understand that the world which constantly exists for us through the flowing alteration of manners of givenness is a universal mental acquisition, having developed as such and at the same time continuing to develop as the unity of a mental configuration, as a meaning-construct [*Sinngebilde*] – as the construct of a universal, ultimately functioning[7] subjectivity. It belongs essentially to this world-constituting accomplishment that subjectivity objectifies itself as human subjectivity, as an element of the world. All objective consideration of the world is consideration of the "exterior" and grasps only "externals," objective entities [*Objektivitäten*]. The radical consideration of the world is the systematic and purely internal consideration of the subjectivity which "expresses" [or "externalizes"][8] itself in the exterior. It is like the unity of a living organism, which one can certainly consider and dissect from the outside but which one can understand only if one goes back to its hidden roots and systematically pursues the life which, in all its accomplishments, is in them and strives upward from them, shaping from within. But is this not simply a metaphor? Is it not in the end our human being, and the life of consciousness belonging to it, with its most profound world-problematics, which is the place where all problems of living inner being and external exhibition are to be decided?

§30 The lack of an intuitive exhibiting method as the reason for Kant's mythical constructions

There is some complaint about the obscurities of the Kantian philosophy, about the incomprehensibility of the evidences of his regressive method, his transcendental-subjective "faculties," "functions," "formations," about the difficulty of understanding what transcendental subjectivity actually is, how its function, its accomplishment, comes about, how this is to make all objective science understandable. And in fact Kant does get involved in his own sort of mythical talk, whose literal meaning points to something subjective, but a mode of the subjective which we are in principle unable to make intuitive to ourselves, whether through factual examples or through genuine analogy. If we try to do it with the intuitively negotiable meaning to which the words refer, we find ourselves in the psychological sphere of the human person, the soul. But then we remember the Kantian doctrine of inner sense, according to which everything that can be exhibited in the self-evidence of inner experience has already been formed by a transcendental function, that of temporalization [*Zeitigung*]. But how are we supposed to arrive at a clear meaning for concepts of something transcendentally subjective, out of which the scientifically true world constitutes itself as objective "appearance," if we cannot give to "inner perception" some meaning other than the psychological one – if it is not a truly apodictic meaning which ultimately furnishes the experiential ground (a ground like that of the Cartesian *ego cogito*), [available to us] through a type of experience which is not Kantian scientific experience and does not have the certainty of objective being in the sense of science, as in physics, but is a truly apodictic certainty, that of a universal ground which finally can be exhibited as the apodictically necessary and ultimate ground of all scientific objectivity and makes the latter understandable? This is where the source of all ultimate concepts of knowledge must lie; here is the source of essential, general insights through which any objective world can become scientifically understandable and through which an absolutely self-supporting philosophy can achieve systematic development.

Perhaps a deeper critique could show that Kant, though he attacks empiricism, still remains dependent upon this very empiricism in his conception of the soul and the range of tasks of a psychology, that what counts for him as the soul is the soul which is made part of nature and conceived of as a component of the psychophysical human being within the time of nature, within space-time. Hence the transcendentally subjective could certainly not be [identical with] the psychic. But is truly apodictic inner perception (self-perception reduced to the truly apodictic) to be identified with the self-perception of this naturalized soul, with its [supposed] self-evidence of the "writing tablet" and its data and even of its faculties as the powers ascribed to it in the manner of natural powers? Because he understands inner perception in this empiricist, psychological sense and because, warned by Hume's skepticism, he fears every recourse to the psychological as an absurd perversion of the genuine problem of the understanding, Kant gets involved in his mythical concept-formation. He forbids his readers to transpose the results of his regressive procedure into intuitive concepts, forbids every attempt to carry out a progressive construction which begins with original and purely self-evident intuitions and proceeds through truly self-evident individual steps. His transcendental concepts are thus unclear in a quite peculiar way, such that for reasons of principle they can never be transposed into clarity, can never be transformed into a formation of meaning which is direct and procures self-evidence.

The clarity of all [these] concepts and problems posed would have been quite different if Kant, instead of being a child of his time, completely bound by its naturalistic psychology (as patterned after natural science and as its parallel), had tackled in a truly radical way the problem of a priori knowledge and its methodical function in rational objective knowledge. This would have required a fundamentally and essentially different regressive method from that of Kant, which rests on those unquestioned assumptions: not a mythically, constructively inferring [schliessende] method, but a thoroughly intuitively disclosing [erschliessende] method, intuitive in its point of departure and in everything it discloses – even though the concept of intuitiveness may have to undergo a considerable expansion in comparison to the Kantian one, and indeed even though intuition, here, may lose its usual sense altogether through a new attitude, taking on only the general sense of original self-exhibition, but precisely only within the new sphere of being.

Thus one must quite systematically inquire back into those things taken for granted which, not only for Kant but for all philosophers, all scientists, make up an unspoken ground [Grund] of their cognitive accomplishments, hidden in respect to its deeper mediating functions. Further, there must be a systematic disclosure of the intentionality which vitally holds sway and is sedimented in this ground – in other words, there must be a genuine, i.e., an "intentional analysis" of mental being in its absolute ultimate peculiarity and of that which has come to be in and through the mind, an analysis which does not permit the reigning psychology to substitute for it a realistic [*reale*] analysis of a naturalistically conceived soul, [which would be] alien to the essence of the mental.

§31 Kant and the inadequacy of the psychology of his day. The opaqueness of the distinction between transcendental subjectivity and soul

In order to make palpably understandable what is concretely meant here and in this way to illuminate the situation which was peculiarly opaque to that whole historical epoch, we shall initiate a reflection which admittedly belongs to a very late fulfillment of the sense of the historical process.

The pregiven point of departure for all the enigmas of knowledge was that of the development of a modern philosophy in accord with its own peculiar rationalistic ideal of science (systematically expanding itself into its special sciences). This thrust in the development of sometimes clearly successful, sometimes hopefully attempted special sciences was suddenly checked. In the construction of one of these sciences, psychology, enigmas emerged which put all of philosophy in question.

Naturally, the psychology of Locke – with the natural science of a Newton before it as a model – found particularly interesting subjects for study in the merely subjective aspects of the appearances (which had been maligned since Galileo) and likewise generally in everything coming from the subjective side that interfered with rationality: the lack of clarity in concepts, the vagueness of judgmental thinking, the faculties of the understanding and of reason in all their forms. It was, of course, a matter of the human being's faculties for psychic accomplishments – precisely those accomplishments which were supposed to procure genuine science and with it a genuine practical life of reason. Thus, questions of the essence and the objective validity of purely rational knowledge, of logical and mathematical knowledge, and the peculiar nature of natural-scientific and metaphysical knowledge belong in this sphere. Looked at in this general way, was this not actually required? Without doubt it was right and a good thing that Locke understood the sciences as psychic accomplishments (though he also directed his gaze too much at what occurs in the individual soul) and everywhere posed questions of origin. After all, accomplishments can be understood only in terms of the activity that accomplishes them. To be sure, in Locke this was done with a superficiality, an unmethodical confusion, and indeed even a naturalism that resulted precisely in Humean fictionalism.

Thus, obviously, Kant could not simply go back and take up the psychology of Locke. But was it for this reason correct to drop the general idea of the Lockean – the psychological-epistemological – approach? Was not every question inspired by Hume first and quite correctly to be taken as a psychological question? If rational science becomes a problem, if the claim of the purely a priori sciences to have unconditional objective validity, and thus to be the possible and necessary method for rational sciences of fact, becomes a problem, it should first betaken into consideration (as we emphasized above) that science in general is a human accomplishment, an accomplishment of human beings who find themselves in the world, the world of general experience, [and that it is] one among other types of practical accomplishments which is aimed at spiritual structures of a certain sort called theoretical. Like all praxis, this one is related, in a sense which is its own and of which the practitioner of it is conscious, to the pregiven world of experience and at the same time takes its ordered place within this world. Thus enigmas about how a spiritual accomplishment comes to pass can be clarified, one will say, only through psychological demonstrations, and they remain thus within the pregiven world. If Kant, on the other hand, in the questions he posed and in his regressive method, also naturally makes use of the pregiven world but at the same time constructs a transcendental subjectivity through whose concealed transcendental functions, with unswerving necessity, the world of experience is formed, he runs into the difficulty that a particular quality of the human soul (which itself belongs to the world and is thus presupposed with it) is supposed to accomplish and to have already accomplished a formative process which shapes this whole world. But as soon as we distinguish this transcendental subjectivity from the soul, we get involved in something incomprehensibly mythical.

§32 The possibility of a hidden truth in Kant's transcendental philosophy: the problem of a "new dimension." The antagonism between the "life of the plane" and the "life of depth"

Were the Kantian theory nevertheless to contain some truth, a truth to be made actually accessible to insight – which is indeed the case – it would be possible only through the fact that the transcendental functions which are supposed to explain the above-mentioned enigmas concerning objectively valid knowledge belong to a dimension of the living spirit that had to remain hidden, because of very natural inhibitions, from humanity and even from the scientists of the ages – whereas this dimension *can* be made accessible to scientific understanding, through a method of disclosure appropriate to it, as a realm of experiential and theoretical self-evidence. The fact that this dimension remained hidden through the ages, the fact that, even after it made itself felt, it never aroused a habitual and consistent theoretical interest, can (and will) be explained by displaying a peculiar antagonism between the entry into this dimension and the preoccupations involved in all the interests which make up the naturally normal human world-life.

Since this is to be a matter of spiritual functions which exercise their accomplishments in all experiencing and thinking, indeed in each and every preoccupation of the human world-life, functions through which the world of experience, as the constant horizon of existing things, values, practical plans, works, etc., has meaning and validity for us, it would certainly be understandable that all objective sciences would lack precisely the knowledge of what is most fundamental, namely, the knowledge of what could procure meaning and validity for the theoretical constructs of objective knowledge and [which] thus first gives them the dignity of a knowledge which is ultimately grounded.

This schema for a possible clarification of the problem of objective science reminds us of Helmholtz's well-known image of the plane-beings, who have no idea of the dimension of depth, in which their plane-world is a mere projection. Everything of which men – the scientists and all the others – can become conscious in their natural world-life (experiencing, knowing, practically planning, acting) as a field of external objects – as ends, means, processes of action, and final results related to these objects – and on the other hand, also, in self-reflection, as the spiritual life which functions thereby – all this remains on the "plane," which is, though unnoticed, nevertheless only a plane within an infinitely richer dimension of depth. But this [image] is universally valid whether it concerns a life which is merely practical in the usual sense or a theoretical life, [i.e.,] scientific experiencing, thinking, planning, acting, or scientific experiential data, ideas, goals of thinking, premises, true results.

This explanatory schema, of course, leaves several pressing questions open. How could the development of the positive sciences purely upon the "plane" appear for so long in the form of a superabundant success? Why was it so late before, in the need for complete transparency in its methodical accomplishments, the difficulties, indeed incomprehensibilities, announced themselves, such that not even the most painstaking construction of logical technique could improve the situation? Why did the later attempts at an "intuitionistic" deepening, which in fact touched upon the higher dimension, and all efforts to clarify the situation in this way not lead to unanimously accepted, truly compelling scientific results? It is *not* the case that this is a matter of merely turning our gaze toward a sphere which up to now has simply not been noticed but which is accessible without further effort to theoretical experience and experiential knowledge. Everything experienceable in this way is the object and domain of possible positive knowledge; it lies on the "plane," in the world of actual and possible experience, experience in the natural sense of the word. We shall soon understand what extraordinary difficulties – grounded in the essence of the matters involved – greeted the methodical efforts actually to approach the depth-sphere, to approach first of all the possibility of its pure grasp of itself in the manner of experiencing proper to it; and it will become clear thereby how great the antagonism is between the "patent" life of the plane and the "latent" life of depth. Of course the power of historical prejudices also plays a constant role here, especially of those which, coming from the origin of the modern positive sciences, dominate us all. It is of the very essence of such prejudices, drilled into the souls even of children, that they are concealed in their immediate effects. The abstract general will to be without prejudice changes nothing about them.

Nevertheless, these are the slightest difficulties compared to those which have their ground in the essence of the new dimension and its relation to the old familiar field of life. Nowhere else is the distance so great from unclearly arising needs to goal-determined plans, from vague questionings to first working problems – through which actual working science first begins. Nowhere else is it so frequent that the explorer is met by logical ghosts emerging out of the dark, formed in the old familiar and effective conceptual patterns, as paradoxical antinomies, logical absurdities. Thus nowhere is the temptation so great to slide into logical aporetics and disputation, priding oneself on one's scientific discipline, while the actual substratum of the work, the phenomena themselves, is forever lost from view.

All this will be confirmed as I now leave the reference to Kant behind and attempt to show, to those willing to understand, one of the paths I have actually taken; *as* a path actually taken, it offers itself as one that can at any time be taken again. Indeed, it is a path which at every step allows just this self-evidence to be renewed and tested as apodictic, i.e., the self-evidence of a path capable of being taken repeatedly at will and capable of being followed further at will in repeatedly verifiable experiences and cognitions.

§33 The problem of the "life-world" as a partial problem within the general problem of objective science

Briefly reminding ourselves of our earlier discussions, let us recall the fact we have emphasized, namely, that science is a human spiritual accomplishment which presupposes as its point of departure, both historically and for each new student, the intuitive surrounding world of life, pregiven as existing for all in common. Furthermore, it is an accomplishment which, in being practiced and carried forward, continues to presuppose this surrounding world as it is given in its particularity to the scientist. For example, for the physicist it is the world in which he sees his measuring instruments, hears time-beats, estimates visible magnitudes, etc. – the world in which, furthermore, he knows himself to be included with all his activity and all his theoretical ideas.

When science poses and answers questions, these are from the start, and hence from then on, questions resting upon the ground of, and addressed to, the elements of this pregiven world in which science and every other life-praxis is engaged. In this life-praxis, knowledge, as prescientific knowledge, plays a constant role, together with its goals, which are in general satisfactorily achieved in the sense which is intended and in each case usually in order to make practical life possible. But a new civilization (philosophical, scientific civilization), rising up in Greece, saw fit to recast the idea of "knowledge" and "truth" in natural existence and to ascribe to the newly formed idea of "objective truth" a higher dignity, that of a norm for all knowledge. In relation to this, finally, arises the idea of a universal science encompassing all possible knowledge in its infinity, the bold guiding idea of the modern period. If we have made this clear to ourselves, then obviously an explicit elucidation of the objective validity and of the whole task of science requires that we first inquire back into the pregiven world. It is pregiven to us all quite naturally, as persons within the horizon of our fellow men, i.e., in every actual connection with others, as "the" world common to us all. Thus it is, as we have explained in detail, the constant ground of validity, an ever available source of what is taken for granted, to which we, whether as practical men or as scientists, lay claim as a matter of course.

Now if this pregiven world is to become a subject of investigation in its own right, so that we can arrive, of course, at scientifically defensible assertions, this requires special care in preparatory reflections. It is not easy to achieve clarity about what kind of peculiar scientific and hence universal tasks are to be posed under the title "life-world" and about whether something philosophically significant will arise here. Even the first attempt to understand the peculiar ontic sense of the life-world, which can be taken now as a narrower, now as a broader one, causes difficulties.

The manner in which we here come to the life-world as a subject for scientific investigation makes this subject appear an ancillary and partial one within the full subject of objective science in general. The latter has become generally, that is, in all its particular forms (the particular positive sciences), incomprehensible as regards the possibility of its objective accomplishment. If science becomes a problem in this way, then we must withdraw from the operation of it and take up a standpoint above it, surveying in generality its theories and results in the systematic context of predicative thoughts and statements, and, on the other side we must also survey the life of acts practiced by working scientists, working with one another – their setting of goals, their termination in a given goal, and the terminating self-evidence. And what also comes under consideration here is precisely the scientists' repeated recourse, in different general manners, to the life-world with its ever available intuited data; to this we can immediately add the scientists' statements, in each case simply adapted to this world, statements made purely descriptively in the same prescientific manner of judging which is proper to the "occasional"[9] statements of practical, everyday life. Thus the problem of the life-world, or rather of the manner in which it functions and must function for scientists, is only a partial subject within the above-designated whole of objective science (namely, in the service of its full grounding).

It is clear, however, that prior to the general question of its function for a self-evident grounding of the objective sciences there is good reason to ask about the life-world's own and constant ontic meaning for the human beings who live in it. These human beings do not always have scientific interests, and even scientists are not always involved in scientific work; also, as history teaches us, there was not always in the world a civilization that lived habitually with long-established scientific interests. The life-world was always there for mankind before science, then, just as it continues its manner of being in the epoch of science. Thus one can put forward by itself the problem of the manner of being of the life-world; one can place oneself completely upon the ground of this straightforwardly intuited world, putting out of play all objective-scientific opinions and cognitions, in order to consider generally what kind of "scientific" tasks, i.e., tasks to be resolved with universal validity, arise in respect to this world's own manner of being. Might this not yield a vast theme for study? Is it not the case that, in the end, through what first appears as a special subject in the theory of science, that "third dimension" is opening up, immediately destined in advance to engulf the whole subject matter of objective science (as well as all other subject matters on the "plane")? At first this must appear peculiar and unbelievable. Many paradoxes will arise; yet they will be resolved. What imposes itself here and must be considered before everything else is the correct comprehension of the essence of the life-world and the method of a "scientific" treatment appropriate to it, from which "objective" scientific treatment, however, is excluded.

§34 Exposition of the problem of a science of the life-world

a. The difference between objective science and science in general

Is not the life-world as such what we know best, what is always taken for granted in all human life, always familiar to us in its typology through experience? Are not all its horizons of the unknown simply horizons of what is just incompletely known, i.e., known in advance in respect of its most general typology? For prescientific life, of course, this type of acquaintance suffices, as does its manner of converting the unknown into the known, gaining "occasional" knowledge on the basis of experience (verifying itself internally and thereby excluding illusion) and induction. This suffices for everyday praxis. If, now, something more can be and is to be accomplished, if a "scientific" knowledge is supposed to come about, what can be meant other than what objective science has in view and does anyway? Is scientific knowledge as such not "objective" knowledge, aimed at a knowledge substratum which is valid for everyone with unconditioned generality? And yet, paradoxically, we uphold our assertion and require that one not let the handed-down concept of objective science be substituted, because of the century-old tradition in which we have all been raised, for the concept of science in general.

The[10] title "life-world" makes possible and demands perhaps various different, though essentially interrelated, scientific undertakings; and perhaps it is part of genuine and full scientific discipline that we must treat these all together, though following their essential order of founding, rather than treating, say, just the one, the objective-logical one (this particular accomplishment within the life-world) by itself, leaving the others completely out of scientific consideration. There has never been a scientific inquiry into the way in which the life-world constantly functions as subsoil, into how its manifold prelogical validities act as grounds for the logical ones, for theoretical truths.[11] And perhaps the scientific discipline which this life-world as such, in its universality, requires is a peculiar one, one which is precisely not objective and logical but which, as the ultimately grounding one, is not inferior but superior in value. But how is this completely different sort of scientific discipline, for which the objective sort has always been substituted up to now, to be realized? The idea of objective truth is predetermined in its whole meaning by the contrast with the idea of the truth in pre- and extra-scientific life. This latter truth has its ultimate and deepest source of verification in experience which is "pure" in the sense designated above, in all its modes of perception, memory, etc. These words, however, must be understood actually as prescientific life understands them; thus one must not inject into them, from current objective science, any psychophysical, psychological interpretation. And above all – to dispose of an important point right away – one must not go straight back to the supposedly immediately given "sense-data," as if *they* were immediately characteristic of the purely intuitive data of the life-world. What is actually first is the "merely subjective-relative" intuition of prescientific world-life. For us, to be sure, this "merely" has, as an old inheritance, the disdainful coloring of the δόξα. In prescientific life itself, of course, it has nothing of this; there it is a realm of good verification and, based on this, of well-verified predicative cognitions and of truths which are just as secure as is necessary for the practical projects of life that determine their sense. The disdain with which everything "merely subjective and relative" is treated by those scientists who pursue the modern ideal of objectivity changes nothing of its own manner of being, just as it does not change the fact that the scientist himself must be satisfied with this realm whenever he has recourse, as he unavoidably must have recourse, to it.

b. The use of subjective-relative experiences for the objective sciences, and the science of them

The sciences build upon the life-world as taken for granted in that they make use of whatever in it happens to be necessary for their particular ends. But to use the life-world in this way is not to know it scientifically in its own manner of being. For example, Einstein uses the Michelson experiments and the corroboration of them by other researchers, with apparatus copied from Michelson's, with everything required in the way of scales of measurement, coincidences established, etc. There is no doubt that everything that enters in here – the persons, the apparatus, the room in the institute, etc. – can itself become a subject of investigation in the usual sense of objective inquiry, that of the positive sciences. But Einstein could make no use whatever of a theoretical psychological-psychophysical construction of the objective being of Mr. Michelson; rather, he made use of the human being who was accessible to him, as to everyone else in the prescientific world, as an object of straightforward experience, the human being whose existence, with this vitality, in these activities and creations within the common life-world, is always the presupposition for all of Einstein's objective-scientific lines of inquiry, projects, and accomplishments pertaining to Michelson's experiments. It is, of course, the one world of experience, common to all, that Einstein and every other researcher knows he is in as a human being, even throughout all his activity of research. [But] precisely this world and everything that happens in it, used as needed for scientific and other ends, bears, on the other hand, for every natural scientist in his thematic orientation toward its "objective truth," the stamp "merely subjective and relative." The contrast to this determines, as we said, the sense of the "objective" task. This "subjective-relative" is supposed to be "overcome"; one can and should correlate with it a hypothetical being-in-itself, a substrate for logical-mathematical "truths-in-themselves" that one can approximate through ever newer and better hypothetical approaches, always justifying them through experiential verification. This is the one side. But while the natural scientist is thus interested in the objective and is involved in his activity, the subjective-relative is on the other hand still functioning for him, not as something irrelevant that must be passed through but as that which ultimately grounds the theoretical-logical ontic validity for all objective verification, i.e., as the source of self-evidence, the source of verification. The visible measuring scales, scale-markings, etc., are used as actually existing things, not as illusions; thus that which actually exists in the life-world, as something valid, is a premise.

c. Is the subjective-relative an object for psychology?

Now the question of the manner of being of this subjective sphere, or the question of the science which is to deal with it in its own universe of being, is normally disposed of by the natural scientist by referring to psychology. But again one must not allow the intrusion of what exists in the sense of objective science when it is a question of what exists in the life-world. For what has always gone under the name of psychology, at any rate since the founding of modern objectivism regarding knowledge of the world, naturally has the meaning of an "objective" science of the subjective, no matter which of the attempted historical psychologies we may choose. Now in our subsequent reflections the problem of making possible an objective psychology will have to become the object of more detailed discussions. But first we must grasp clearly the contrast between objectivity and the subjectivity of the life-world as a contrast which determines the fundamental sense of objective-scientific discipline itself, and we must secure this contrast against the great temptations to misconstrue it.

d. The life-world as universe of what is intuitable in principle; the "objective-true" world as in principle nonintuitable "logical" substruction

Whatever may be the chances for realizing, or the capacity for realizing, the idea of objective science in respect to the mental world (i.e., not only in respect to nature), this idea of objectivity dominates the whole *universitas* of the positive sciences in the modern period, and in the general usage it dominates the meaning of the word "science." This already involves a naturalism insofar as this concept is taken from Galilean natural science, such that the scientifically "true," the objective, world is always thought of in advance as nature, in an expanded sense of the word. The contrast between the subjectivity of the life-world and the "objective," the "true" world, lies in the fact that the latter is a theoretical-logical substruction, the substruction of something that is in principle not perceivable, in principle not experienceable in its own proper being, whereas the subjective, in the life-world, is distinguished in all respects precisely by its being actually experienceable.[12]

The life-world is a realm of original self-evidences.[13] That which is self-evidently given is, in perception, experienced as "the thing itself,"[14] in immediate presence, or, in memory, remembered as the thing itself; and every other manner of intuition is a presentification of the thing itself. Every mediate cognition belonging in this sphere – broadly speaking, every manner of induction – has the sense of an induction of something intuitable, something possibly perceivable as the thing itself or rememberable as having-been-perceived, etc. All conceivable verification leads back to these modes of self-evidence because the "thing itself" (in the particular mode) lies in these intuitions themselves as that which is actually, intersubjectively experienceable and verifiable and is not a substruction of thought; whereas such a substruction, insofar as it makes a claim to truth, can have actual truth only by being related back to such self-evidence.

It is of course itself a highly important task, for the scientific opening-up of the life-world, to bring to recognition the primal validity of these self-evidences and indeed their higher dignity in the grounding of knowledge compared to that of the objective-logical self-evidences. One must fully clarify, i.e., bring to ultimate self-evidence, how all the self-evidence of objective-logical accomplishments, through which objective theory (thus mathematical and natural-scientific theory) is grounded in respect of form and content, has its hidden sources of grounding in the ultimately accomplishing life, the life in which the self-evident givenness of the life-world forever has, has attained, and attains anew its prescientific ontic meaning. From objective-logical self-evidence (mathematical "insight," natural-scientific, positive-scientific "insight," as it is being accomplished by the inquiring and grounding mathematician, etc.), the path leads back, here, to the primal self-evidence in which the life-world is ever pregiven.

167

One may at first find strange and even questionable what has been simply asserted here, but the general features of the contrast among levels of self-evidence are unmistakable. The empiricist talk of natural scientists often, if not for the most part, gives the impression that the natural sciences are based on the experience of objective nature. But it is not in this sense true that these sciences are experiential sciences, that they follow experience in principle, that they all begin with experiences, that all their inductions must finally be verified through experiences; rather, this is true only in that other sense whereby experience [yields] a self-evidence taking place purely in the life-world and as such is the source of self-evidence for what is objectively established in the sciences, the latter never themselves being experiences of the objective. The objective is precisely never experienceable as itself; and scientists themselves, by the way, consider it in this way whenever they interpret it as something metaphysically transcendent, in contrast to their confusing empiricist talk. The experienceability of something objective is no different from that of an infinitely distant geometrical construct and in general no different from that of all infinite "ideas," including, for example, the infinity of the number series. Naturally, "rendering ideas intuitive" in the manner of mathematical or natural-scientific "models" is hardly intuition of the objective itself but rather a matter of life-world intuitions which are suited to make easier the conception of the objective ideals in question. Many [such] conceptual intermediaries are often involved, [especially since] the conception itself does not always occur so immediately, cannot always be made so self-evident in its way, as is the case in conceiving of geometrical straight lines on the basis of the life-world self-evidence of straight table-edges and the like.

As can be seen, a great deal of effort is involved here in order to secure even the presuppositions for a proper inquiry, i.e., in order first to free ourselves from the constant misconstructions which mislead us all because of the scholastic dominance of objective-scientific ways of thinking.

e. The objective sciences as subjective constructs – those of a particular praxis, namely, the theoretical-logical, which itself belongs to the full concreteness of the life-world

If the contrast [under discussion] has been purified, we must now do justice to the essential interrelatedness [of the elements contrasted]: objective theory in its logical sense (taken universally: science as the totality of predicative theory, of the system of statements meant "logically" as "propositions in themselves," "truths in themselves," and in this sense logically joined) is rooted, grounded in the life-world, in the original self-evidences belonging to it. Thanks to this rootedness objective science has a constant reference of meaning to the world in which we always live, even as scientists and also in the total community of scientists – a reference, that is, to the general life-world. But at the same time, as an accomplishment of scientific[15] persons, as individuals and as joined in the community of scientific activity, objective science itself belongs to the life-world. Its theories, the logical constructs, are of course not things in the life-world like stones, houses, or trees. They are logical wholes and logical parts made up of ultimate logical elements. To speak with Bolzano, they are "representations-in-themselves" ["*Vorstellungen an sich*"] "propositions in themselves," inferences and proofs "in themselves," ideal unities of signification whose logical ideality is determined by their *telos*, "truth in itself."

But this or any other ideality does not change in the least the fact that these are human formations, essentially related to human actualities and potentialities, and thus belong to this concrete unity of the life-world, whose concreteness thus extends farther than that of "things." Exactly the same thing is true, correlative to this, of scientific activities – those of experiencing, those of arriving at logical formations "on the basis of" experience – activities through which these formations appear in original form and original modes of variation in the individual scientists and in the community of scientists: the original status of the proposition or demonstration dealt with by all.

But here we enter an uncomfortable situation. If we have made our contrast with all necessary care, then we have two different things: life-world and objective-scientific world, though of course [they are] related to each other. The knowledge of the objective-scientific world is "grounded" in the self-evidence of the life-world. The latter is pregiven to the scientific worker, or the working community, as ground; yet, as they build upon this, what is built is something new, something different. If we cease being immersed in our scientific thinking, we become aware that we scientists are, after all, human beings and as such are among the components of the life-world which always exists for us, ever pregiven; and thus all of science is pulled, along with us, into the – merely "subjective-relative" – life-world. And what becomes of the objective world itself? What happens to the hypothesis of being-in-itself, related first to the "things" of the life-world, the "objects," the "real" bodies, real animals, plants, and also human beings within the "space-time" of the life-world – all these concepts being understood, now, not from the point of view of the objective sciences but as they are in prescientific life?

Is it not the case that this hypothesis, which in spite of the ideality of scientific theories has direct validity for the scientific subjects (the scientists as human beings), is but *one* among the many practical hypotheses and projects which make up the life of human beings in this life-world – which is at all times consciously pregiven to them as available? Do not all goals, whether they are "practical" in some other, extrascientific sense or are practical under the title of "theory," belong *eo ipso* to the unity of the life-world, if only we take the latter in its complete and full concreteness?

On the other hand, we have seen also that the propositions, the theories, the whole edifice of doctrine in the objective sciences are structures attained through certain activities of scientists bound together in their collaborative work – or, to speak more exactly, attained through a continued building-up of activities, the later of which always presuppose the results of the earlier. And we see further that all these theoretical results have the character of validities for the life-world, adding themselves as such to its own composition and belonging to it even before that as a horizon of possible accomplishments for developing science. The concrete life-world, then, is the grounding soil [*der gründende Boden*] of the "scientifically true" world and at the same time encompasses it in its own universal concreteness. How is this to be understood? How are we to do justice systematically – that is, with appropriate scientific discipline – to the all-encompassing, so paradoxically demanding, manner of being of the life-world?

We are posing questions whose clarifying answers are by no means obvious.

The contrast and the inseparable union [we have been exploring] draw us into a reflection which entangles us in more and more troublesome difficulties. The paradoxical interrelationships of the "objectively true world" and the "life-world" make enigmatic the manner of being of both. Thus [the idea of a] true world in any sense, and within it our own being, becomes an enigma in respect to the sense of this being. In our attempts to attain clarity we shall suddenly become aware, in the face of emerging paradoxes, that all of our philosophizing up to now has been without a ground. How can we now truly become philosophers?

We cannot escape the force of this motivation. It is impossible for us to evade the issue here through a preoccupation with aporia and argumentation nourished by Kant or Hegel, Aristotle or Thomas.

f. The problem of the life-world not as a partial problem but rather as a universal problem for philosophy

Of course, it is a new sort of scientific discipline that is required for the solution of the enigmas which now disquiet us: it is not mathematical, nor logical at all in the historical sense; it cannot already have before it, as an available norm, a finished mathematics, logic, or logistic, since these are themselves objective sciences in the sense which is presently problematical and, as included in the problem, cannot be presuppositions used as premises. At first, as long as one only makes contrasts, is only concerned with oppositions, it could appear that nothing more than or different from objective science is needed, just as everyday practical life undertakes its rational reflections, both particular and general, without needing a science for them. It just *is* this way, a fact familiar to all, unthinkingly accepted rather than being formulated as a fundamental fact and thought through as a subject for thinking in its own right – namely, that there are two sorts of truth: on the one side, everyday practical situational truths, relative, to be sure, but, as we have already emphasized, exactly what praxis, in its particular projects, seeks and needs; on the other side there are scientific truths, and their grounding leads back precisely to the situational truths, but in such a way that scientific method does not suffer thereby in respect to its own meaning, since it wants to use and must use precisely these truths.

Thus it could appear – if one allows oneself to be carried along by the thoughtless naïveté of life even in the transition from the extralogical to the logical, to the objective-scientific praxis of thinking – that a separate investigation under the title "life-world" is an intellectualistic enterprise born of a mania, peculiar to modern life, to theorize everything. But, on the other hand, it has at least become apparent that we cannot let the matter end with this naïveté, that paradoxical enigmas announce themselves here: merely subjective relativity is supposedly overcome by objective-logical theory, yet the latter belongs, as the theoretical praxis of human beings, to the merely subjective and relative and at the same time must have its premises, its sources of self-evidence, in the subjective and relative. From here on this much is certain: that all problems of truth and of being, all methods, hypotheses, and results conceivable for these problems – whether for worlds of experience or for metaphysical higher worlds – can attain their ultimate clarity, their evident sense or the evidence of their nonsense, only through this supposed intellectualistic hypertrophy. This will then include, certainly, all ultimate questions of legitimate sense and of nonsense in the busy routine of the "resurrected metaphysics" that has become so vocal and so bewitching of late.

Through this last series of considerations the magnitude, the universal and independent significance, of the problem of the life-world has become intelligible to us in an anticipatory insight. In comparison with this the problem of the "objectively true" world or that of objective-logical science – no matter how pressing it may repeatedly become, and properly so – appears now as a problem of secondary and more specialized interest. Though the peculiar accomplishment of our modern objective science may still not be understood, nothing changes the fact that it is a validity for the life-world, arising out of particular activities, and that it belongs itself to the concreteness of the life-world. Thus in any case, for the sake of clarifying this and all other acquisitions of human activity, the concrete life-world must first be taken into consideration; and it must be considered in terms of the truly concrete universality whereby it embraces, both directly and in the manner of horizons, all the built-up levels of validity acquired by men for the world of their common life and whereby it has the totality of these levels related in the end to a world-nucleus to be distilled by abstraction, namely, the world of straightforward intersubjective experiences. To be sure, we do not yet know how the life-world is to become an independent, totally self-sufficient subject of investigation, how it is supposed to make possible scientific statements – which as such, after all, must have their own "objectivity," even if it is in a manner different from that of our sciences, i.e., a necessary validity to be appropriated purely methodically, which we and everyone can verify precisely through this method. We are absolute beginners, here, and have nothing in the way of a logic designed to provide norms; we can do nothing but reflect, engross ourselves in the still not unfolded sense of our task, and thus secure, with the utmost care, freedom from prejudice, keeping our undertaking free of alien interferences (and we have already made several important contributions to this); and this, as in the case of every new undertaking, must supply us with our method. The clarification of the sense of the task is, indeed, the self-evidence of the goal *qua* goal; and to this self-evidence belongs essentially the self-evidence of the possible "ways" to it. The intricacy and difficulty of the preliminary reflections which are still before us will justify themselves, not only because of the magnitude of the goal, but also because of the essential strangeness and precariousness of the ideas which will necessarily become involved.

Thus what appeared to be merely a problem of the fundamental basis of the objective sciences or a partial problem within the universal problem of objective science has indeed (just as we announced in advance that it would) proven to be the genuine and most universal problem. It can also be put this way: the problem first appears as the question of the relation between objective-scientific thinking and intuition; it concerns, on the one hand, then, logical thinking as the thinking of logical thoughts, e.g., the physicist's thinking of physical theory, or purely mathematical thinking, in which mathematics has its place as a system of doctrine, as a theory. And, on the other hand, we have intuiting and the intuited, in the life-world prior to theory. Here arises the ineradicable illusion of a pure thinking which, unconcerned in its purity about intuition, already has its self-evident truth, even truth about the world – the illusion which makes the sense and the possibility, the "scope," of objective science questionable. Here one concentrates on the separateness of intuiting and thinking and generally interprets the nature of the "theory of knowledge" as theory of science, carried out in respect to two correlative sides[16] (whereby science is always understood in terms of the only concept of science available, that of objective science). But as soon as the empty and vague notion of intuition – instead of being something negligible and insignificant compared to the supremely significant logical sphere in which one supposedly already has genuine truth – has become the problem of the life-world, as soon as the magnitude and difficulty of this investigation take on enormous proportions as one seriously penetrates it, there occurs the great transformation of the "theory of knowledge" and the theory of science whereby, in the end, science as a problem and as an accomplishment loses its self-sufficiency and becomes a mere partial problem.

What we have said also naturally applies to logic, as the a priori theory of norms for everything "logical" – in the overarching sense of what is logical, according to which logic is a logic of strict objectivity, of objective-logical truths. No one ever thinks about the predications and truths which precede science, about the "logic" which provides norms within this sphere of relativity, or about the possibility, even in the case of these logical structures conforming purely descriptively to the life-world, of inquiring into the system of principles that give them their norms a priori. As a matter of course, traditional objective logic is substituted as the a priori norm even for this subjective-relative sphere of truth.

§35 Analysis of the transcendental epochē.
First step: The epochē of objective science

Because of the peculiar nature of the task which has arisen for us, the method of access to the new science's field of work – which must be attained before the working problems of the science are given – is articulated into a multiplicity of steps, each of which has, in a new way, the character of an *epochē*, a withholding of natural, naïve validities and in general of validities already in effect. The first necessary *epochē*, i.e., the first methodical step, has already come into view through the preliminary reflections hitherto carried out. But an explicit, universal formulation is needed. Clearly required before everything else is the *epochē* in respect to all objective sciences. This means not merely an abstraction from them, such as an imaginary transformation, in thought, of present human existence, such that no science appeared in the picture. What is meant is rather an *epochē* of all participation in the cognitions of the objective sciences, an *epochē* of any critical position-taking which is interested in their truth or falsity, even any position on their guiding idea of an objective knowledge of the world. In short, we carry out an *epochē* in regard to all objective theoretical interests, all aims and activities belonging to us as objective scientists or even simply as [ordinary] people desirous of [this kind of] knowledge.

Within this *epochē*, however, neither the sciences nor the scientists have disappeared for us who practice the *epochē*. They continue to be what they were before, in any case: facts in the unified context of the pregiven life-world; except that, because of the *epochē*, we do not function as sharing these interests, as coworkers, etc. We establish in ourselves just one particular habitual direction of interest, with a certain vocational attitude, to which there belongs a particular "vocational time."[17] We find the same thing here as elsewhere: when we actualize one of our habitual interests and are thus involved in our vocational activity (in the accomplishment of our work), we assume a posture of *epochē* toward our other life-interests, even though these still exist and are still ours. Everything has "its proper time," and in shifting [activities] we say something like: "Now it is time to go to the meeting, to the election," and the like.

In a special sense, of course, we call science, art, military service, etc., our "vocation," but as normal human beings we are constantly (in a broadened sense) involved in many "vocations" (interested attitudes) at the same time: we are at once fathers, citizens, etc. Every such vocation has its time of actualizing activities. Accordingly, this newly established vocational interest, whose universal subject matter is called the "life-world," finds its place among the other life-interests or vocations and it has "its proper time" within the one personal time, the form of the various exercised vocational times.

Of course, to equate the new science in this way with all "bourgeois" [*bürgerliche*] vocations, or even with the objective sciences, is a sort of trivialization, a disregard for the greatest value-distinction there can be between sciences. Understood in this way, it was so happily criticized by the modern irrationalistic philosophers. This way of looking at it makes it appear as if, once again, a new, purely theoretical interest, a new "science" with a new vocational technique, is to be established, carried on either as an intellectualistic game with very ideal pretensions or as a higher-level intellectual technique in the service of the positive sciences, useful for them, while they themselves, in turn, have their only real value in their usefulness for life. One is powerless against the misrepresentations of hurried readers and listeners who in the end hear only what they want to hear; but in any case they are part of the indifferent mass audience of the philosopher. The few, for whom one [really] speaks, will know how to restrain such a suspicion, especially after what we have said in earlier lectures. They will at least wait to see where our path leads them.

There are good reasons for my stressing so sharply the vocational character of even the "phenomenologist's" attitude. One of the first things to be described about the *epochē* in question is that it is a habitual *epochē* of accomplishment, one with periods of time in which it results in work, while other times are devoted to other interests of work or play; furthermore, and most important, the suspension of its accomplishment in no way changes the interest which continues and remains valid within personal subjectivity – i.e., its habitual directedness toward goals which persist as its validities – and it is for this very reason that it can be actualized again and again, at different times, in this identical sense. This by no means implies, however, that the life-world *epochē* – to which further significant moments belong, as we shall show – means no more for human existence, practically and "existentially," than the vocational *epochē* of the cobbler, or that it is basically a matter of indifference whether one is a cobbler or a phenomenologist, or, also, whether one is a phenomenologist or a positive scientist. Perhaps it will even become manifest that the total phenomenological attitude and the *epochē* belonging to it are destined in essence to effect, at first, a complete personal transformation, comparable in the beginning to a religious conversion, which then, however, over and above this, bears within itself the significance of the greatest existential transformation which is assigned as a task to mankind as such.

Notes

1 Reading ". . . ist der hinsichtlich der Natur doppelt fungierende Verstand . . ."
2 *Vergegenwärtigungen*, i.e., modifications of *Gegenwärtigungen*. The former are explicit acts of rendering consciously present that which is not "itself present," as in the case of recollection or imagination.
3 *Walten*. "Holding sway" is somewhat awkward in English, but it seems to best approximate Husserl's use of this archaic term. The latter is often used in religious language (*Gottes Walten*) to signify God's rule and power over the world and his intervention in its affairs. The English "wield" is related to it but is transitive. Husserl uses the term primarily in connection with the living body (unlike Heidegger, who resurrected it for a different purpose), meaning one's "wielding" of the body and its organs so as to have some control of one's surroundings.
4 *Körper* means body in the geometric or physical sense; *Leib* refers to the body of a person or animal. Where possible, I have translated *Leib* as "living body" (*Leib* is related to *Leben*); *Körper* is translated as "body" or sometimes "physical body".
5 i.e., as a physical body (*Körper*).
6 Naturally all activity, and thus also this reflecting activity, gives rise to its habitual acquisitions. In observing, we attain habitual knowledge, acquaintance with the object which exists for us in terms of its previously unknown characteristics – and the same is true of self-knowledge through self-observation. In the evaluation of ourselves and the plans and actions related to ourselves and our fellows, we likewise attain self-values and ends concerning ourselves [which become] our habitually persisting validities. But all knowledge in general, all value-validities and ends in general, are, as having been acquired through our activity, at the same time persisting properties of ourselves as ego-subjects, as persons, and can be found in the reflective attitude as making up our own being.
7 *letztfungierende*, i.e., functioning at the ultimate or deepest level.
8 *der sich selbst im Aussen "äussernden" Subjektivität*.
9 *okkasionelle*. A term from the First Logical Investigation §26 an expression is "essentially subjective and occasional" if its actual meaning depends "on the occasion [*Gelegenheit*], the person speaking, and his situation."
10 This whole paragraph is crossed out in the MS.
11 This sentence was added by Fink. It does not seem to fit in, and it breaks the continuity between the preceding and following sentences.
12 In life the verification of being, terminating in experience, yields a full conviction. Even when it is inductive, the inductive anticipation is of a possible experienceability which is ultimately decisive. Inductions can be verified by other inductions, working together. Because of their anticipations of experienceability, and because every direct perception itself includes inductive moments (anticipation of the sides of the object which are not yet experienced), everything is contained in the broader concept of "experience" or "induction." [Husserl's own note].
13 Husserl's use of *Evidenz* does not permit of its always being translated in the same way. But when used in its most special or technical sense, as it is here, "self-evidence" is better than simply "evidence." As can be seen from the context here, it means "self-givenness"; whereas the English word "evidence" usually has a very different meaning, that of something testifying to the existence of something else (e.g., evidence in a trial).
14 "*es selbst*." The use of the word "thing" in this expression is not out of place as long as Husserl is talking about perception. But in another context that which is "itself" given might not be a "thing"; it could be an ideal state of affairs, for example in mathematical or logical intuition.
15 The text reads "prescientific persons," which must be a mistake.
16 i.e., the subjective and the objective.
17 *Berufszeit*, colloq., "working hours." But it has been translated literally as "vocational time" in order to preserve the notion of *Beruf*, a "calling."

Part III

ADOLF REINACH
The Phenomenology of Social Acts

ADOLF REINACH (1883–1917)

Introduction

Adolf Reinach was born in Mainz, Germany, in 1883. He entered the University of Munich in 1901 to study political economy and law, but, inspired by Theodor Lipps' lectures, soon became interested in psychology and philosophy. He was drawn to the new way of doing philosophy offered by Husserl's *Investigations* and participated in the Munich philosophical circle, which included Moritz Geiger, Johannes Daubert, and others (including Max Scheler after 1906). He completed his doctorate in 1904 under Lipps on the concept of cause in law. He then went to Göttingen to study with Husserl, but soon after returned to Munich, and completed his law training in Tübingen. In 1909 he returned to Göttingen to complete his *Habilitation* with Husserl, eventually becoming his assistant. At Göttingen, Reinach was known as a brilliant teacher (acknowledged by Stein) who was able to distil Husserl's insights in a clear and rigorous manner. Along with his friends in the Munich circle and the Göttingen group, which included Edith Stein, Reinach was intent on developing Husserl's earlier realist phenomenology, as the identification and description of the essences of all kinds of phenomena, and the overall pursuit of a priori synthetic knowledge of various material regions. In 1914, however, the First World War broke out and Reinach was called up. He was killed in Flanders in 1917. Husserl regarded Reinach as the most gifted of his students and was deeply affected by his death, writing an obituary for Reinach in *Kant Studien* in 1919. Reinach's former students put together a collection of his papers, with a Foreword by Hedwig Conrad-Martius, in 1921.

Reinach's short life and untimely end meant that he never managed to produce a book, but he had a deep interest and was widely read in philosophy, especially, Hume, Kant and William James. He was the first phenomenologist after Husserl to take serious notice of Frege. Overall, Reinach wrote in a clear, precise manner, and developed an approach similar to analytic philosophy. He was interested in Husserl's theory of judgement and in the analysis of subjectless sentences (e.g. 'it is raining'). He was especially known as a brilliant philosopher of law, with insights into the social context of utterances. His treatise, *Die apriorischen Grundlagen des bürgerlichen Rechtes* ("The A Priori Foundations of Civil Law"), appeared in the first volume of Husserl's *Jahrbuch* in 1913. Here Reinach takes promising to be the basis of social interaction and criticises Hume's account which sees promising as an act of will. Reinach offers a first attempt at a systematic theory of the phenomena of promising, questioning, commanding, threatening, accusing, enacting, requesting and other such acts, which he terms 'social acts', thereby anticipating the speech act theory more recently developed by John Austin and systematised by John Searle.

According to Reinach, social acts are not just externalisations of inner mental acts, but are actually performances to whose essence belongs the possibility of being grasped by another. They are to be distinguished from statements ('I am angry'), what Austin calls *constatives*. Social acts are executed in the very act of speaking or announcing them, and similarly they announce themselves to another by the same means. Thus when I promise to marry someone, the very utterance enacts the promise and also communicates it as a promise to the hearer. Reinach sees these social acts as making up new parts of reality, despite being complexes which bring together human agents, acts and certain articulations to others. In this sense, Reinach was interested in the ontology of the social (and legal) world.

Reinach also analysed the nature and composition of 'states of affair' (*Sachverhalte*), complex combinations of objects internally related to one another, which were the objects of judgements. The discussion of states of affairs had been prominent among Brentano's students but was later made famous by Wittgenstein in the *Tractatus*. Reinach's reading of Hume as a phenomenologist was close to that of Husserl, whom he may have influenced in this regard.

Our selection is an essay "Concerning Phenomenology", originally a lecture delivered at Marburg, the home of neo-Kantianism, in 1914. Reinach offers a clear and original portrait of the nature of phenomenology, notable for its extended discussion of Frege. Reinach emphasises that phenomenology is a way of doing philosophy and not a particular doctrine. It is aimed at seeing essences, making essential distinctions and repudiating existing distinctions where they are not validly drawn. In this respect phenomenology aims at conceptual clarification or meaning analysis (*Bedeutungsanalyse*). However, Reinach insists that the clarification of meaning is not the aim of phenomenology but rather only one means. The real aim of phenomenology is the intuition of essences and the essential laws governing them. Here Reinach shows how such essential seeing can have an extraordinary impact on the understanding of other areas of knowledge. He argues that phenomenology is concerned with essences in a manner in which other sciences (e.g. mathematics) are not. This leads him to show how a careful attention to 'the matters themselves' (*die Sachen selbst*) helps clarify the understanding of the nature of number. A classical dispute in mathematics centred around the issue of whether cardinal or ordinal numbers were basic in arithmetic. Reinach uses essential seeing to argue that numbers cannot be properties of objects or groups nor of concepts, and indeed the whole question of 'of what are numbers predicated?' is itself invalid. Numbers are based on predications but are not themselves predicated of anything. They are categorial forms like the quantifiers in logic. Similarly, Reinach argues that the notion of ordinality has nothing to do with number as such. That something comes fifth in a sequence has nothing essentially to do with the number five, and similarly being first and being one are not identical. Reinach then turns to clarifying the kind of a priori knowledge that belongs properly to phenomenology.

Further reading

Reinach, Adolf. "Kants Auffassung des humeschen Problems", *Zeitschrift für Philosophie und philosophische Kritik* 141 (1911), pp. 176–209.
Reinach, Adolf. *Gesammelte Schriften*. Halle: Max Niemeyer, 1921.

Reinach, Adolf. "Concerning Phenomenology", trans. Dallas Willard, *The Personalist* 50 (1969), pp. 194–221.

Reinach, Adolf. "Kant's Intepetation of Hume's Problem", trans. J. N. Mohanty, *Southwestern Journal of Philosophy* 7 (1976), pp. 161–188.

Reinach, Adolf. "On the Theory of the Negative Judgement", trans. B. Smith, in Barry Smith, ed. *Parts and Moments. Studies in Logic and Formal Ontology*. Munich: Philosophia, 1982, pp. 315–377.

Reinach, Adolf. "The A Priori Foundations of Civil Law", trans. John Crosby, *Aletheia* 3 (1983), pp. 1–142.

Reinach, Adolf. *Sämtliche Werke*, ed. Karl Schuhmann and Barry Smith, 2 vols. Munich: Philosophia Verlag, 1989.

Reinach, Adolf. "The Supreme Rules of Rational Inference According to Kant", trans. James M. DuBois, *Aletheia* 6 (1993–1994), pp. 81–97.

Husserl, Edmund. "Adolf Reinach", *Kant Studien* 23 (1919), pp. 147–149.

Mulligan, K. Ed. *Speech Act and Sachverhalt. Reinach and the Foundations of Realist Phenomenology*. Dordrecht: Nijhoff, 1987.

Smith, Barry. Ed. *Parts and Moments. Studies in Logic and Formal Ontology*. Munich: Philosophia, 1982.

Smith, Barry. "Realistic Phenomenology", in L. Embree *et al.* eds. *Encyclopedia of Phenomenology*. Dordrecht: Kluwer, 1997, pp. 586–590.

1

CONCERNING PHENOMENOLOGY

I have not set myself the task of telling you what phenomenology is. Rather I would like to try to *think* with you in the phenomenological manner.[1] To talk about phenomenology is the most idle thing in the world, so long as that is lacking which alone can give talk concrete fullness and intuitiveness, namely, the phenomenological *way of seeing* and the phenomenological *attitude*. For the essential point is this, that phenomenology is not a system of philosophical propositions and truths – a system of propositions in which all who call themselves phenomenologists must believe, and which I could prove to you – but rather it is a method of philosophizing which is required by the problems of philosophy, which is very different from the manner of viewing and verifying in life, and which is even more different from the way in which one does and must work in most sciences. And so today my aim is to touch upon a series of philosophical problems with you, in the hope that, at this or that point, it will become clear to you what the peculiarity of the phenomenological attitude is. Only then is the basis for further discussions given.

There are all sorts of ways in which we relate to objects – to existing and to nonexisting objects. We stand in the world as practically active beings. We see it, and yet we do not see it; we see it more or less exactly, and what we see of it is, in general, determined by our needs and purposes. We all know how laborious a task it is to learn to really see; what work is required, for example, to really see the colors which all along fall in our visual field and are swept over by our glance. What is true in this case is true, to an even higher degree, of the stream of psychic events – of that which we call 'experiencing' (*Erleben*), which, as such, does not, like the sensible world, stand over against us as something foreign, but rather is in essence selfly (*ichzugehörig*) – in short, of the states, acts, and functions of the ego. This 'experiencing' is just as remote and difficult to comprehend in its qualitative structure or nature as it is certain for us in its existence. What the normal man views of it – in fact, what he even merely notices about it – is little enough. Joy and pain, love and hate, yearning, homesickness, etc., certainly present themselves to him. But in the last analysis these are only crudely-cut sections within an infinitely nuanced domain. Even the poorest conscious life is yet much too rich to be wholly comprehensible to its bearer. Also here we can *learn* to look; also here it is art which teaches the normal person to comprehend, for the first time, what he

A. Reinach, "Concerning Phenomenology", trans. Dallas Willard, *The Personalist*, 1969, Vol. 50, pp. 194–221.

had hitherto overlooked. This does not mean merely that, by means of art or technique, experiences are evoked within us which we would not have otherwise had, but also that, out of the fullness of experience, art allows us to view what was, indeed, *there already*, but without our being conscious of it.

Difficulties increase when we turn to other matters yet further from us – to time, space, number, concepts, propositions, etc. Of all these things we speak; and when we so speak, we have reference to them, we *mean* or *intend* (*meinen*) them. But in this intending (*Meinung*) we stand infinitely far from them. We still stand afar off from them when we have *definitionally* delimited them. If we wish to delimit the class of judgmental propositions (*Urteils-sätze*) by saying, for example, that it consists of all of those propositions which are either true or false, then the essence of the proposition and of the judgmental proposition – that which it is, its "whatness" – has come no closer to us thereby. If we aim to grasp the essence of red or of color, then, in the last analysis, we need only to look upon some perceived, imagined, or represented color, and, in what is so presented, lift the essence (*So-Sein*), the "whatness" (*Was*), of the color away from that which, as singular or actual, is of no interest to us.

If, now, the experiences in the ego are to be approached in this way, the difficulties are considerably greater. We well know that there are such things as feelings, acts of will, and convictions. We also know that they, like all that is, can be brought to adequate intuition. But if we try to conceptualize them, to bring them to us by means of their specific characteristics, then they seep away from us. It is as though we grasped in a void. Psychologists know how years of practice are required in order to master the difficulties involved here. But right at the beginning of this task we have wholly to do with ideal objects (*Ideelles*). Surely we do speak of numbers and the like; we operate with them; and the designations and rules with which we are familiar are quite adequate to enable us to attain the goals of practical life. But the essence of such things is yet infinitely removed from us. And if we are earnest enough not to be satisfied with definitions – which, after all, cannot bring the fact itself (*die Sache selbst*) a hair closer to us – then we must say, as Augustine said of time: "If you do not ask me what it is, I believe that I know. But if you ask me, then I no longer know."

It is an oppressive and disastrous error to suppose that this natural distance from objects, which is so hard to overcome, is suppressed by science. Many sciences, by their very nature, do not involve direct intuition of essences (*Wesenschau*). These sciences can be and are satisfied by definitions and derivations from definitions. Other sciences are indeed by nature allotted the task of direct essential intuition, but in their factual development have avoided that task. The significant – in fact, the frightening – example of this latter type of science is Psychology. I am not here speaking of it insofar as it is a science of lawlike regularities (*Gesetzes-wissenschaft*), i.e., insofar as it attempts to formulate laws of the actual, real course of consciousness. Here the case is quite different. I am speaking of what is called "descriptive psychology," of that discipline which strives to take an inventory of consciousness, and to fix upon the various species of experience as such. This has nothing to do with establishing existence, or with the singular experience, with its occurrence in the world at some point of objective time, and with its union with a spatially localized body. In the sphere of Descriptive Psychology, all of this is indifferent. There the question is not about existence, but about essence, about the possible species of consciousness *as such*, indifferently of whether, or where, or when they occur. But it will surely be said that we nonetheless could not know experience-essences were they not real-ized in the world. Now this objection is mistaken, as it stands. We do in fact have knowledge of species of experience of which we also know that, in the purity that they have as conceived by us, they perhaps have never been real-ized in the world. But even if the objection were wholly correct, it could only indicate that we men are limited in the species of experience accessible to us, and limited by what we are ourselves permitted to experience. But the dependence of essence itself upon its possible real-ization in consciousness is, naturally, not thereby established.

If we take a look at the factually existing Psychology, we see that it has not yet once succeeded in getting clear about its supreme and delimiting essence; the essence of the psychic itself. We do not mean that the opposition between the psychic and non-psychic is first constituted by means of our determining and defining. Rather, to the contrary, our determining must be directed by the distinctions of essence which are ultimately given and found before us. All of that which can enter into the stream of our experience, that which belongs, in the genuine sense, to the ego (e.g. our feeling, willing, perceiving, and the like), is essentially distinguished from all of that which transcends the stream of consciousness, standing over against it as ego-foreign (e.g. houses, or concepts, or numbers). Taking the case where I see a material, colored object in the world, the object – with its properties and modalities – is then something physical; but my perception of the object, my turning to it and attending to it, the joy over it which I feel, my admiration and, in short, all that presents itself as an activity or state or function of the ego – all of *that* is psychical. And now as to the present-day Psychology, it deals with colors, tones, odors, and the like, just as if with these we have to do with conscious experiences, just as if these did not foreignly stand over against us as much as does the highest and thickest of trees. We are assured that colors and tones are, after all, not real (*wirklich*), and thus are subjective and psychical. But this assurance is only obscure words. Leaving the unreality of colors and tones undecided – let us assume that they are unreal – do they perchance thereby become something psychical? Can the distinction between essence and existence be so far misunderstood that the denial of existence is confused with a modification of essence, of the essential characteristics? Concretely expressed: does a gigantic house of five floors, which I suppose myself to be perceiving, by any chance become an experience when this perceiving turns out to be an hallucination? Thus, all of those investigations of tone and color and odor must not be claimed for psychology. One has to say of the investigators who deal solely with sense qualities, that the genuinely psychic has remained foreign to them, even if they do call themselves "*Psycho*-logists." Certainly the *seeing* of color and the *hearing* of tones are functions of the ego, and *they* belong to Psychology. But how can the hearing of tones, which has its proper essence and follows its proper laws, be taken for the heard tones? There is, after all, such a thing as the unclear hearing of a strong tone. The strength here belongs to the tone; clarity and unclarity, on the other hand, are modifications of the function of hearing.

Of course, not all psychologists have misunderstood the sphere of the psychic in this way; but the tasks of pure essence-apprehension have been conceived of only by a very few. People want to learn from the natural sciences, and want to "reduce" experience to the furthest possible extent. And yet this way of putting the problem is senseless from the very outset. When the physicist reduces colors and tones to waves of determinate kinds, he is dealing with real existence, whose factuality he intends to explain. Leaving the broader sense of reduction undecided, reduction certainly has no application to essences. Would one perhaps wish to reduce the essence of red, which I can view in any instance of red, to the essence of waves, which nonetheless is an evidently different essence? Now it is precisely with *facts* that descriptive psychology has nothing to do. It has nothing to do with explanation of existences and the reduction of them to other existences. When it forgets that, there arise those reduction attempts which are in truth an impoverishment and falsification of consciousness. Then one comes to posit, as the fundamental essences of consciousness, feeling, willing, and thinking, let us say; or to propose some other such insufficient division of consciousness as that into representing, judging, and feeling. And then, when one gets hold of one of the infinitely many experience-types not covered by these classifications, it must be twisted into something which it, nonetheless, is not. Suppose that the experience is that of pardoning – a deep-seated and noteworthy act of a peculiar kind. Well, it certainly is not an act of *representing*. So people have attempted to maintain that this act is a judgment: the judgment that the injustice done is, after all, not so serious, or really is no injustice at all – thus rendering absolutely impossible any meaningful pardoning. Or, one says that pardoning is the cessation of a *feeling*, the cessation of wrath, as if pardoning were not something peculiar and positive, and much more than a mere forgetting or disappearing. Descriptive Psychology is not to explain and reduce to other things. Rather its aim is to illuminate and expose. It intends to bring to ultimate, intuitive giveness the "whatness" of experience, from which, in itself, we are so remote. It intends to determine this "whatness" as it is in itself, and to distinguish and mark it off from other "whatnesses." Thereby, to be sure, no final stopping place is attained. Of these essences laws hold: laws of a peculiarity and dignity which distinguishes them absolutely from all empirical connections and empirical uniformities. Pure intuition of essences is the means whereby one attains to insight into, and adequate comprehension of, these laws. But concerning such intuition I do not wish to speak until the second part of these remarks.

Essence intuition is also required in other disciplines. Not only the essence of that which can be realized arbitrarily many times, but also the essence of what is by nature singular and solitary, requires illumination and analysis. We see that the historian endeavors, not only to bring the unknown to light, but also to bring the known closer to us, to bring it to adequate intuition in its very nature. Here it is a matter of other goals and other methods. But we also see here great difficulties, and the danger of deviations and constructions. We see how, again and again, development is spoken of, while the question about the "what" of that which develops is neglected. We see how the environment of a thing is anxiously inquired into, only in order not to have to analyze *the thing itself*; how questions about the essence of a thing are believed resolved by answers to questions about its origination or its effect. How characteristic here [in historical studies] are the frequent juxtapositions of Goethe and Schiller, of Keller and Meyer, and so on – characteristic of the hopeless attempts to define something by means of that which it is not!

That a direct apprehension of essence is so unusual and difficult that to many it appears impossible may be once explained by the deeply rooted attitude of practical life, which more possesses and operates with objects than it contemplatively views them and penetrates into their peculiar being. But it is fully explained once again from the fact that many scientific disciplines – in contrast to those hitherto discussed – have *as a matter of principle* nothing to do with direct intuition of essences, and consequently produce in all who are devoted to them a profound disinclination toward any direct intuition of essences. Here, of course, Mathematics is to be named before all. It is the pride of mathematicians not to know – in its material essence – that of which they speak. I refer you to how David Hilbert introduces the numbers: "We conceive of a system of things, call them numbers, and designate them as a, b, c, ... We conceive of these numbers as having certain reciprocal relations, the description of which is done by the following axioms." "We conceive of a system of propositions which are to hold true of these things." Of the "what," the essence of these things, nothing is said. In fact, even the expression "thing" says too much. It must not be taken in the philosophical sense in which it designates a determinate categorial form; it only stands for the most general and absolutely contentless concept of something in general. Of this "something," then, all sorts of things are said – better, they are "ascribed" to it, e.g., $a + b = b + a$; and out of this and a number of other propositions – without touching upon the essence of objects – conclusively and cogently, in purely logical sequence, a system is constructed.

Departures from objects cannot be pushed further than is found here. An insight into their structure, and all *Evidenz* for the ultimate principles, is given up *as a matter of principle*. That insight which does have play here is a purely logical insight: – it is the *Evidenz*, let us say, for the fact that an A which is B must be C, if all B is C, an *Evidenz* which comes without the natures which stand back of the A, B, C being examined. The axioms which are presupposed [in number theory] are not themselves tested and verified as true. The only means of verification available in Mathematics, that of proof, is not at our disposal here. The axioms are suppositions, besides which other contrary axioms are possible upon which one can also attempt to construct self-consistent systems of propositions. Yet more! Not only has the mathematician no need, within his discipline, to verify the assumed axioms; he also does not need to understand their ultimate material content. What does "$a + b = b + a$" really mean? What is the sense of this proposition? The mathematician can decline the question. The possibility of sign commutation suffices him. Beyond this the information gotten from him is unsatisfactory for the most part. In fact, the proposition certainly does not refer to the spatial arrangement of signs on the paper. But it also cannot refer to the temporal order of psychical acts – not to the fact that it is indifferent whether I, or some subject or other, adds b to a or a to b. For it is a proposition which says nothing at all about subjects and their acts and the temporal course of those acts. Rather it states that it is indifferent whether a be added to b or b be added to a. But what is to be understood by "adding," since it is nothing spatial or temporal – *that* is now the problem, and a problem to which the mathematician can be indifferent, but upon which the philosopher, who must not stop at the signs but push on to the essence of that which the signs designate, must employ himself most intensively.

Or, take the law of association: $a + (b + c) = (a + b) + c$. This proposition surely has a sense, a sense of the most extreme importance, even; and it certainly does not, in the last analysis, have to do with the fact that the bracket signs can be written differently. The bracket does have a signification, and this signification must be fathomable. It certainly stands, as a sign, on a different level from "=" and "+". It signifies no relation or operation, but rather indicates the type and scope of relations and operations, as is also done by means of punctuation marks. But by means of *this* indication, or by means of *that*, now these, now those signs are taken together and marked off from the other; and the *signification* of the whole expression is modified accordingly. To understand just this modification of signification and its possibility is a problem which also may fall to the mathematician. That is the question about *sense*. Beside it stands the question about *being*, i.e., the problem of bringing to intuition, and, if possible, to the ultimate degree of insight, whether or not the postulate is correct; whether or not that which the proposition, "$a + b = b + a$," expresses can prove out valid and as grounded in the essence of numbers. Precisely such considerations lie especially remote from the mathematician. He formulates his postulates, and the postulates of different systems may be contradictory to each other. Perhaps he postulates, as an axiom, that through a point not on a given straight line one and only one straight line in the same plane can be drawn which does not cross the first-mentioned straight line. But he could also posit that, through the point not on the given straight line, several straight lines, or no such a straight line, can be drawn; and on these postulates also a system of consistent propositions may be founded. The mathematician as such must contend for the equal worth of all such systems. For him, there are only the postulates and the logically complete and consistent deductive consequents built thereon.

But the systems *are not* of equal worth. There in fact *are* such things as points and lines, even if they do not exist as real things in the world. And, in acts of a particular sort, we can bring these items to adequate intuition. But if we do that, then we *see* (*sehen wir ein*) that, in fact, through a point not on a given straight line, one straight line on the same plane can be drawn which does not cross the first-mentioned straight line, and that it is false that none such can be drawn. Thus, either in this latter postulate mentioned above the same terms mean something different than in the former, or it is a matter of a system of propositions which is built upon an *invalid* postulate, and which, as such, also is able to have a value: – in particular, a mathematical value. If one understands by "points" and "lines" things which have to satisfy such postulates, then there are no things such that the resulting axiom system could apply to them. The removal from all that one finds intuitively becomes crystal clear at this point.

This peculiarity of mathematics renders intelligible the peculiar character of those solely mathematical minds which have done certain great things within mathematics, but which have done more harm to philosophy than can be shortly said. They are of that type which only formulates postulates and carries out derivations therefrom. In this way they lose the sense for ultimate and absolute being. They have unlearned how to view, and can only prove. But philosophy has to do precisely with that for which they have no concern. It is therefore that a philosophy in the geometrical style (*more geometrico*) is, when taken literally, a flat self-contradiction. On the other hand, only from philosophy can mathematics receive its ultimate elucidation (*Aufklärung*). It was from philosophy that there first issued the investigation of the fundamental mathematical essences and the ultimate laws grounded in those essences. Also, philosophy can make completely intelligible the way in which mathematics is to proceed on from these elements only, by repeatedly leading it back to the intuitive essence-content from which it is so far removed. Here our first task must surely be to learn to see the problems once again, through the thicket of signs and rules which operate so admirably: to penetrate through to the material content. Concerning negative numbers, for example, most of us have genuinely thought only when young. *Then* we stood before something puzzling. *Now* these doubts have been put to rest: – but on quite a dubious basis, for the most part. Many today appear to have almost lost the consciousness that, while there indeed are numbers, the contrast between positive and negative numbers rests upon a postulate of technique, the justification of which is not easily seen into. This is similar to the way lawyers are about the postulates of civil rights.

If we bring ourselves to the point where, as philosophers, we must bring ourselves – through all signs, definitions and rules – to the facts themselves (*zu den Sachen selbst*), things will present themselves to us quite differently than is today believed. Permit me to show this my means of a simple example which is rather easy to take in. The division of numbers into ordinal and cardinal is generally accepted today. But people do not agree on which type of number, the ordinal or the cardinal, is the primitive, and on whether we may or may not designate one as more primitive than the other. If one takes the ordinal as primitive, Helmholtz and Kronecker are usually invoked for support. And it is very instructive, for our purposes, to go back to what these mathematicians actually said. Kronecker states that he finds in the ordinal the natural starting point for the development of the number concept. The ordinals present us with a supply of ordered designations which we can assign to a determinate group of objects. Suppose we have the series of letters, *a, b, c, d, e*. Now, in sequence, we designate them as first, second, third, fourth, and finally fifth. If we wish to designate the total of the ordinal numbers used, or the number of letters, we use the last of the ordinal numbers used in order to do it. But, now, it should be clear that Kronecker here introduces certain signs, not numbers. And he first introduces the ordinal signs, because he can then use the last of these signs for a designation of number. For the philosopher, *this* is where the problem first begins. How is it to be understood that the ordinal sign can at the same time indicate the number of all the designated things? What, after all, *is* the ordinal number, and what is the cardinal number? Let us now take a few steps on the road which leads to an elucidation of these concepts.

The question has been raised about the sense of numerical assertions. More precisely, the question is: *Of what are numbers predicated?* To this question very many diverse answers have been given. Let us look a little closer at some of these answers? One of them requires little consideration. That is Mill's view that number is asserted of the enumerated things. Were the number three really attributed to the enumerated things, as, for example the color red is attributed to them, then each of them would be three, just as each of them is red. So it has been said that the number is not asserted of the enumerated things, but of the totality, of the group or set, which is composed of the enumerated things. But we must also argue against that. Groups can have many sorts of properties, depending upon the objects which compose them. One group of trees can be next to another, or can be greater or smaller in size than another. But a group cannot be four or five. To be sure, a group can contain four or five objects. But then it is the *containing* of four objects which is predicated of the group, and not the *four*. A group which contains four objects is just as little itself four as a group containing only red objects is itself therefore red. Perhaps one may *assign* the number four to the group which has four elements; but one cannot *predicate* the number four of that group. And since the number cannot, as has been shown, even be predicated of the objects which the group contains, we find ourselves in a difficult position.

These difficulties have caused Frege to conceive of the numerical statement as an assertion made about a *concept* (*Begriffe*). "The Kaiser's coach is drawn by four horses" is to signify, then, that under the concept of *the horses which draw the Kaiser's coach* four objects fall. But, of course, no advantage is gained by this move. It is asserted of the concept that four objects fall under it, but the four is not asserted of *it*. A concept which subsumes four objects is just as little four as a concept which subsumes material objects is, therefore, itself material. I will not go into the many other attempts to solve this problem.

In such situations there is one question which, for philosophy, is obvious: – Is there not to be found in the very problem posed a certain pre-judgment? Doubtless there is in the case just discussed. The pre-judgment is already essentially contained in the way the problem is put. The subject of which the number is predicated is inquired after. But how, indeed, does one know that the number really is *predicated* of something? Can one presuppose that every element of our thinking must be predicable? Certainly not! We need only consider a simple example to see that. For example, we often say: "Only *A* is *B*." In the assertion there corresponds to the "only" an important element; but obviously it would be completely absurd to ask: "Of what is the 'only' predicated?" The "only" concerns the *A* in a certain manner; but it can neither be predicated of it, nor of any other thing whatever. The same is true of "All *A*'s are *B*," or "Some *A*'s are *B*," and so on. All categorial elements ["all," "some," etc] are impredicable. They simply give the range of objects with which the predication, the being-*B*, has to do. This also sheds light on number. Two things about it: – First, in and for itself it is impredicable. And, second, it presupposes predication, insofar as it determines the quantitative range of somewhats, the multiplicity of the somewhats, which are affected by a predication. A number does not answer the question, "How many?" But it does answer the question, "How many *A*'s are *B*?" For category theory, this point is of the very greatest importance. Insofar as numerical determinateness presupposes a predication upon certain things, it resides in a quite different sphere from, let us say, the category of causality. It resides in a sphere which we shall later come to know as that of the "state of affairs" (*Sachverhalt*). Moreover, from here on, further differentiations very easily yield themselves. For example, it is possible that the predication concerned has to do with each single object of the domain it determines, or only with these objects taken together. If we say that five trees are green, it is meant that each single tree is green. If, by contrast, we say that four horses suffice to draw the coach, then certainly *each* horse does not suffice. Such differences can be rendered intelligible only by the view of number here represented, according to which, as was said, numbers themselves are not predicable, but presuppose a predication upon certain things, the range of which the number then determines.

This must suffice for now as a determination of cardinal number (*Anzahl*). But then there is supposed to be yet another sort of number (*Zahlen*), the ordinal numbers. Let us take a closer look at them. The cardinal number turned out to be impredicable. By contrast, there appears at first glance to be no doubt about the predicability of the ordinal. Obviously it is affirmed, and, indeed, affirmed of a term of an ordered set. It appears to assign to this term its position within the set. It seems obvious that the ordinal is what determines the respective positions of elements in ordered sets. But that does not hold up, once we forsake words and signs, and turn to *the facts themselves*. What then is truly the case with the terms of the series and their positions? We have, first, the opening term, the first term of the series; and, corresponding to that term, there is the closing term, the last. Then there is a term which follows the first one, then one following the term following the first one, and so on. So the position of any term can be defined by referring back to the term which opens the series. Of a number, or of something numerical, nothing has yet been said. One does not show the contrary by pointing out that we have spoken of the "first" term. The "first" has exactly as little to do with "one" as the "last" has to do with "five" or "seven." And further, there is absolutely-nothing more in the series – no peculiarity of series terms as such, nothing numerical – which might be dragged out by us. The elements have their positions in the series, and these positions can be defined by the successor relation to the opening term. Nothing is said of number.

But if this is so, why those ordinal designations which, nonetheless, suggest numbers? Very simple! The position designations were rather complicated from the beginning. Already the *c* term must be designated as the term following the term following the first term. The complication finally becomes unbearable, and one has to invent a more convenient mode of designation. Now of course there are relations between the set and its terms, on the one hand, and the numbers (*Anzahlen*) – note well, the *numbers* – on the other hand. The series contains a number of terms, and the same goes for each part of the series. The term *c* is that term up to which the series contains three terms. Therefore we call it the third. Likewise, *d* is the fourth; and so we can coordinate to each term of the series such a designation, just because at each of its terms the series contains a determinate and always different number of terms.

But now consider the error occasioned by remaining at the level of signs. In addition to numbers – cardinal numbers, that is – there is said to be a second type of number, the ordinal number. Well, where are they then? Seek as long as you wish, they will not be found. There are numbers (*Anzahlen*) and designations of numbers. There are, further, ordinal designations, which, with the aid of cardinal numbers (*Kardinalzahlen*), can define the position of elements in ordered sets. But there are no ordinal *numbers*. Philosophy has possibly been flustered here because it blindly followed the sign-makings of the mathematicians, and thereby took words for facts. Is anyone so far gone as to wish to derive the cardinal numbers (*Anzahl*) from a mode of designation which, moreover, has the cardinal numbers as a presupposition? As to this mode of designation, one of course must not be misled into straightway equating the word-designation with the number-designation. In fact, the word-designation certainly does not always use the number: – the *first* is not the *once* (*einste*). Whether or not there is a linguistic system in which is expressed the fact that the opening term is at the same time that term up to which the series contains one term, I do not know. Also, the term following the first need not be designated with the aid of a number. We, indeed, say "zweite," but the Latin says "secundus." So not all ordinal designations are ordinal number-designations. Further investigation of this must, of course, be left to the linguist.

When we aspire to essence-analysis, we will naturally set out from words and their significations. It is no accident that Husserl's *Logische Untersuchungen* begins with an analysis of the concepts *word, expression, signification*, and so on. Right away it turns out that scarcely believable equivocations are dominant here, and especially in philosophical terminology. Husserl has exhibited fourteen different significations of the concept *representation*, and in so doing he has in no wise exhausted the equivocations in that concept – mostly undetected – which play a role in philosophy. It has been very unjustly objected that these signification differentiations are overly subtle. A minute and intrinsically obvious difference can lead to the subversion of a whole philosophical theory, if the great philosopher concerned has not paid attention to it. An instructive example of this is, precisely, the term "representation," or the term "concept," with its numerous and basically different significations.

But further – and this aspect we ourselves have just now worked out – the analysis of signification not only can lead to the making of distinctions, but also to the suppressing of unjustified distinctions. It is understandable that the young Phenomenology should at first have gazed in astonishment at the infinite richness of that which, so far, had been interpreted away or overlooked. But in its progress it will also have to do away with many things which have been falsely claimed as distinct realities (*Eigengebilder*) – an example of which seems to me to be the ordinal number.

Moreover, I no longer need to especially stress the fact that the essence-analysis which is required is in no wise exhausted by investigations of significations. Though we do begin with words and word-significations, that is only supposed to lead us to *the facts themselves*, which are to be illumined (*aufzuklären*). But direct access to the facts is also possible, without guidance through word-significations. Indeed, not only the 'already' intended (*Intendierte*), but new essences also, must be discovered and brought to view. To a certain degree, the step from Socrates to Plato is what is in question here. Socrates did signification analysis when, in the streets of Athens, he put his question: – "You talk of such and such. Now just what do you mean?" Here it is a question of clearing up the obscurities and contradictions of significations – a procedure which, moreover, really has nothing to do with definition, and certainly not with induction. By contrast, Plato does not start with words and significations. He aims at the *direct* view of the ideas (*Ideen*), the *unmediated* grasp of essences as such.

I have already indicated that essence analysis is no ultimate goal, but rather is a means. Of essences laws hold true, and these laws are incomparable with any fact or factual connection of which sense perception informs us. The laws in question hold of the essences as such, in virtue of their nature (*Wesen*). There is no accidentally-being-so in essences, but rather a necessarily-having-to-be-so, and an essentially-cannot-be-otherwise. That there *are* these laws is one of the most important things for philosophy and – if one thinks it out completely – for the world at large. To present them in their purity is, therefore, a significant task of philosophy. But one cannot deny that this task has not been executed. True, the *a priori* has always been acknowledged. Plato discovered it, and since then it has never disappeared from sight in the history of philosophy. But it has been misunderstood and restricted, even by those who have maintained it right; and there are two motifs which we must, above all others, protest: – that of the subjectification of the *a priori*, and that of the arbitrary restriction of it to a few realms, in spite of the fact that its governing influence extends absolutely everywhere.

We must first discuss the subjectification of the *a priori*. About one thing there has been constant agreement: *a priori* knowledge is not derived from experience. For us that results from earlier discussions, without saying anything further. Experience refers, as sense perception, to the singular, to the "that-right-there," and seeks to grasp it as *this*. The subject tries, as it were, to draw to itself what is about to be experienced. Sense perception, in fact, is essentially possible only from some point of view; and, for us men, this point of departure for perception must be in the proximity of the perceived. With the *a priori*, by contrast, we have to do with the viewing and the knowing of essences. But no sense perception is required in order to grasp essence. Here are involved intuitional acts of a wholly different sort, which can be realized at anytime, and wherever the representing subject may be. To take a quite simple and trivial example, I can now, in this moment, convince myself with complete certainty of the fact that orange lies qualitatively between red and yellow, if only I succeed in bringing to clear intuition for myself the corresponding natures (*Wesheiten*). I need not be referred to some sense perception, which would have to lead me to a place in the world where a case of orange, red, and yellow could be found. Because of this, not only – as is often said – does one need to perceive merely a single case in order to apprehend the *a priori* laws involved; in truth, one also does not need to perceive or "experience" the single case. One need perceive nothing at all. Pure imagination suffices. Wherever in the world we find ourselves, the doorway to the world of essences and their laws always stands open to us.

But right here at this undeniable point, the most harmful of misunderstandings have set in. What does not, as it were, enter into us from the outside by means of sense perception appears necessarily to be present 'on the inside.' So *a priori* knowledge is marked as a possession of the soul, as something innate – even though only virtually – to which the subject need only turn its glance in order to become conscious of it. According to this particular picture of human knowledge, which has been so effective historically, all men are ultimately equal in their "knowledge-holdings," and are distinguished only by the manner in which they improve upon the common supply. Many live and struggle along without the slightest suspicion of their riches. But if a piece of *a priori* knowledge is once drawn to light, then insight into it can be avoided by no one. Vis-à-vis such knowledge there is discovery, but never deception and error. For this point of view, the pedagogical ideal is the Platonic Socrates, as understood by the philosophy of the Enlightenment (*Aufklärungsphilosophie*), who unlocked mathematical truths in the slave merely by questioning, to which end only the awakening of memories was required.

One corollary of this view is the doctrine of *consensus omnium* as the indubitable guarantee for the highest axioms of knowledge. A further corollary of it is the talk of *a priori* knowledge as necessities of our thought, as an emanation of having-to-think-so and of not-being-able-to-think-otherwise. But all of this is fundamentally false and wrong; and, against such views, Empiricism has had an easy go of it. *A priori* connections obtain indifferently of whether or not all, many, or none whatsoever of men or other subjects acknowledge them. But that is characteristic of all truth whatsoever, and not of *a priori* truths only. Even the most highly empirical of truths, e.g. that to some man at some time a piece of sugar tastes sweet, has general validity in that sense.

We must totally reject the idea of thought-necessity being the essential earmark of the *a priori*. If I ask myself which was earlier, the Thirty-year War or the Seven-year War, then I become aware of a necessity to think of the first as earlier; and yet what we have here is *empirical* knowledge. On the other hand, whoever has negated an *a priori* connection, has denied the principle of contradiction, or did not regard as true the principle of the univocal determination of all events, apparently noticed no thought necessity in these.

What then do all of these Psychologistic distortions mean? Certainly necessity has a role to play in the *a priori*, but the necessity is not one of thought. Rather, it is a necessity of being. Just consider these situations. One object lies somewhere in space beside another. That is an accidental existence – accidental in the sense that the essence of each object permits it to be removed from the other. But by contrast: The straight line is the shortest line of connection between two points. Here it makes no sense to say that matters could also be otherwise. It is grounded in the nature of the straight line as straight to be the shortest line of connection. Here is a necessary-being-so. Hence, this is the essential point: *States of affairs (Sachverhalte) are a priori*, in that the predication in them – the being-*B*, let us say – is required by the nature of the *A*; that is, in that the predication is necessarily grounded in that nature. But "states of affairs" obtain (*bestehen*) indifferently of what consciousness apprehends them, and of whether they are apprehended by any consciousness at all. In and for itself, the *a priori* has not even the least thing to do with thinking and knowing. That admits of clear insight. But if one has insight into (*eingesehen*) it, then one can also avoid the false questions (*Scheinprobleme*) which have arisen in connection with the *a priori*, and which have led to the most amazing constructions in the history of philosophy. *A priori* connections find an application, for example, in the events of nature. If these connections are conceived of as thought-laws, then the question of how this application is possible arises. How does it happen that nature complies with the laws of our thought? Are we to assume here an enigmatic, pre-established harmony? Or are we perhaps to say that nature can lay no claim to a peculiar and intrinsic being of its own? That it is to be in some way thought of as being functionally dependent upon thinking and positing acts? The reason why nature should accommodate itself to the laws of our thought cannot be given to our insight. But, in truth, our problem has nothing to do with laws of thought. Rather, here we have to do with the fact that such and such a property or event is grounded in the nature of something. Is it then to be wondered at if all things which share this nature are subject to the same predication? Let us speak concretely and as simply as possible. If it is grounded in the essence of change to stand in a univocal dependence upon temporally previous events – not, if we must *think* this, but if, rather, this must *be* – then is it to be wondered as if the same is true of every particular, concrete change in the world? That it should be otherwise is inconceivable, it seems to me. Or, better said, it is *evident* that it could not be otherwise.

When one has fixed upon the peculiar character of *a priori* connections as such – as forms of 'states of affairs,' not as forms of thinking – then, and only then, can there be raised, as a second problem, the question of how these 'states of affairs' genuinely come to givenness, of how they are thought of or, better, known. The immediate *Evidenz* of the *a priori* has been spoken of as opposed to the non-*Evidenz* of the empirical. But such an opposition is not tenable. What is meant by it is, indeed, quite clear. That that which stands over against me in the sense world as obtaining (*bestehend*) and existing (*existierend*) really obtains and exists: – for *this*, acts of perception themselves do indeed provide a basis, but no irrefutable guarantee. The possibility that the houses and trees which I percieve do not exist always remains open in the very face of this perceiving. An ultimate and absolute *Evidenz* is not to be found here. Were it therefore said that judgments about the real existence of physical things cannot lay claim to ultimate *Evidenz*, that would be quite correct. But this is also said, quite generally, of *empirical* judgments; and there one goes wrong. If we assume that the perception of the house, of which I just spoke, is an illusion, and that the perceived house therefore does not exist, it of course by that very fact remains that I do have such a perception, even though illusory. How otherwise could we speak of an illusion at all? In contrast to the judgment, "There stands a house," the judgment, "I see a house," possesses ultimate, irrefutable *Evidenz*. But it is obviously an empirical judgment. That I see a house certainly is not grounded in the nature of the ego. So the lack of *Evidenz* is not an earmark of empirical knowledge. But it is correct to say that all *a priori* knowledge is without exception capable of irrefutable *Evidenz*: that is, it is capable of having its content intuitively given in the strongest sense. What is grounded in the essence of objects can be brought to ultimate givenness in essence intuition. Certainly there is *a priori* knowledge which cannot be known in isolation, but rather requires derivation from other *a priori* knowledge. But this also finally leads one back to ultimate connections which are insightful (*einsichtige*) by themselves. It certainly is not to be blindly accepted, nor built upon a fabulous *consensus omnium* or vague necessities of thought. Nothing lies further from phenomenology than that. This derivative knowledge must rather be brought to luminosity, to the highest sort of intuitive givenness; and we precisely stress that for this purpose a special effort and methodology are required. However, with the utmost rigor we must contest the attempt to further justify the ultimate *a priori* connections: to show their right by reference to something else. We contest the attempt to ground the absolutely clear and insightful sources of knowledge by reference to brute, uninsightful facts, which themselves can be grounded only through those sources. Here, it seems to me, is again validated what we earlier said about the anxiety over facing up to ultimate connections themselves, about the blind grasping after something else to support them: – as if such an attempt at grounding, if it is not to be quite arbitrary, did not also have to finally come to rest on connections given only through underivative insight.

Up to now I have been dealing with the subjectification of the *a priori*. No less an evil is what I have previously called the "impoverishment" of the *a priori*. There are few philosophers who have not in some way acknowledged the fact of the *a priori*; but there are none but what have in some way reduced it to a small province of its actual kingdom. Hume enumerates a few relations of ideas. They *are*, surely, *a priori* connections. But why he restricted such connections to *relations*, and then only to some few of them, is not clear. And, finally, the restrictiveness with which Kant conceived of the *a priori* could not but become disastrous for subsequent philosophy.

In truth, the realm of the *a priori* is incalculably large. All objects known have their "what," their "essence"; and of all essences there hold essence-laws. All restriction, and all reason for restriction, of the *a priori* to the, in some sense, 'formal' is lacking. *A priori* laws also hold true of the material – in fact, of the sensible, of tones and colors. With that there opens up for investigation an area so large and rich that yet today we cannot see its boundaries. Allow me to mention only a few things from it.

Our psychology is so proud of being *empirical* psychology. The result is that it neglects the vast stock of knowledge which is grounded in the essence of experience, in the essence of perceiving and representing, of judging feeling, willing, and so on. When it does bump into essence-laws, they are misinterpreted as empirical laws. I mention to you David Hume as a classical example of this. At the beginning of his main work he speaks of impressions (*Wahrnehmung*) and ideas (*Vorstellung*), and says that to each impression there corresponds an idea of the same object. This Hume takes as one cornerstone of his philosophy. But how are we to understand this proposition? Does it mean that in each consciousness in which the impression of an object is realized an idea of that same object must also be realized? That would be a very dubious claim. We certainly have impressions of many things without any idea of them – things of which perhaps no one at all has ever had idea. In any case, we certainly have no reason to maintain the contrary. But how then did Hume come to set such a proposition right at the head of his discussions? Where does the proposition get that power to convince which it certainly has? Well, of course it is correct to say that to every impression there corresponds an idea, and conversely – in the sense, say, that to any straight line there corresponds a circle of which it is the radius. It is here no question of real existence, of being realized in empirical consciousness, but rather is one of an ideal correlation. And so, likewise, the connection which Hume contends is empirical is in truth *a priori*, grounded in the nature of impressions and ideas. The same goes for the second proposition which forms a foundation of Hume's epistemology, *viz.*, that in its elements every idea presupposes an earlier impression of the same subject, and that we therefore can have an idea only of something the elements of which have already been perceived by us. This proposition presents serious difficulties, but from the outset one is certain that it cannot be an empirical proposition. How could we know whether the new-born child has impressions first, or ideas? One must not say: "*Obviously* he must first have impressions before he can have ideas." Right where claims to such 'obviousness' are raised is where we must lay hold. These claims always indicate essence connections which are begging for scientific elucidation.

Up to here we have dealt with peripheral experiences, but in the deeper psychic levels things are not otherwise. Above all, just think of the motivation connections which we follow with such clarity both in practical life and in the historical disciplines. We *understand* (*verstehen*) that out of this or that disposition, out of this experience, this or that action could arise or must arise. It is not as if we have a certain number of times had the experience that men upon certain occasions have acted with this or that intention, and now we say: "Probably this man will act in the same way." Rather we just understand that things are and must be so. We understand it from the motive. But bare empirical fact never yields *understanding*. The historian who sympathetically follows a motivation connection, the psychiatrist who follows out the process of an illness: – they *understand*. Even when the development in question first confronted them, they were guided by essence connections. And this is not voided by the fact they perhaps never have, or that they even *could* not have, formulated the essence connections involved. Here lies the connection between psychology and history, which is so often spoken of: a connection which empirical psychology does not touch upon, but which, rather, is the subject matter of *a priori* psychology, the beginning of which is an affair of the future. Empirical psychology is in no wise independent of the *a priori*. The laws grounded in the nature of perception and representation, thought and judgment, are constantly presupposed, when the empirical course of these events in consciousness is investigated.

Today psychology concludes these laws under the obscure idea of the natural life. They belong to that region of dreary truisms with which it no longer bothers. And yet a thoroughly worked out theory of psychic essences could have a significance for empirical psychology similar to that which geometry possesses for natural science. Just consider the laws of association. How their true sense has been misunderstood! In fact, their formulation is usually a flat falsehood. It is not correct to say that, when I have at the same time perceived A and B, and now represent A, a tendency exists also to represent B. I must have perceived A and B together in a phenomenal unity – even if it is only the loosest of relations – in order for that distinct tendency to arise. Where two objects appear to us *as related*, an association sets in. Further, if the relation is one which is grounded in ideas (*Ideen*) themselves, e.g., similarity or contrast, then not even such a previous appearance is necessary. The representation of an A, already as such, leads to the representation of the similar or contrasting B, without my ever needing to have perceived A and B together at any time. It is wholly arbitrary to base association on a certain few relations, as today is done, for example, with spatial or temporal contiguity or similarity. Any relation at all is capable of setting up associations. But above all it must be said that in association we have to do, not with empirically collocated facts, but rather with rational (*verstehbare*) connections, grounded in the nature of things. To be sure, here we have a new sort of essential connection: not one of necessity, but one of possibility. It is intelligible that the representation of an A *can* lead to the representation of a B similar to it, not that it *must* so lead. Motivation connections likewise are largely those which involve an essentially-can-be-so, not an essentially-must-be-so.

As there is required a theory of psychic essence, so also a theory of natural essence is required. To get that theory one certainly has to give up the peculiar attitude of the natural sciences, an attitude which in fact follows after quite determinate purposes and goals; and the difficulty of this is so great that we are apt to sink under it. But here also we must succeed in grasping the phenomena purely, in working out its essence without preconceptions and prejudgments: – the essence of color, extension and matter, light and dark, tones, and so on. We must also investigate the constitution of the phenomenal thing, purely in itself and according to its essential structure. In that structure, color, for example, certainly plays another role than does extension or matter. Everywhere it is essence laws that are in question. Existence is never posited.

In all of this we are not working against science. Rather we are creating the basis upon which its structure can be *understood for the first time*. But I can go no further into this. The first effort of phenomenology has been to trace out the most diverse of the domains of essence relations – psychology and aesthetics, ethics and law, etc. Everywhere new domains of such relations open up to us.

But let us look away from the new problems. From the standpoint of essence inspection, new light is thrown upon the old problems supplied by the history of philosophy, especially the "problem of knowledge." What sense is there in defining knowledge, reinterpreting it, reducing it, even removing the very possibility of it, in order then to be able to replace it with something which it just is not. We all do speak of knowing (*Erkennen*), and we mean something by our talk. If this meaning is too indeterminate, then we can orient ourselves by some case where knowing is present: a certain and indubitable knowing, and the most uncomplicated and trivial, is the very best. Consider the case where we know ourselves to be filled with joy, or where we know we are seeing a red thing, or where we know that tone and color are different, or other such things. Here it is not a matter of the singular case of knowing, and of its existence; but in the singular we view, as always, the "What," the nature or essence of knowing, which consists in an accepting or receiving, in a making one's own something presenting itself. To this essence we must go. It we must investigate. But we must not substitute for it something other. For example, we must not say that knowing is really defining or positing (*Setzen*) or some other such thing. We must not do it because, while colors can indeed be 'reduced' to waves, essences cannot be reduced to other essences. Indeed, there *are* such things as acts of positing and defining, and their essence also must be illumined. There is the judgment – specifically, the assertion – as a spontaneous, discrete, positings act. Then there are certain assertions which prove out as positings of determinate kinds. Thus we have assertions of the form, *A is B*. But by realizing in ourselves an act of defining, and bringing its essence near to us, we see very clearly that its essence is not identical with the essence of knowing. In fact, we see that every definition essentially refers back to a knowing, from which alone it can receive its justification and verification. Should one say that *man* can actualize no knowledge acts, but only acts of definition, that would be a bold contention, which is certainly untenable; but it would not be intrinsically absurd. However, if one said that knowledge is in truth definition, that would be just like saying that tones are really colors.

Certainly essence analysis is not exhausted in distinguishing what must not be confused with the subject of investigation. Rather it only starts at that point. And this is what I really wish to impress upon you as vigorously as possible. If in phenomenology we want to break with theories and constructions, and if we strive to return to 'the facts themselves,' to pure, unobscured intuition of essences, that does not mean that intuition is thought of as a sudden inspiration and illumination. Today I have continuously stressed the fact that a peculiar and immense effort is required in order to surmount the distance which naturally separates us from objects and to attain to clear apprehension of them. It is precisely in this respect that we speak of phenomenological *method*. Here there is a gradual approximation to the object, as well as all of the possibilities of deception which come with any form of knowing. The intuition of essence is also something which requires to be worked out; and this 'work' stands under the model sketched by Plato in the *Phaedrus*, that of the soul having to *rise up*, with its team, to heaven in order to view the ideas (*Ideen*).

At the moment when, in place of momentary brainstorms, there sets in the laborious effort at illumination, *there* philosophical work is taken out of the hands of individuals and laid in the hands of ongoing generations of relief workers. To future generations it will be just as unintelligible that an individual should project a philosophy as today it is that an individual should project natural science. When continuity within philosophical work is attained, then that developmental process within world history, in which one science after another peeled off from philosophy, will be realized within philosophy itself. Philosophy will become a rigorous science – not in that it imitates other rigorous sciences, but rather in that it senses the fact that its problems require a peculiar procedure, the working out of which is the task of the centuries.

Translator's Note

1 Reinach (1883–1917) was perhaps Edmund Husserl's first real co-worker in the development of the phenomenological movement. He came to Göttingen in 1905 to study with Husserl, and later joined him there as a teacher and co-editor of the *Jahrbuch für Philosophie und phänomenologische Forschung*. Husserl said of him that "he was among the first who could understand, creatively and perfectly, the peculiar meaning of the phenomenological method and could view in its entire philosophical range." On one occasion he even remarked that "It was really Reinach who introduced me to my *Logische Untersuchungen*, and in an excellent way." Much later, Hedwig Conrad-Martius, another early student of Husserl's, stated that "Adolf Reinach was the phenomenologist among the phenomenologists: – the phenomenologist in itself and as such." Although Husserl was clearly the originator and principal sustainer of the phenomenological movement, Reinach's clear and careful thought and statement makes him the best introduction to this line of thought. All of which must not be taken to mean that his views *precisely* coincide with the views of Husserl or any other phenomenologist.

The lecture, "Über Phänomenologie," which is here translated into English, was read in Marburg during January of 1914. It was first published in Reinach's *Gesammelte Schriften* (Halle, 1921), and was later published separately under the title *Was ist Phänomenologie?* (München, 1951). Translation and publication are by permission of the Reinach heirs and Kösel-Verlag, München.

Part IV

MAX SCHELER
Phenomenology of the Person

MAX SCHELER (1874–1928)

Introduction

Max Scheler was born in Munich on 22 August 1874. His father was Lutheran, his mother orthodox Jewish, but Scheler himself converted to Catholicism in his teenage years, although he became less orthodox during his life, and in 1926, in the Preface to the Third Edition of his chief work, *Formalism in Ethics*, he wrote that he could no longer call himself a theist in the usual sense. He first studied medicine in Munich and Berlin, but in 1895 was attracted to the lectures in philosophy and sociology given by Wilhelm Dilthey and Georg Simmel. He then moved to Jena to study with Rudolf Eucken (1846–1926), an extraordinarily influential writer (awarded the Nobel Prize for Literature in 1908), who argued for the independent value of religion and the spiritual life, and the value of studying man's place in nature. Eucken introduced Scheler to the writings of St Augustine. Scheler was awarded his doctorate from Jena in 1897 for a study of the relations between logical and ethical principles, and completed his *Habilitation* thesis there in 1899 for a study of the transcendental and the psychological methods in philosophy (*The Transcendental and the Psychological Method*).

Scheler lectured as *Privatdozent* at the University of Jena from 1900 to 1906, and was interested in logic and in the dominant neo-Kantian tradition of philosophy. In 1901 he met Husserl for the first time in Halle, shortly before the publication of the *Logical Investigations*, and, in conversation, was impressed by Husserl's concept of categorial intuition (as developed in the Sixth Investigation) which he saw as similar to the wider notion of intuition he himself was proposing in critique of Kant. Although Scheler would later criticise Husserl for the excessive Platonism of the *Investigations*, nevertheless he embraced his notion of intuition of essences, and in his Preface to *Formalism in Ethics* (*Der Formalismus in der Ethik*, 1916), Scheler wrote: "I owe to the significant works of Edmund Husserl the methodological consciousness of the unity and sense of the phenomenological attitude." As he would write in the Preface to the First Edition of *On the Eternal in Man* (*Vom Ewigen in Menschen*, 1921): "Phenomenological philosophy is one which undertakes to look on the essential fundamentals of all existence with rinsed eyes, and redeem the bills of exchange which an over-complex civilization has drawn on them in terms of symbol upon symbol." For Scheler, something can be self-given when it is no longer given through any kind of symbol: "phenomenological philosophy is a continual *desymbolization of the world*" ("Phenomenology and the Theory of Cognition", 1913).

With a recommendation from Husserl, Scheler transferred to the University of Munich in 1907, becoming Theodor Lipps' assistant. Scheler was an active participant in the phenomenological circle around Lipps, which included Johannes Daubert,

Moritz Geiger, Theodor Conrad, Dietrich von Hildebrand and Alexander Pfänder. Due to personal matters, including his very public divorce, he was forced to resign from his position at Munich in 1910. Husserl was able to provide him with lectures at Göttingen. In these lectures, Scheler explicitly repudiated Husserl's conception of philosophy as a rigorous science. In 1913 Husserl appointed him as one of the editors of the new *Yearbook for Philosophy and Phenomenological Research*, but Scheler did not approve of Husserl's turn towards a Fichtean transcendental idealism, although he continued to maintain that phenomenology sought to achieve self-evident knowledge of essences. Scheler argued that the sphere of a priori essential knowledge extended beyond the purely formal and rational domains to include the essential forms of cultural and spiritual life (love, hate, sympathy, resentment and so on).

Without a university position, Scheler moved to Berlin with his wife and began to attempt to make a living as a writer and occasional lecturer. He became very productive, writing his famous essay *On Ressentiment and Moral Value Judgement* (*Über Ressentiment und moralisches Werturteil*) in 1912. The first part of his major treatise, *Formalism in Ethics and the Material Ethics of Value* appeared along with Husserl's *Ideas* I in the first volume of the *Yearbook* in 1913, the second part appearing in 1916. This work argued against Kantian formalism as a distortion of the true meaning of ethics, and as a falsification of human nature. In contrast Scheler argued for the objectivity of values (he acknowledged that G. E. Moore defended a similar position), which are encountered as the intentional objects of feelings (*Wertfühlen*). We apprehend values in feeling in exactly the same way as we apprehend colours in perception. The following year he published *On Phenomenology and the Theory of Sympathy* (*Zur Phänomenologie und Theorie der Sympathiegefühle*, 1914). Scheler expressed his relation to Husserl and phenomenology in several writings, including *German Philosophy Today* (*Die Deutsche Philosophie der Gegenwart*, 1922). In 1913 he wrote an important essay on phenomenology, "Phenomenology and the Theory of Knowledge" intended for publication in a philosophy journal that was suspended due to the outbreak of war. During the First World War, Scheler was called up, but discharged because of eye problems. Having married again, to provide an income for his family, he wrote a huge number of popular writings, including patriotic pamphlets analysing the nature of what he saw as the world's hatred against Germany (*The Causes of Germanophobia*, 1917), and suggesting the kind of moral attitude needed in times of spiritual disintegration. In 1919 he was appointed to a special professorship of philosophy and sociology at the University of Cologne, where he remained until 1928, when he was appointed to the University of Frankfurt, where he had just begun teaching when he died following a stroke on 19 May 1928. After 1922 he again abandoned Catholicism and, in the late 1920s, he actively opposed both the emerging Nazism as well as Marxism. His work was suppressed during the Nazi period. The complete edition of his works began in 1954.

Scheler was a prolific and eclectic author, amassing eleven books and a considerable number of articles by the time of his death, writing on ethics, metaphysics, sociology, politics, religion, anthropology and epistemology. He offered analyses of the nature of culture and critiques of nationalism, capitalism, relativism and moral bankruptcy, as well as an analysis of pacifism. He was also a flamboyant personality, a remarkable orator and popular lecturer, who drew large crowds, and was, in the decade after the First World War, the best known philosopher in Germany. He

MAX SCHELER (1874–1928)

decisively influenced Edith Stein and Martin Heidegger, and had an important influ-ence on Merleau-Ponty. Like Husserl, he was a dynamic thinker who constantly changed direction, announced new projects, then often left them uncompleted. He championed the notion of phenomenology as an *attitude* rather than a method, a *moral attitude* of radical honesty – a return to living intuition – specifically, an 'atti-tude of spiritual seeing' (as he calls it in his essay "Phenomenology and the Theory of Cognition", written in 1913) in 'vital and most immediate contact with the world itself'. He was a realist who argued for the independent objectivity of values inter-connected in precise ways. Reality is characterised by a quality of resistance, whereby it cannot be encompassed by the intentional act relating to it. He combined an interest in exact and systematic philosophising with a recognition of the specific existential and human situation.

Scheler emphasised the importance of concrete lived experience as the experi-ence of the *whole* person entering into acts, focusing on matters such as the role of the emotions, and the need to sympathise with others, as opposed to the will to domination. For Scheler, the phenomenologist attends to the personal way of viewing things and hence must purify his own heart before he can attend properly to intuiting things (he acknowledged the influence of Augustine). As he put it, self-evidence may also be at the same time the most individually personal evidence. It may be that certain objective values are accessible to only one person in a particular historical setting (e.g. Socrates articulating a genuine value not understood by his contemporaries).

Because of Scheler's interest in ethical matters, he was particularly conscious of the importance of the *person*, which he felt had been neglected both in Kant and in Husserlian phenomenology. For Scheler, the sciences engage only aspects of the mind, whereas philosophy requires the whole person. To be a person is not the same as to be a self (and ego) or to have a soul. The person is revealed in acts but in such a way that the whole person is in each act and yet the person is not exhausted in the act or even in the sum of all of his or her acts. Scheler also developed both the notions of the need for a phenomenology of the natural world in which we live, the human environment, and the manner of our embodiment in it and the individual world correlated with each of us, in parallel with Husserl, and placing a rather differ-ent emphasis on the notion of the reduction. In his later writings Scheler moved away from phenomenology to write on issues of anthropology and spirituality, but con-tinued to agree with Husserl's critique of a philosophical attitude founded on mod-ern science, which for him could be only a kind of *Weltanschauung*, as he argues in *On the Eternal in Man*.

Our reading is drawn from Scheler's key work, *Formalism in Ethics*, where he dis-cusses the concept of the person beginning with a critique of the Kantian conception of the person as a rational being, a purely logical subject of rational acts, and hence as anonymous instead of uniquely individual. Scheler wants to emphasise that the person must be understood as a concrete, individual, self-sufficient entity (as dis-tinct from the ego), a foundational source of intentional acts, but in such a way that the person *as a whole* is involved in each of the acts, permeating that act with a unique character. Person is correlated with *world*, there is an individual world for each person. Scheler goes on to give a very interesting account of his understanding of the nature of human embodiment in the world. The person is not constituted through temporal connection between successive stages, but 'lives into' time. Nor is

201

a person the product of a transcendental ego. Embodiment is a mode of experiencing the world, but there are a variety of modes of givenness – being sad is in a different relation to the body than being hungry, in that hunger has a certain bodily relatedness and location which is not the case with the experienced sadness.

Further reading

Scheler, Max. *Formalism in Ethics and Non-Formal Ethics of Values. A New Attempt Toward A Foundation of An Ethical Personalism*, trans. Manfred S. Frings and Roger L. Funk. Evanston, IL: Northwestern University Press, 1973.

Scheler, Max. *Gesammelte Werke*, 16 Vols. Bonn: Bouvier, 1998.

Scheler, Max. *Man's Place in Nature*, trans. H. Meyeroff. Boston, MA: Beacon Press, 1961.

Scheler, Max. *On the Eternal in Man*, trans. Bernard Noble. London: SCM Press, 1960.

Scheler, Max. *Philosophical Perspectives*, trans. Oscar Haac. Boston, MA: Beacon Press, 1958.

Scheler, Max. *Problems of a Sociology of Knowledge*, trans. Manfred S. Frings, ed. and Introduction by Kenneth W. Stikkers. London: Routledge & Kegan Paul, 1980.

Scheler, Max. *Ressentiment*, trans. William W. Holdheim. Second Edition, Introduction by Manfred S. Frings. Milwaukee, WI: Marquette University Press, 1994.

Scheler, Max. *Selected Philosophical Writings*, trans. David R. Lachterman. Evanston, IL: Northwestern University Press, 1973.

Scheler, Max. *The Nature of Sympathy*, trans. Peter Heath. New Haven, CT: Yale University Press, 1954.

Barber, Michael. *Guardian of Dialogue: Max Scheler's Phenomenology, Sociology of Knowledge, and Philosophy of Love*. Lewisburg, PA: Bucknell University Press, 1993.

Bershshady, Harold. *Max Scheler on Feeling, Knowing and Valuing*. Chicago, IL: University of Chicago Press, 1992.

Blosser, Philip. *Scheler's Critique of Kant's Ethics*. Athens: Ohio University Press, 1995.

Frings, Max. *Max Scheler: A Concise Introduction into the World of a Great Thinker*. Pittsburgh, PA: Duquesne University Press, 1965.

Frings, Manfred S. "Max Scheler. Rarely Seen Complexities of Phenomenology", in J. F. Smith, Ed. *Phenomenology in Perspective*. Den Haag: Nijhoff, 1970, pp. 32–53.

Frings, Manfred S. "Husserl and Scheler: Two Views on Inter-Subjectivity", *The Journal of the British Society for Phenomenology* 9 (1978), pp. 143–149.

Spader, Peter H. "Phenomenology and the Claiming of Essences", *Husserl Studies* 11 (1994/95), pp. 169–199.

Staude, John Raphael. *Max Scheler: An Intellectual Portrait*. New York: Free Press, 1967.

1

THE BEING OF THE PERSON

a. Person and act

Neither the being nor the problem of the "*person*" would exist if there were beings (whose natural organization we set aside in the reduction) endowed *only with knowing* (as thought and intuition) and those acts belonging to this (specifically theoretical) sphere. (Let us call such beings purely rational beings.) Of course these beings would still be (logical) subjects that execute rational acts: but they would not be "persons." Nor would they be persons if they had both inner and outer perception and often dealt with knowledge of the soul and nature, that is, even if they found an object "ego" in themselves and others and could perfectly observe, describe, and explicate experiences of "the ego" as well as all individual egos. The same would hold for beings whose entire contents were given only as projects of willing. They would be (logical) subjects of a willing, but not persons. For the person is precisely that unity which exists for acts of all possible *essential differences* insofar as these acts are thought to be executed.[1] Hence, by saying that it belongs to the nature of the differences of acts to be in a *person* and *only* in a person, we imply that the *different logical subjects* of essentially different acts (which are different only as otherwise identical subjects of such act-differences) can only *be in a form of unity* insofar as we reflect on the possible "being" of these subjects and not merely on their nature.

We can now enunciate the essential definition in the above sense: *the person is the concrete and essential unity of being of acts of different essences* which in itself (and therefore not πρὸς ἡμᾶς) precedes all essential act-differences (especially the difference between inner and outer perception, inner and outer willing, inner and outer feeling, loving and hating, etc.). *The being of the person is therefore the "foundation" of all essentially different acts.*

But all of this depends on a correct understanding of the relation which we call foundation.

Above all, it must be made clear that in *all* investigations of acts made in pure phenomenology we are concerned with *genuine intuitive essences*, never with empirical abstractions, which always presuppose the intuition of such essences in that these essences delineate the possible scope of the inductive abstraction of possible "common characteristics." Nevertheless in all act-investigations we are

M. Scheler, *Formalism in Ethics and Non-Formal Ethics of Values*, 1973, trans. Manfred Frings and Roger L. Funk, pp. 382–415. Evanston: Northwestern University Press.

also concerned with *abstract intuitive essences.*[2] These are "abstract," not because they have been "abstracted," but because they require supplementation insofar as they are to *be*. As opposed to abstract essences, *concrete essences* are a second kind of genuine intuitive essences.[3] If an act-essence is to be concrete, its full intuitable givenness *presupposes* a reference to the essence of the *person*, who is the executor of acts.[4]

From this it clearly follows that the person can never be reduced to the X of a mere "point of departure" of acts or to some kind of mere "interconnective complex" or network of acts, as a form of the so-called actualistic theories which conceives of the being of the person in terms of his doings (*ex operari sequitur esse*) would have it. The person is not an empty "point of departure" of acts; he is, rather, a concrete being. Unless we keep this in mind, all of our talk about acts can never catch the fully adequate essence of any act, but only an abstract essence. Abstract act-essences concretize into concrete act-essences only by belonging to the essence of this or that individual person. Therefore a concrete act can never be fully and adequately comprehended without the antecedent intending of the essence of the person. Any "interconnective complex" will remain a mere complex of abstract act-essences if the person "himself" in whom such an interconnective complex exists is not given.[5] Of course the actualistic theory is correct to maintain that the person is not a "thing" or a "substance" which executes acts in the sense of a substance-causality. For such "things" could in fact be randomly obliterated or exchanged, if there is a multiplicity (one thinks of Kant's picture of electric spheres, which are dynamically unified), with no change at all in immediate experience. In addition, everyone would carry the same "substance" with him, which – since *every* kind of manifold, e.g., time, space, number, plurality, would be missing – could not yield differences between one and the other.[6] The conclusion that the person must be only an "interconnective complex" of acts (even if only the intentional interconnection of meaning) is quite false.[7] Surely the person *is* and experiences himself only as a being that *executes acts*, and he is in no sense "behind" or "above" acts, or something standing "above" the execution and processes of acts, like a point at rest. For all of this is a picture taken from a spatio-temporal sphere; and it stands to reason that this does not hold for the relation between *person* and *acts*. This picture always leads to a substantialization of the person.[8] But the *whole person* is contained in *every* fully concrete act, and the whole person "*varies*" in and through every act – without being exhausted in his being in any of these acts, and without "changing" like a thing in time. But this concept of "variation" as a pure "becoming different" implies no time that makes change possible, nor does it imply a fortiori any thinglike changes. Nor is anything given here of a "succession" in this becoming different (we can comprehend succession without comprehending a change and without comprehending a thinglike arrangement of a given material, e.g., succession in the phenomenon of "oscillation"). And for this very reason there is *no* necessity for an *enduring being* that subsists in this succession in order to safeguard the "identity of the individual person." Identity lies solely in the qualitative direction of this pure becoming different. In trying to bring this most hidden of all phenomena to givenness, we can guide the reader to the direction of the phenomenon only by way of images. Thus we can say that the person lives *into* time and executes his acts into time in becoming different. But the person does not live within phenomenal time, which is immediately given in the flow of inwardly perceived psychic processes, nor does he live in the objective time of physics. In the latter there is nothing like fast and slow, endurance (which figures here only as a limiting case of succession),[9] or the phenomenal time dimensions of present, past, and future, because the past and future points of phenomenal time are treated "as" possible points of the present. Because the person lives his existence precisely in the *experiencing* of his possible *experiences*, it makes no sense to try to grasp the person in past lived experiences. As long as we look only at the so-called experiences and not at their *being* experienced, the person remains completely transcendent. But every experiencing, or, as we can also say, every *concrete act*, contains all act-essences that can be distinguished in phenomenological investigations. It contains them according to a priori orders of foundation, which are established by the results concerning act-founding. Therefore every concrete act always contains inner and outer perception, lived-body consciousness, loving and hating, feeling and preferring, willing and not willing, judging, remembering, representing, etc. All these divisions, necessary as they are, yield only abstract traits of the concrete act of the person – if we are looking at the person. The concrete act of the person can be understood as a mere sum or a mere construct of such abstract actessences no more than the person can be understood as a mere interconnective complex of acts. Rather, it is the person himself, living in each of his acts, who permeates every act with his peculiar character. No knowledge of the nature of love, for instance, or of the nature of judgment, can bring us one step nearer to the knowledge of how person *A* loves or judges person *B*; nor can a reference to the contents (values, states of affairs) given in each of these acts furnish this knowledge. But, on the other hand, a glance at the person himself and his essence immediately yields a peculiarity for every act that we know him to execute, and the knowledge of his "world" yields a peculiarity for the contents of his acts.

b. The being of the person is never an object. The psychophysical indifference of the person and his acts. The relation of the person to "consciousness"

The "ego," as we have shown, is an object in every sense of the term: egoness is an object of formless intuition, and the individual ego an object of inner perception. In contrast to this, an *act* is never an object. No matter how much knowledge we have of an act, our reflecting on its naïve execution (in the moment of such execution or in reflective, immediate memory) contains nothing like the objectification which marks, e.g., all inner perception, especially all inner observation.[10]

If an act can therefore never be an object, then the *person* who lives in the execution of acts can a fortiori never be an object. The only and exclusive kind of givenness of the person is his *execution of acts* (including the execution of acts reflecting on acts). It is through this execution of acts that the person experiences himself at the same time. Or, if we are concerned with other persons, the person is experienced in terms of post-execution, coexecution, or pre-execution of acts. In these cases of the execution of acts of other persons, there is no objectification.

If one understands *psychology* (in the way that it usually is understood) as a science of (the observation, description, and explanation of accessible) "happenings," and, indeed, happenings in inner perception, everything that deserves the name *act*, as well as everything that deserves the name *person*, must, for this reason, remain *transcendent* to psychology. Hence we are compelled to regard the attempt to assign to psychology studies of *acts*, for example, acts of judging, representing, feeling, etc., and to other sciences studies of "*appearances*" and "*contents*" (according to Franz Brentano, natural science; according to Carl Stumpf, "phenomenology") as completely mistaken. What is regarded as content and object, as opposed to "act," contains, among many other things, all possible facts of psychological research. In the case of that which is given according to essential laws only in the person-act of inner perception, the act must be executed-with by the researcher who "understands," for example, what his subject has perceived and observed, for it cannot be objectified. This does not imply, however, that within the series of objectively given phenomena of inner perception, the *contents* and *functions* of appearances are not to be distinguished, as they are in Stumpf's valuable studies.[11] Indeed, we regard this distinction as both necessary and irreducible. Associative psychology was mistaken in its failure to take this differentiation into account. Nevertheless these "*functions*" have nothing to do with "*acts*." First, all functions are ego-functions; they never belong to the sphere of the person. Functions are psychic; acts are non-psychic. Acts are executed; functions happen by themselves. Functions necessarily require a lived body and an environment to which the "appearances" of functions belong. But with the person and acts we do not posit a lived body; and to the person there corresponds a world, not an environment. Acts spring from the person into time; functions are facts in phenomenal time and can be measured indirectly by coordinating their phenomenal time-relations with measurable lengths of time of appearances given in functions themselves. For example, seeing, hearing, tasting, and smelling belong to functions, as do *all* kinds of noticing, noting, and taking notice of (and not only so-called sensible attention to) vital feeling, etc. However, genuine acts, in which something is "meant," and which among themselves possess an immediate complex of meaning, are not functions. *Functions* can have a twofold relation to *acts*. They can be objects of acts, e.g., when I try to bring my seeing to intuitive givenness; and they can also be that "through" which an act is directed toward something objectified, though without this function's becoming an object in the process. The latter happens when I perform the "same" act of judging in both seeing an object and hearing it at another time (that is, an act of judging of identical sense and about the same state of affairs). Stumpf properly stresses that the variation of an object's "appearances" is independent of the variation of functions, that the latter is independent of the former, and that together these are *in concreto* a criterion of the distinction between functions and appearances. This criterion also holds for the differentiation of functions and acts, but with this difference: the same acts can be conjoined with all possible combinations and variations of functions, and vice versa. On the other hand, laws of acts and their interconnections of foundations are transferable, for example, to beings of quite a different *functional* character. But it is impossible for laws of functions, which are in principle empirical and inductive, to set limits on laws of acts, which are a priori in nature.[12]

This means that the opposition of function and appearance is still contained as a part within person and world and therefore does not coincide with the opposition of person and world. Stumpf's "functions" and their counterparts, "appearances," can become given only when we focus, from among the givens of the act of intuition which is separated from the concrete person-act, on the givenness "lived body" and its corresponding "environment," and think of the act of "inner perception" as having been executed.

Our claim that acts (and especially the person) do not belong to the psychic sphere does not imply that they are physical. We maintain only that both act and person are psychophysically *indifferent*. We are not at all troubled by the old Cartesian alternative, which requires that everything be either psychic or physical. For such a long time this alternative concealed ideal objects and the fact "lived body" (as distinct from thing-bodies) and thus the true object of biology, and it also led to the vain attempt to place the whole sphere of law and the state, that of art and religious objects, and many other domains into the ontological categories "recognized" by philosophers.

Still, we use the term *mind* [*Geist*] for the entire sphere of acts (following our procedure of many years).[13] With this term we designate all things that possess the nature of act, intentionality, and fulfillment of meaning, wherever we may find them. This of course implies at once that all mind is by essential necessity "*personal*," and that the idea of a "non-personal mind" is "contradictory." But no "*ego*" at all belongs to the essence of mind, and hence no division between "*ego*" and *outer world*."[14] It is, rather, the *person* that is the single and necessary existential form of mind insofar as we are concerned with concrete mind.

The use of the word *person* in *language* already reveals that the form of unity meant by this term has nothing to do with the form of unity of the "consciousness"-object of inner perception or consequently the "ego" (either the "ego" in opposition to a "thou" or the "ego" in opposition to the "outer world"). For *person*, unlike these terms, is an absolute, not a feeably *relative*, name. The word *I* is always connected with a "thou" on the one hand and an "outer world" on the other. This is not the case with the title *person*. God, for example, can be a person, but not an "I," because for him there is neither a "thou" nor an "outer world." What we mean by the term *person*, in contrast to the ego, is something of a self-sufficient *totality*. A person acts, for example. He "takes a walk," etc. True, language permits such expressions as "I act," "I go for a walk." But here the word *I* does not designate a psychic fact of experience; it is, rather, an occasional expression, changing its meaning from speaker to speaker, and merely a linguistic form of address. The "I" does not speak. The man does. All of this clearly shows that *person* means something that is completely indifferent to the oppositions "I–thou," "psychic–physical," and "ego–outer world." If I say, "*I* perceive myself," the "I" is the form of address, not the psychic ego of experience. "Myself," however, does not mean "my I": it does not answer the question of whether I perceive "myself" in an outer or inner fashion. If, on the other hand, I say, "I perceive my ego," again the "I" and the "ego" have different senses. The "I" has the same sense as in "I go for a walk"; i.e., it is the form of address. The "ego," however, is the psychic ego of experiencing. It is the object of *inner perception*. Hence, just as a person can "go for a walk," so also can he "perceive" his ego, e.g., when he is working in psychology. However, this psychic ego that the person perceives can no more perceive than it can go for a walk or act. Although the person can perceive his ego as well as his lived body and the outer world, it is not possible for him to become an object of representation or perception, either for himself or for others.

It *belongs to the essence of the person* to exist and to live solely in the *execution of intentional acts*. The person is therefore essentially never an "object." On the contrary, any objectifying attitude (be it perception, representation, thinking, remembering, or expectation) makes the person immediately transcendent.

The psychophysical indifference of acts is also clearly given in the fact that all acts and act-differences can have as their objects both the psychic and the physical. Thus, representing and perceiving, remembering and expecting, feeling and preferring, willing and not willing, loving and hating, judging, etc., can have psychic as well as physical "contents." I can, for instance, "remember" an appearance of nature and a psychic experience, and I can feel my own value or that of an object of the outer world, etc. We therefore expressly reject those curious theories which hold that when I remember an experience, there must be an element of the psychic stream coming from it in order to bend back intentionally to another part. Acts can be objects no more than psychic happenings or "events" can "mean" something or relate to each other intentionally. Acts either are or are not, and are of either this or that quality. On the other hand, we do not need any passageway through the psychic sphere in order to love physical appearances or to will or to do something in the physical world. As the person wills or does something, whatever happens in his psychic sphere is quite indifferent to the meaning and being of this willing or doing. But no matter how wrong it is to smuggle intentional factors into the psychic sphere, as the theories that we have criticized do, it is also wrong to deny completely the intentional factor and to say, for example, as Theodor Ziehen does, that every memory of a representation is a new representation or merely a new element in the psychic stream. The former theory falsely spiritualizes the psychic and ruins psychology. The latter psychologizes the mind and ruins philosophy.

Psychology can deal neither with (abstract) essences of remembering, expecting, loving, etc., nor with these acts as abstract parts of a concrete person-act. Even less can it deal with the a priori orders of foundation of these acts. What concerns psychology is simply what happens in the sphere of inner perception on the occasion of the execution of such acts, and the interconnections that such executions have among themselves and with the lived body (in causal terms). As in all other inductive sciences, there is no sharp distinction between description and explanation. Thus, for example, association, reproduction, perseveration, and the aftereffect of a determining tendency toward the processes of representation, i.e., as a condition of the origin of an act of representing or remembering a "content" (which is determined by its object, which is presupposed as real), become problems for psychology. But the essence of remembering and representing, etc., and the phenomenology of these things remain inaccessible to psychology, and so does the origin of these acts in the person, as well as the a priori laws of this origin. For both the origin and the laws obtain for *any* imaginable phase of this stream, whose changing complexes of contents psychology studies inductively. This stream, whose parts a psychologist sees, "originates" at *every* point according to a priori laws of origin and, within the scope of these, in the concrete nature of the person. If the content of this stream could teach us anything at all about this "origin," *any* random phase and *any* random cross-section of this stream would suffice, and no "induction" would be needed. For the origin of an experience out of a person and the rise of an experience within a person are basically two different things.

If we take the word *consciousness* to mean everything that comes to appearance in inner perception, as we do when we define psychology as the "science of appearances in consciousness," (and it seems to me that this is the only usage which makes any sense), then both the *person* and his acts must be designated as *supraconscious being*, whereas the appearances in consciousness themselves divide into *surconscious* and *subconscious* ones. And all psychic real being corresponding to these appearances – i.e., so-called psychic events and processes and their caus-ality, the psychic dispositions that are hypothetically assumed for the production of a causal nexus, etc. – must be called *unconscious*.[15] But one who uses the term *consciousness* to designate all "*consciousness of something*," who carefully avoids contaminating the usage of the term with the introduction of the intellectualistic theory according to which "representation" must be the basis of all intentional acts (including judging, loving, hating, feeling, willing) as the basic act of object-ification, and who therefore understands by "consciousness of something" (first without any theory of foundations) all intentionally directed acts filled with meaning (also feeling of something [e.g., values], willing of something [projects], judging of something [states of affairs], etc.), may also call the person the concrete "consciousness-of." But this cannot be allowed when this "conscious-ness of something" is taken to mean and imply (in a Cartesian fashion) only the *cogitare*, so that loving, hating, feeling, willing, and their own lawfulness have their foundations in the union of the person so defined (*res cogitans*) with a body. This is also Kant's presupposition with regard to all emotional and voluntary acts with the curious exception of the "feeling of reverence."[16] We shall prefer in the following to use the term *consciousness* only in the sense of either a specific consciousness-of of inner perception or appearances in consciousness (the psychic), because the term *consciousness* in the sense of "consciousness of something" is closely connected historically with Cartesian rationalism and its thousand modifications (among which, in this case, we may include Kant).

c. Person and world

In the foregoing we called the *world* the correlate [*Sachkorrelat*] of the person. Hence there is an *individual world* corresponding to every individual person. Just as every act belongs to a person, so also every object "belongs" by essential neces-sity to a *world*. But every world is in its essential structure a priori bound to the interconnections of essence and structure that exist for essences of things [*Sach-wesenheiten*]. Every world is at the same time a concrete world, but only as the *world* of a *person*. No matter which realms of objects we may distinguish – the realm of objects of the inner world, of the outer world, of bodiliness (and thereby the total possible realm of life), the realm of ideal objects, or the realm of values – they all have an abstract objectivity. They become fully concrete only as part of a world, the world of a person. But the *person* is never a "part" of a world; the person is always the *correlate* of a "world," namely, the world in which he experi-ences himself. If we consider only one concrete act of a person, this act contains in itself all possible act-essences, and its objective correlate contains all essential factors of world – e.g., egoness, the individual ego, and all essential constituents of the psychic, as well as the outer world, spatiality, temporality, the phenomenon of the lived body, thingness, effecting, etc. – on the basis of an a priori and lawful structure, valid without exception for all possible persons and all possible acts of all persons. This structure is valid not only for the real world but also for all possible worlds. This correlate also contains an ultimate peculiarity, an original trait, belonging only to the "world" of this person and nobody else. This peculiarity cannot be grasped in terms of essential concepts pertaining to general essences. The fact that this is so is not empirically found,[17] nor is it this individual a priori essence itself. It is, rather, a general essential trait of all *possible worlds*. Therefore, if we reduce everything that is "given" to a concrete person in general to the phenomenal essences that are purely *self*-given to the person (i.e., to facts that are perfectly what they are), so that even all abstract qualities, forms, and directions of acts, and what we distinguish among acts, enter into the sphere of *givenness* for a pure and formless act of the person, here alone we have a world that is *not relative* to life [*daseins-absolut*], and we find ourselves in the realm of things themselves. However, so long as a *single* world exists for different individual persons, a world that is regarded as "self-given" and "absolute," its singularity and sameness are necessarily an *illusion* [*Schein*]. Here, in fact, only realms of objects that are relative to the types of bearers of concrete personalities (e.g., living beings, men, races, etc.) are given. Or it is "the world," i.e., the *one* concrete world encompassing all concrete worlds, that is "given"; but it is not "self-given," only meant. That is, "*the world*" becomes in this case a mere "idea" in Kant's sense of the term (but not with the token of reality that he attributes to it). For Kant believed he could degrade the nature of "world" itself to an "idea." But "*the world*" is by no means an idea. It is an absolute, always concrete, individual being. The intention toward it becomes an idea that is in principle unfulfillable, something only meant, as soon as we demand that it be "given" to a *plurality* of individual persons and thus self-given. This is also the case when we allow ourselves to believe that we can make the "universal validity" of the establishment and the determination of its being and content the condition of its own and every kind of existence through general concepts and propositions. For such a determination of the world is in principle not possible. As we showed earlier, the so-called transcendental concept of truth, existence, and object, which volatilizes the object in a necessary and universally valid combination of representations, is in fact a subjectivistic falsification. And it is this falsification which *entails* that absolute being become an unrecognizable X of a "thing in itself." Hence metaphysical truth, or "the" truth itself, *must* have a different content, within the limits of the a priori structure of world, for each person because the content of world-*being* is, in every case, different for each person. Therefore, the fact that truth about the world and the absolute world is, in a certain sense, a "personal truth" (as the absolute good is a "personal good," as we shall see later) is due not to any supposed "relativity" and "subjectivity," or "humanness," of the idea of truth, but to the essential interconnection between person and world. The fact that this is so and not otherwise has its foundation in the essence of *Being, not* in the essence of the "truth." Of course one who from the very beginning looks on personality as something "negative," for instance, as a contingent bodily or egological limitation of a "transcendental reason," will not see this point, nor will one who regards the person merely as a factual part of the empirical world or a world in general, one who does not regard the person as having his foundation in *absolute* Being and as representing absolute Being (and world). He will always believe that in order to reach Being itself, one must set the person *aside*, "rise above" him, or "get rid" of him. In fact, he has only to "overcome" his ego, his bodiliness, and his prejudices – above all, his prejudices of genus and race – which limit the nature of his personality because he regards them all as objective, so that the absolute world belonging essentially to his person can gradually emerge from the empty web of mere "world relations." For if person and world are absolute being, and if they are reciprocally related essentially, absolute truth can only be personal. And insofar as truth is impersonal, and insofar as it is "universal" and not personally valid, there *must* be either falsehood or merely truth about objects relative to life. Only those subjectivists and transcendental psychologists who believe that they can *define* "truth" merely as the "universal validity" of a proposition hold that a personally valid truth cannot be a "truth" in the (strictest and "transcendentally" unspoiled) sense of an agreement between a judged proposition and its state of affairs, and that personally valid truth (and, analogously, a good) is a "*contradictio in adjecto.*"

If personality were a concept having its foundation in the "*ego*" – in any sense of the term – or in a "transcendental ego" or in "consciousness in general," what we call a personal truth would of course be a contradictory notion. It is Fichte's "ego" and its numerous modern forms, as well as Kant's infinitely more profound and more carefully explained "transcendental apperception," which dissolve the basis of a strict and objective idea of truth, and which represent the first steps on a path that ends in the pragmatistic conversion of all philosophy into a bog.

d. Microcosm, macrocosm, and the idea of God

If to every "person" there corresponds a "world," and to every "world," a "person," we must ask – because concreteness belongs to the essence of the real, not only to its empirical being-real – whether the "idea" of *one identical real world*, surpassing the a priori essential structure that binds "all possible worlds," has phenomenal fulfillment, or whether we must stay on the level of a plurality of personal worlds. We are not referring to the idea of "a" concrete, real, absolute world, one that is accessible to each person in principle as "his world." Let us call this idea of one identical real world the idea of the *macrocosm*, following an old philosophical tradition, but without committing ourselves to what various writers have meant by this notion. If there is such a macrocosm, there is something familiar about and in it: namely, its a priori essential structure, which phenomenology brings to prominence in all regions. This structure holds for all *possible worlds* because it holds for the general essence of "world." All microcosms, i.e., all individual "personal worlds," are, notwithstanding their totality, parts of the macrocosm – if there is one concrete world into which all persons look [*hinblicken*]. And the personal correlate of the macrocosm would be the idea of an infinite and perfect person of spirit, one whose acts would be given to us in their essential determinations in act-phenomenology, which pertains to the acts of all possible persons. But this "person" would have to be concrete simply to fulfill the essential condition of a reality. Thus the *idea of God* is *cogiven* with the unity and identity and singularity of the world on the basis of an essential interconnection of complexes. Therefore, if we posit one concrete world as real, it would be absurd (though not "contradictory") not to posit the idea of a concrete spirit [*Geistes*]. However, only a concrete person who is in immediate communication with something corresponding to this idea, and to whom its concrete being is "self-given," can posit the idea of God as real; philosophy can never do so. The reality of "God" therefore has its only foundation in a possible positive revelation of God in a concrete person. Without going into this question in detail, we would like to stress one point: every "unity of the world" (including all kinds of monism and pantheism) without regress to the essence of a *personal* God, and, similarly, every kind of "substitute" for a personal "God," be it a "universal world-reason," a "transcendental rational ego," a "moral governor of the world" (Kant), an *ordo ordinans* (Fichte in his earlier period), an infinite logical "subject" (Hegel), or an impersonal or self-styled "suprapersonal unconscious," etc., is an "absurd" philosophical assumption. For such assumptions do not agree with evidential essential interconnections. One who speaks of *concrete* thought or *concrete* willing posits at the same time the totality of personality. For otherwise he would be concerned only with abstract act-essences. But concreteness itself belongs to the essence of reality, not only to reality's being posited. One who speaks about and posits "the" concrete absolute world, and does not mean simply his own, necessarily posits the concrete person of God, also. If, on the other hand, the essence of personality were based in the "ego," e.g., as Eduard von Hartmann presupposes in his subtle but purely dialectical investigations of the question, the idea of a divine person would be nonsense. For to every "ego" there belongs by essential necessity an "outer world" and a "thou" and a "lived body," all of which it would be a priori nonsensical to attribute to God. Conversely, it is the meaningful idea of a personal God which shows that the idea of the person is not founded in the "ego."

If, however, the unity and singularity of world are not founded in the unity of the logical consciousness (in which only the unity of objects of cognition is founded, objects which in turn essentially require belongingness to a world), and if it is a fortiori not founded in "science" (as a special symbolic and universal type of cognition of objects relative to life) or in any other spiritual root of culture, but in the essence of a concrete personal God, then we must also say that all essential communities of individual persons are not founded in some "rational lawfulness" or in an abstract idea of reason, but solely in the possible community of these persons and the person of persons, i.e., in the *community with God*. All other communities of a moral and legal character have this community as their *foundation*. Hence, all *amare, contemplare, cogitare,* and *velle* are intentionally interwoven with the *one concrete world*, the macrocosm, by way of *amare, contemplare, cogitare,* and *velle* "*in Deo*." But this is not the place to pursue this matter further.

e. Lived body and environment

We have already touched upon the concepts of the *lived body* [*Leib*] and the *environment* [*Umwelt*] in our analysis of deeds. We sharply distinguished these from the oppositions of ego and external world, and person and world. We are now concerned with an explanation of their relation or the relation of their corresponding givens to the givens of the person and the world. We will not, however, furnish an exhaustive explanation of these data as such.

First, there can be no doubt that the *lived body* does *not* belong to the *sphere of the person* or the *sphere of acts*. It belongs to the *object sphere* of any "consciousness of something" and its kind and ways of being. The lived body's phenomenal mode of givenness, with its foundations, is essentially different from that of the *ego*, with its states and experiences.

In order to arrive at correct knowledge of these states of affairs, let us begin with a critique of major types of prevailing opinions on this matter. We will then pursue a positive investigation of the facts involved.

It is our contention that "*lived bodiliness*" [*Leiblichkeit*] represents a special non-formal essential given (for pure phenomenological intuition), which, in any factual perception of a lived body, functions as a form of perception (we can also say that it functions as a category, in the sense of the aforementioned precise characteristic of anything categorial). This implies that its *givenness* is not reducible to a form of outer or inner perception, to a coordination of the contents of these, or a fortiori to a fact of inductive experience, i.e., the perception of an individual thing. This also implies that the lived body must never be considered a primary given on whose foundation some psychophysically indifferent thing that we "come upon" differentiates itself and sets itself off as "psychic" or "physical" according to different relations with the lived body. If the psychic and the physical have been shown to belong to two irreducible perceptual directions (inner and outer perception), the lived double relationship of their series of contents to the datum "lived body" must lead to two sciences, whose proper characteristics will clearly be revealed to us at this time.

We wish to make a sharp distinction between "*lived body*" and "*thing-body*" [*der* "Leib" *und der* "Körper"], a distinction which, unfortunately, is not found nowadays in scientific terminology. If, in thinking, we suppressed the functions of all the external senses by which we perceive the external world, then all possible perception of our own "thing-body" would be abolished, along with the perception of all other different bodies. We would not be able to touch ourselves or have any access to the forms of our chest, hands, legs, etc., as in the case of external bodies, e.g., inanimate ones; nor would we be able to look at ourselves (with or without mirrors). We would not be able to hear any sounds of our voice or those otherwise produced, nor would we be able to taste anything, smell ourselves, etc. But the phenomenon of our "lived body" would by no means be annihilated in this case. For – no matter how closely one may focus on this point – in the case of our lived body we have, in addition to its possible external consciousness, an inner consciousness that we lack in regard to inanimate bodies. There is a customary interpretation of this inner consciousness of our lived body: (1) it is identified with the sum or the product of the fusion of so-called "*organic sensations*" (e.g., sensations of muscles, of moving joints, of pain, of itching); and (2) these "sensations" are distinguished from those of our outer senses, such as the so-called sensations of colors and sounds, only with regard to *quality* and *location*. And this, in turn, leads to a terminology in the sciences – one most curious, indeed, to the unsophisticated – according to which a painful sensation in the forehead or an occurrence of "itching" is referred to as a psychic phenomenon and is thus included with woe and sadness, for instance, in a basic class of phenomena, namely, the so-called psychic phenomena. Of course, from this point of view there is no irreducible, unanalyzable sphere of consciousness which is lived-body consciousness; nor is there any corresponding phenomenon of "lived body." Rather, there is on the one hand only my own "body" [*Körper*], which I "think into" the sense-contents of optical, tactile, and other outer perceptions in the same manner in which I think other "bodies" into other sense-contents (e.g., the body of the inkwell standing in front of me into my own optical picture of it). There are on the other hand certain components of my psychic stream of consciousness which are coordinated with such sense-contents only through the outer observation of their appearance and disappearance that depends on changes in my body and changing states of certain organs (e.g., hands, legs, muscles, joints, etc.). According to this interpretation the coordination would, of course, result in a *justification* for calling the above sense-contents "sensations," e.g., "organic sensations," "muscular sensations," "articular sensations," etc., whereas according to their phenomenal facticity there would be nothing in them which could betray the existence of a muscle, a stomach, etc. In short, the "lived body" is reduced to the fact of an animated body, and lived-body consciousness either to a mere coordination of psychic and corporal facticities or to a more relation and order between them.

Who cannot at first glance see – insofar as he is still unsophisticated and can see the visible – that this way of conjuring away the lived body is nothing but a totally empty and irrelevant construction alien to intuitive comprehension?

The first thing that remains wholly unintelligible here is the indubitable fact that there exists a strict and *immediate unity of identity* of the *inner consciousness* which everyone has "of" the existence and the "hereness" [*Befinden*] of the lived body – first of all, of one's own lived body – and the *outer perception* of one's lived body (as the body-thing [*Leibkörper*]), e.g., through the senses of sight and touch. It may be true that some *learning* and a gradual and progressive "development" are required in order to recognize my right hand, whose being, Gestalt, and finger movements I possess as elements of my inner lived-body consciousness, and which now, e.g., "aches," as the *same thing* which I now touch with my hand, and which corresponds to my own optical picture. Analogously, there is a thing-like identification of the place in which I feel hungry with what to the anatomist represents a stomach. But this process of learning refers to only two factors: (1) the coordination of the *corresponding parts* of the "sides" of this one "lived body" (seen from within and without), in which the *immediate identity* of the whole lived-body object, given from within and without, is already *pregiven*; and (2) not the relationship of immediately given appearances to the same objective thing as such, but only those appearances of *thinglike* significance or those which cofunction as symbols for *certain things*, e.g., this *thing* "hand," this *thing* "stomach," etc. That is, everything here is analogous to the fact that we must learn to relate the *differences* among depths in which simple things of sight are given – and, indeed, given in an original manner – to the objective proportions of distances of real bodies (including also the body "eye") as a kind of system of signs for such distances (Hering). By no means do we have to "learn" the seeing of depths themselves, nor does this seeing "originate" in so-called sensations which do not yet contain anything like depths and their differences. Hence we do not have to learn the identity of the same "*lived body*" given in inner and outer consciousness – given, we might say, in the former as a "*lived-body soul*," in the latter as a "*body-thing*." The lived body is given, rather, as a totally uniform, phenomenal fact and as a subject of "being-here" thus and otherwise. This fact is independent of and, in order of givenness, prior to any special so-called organic sensations and any special kinds of outer perception. It, or its immediate and total perception, *founds* the givenness of the lived-body soul, as well as that of the body-thing. It is precisely *this* basic founding phenomenon which is the "*lived body*" in the strictest sense of the term.

In contrast to this, the above-mentioned theory would prove that an identically meant lived body is only a fiction: that *in practice* there is only one class of purely psychic sensations (later termed organic sensations) and an increasingly more fixed coordination of them, their unities, and their changes to other classes of sensations, which have no relation to a body-thing other than what they have to inanimate physical bodies not belonging to it. The *difference* between the two groups of "sensations" lies only in a certain constancy in the first group and frequent appearances of "double sensations." (Such a double sensation occurs, for example, when I touch my body, but not when I see my body;[18] in hearing my voice, experiences in the larynx, mouth, etc., are connected with acoustical contents.) The theory also implies that an immediately given identity of the lived body, which alone makes such a constancy and coordination something meaningful, can be reduced to a mere constancy of a part of my experiences (something totally "incomprehensible") and a mere "coordination," which is supposed to be nothing more than a "fixed" association. Apart from the deficiencies in the bases of this theory, the criteria for separating sensations related to the "lived body" and to extrabodily objects are insufficient. To someone sentenced to life imprisonment, the walls of a prison are no less "constant" than, say, the image that he has of his hands. Yet, it is impossible for him to confuse them for an instant with his lived body. A so-called double sensation is not at all given in the phenomena on the occasion of touching; it is only by looking at a finger and by touching the palm of the hand with it that we are able to relate two functional processes of *sensing* to the *same* content. But in this the differences between a lived body (and its parts) and other bodies are already presupposed.

Let me summarize the various errors of these traditional theories. It is erroneous (1) to consider inner "lived-body consciousness" only a group of sensations; (2) to think that *lived-body sensations* are different only in degree from "organic sensations," and to hold that certain organic sensations as states of a lived body are different only in degree and content from "sensations" of sound, color, taste, and smell, rather than in the kind of givenness which belongs essentially to them; (3) to believe that the *lived-body-thing* is originally encountered in the same fashion as *other bodies*;[19] (4) to consider *lived-body sensations* "psychic phenomena"; (5) to consider inner *lived-body consciousness* something originally unarticulated which is articulated only according to the parts of the body to which it is secondarily related (the converse assertion would be equally wrong); (6) to hold that the contents of inner lived-body consciousness are more deceptive than those of outer consciousness (inner diagnostics); (7) to think that inner lived-body consciousness is originally non-extended and without any spatio-temporal order; (8) to think that there is no fundamental essential difference between volitional control over the lived body and over external objects; and (9) to hold that the unity of the lived body has only an associative character (this is erroneous because it is the lived body that first of all makes associative combinations possible).

Let us return for a moment to the first of these errors.[20]

The *first* error of this theory consists in the assumption that it is possible simply to equate the inner consciousness of our lived body with the sum of sensations experienced as localized in specific organs. In fact, consciousness of our lived body is always given as a consciousness of a whole that is more or less vaguely articulated, and it is given independent of and *prior to* the givenness of any special complex of "organic sensations." But the relation between this consciousness of a lived body and organic sensations is not comparable to that between a whole and its parts, or to a relation between two "terms." It is a relation of *form* to its *content*. Just as all psychic experiences are experienced together only in an "ego" in which they are joined into a unity of a special kind, so all organic sensations are necessarily given "together" in a lived body. Just as the "ego" must accompany all our (psychic) experiences (as Kant observed), so must our lived body accompany all organic sensations. The lived body is therefore the underlying form through which all organic sensations are conjoined, and through which they are organic sensations of *this* lived body and not of any other. When special organic sensations are observed or otherwise more sharply set off, as in the case of painful sensations, the vague whole of the lived body is coexperienced as their "background"; but the lived body as a whole is cointended in any *organic sensation* as a special kind of sensation. From this it clearly follows that we do not have to "learn" by "experience" – in the sense of progressive induction – that we are *not angels*, that we possess a body. We only "learn" the orientation in the manifold of our given body, as well as the "sense and meaning" of the vicissitudes in this manifold for the states of limb-units, which are likewise given in inner fashion, of the lived body or the body organs. However, for any finite consciousness there is an essential interconnection between *"ego"* and *"lived body."* This interconnection is not an inductive-empirical or associative one. Otherwise correct observations of infants have often been falsely interpreted in this regard. An infant is certainly "amazed" when he sees his feet for the first time. He may kick his feet as if they were strange external bodies; and there may come a time when he must learn that the optical picture of the far corner of his bed does not have the same relation to his body as the picture of his feet. But the difference between the spheres "lived body" and "external world" is *presupposed* here as given. The child does not learn how to distinguish these spheres as such; he only "learns" that some *seen things* belong to this sphere, some to that one.

"Lived Body" and "Environment" Are Not Presupposed by the Distinction between "Psychic" and "Physical." Among modern scholars it was Avenarius and, quite independent of him, Ernst Mach ("coming from the idealistic camp," as he himself said) who most successfully elaborated a theory of knowledge in which it is maintained that a distinction between psychic and physical phenomena is possible only on the basis of a pregiven lived body and environment. Avenarius asserts that there is a plain *"coming upon"* [*Vorfinden*] (which neither presupposes nor contains either an "ego" or a distinction of act, object, and content), and that the content of this plain *"coming upon"* represents the datum of the "natural conception of the world." But this datum, he says, contains nothing more than a lived body and its environment, whose contents exhibit certain dependencies in their variations. Dependencies existing between the parts of the environment are said to represent the subject matter of the natural sciences – physics, chemistry,

etc. Dependencies between the facts of the above order of dependencies and the parts and processes of the body are said to form the subject matter of biology. The subject matter of psychology is said to be the dependencies among the alterations of contents lying between environmental parts and the parts of the body, not the dependencies among the contents themselves. Avenarius further maintains that a false and "artificial" concept of the world results when the variational relationship between the content that one "comes upon" in the environment (e.g., this "tree") and a lived body (which is reduced to "system *C*," i.e., the brain with its spinal continuation) is made a special object, an object that is said to be "introjected" into the lived bodies of our "fellow men" so that in these lived bodies one imagines the "perception" or "representation" of the tree and in these new "psychic forms" or "contents of consciousness," etc., a special "subject," a "soul," etc. In this fashion, so runs the argument, there arises the "concept of the soul" and the concept of the "psychic," as well as the assumption of a special perceptual source of such fictitious objects, namely, the concept of an "inner perception." For other scholars this was the basis for the distinction between (psychic) acts and the (physical) objects corresponding to them, as well as for analogous distinctions.

These assertions (and, *mutatis mutandis*, Mach's also) do not require a serious refutation. They have been judged by their inevitable consequences: one is forced to reduce *all* feeling-states to organic sensations and their (sensible) character, and to reduce the experience of the ego, and even that of the person, to complexes and derivatives of such experiences; one is also forced to reduce all pictorial recollections to the reappearance of faint ("shadowlike") elements of the environment, and all "thinking" to mere economy, to the most parsimonious use of images and their contents. For a psychology dealing with at least some facts, such inadmissible consequences are not even debatable.

We are interested in these (now antiquated) theories only in regard to the *lived body*. Avenarius' premise is that the "lived bodies of our fellow men," their "environments," and their "statements" are all "come upon" in fully identical ways. From the outset, however, he fails to see that there is not the least clue in this primary material that we are supposed to "come upon" which would distinguish anything like "*lived body*," "*environment*," or "*statement*." What is it that distinguishes the "lived body" from an "element of the environment," e.g., some inanimate object in the same sensible content? What is it that distinguishes a "statement" from any combination of sounds or noises? What makes it a "statement," or even only a "phenomenal expression"? That the "lived body" is not simply *one* thing-body among others; that it is given, rather, as a "center" of thing-bodies functioning as its "environment"; that "expressions," or even "statements," are not simple changes in thing-bodies determined by changing relationships to other thing-bodies, as is the case with the sound of a piece of steel hitting the ground, but that they always exist in terms of a twofold symbolic relation[21] – where could one find all of this in the *givenness* of such plain "coming upon"? The alternative is simple: either this plain and indifferent "coming upon" of Avenarius' is not plain at all but possesses *different modes* and *forms* for a lived body, an environment, and a statement (all of which can contain the *same* sensible material), in which case what one "comes upon" must have different (intuitive but non-sensible) structures corresponding to such forms; or the above *distinctions* cannot be accounted for at all. Avenarius makes the obvious mistake of identifying the "*lived body*" with the body-thing; and instead of recognizing an essential interconnection according to which the *same* lived body is capable of a totally different (inner) givenness (e.g., in hunger, lust, pain), he understands this latter on the basis of an "introjection" analogous to the introjection of the environmental "tree" "into" the lived body as the "perception" of the tree. Let us *suppose* that there is such an "introjection." If, on this premise, we assume that something "psychic" arises which has the fictitious structure of a thing-like "relation" in a "perception" or a "representation" belonging to an "ego," and if we further assume a special source of knowledge belonging to this "ego," namely, "inner perception," nothing like "being hungry" or "tickling" could ever be "introjected" in an analogous fashion. Where could we find the "environmental element" for this, or what would the introjected "character" be like? The occurrence of such an "introjection," which does not occur in inanimate objects, would presuppose a unity of a lived body that is essentially distinct from such environmental elements. (No animist would hold that a stone "perceives" an animal in the same way that an animal perceives a stone.)[22] We consider this "theory of introjection," insofar as it goes beyond the dismissal of the old, well-known "projection theories" of sensation, to have no basis whatsoever in fact. On one point, however, we agree with Avenarius, and not with his many critics: no matter how we arrive at the idea of the "ego," no matter how the "ego" of our fellow man is "given," the perception of a factual reality of the essence "lived-bodiliness" is *not* based on the assumption that there is an "ego" or psychic facts in what we come upon, and that this "ego" (our own or that of another) must be given to us before we can consider any appearances to be appearances of a "lived body."[23] Although every given lived body of a human being is given (to the human being himself) as "my" body or (to someone else) as "his" body, it is not this relation to the ego that makes this a "lived body," or that detaches the lived body as a unit from the manifold of other "given" contents. It is on the *basis* of the independence of the givenness of a lived body that its unity must be different in essence from that of inanimate things.[24] The facts apply analogously to Ernst Mach's theory. According to Mach, "*elements of being*" are "sensations" if their givenness and their absence prove to be dependent on the being of an "organism." If, for instance, a sphere is "yellow," not because of sodium light, but because a person has taken santonin, the element of being "yellow" is psychic. But how does the mass of these elements L, representing a *lived body*, differ from other such elements E, representing an environment, so that the variations in E and their mutual "dependencies" can be differentiated from the variations in L and their respective mutual dependencies? What is the phenomenal difference between "sensations," which are elements of being *as* related to the lived body, and the elements *of which* the lived body is supposed to consist? There are no answers to these questions. Both Avenarius and Mach fail to see that there is an essence "*lived-bodiliness*" that is not inductively abstracted from factual lived bodies, an essence whose possible intuition in the presence of an empirical object (e.g., my lived body at this moment, that of someone else, etc.) presents the object to me as one that is different from inanimate objects and as an *essentially* different lived-body object. They both equate lived-bodiliness with the lived body (*in concreto*) and the latter with a mere body-thing, i.e. (in our terminology), the lived body as an object of outer perception alone. Avenarius maintains that there is no difference between "outer" and "inner" perception with regard to what we come upon; but his mistaken polemic against the concept of "inner perception" merely reveals that he reduces all perception to the concept of "outer perception." Avenarius tries to show that facts of inner perception consist of the same elements as the "simplest" complexities of outer perception, and, like Berkeley, he falls victim to an erroneous, one-sided artificiality. Berkeley attempted to show that Locke's "sensation" is merely a limiting case of "reflection" – as if colors and sounds (supposedly related to an ego and experienced only as ego-related) were given in the same fashion as pain or muscular tension, as if outer sense-perception were nothing but a strong representation. Avenarius also tries to do away with the perceptual *direction* of "inner perception" by assuming that this expression refers to a perception of something psychic "in" an objective thing-body, and that there is no "blue in the head" or "pain in the (anatomic) arm" when one senses "blue" or "pain." These assumptions result in his theory (which later was widely accepted) that all specific lived-body phenomena, or phenomena experienced as belonging to the lived body, e.g., pain, tickling, tension, relaxing, and even all experienced active motor impulses, as opposed to so-called kinesthetic passive phenomena, are complexes of "sensations" which can also occur as "elements" of the content of outer perception. (Kinesthetic passive sensations are, in fact, only consequences of tactile sensations in sinews and joints and the phenomena of position and form built on the basis of these. They can be "interpreted" as "sensations of movements" only on the basis of previously experienced impulses of movements.) All of this also results in the opinion that there are no non-extensive psychic experiences at all – e.g., in spiritual feelings and especially the experience of the ego – which are unquestionably experiences of this particular kind. Indeed, Avenarius did not even see that the difference in direction between "inner" and "outer" perception is not at all relative to what is (in a spatial sense) "inner" and "outer" for a body-thing. But there is in fact a difference in *act-direction*, one that is essentially conjoined with a special form of the manifold of the given. This difference in direction and form remains as a residuum, even when the lived body is completely bracketed. Once this difference in direction and form is related to a uniformly "given" lived body – one that is given in principle *without* this directional differentiation of perceptual acts – it projects two entirely different "aspects" of the lived body; but it is nevertheless evident that it relates to the *"same"* facticity *"lived body."*[25]

It is equally erroneous to assume, as both Avenarius and Mach do, that the difference between the "psychic" and the "physical" is a difference in the *"connection"* and *"order"* of the *"same"* contents and *elements*. In fact, they always consider physical elements the primary factors of givenness (as elements of *outer* perception which are not yet comprehended as thing like or a fortiori as corporeal). Much as Mach, like Hume, endeavors to derive the thing-category from his "elements of being" as a relatively stable complex of them,[26] his "elements of being" are in fact true and genuine *physical things* (i.e., things of the senses of sight, touch, etc.), having all the phenomenological determinations of essence belonging to things (like Hume's "impressions"). As *"sensations,"* i.e., as "related to an organism," such "elements" are not pure "contents" of sensation, but are already things-of-sensation. It is precisely at this point that we encounter the formal "materialism" of this philosophy; and it is as much a qualitative materialism as any. Moreover, every other possible form of an *"order theory,"* which would have to avoid this mistake, would also fail. An "element" of sorrow or woe can never occur "also" as an element of a physical appearance (even if this concept were expanded to include so-called organic sensations). Nor can it ever occur as a "character" of, say, a landscape. For what is qualitatively identical in the feeling-state of sorrow – when "I am sad" – and in the "character" of a "sorrowful landscape" represents no *real* element in either case. If the order theory were to hold only that the "psychic" and the "physical" are not *empirically definable* objective unities (i.e., definable *per genus proximum* and *differentia specifica*), then it would be completely correct. For these unities taken in that sense would not imply a difference in *essence*. The criterion of such essential differences is precisely this: in attempting to define them, we must presuppose them, and we therefore are necessarily trapped in a *circulus in definiendo*. The above assumption does not afford a reason to posit *two different modes* and directions of perception instead of one kind of perception plus two different empirical concepts of objects (as in "I perceive trees," "I perceive houses," etc.).[27] However, it does not follow from such a negatively correct assertion of the "order theory" that there are no non-formal differences at all in the phenomena of the psychic, the physical, and the lived body, or that we are concerned only with *differences in order* from a logicoformal point of view. For it merely follows that different non-formal contents already residing in the essence of psychic and physical objects are essentially connected with both perceptual directions.[28]

It is therefore out of the question to think that *"egoness" itself* and *"individual ego-being"* are somehow based on genetically and historically explicable processes like that of *"introjection,"* instead of considering them data of immediate intuition (corresponding to the "materiality" of objects of outer perception, which does not presuppose any hypothetical positing of a specific thing like "matter"). The thousands of beliefs and superstitions concerning a substantial soul can be reduced to analogous processes – but only on the *assumption* of intuitive facts. The essence "egoness," however, is *constitutive* of the essence "psychic" and is *essentially connected* with the direction of inner perception; this interconnection is given in both factors in formless, *pure* intuition itself. The "projective theory of sensations," which Avenarius rightly refutes, and the quite similar "empathic theory" of "values," "characters," forces, and phenomena of life are invalid and cannot establish a basis for the phenomenon of an "external world" (with or without the unconscious causal inferences subscribed to by Schopenhauer and Helmholtz), just as "introjection" cannot make the assumption of a psychic sphere, an ego, etc., comprehensible. Whenever such processes in fact occur, they presuppose both spheres and regions of being, as well as their essential contents, which are projected, empathized, and introjected into.[29]

Although we emphasized that *"lived-bodiliness"* "can be given" without regard to a psychic ego belonging to it (we are in agreement with Avenarius on this point), we must point out on the other hand that we do not in principle have to *pass through* any givenness of the *lived body* in order to comprehend an *egoness* in each psychic experience, and that a fortiori we do not have to pass through the perception of another, alien lived body or that of a fellow man. Nor is there any need to pass through the perception of one's own ego and lived body in order to comprehend another's ego and lived body as such.[30] Even if in imagination we reduce organic sensations of our lived body to a zero point, the ego and, for example, its spiritual feelings remain "given" (for there are in fact moments in our lives when only the schema of our lived body immediately exists for us – almost without positive contents – moments in which we seem to be lifted "from all earthly heaviness" [*Erdenschwere*], and there are also cases of deeply pathological anesthesia of bodily sensations and feelings). There is an essential difference between the manner in which I "am sad," i.e., the way in which sadness is related to the ego and "fills" it, and the manner in which I "feel *myself*" weak or strong, hungry or appeased, ill or healthy, or even the way in which I "feel my leg hurt" or "feel my skin itch." The modal diversity of the givenness in the phenomenal essence is not affected in the least by the fact that it is often difficult, sometimes even impossible, to distinguish *in concreto* the modes of the vital feeling-states belonging to a concrete global state and to lived-body sensations from a fact that is experienced as an ego-determination or one that is immediately related to the ego. Although self-deceptions are obviously possible here (especially regarding affections, which are always admixtures of the psychic, the body, and outer sensations), again, the modal diversity of the givenness in the phenomenal essence is by no means affected by this. One could come to believe that he finds a "bridge," e.g., from colors and sounds to feelings of hunger, or that he understands facts like "to be hungry" in exactly the same terms as sensations of the inner body, since sensations of colors are supposedly "sensations" of extrabodily objects. But one could do this only by making an insufficient distinction between inner bodily sensations of touch (possessing the quality of contents of touch), e.g., sensations of joints or sinews, which belong to the exterior sphere of the senses, and genuine bodily sensations and feeling-states, as well as drive-impulses, e.g., pain, tickling, and the feeling and impulses of hunger. However, the experienced *states* of the lived body are absolutely distinct from the contents and qualities of functions of the outer senses, and these (e.g., colors and sounds), in turn, from their "sensing" and its main types (e.g., seeing and hearing). Although the same contents of touching, for example, can serve as the basis for phenomenal body-determinations, such as smoothness, softness, and hardness, which are the phenomena to which we refer when we say that something feels "soft," "hard," "rough," or "smooth," as well as the basis for experiences that are more than sensuous states, this is *totally impossible* with respect to pain, tickling, and being hungry. These can never be "given" as determinations of inanimate bodies, but, at best, as experienced effects on a lived body. There are also no "elements" in them which can be given as such determinations.

Of course, what is always and by evident necessity given in an act of the essence of *inner perception* is only the essence and individuality of the ego and "any" of its *experiences* and *determinations*. For every factual comprehension of these and their special contents, the following proposition holds: All contents in the sphere of inner intuition also become, *in all degrees of clarity and distinctness*, contents of real perception only insofar as their being or non-being and their being-so or being-other-than-so posit some *variation* of the *lived body*. This fact is described in the following manner: All *inner perception is executed through an "inner sense,"* according to which all contents of possible inner perception that do *not* posit a variation of the lived body remain in the sphere of the "subconscious," and according to which it is not the inwardly perceived itself but the form of givenness of "appearances" presented in factual perceiving that acquires the forms of the manifold that are essential for facts of a phenomenal "*lived body*." Hence the factual perception of the ego and of the sphere of "pure" psychic facts is *not* an immediate perception that gives such facts themselves; it is, rather, a perception that is *mediated* through a *sensible lived body*. Factual perception of the ego and of psychic facts is, for this reason, as subject to deception as factual outer perception through outer "sensibility" is.[31] In both cases "sensibility" neither "creates" nor "produces" anything at all. It only suppresses or selects in accordance with the significance of psychic experiences (or possible contents of outer perception) for a lived body and the immanent goal-direction of its activity.

From this it becomes clear why the pure "*interwovenness*" [*Ineinander*] of experiences in the ego acquires, for factual perception, a *sequential* and *extensional* character [Nacheinander-*sein und* Aussereinander*sein*], which already belongs to the manifoldness of the phenomenal lived body (but without any trace of temporality or spatiality); and it also becomes clear how psychic experiences divide into "present," "past," and "future" ones.

No characteristic distinguishes all essentially *lived-body* phenomena from purely psychic phenomena more sharply than their being *extensive* and *non-extensive*. Moreover, both types of phenomena have a "position" that is "different in kind" in relation to the ego; this also holds for their subdivisions. For instance, pain is clearly extended: it "spreads" "across the back" or changes its place. "Hunger" is something that occurs in the area of the stomach and the chest. Even "fatigue," though it has no specific area of localization, as does tickling or, for example, "tiredness in the legs," is "spread" over and in the extended whole of a lived body. Such characteristics are completely nonsensical with regard to "sorrow," "woe," "serenity," etc. Nevertheless, such lived-body phenomena are by no means "in" space, neither in an objective space (e.g., in an arm as an anatomic, objective form-unity) nor even in a phenomenal space. On the contrary, they share "non-spatiality" with everything belonging to the purely psychic.

However, not only are lived-body phenomena of an extended nature. They also reveal "*extensionality*" [*Aussereinandersein*] and, within this form of manifoldness, in turn, a *side-by-side* as well as a *sequential* character [Nebeneinander- *und* Nacheinander*sein*]. There is also an appearance of "*oscillation*" within this form of manifoldness. Neither the side-by-side nor the sequential character is a relation in space and time, i.e., in *one* space and *one* time; and a fortiori they are not measurable relations. There is here, however, something like a "more" or "less" of this extensionality in terms of the side-by-side and sequential characters of, e.g., the tickle coming from a pain. But there are no spatial or temporal lines that would serve to connect these phenomena. Nor is there any fixed order in space or time. Pain may "alternate" with tickling in the same area. But in such a case it is senseless to say that a specific area of the body "changed" from a painful one into a ticklish one. Pain spreads "out" or afflicts first this and then that limb (e.g., in a case of gout), but there is no trace of "pain moving from one area to another." This particular manifold is therefore totally different from that of *extra*-lived-body phenomena.

This manifold is no less different from the above "*interwovenness in the ego*," which (purely) *psychic* facts possess. It would be senseless to assert that a thought, a spiritual feeling, or an expectation is "extensional" or "sequential," or that thoughts, etc., stand "side by side." The fact that one attributes a "sequential" character to them more often than a "side-by-side" character is only a consequence of identifying the type of *givenness* through which they come before the inner sense with an *element* of their content. It is not the "purely" psychic phenomena, from which every state of a lived body that is the condition of their factual perception is taken, but their *appearing in this and that content* of a plurality of acts of the type and form of "inner intuition," that brings about the "sequential character." Doubtless an act A of inner perception can possess more fullness in its content than another act B. But this difference in *fullness* is not the manifold of the "sequential." True, a third act C of inner intuition may even *encompass* the fullness of A and B in its content. In this case the fullness of A and B (F and F_1) may appear "sequentially" within the fullness of act C (F_2), but this is because F and F_1 were coordinated to *factually sequential* states of the lived body. This sequence of F and F_1 within the act C is only a part of the *content* of this act's fullness, whereas F and F_1 possess no existence as separate units of fullness. Thus the inner field of view overlooking one's own (or another's) ego may wax and wane, but without any manifestation of sequence in the contents of this field. It is therefore not what appears there but *how* it appears that reveals a "sequence." If a light is moved along a dark wall (the source of light being unknown), various areas of the wall are successively illuminated; however, there is no sequence of parts of the wall, but only the sequence of their illumination. One who is ignorant of the mechanism involved is led to believe that there is a sequence of parts. In this manner the factually sequential lived-body states illuminate interwoven determinations of the ego for inner perception according to specific laws of direction. It may seem that these determinations are *in themselves* sequential, but they are only coordinated to different, successively appearing lived-body states and are at the same time conditioned by them.

In this sense all that we experience (and also all that appears from the point of view of a given lived body as past) is experienced as "*together and interwoven*" in the ego. We cannot say that what appears as "past" lasts in objective time and is simply not perceived now (or that a "disposition," a psychic disposition, of it lasts). Nor can we say that it does *not* last but is annihilated, or that what lasts is only a physiological disposition to bring it back to life (epiphenomenalism of the psychic). Although these theories are strongly opposed to each other, they suffer from the *same πρῶτον ψεῦδος*: they construe the ego and its determinations and manifoldness as originally *sequential*, whereas in reality we are concerned with a totally different, positive manifoldness, namely, that of an *interwovenness* whose elements, as the elements which appear in inner perception to an embodied being, are coordinated by this being to the sequence of its lived-body states and are in their appearance conditioned by these states. These theories are bootless precisely because each psychic experience determines the *totality* of the "ego" in a *different* manner. The ego itself, however, which is neither sequential nor extensional, neither endures nor ceases to be (i.e., it cannot be or cease to be in a second point of time – *if* it existed in a preceding point of time).

Notes

1 Therefore a *"being which thinks itself"* (e.g., Aristotle's God, according to many interpreters, although not Franz Brentano) is not a "person." For "self-consciousness" is not a person if, in this consciousness "of" itself, all possible kinds of conscious activities (e.g., the knowing, willing, feeling, loving, and hating kinds) are not uniformly contained in it.

2 A nuance of red on the surface of a cloth, for example, is truly intuitable; and, as this nuance, it is also "individual." That is, it is not individual because of the complex it enters into, but at the same time it is something *abstract* belonging to the *concretum* of this surface.

3 Just because something is concrete does not mean that it is "real." Thus "the" number 3 is a single concrete existence, but ideal and not real, insofar as it functions neither as a quantity nor as an ordinal number fulfilling all possible equations (e.g., $4 - 1 = ?, 2 + 1 = ?, 17 - 14 = ?$; or $2 + 1 = +?, 4 - 7 = -?$). The *possible fulfillments* of the 3s meant in such equations represent only *abstracta* of this concrete 3.

4 One can also form classes of persons that lead to a more complete essential cognition of the acts concerned, which cognition is completed in the cognition of the personal individual who executed an act.

5 A theory of acts which neglects this turns the person into a mosaic of acts and so arrives at another version of the atomistic conception of the mind, a version similar to that of association psychology.

6 This was Spinoza's deep insight, insofar as he broke away from the Cartesian theory of substance. Thus soul-substances became modes of the attribute "thinking" of a substance. Spinoza correctly saw that there is no place for the *person* on the presupposition that the mind's essence is only "thinking," and he saw as well that the individualization of thinking beings would have to be shifted to mere differences among human bodies (as in the philosophy of Averroes). Thus Spinoza drew correct conclusions from Descartes's false presuppositions.

7 Needless to say, there is no causal relationship here. For the latter exists only for real correlates of experience of what is given in inner perception.

8 Pictures of this kind also lead to questions characteristic of the seventeenth century: whether the *soul always* thinks, whether it executes acts even in dreamless sleep, etc., whether it "remains unchanged" throughout life.

9 "Objective" time is deformed and dequalified phenomenal time. Whereas duration and succession within phenomenal time are positive qualities, duration in objective time consists only in successive phases of the being of an object in which the object does not change. Although there is no "present" in objective time, since there is neither past nor future (a distinction which is relative to a lived body), present points of phenomenal time (and these exclusively) do correspond to points of objective time.

10 The difference between reflection and inner perception is also made clear by the fact that an act of outer perception can definitely be given in reflection, but, of course, never in inner perception. One who does not see this is bound to declare the entire content of outer perception a partial content of the act of outer perception given (on this premise) in inner perception; i.e., he will fall victim to idealistic psychologism.

11 See Carl Stumpf, "Erscheinungen und psychische Funktionen," in *Abhandlungen der preussischen Akademie der Wissenschaften vom Jahre 1906* (Berlin, 1907).

12 See my critique of Brentano's and Stumpf's division of the psychic and the physical in "Idole der Selbsterkenntnis."

13 See "Die transzendentale und die psychologische Methode".

14 Hence the spheres of person and world, egoness and outer world, individual ego and community, and lived body and environment are not reducible, one to the other.

15 By "subconscious" sphere of inner perception, I do not mean, say, "unnoticed" or "unrecognized." I mean everything whose presence, absence, or variation produces in the totality of what is inwardly perceived a "change" in a specific direction, but which is not necessarily given (even in an attitude of maximal noticing). For these "subconscious" facts, all of which belong to the *phenomenal* sphere, there is the real plus dispositions, just as in the case of surconscious appearances. Thus the sphere of the

unconscious divides into what is unconscious in the subconscious sphere and what is unconscious in the surconscious sphere. In Benno Erdmann's terminology (of association psychology), our sphere of what is unconscious in the subconscious sphere coincides with the "dispositionally excited."

16 His pure will is simply "reason as practical," i.e., thinking related to the realization of a content by means of actions (πράττειν). The fact that Kant actually denies a pure "will" was emphasized first by Herman Schwarz. See his *Psychologie des Willens* (Leipzig: Engelmann, 1900).

17 The "contingency" of the real world, the fact that it cannot be deduced from the laws of "possible worlds," is given with this alone.

18 Insofar as one does not wish to regard as such the sensations of tension and position mediated by muscles of the eyes when the eyes are open and at rest.

19 Lipps's argument against an original depth-dimension of vision can be understood on the basis of the following presupposition: Every comprehension of distance presupposes that the two bodies at a distance from each other are perceived, but the eye itself is not perceived; hence . . .

20 It is not my intention in this connection to clarify completely the difficult problem of the givenness of the lived body. But I intend to return to this in a later work dealing with a phenomenological examination of basic concepts of biology with which I dealt earlier. In the present context I am concerned only with the systematic determination of limits of the givenness of the lived body within the interconnection of the givenness of the body and the ego.

21 With respect to both the expressed experience and the object meant in the expression. An object is always comeant in statements.

22 Animism, as referred to by Avenarius, presupposes the formation of the idea "ego" or "soul" with regard to the inanimate world.

23 As, for instance, Lipps and Ettlinger hold.

24 The idea at the basis of Avenarius' critique of pure experience, that his system *C*, with all its excitations, aims at a maximum of "self-preservation" and therefore works according to the principle of the "smallest amount of force," *presupposes* "amechanical" factors. No matter how justified this may be in our view, it has no justification in his theory of knowledge, according to which the lived body is found like any other thing-body. If one were to make the quite impossible *attempt* to derive the logical principles from the principle of the economy of thought, which would mean, of course, to demonstrate their validity as "conditions of preservation of the lived body" (even of a "system *C*"), one would have to attribute to the lived body a *teleological* principle which is effective in it and which determines its *unity*, i.e., a tendency toward self-preservation with the fewest means. But then one cannot *also* be a mechanist in biology.

25 The following is to be said against Avenarius' assertion that one implicitly thinks of a perception of the "interior" of something corporeal on the occasion of an "inner" perception. There is, strictly speaking, no "interior" or "exterior" to the spatiality of outer perception. There is *extensionality*, but no genuine "interwovenness" [*Ineinander*]. It is only on the basis of a lived-embodying [*Verleiblichung*] of even inanimate things, which is so typical of the natural standpoint, that we can say, for example, that a ball is "in" a box, or even that a box is "in" space. For both cases presuppose that we first *add* the spatial form of the ball to the box in intuition and then subtract the form (as belonging to the ball) from the "box." The evident a priori proposition of the impenetrability of a "body" makes every "in" merely "apparent." Hence things are just the *reverse* of what Avenarius believes. Any *interwovenness* is analogous to the way in which elements can be with one another in the manifold of inner perception. This "analogy" holds even when we say: My heart is "in" my lived-body-thing [*Leibkörper*].

26 E. Mach, *Die Analyse der Empfindungen* (Jena, 1903), Vol. I, sec. 7–8.

27 If there were a property *X* that physical objects could have, but psychic objects could not, one could maintain only that there is one and the same perception of physical objects on the one hand and psychic objects on the other, like a perception of tables and chairs; one could not maintain that there are two different perceptual directions, like inner and outer perception.

28 Just as Husserl's "noema" and "noesis" are mutually interdependent in their qualitative nature.

29 The old theory of projection and its opposite, the theory of introjection, make the same basic mistake of not distinguishing between psychic, physical, and lived-body phenomena and the types of perception which belong to them.

30 See *Zur Phänomenologie und Theorie der Sympathiegefühle*.

31 The failure to see that factual psychic self-perception is mediated by the lived body and sensibility leads to difficulties in understanding the cognition of the alter psychic. I have shown this in *Zur Phänomenologie und Theorie der Sympathiegefühle*, p. 133.

Part V

EDITH STEIN
Phenomenology and the Interpersonal

EDITH STEIN (1891–1942)

Introduction

Husserl's phenomenology in its early Göttingen years attracted a significant number of women philosophers, including Hedwig Conrad-Martius (1888–1966), Gerda Walther (1897–1977), and, the most significant for phenomenology, Edith Stein (1891–1942). Stein was born in 1891 in Breslau, Prussia (now Wroclaw, Poland), and attended local schools and gymnasia. She was precocious, and, at an early age, declared herself an atheist. She enrolled at the University of Breslau to study literature and philosophy, but, having read Husserl's *Logical Investigations*, she transferred to the University of Göttingen, interrupting her studies in 1915 to serve in the Red Cross. She was an active member of the Göttingen Philosophical Society, which included Adolf Reinach, Roman Ingarden and Hedwig Conrad-Martius. She attended Scheler's lectures from 1910 to 1911. In 1916, she completed her doctoral thesis with Husserl, published as *On the Problem of Empathy* (1917). Being one of the first women to gain a doctorate in philosophy from a German university, she campaigned to be allowed to register for a *Habilitation*, hitherto denied to women.

When Husserl moved to Freiburg in 1916, he invited Stein to work as his private assistant. She transcribed and edited Husserl's research manuscripts, including the manuscript of *Ideas* II, which shows considerable evidence of her editorial interventions. She also laboured on Husserl's *Lectures on the Consciousness of Internal Time* (1905–1917), although these were eventually brought to press by Heidegger in 1928 (with only the slightest reference to Stein's labours on them). Her letters to Ingarden show that she was unable to interest Husserl in her revisions of his manuscripts, including the draft revision of the Sixth Investigation. Inspired by reading St Theresa of Avila, she converted to Catholicism in 1921 and was baptised in 1922. Having been initially denied permission to follow a *Habilitation*, she taught at a Dominican school in Speyer until 1932, when she moved to teach at the Institute of Pedagogy in Münster. She continued to correspond with Husserl, Ingarden and others, and contributed an article to Husserl's *Festschrift* (1929) on "Husserl's Phenomenology and the Philosophy of St. Thomas Aquinas". Meanwhile, she began reading Thomas Aquinas, and even translated his *De Veritate* (*On Truth*). She also wrote an important work *On Finite and Eternal Being*, an attempt to relate Thomism and Husserlian phenomenology. She campaigned on women's issues and was a prominent feminist in the early 1930s.

In 1933, Stein was forced to resign her teaching position, because of the Nazi laws against Jews. She entered a Carmelite convent in Cologne and became Sister Teresa Benedicta a Cruce in 1934. In 1938, because of Nazi persecution, she transferred to a convent at Echt in Holland, where she wrote her study on St John of the

Cross, *The Science of the Cross*. In 1942, her convent was raided by the Nazis, and she was arrested and deported to Auschwitz concentration camp in Poland, where she perished on 9 August 1942. In 1988, she was beatified and in 1998, she was canonised by Pope John Paul II. Her autobiographical *Life in a Jewish Family* was published posthumously in 1965.

Stein wrote primarily on issues of psychology, spirituality and religious philosophy. From the point of view of phenomenology, she contributed a number of important studies, including her study of empathy (*Einfühlung*) and a long treatise, *Contributions to the Philosophical Grounding of Psychology and the Human Sciences* (1922), published in Husserl's *Yearbook for Philosophy and Phenomenological Research*. Her conversion to Catholicism in 1922 meant that her later writings moved away from phenomenology, but she still published a political text, *An Investigation on the State* in the *Yearbook* in 1925. Her critical developments of key Husserlian concepts show that she was no mere follower but an independent thinker in her own right.

Stein was initially attracted to phenomenology as a way of overcoming neo-Kantianism and gaining objective truth about reality. Her discussion of empathy develops and sharpens the meditations of Husserl in his draft manuscripts of *Ideas* II and other research notes on intersubjectivity. Following Husserl, Stein distinguishes between primordial and non-primordial experiences within the individual in order to understand the constitution of the other. I constitute myself in primordial acts and the other in non-primordial acts. I recognise the other through perceiving the other's body.

Our reading is a discussion of our first-person experience of the body, which is not experienced simply as a physical object but is constituted in our experience in a complex way. Stein's concern is with the psychophysical being, the manner in which the psychological features of the human subject are embodied. In this reading, Stein describes the peculiar way in which sensations and feelings present themselves, at a distance for the ego which is experienced at the heart of judgings or willings. Stein discusses the different kinds of distance involved in the way in which we map sensations, feelings and emotions in our bodies.

Further reading

Stein, Edith. *Collected Works of Edith Stein*. Washington, DC: ICS Publications, ongoing.
Stein, Edith. *Kreuzeswissenschaft. The Science of the Cross*, trans. Hilda Graef. Chicago, IL: Henry Regnery, 1960.
Stein, Edith. *Life in a Jewish Family*, trans. Joesephine Koeppel. Washington, DC: ICS Publications, 1986.
Stein, Edith. *On the Problem of Empathy*, trans. Waltraut Stein. The Hague: Nijhoff, 1964. Reprinted Washington, DC: ICS Publications, 1989.
Stein, Edith. *On Woman*, trans. Freda Mary Oben. Washington, DC: ICS Publications, 1987.
Stein, Edith. *Writings of Edith Stein*. Ed. and trans. Hilda Graef. Westminster, MD: Newman Press, 1986.
Graef, Hilda. *The Scholar and the Cross*. Westminster, MD: Newman Press, 1955.
Haney, Kathleen. "Edith Stein", in Lester Embree *et al.* (eds), *Encyclopedia of Phenomenology*. Dordrecht: Kluwer, 1997.

1

ON THE PROBLEM OF EMPATHY

(a) The givenness of the living body

We again proceed from the sphere forming the basis of all our investigations: that of pure consciousness. How is my body [*Leib*] constituted within consciousness? I have my physical body [*Körper*] given once in acts of outer perception. But if we suppose it to be given to us in this manner alone, we have the strangest object. This would be a real thing, a physical body, whose motivated successive appearances exhibit striking gaps. It would withhold its rear side with more stubbornness than the moon and invite me continually to consider it from new sides. Yet as soon as I am about to carry out its invitation, it hides these sides from me. To be sure, things that withdraw from the glance are accessible to touch. But precisely the relationship between seeing and touching is different here than anywhere else. Everything else I see says to me, "Touch me. I am really what I seem to be, am tangible, and not a phantom." And what I touch calls to me, "Open your eyes and you will see me." The tactile and visual senses (as one can speak of sense in the pure sphere) call each other as witnesses, though they do not shift the responsibility on one another.

This unique defect of the outwardly perceived physical body is in contrast with another peculiarity. I can approach and withdraw from any other thing, can turn toward or away from it. In the latter case, it vanishes from my sight. This approaching and withdrawing, the movement of my physical body and of other things, is documented by an alteration of their successive appearances. A distinction between these two cases: the movement of other things and the movement of my physical body, is inconceivable. Nor is it possible to see how we comprehend the movement of our own physical bodies at all as long as we maintain the fiction that our physical body is only constituted in outer perception and not as a characteristically living body. Thus we must say, more precisely, that every other object is given to me in an infinitely variable multiplicity of appearances and of changing positions, and there are also times when it is not given to me. But this one object (my physical body) is given to me in successive appearances only variable within very narrow limits. As long as I have my eyes open at all, it is continually there with a steadfast obtrusiveness, always having the same tangible nearness as no other object has. It is always "here" while other objects are always "there."

E. Stein, *On the Problem of Empathy*, 1989, trans. Waltraut Stein, pp. 41–56. Washington, DC: ICS Publications.

But this brings us to the limit of our supposition and we must suspend it. For even if we shut our eyes tightly and stretch out our arms, in fact allowing no limb to contact another so that we can neither touch nor see our physical body, even then we are not rid of it. Even then it stands there inescapably in full embodiment (hence the name), and we find ourselves bound to it perpetually. Precisely this affiliation, this belonging to me, could never be constituted in outer perception. A living body [*Leib*] only perceived outwardly would always be only a particularly disposed, actually unique, physical body, but never "my living body."

Now let us observe how this new givenness occurs. As an instance of the supreme category of "experience," sensations are among the real constituents of consciousness, of this domain impossible to cancel. The sensation of pressure or pain or cold is just as absolutely given as the experience of judging, willing, perceiving, etc. Yet, in contrast with these acts, sensation is peculiarly characterized. It does not issue from the pure "I" as they do, and it never takes on the form of the "cogito" in which the "I" turns toward an object. Since sensation is always spatially localized "somewhere" at a distance from the "I" (perhaps very near to it but never in it), I can never find the "I" in it by reflection. And this "somewhere" is not an empty point in space, but something filling up space. All these entities from which my sensations arise are amalgamated into a unity, the unity of my living body, and they are themselves places in the living body.

There are differences in this unified givenness in which the living body is always there for me as a whole. The various parts of the living body constituted for me in terms of sensation are various distances from me. Thus my torso is nearer to me than my extremities, and it makes good sense to say that I bring my hands near or move them away. To speak of distance from "me" is inexact because I cannot really establish an interval from the "I," for it is non-spatial and cannot be localized. But I relate the parts of my living body, together with everything spatial outside of it, to a "zero point of orientation" which my living body surrounds. This zero point is not to be geometrically localized at one point in my physical body; nor is it the same for all data. It is localized in the head for visual data and in mid-body for tactile data. Thus, whatever refers to the "I" has no distance from the zero point, and all that is given at a distance from the zero point is also given at a distance from the "I."

However, this distance of bodily parts from me is fundamentally different from the distance of other things from each other and from me. Two things in space are at a specific distance from each other. They can approach each other and even come into contact, whereupon their distance disappears. It is also possible (if the objects are not materially impenetrable, but, for instance, are hallucinatory objects of different visual hallucinators) for them to occupy the same portion of space. Similarly, a thing can approach me, its distance from me can decrease, and it can contact not me, but my physical body. Then the distance from my physical body, but not from me, becomes zero. Nor does the distance of the thing from the zero point become the same as the distance of the contacted part of the physical body from the zero point. I could never say that the stone I hold in my hand is the same distance or "only a tiny bit farther" from the zero point than the hand itself.

The distance of the parts of my living body from me is completely incomparable with the distance of foreign physical bodies from me. The living body as a whole is at the zero point of orientation with all physical bodies outside of it.

"Body space" [*Leibraum*] and "outer space" are completely different from each other. Merely perceiving outwardly, I would not arrive at the living body, nor merely "perceiving bodily" [*leibwahrnehmend*], at the outer world. But the living body is constituted in a two-fold manner as a sensed (bodily perceived) living body and as an outwardly perceived physical body of the outer world. And in this doubled givenness it is experienced as the same. Therefore, it has a location in outer space and fills up a portion of this space.

There is still something to say about the relationship between sensation and "bodily perception." The analysis of sensations usually comes up in other contexts. We usually look at sensations as what "give" us the outer world, and in this sense we separate "sensation" from "what is sensed" or "content of sensation" from "sensation as function" in Stumpf's sense. We separate, for example, the seen red and the possessing of this red. I cannot agree with him. The object's red is "perceived" and I must distinguish between perception and what is perceived. The analysis of perception leads me to "sensory data" so that I can look at the perception of qualities as an "objectification of sensory data." But this does not make qualities into perceptions nor perceptions into qualities or giving acts. As constituents of outer perception, both are elements not further analyzable.

Now if we consider sensation in terms of the side turned toward the living body, we find an entirely analogous phenomenal state of affairs. I can speak of a "sensed" living body as little as of a "sensed" object in the outer world. However, this also requires an objectifying apprehension. If my fingertips contact the table, I have to distinguish, first, the sensation of touch, the tactile datum not further divisible. Secondly, there is the hardness of the table with its correlative act of outer perception and, thirdly, the touching fingertip and the correlative act of "bodily perception." What makes the connection between sensation and bodily perception particularly intimate is the fact that sensations are given at the living body to the living body as senser.

An investigation of all kinds of sensations in their meaning for bodily perception would be beyond the scope of this work. But we must discuss one more point. We said that the "outer" and "bodily perceived" living body is given as the same. This requires still further elucidation. I not only see my hand and bodily perceive it as sensing, but I also "see" its fields of sensation constituted for me in bodily perception. On the other hand, if I consciously emphasize certain parts of my living body, I have an "image" of this part of the physical body. The one is given with the other, though they are not perceived together. This is exactly analogous to the province of outer perception. We not only see the table and feel its hardness, but we also "see" its hardness. The robes in Van Dyck's paintings are not only as shiny as silk but also as smooth and as soft as silk. Psychologists call this phenomenon fusion and usually reduce it to "mere association." This "mere" indicates psychology's tendency to look at explanation as an explaining away, so that the explained phenomenon becomes a "subjective creation" without "objective meaning." We cannot accept this interpretation. Phenomenon remains phenomenon. An explanation is very desirable, but this explanation adds nothing to or subtracts nothing from it. Thus the certainty of tactile qualities would continue to exist and lose none of its merit whether or not association can explain it.

To be sure, we do not think such an explanation possible because it contradicts the "phenomenon" of association. Association is typically experienced as "something reminding me of something." For example, the sight of the table corner reminds me I once bumped myself on it. However, this corner's sharpness is not remembered, but seen. Here is another instructive example: I see a rough lump of sugar and know or remember that it is sweet. I do not remember it is rough (or only incidentally), nor see its sweetness. By contrast, the flower's fragrance is really sweet and does not remind me of a sweet taste. This begins to open up perspectives for a phenomenology of the senses and of sense perceptions that, of course, we cannot go into here. At this point we are only interested in applying these insights to our case. The seen living body does not remind us it can be the scene of manifold sensations. Neither is it merely a physical thing taking up the same space as the living body given as sensitive in bodily perception. It is given as a sensing, living body.

So far we have only considered the living body at rest. Now we can go a step farther. Let us suppose that I (i.e., my living body as a whole) move through the room. As long as we disregarded the constitution of the living body, this was not a peculiarly characterized phenomenon. It was no different than the kaleidoscopic shifting of the surrounding outer world. Now the experience that "I move" becomes entirely new. It becomes the apperception of our own movement based on manifold sensations and is entirely different from the outwardly perceived movement of physical bodies. Now the comprehension of our own movement and the alteration of the outer world are combined in the form of "if . . . then." "If I move, then the picture of my environment shifts." This is just as true for the perception of the single spatial thing as for the cohesive spatial world, and, similarly, for movements of parts of the living body as for its movement as a whole. If I rest my hand on a rotating ball, this ball and its movement are given to me as a succession of changing tactile data merging into an intention permeating the whole. These data can be comprehended together in an "apperceptive grasp," a unified act of outer perception. Data have the same sequence if my hand glides over the still ball, but the experience that "I move" supervenes anew and, with the apperception of the ball, goes into the form of "if . . . then." Visual data are analogous. While being still, I can see the changing appearances of a rolling ball: and the "shades of the ball" can look the same if the ball is still and I move my head or only my eyes. This movement, again, is given to me in "bodily perception."

This is how parts of the living body are constituted as moving organs and the perception of the spatial world as dependent on the behavior of these organs. But this does not yet show us how we comprehend the movements of living bodies as movements of physical bodies. When I move one of my limbs, besides becoming bodily aware of my own movement, I have an outer visual or tactile perception of physical body movements to which the limb's changed appearances testify. As the bodily perceived and outwardly perceived limb are interpreted as the same, so there also arises an identical coincidence of the living and physical body's movement. The moving living body becomes the moved physical body. And the fact that "I move" is "seen with" the movement of a part of my physical body. The unseen movement of the physical body in the experience of "I move" is comprehended jointly.

The affiliation of the "I" with the perceiving body requires some further elucidation. The impossibility of being rid of the body indicates its special givenness.

This union cannot be shaken; the bonds tying us to our bodies are indissoluble. Nevertheless, we are permitted certain liberties. All the objects in the outer world have a certain distance from me. They are always "there" while I am always here. They are grouped around me, around my "here." This grouping is not rigid and unchangeable. Objects approach and withdraw from me and from one another, and I myself can undertake a regrouping by moving things farther or nearer or exchanging their places. Or else I can take another "standpoint" so that I change my "here" instead of their "there." Every step I take discloses a new bit of the world to me or I see the old one from a new side. In so doing I always take my living body along. Not only I am always "here" but also it is; the various "distances" of its parts from me are only variations within this "here."

Now, instead of in reality, I can also "regroup" my environment "in thought alone." I can fantasize. For example, I can fantasize my room empty of furniture and "imagine" how it would look then. I can also take an excursion through the world of fantasy. "In thought" I can get up from my desk, go into a corner of the room, and regard it from there. Here I do not take my living body along. Perhaps the "I" standing there in the corner has a fantasized living body, i.e., one seen in "bodily fantasy," if I may say so. Moreover, this body can look at the living body [Leibkörper] at the desk it has left just as well as at other things in the room. Of course, this living body then also is a represented object, i.e., one given in representing outer intuition. Finally, the real living body [Leib] has not disappeared, but I actually continue to sit at my desk unsevered from my living body. Thus my "I" has been doubled, and, even though the real "I" cannot be released from its body, there is at least the possibility of "slipping out of one's skin" in fantasy.

An "I" without a body is a possibility. But a body without an "I" is utterly impossible. To fantasize my body forsaken by my "I" means to fantasize my living body no longer, but a completely parallel physical body, to fantasize my corpse. If I leave my living body, it becomes for me a physical body like others. And, instead of my leaving it, should I think of it away from me, this removal is not "one's own movement" but a pure movement of the physical body. There is still another way of showing this. A "withered" limb without sensations is not part of my living body. A foot "gone to sleep" is an appendage like a foreign physical body that I cannot shake off. It lies beyond the spatial zone of my living body into which it is once more drawn when it "awakens." Every movement I make of it in this condition is like "moving an object," i.e., my alive movement evokes a mechanical movement. And this moving itself is not given as the living moving of a living body. For the living body is essentially constituted through sensations: sensations are real constituents of consciousness and, as such, belong to the "I." Thus how could there be a living body not the body of an "I"!

Whether a sensing "I" is conceivable without a living body is another question. This is the question of whether there could be sensations in which no living body is constituted. The answer can be given without further ado because, as already stated, the sensations of the various sensory provinces do not share in the structure of the living body in the same manner. Thus we have to assay whether the localization of the senses clearly experienced at places in the living body – of taste, temperature, or pain – is necessary and incommutable. If this is the case, it would make them possible only for a living bodily "I" so that another analysis of the senses of sight, hearing, etc. would still seem to be necessary.

We need not decide these questions here, though a phenomenology of outer perception would not be able to avoid them. Nevertheless, the senses have already constituted the unity of "I" and living body for us, even though not the complete range of reciprocal relationships as yet. Also the causal relationship between the psychic and the physical already confronts us in the province of the senses. Purely physical events such as a foreign body being forced under my skin or a certain amount of heat coming into contact with the surface of my physical body is the phenomenal cause [*Ursache*] of sensations of pain and of temperature. It turns out to be "stimulation." We shall come upon such phenomenal causal relationships often now as we further pursue the relationships between soul and living body.

(b) The living body and feelings

Sensations of feelings [*Gefühlsempfindungen*] or sensual feelings [*sinnliche Gefühle*] are inseparable from their founding sensations. The pleasantness of a savory dish, the agony of a sensual pain, the comfort of a soft garment are noticed where the food is tasted, where the pain pierces, where the garment clings to the body's surface. However, sensual feelings not only are there but at the same time also in me; they issue from my "I." General feelings have a hybrid position similar to sensual feelings. Not only the "I" feels vigorous or sluggish, but I "notice this in all my limbs." Every mental act, every joy, every pain, every activity of thought, together with every bodily action, every movement I make, is sluggish and colorless when "I" feel sluggish. My living body and all its parts are sluggish with me. Thus our familiar phenomenon of fusion again appears. Not only do I see my hand's movement and feel its sluggishness at the same time, but I also see the sluggish movement and the hand's sluggishness. We always experience general feelings as coming from the living body with an accelerating or hindering influence on the course of experience. This is true even when these general feelings arise in connection with a "spiritual feeling."

Moods are "general feelings" of a non-somatic nature, and so we separate them from strictly general feeling as a species of their own. Cheerfulness and melancholy do not fill the living body. It is not cheerful or melancholy as it is vigorous or sluggish, nor could a purely spiritual being be subject to moods. But this does not imply that psychic and bodily general feelings run beside one another undisturbed. Rather, one seems to have a reciprocal "influence" on the other. For instance, suppose I take a trip to recuperate and arrive at a sunny, pleasant spot. While looking at the view, I feel that a cheerful mood wants to take possession of me, but cannot prevail because I feel sluggish and tired. "I shall be cheerful here as soon as I have rested up." I say to myself, I may know this from "previous experience," yet its foundation is always in the phenomenon of the reciprocal action of psychic and somatic experiences.

(c) Soul and living body, psycho-physical causality

The psychic is in essence characterized by this dependence of experiences on somatic influences. Everything psychic is body-bound consciousness, and in this area essentially psychic experiences, body-bound sensations, etc., are distinguished from accidental physical experiences, the "realizations" of spiritual life. As the substantial unity announced in single psychic experiences, the soul is based on the living body. This is shown in the phenomenon of "psycho-physical causality" we have delineated and in the nature of sensations. And the soul together with the living body forms the "psycho-physical" individual.

Now we must consider the character of so-called "spiritual feelings." The term already indicates to us that spiritual feelings are accidentally psychic and not body-bound (even if psychologists would not like to acknowledge this consequence.) Anyone who brings the pure essence of a bodiless subject to givenness would contend that such a subject experiences no pleasure, grief, or aesthetic values. By contrast, many noted psychologists see "complexes of organic sensations" in feelings. As absurd as this definition may seem as long as we consider feelings in their pure essence, in concrete psychic contexts we actually do find phenomena which do not ground feelings, to be sure, though they can make them intelligible. "Our heart stops beating" for joy; we "wince" in pain; our pulse races in alarm; and we are breathless. Examples which all deal with psycho-physical causality, with effects of psychic experience on body functions, can be multiplied at will. When we think the living body away, these phenomena disappear, though the spiritual act remains. It must be conceded that God rejoices over the repentance of a sinner without feeling His heart pound or other "organic sensations," an observation that is possible whether one believes in God or not. People can be convinced that in reality feelings are impossible without such sensations and that no existing being experiences them in their purity. However, feelings can be comprehended in their purity, and this appearance of accompaniment is experienced exactly as such, as neither a feeling nor a component of one. The same thing can also be shown in cases of purely psychic causality. "I lose my wits" for fright, i.e., I notice my thoughts are paralyzed. Or "my head spins" for joy so that I do not know what I am doing and do pointless things. A pure spirit can also become frightened but it does not lose its wits. [Its understanding does not stand still.] It feels pleasure and pain in all their depth without these feelings exerting any effect.

I can expand these considerations. As I "observe" myself, I also discover causal relationships between my experiences with their announced capacities and the attributes of my soul. Capacities can be developed and sharpened by use as well as worn out and dulled. Thus my "power of observation" increases as I work in natural science; for example, my power for distinguishing colors as I work with sorting threads of finely shaded colors, my "capacity for enjoyment" as I have pleasures. Every capacity can be strengthened by "training." On the other hand, at a certain "habituation" point the opposite effect takes place. I "get enough of" an "object of pleasure" continually placed before me. It eventually arouses boredom, disgust, etc. In all these cases the physical is phenomenally having an effect on the psychic. But it is a question of what kind of an "effect" this is and of whether this phenomenon of causality enables us to arrive at an exact concept of causality for natural science and at a general law of cause. Exact natural science is based on this concept, while descriptive science deals only with the phenomenal concept of causality. It is also the case that an exact concept of causality and unbroken causal precision are a presupposition of the exact causal-genetic psychology to which psychologists aspire in conjunction with the example set by the modern science of physical nature. We must content ourselves here with pointing out these problems without going into their solution.

(d) The phenomenon of expression

The consideration of the causal operation of feelings has led us further than we anticipated. Nevertheless, we have not exhausted what feelings can teach us. There arises a new phenomenon of the expression of feeling beside this appearance of accompaniment. I blush for shame, I irately clench my fist, I angrily furrow my brow, I groan with pain, am jubilant with joy. The relationship of feeling to expression is completely different from that of feeling to the appearance of physical accompaniment. In the former case I do not notice physical experiences issuing out of psychic ones, much less their mere simultaneity. Rather, as I live through the feeling, I feel it terminate in an expression or release expression out of itself. Feeling in its pure essence is not something complete in itself. As it were, it is loaded with an energy which must be unloaded.

This unloading is possible in different ways. We know one kind of unloading very well. Feelings release or motivate volitions and actions, so to speak. Feeling is related to the appearance of expression in exactly the same way. The same feeling that motivates a volition can also motivate an appearance of expression. And feeling by its nature prescribes what expression and what volition it can motivate. By nature it must always motivate something, must always be "expressed." Only different forms of expression are possible.

It could be objected here that in life feelings often arise without motivating a volition or bodily expression. As is well-known, we civilized people must "control" ourselves and hold back the bodily expression of our feelings. We are similarly restricted in our activities and thus in our volitions. There is, of course, still the loophole of "airing" one's wishes. The employee who is allowed neither to tell his superior by contemptuous looks he thinks him a scoundrel or a fool nor to decide to remove him, can still wish secretly that he would go to the devil. Or one can carry out deeds in fantasy that are blocked in reality. One who is born into restricted circumstances and cannot fulfill himself in reality carries out his desire for great things by winning battles and performing wonders of valor in imagination. The creation of another world where I can do what is forbidden to me here is itself a form of expression. Thus the man dying of thirst sees in the distance before him oases with bubbling springs or seas that revive him, as Gebsattel reports.

The joy filling us is not a meditative devotion to the pleasing object. Rather, it is externalized in other situations as we entirely surround ourselves with what is enjoyable. We seek it in our real surrounding world or induce it by memory or freely fantasizing representation. We neglect everything that does not fit in with it until our frame of mind is in complete harmony with our surrounding world.

This peculiarity of expression requires a comprehensive clarification. It is not enough to state that feelings influence the "reproduction of ideas" and how frequently this occurs, as psychology usually does.

But expression or its surrogate is possible in still another way, and to this the "controlled" person who for social, aesthetic, or ethical reasons puts on a uniform countenance in public usually retreats. Feeling can release an act of reflection that makes the feeling itself objective. The experience "terminates" in this act of reflection just as in a volition or bodily expression. We usually say that reflection weakens feeling and that the reflecting man is incapable of intense feelings. This inference is completely unjustified. The feeling "terminates" in "passionate" expression just as in "cool" reflection. The type of expression signifies nothing about the intensity of the feeling expressed.

So far, we can conclude that feeling by its nature demands expression. The various types of expression are various essential possibilities. Feelings and expression are related by nature and meaning, not causally. The bodily expression, like other possible forms issuing from feeling and its meaning, is therefore also definitely experienced. For I not only feel how feeling is poured into expression and "unloaded" in it, but at the same time I have this expression given in bodily perception. The smile in which my pleasure is experientially externalized is at the same time given to me as a stretching of my lips. As I live in the joy, I also experience its expression in the mode of actuality and carry out the simultaneous bodily perception in the mode of non-actuality. I am not, so to speak, conscious of it. Should I then turn my attention to the perceived change of my living body, I see it as effected through a feeling. Thus a causal connection between feeling and expression has been constituted beside the sensory unity. Expression uses psycho-physical causality to become realized in a psycho-physical individual. The experienced unity of experience and expression is taken apart in bodily perception, and expression is separated as a relatively independent phenomenon. At the same time it itself becomes productive. I can stretch my mouth so that it could be "taken for" a smile but actually not be a smile.

Similar perceptual phenomena are also seen as different phenomena of expression independently of the will. I blush in anger, for shame, or from exertion. In all these cases I have the same perception of my "blood rising into my face." But in one instance I experience this as an expression of anger, in another I experience the same occurrence as an expression of shame, and, again, not as an expression at all but as a causal result of exertion. We have said that it requires an observant glance to make the bodily perceived expression into an intentional object in the pregnant sense. Yet the felt expression, even though experienced in the mode of actuality, also requires a particular turning of the glance to become a comprehended object. This turning of the glance is not the transition from non-actuality to actuality that is characteristic of all non-theoretical acts and their correlates.

The fact that I can objectify experienced phenomena of expression and comprehend them as expression is a further condition of the possibility of voluntarily producing them. Nevertheless, the bodily change resembling an expression is not really given as the same. The furrowing of the brow in anger and the furrowing of the brow to simulate anger are clearly distinguishable in themselves even when I pass over from bodily perception to outer perception. Since phenomena of expression appear as the outpouring of feelings, they are simultaneously the expression of the psychic characteristics they announce. For example, the furious glance reveals a vehement state of mind. We shall conclude this investigation by a consideration of experiences of will.

(e) Will and living body

Experiences of will also have an important meaning for the constitution of psycho-physical unity. For one thing, they are important because of accompanying physical manifestations (sensations of tension, etc.), though we shall not consider these further because we are already familiar with them from our discussion of feelings.

Other phenomena of bodily expression being considered do not appear to be the expression of volition itself, but to be feeling components of complex volitional experiences. I may sit here quietly weighing two practical possibilities. Then I have chosen, have made a decision. I plant my feet on the floor and spring up vivaciously. These movements do not express a volitional decision, but the resulting feeling of decisiveness, of activity, of unrest that fills me. Will itself is not expressed in this sense, but, like feeling, neither is it isolated in itself, having to work itself out. Just as feeling releases or motivates volition from itself (or another possible "expression" in a wider sense), so will externalizes itself in action. To act is always to produce what is not present. The "fieri" ['to be done'] of what is willed conforms to the "fiat!" ['let it be done!'] of the volitional decision and to the "facere" ['doing'] of the subject of the will in action. This action can be physical. I can decide to climb a mountain and carry out my decision. It seems that the action is called forth entirely by the will and is fulfilling the will. But the action as a whole is willed, not each step. I will to climb the mountain. What is "necessary" for this takes care "of itself." The will employs a psycho-physical mechanism to fulfill itself, to realize what is willed, just as feeling uses such a mechanism to realize its expression.

At the same time the control of the mechanism or at least the "switching on of the machine" is experienced. It may be experienced step by step if it means overcoming a resistance at the same time. If I become tired halfway up, this causes a resistance to the movement to seize my feet and they stop serving my will. Willing and striving oppose each other and fight for control of the organism. Should the will become master, then every step may now be willed singly and the effective movement experienced by overcoming the countereffect.

The same thing applies in purely psychic domains. I decide to take an examination and almost automatically do the required preparation. Or my strength may give out before I reach my goal, and I must call to life each requisite mental act by a volition to overcome a strong resistance. The will is thus master of the soul as of the living body, even though not experienced absolutely nor without the soul refusing obedience. The world of objects disclosed in experience sets a limit to the will. The will can turn toward an object that is perceived, felt, or otherwise given as being present, but it cannot comprehend an object not present. This does not mean that the world of objects itself is beyond the range of my will. I can bring about a change in the world of objects but I cannot deliberately bring about its perception if it itself is not present. The will is further limited by countereffective tendencies which are themselves in part body-bound (when they are caused by sensory feelings) and in part not.

Is this effect of willing and tending on the soul and on the living body psycho-physical causality or is it that much-talked-about causality in freedom, the severing of the "continuous" chain of causality? Action is always the creation of what is not. This process can be carried out in causal succession, but the initiation of the process, the true intervention of the will is not experienced as causal but as a special effect. This does not mean that the will has nothing to do with causality. We find it causally conditioned when we feel how a tiredness of body prevents a volition from prevailing. The will is causally effective when we feel a victorious will overcome the tiredness, even making it disappear. The will's fulfillment is also linked to causal conditions, since it carries out all its effects through a causally regulated instrument. But what is truly creative about volition is not a causal effect. All these causal relationships are external to the essence of the will. The will disregards them as soon as it is no longer the will of a psycho-physical individual and yet will. Tending also has a similar structure, and action progressing from a tendency does not appear as a causal succession, either. The difference is that in tending the "I" is drawn into the action, does not step into it freely, and no creative strength is lived out in it. Every creative act in the true sense is a volitional action. Willing and tending both have the capacity to make use of psycho-physical causality, but it can only be said that the willing "I" is the master of the living body.

Part VI

MARTIN HEIDEGGER
Hermeneutical Phenomenology and
Fundamental Ontology

MARTIN HEIDEGGER (1889–1976)
Introduction

Martin Heidegger was born in 1889 in Messkirch, Baden-Württemburg, Germany, a small village where his father was a cooper and local sexton. Heidegger attended gymnasia in Constance (1903–1906), and Freiburg (1906–1909). He entered the Jesuit novitiate for a brief period, but then moved to the University of Freiburg as a theology student and seminarian (1909–1911). Having been introduced to Brentano's work on Aristotle while still at Constance, during his first semester at Freiburg Heidegger encountered Husserl's *Logical Investigations*, a work that challenged him deeply. Around the same time he was discovering hermeneutics through the writings of Schleiermacher, and reading Hölderlin, Georg Trakl, Rilke, Kierkegaard and Nietzsche. In 1911, he left the seminary and re-enrolled in Freiburg to study philosophy, completing his doctorate, *The Doctrine of Judgement in Psychologism* (1914) and his *Habilitation* in 1915 on *The Categories and the Doctrine of Meaning in Duns Scotus*, supervised by Heinrich Rickert.

In 1915 Heidegger began lecturing as *Privatdozent* at Freiburg, and, when Husserl arrived as professor in 1916, the two soon became friends. Following his military service, after the First World War in 1919, Heidegger returned to Freiburg as Husserl's personal assistant. He lectured at Freiburg until 1923, then transferred to Marburg (1923–1928), where he developed a reputation as an extraordinary teacher, and moved in an intellectual circle which included Natorp and Bultmann, among others, and met Hannah Arendt. He also was deeply influenced by Max Scheler. In 1923 he began writing *Being and Time*, which was published in 1927. On the basis of this work, and with Husserl's support, he succeeded Husserl to the Professorship of Philosophy at Freiburg on the latter's retirement in 1928. In 1929, he delivered his inaugural lecture at Freiburg "What is Metaphysics?", which argued that the sciences study everything and what is left over for the philosopher to study is literally nothing, but it is this 'nothing' which deserves attention. The controversial claim in the lecture that 'nothing nothings' was attacked as nonsense by Rudolf Carnap. Heidegger also engaged in a famous debate with Cassirer concerning the nature of neo-Kantianism.

Shortly after *Being and Time*, Heidegger abandoned the transcendental approach and his thought underwent what he later described as a 'turning' (*Kehre*), wherein he sought to express his insights in a more poetic, meditative way, struggling against 'the language of metaphysics'. Among the most important lectures he gave during the 1930s were his 1935 lectures "Introduction to Metaphysics" and his 1935–1936 lectures on "The Origin of the Work of Art", which defend an ontological approach to the nature of the artwork as an event which discloses truth and founds a world.

During the 1930s, Heidegger became a supporter and member of the Nazi Party and served as Rector of Freiburg University from 1933 to 1934. After the war, he was stripped of his teaching duties by the Allied De-Nazification Committee and thereafter conducted his philosophy mainly in the form of private seminars. His later thinking focused more and more on Nietzsche, Hölderlin and other poetic thinkers whose 'saying' (die Sage) of being lay outside technical philosophical discourse. He wrote some extraordinary essays on the nature of language, and about the manner in which things appear in language (consider his assertion "language is the house of Being"). More and more, he saw poetic saying (Dichtung) as revealing the truth of being obscured and distorted by the metaphysical tradition of the West which had culminated in a kind of global nihilism. Heidegger moved away from the project of fundamental ontology into a quasi mytho-poetic reflection of the nature of the fundamental elements that make up the human world. In later essays he draws both on Greek mythology and on Hölderlin's poetry to speak of the dimensions of 'mortals' and 'gods' and the 'fourfold' (das Geviert) of earth, sky, mortals and gods (see e.g. his essay, "Building, Dwelling, Thinking", 1951). In 1947 Heidegger wrote his famous "Letter on Humanism", in the form of a letter to Jean Beaufret, replying to Sartre's 1945 essay "Existentialism is a Humanism". In this essay Heidegger states: "Language is the house of Being. In its home man dwells", and emphasises the importance in going beyond subjectivity in order to understand the essence of human being.

His 1953 lecture to the Bavarian Academy, "Die Frage nach der Technik" ("The Question Concerning Technology") is perhaps the apex of his assessment of the new technological, global culture, and this essay has been hugely influential in the philosophy of technology and in the development of eco-philosophy. Heidegger's obsession with the 'framework' (die Stelle, das Gestell) of technological society was such that, in one lecture, he equated the Nazi concentration camps with the horrors of mechanised farming. In a late essay, Heidegger offered a meditation on the nature of 'letting-be' (Gelassenheit), a concept drawn from the medieval German mystic Meister Eckhart. Heidegger died on 26 May 1976. Since his death, his collected works (Gesamtausgabe) of more than eighty projected volumes have been appearing in an uncritical and somewhat controversial edition, supposedly on the basis of Heidegger's last wishes.

According to Heidegger's own account of his intellectual formation, it was his first encounter with Brentano that stimulated him to rethink the question of Being (die Seinsfrage) originally raised by Plato and Aristotle but forgotten in contemporary philosophy. In Being and Time (1927), Heidegger announces that he proposes to investigate the "question of the meaning of Being" (die Frage nach dem Sinn von Sein), that is, to do 'fundamental ontology'. Heidegger begins with the phenomenon of the 'forgetting of Being' (Seinsvergessenheit) in contemporary thought. He wants to break through this covering up of being by freeing up original experiences encrusted in tradition through a kind of 'destruction' (Destruktion), 'dismantling' (Abbau) or 'deconstruction' of the philosophical tradition. This requires a critique of Kant, Descartes and others, in order to uncover the genuine experiential sources of philosophy as understood by the early Greeks in particular. In the metaphysical tradition stemming from Plato and Aristotle, Being has been understood as *presence*

(*Anwesenheit*, which contains the word '*Wesen*' which means 'essence', the Greek *ousia*), understood as static permanence. Heidegger, on the other hand, sees human existence as essentially taking place in time, spread out between past and future and radically limited by death. Being must be understood in terms of time.

This radical inquiry into the meaning of Being begins with an account of the fundamental structures of human existence, which Heidegger calls '*Dasein*' (existence). Heidegger's existential analytic of *Dasein* reveals that the ultimate context of all understanding and action is the 'world'. *Dasein* is essentially 'being-in-the-world' (*In-der-Welt-sein*). We are thrust into a world, and are involved in a kind of caring involvement with things.

Heidegger claims that he understands phenomenology in a more radical way than Husserl. While he admired Husserl's account of categorial intuition in the Sixth Logical Investigation, he thought Husserlian phenomenology had become yet another idealist philosophy which ignored the essential historicity of human existence. In his 1962 letter to William Richardson, Heidegger sees Husserl's phenomenology as a distinctively modern philosophical position (following Descartes, Kant and Fichte), which ignored historicity, whereas his own approach involves a radical reawakening of covered up experiences that lie beneath the encrusted metaphysical tradition. Husserl in fact valued Scheler's version of phenomenology and Dilthey's hermeneutics over Husserl's transcendental idealism, and thus proposes that hermeneutics and phenomenology should be joined together.

Our first reading, "My Way to Phenomenology", where Heidegger recounts his first encounter with Husserl's phenomenology and his recognition that, with his transcendental turn, Husserl had embraced the tradition of modern philosophy. Heidegger in contrast began to see Aristotle as the more original phenomenologist who understood truth in terms of what is self-revealing. Heidegger articulates his view that phenomenology represents a promise, a possibility of thinking rather than naming a method or identifying a school.

Our second reading is taken from Heidegger's 1925 lectures on the *History of the Concept of Time*, which offered a first draft of the investigations which later appeared as *Being and Time*. In this extract, Heidegger is acknowledging the achievements of Brentano and Husserl in terms of their recognition of intentionality. He singles out three fundamental discoveries of Husserlian phenomenology: intentionality, categorial intuition, and the original sense of the a priori. Heidegger gives a clear and insightful account of Brentano's and Husserl's conceptions of intentionality and rejects a misinterpretation from Heinrich Rickert. Heidegger emphasises that intentionality should not be construed in a representationalist manner as stating that the object intended is somehow 'in' the subject, or as somehow expressing a relation between the physical and the psychical, but rather signals the fact that the very essence of consciousness – or of 'comportment', as Heidegger prefers to say – is its directedness towards the object: "the very being of comporting is a directing-itself-toward." Heidegger goes on to discuss the various ways of comporting oneself towards an object; for example, we perceive the hardness of a chair through our experience of discomfort in sitting on it. There are manifold ways of comporting towards an object, from direct engagement with it in our practical doings, to our remembering, imagining or simply talking about an absent entity. Heidegger then goes on to give an interesting account of the synthesis of identification involved in knowledge and the experience of truth.

Our third reading is taken from paragraph 7 of the Introduction to *Being and Time* where Heidegger outlines his own conception of phenomenology, paying very close attention to the linguistic meanings involved in talking about phenomena, appearances, semblances, manifestations and so on. Heidegger wants to suggest that phenomenology is the science of the manifest, of what shows itself, in all senses of that showing, which includes seeming and dissembling. Heidegger also invokes the ancient Greeks to suggest that the Greek study of Being was also a study of what manifests itself, of what lays itself open to view, and hence that appearances cannot be contrasted with being in itself.

Our final reading is taken the first Section of Part One of Heidegger's classic *Being and Time* where he discusses the nature of the 'worldhood' involved in his characterisation of *Dasein* as 'being-in-the-world', part of his existential analysis of *Dasein* which was to serve as a preparation for approaching the question of Being. Being-in-the-world is a unitary phenomenon, but humans are not in the world as tables and chairs are in a room. Rather humans *dwell* in the world, and are concerned about projects within, but often in such a way that they are completely absorbed in them and no longer notice the world at all. It has become so familiar, essentially disguised, and certainly it has never been treated properly by previous ontologies. Being-in-the-world must be made visible and this is the task of our selection. Following Husserl and Scheler, Heidegger emphasises the a priori structure that belongs to the world correlated to human endeavour. Indeed, it belongs to the essence of our relation to world, that world is passed over as unnoticed. Heidegger makes the point that the special kind of human relation to the environment normally gets interpreted as primarily a spatial relation (taken to an extreme in Descartes' metaphysical analysis of *res extensa*). Influenced by Aristotle, Heidegger begins with our pragmatic encounters with things in which what is of primary interest is not the things or ourselves, but the goals of the projects in which we are engaged. We want to meet someone, so we open the door. The door itself is not explicitly in view in this kind of act, the entities are hidden in this kind of encounter, or mode of concern. For Heidegger, one of the Greek words for 'things' – *pragmata* – sums up this kind of practical engagement; Heidegger himself proposes the term '*Zeug*' (equipment), something which emerges only within the context of some use. A hammer's functionality is experienced (and thus uncovered or revealed) in the act of successful hammering of something for a particular purpose (e.g. hanging a picture). Our manipulating of things in this useful way has its own kind of sight, Heidegger says. These things in general have the character of being 'ready to hand', 'handy', (*Zuhanden*), but this ontological understanding of things is normally only uncovered when they become unserviceable as equipment, when things break down. At this point, the obstinacy of the thing (perhaps an echo of Scheler here), the sheer presence or 'presence at hand' (*Vorhandensein*) of the thing comes into view. Thus the complexity of the layers of being of things in the world becomes revealed to us. Our 'being-in-the-world' is normally just this unthematised 'circumspective absorption' into the system of references and assignments in which we put things to use for certain purposes. Moreover, in this 'involvement' (*Bewandtnis*) lies the very being of the ready to hand according to Heidegger. The system of such involvements is the 'world' as Heidegger understands it.

Further readings

Heidegger, Martin. *An Introduction to Metaphysics*, trans. R. Manheim. New York: Doubleday, 1961.

Heidegger, Martin. *Basic Concepts*, trans. G. E. Aylesworth. Bloomington: Indiana University Press, 1993.

Heidegger, Martin. *Basic Questions in Philosophy*, trans. R. Rojcewicz and A. Schuwer. Bloomington: Indiana University Press, 1994.

Heidegger, Martin. *Basic Writings*, ed. D. F. Krell, Second Revised Edition. London: Routledge & Kegan Paul, 1978.

Heidegger, Martin. *Being and Time*, trans. John Macquarrie and E. Robinson. New York: Harper and Row, 1962.

Heidegger, Martin. *Being and Time*, trans. Joan Stambaugh. Albany, NY: SUNY Press, 1996.

Heidegger, Martin. *Discourse on Thinking*, trans. J. M. Anderson and E. H. Freund. London: Harper and Row, 1969.

Heidegger, Martin. *Early Greek Thinking*, trans. D. F. Krell and F. A. Capuzzi. London: Harper and Row, 1975.

Heidegger, Martin. *Existence and Being*, Introduction by W. Brock. London: Vision, 1968.

Heidegger, Martin. *Hegel's Concept of Experience*. London: Harper and Row, 1970.

Heidegger, Martin. *History of the Concept of Time: Prolegomena*, trans. T. Kisiel. Bloomington: Indiana University Press, 1985.

Heidegger. Martin. *Introduction to Metaphysics*. New Haven: Yale University Press, 2000.

Heidegger, Martin. *Kant and the Problem of Metaphysics*, trans. J. S. Churchill. Bloomington: Indiana University Press, 1962.

Heidegger, Martin. *Nietzsche* (2 vols.), trans. D. F. Krell. San Francisco, CA: Harper, 1991.

Heidegger, Martin. *On the Way to Language*, trans. P. D. Hertz. New York: Harper and Row, 1971.

Heidegger, Martin. *On Time and Being*, trans. J. Macquarrie and E. Robinson. SCM Press Ltd, 1962.

Heidegger, Martin. *Pathmarks*, trans. William McNeill. Cambridge: Cambridge University Press, 1998.

Heidegger, Martin. *Phenomenological Interpretation of Kant's "Critique of Pure Reason"*, trans. P. Emad and K. Maly. Bloomington: Indiana University Press, 1997.

Heidegger, Martin. *Plato's Sophist*, trans. R. Rojcewicz and A. Schuwer. Bloomington: Indiana University Press, 1997.

Heidegger, Martin. *Poetry, Language and Thought*, trans. A. Hofstadter. New York: Harper and Row, 1975.

Heidegger, Martin. *The Basic Problems of Phenomenology*, trans. A. Hofstadter. Bloomington: Indiana University Press, 1982.

Heidegger, Martin. *The Concept of Time*, trans. W. McNeill. Oxford: Blackwell, 1992.

Heidegger, Martin. *The End of Philosophy*, trans. J. Stambaugh. London: Souvenir Press, 1975.

Heidegger, Martin. *The Fundamental Concepts of Metaphysics: World, Finitude, Solitude*, trans. W. McNeill and N. Walker. Bloomington: Indiana U.P., 1995.

Heidegger, Martin. *The Metaphysical Foundations of Logic*, trans. M. Heim. Bloomington: Indiana University Press, 1984.

Heidegger, Martin. *The Piety of Thinking: Essays*, trans. J. G. Hart and J. C. Maraldo. Bloomington: Indiana University Press, 1976.

Heidegger, Martin. *The Principle of Reason*, trans. R. Lilly. Bloomington: Indiana University Press, 1991.

Heidegger, Martin. *The Question Concerning Technology and Other Essays*, trans. W. Lovitt. New York: Harper and Row, 1977.

Heidegger, Martin. "The Rectorate 1933/4: Facts and Thoughts", trans. K. Harries. *Review of Metaphysics* 38 (March) pp. 481–502, 1985.

Heidegger, Martin. *What is Philosophy?*, trans. W. Kluback and J.T. Wilde. New York: Twayne Publishers, 1958.

Adorno, T. *The Jargon of Authenticity*, trans. J. Tarnwoski and F. Will. Evanston: Northwestern University Press, 1973.

Dreyfus, Hubert L. *Being-In-the-World. A Commentary on Heidegger's Being and Time, Division I.* Cambridge, MA: MIT Press, 1991.

Dreyfus, Hubert L. and Harrison Hall. Eds. *Heidegger: A Critical Reader*. Oxford: Blackwell, 1992.

Farias, Victor. *Heidegger and Nazism*, trans. J. Margolis and T. Rockmore. Philadelphia, PA: Temple University Press, 1989.

Guignon, C. (ed.). *The Cambridge Companion to Heidegger*. Cambridge: Cambridge University Press, 1993.

Harries, K. and C. Jamme (eds). *Martin Heidegger. Politics, Art and Technology*. New York: Holmes and Meier, 1994.

Kisiel, Theodore. *The Genesis of Heidegger's Being and Time*. Berkeley: University of California Press, 1993.

Kisiel, Theodore and John Van Buren (eds). *Reading Heidegger from the Start: Essays in his Earliest Thought*. Albany, NY: SUNY Press, 1994, pp. 19–34.

Murray, Michael (ed.). *Heidegger and Modern Philosophy*. New Haven, CT: Yale University Press, 1978.

Ott, Hugo. *Martin Heidegger. A Political Life*, trans. Allan Blunden. London: HarperCollins, 1993.

Philipse, Herman. *Heidegger's Philosophy of Being*. Princeton, NJ: Princeton University Press, 1988.

Pöggeler, Otto. *Martin Heidegger's Path of Thinking*. Athlantic Highlands, NJ: Humanities Press, 1989.

Richardson, William. *Heidegger: Through Phenomenology to Thought*. The Hague: Nijhoff, 1963.

Rorty, Richard. *Essays on Heidegger and Others. Philosophical Papers*, Vol. 2. Cambridge: Cambridge University Press, 1991.

Sheehan, Thomas (ed.). *Heidegger: The Man and the Thinker*. Chicago, IL: Precedent, 1981.

Taminiaux, Jacques. *Heidegger and the Project of Fundamental Ontology*. Albany, NY: SUNY Press, 1991.

Van Buren, John. *The Young Heidegger. Rumor of the Hidden King*. Bloomington: Indiana University Press, 1994.

Wolin, Richard (ed.). *The Heidegger Controversy. A Critical Reader*. Cambridge, MA: MIT Press, 1993.

1

MY WAY TO PHENOMENOLOGY

My academic studies began in the winter of 1909–10 in theology at the University of Freiburg. But the chief work for the study in theology still left enough time for philosophy which belonged to the curriculum anyhow. Thus both volumes of Husserl's *Logical Investigations* lay on my desk in the theological seminary ever since my first semester there. These volumes belonged to the university library. The date due could be easily renewed again and again. The work was obviously of little interest to the students. But how did it get into this environment so foreign to it?

I had learned from many references in philosophical periodicals that Husserl's thought was determined by Franz Brentano. Ever since 1907, Brentano's dissertation "On the manifold meaning of being since Aristotle" (1862) had been the chief help and guide of my first awkward attempts to penetrate into philosophy. The following question concerned me in a quite vague manner: If being is predicated in manifold meanings, then what is its leading fundamental meaning? What does Being mean? In the last year of my stay at the *Gymnasium*, I stumbled upon the book of Carl Braig, then professor for dogmatics at Freiburg University: "On Being. Outline of Ontology." It had been published in 1896 at the time when he was an associate professor at Freiburg's theological faculty. The larger sections of the work give extensive text passages from Aristotle, Thomas of Aquinas and Suarez, always at the end, and in addition the etymology for fundamental ontological concepts.

From Husserl's *Logical Investigations*, I expected a decisive aid in the questions stimulated by Brentano's dissertation. Yet my efforts were in vain because I was not searching in the right way. I realized this only very much later. Still, I remained so fascinated by Husserl's work that I read in it again and again in the years to follow without gaining sufficient insight into what fascinated me. The spell emanating from the work extended to the outer appearance of the sentence structure and the title page. On that title page I encountered the name of the publisher Max Niemeyer. This encounter is before my eyes as vividly today as then. His name was connected with that of "Phenomenology," then foreign to me, which appears in the subtitle of the second volume. My understanding of the term "phenomenology" was just as limited and vacillating as my knowledge in those years of the publisher Max Niemeyer and his work. Why and how both

M. Heidegger, *On Time and Being*, 1962, trans. John Macquarrie and Edward Robinson. SCM Press Ltd.

names – Niemeyer Publishing House and Phenomenology – belong together would soon become clearer.

After four semesters I gave up my theological studies and dedicated myself entirely to philosophy. I still attended theological lectures in the years following 1911, Carl Braig's lecture course on dogmatics. My interest in speculative theology led me to do this, above all the penetrating kind of thinking which this teacher concretely demonstrated in every lecture hour. On a few walks when I was allowed to accompany him, I first heard of Schelling's and Hegel's significance for speculative theology as distinguished from the dogmatic system of Scholasticism. Thus the tension between ontology and speculative theology as the structure of metaphysics entered the field of my search.

Yet at times this realm faded to the background compared with that which Heinrich Rickert treated in his seminars: the two writings of his pupil Emil Lask who was killed as a simple soldier on the Galician front in 1915. Rickert dedicated the third fully revised edition of his work *The Object of Knowledge, Introduction to Transcendental Philosophy*, which was published the same year, "to my dear friend." The dedication was supposed to testify to the teacher's benefit derived from this pupil. Both of Emil Lask's writings – *The Logic of Philosophy and the Doctrine of Categories. A Study of the Dominant Realm of Logical Form* (1911) and *The Doctrine of Judgment* (1912) – themselves showed clearly enough the influence of Husserl's *Logical Investigations*.

These circumstances forced me to delve into Husserl's work anew. However, my repeated beginning also remained unsatisfactory, because I couldn't get over a main difficulty. It concerned the simple question how thinking's manner of procedure which called itself "phenomenology" was to be carried out. What worried me about this question came from the ambiguity which Husserl's work showed at first glance.

The first volume of the work, published in 1900, brings the refutation of psychologism in logic by showing that the doctrine of thought and knowledge cannot be based on psychology. In contrast, the second volume, which was published the following year and was three times as long, contains the description of the acts of consciousness essential for the constitution of knowledge. So it is a psychology after all. What else is section 9 of the fifth investigation concerning "The Meaning of Brentano's Delimitation of 'psychical phenomena'"? Accordingly, Husserl falls back with his phenomenological description of the phenomena of consciousness into the position of psychologism which he had just refuted. But if such a gross error cannot be attributed to Husserl's work, then what is the phenomenological description of the acts of consciousness? Wherein does what is peculiar to phenomenology consist if it is neither logic nor psychology? Does a quite new discipline of philosophy appear here, even one with its own rank and precedence?

I could not disentangle these questions. I remained without knowing what to do or where to go. I could hardly even formulate the questions with the clarity in which they are expressed here.

The year 1913 brought an answer. The *Yearbook for Philosophy and Phenomenological Investigation* which Husserl edited began to be published by the publisher Max Niemeyer. The first volume begins with Husserl's treatise *Ideas*.

"Pure phenomenology" is the "fundamental science" of philosophy which is characterized by that phenomenology. "Pure" means: "transcendental phenomenology." However, the "subjectivity" of the knowing, acting and valuing subject is posited as "transcendental." Both terms, "subjectivity" and "transcendental," show that "phenomenology" consciously and decidedly moved into the tradition of modern philosophy but in such a way that "transcendental subjectivity" attains a more original and universal determination through phenomenology. Phenomenology retained "experiences of consciousness" as its thematic realm, but now in the systematically planned and secured investigation of the structure of acts of experience together with the investigation of the objects experienced in those acts with regard to their objectivity.

In this universal project for a phenomenological philosophy, the *Logical Investigations*, too – which had so to speak remained philosophically neutral – could be assigned their systematic place. They were published in the same year (1913) in a second edition by the same publisher. Most of the investigations had in the meantime undergone "profound revisions." The sixth investigation, "the most important with regard to phenomenology" (preface to the second edition) was, however, withheld. But the essay "Philosophy as Exact Science" (1910–11) which Husserl contributed to the first volume of the new journal *Logos* also only now acquired a sufficient basis for its programmatical theses through the *Ideas*.

In virtue of these publications, Niemeyer's work attained the foremost rank of philosophical publishers. At that time the rather obvious idea was current that with "phenomenology" a new school had arisen in European philosophy. Who could have denied the correctness of this statement?

But such historical calculation did not comprehend what had happened in virtue of "phenomenology," that is, already with the *Logical Investigations*. This remained unspoken, and can hardly even be rightly expressed today. Husserl's own programmatical explanations and methodological presentations rather strengthened the misunderstanding that through "phenomenology" a beginning of philosophy was claimed which denied all previous thinking.

Even after the *Ideas* was published, I was still captivated by the never-ceasing spell of the *Logical Investigations*. That magic brought about anew an unrest unaware of its own reason, although it made one suspect that it came from the inability to attain the act of philosophical thinking called "phenomenology" simply by reading the philosophical literature.

My perplexity decreased slowly, my confusion dissolved laboriously, only after I met Husserl personally in his workshop.

Husserl came to Freiburg in 1916 as Heinrich Rickert's successor. Rickert had taken over Windelband's chair in Heidelberg. Husserl's teaching took place in the form of a step-by-step training in phenomenological "seeing" which at the same time demanded that one relinquish the untested use of philosophical knowledge. But it also demanded that one give up introducing the authority of the great thinkers into the conversation. However, the clearer it became to me that the increasing familiarity with phenomenological seeing was fruitful for the interpretation of Aristotle's writing, the less I could separate myself from Aristotle and the other Greek thinkers. Of course I could not immediately see what decisive consequences my renewed occupation with Aristotle was to have.

As I myself practiced phenomenological seeing, teaching and learning in Husserl's proximity after 1919 and at the same time tried out a transformed understanding of Aristotle in a seminar, my interest leaned anew toward the *Logical Investigations*, above all the sixth investigation in the first edition. The distinction which is worked out there between sensuous and categorial intuition revealed itself to me in its scope for the determination of the "manifold meaning of being."

For this reason we – friends and pupils – begged the master again and again to republish the sixth investigation which was then difficult to obtain. True to his dedication to the cause of phenomenology, the publisher Niemeyer published the last chapter of the *Logical Investigations* again in 1922. Husserl notes in the preface: "As things stand, I had to give in to the wishes of the friends of this work and decide to make its last chapter available again in its old form." With the phrase "the friends of this work," Husserl also wanted to say that he himself could not quite get close to the *Logical Investigations* after the publication of the *Ideas*. At the new place of his academic activity, the passion and effort of his thought turned toward the systematic development of the plan presented in the *Ideas* more than ever. Thus Husserl could write in the preface mentioned to the sixth investigation: "My teaching activity in Freiburg, too, furthered the direction of my interest toward general problems and the system."

Thus Husserl watched me in a generous fashion, but at the bottom in disagreement, as I worked on the *Logical Investigations* every week in special seminars with advanced students in addition to my lectures and regular seminars. Especially the preparation for this work was fruitful for me. There I learned one thing – at first rather led by surmise than guided by founded insight: What occurs for the phenomenology of the acts of consciousness as the self-manifestation of phenomena is thought more originally by Aristotle and in all Greek thinking and existence as *aletheia*, as the unconcealedness of what-is present, its being revealed, its showing itself. That which phenomenological investigations rediscovered as the supporting attitude of thought proves to be the fundamental trait of Greek thinking, if not indeed of philosophy as such.

The more decisively this insight became clear to me, the more pressing the question became: Whence and how is it determined what must be experienced as "the things themselves" in accordance with the principle of phenomenology? Is it consciousness and its objectivity or is it the Being of beings in its unconcealedness and concealment?

Thus I was brought to the path of the question of Being, illumined by the phenomenological attitude, again made uneasy in a different way than previously by the questions prompted by Brentano's dissertation. But the path of questioning became longer than I suspected. It demanded many stops, detours and wrong paths. What the first lectures in Freiburg and then in Marburg attempted shows the path only indirectly.

"Professor Heidegger – you have got to publish something now. Do you have a manuscript?" With these words the dean of the philosophical faculty in Marburg came into my study one day in the winter semester of 1925–26. "Certainly," I answered. Then the dean said: "But it must be printed quickly." The faculty proposed me *unico loco* as Nicolai Hartmann's successor for the chief philosophical chair. Meanwhile, the ministry in Berlin had rejected the proposal with the explanation that I had not published anything in the last ten years.

Now I had to submit my closely protected work to the public. On account of Husserl's intervention, the publishing house Max Niemeyer was ready to print immediately the first fifteen proof sheets of the work which was to appear in Husserl's *Jahrbuch*. Two copies of the finished page proofs were sent to the ministry by the faculty right away. But after some time, they were returned to the faculty with the remark: "Inadequate." In February of the following year (1927), the complete text of *Being and Time* was published in the eighth volume of the *Jahrbuch* and as a separate publication. After that the ministry reversed its negative judgment half a year later and made the offer for the chair.

On the occasion of the strange publication of *Being and Time*, I came first into direct relationship with the publishing house Max Niemeyer. What was a mere name on the title page of Husserl's fascinating work during the first semester of my academic studies became evident now and in the future in all the thoroughness and reliability, generosity and simplicity, of publication work.

In the summer of 1928, during my last semester in Marburg, the *Festschrift* for Husserl's seventieth birthday was in preparation. At the beginning of this semester Max Scheler died unexpectedly. He was one of the co-editors of Husserl's *Jahrbuch* where he published his great investigation *Formalism in Ethics and Material Ethics of Value* in the first and second volume (1916). Along with Husserl's *Ideas*, it must count as the most significant contribution to the *Jahrbuch*. Through its far-reaching effects, it placed the scope and effectiveness of the Niemeyer publishing house in a new light.

The *Festschrift* for Edmund Husserl appeared punctually for his birthday as a supplement to the *Jahrbuch*. I had the honor of presenting it to the celebrated teacher within a circle of his pupils and friends on April 8, 1929.

During the following decade all more extensive publications were withheld until the publishing house Niemeyer dared to print my interpretation of Hölderlin's hymn "As on a Holiday" in 1941 without giving the year of publication. I had given this lecture in May of the same year as a public guest lecture at the university of Leipzig. The owner of the publishing house, Mr. Hermann Niemeyer, had come from Halle to hear this lecture. Afterward we discussed the publication.

When I decided twelve years later to publish earlier lecture series, I chose the Niemeyer publishing house for this purpose. It no longer bore the designation "Halle a.d. Saale." Following great losses and manifold difficulties, and visited by hard personal suffering, the present owner had re-established the firm in Tübingen.

"Halle a.d. Saale" – in the same city, the former *Privatdozent* Edmund Husserl taught during the '90's of the last century at that university. Later in Freiburg, he often told the story of how the *Logical Investigations* came to be. He never forgot to remember the Max Niemeyer publishing house with gratitude and admiration, the house which took upon itself the venture of publishing, at the turn of the century, an extensive work of a little-known instructor who went his own new ways and thus had to estrange contemporary philosophy, which ignored the work for years after its appearance, until Wilhelm Dilthey recognized its significance. The publishing house could not know at that time that his name would remain tied to that of phenomenology in the future, that phenomenology would soon determine the spirit of the age in the most various realms – mostly in a tacit manner.

And today? The age of phenomenological philosophy seems to be over. It is already taken as something past which is only recorded historically along with other schools of philosophy. But in what is most its own, phenomenology is not a school. It is the possibility of thinking, at times changing and only thus persisting, of corresponding to the claim of what is to be thought. If phenomenology is thus experienced and retained, it can disappear as a designation in favor of the matter of thinking whose manifestness remains a mystery.

Supplement 1969

In the sense of the last sentence, one can already read in *Being and Time* (1927) pp. 62–63: "Its (phenomenology's) essential character does not consist in being *actual* as a philosophical school. Higher than actuality stands *possibility*. The comprehension of phenomenology consists solely in grasping it as possibility."

2

THE FUNDAMENTAL DISCOVERIES
OF PHENOMENOLOGY,
ITS PRINCIPLE, AND THE
CLARIFICATION OF ITS NAME

We shall detail these discoveries and then supplement this account with an elucidation of the principle of phenomenological research. On this basis we shall try to
interpret the name given to this research and thus define 'phenomenology.'

Of the decisive discoveries, we intend to discuss three: 1) *intentionality*, 2) *categorial intuition*, and 3) the *original sense of the apriori*. These considerations are
indispensable in their content as well as in the way it is considered. Only in this
way can '*time*' be brought into view phenomenologically. Only in this way is the
possibility given for an orderly procedure in the analysis of time as it shows itself.

§5 Intentionality

We want to consider intentionality first, precisely because contemporary philosophy then and even now actually finds this phenomenon offensive, because
intentionality is precisely what prevents an immediate and unprejudiced reception
of what phenomenology wants to do. Intentionality was already alluded to in our
account of how Brentano sought to classify the totality of psychic phenomena in
strict accord with it. Brentano discerned in intentionality the structure which
constitutes the true nature of a psychic phenomenon. Intentionality thus became
for him the criterion for the distinction of psychic from physical phenomena. But
at the same time this structure is the criterion and principle of a natural division
among psychic phenomena themselves, inasmuch as it is already found in the
essence which appears in these phenomena. Brentano expressly emphasizes that
he is only taking up what Aristotle and the Scholastics were already acquainted
with. It was through Brentano that Husserl learned to see intentionality.

But by what right do we then still speak of the discovery of intentionality by
phenomenology? Because there is a difference between the rough and ready
acquaintance with a structure and the understanding of its inherent sense and its
implications, from which we derive the possibilities and horizons of an investigation directed toward it in a sure way. From a rough acquaintance and an

M. Heidegger, *History of the Concept of Time: Prolegomena*, 1992, trans. Theodore Kisiel, pp. 27–53.
Bloomington: Indiana University Press.

application aimed at classification to a fundamental understanding and thematic elaboration is a very long road calling for novel considerations and radical transpositions. On this point Husserl writes: "Nevertheless, from an initial apprehension of a distinction in consciousness to its correct, phenomenologically pure determination and concrete appreciation there is a mighty step – and it is just this step, crucial for a consistent and fruitful phenomenology, which was not taken."[1]

In the popular philosophical literature, phenomenology tends to be characterized in the following manner: Husserl took over the concept of intentionality from Brentano; as is well known, intentionality goes back to Scholasticism; it is notoriously obscure, metaphysical, and dogmatic. Consequently, the concept of intentionality is scientifically useless and phenomenology, which employs it, is fraught with metaphysical presuppositions and therefore not at all based upon immediate data. Thus, in "The Method of Philosophy and the Immediate," H. Rickert writes:

> Especially where the concept of 'intentionality,' Scholastic in origin but mediated by Brentano, plays a role, there the concept of the immediate still seems to be left largely unclarified and the train of thought of most phenomenologists seems steeped in traditional metaphysical dogmas, which make it impossible for its adherents to see impartially what is before their very eyes.[2]

This article contains a fundamental polemic against phenomenology. Elsewhere also, and right in the Introduction to the new edition of Brentano's *Psychology* by O. Kraus,[3] it is stated that Husserl had simply taken over Brentano's concept of intentionality. For the Marburg School as well, intentionality remained the real stumbling block, obstructing its access to phenomenology.

We expressly reject such opinions, not in order to preserve Husserl's originality against Brentano, but to guard against having the most elementary considerations and steps necessary for the understanding of phenomenology thwarted in advance by such characterizations.

a) Intentionality as the structure of lived experiences: exposition and initial elucidation

We will try to show that intentionality is a structure of lived experiences as such and not a coordination relative to other realities, something added to the experiences taken as psychic states. It should first be noted that this attempt to make intentionality clear, to see it and in so doing to apprehend what it is, cannot hope to succeed in a single move. We must free ourselves from the prejudice that, because phenomenology calls upon us to apprehend the matters themselves, these matters must be apprehended all at once, without any preparation. Rather, the movement toward the matters themselves is a long and involved process which, before anything else, has to remove the prejudices which obscure them.

Intentio literally means *directing-itself-toward*. Every lived experience, every psychic comportment, directs itself toward something. Representing is a representing of something, recalling is a recalling of something, judging is judging about something, presuming, expecting, hoping, loving, hating – of something.

But, one will object, this is a triviality hardly in need of explicit emphasis, certainly no special achievement meriting the designation of discovery. Notwithstanding, let us pursue this triviality a bit and bring out what it means phenomenologically.

The following considerations call for no special talent. They do demand that we set aside our prejudices, learn to see directly and simply and to abide by what we see without asking, out of curiosity, what we can do with it. In the face of the most obvious of matters, the very fact of the matter is the most difficult thing we may hope to attain, because man's element of existence is the artificial and mendacious, where he is always already cajoled by others. It is erroneous to think that phenomenologists are models of excellence who stand out in their resolve to wage an all-out war with this element, in their positive will-to-disclose and nothing else.

Let us envisage an exemplary and readily available case of 'psychic comportment': a concrete and natural perception, the perception of a chair which I find upon entering a room and push aside, since it stands in my way. I stress the latter in order to indicate that we are after the most common kind of everyday perception and not a perception in the emphatic sense, in which we observe only for the sake of observing. Natural perception as I live in it in moving about my world is for the most part not a detached observation and scrutiny of things, but is rather absorbed in dealing with the matters at hand concretely and practically. It is not self-contained; I do not perceive in order to perceive but in order to orient myself, to pave the way in dealing with something. This is a wholly natural way of looking in which I continually live.

A crude interpretation tends to depict the perception of the chair in this way: a specific psychic event occurs within me; to this psychic occurrence 'inside,' 'in consciousness,' there corresponds a physically real thing 'outside.' A coordination thus arises between the reality of consciousness (the subject) and a reality outside of consciousness (the object). The psychic event enters into a relationship with something else, outside of it. But in itself it is not necessary for this relationship to occur, since this perception can be an illusion, a hallucination. It is a psychological fact that psychic processes occur in which something is perceived – presumably – which does not even exist. It is possible for my psychic process to be beset by a hallucination such that I now perceive an automobile being driven through the room over your heads. In this case, no real object corresponds to the psychic process in the subject. Here we have a perceiving without the occurrence of a relationship to something outside of it. Or consider the case of a deceptive perception: I am walking in a dark forest and see a man coming toward me; but upon closer inspection it turns out to be a tree. Here also the object supposedly perceived in this deceptive perception is absent. In view of these indisputable facts which show that the real object can in fact be missing in perception, it can *not* be said that every perception is the perception of something. In other words, intentionality, directing itself toward something, is not a necessary mark of every perception. And even if some physical object should correspond to every psychic event which I call a perception, it would still be a dogmatic assertion; for it is by no means established that I ever get to a reality beyond my consciousness.

Since Descartes, everyone knows and every critical philosophy maintains that I actually only apprehend 'contents of consciousness.' Accordingly, the application of the concept of intentionality to the comportment of perception, for example, already implies a double presupposition. First, there is the metaphysical presupposition that the psychic comes out of itself toward something physical. With Descartes, as everyone knows, this became a forbidden presupposition. Second, there is in intentionality the presupposition that a real object always corresponds to a psychic process. The facts of deceptive perception and hallucination speak against this. This is what Rickert maintains and many others, when they say that the concept of intentionality harbors latent metaphysical dogmas. And yet, with this interpretation of perception as hallucination and deceptive perception, do we really have intentionality in our sights? Are we talking about what phenomenology means by this term? In no way! So little, in fact, that use of the interpretation just given as a basis for a discussion of intentionality would hopelessly block access to what the term really means phenomenologically. Let us therefore clear the air by going through the interpretation once again and regarding it more pointedly. For its ostensible triviality is not at all comprehensible without further effort. But first, the base triviality of spurious but common epistemological questions must be laid to rest.

Let us recall the hallucination. It will be said that the automobile here is in reality not present and on hand. Accordingly, there is no coordination between psychic and physical. Only the psychic is given. Nonetheless, is not the hallucination in its own right a hallucination, a presumed perception of an automobile? Is it not also the case that this presumed perception, which is without real relationship to a real object, precisely as such is a directing-itself-toward something presumably perceived? Is not the deception itself as such a directing-itself-toward, even if the real object is in fact not there?

It is not the case that a perception first becomes intentional by having something physical enter into relation with the psychic, and that it would no longer be intentional if this reality did not exist. It is rather the case that perception, correct or deceptive, is in itself intentional. Intentionality is not a property which would accrue to perception and belongs to it in certain instances. As perception, it is *intrinsically intentional*, regardless of whether the perceived is in reality on hand or not. Indeed, it is really only because perception as such is a directing-itself-toward something, because intentionality constitutes the very structure of comportment itself, that there can be anything like deceptive perception and hallucination.

When all epistemological assumptions are set aside, it becomes clear that comportment itself – as yet quite apart from the question of its correctness or incorrectness – is in its very structure a directing-itself-toward. It is not the case that at first only a psychic process occurs as a nonintentional state (complex of sensations, memory relations, mental image and thought processes through which an image is evoked, where one then asks whether something corresponds to it) and subsequently becomes intentional in certain instances. Rather, the very being of comporting is a directing-itself-toward. Intentionality is not a relationship to the non-experiential added to experiences, occasionally present along with them. Rather, the lived experiences themselves are as such intentional. This is our first specification, perhaps still quite empty, but already important enough to provide the footing for holding metaphysical prejudices at bay.

b) Rickert's misunderstanding of phenomenology and intentionality

In the reception of intentionality as well as in the way in which Brentano was interpreted and developed, everyone saw not so much the exposition of this composition of the structure of lived experience as what they suspected in Brentano: metaphysical dogmas. The decisive thing about Husserl was that he did not look to the dogmas and presuppositions, so far as these were there, but to the phenomenon itself, that *perceiving is a directing-itself-toward*. But now this structure cannot be disregarded in the other forms of comportment as well. Rickert makes this the basis of his argument and disputes seeing such a thing in these comportments. He reserves intentionality for the comportment relating to judgment but drops it for representing. He says representing is not knowing. He comes to this because he is trapped in dogmas, in this case the dogma that my representing involves no transcendence, that it does not get out to the object. Descartes in fact said that representing (*perceptio*) remains in the consciousness. And Rickert thinks that the transcendence of judging, whose object he specifies as a *value*, is less puzzling than the transcendence which is in representing, understood as getting out to a real thing. He comes to this view because he thinks that in judgment something is acknowledged which has the character of value and so does not exist in reality. He identifies it with the mental which consciousness itself is, and thinks that value is something immanent. When I acknowledge a value, I do not go outside of consciousness.

The essential point for us is not to prove that Rickert is involved in contradictions, that he now uses the phenomenological concept of representing and now a mythical one from psychology. The point is rather that he lays claim to intentionality in his own starting point to the extent that it fits his theory but casts it aside when it contravenes his theory that representing is not knowing. What is characteristic is that, in spite of all the sagacity, the most primitive of requirements is nevertheless missing: admission of the matters of fact as they are given. The thinking thus becomes groundless. The constraint of the facts cannot in one case be heeded and in others not; heeded when they fit into a preconceived theory and not heeded when they explode it. A typical example of this kind of thinking is Rickert's theory of knowledge and of judgment as it takes its starting point from Brentano. We shall review it in order to see how judgments depend upon the apprehension of the matters themselves.

Rickert takes from Brentano the definition of judgment as *acknowledging*. We can trace the exact place where he makes use of intentionality as exhibited by Brentano and at the same time shuts his eyes to it and falls into theory construction. Let us briefly recall the theory which he bases upon Brentano's account of judgment.

When we judge, Rickert says, we concur with the representations or we reject them. Invested in the judgment as its essential element is a 'practical' comportment. "Since what is valid for judgment must also be valid for knowing, it follows, from the kinship that judgment has with willing and feeling, that also *in pure theoretical knowing what is involved is taking a position toward a value* . . . Only in relation to values does the alternative comportment of approval and disapproval make any sense."[4] Rickert thus arrives at his theory that *the object of knowledge is a value*. When I perceive a chair and say, "The chair has four legs," the sense of this knowledge according to Rickert is the *acknowledging of a value*. Even with the best of intentions one cannot find anything like this in the structure of this perceptual assertion. For I am not directed toward representations and less still toward value but instead toward the chair which is in fact given.

Acknowledging is not imposed upon representations; representing is itself directing-itself-toward. Representing as such gives the potential about-which of judging, and the affirmation in judging is founded in representing. There is an intentional connection between representing and judging. If Rickert had seen the intentionality of representing, he would not have fallen into the mythology of the connection between judgment and representation, as though judgment comes as an 'aside.' *The relations between intentionalities are themselves intentional.*

Hence Rickert arrived at this theory not from a study of the matters themselves but by an unfounded deduction fraught with dogmatic judgments. The last vestige of the composition of this matter is solely what Rickert took from Brentano. But even here it is questionable whether it is brought to bear upon the full composition of judgment. "When we characterize judgment as a comportment which is not like representation, this does not mean that, with Brentano, we see in it another kind of relation of consciousness to its object than the kind involved in representation. This claim is for us far too full of presuppositions."[5] Here Rickert rejects intentionality, in Brentano's sense, as a criterion distinguishing the comportments of representation and judgment. What does he put in its place? How does he define and ground the distinction?

We are investigating

> in what genus of psychic processes the complete judgment belongs when we generally distinguish those states in which we comport ourselves impassively and contemplatively from those in which we take an interest in the content of our consciousness, as a content *of value* to us . . . We thus simply wish to establish a fact which even a pure sensualistic theory cannot dispute.[5a]

One would have to be blind not to see that this is word for word the position of Brentano, who wanted nothing other than to subdivide the genus of psychic processes according to the mode of our comportment, whether we contemplate them impassively or take an active interest in them. Rickert first takes his theory from a basis which is exposed by Brentano's description but does not see that he lays claim to intentionality as the foundation of his theory of judgment and knowledge. The proof for this is that while he lays claim to this descriptive distinction Rickert at the same time employs a concept of representation which runs counter to that which he uses as a basis for securing the definition of judgment, here impassive directing-itself-toward – accordingly representing as the manner of representing – and there representation as the represented, where the represented is in fact the content of consciousness. Wherever Rickert refutes the idealism of representation and wants to prove that knowing is not representing, he does not restrict himself to the direct and simple sense of representing but bases himself upon a mythical concept. Rickert says that as long as the representations are only represented, they come and go.[6] Representing is now not direct representational comportment; the representations now get represented. "A knowing that represents needs a reality independent of the knowing subject because with representations we are capable of apprehending something independent of the knowing subject only by their being images or signs of a reality."[7] In such a concept of representation it can of course be shown that representing is not a knowing if the directing-itself-toward can tend only toward signs.

But how does it stand with the concept of representation which Rickert uses when he differentiates the judgment from representing understood as a comportment that simply contemplates? Why does Rickert not take the concept of representation in a descriptive sense as he does the concept of judgment, which has accrued to description? Why does he not go straight to the sense of its implication, namely, a comportment which contemplates impassively?

It is because Rickert is guided by the presumption, the thesis that *knowing cannot be representing*. For if it were, then his own theory that knowing is acknowledging and the object of knowledge is a value would be superfluous and perhaps wrong. Representing cannot be knowledge. This prejudice is given further weight by an appeal to Aristotle's thesis that knowing is judging. Knowledge is always true or false, and according to Aristotle only judgments are true or false. In this appeal to Aristotle, Rickert supposes that Aristotle means the same by judgment – whereas Aristotle means precisely that which Rickert is not willing to see in the simple composition of representing as such – "*letting something be seen*." Rickert does not see that the simple sense of representing actually includes knowing.

He is prevented from seeing the primary cognitive character of representation because he presupposes a mythical concept of representing from the philosophy of natural science and so comes to the formulation that in representing the representations get represented. But in the case of a representation on the level of simple perception a representation is not represented; I simply see the chair. This is implied in the very sense of representing. When I look, I am not intent upon seeing a representation of something, but the chair. Take for example mere envisaging or bringing to mind, which is also characterized as a representation of something which is not on hand,[7] as when I now envisage my writing table. Even in such a case of merely thinking of something, what is represented is not a representation, not a content of consciousness, but the matter itself. The same applies to the recollective representation of, for example, a sailboat trip. I do not remember representations but the boat and the trip itself. The most primitive matters of fact which are in the structures themselves are overlooked simply for the sake of a theory. Knowing cannot be representing, for only then is the theory justified that the object of knowledge is and must be a value, because there must be a philosophy of value.

What makes us blind to intentionality is the presumption that what we have here is a theory of the relation between physical and psychic, whereas what is really exhibited is simply a structure of the psychic itself. Whether that toward which representing directs itself is a real material thing or merely something fancied, whether acknowledging acknowledges a value or whether judging directs itself toward something else which is not real, the first thing to see is this directing-itself-toward as such. The structure of comportments, we might say, is to be made secure without any epistemological dogma. It is only when we have rightly seen this that we can, by means of it, come to a sharper formulation and perhaps a critique of intentionality as it has been interpreted up to now. We shall learn that in fact even in phenomenology there are still unclarified assumptions associated with intentionality which admittedly make it truly difficult for a philosophy so burdened with dogmas as Neo-Kantianism to see plainly what has been exhibited here. As long as we think in dogmas and directions, we first tend to assume something along the same lines. And we hold to what we assume all the more so as the phenomena are not in fact exhaustively brought out into the open.

When it comes to comportments, we must keep a steady eye solely upon the structure of directing-itself-toward in them. All theories about the psychic, consciousness, person, and the like must be held in abeyance.

c) The basic constitution of intentionality as such

What we have learned about intentionality so far is, to put it formally, empty. But one thing is already clear: before anything else, its structural coherence must be envisaged freely, without the background presence of any realistic or idealistic theories of consciousness. We must learn to see the data as such and to see that relations between comportments, between lived experiences, are themselves not complexions of things but in turn are of an intentional character. We must thus come to see that all the relations of life are intrinsically defined by this structure. In the process we shall see that there are persistent difficulties here which cannot be easily dispelled. But in order to see this, we must first take a look at intentionality itself. From this point on we can also fix our terminology in order to come to understand an expression which is often used in phenomenology and is just as often misunderstood, namely, the concept of *act*. The comportments of life are also called acts: perception, judgment, love, hate. . . . What does act mean here? Not activity, process, or some kind of power. No, act simply means *intentional relation*. Acts refer to those lived experiences which have the character of intentionality. We must adhere to this concept of act and not confuse it with others.

As fundamental as intentionality is, it also seems empty at first glance. We are simply saying that representing is the representing of something, judging is judging about something, and the like. It is hard to see just how a science is to be made possible from such structures. This science is evidently at its end before it has really begun. In fact, it seems as if this phenomenological statement of intentionality is merely a tautology. Thus Wundt early on observed that all phenomenological knowledge can be reduced to the proposition A = A. We will try to see whether there is not very much to say and whether in the end most of it has not yet even been said. By holding to this first discovery of phenomenology that intentionality is a structure of lived experiences and not just a supplementary relation, we already have an initial instruction on how we must proceed in order to see this structure and constitution.

α) The perceived of perceiving: the entity in itself (environmental thing, natural thing, thinghood)

In maintaining that intentionality is the structure found in comportments, we have in any case avoided the danger of lapsing into construction and into a theory which goes beyond what is before us. But at the same time the necessity of this structure, in order to be equally impartial in our pursuit of it, is decided within it. We shall now try to shed some light upon the basic structure of intentionality. The preliminary designation of directing-itself-toward is only an initial moment in this structure, far removed from its full constitution as well as wholly formal and empty.

In order to clarify the basic constitution of intentionality, let us turn once again to the exemplary case of naturally perceiving a thing. By intentionality we do not mean an objective relation which occasionally and subsequently takes place between a physical thing and a psychic process, but the structure of a comportment as comporting to, directing itself toward. With this, we are not just characterizing this one particular perception (of the chair) here and now, but the *perceived as such*. If we are after the basic constitution of intentionality, the best way to do it is to go after it itself – directing-itself-toward. Let us now focus not on the directing-itself but on the *toward-which*. We will not look at the perceiving but at the perceived, and in fact at the *perceived of this perception*. What is this?

If I answer without prejudice, I say the chair itself. I see no 'representations' of the chair, register no image of the chair, sense no sensations of the chair. I simply see *it* – it itself. This is the most immediate sense that perceiving offers. More precisely, I must ask: *What* do I see in my 'natural' perception, in which I now live and dwell and am here in this room; what can I say about the chair? I would say that it stands in Room 24 next to the desk, and it is probably used by lecturers who prefer to sit while they lecture. It is not just any chair but a very particular one, the desk chair in Room 24 at Marburg University, perhaps somewhat worse for wear and poorly painted in the factory from which it evidently came. Something like this could be said of the chair when I describe it quite naturally, without elaborate constructions and advance preparations. What would I then be saying? I would simply be recounting the very particular as well as trivial story of the chair as it is here and now and day after day. What is perceived in this 'natural' perception we shall designate as a thing of the environing world, or simply the *environmental thing*.

I can dwell upon this perception and further describe what I find in it, the chair itself, and can say: it is so heavy, so colored, so high, and so wide; it can be pushed from one place to another; if I lift it and let go, it falls; it can be chopped into pieces with a hatchet; if ignited, it burns. Here again we have plain statements in which I speak of the perceived itself and not of representations or sensations of the chair. But now it is a matter of other determinations of the chair than those we began with. What we have just said of the perceived can be said of any piece of wood whatsoever. What we have elicited in the chair does not define it as a chair. Something is indeed asserted about the chair, not qua chair-thing, but rather as a thing of nature, as *natural thing*. The fact that what is perceived is a chair is now of no account.

The perceived is an environmental thing, but it is also a natural thing. For this distinction, we have in our language very fine distinctions in the way in which language itself forms its meanings and expressions. We say, "I am giving roses." I can also say, "I am giving flowers," but not "I am giving plants." Botany, on the other hand, does not analyze flowers but rather plants. The distinction between plant and flower, both of which can be said of the same rose, is the distinction between natural and environmental thing. The rose as flower is an environmental thing, the rose as plant is a natural thing.

The perceived in itself is both. And still the question arises whether this description eliciting what is given in the perceived thing itself already gives us what phenomenology strictly means by the perceived. When we consider that these two thing-structures – environmental thing and natural thing – apply to one and the same chair, one obvious difficulty already arises: how are we to understand the relationship of these two structures of a thing? We shall arrive at a more precise knowledge of this later in other contexts. At the moment, I only maintain that when I say in ordinary language and not upon reflection and theoretical study of the chair, "The chair is hard," my aim is not to state the degree of resistance and density of this thing as material thing. I simply want to say, "The chair is uncomfortable." Already here we can see that specific structures belonging to a natural thing and which as such can be regarded separately – hardness, weight – present themselves first of all in well-defined environmental characteristics. Hardness, material resistance, is itself present in the feature of discomfort and even only present in this way, and not just inferred from it or derived through it. The perceived gives itself in itself and not by virtue of points of view, say, which are brought to the thing. It is the specific environmental thing, even when it remains concealed from many.

I can go still further into what is found in perceiving, this natural thing here. By applying an appropriate form of research to it, I can show that, as a natural thing, something like materiality and extension belong to it, that anything extended is as such colored, and further, that every color as color has its extension, and that a material and extended thing is displaceable, subject to change of place. Thus once again I have elicited something found in this thing itself, but now it is no longer in the perceived (chair) as environmental thing or as natural thing. Now I am concerned with *thingness* as such. I speak of materiality, extension, coloration, local mobility, and other determinations of this kind which do not belong to the chair as this peculiar chair but to any natural thing whatsoever. These are structures which constitute the thingness of the thing, structural moments of the natural thing itself, contents which can be read out from the given itself.

In all three cases we were concerned with the perceived entity in itself, with what can be found in it through a cognizance of it. Perceiving is here taken in a broad but natural sense. The typical epistemology as well as psychology will say that these descriptions of the natural thing and environmental thing are quite naïve and as such essentially unscientific. For in the first instance and in actuality, with my eyes I merely see something colored, in the first instance I merely have sensations of yellow, to which I then add other such elements.

In opposition to this scientific account, what we want is precisely naïveté, pure naïveté, which in the first instance and in actuality sees the chair. When we say 'we see,' 'seeing' here is not understood in the narrow sense of optical sensing. Here it means nothing other than 'simple cognizance of what is found.' When we hold to this expression, then we also understand and have no difficulty in taking the immediately given just as it shows itself. We thus say that one sees in the chair itself that it came from a factory. We draw no conclusions, make no investigations, but we simply see this in it, even though we have no sensation of a factory or anything like it. The field of what is found in simple cognizance is in principle much broader than what any particular epistemology or psychology could establish on the basis of a theory of perception. In this broad sense of perceiving and seeing, what is perceived even includes, as we shall see later, all of what I have said about thingness, that this thing itself includes materiality, that to materiality belongs extension as well as coloration, which in turn has its own kind of extension. These are not matters that I discover here in this classroom; they are correlations between general features. But they are not invented or constructed. I can also see these structures and their specific correlations in an adequately and sufficiently cultivated form of simple finding – seeing not in the sense of a mystical act or inspiration but in the sense of a simple envisaging of structures which can be read off in what is given.

β) The perceived of perceiving: the how of being-intended (the perceivedness of the entity, the feature of bodily-there)

But we have still not arrived at what we have called the perceived in the strict sense. The perceived in the strict sense for phenomenology is not the perceived *entity* in itself but the *perceived* entity insofar as it is perceived, *as* it shows itself in concrete perception. The perceived in the strict sense is the perceived as such or, more precisely expressed, the *perceivedness*, of this chair for example, the way and manner, the structure in which the chair is perceived. The way and manner of how this chair is perceived is to be distinguished from the structure of how it is represented. The expression *the perceived as such* now refers [not to the perceived entity in itself but] *to this entity in the way and manner of its being-perceived*. With this we have, as a start, only suggested a completely new structure, a structure to which I cannot now attribute all those determinations which I have thus far attributed to the chair.

The being-perceived of the chair is not something which belongs to the chair as chair, for a stone or house or tree or the like can also be perceived. Being-perceived and the structure of perceivedness consequently belong to perceiving as such, i.e., to intentionality. Accordingly, we can distinguish along the following lines: *the entity itself*: the environmental thing, the natural thing, or the thingness; and *the entity in the manner of its being intended*: its being-perceived, being-represented, being-judged, being-loved, being-hated, being-thought in the broadest sense. In the first three cases we have to do with the entity in itself, in the latter with its being-intended, the perceivedness of the entity.

What is perceivedness? Is there really anything like this? Can anything be said about the perceivedness of the chair? Independent of any theories, we must regard these structures in their distinction from the structures that pertain to the thing and to the entity as an entity. This provisional specification and differentiation from thingness already give us an initial indication as to where we should look: manifestly not at the chair itself as it is intended in perceiving, but rather at it *in the how of its being-intended*. What shows itself there? The perceived as such has the feature of *bodily presence* [*Leibhaftigkeit*]. In other words, the entity which presents itself as perceived has the feature of being *bodily-there*. Not only is it given as itself, but as itself in its bodily presence. There is a distinction in mode of givenness to be made between the *bodily-given* and the *self-given*. Let us clarify this distinction for ourselves by setting it off from the way in which something merely represented is there. Representing is here understood in the sense of simple envisaging, simply bringing something to mind.

I can now envisage the Weidenhauser bridge; I place myself before it, as it were. Thus the bridge is itself given. I intend the bridge itself and not an image of it, no fantasy, but it itself. And yet it is not bodily given to me. It would be bodily given if I go down the hill and place myself before the bridge itself. This means that what is itself given need not be bodily given, while conversely anything which is bodily given is itself given. *Bodily presence is a superlative mode of the self-givenness of an entity*. This self-givenness becomes clearer still by setting it off from another possible mode of representing, which in phenomenology is understood as *empty intending*.

Empty intending is the mode of representing something in the manner of thinking of something, of recalling it, which for example can take place in a conversation about the bridge. I intend the bridge itself without thereby seeing it simply in its outward appearance, but I intend it in an empty intending [which in this conversation is left intuitively unfulfilled]. A large part of our ordinary talk goes on in this way. We mean the matters themselves and not images or representations of them, yet we do not have them intuitively given. In empty intending as well, the intended is itself directly and simply intended, but merely emptily, which means without any intuitive fulfillment. Intuitive fulfillment is found once again in simple envisaging; this indeed gives the entity itself but does not give it bodily.

This distinction between empty intending and intuitive representing applies not only to sense perception but to the modifications of all acts. Take the sentence: 1 + 2 is 2 + 1. One can repeat it thoughtlessly but still understand it and know that one is not talking nonsense. But it can also be carried out with insight, so that every step is performed by envisaging what is intended. In the first instance it is uttered to some extent blindly, but in the second it is seen. In the latter case, the intended is envisaged in an originary envisaging, in that I make present to myself 2 + 1 . . . , i.e., all determinations in their original meanings. This mode of intuitive thinking demonstrates the determinations in the matters themselves. But it is only on rare occasions that we operate in this mode of intuitive thinking. For the most part we operate in foreshortened and blind thinking.

Another type of representing in the broadest sense is the *perception of a picture*. If we analyze a perception of a picture, we see clearly how what is perceived in the consciousness of a picture has a totally different structure from what is perceived in simple perception or what is represented in simple envisaging. I can look at a picture postcard of the Weidenhauser bridge. Here we have a new type of representing. What is now bodily given is the postcard itself. This card itself is a thing, an object, just as much as the bridge or a tree or the like. But it is not a simple thing like the bridge. As we have said, it is a picture-thing. Rather, when I see a picture postcard, I see – in the natural attitude – what is pictured on it, the bridge, [which is now seen as] what is pictured on the card. In this case, the bridge is not emptily presumed or merely envisaged or originarily perceived, but apprehended in this characteristic layered structure of the portrayal of something. The bridge itself is now the represented in the sense of being represented by way of being depicted through something. This apprehension of a picture, the apprehension of something as something pictured through a picture-thing, has a structure totally different from that of a direct perception. This must be brought home quite forcefully because of the efforts once made, and once again being made today, to take the apprehension of a picture as the paradigm by means of which, it is believed, any perception of any object can be illuminated. In the consciousness of a picture, there is the picture-thing and the pictured. The picture-thing can be a concrete thing – the blackboard on the wall – but the picture-thing is not merely a thing like a natural thing or another environmental thing. For it shows something, what is pictured itself. In simple perception, by contrast, in the simple apprehension of an object, nothing like a consciousness of a picture can be found. It goes against all the plain and simple findings about the simple apprehension of an object to interpret them as if I first perceive a picture in my consciousness when I see that house there, as if a picture-thing were first given and thereupon apprehended as picturing that house out there. There would thus be a subjective picture within and that which is pictured outside, transcendent. Nothing of the sort is to be found. Rather, in the simple sense of perception I see the house itself. Even aside from the fact that this transposition of the consciousness of a picture, which is constituted in a totally different way, onto the simple apprehension of an object explains nothing and leads to untenable theories, we must keep in mind the real reason for rejecting this transposition: it does not correspond to the simple phenomenological findings. There is also the following difficulty, which we shall only mention without exploring. If knowledge in general is an apprehension of an object-picture as an immanent picture of a transcendent thing outside, how then is the transcendent object itself to be apprehended? If every apprehension of an object is a consciousness of a picture, then for the immanent picture I once again need a picture-thing which depicts the immanent picture for me etc. etc. This is a secondary factor which argues against this theory. But the main thing is this: not only is there nothing of the pictorial and picturing in the course of simple apprehension; there is in particular nothing like a consciousness of a picture in the very act of apprehending an object. It is not because we fall into an infinite regress, and so explain nothing, that the infrastructure of the consciousness of a picture for the apprehension of an object is to be rejected. It is not because we arrive at no genuine and tenable theory with this infrastructure. It is rather because this is already contrary to every phenomenological finding. It is a theory without phenomenology. Hence perceiving must be considered totally distinct from the consciousness of a picture. Consciousness of a picture is possible at all first only as perceiving, but only in such a way that the picture-thing is actually apprehended beginning with what is pictured on it.

When we start from simple perception, let us reaffirm that the authentic moment in the perceivedness of the perceived is that *in perception the perceived entity is bodily there*. In addition to this feature, another moment of every concrete perception of a thing in regard to its perceivedness is that the perceived thing is always presumed in its *thing-totality*. When I see a sensibly perceptible object, this familiar chair here, I always see – understood as a particular way of seeing – only one particular side and one aspect. I see, for example, the upper part of the seat but not the lower surface. And yet, when I see the chair in this way or see only the legs, I do not think that the chair has its legs sawed off. When I go into a room and see a cupboard, I do not see the door of the cupboard or a mere surface. Rather, the very sense of perception implies that I see the cupboard. When I walk around it, I always have new aspects. But in each moment I am intent, in the sense of natural intending, upon seeing the cupboard itself and not just an aspect of it. These aspects can change continually with the multiplicity of aspects being offered to me. But the bodily selfsameness of the perceived persists throughout my circling of the thing. The thing *adumbrates*, shades off in its aspects. But it is not an *adumbration* which is intended, but the perceived thing itself, in each case in an adumbration. In the multiplicity of changing perceptions the selfsameness of the perceived persists. I have no other perception in the sense of something else perceived. The content of perception is different, but the perceived is presumed as the same.

In view of the apprehension of the whole and its adumbrations, there is one further structure of the perceived in the narrow sense to be considered in the perception of a picture. What is bodily perceived is the picture-thing itself, but this too is perceived in each instance in an aspect. To some extent, however, the perception of a picture-thing does not come to completion in the normal and natural perception of a picture. Contrariwise, for example, the postman can take the picture-thing (the *picture* postcard) simply as an environmental thing, as a *post*card. Not only does such a perception not come to completion, but it is also not the case that I first merely see a thing and then conclude "it is a picture of . . ." Instead, I see in a flash something pictured and not really the picture-thing, the strokes and patches of the drawing, in the first instance and in thematic isolation. To see these as pure moments of the thing already calls for a modification of our natural regard, a kind of *depicturization*. The natural tendency of perception in this sense proceeds in the direction of apprehending the picture.

γ) Initial indication of the basic mode of intentionality as the belonging-together of intentio *and* intentum

Within this manifold of modes of representation we have at the same time a specific interrelation. Empty intending, envisaging, apprehending a picture and simple perceiving are not merely juxtaposed, but inherently have a specific structural interrelation. Empty intending, for example, can be intuitively fulfilled in intuitive envisaging. In thoughtless thought, in empty intending, the intended is intuitively unfulfilled, it lacks the fullness of intuition. Envisaging has the possibility of intuitive fulfillment up to a certain level, since envisaging is never capable of giving the matter itself in its bodily givenness.

Instead of talking about it in this way, I can talk about what is envisaged from the simple and persistent envisaging of something, or I can even, if for example a dispute arises over the number of arches and pillars in the bridge, fill the envisaged in a new way through bodily givenness itself. Perception, with its kind of givenness, is a superlative case of intentional fulfillment. Every intention has within it a tendency toward fulfillment and its specifically proper way of possible fulfillment: perception in general only through perception; remembrance never through expectation but through an envisaging that remembers or through perception. There are very specific laws which govern the connections among the possibilities of fulfilling an already given empty intention. This is also true in the realm of perceiving pictures. It is possible to arrange these connections in more complicated ways. I can place, next to the original picture, a copy of it. If I have a copy, that is, a copied picture of something, I have a specific structural continuity running from copy to picture (original) to model [what is pictured], so that what is actually pictured shows through the depicting function of the copy (picture to model). But if the copy is to furnish evidence of its genuineness as a copy, then I cannot compare it to the model. Instead, the intuitive demonstration of the copy is given by the copied picture (original) which, as the picture of the model, is in itself a model. These characteristic structures of demonstration and their possibility run through all acts of apprehending, even if we now totally disregard this specific act of perceptual apprehension. Thus the perceived shows itself in its perceivedness (this is the most important), what we are conscious of as a picture shows itself in its pictoriality, the simply envisaged shows itself in the way of envisaging, the emptily intended shows itself in the way of empty intending. All of these distinctions are different ways in which their objects are intended.

These structural continuities and levels of fulfillment, demonstration, and verification are relatively easy to see in the field of intuitive representation. But they are to be found without exception in all acts, for example, in the domain of pure theoretical comportment, determination, and speech. Without the possibility here of following the structures of every pertinent intention to its intended as such, the scientific elaboration of a genuine phenomenology (drawn from the phenomena themselves) of concept formation – the genesis of the concept from raw meaning – cannot even be considered. But without this foundation every logic remains a matter for dilettantes or a construction.

We thus have an inherent affinity between the way something is intended, the *intentio*, and the *intentum*, whereby *intentum*, the intended, is to be understood in the sense just developed, not the perceived as an entity, but the entity in the how of its being-perceived, the *intentum* in the how of its being-intended. Only with the how of the being-intended belonging to every *intentio* as such does the basic constitution of intentionality come into view at all, even though only provisionally.

Intentio in phenomenology is also understood as the act of presuming [*Vermeinen*]. There is a connection between presuming and presumed, or *noesis* and *noema*. Noειν means to perceive [*vernehmen*] or come to awareness, to apprehend simply, the perceiving itself and the perceived in the way it is perceived. I refer to these terms because they involve not only a terminology but also a particular interpretation of directing-itself-toward. Every directing-itself-toward (fear, hope, love) has the feature of directing-itself-toward which Husserl calls *noesis*. Inasmuch as νοειν is taken from the sphere of theoretical knowing, any exposition of the practical sphere here is drawn from the theoretical. For our purposes this terminology is not dangerous, since we are using it to make it clear that intentionality is fully determined only when it is seen as this belonging together of *intentio* and *intentum*. By way of summary let us therefore say: just as intentionality is not a subsequent coordination of at first unintentional lived experience and objects but is rather a structure, so inherent in the basic constitution of the structure in each of its manifestations must always be found its own intentional toward-which, the *intentum*. This provisional exposition of the *basic constitution of intentionality as a reciprocal belonging-together of intentio and intentum* is not the last word, but only an initial indication and exhibition of a thematic field for consideration.

How is this analysis of intentionality different from Brentano's? In intentionality Brentano saw the *intentio, noesis*, and the diversity of its modes, but not the *noema*, the *intentum*. He remained uncertain in his analysis of what he called "intentional object." The four meanings of the object of perception – the perceived – already indicate that the sense of 'something' in the representation of something is not transparently obvious. Brentano wavers in two directions. On the one hand, he takes the "intentional object" to be the entity itself in its being. Then again it is taken as the how of its being-apprehended unseparated from the entity. Brentano never clearly brings out and highlights the how of being-intended. In short, he never brings into relief intentionality as such, as a structural totality. But this further implies that intentionality, defined as a character of a certain entity, is at one with the entity; intentionality is identified with the psychic. Brentano also left undiscussed just what intentionality is to be the structure of, since his theory of the psychic assumed its traditional sense of the immanently perceptible, the immanently conscious along the lines of Descartes's theory. The character of the psychic itself was left undetermined, so that that of which intentionality is the structure was not brought out in the original manner demanded by intentionality. This is a phase which phenomenology has not yet overcome. Even today intentionality is taken simply as a structure of consciousness or of acts, of the person, in which these two realities of which intentionality is supposed to be the structure are again assumed in a traditional way. Phenomenology – Husserl along with Scheler – tries to get beyond the psychic restriction and psychic character of intentionality in two very different directions. Husserl conceives intentionality as the universal structure of reason (where reason is not understood as the psychic but as differentiated from the psychic). Scheler conceives intentionality as the structure of the spirit or the person, again differentiated from the psychic. But we shall see that what is meant by reason, spirit, *anima* does not overcome the approach operative in these theories. I point this out because we shall see how phenomenology, with this analysis of intentionality, calls for a more radical internal development. To refute phenomenological intentionality, one cannot simply criticize Brentano! One thus loses touch with the issue from the very beginning.

It is not intentionality as such that is metaphysically dogmatic but what is built under its structure, or is left at this level because of a traditional tendency not to question that of which it is presumably the structure, and what this sense of structure itself means. Yet the methodological rule for the initial apprehension of intentionality is really not to be concerned with interpretations but only to keep strictly to that which shows itself, regardless of how meager it may be. Only in this way will it be possible to see, in intentionality itself and through it directly into the heart of the matter, that of which it is the structure and how it is that structure. Intentionality is not an ultimate explanation of the psychic but an initial approach toward overcoming the uncritical application of traditionally defined realities such as the psychic, consciousness, continuity of lived experience, reason. But if such a task is implicit in this basic concept of phenomenology, then "intentionality" is the very last word to be used as a phenomenological slogan. Quite the contrary, it identifies that whose disclosure would allow phenomenology to find itself in its possibilities. It must therefore be flatly stated that what the belonging of the *intentum* to the *intentio* implies is obscure. How the being-intended of an entity is related to that entity remains puzzling. It is even questionable whether one may question in this way at all. But we cannot inquire into these puzzles as long as we cover up their puzzling character with theories for and against intentionality. Our understanding of intentionality is therefore not advanced by our speculations about it. We shall advance only by following intentionality in its concretion. An occasion for this is to be found in our effort to clarify the second discovery of phenomenology, the discovery of *categorical intuition*.

§6. Categorial intuition

What calls for clarification under this heading could be discovered only after the exposition of *intentionality* as a structure. The term 'intuition' corresponds in its meaning to what above was already defined as 'seeing' in the broad sense of that word. *Intuition* means: simple apprehension of what is itself bodily found just as it shows itself. First, this concept carries no prejudice as to whether sense perception is the sole and most original form of intuiting or whether there are further possibilities of intuition regarding other fields and constituents. Second, nothing should be read into its meaning other than what the phenomenological use of the term specifies: *simply apprehending the bodily given as it shows itself*. Intuition in the phenomenological sense implies no special capacity, no exceptional way of transposing oneself into otherwise closed domains and depths of the world, not even the kind of intuition employed by Bergson. It is therefore a cheap characterization of phenomenology to suggest that it is somehow connected with modern intuitionism. It simply has nothing to do with it.

The discovery of categorical intuition is the demonstration, first, that there is a simple apprehension of the *categorical*, such constituents in entities which in traditional fashion are designated as *categories* and were seen in crude form quite early [in Greek philosophy, especially by Plato and Aristotle]. Second, it is above all the demonstration that this apprehension is invested in the most everyday of perceptions and in every experience. This only clarifies the meaning of the term. What matters is to exhibit this kind of intuition itself, to bring it to givenness as intentionality, and to make clear *what* is intuited in it and *how*.

It was already suggested that categorical intuition is found in every concrete perception (perception of a thing), as it were, as an inclusion. In order to show this we shall return to our exemplary case of the perception of this chair. But in order to see the categorical intuition in it, we must be adequately prepared. This calls for two more general considerations. We shall deal with 1) intentional presuming and its intentional fulfillment and 2) intentional compartments as expressed – *intuition and expression*.

We shall see that our comportments, lived experiences taken in the broadest sense, are through and through *expressed* experiences; even if they are not uttered in words, they are nonetheless expressed in a definite articulation by an understanding that I have of them as I simply live in them without regarding them thematically.

a) Intentional presuming and intentional fulfillment

α) Identification as demonstrative fulfillment

Our account of the interrelation of the modes of representation manifested a distinct sequence of levels ranging from mere empty intending (signitive acts) to originarily giving perception (intuitive act in the narrowest sense). Empty intending is unfulfilled in its sense; what is presumed in it is there in the how of non-fulfillment. Empty intending or what is presumed in it can in a certain sense be fulfilled in intuitive envisaging. The presumed (envisaged) is thus given in greater or lesser completeness (bridge: columns – railings – type of arches – arrangements of the building stones). But however great the perfection of the fullness may be, it always manifests a difference from the fullness of perception, which gives the entity bodily. But even here, if we restrict ourselves to the sense perception of material things, the fullness is not total. Sense perception indeed gives the entity originarily, but always only from one side. However adequate a perception may be, the perceived entity always shows itself only in a particular adumbration. There are thus distinctions with regard to the definitiveness and completeness of the fullness which a fulfilling intuition is capable of giving. We accordingly speak of a *definitive and thoroughgoing fulfillment* when on the side of presuming *all the partial intentions are fulfilled* and, on the side of the intuition which bestows fulfillment, that intuition presents the *whole matter in its totality*.

The interrelation of these modes of representations is a functional interrelation which is always prefigured in their intentionality. Empty intending, envisaging, sense perception are not simply coordinated as species in a genus, as when I say that apples, pears, peaches, and plums are fruits. Rather, these modes stand to one another in functional relation, and the fulfillment itself is of an intentional character. Fulfillment means having the entity present in its intuitive content so that what is at first only emptily presumed in it demonstrates itself as grounded in the matters. Perception, or *what* it gives, *points out, de-monstrates*. The empty intention is demonstrated in the state of affairs given in intuition; the originary perception gives the demonstration.

The peculiar thing is that there is a correlation in such demonstration or fulfillment. Let us look at this more concretely. I can in an empty way now think of my desk at home simply in order to talk about it. I can fulfill this empty intention in a way by envisaging it to myself, and finally by going home and seeing it itself in an authentic and final experience. In such a demonstrative fulfillment the emptily intended and the originarily intuited come into coincidence. This bringing-into-coincidence – the intended being experienced in the intuited as itself and selfsame – is an *act of identification*. The intended identifies itself in the intuited; selfsameness is *experienced* [*erfahren*]. Here it is well to note that in this act of identification the identity is not apprehended thematically as selfsameness. Identification is for its part not already an apprehension of identity but solely of the identical. Inasmuch as intuition is bodily originary, it gives the entity itself, the matter itself. The emptily presumed is compared to the matter itself, so that in fulfillment I obtain insight into the matter itself. More precisely, I obtain insight into the groundedness in the matter of what was before only presumed. This fulfillment as an act of identification includes obtaining insight into the grounding of what is presumed in the matter. This act of obtaining insight, as identifying fulfillment, is called *evidence*.

β) Evidence as identifying fulfillment

Identifying fulfillment is what we call evidence. Evidence is a specific intentional act, that of identifying the presumed and the intuited; the presumed is itself illuminated in the matter. This elaboration of evidence was for the first time brought to a successful resolution by Husserl, who thus made an essential advance beyond all the obscurities prevalent in the tradition of logic and epistemology. But it has not had much of an effect. Even today we still adhere to the traditional mythological account of evidence in regarding it as a peculiar indicator of certain lived experiences, especially experiences of judgment. It is something like a sign which wells up at times in the soul and announces that the psychic process with which it is associated is true. To some extent, it is as if a psychic datum announces that there is something real outside which corresponds to the judging. As everyone knows, this transcendent reality cannot itself become immanent. So there must be a way in which it can be announced on the 'inside.' This is the so-called "*feeling of evidence*" of Rickert.

But if we see that the acts of identifying apprehension are defined by intentionality, then we do not resort to the mythological account of evidence as psychic feeling or psychic datum, as though a pressure were first exerted and then it dawns on one that the truth is indeed there.

It is further customary to regard evidence as an addition to a specific class of lived experiences, that of judgments. This restriction along with the concept of evidence as a possible addition to [psychic] processes do not correspond to the findings. It is readily seen that evidence in general is comprehensible only if we regard the intentionality in it [now understood as identifying apprehension]. But this at the same time yields a fundamental insight of great significance. Since the act of evidence connotes an identifying vision that selects a state of affairs from the originarily intuited matter, evidence is in its sense always of a sort and rigor which varies according to the ontological character [*Seinscharakter*] of the field of subject matter, the intentional structure of the kind of apprehensive access, and the possibility of fulfillment grounded therein. We therefore speak of the *regionality of evidence*. All evidence is in its sense geared to a corresponding region of subject matter. It is absurd to want to transpose one possibility of evidence, for example, the mathematical, into other kinds of apprehension. The same holds for the idea of rigor of theoretical demonstration, which in its sense is built upon the concept of evidence peculiar to each type: philosophical, theological, physical. With all this regionality, on the other hand, the *universality of evidence* must again be stressed. *Evidence is a universal function, first, of all acts which give their objects, and then, of all acts* (evidence of willing and wishing, of loving and hoping). It is not restricted to assertions, predications, judgments. In this universality it at the same time varies according to the region of subject matter and the kind of access to it.

We have thus arrived at 1) the idea of pure and absolute evidence, '*apodicticity*' as insight into essential states of affairs; 2) the idea of insight into 'individual' states of affairs, 'subject matters,' *assertoric* evidence; 3) the idea of the connection of these two, the insight into the necessity of an individual state of affairs "being so" [*Sosein*] based upon the essential grounds of the 'posited individual.'

γ) Truth as demonstrative identification

From what has now been brought out about the supreme and total fulfillment come two phenomenological concepts, those of *truth* and *being*. Definitive and thoroughgoing fulfillment means commensuration (*adaequatio*) of what is presumed (*intellectus*) with the intuited subject matter itself (*res*). We thus obtain a phenomenological interpretation of the old scholastic definition of truth: *veritas est adaequatio rei et intellectus*. In the context of presuming, this means that there is no partial intention in what is objectively given which would not be fulfilled intuitively, i.e., from the originarily intuited matter. Phenomenologically understood, *adaequatio* refers to this commensuration in the sense of bringing-into-coincidence. Now what does the term "truth" mean in the full structural context of knowledge?

The demonstration of the presumed in the intuited is identification, an act which is phenomenologically specified in terms of intentionality, directing-itself-toward. This means that every act has its intentional correlate, perception the perceived, and identification the identified, here the being-identical of presumed and intuited as the intentional correlate of the act of identification. Truth can be designated in a threefold way. The *first* concept of truth is this *being-identical of presumed and intuited*. Being-true is then equivalent to this being-identical, *the subsistence [Bestand] of this identity*. We obtain this first concept of truth by referring to the correlate of the act of identification: subsistence of the identity of presumed and intuited. Here it should be noted that in the living act of concrete perceiving and in the demonstration of what is presumed, this perceiving lives in the apprehension of the matter as such, in the performance of the act. In the coming into coincidence of the presumed with the intuited, I am solely and primarily directed toward the subject matter itself, and yet – this is the peculiarity of this structural correlation – evidence is experienced in this apprehension of the intuited matter itself. The correlation is peculiar in that *something is experienced but not apprehended*. So it is really only in apprehending the object as such, which amounts to not apprehending the identity, that this identity is experienced. This act of bringing into coincidence is in touch with the subject matter; it is precisely through this particular intentionality of being-in-touch-with-the-subject-matter [*Bei-der-Sache-sein*] that this intentionality, itself unthematic in its performance, is immediately and transparently experienced as true. This is the phenomenological sense of saying that in evident perception I do not thematically study the truth of this perception itself, but rather live *in* the truth. Being-true is experienced as a distinctive *relation, a comportmental* relation [*Verhalt*] between presumed and intuited specifically in the sense of identity. We call this distinctive relation the *truth-relation*; being-*true* consists precisely in this relation. Truth in this sense is seen with respect to the correlate of the act of identification, that is, by way of intentionality with reference to the *intentum*.

Correlatively, we can obtain a *second* concept of truth commensurate to the *intentio*, not to the content of the act but to the act itself. What is now thematic is not the being-identical of what is intended in presuming and intuiting but *the act-structure of evidence itself as this coincident identification*. Formulated differently, under consideration now is the idea of the structural relationship of the acts of presuming and intuiting, the structure of the intentionality of evidence itself, *adaequatio* understood as *adaequare*. Truth is now taken as a character of knowledge, as an act, which means as intentionality.

The concept of truth as *adaequatio* can be taken in a double sense, as it always has been in history: on the one hand as the correlate of identification, of the bringing into coincidence, and on the other as a specification of this very act of bringing into coincidence. The controversy over the concept of truth goes back and forth between the thesis, *Truth is a relationship of the state of affairs to the subject matter*, and the thesis, *Truth is a specific correlation of acts*, for I can really only assert truth about knowing. Both conceptions try to direct the concept of truth to one side and so are incomplete. Neither the one oriented toward the state of affairs nor the one oriented toward the act captures the original sense of truth.

We obtain a *third* concept of truth by turning once again to the intuited entity itself. The true can also be understood in terms of the very object which is. As the originarily intuited it provides the demonstration, it gives the identification its ground and legitimacy. Here, the true amounts to that which *makes* knowledge *true* [i.e., the true-making matter, the entity itself as an intuited matter]. Truth here comes down to *being, being-real*. This is a concept of truth which also emerged very early in Greek philosophy and was constantly being confused with the first two concepts.

Notes

1 Edmund Husserl, *Ideen zu einer reinen Phänomenologie und phänomenologischen Philoso-phie*, in the *Jahrbuch für Philosophie und phänomenologische Forschung*, Vol. 1, Part 1 (Halle: Niemeyer, 1913), p. 185. Editor's note: cited as *Ideen I*; cf. Husserliana Vol. III, First Book, ed. Walter Biemel (The Hague: Nijhoff, 1950), pp. 223f. [English translation by Fred Kersten, *Ideas Pertaining to a Pure Phenomenology and to a Phenomenological Philosophy. First Book: General Introduction to a Pure Phenomenology* (The Hague/Boston/London: Nijhoff, 1982), §90, p. 218.]

2 Heinrich Rickert, "Die Methode der Philosophie und das Unmittelbare. Eine Problem-stellung," *Logos* XII (1923/24), p. 242 n.

3 Cf. the *Philosophische Bibliothek* edition (Hamburg: Meiner, 1925).

4 Heinrich Rickert, *Der Gegenstand der Erkenntnis. Ein Beitrag zum Problem der philoso-phischen Transzendenz* (Freiburg i. Br.: Wagner, 1892), p. 57. Editor's note: 2nd Edition, 1904, p. 106.

5 Ibid., p. 56; 2nd edn, p. 104.

5a Ibid., 2nd edn, p. 105.

6 Ibid., p. 57; 2nd edn, p. 105.

7 Ibid., p. 47; 2nd edn, p. 78.

3

THE PHENOMENOLOGICAL
METHOD OF INVESTIGATION

In provisionally characterizing the object which serves as the theme of our investigation (the Being of entities, or the meaning of Being in general), it seems that we have also delineated the method to be employed. The task of ontology is to explain Being itself and to make the Being of entities stand out in full relief. And the method of ontology remains questionable in the highest degree as long as we merely consult those ontologies which have come down to us historically, or other essays of that character. Since the term "ontology" is used in this investigation in a sense which is formally broad, any attempt to clarify the method of ontology by tracing its history is automatically ruled out.

When, moreover, we use the term "ontology", we are not talking about some definite philosophical discipline standing in interconnection with the others. Here one does not have to measure up to the tasks of some discipline that has been presented beforehand; on the contrary, only in terms of the objective necessities of definite questions and the kind of treatment which the 'things themselves' require, can one develop such a discipline.

With the question of the meaning of Being, our investigation comes up against the fundamental question of philosophy. This is one that must be treated *phenomenologically*. Thus our treatise does not subscribe to a 'standpoint' or represent any special 'direction'; for phenomenology is nothing of either sort, nor can it become so as long as it understands itself. The expression 'phenomenology' signifies primarily a *methodological conception*. This expression does not characterize the what of the objects of philosophical research as subject-matter, but rather the *how* of that research. The more genuinely a methodological concept is worked out and the more comprehensively it determines the principles on which a science is to be conducted, all the more primordially is it rooted in the way we come to terms with the things themselves, and the farther is it removed from what we call "technical devices", though there are many such devices even in the theoretical disciplines.

Thus the term 'phenomenology' expresses a maxim which can be formulated as 'To the things themselves!' It is opposed to all free-floating constructions and accidental findings; it is opposed to taking over any conceptions which only seem to have been demonstrated; it is opposed to those pseudo-questions which parade

M. Heidegger, *Being and Time*, 1962, trans. John Macquarrie and Edward Robinson, pp. 49–63, Oxford/New York: Blackwell/Harper & Row.

themselves as 'problems', often for generations at a time. Yet this maxim, one may rejoin, is abundantly self-evident, and it expresses, moreover, the underlying principle of any scientific knowledge whatsoever. Why should anything so self-evident be taken up explicitly in giving a title to a branch of research? In point of fact, the issue here is a kind of 'self-evidence' which we should like to bring closer to us, so far as it is important to do so in casting light upon the procedure of our treatise. We shall expound only the preliminary conception [*Vorbegriff*] of phenomenology.

This expression has two components: "phenomenon" and "logos". Both of these go back to terms from the Greek: φαινόμενον and λόγος. Taken superficially, the term "phenomenology" is formed like "theology", "biology", "sociology" – names which may be translated as "science of God", "science of life", "science of society". This would make phenomenology the *science of phenomena*. We shall set forth the preliminary conception of phenomenology by characterizing what one has in mind in the term's two components, 'phenomenon' and 'logos', and by establishing the meaning of the name in which these are *put together*. The history of the word itself, which presumably arose in the Wolffian school, is here of no significance.

A. The concept of phenomenon

The Greek expression φαινόμενον, to which the term 'phenomenon' goes back, is derived from the verb φαίνεσθαι, which signifies "to show itself". Thus φαινόμενον means that which shows itself, the manifest [*das, was sich zeigt, das Sichzeigende, das Offenbare*]. Φαίνεσθαι itself is a *middle-voiced* form which comes from φαίνω – to bring to the light of day, to put in the light. Φαίνω comes from the stem φα –, like φῶς, the light, that which is bright – in other words, that wherein something can become manifest, visible in itself. Thus we must *keep in mind* that the expression '*phenomenon*' signifies *that which shows itself in itself*, the manifest. Accordingly the φαινόμενα or 'phenomena' are the totality of what lies in the light of day or can be brought to the light – what the Greeks sometimes identified simply with τὰ ὄντα (entities). Now an entity can show itself from itself in many ways, depending in each case on the kind of access we have to it. Indeed it is even possible for an entity to show itself as something which in itself it is *not*. When it shows itself in this way, it 'looks like something or other'. This kind of showing-itself is what we call "*seeming*" [*Scheinen*]. Thus in Greek too the expression φαινόμενον ("phenomenon") signifies that which looks like something, that which is 'semblant', 'semblance' [*das "Scheinbare", der "Schein"*]. Φαινόμενον ἀγαθόν means something good which looks like, but 'in actuality' is not, what it gives itself out to be. If we are to have any further understanding of the concept of phenomenon, everything depends on our seeing how what is designated in the first signification of φαινόμενον ('phenomenon' as that which shows itself) and what is designated in the second ('phenomenon' as semblance) are structurally interconnected. Only when the meaning of something is such that it makes a pretension of showing itself – that is, of being a phenomenon – *can* it show itself *as* something which it is *not*; only then *can* it 'merely look like so-and-so'. When φαινόμενον signifies 'semblance', the primordial signification (the phenomenon as the manifest) is already included as that upon which the second signification is founded. We shall allot the term 'phenomenon' to this positive and primordial signification of φαινόμενον, and distinguish "phenomenon" from "semblance", which is the privative modification of "phenomenon" as thus defined. But what *both* these terms express has proximally nothing at all to do with what is called an 'appearance', or still less a 'mere appearance'.

This is what one is talking about when one speaks of the 'symptoms of a disease'. Here one has in mind certain occurrences in the body which show themselves and which, in showing themselves as thus showing themselves, 'indicate' something which does *not* show itself. The emergence of such occurrences, their showing-themselves, goes together with the Being-present-at-hand of disturbances which do not show themselves. Thus appearance, as the appearance 'of something', does *not* mean showing-itself; it means rather the announcing-itself by something which does not show itself, but which announces itself through something which does show itself. Appearing is a *not-showing-itself*. But the 'not' we find here is by no means to be confused with the privative "not" which we used in defining the structure of semblance. What appears does *not* show itself; and anything which thus fails to show itself, is also something which can never seem. All indications, presentations, symptoms, and symbols have this basic formal structure of appearing, even though they differ among themselves.

In spite of the fact that 'appearing' is never a showing-itself in the sense of "phenomenon", appearing is possible only *by reason of a showing-itself* of something. But this showing-itself, which helps to make possible the appearing, is not the appearing itself. Appearing is an *announcing*-itself [das Sich-*melden*] through something that shows itself. If one then says that with the word 'appearance' we allude to something wherein something appears without being itself an appearance, one has not thereby defined the concept of phenomenon: one has rather *presupposed* it. This presupposition, however, remains concealed; for when one says this sort of thing about 'appearance', the expression 'appear' gets used in two ways. "That wherein something 'appears'" means that wherein something announces itself, and therefore does not show itself; and in the words [*Rede*] 'without being itself an "appearance"', "appearance" signifies the *showing-itself*. But this showing-itself belongs essentially to the 'wherein' in which something announces itself. According to this, phenomena are *never* appearances, though on the other hand every appearance is dependent on phenomena. If one defines "phenomenon" with the aid of a conception of 'appearance' which is still unclear, then everything is stood on its head, and a 'critique' of phenomenology on this basis is surely a remarkable undertaking.

So again the expression 'appearance' itself can have a double signification: first, *appearing*, in the sense of announcing-itself, as not-showing-itself; and next, that which does the announcing [*das Meldende selbst*] – that which in its showing-itself indicates something which does not show itself. And finally one can use "appearing" as a term for the genuine sense of "phenomenon" as showing-itself. If one designates these three different things as 'appearance', bewilderment is unavoidable.

But this bewilderment is essentially increased by the fact that 'appearance' can take on still another signification. That which does the announcing – that which, in its showing-itself, indicates something non-manifest – may be taken as that which emerges in what is itself non-manifest, and which emanates [*ausstrahlt*] from it in such a way indeed that the non-manifest gets thought of as something that is essentially *never* manifest. When that which does the announcing is taken this way, "appearance" is tantamount to a "bringing forth" or "something brought forth", but something which does not make up the real Being of what brings it forth: here we have an appearance in the sense of 'mere appearance'. That which does the announcing and is brought forth does, of course, show itself, and in such a way that, as an emanation of what it announces, it keeps this very thing constantly veiled in itself. On the other hand, this not-showing which veils is not a semblance. Kant uses the term "appearance" in this twofold way. According to him "appearances" are, in the first place, the 'objects of empirical intuition': they are what shows itself in such intuition. But what thus shows itself (the "phenomenon" in the genuine primordial sense) is at the same time an 'appearance' as an emanation of something which *hides* itself in that appearance – an emanation which announces.

In so far as a phenomenon is constitutive for 'appearance' in the signification of announcing itself through something which shows itself, though such a phenomenon can privatively take the variant form of semblance, appearance too can become mere semblance. In a certain kind of lighting someone can look as if his cheeks were flushed with red; and the redness which shows itself can be taken as an announcement of the Being-present-at-hand of a fever, which in turn indicates some disturbance in the organism.

"*Phenomenon*", the showing-itself-in-itself, signifies a distinctive way in which something can be encountered. "*Appearance*", on the other hand, means a reference-relationship which is in an entity itself, and which is such that what *does the referring* (or the announcing) can fulfil its possible function only if it shows itself in itself and is thus a 'phenomenon'. Both appearance and semblance are founded upon the phenomenon, though in different ways. The bewildering multiplicity of 'phenomena' designated by the words "phenomenon", "semblance", "appearance", "mere appearance", cannot be disentangled unless the concept of the phenomenon is understood from the beginning as that which shows itself in itself.

If in taking the concept of "phenomenon" this way, we leave indefinite which entities we consider as "phenomena", and leave it open whether what shows itself is an entity or rather some characteristic which an entity may have in its Being, then we have merely arrived at the *formal* conception of "phenomenon". If by "that which shows itself" we understand those entities which are accessible through the empirical "intuition" in, let us say, Kant's sense, then the formal conception of "phenomenon" will indeed be legitimately employed. In this usage "phenomenon" has the signification of the *ordinary* conception of phenomenon. But this ordinary conception is not the phenomenological conception. If we keep within the horizon of the Kantian problematic, we can give an illustration of what is conceived phenomenologically as a "phenomenon", with reservations as to other differences; for we may then say that that which already shows itself in the appearance as prior to the "phenomenon" as ordinarily understood and as accompanying it in every case, can, even though it thus shows itself unthematically, be brought thematically to show itself; and what thus shows itself in itself (the 'forms of the intuition') will be the "phenomena" of phenomenology. For manifestly space and time must be able to show themselves in this way – they must be able to become phenomena – if Kant is claiming to make a transcendental assertion grounded in the facts when he says that space is the *a priori* "inside-which" of an ordering.[1]

If, however, the phenomenological conception of phenomenon is to be understood at all, regardless of how much closer we may come to determining the nature of that which shows itself, this presupposes inevitably that we must have an insight into the meaning of the formal conception of phenomenon and its legitimate employment in an ordinary signification. – But before setting up our preliminary conception of phenomenology, we must also define the signification of λόγος so as to make clear in what sense phenomenology can be a 'science of' phenomena at all.

B. The concept of the *logos*

In Plato and Aristotle the concept of the λόγος has many competing significations, with no basic signification positively taking the lead. In fact, however, this is only a semblance, which will maintain itself as long as our Interpretation is unable to grasp the basic signification properly in its primary content. If we say that the basic signification of λόγος is "discourse", then this word-for-word translation will not be validated until we have determined what is meant by "discourse" itself. The real signification of "discourse", which is obvious enough, gets constantly covered up by the later history of the word λόγος, and especially by the numerous and arbitrary Interpretations which subsequent philosophy has provided. Λόγος gets 'translated' (and this means that it is always getting interpreted) as "reason", "judgment", "concept", "definition", "ground", or "relationship". But how can 'discourse' be so susceptible of modification that λόγος can signify all the things we have listed, and in good scholarly usage? Even if λόγος is understood in the sense of "assertion", but of "assertion" as 'judgment', this seemingly legitimate translation may still miss the fundamental signification, especially if "judgment" is conceived in a sense taken over from some contemporary 'theory of judgment'. Λόγος does not mean "judgment", and it certainly does not mean this primarily – if one understands by "judgment" a way of 'binding' something with something else, or the 'taking of a stand' (whether by acceptance or by rejection).

Λόγος as "discourse" means rather the same as δηλοῦν: to make manifest what one is 'talking about' in one's discourse. Aristotle has explicated this function of discourse more precisely as ἀποφαίνεσθαι. The λόγος lets something be seen (φαίνεσθαι), namely, what the discourse is about; and it does so either *for* the one who is doing the talking (the *medium*) or for persons who are talking with one another, as the case may be. Discourse 'lets something be seen' ἀπό . . . : that is, it lets us see something from the very thing which the discourse is about. In discourse (ἀπόφανσις), so far as it is genuine, *what* is said [*was* geredet ist] is drawn *from* what the talk is about, so that discursive communication, in what it says, makes manifest what it is talking about, and thus makes this accessible to the other party. This is the structure of the λόγος as ἀπόφανσις. This mode of making manifest in the sense of letting something be seen by pointing it out, does not go with all kinds of 'discourse'. Requesting (εὐχή), for instance, also makes manifest, but in a different way.

When fully concrete, discoursing (letting something be seen) has the character of speaking – vocal proclamation in words. The λόγος is φωνή, and indeed, φωνὴ μετὰ φαντασίας – an utterance in which something is sighted in each case.

And only *because* the function of the λόγος as ἀπόφανσις lies in letting something be seen by pointing it out, can the λόγος have the structural form of σύνθεσις. Here "synthesis" does not mean a binding and linking together of representations, a manipulation of psychical occurrences where the 'problem' arises of how these bindings, as something inside, agree with something physical outside. Here the συν has a purely apophantical signification and means letting something be seen in its *togetherness* with something – letting it be seen *as* something.

Furthermore, because the λόγος is a letting-something-be-seen, it can *therefore* be true or false. But here everything depends on our steering clear of any conception of truth which is construed in the sense of 'agreement'. This idea is by no means the primary one in the concept of ἀλήθεια. The 'Being-true' of the λόγος as ἀληθεύειν means that in λέγειν as ἀποφαίνεσθαι the entities *of which* one is talking must be taken out of their hiddenness; one must let them be seen as something unhidden (ἀληθές); that is, they must be *discovered*. Similarly, 'Being false' (ψεύδεσθαι) amounts to deceiving in the sense of *covering up* [*verdecken*]: putting something in front of something (in such a way as to let it be seen) and thereby passing it off *as* something which it is *not*.

But because 'truth' has this meaning, and because the λόγος is a definite mode of letting something be seen, the λόγος is just *not* the kind of thing that can be considered as the primary 'locus' of truth. If, as has become quite customary nowadays, one defines "truth" as something that 'really' pertains to judgment, and if one then invokes the support of Aristotle with this thesis, not only is this unjustified, but, above all, the Greek conception of truth has been misunderstood. Αἴσθησις, the sheer sensory perception of something, is 'true' in the Greek sense, and indeed more primordially than the λόγος which we have been discussing. Just as seeing aims at colours, any αἴσθησις aims at its ἴδια (those entities which are genuinely accessible only *through* it and *for* it); and to that extent this perception is always true. This means that seeing always discovers colours, and hearing always discovers sounds. Pure νοεῖν is the perception of the simplest determinate ways of Being which entities as such may possess, and it perceives them just by looking at them. This νοεῖν is what is 'true' in the purest and most primordial sense; that is to say, it merely discovers, and it does so in such a way that it can never cover up. This νοεῖν can never cover up; it can never be false; it can at worst remain a *non-perceiving*, ἀγνοεῖν, not sufficing for straightforward and appropriate access.

When something no longer takes the form of just letting something be seen, but is always harking back to something else to which it points, so that it lets something be seen *as* something, it thus acquires a synthesis-structure, and with this it takes over the possibility of covering up. The 'truth of judgments', however, is merely the opposite of this covering-up, a secondary phenomenon of truth, *with more than one kind of foundation*. Both realism and idealism have – with equal thoroughness – missed the meaning of the Greek conception of truth, in terms of which only the possibility of something like a 'doctrine of ideas' can be understood as philosophical *knowledge*.

And because the function of the λόγος lies in merely letting something be seen, in *letting* entities be *perceived*, λόγος can signify the *reason* [*Vernunft*]. And because, moreover, λόγος is used not only with the signification of λέγειν but also with that of λεγόμενον (that which is exhibited, as such), and because the latter is nothing else than the ὑποκείμενον which, as present-at-hand, already lies at the *bottom* [zum *Grunde*] of any procedure of addressing oneself to it or discussing it, λόγος *qua* λεγόμενον means the ground, the *ratio*. And finally, because λόγος as λεγόμενον can also signify that which, as something to which one addresses oneself, becomes visible in its relation to something in its 'relatedness', λόγος acquires the signification of *relation* and *relationship*.

This Interpretation of 'apophantical discourse' may suffice to clarify the primary function of the λόγος.

C. The preliminary conception of phenomenology

When we envisage concretely what we have set forth in our Interpretation of 'phenomenon' and 'logos', we are struck by an inner relationship between the things meant by these terms. The expression "phenomenology" may be formulated in Greek as λέγειν τὰ φαινόμενα, where λέγειν means ἀποφαίνεσθαι. Thus "phenomenology" means ἀποφαίνεσθαι τὰ φαινόμενα – to let that which shows itself be seen from itself in the very way in which it shows itself from itself. This is the formal meaning of that branch of research which calls itself "phenomenology". But here we are expressing nothing else than the maxim formulated above: 'To the things themselves!'

Thus the term "phenomenology" is quite different in its meaning from expressions such as "theology" and the like. Those terms designate the objects of their respective sciences according to the subject-matter which they comprise at the time [*in ihrer jeweiligen Sachhaltigkeit*]. "Phenomenology" neither designates the object of its researches, nor characterizes the subject-matter thus comprised. The word merely informs us of the "*how*" with which *what* is to be treated in this science gets exhibited and handled. To have a science 'of' phenomena means to grasp its objects *in such a way* that everything about them which is up for discussion must be treated by exhibiting it directly and demonstrating it directly. The expression 'descriptive phenomenology', which is at bottom tautological, has the same meaning. Here "description" does not signify such a procedure as we find, let us say, in botanical morphology; the term has rather the sense of a prohibition – the avoidance of characterizing anything without such demonstration. The character of this description itself, the specific meaning of the λόγος, can be established first of all in terms of the 'thinghood' ["*Sachheit*"] of what is to be 'described' – that is to say, of what is to be given scientific definiteness as we encounter it phenomenally. The signification of "phenomenon", as conceived both formally and in the ordinary manner, is such that any exhibiting of an entity as it shows itself in itself, may be called "phenomenology" with formal justification.

Now what must be taken into account if the formal conception of phenomenon is to be deformalized into the phenomenological one, and how is this latter to be distinguished from the ordinary conception? What is it that phenomenology is to 'let us see'? What is it that must be called a 'phenomenon' in a distinctive sense? What is it that by its very essence is *necessarily* the theme whenever we exhibit something *explicitly*? Manifestly, it is something that proximally and for the most part does *not* show itself at all: it is something that lies *hidden*, in contrast to that which proximally and for the most part does show itself; but at the same time it is something that belongs to what thus shows itself, and it belongs to it so essentially as to constitute its meaning and its ground.

Yet that which remains *hidden* in an egregious sense, or which relapses and gets *covered up* again, or which shows itself only '*in disguise*', is not just this entity or that, but rather the *Being* of entities, as our previous observations have shown. This Being can be covered up so extensively that it becomes forgotten and no question arises about it or about its meaning. Thus that which demands that it become a phenomenon, and which demands this in a distinctive sense and in terms of its ownmost content as a thing, is what phenomenology has taken into its grasp thematically as its object.

Phenomenology is our way of access to what is to be the theme of ontology, and it is our way of giving it demonstrative precision. *Only as phenomenology is ontology possible*. In the phenomenological conception of "phenomenon" what one has in mind as that which shows itself is the Being of entities, its meaning, its modifications and derivatives. And this showing-itself is not just any showing-itself, nor is it some such thing as appearing. Least of all can the Being of entities ever be anything such that 'behind it' stands something else 'which does not appear'.

'Behind' the phenomena of phenomenology there is essentially nothing else; on the other hand, what is to become a phenomenon can be hidden. And just because the phenomena are proximally and for the most part *not* given, there is need for phenomenology. Covered-up-ness is the counter-concept to 'phenomenon'.

There are various ways in which phenomena can be covered up. In the first place, a phenomenon can be covered up in the sense that it is still quite *undiscovered*. It is neither known nor unknown. Moreover, a phenomenon can be *buried over* [*verschüttet*]. This means that it has at some time been discovered but has deteriorated to the point of getting covered up again. This covering-up can become complete; or rather – and as a rule – what has been discovered earlier may still be visible, though only as a semblance. Yet so much semblance, so much 'Being'. This covering-up as a 'disguising' is both the most frequent and the most dangerous, for here the possibilities of deceiving and misleading are especially stubborn. Within a 'system', perhaps, those structures of Being – and their concepts – which are still available but veiled in their indigenous character, may claim their rights. For when they have been bound together constructively in a system, they present themselves as something 'clear', requiring no further justification, and thus can serve as the point of departure for a process of deduction.

The covering-up itself, whether in the sense of hiddenness, burying-over, or disguise, has in turn two possibilities. There are coverings-up which are accidental; there are also some which are necessary, grounded in what the thing discovered consists in. Whenever a phenomenological concept is drawn from primordial sources, there is a possibility that it may degenerate if communicated in the form of an assertion. It gets understood in an empty way and is thus passed on, losing its indigenous character, and becoming a free-floating thesis. Even in the concrete work of phenomenology itself there lurks the possibility that what has been primordially 'within our grasp' may become hardened so that we can no longer grasp it. And the difficulty of this kind of research lies in making it self-critical in a positive sense.

The way in which Being and its structures are encountered in the mode of phenomenon is one which must first of all be *wrested* from the objects of phenomenology. Thus the very *point of departure* [*Ausgang*] for our analysis requires that it be secured by the proper method, just as much as does our *access* [*Zugang*] to the phenomenon, or our *passage* [*Durchgang*] through whatever is prevalently covering it up. The idea of grasping and explicating phenomena in a way which is 'original' and 'intuitive' is directly opposed to the *naïveté* of a haphazard, 'immediate', and unreflective 'beholding'. ["*Schauen*"].

Now that we have delimited our preliminary conception of phenomenology, the terms '*phenomenal*' and '*phenomenological*' can also be fixed in their signification. That which is given and explicable in the way the phenomenon is encountered is called 'phenomenal'; this is what we have in mind when we talk about "phenomenal structures". Everything which belongs to the species of exhibiting and explicating and which goes to make up the way of conceiving demanded by this research, is called 'phenomenological'.

Because phenomena, as understood phenomenologically, are never anything but what goes to make up Being, while Being is in every case the Being of some entity, we must first bring forward the entities themselves if it is our aim that Being should be laid bare; and we must do this in the right way. These entities must likewise show themselves with the kind of access which genuinely belongs to them. And in this way the ordinary conception of phenomenon becomes phenomenologically relevant. If our analysis is to be authentic, its aim is such that the prior task of assuring ourselves 'phenomenologically' of that entity which is to serve as our example, has already been prescribed as our point of departure.

With regard to its subject-matter, phenomenology is the science of the Being of entities – ontology. In explaining the tasks of ontology we found it necessary that there should be a fundamental ontology taking as its theme that entity which is ontologico-ontically distinctive, Dasein, in order to confront the cardinal problem – the question of the meaning of Being in general. Our investigation itself will show that the meaning of phenomenological description as a method lies in *interpretation*. The λόγος of the phenomenology of Dasein has the character of a ἑρμηνεύειν, through which the authentic meaning of Being, and also those basic structures of Being which Dasein itself possesses, are *made known* to Dasein's understanding of Being. The phenomenology of Dasein is a *hermeneutic* in the primordial signification of this word, where it designates this business of interpreting. But to the extent that by uncovering the meaning of Being and the basic structures of Dasein in general we may exhibit the horizon for any further ontological study of those entities which do not have the character of Dasein, this hermeneutic also becomes a 'hermeneutic' in the sense of working out the conditions on which the possibility of any ontological investigation depends. And finally, to the extent that Dasein, as an entity with the possibility of existence, has ontological priority over every other entity, 'hermeneutic', as an interpretation of Dasein's Being, has the third and specific sense of an analytic of the existentiality of existence; and this is the sense which is philosophically *primary*. Then so far as this hermeneutic works out Dasein's historicality ontologically as the ontical condition for the possibility of historiology, it contains the roots of what can be called 'hermeneutic' only in a derivative sense: the methodology of those humane sciences which are historiological in character.

Being, as the basic theme of philosophy, is no class or genus of entities; yet it pertains to every entity. Its 'universality' is to be sought higher up. Being and the structure of Being lie beyond every entity and every possible character which an entity may possess. *Being is the transcendens pure and simple.* And the transcendence of Dasein's Being is distinctive in that it implies the possibility and the necessity of the most radical *individuation*. Every disclosure of Being as the *transcendens is transcendental* knowledge. *Phenomenological truth (the disclosedness of Being) is veritas transcendentalis.*

Ontology and phenomenology are not two distinct philosophical disciplines among others. These terms characterize philosophy itself with regard to its object and its way of treating that object. Philosophy is universal phenomenological ontology, and takes its departure from the hermeneutic of Dasein, which, as an analytic of *existence*, has made fast the guiding-line for all philosophical inquiry at the point where it *arises* and to which it *returns*.

The following investigation would not have been possible if the ground had not been prepared by Edmund Husserl, with whose *Logische Untersuchungen* phenomenology first emerged. Our comments on the preliminary conception of phenomenology have shown that what is essential in it does not lie in its *actuality* as a philosophical 'movement' ["*Richtung*"]. Higher than actuality stands *possibility*. We can understand phenomenology only by seizing upon it as a possibility.

With regard to the awkwardness and 'inelegance' of expression in the analyses to come, we may remark that it is one thing to give a report in which we tell about *entities*, but another to grasp entities in their *Being*. For the latter task we lack not only most of the words but, above all, the 'grammar'. If we may allude to some earlier researches on the analysis of Being, incomparable on their own level, we may compare the ontological sections of Plato's *Parmenides* or the fourth chapter of the seventh book of Aristotle's *Metaphysics* with a narrative section from Thucydides; we can then see the altogether unprecedented character of those formulations which were imposed upon the Greeks by their philosophers. And where our powers are essentially weaker, and where moreover the area of Being to be disclosed is ontologically far more difficult than that which was presented to the Greeks, the harshness of our expression will be enhanced, and so will the minuteness of detail with which our concepts are formed.

Note

1 Cf. *Critique of Pure Reason*, 2nd Edition, 'Transcendental Aesthetic', Section 1.

4

THE WORLDHOOD OF THE WORLD

§ 14 The idea of the worldhood of the world in general

Being-in-the-world shall first be made visible with regard to that item of its structure which is the 'world' itself. To accomplish this task seems easy and so trivial as
to make one keep taking for granted that it may be dispensed with. What can be
meant by describing 'the world' as a phenomenon? It means to let us see what
shows itself in 'entities' within the world. Here the first step is to enumerate the
things that are 'in' the world: houses, trees, people, mountains, stars. We can
depict the way such entities 'look', and we can give an *account* of occurrences in
them and with them. This, however, is obviously a pre-phenomenological 'business' which cannot be at all relevant phenomenologically. Such a description is
always confined to entities. It is ontical. But what we are seeking is Being. And we
have formally defined 'phenomenon' in the phenomenological sense as that which
shows itself as Being and as a structure of Being.

Thus, to give a phenomenological description of the 'world' will mean to
exhibit the Being of those entities which are present-at-hand within the world,
and to fix it in concepts which are categorial. Now the entities within the world
are Things – Things of Nature, and Things 'invested with value'. Their Thinghood becomes a problem; and to the extent that the Thinghood of Things
'invested with value' is based upon the Thinghood of Nature, our primary theme
is the Being of Things of Nature – Nature as such. That characteristic of Being
which belongs to Things of Nature (substances), and upon which everything is
founded, is substantiality. What is its ontological meaning? By asking this, we
have given an unequivocal direction to our inquiry.

But is this a way of asking ontologically about the 'world'? The problematic
which we have thus marked out is one which is undoubtedly ontological. But even
if this ontology should itself succeed in explicating the Being of Nature in the
very purest manner, in conformity with the basic assertions about this entity,
which the mathematical natural sciences provide, it will never reach the phenomenon that is the 'world'. Nature is itself an entity which is encountered within the
world and which can be discovered in various ways and at various stages.

Should we then first attach ourselves to those entities with which Dasein proximally and for the most part dwells – Things 'invested with value'? Do not these

M. Heidegger, *Being and Time*, 1962, trans. John Macquarrie and Edward Robinson, pp. 91–119,
Oxford/New York: Blackwell/Harper & Row.

'really' show us the world in which we live? Perhaps, in fact, they show us something like the 'world' more penetratingly. But these Things too are entities 'within' the world.

Neither the ontical depiction of entities within-the-world nor the ontological Interpretation of their Being is such as to reach the phenomenon of the 'world.' In both of these ways of access to 'Objective Being', the 'world' has already been 'presupposed', and indeed in various ways.

Is it possible that ultimately we cannot address ourselves to 'the world' as determining the nature of the entity we have mentioned? Yet we call this entity one which is "within-the-world". Is 'world' perhaps a characteristic of Dasein's Being? And in that case, does every Dasein 'proximally' have its world? Does not 'world' thus become something 'subjective'? How, then, can there be a 'common' world 'in' which, nevertheless, we *are*? And if we raise the question of the 'world', *what* world do we have in view? Neither the common world nor the subjective world, but *the worldhood of the world as such*. By what avenue do we meet this phenomenon?

'Worldhood' is an ontological concept, and stands for the structure of one of the constitutive items of Being-in-the-world. But we know Being-in-the-world as a way in which Dasein's character is defined existentially. Thus worldhood itself is an *existentiele*. If we inquire ontologically about the 'world', we by no means abandon the analytic of Dasein as a field for thematic study. Ontologically, 'world' is not a way of characterizing those entities which Dasein essentially is *not*; it is rather a characteristic of Dasein itself. This does not rule out the possibility that when we investigate the phenomenon of the 'world' we must do so by the avenue of entities within-the-world and the Being which they possess. The task of 'describing' the world phenomenologically is so far from obvious that even if we do no more than determine adequately what form it shall take, essential ontological clarifications will be needed.

This discussion of the word 'world', and our frequent use of it have made it apparent that it is used in several ways. By unravelling these we can get an indication of the different kinds of phenomena that are signified, and of the way in which they are interconnected.

1   "World" is used as an ontical concept, and signifies the totality of those entities which can be present-at-hand within the world.
2   "World" functions as an ontological term, and signifies the Being of those entities which we have just mentioned. And indeed 'world' can become a term for any realm which encompasses a multiplicity of entities: for instance, when one talks of the 'world' of a mathematician, 'world' signifies the realm of possible objects of mathematics.
3   "World" can be understood in another ontical sense – not, however, as those entities which Dasein essentially is not and which can be encountered within-the-world, but rather as that '*wherein*' a factical Dasein as such can be said to 'live'. "World" has here a pre-ontological *existentiell* signification. Here again there are different possibilities: "world" may stand for the 'public' we-world, or one's 'own' closest (domestic) environment.
4   Finally, "world" designates the ontologico-existential concept of *worldhood*. Worldhood itself may have as its modes whatever structural wholes any

special 'worlds' may have at the time; but it embraces in itself the *a priori* character of worldhood in general. We shall reserve the expression "world" as a term for our third signification. If we should sometimes use it in the first of these senses, we shall mark this with single quotation marks.

The derivative form 'worldly' will then apply terminologically to a kind of Being which belongs to Dasein, never to a kind which belongs to entities present-at-hand 'in' the world. We shall designate these latter entities as "belonging to the world" or "within-the-world"

A glance at previous ontology shows that if one fails to see Being-in-the-world as a state of Dasein, the phenomenon of worldhood likewise gets *passed over*. One tries instead to Interpret the world in terms of the Being of those entities which are present-at-hand within-the-world but which are by no means proximally discovered – namely, in terms of Nature. If one understands Nature ontologico-categorially, one finds that Nature is a limiting case of the Being of possible entities within-the-world. Only in some definite mode of its own Being-in-the-world can Dasein discover entities as Nature. This manner of knowing them has the character of depriving the world of its worldhood in a definite way. 'Nature', as the categorial aggregate of those structures of Being which a definite entity encountered within-the-world may possess, can never make *worldhood* intelligible. But even the phenomenon of 'Nature', as it is conceived, for instance, in romanticism, can be grasped ontologically only in terms of the concept of the world – that is to say, in terms of the analytic of Dasein.

When it comes to the problem of analysing the world's worldhood ontologically, traditional ontology operates in a blind alley, if, indeed, it sees this problem at all. On the other hand, if we are to Interpret the worldhood of Dasein and the possible ways in which Dasein is made worldly [*Verweltlichung*], we must show *why* the kind of Being with which Dasein knows the world is such that it passes over the phenomenon of worldhood both ontically and ontologically. But at the same time the very Fact of this passing-over suggests that we must take special precautions to get the right phenomenal point of departure [*Ausgang*] for access [*Zugang*] to the phenomenon of worldhood, so that it will not get passed over.

Our method has already been assigned [*Anweisung*]. The theme of our analytic is to be Being-in-the-world, and accordingly the very world itself; and these are to be considered within the horizon of average everydayness – the kind of Being which is *closest* to Dasein. We must make a study of everyday Being-in-the-world; with the phenomenal support which this gives us, something like the world must come into view.

That world of everyday Dasein which is closest to it, is the *environment*. From this existential character of average Being-in-the-world, our investigation will take its course [*Gang*] towards the idea of worldhood in general. We shall seek the worldhood of the environment (environmentality) by going through an ontological Interpretation of those entities within-the-*environment* which we encounter as closest to us. The expression "environment" [*Umwelt*] contains in the 'environ' ["*um*"] a suggestion of spatiality. Yet the 'around' ["*Umherum*"] which is constitutive for the environment does not have a primarily 'spatial' meaning. Instead, the spatial character which incontestably belongs to any environment, can be clarified only in terms of the structure of worldhood. From this point of view,

Dasein's spatiality, of which we have given an indication in Section 12, becomes phenomenally visible. In ontology, however, an attempt has been made to start with spatiality and then to Interpret the Being of the 'world' as *res extensa*. In Descartes we find the most extreme tendency towards such an ontology of the 'world', with, indeed, a counter-orientation towards the *res cogitans* – which does not coincide with Dasein either ontically or ontologically. The analysis of world-hood which we are here attempting can be made clearer if we show how it differs from such an ontological tendency. Our analysis will be completed in three stages: the analysis of environmentality and worldhood in general; an illustrative contrast between our analysis of worldhood and Descartes' ontology of the 'world'; the aroundness [*das Umhafte*] of the environment, and the 'spatiality' of Dasein.

ANALYSIS OF ENVIRONMENTALITY AND WORLDHOOD IN GENERAL

§ 15 The Being of the entities encountered in the environment

The Being of those entities which we encounter as closest to us can be exhibited phenomenologically if we take as our clue our everyday Being-in-the-world, which we also call our *"dealings"* [*Umgang*] *in* the world and *with* entities within-the-world. Such dealings have already dispersed themselves into manifold ways of concern. The kind of dealing which is closest to us is as we have shown, not a bare perceptual cognition, but rather that kind of concern which manipulates things and puts them to use; and this has its own kind of 'knowledge'. The phenomeno-logical question applies in the first instance to the Being of those entities which we encounter in such concern. To assure the kind of seeing which is here required, we must first make a remark about method.

In the disclosure and explication of Being, entities are in every case our pre-liminary and our accompanying theme [*das Vor und Mitthematische*]; but our real theme is Being. In the domain of the present analysis, the entities we shall take as our preliminary theme are those which show themselves in our concern with the environment. Such entities are not thereby objects for knowing the 'world' theoretically; they are simply what gets used, what gets produced, and so forth. As entities so encountered, they become the preliminary theme for the purview of a 'knowing' which, as phenomenological, looks primarily towards Being, and which, in thus taking Being as its theme, takes these entities as its accompanying theme. This phenomenological interpretation is accordingly not a way of knowing those characteristics of entities which themselves are [*seiender Beschaffenheiten des Seienden*]; it is rather a determination of the structure of the Being which entities possess. But as an investigation of Being, it brings to completion, autonomously and explicitly, that understanding of Being which belongs already to Dasein and which 'comes alive' in any of its dealings with entities. Those entities which serve phenomenologically as our preliminary theme – in this case, those which are used or which are to be found in the course of production – become accessible when we put ourselves into the position of con-cerning ourselves with them in some such way. Taken strictly, this talk about "putting ourselves into such a position" [*Sichversetzen*] is misleading; for the kind of Being which belongs to such concernful dealings is not one into which we need to put ourselves first. This is the way in which everyday Dasein always *is*: when I open the door, for instance, I use the latch. The achieving of phenomenological access to the entities which we encounter, consists rather in thrusting aside our interpretative tendencies, which keep thrusting themselves upon us and running along with us, and which conceal not only the phenomenon of such 'concern', but even more those entities themselves *as* encountered of their own accord *in* our concern with them. These entangling errors become plain if in the course of our investigation we now ask which entities shall be taken as our preliminary theme and established as the pre-phenomenal basis for our study.

One may answer: "Things." But with this obvious answer we have perhaps already missed the pre-phenomenal basis we are seeking. For in addressing these entities as 'Things' (*res*), we have tacitly anticipated their ontological character. When analysis starts with such entities and goes on to inquire about Being, what it meets is Thinghood and Reality. Ontological explication discovers, as it proceeds, such characteristics of Being as substantiality, materiality, extendedness, side-by-side-ness, and so forth. But even pre-ontologically, in such Being as this, the entities which we encounter in concern are proximally hidden. When one designates Things as the entities that are 'proximally given', one goes ontologically astray, even though ontically one has something else in mind. What one really has in mind remains undetermined. But suppose one characterizes these 'Things' as Things 'invested with value'? What does "value" mean ontologically? How are we to categorize this 'investing' and Being-invested? Disregarding the obscurity of this structure of investiture with value, have we thus met that phenomenal characteristic of Being which belongs to what we encounter in our concernful dealings?

The Greeks had an appropriate term for 'Things': πράγματα – that is to say, that which one has to do with in one's concernful dealings (πρᾶξις). But ontologically, the specifically 'pragmatic' character of the πράγματα is just what the Greeks left in obscurity; they thought of these 'proximally' as 'mere Things'. We shall call those entities which we encounter in concern "*equipment*" [*das Zeug*]. In our dealings we come across equipment for writing, sewing, working, transportation, measurement. The kind of Being which equipment possesses must be exhibited. The clue for doing this lies in our first defining what makes an item of equipment – namely, its equipmentality.

Taken strictly, there 'is' no such thing as *an* equipment. To the Being of any equipment there always belongs a totality of equipment, in which it can be this equipment that it is. Equipment is essentially 'something in-order-to . . .' ["*etwas um-zu . . .*"]. A totality of equipment is constituted by various ways of the 'in-order-to', such as serviceability, conduciveness, usability, manipulability.

In the 'in-order-to' as a structure there lies an *assignment* or *reference* [*Verweisung*] of something to something. Only in the analyses which are to follow can the phenomenon which this term 'assignment' indicates be made visible in its ontological genesis. Provisionally, it is enough to take a look phenomenally at a manifold of such assignments. Equipment – in accordance with its equipmentality – always is *in terms of* [*aus*] its belonging to other equipment: ink-stand, pen, ink, paper, blotting pad, table, lamp, furniture, windows, doors, room. These 'Things' never show themselves proximally as they are for themselves, so as to add up to a sum of *realia* and fill up a room. What we encounter as closest to us (though not as something taken as a theme) is the room; and we encounter it not as something 'between four walls' in a geometrical spatial sense, but as equipment for residing. Out of this the 'arrangement' emerges, and it is in this that any 'individual' item of equipment shows itself. *Before* it does so, a totality of equipment has already been discovered.

Equipment can genuinely show itself only in dealings cut to its own measure (hammering with a hammer, for example); but in such dealings an entity of this kind is not *grasped* thematically as an occurring Thing, nor is the equipment-structure known as such even in the using. The hammering does not simply have knowledge about [*um*] the hammer's character as equipment, but it has appropriated this equipment in a way which could not possibly be more suitable. In dealings such as this, where something is put to use, our concern subordinates itself to the "in-order-to" which is constitutive for the equipment we are employing at the time; the less we just stare at the hammer-Thing, and the more we seize hold of it and use it, the more primordial does our relationship to it become, and the more unveiledly is it encountered as that which it is – as equipment. The hammering itself uncovers the specific 'manipulability' ["*Handlichkeit*"] of the hammer. The kind of Being which equipment possesses – in which it manifests itself in its own right – we call "*readiness-to-hand*" [*Zuhandenheit*]. Only because equipment has *this* 'Being-in-itself' and does not merely occur, is it manipulable in the broadest sense and at our disposal. No matter how sharply we just *look* [*Nur-noch-hinsehen*] at the 'outward appearance' ["*Aussehen*]" of Things in whatever form this takes, we cannot discover anything ready-to-hand. If we look at Things just 'theoretically', we can get along without understanding readiness-to-hand. But when we deal with them by using them and manipulating them, this activity is not a blind one; it has its own kind of sight, by which our manipulation is guided and from which it acquires its specific Thingly character. Dealings with equipment subordinate themselves to the manifold assignments of the 'in-order-to'. And the sight with which they thus accommodate themselves is *circumspection* [*Umsicht*].

'Practical' behaviour is not 'atheoretical' in the sense of "sightlessness". The way it differs from theoretical behaviour does not lie simply in the fact that in theoretical behaviour one observes, while in practical behaviour one *acts* [*gehandelt wird*], and that action must employ theoretical cognition if it is not to remain blind; for the fact that observation is a kind of concern is just as primordial as the fact that action has *its own* kind of sight. Theoretical behaviour is just looking, without circumspection. But the fact that this looking is non-circumspective does not mean that it follows no rules: it constructs a canon for itself in the form of *method*.

The ready-to-hand is not grasped theoretically at all, nor is it itself the sort of thing that circumspection takes proximally as a circumspective theme. The peculiarity of what is proximally ready-to-hand is that, in its readiness-to-hand, it must, as it were, withdraw [*zurückzuziehen*] in order to be ready-to-hand quite authentically. That with which our everyday dealings proximally dwell is not the tools themselves [*die Werkzeuge selbst*]. On the contrary, that with which we concern ourselves primarily is the work – that which is to be produced at the time; and this is accordingly ready-to-hand too. The work bears with it that referential totality within which the equipment is encountered.

The work to be produced, as the "*towards-which*" of such things as the hammer, the plane, and the needle, likewise has the kind of Being that belongs to equipment. The shoe which is to be produced is for wearing (footgear) [*Schuhzeug*]; the clock is manufactured for telling the time. The work which we chiefly encounter in our concernful dealings – the work that is to be found when one is "at work" on something [*das in Arbeit befindliche*] – has a usability which belongs to it essentially; in this usability it lets us encounter already the "towards-which" for which *it* is usable. A work that someone has ordered [*das bestellte Werk*] is only by reason of its use and the assignment-context of entities which is discovered in using it.

But the work to be produced is not merely usable for something. The production itself is a using *of* something for something. In the work there is also a reference or assignment to 'materials': the work is dependent on [*angewiesen auf*] leather, thread, needles, and the like. Leather, moreover is produced from hides. These are taken from animals, which someone else has raised. Animals also occur within the world without having been raised at all; and, in a way, these entities still produce themselves even when they have been raised. So in the environment certain entities become accessible which are always ready-to-hand, but which, in themselves, do not need to be produced. Hammer, tongs, and needle, refer in themselves to steel, iron, metal, mineral, wood, in that they consist of these. In equipment that is used, 'Nature' is discovered along with it by that use – the 'Nature' we find in natural products.

Here, however, "Nature" is not to be understood as that which is just present-at-hand, nor as the *power of Nature*. The wood is a forest of timber, the mountain a quarry of rock; the river is water-power, the wind is wind 'in the sails'. As the 'environment' is discovered, the 'Nature' thus discovered is encountered too. If its kind of Being as ready-to-hand is disregarded, this 'Nature' itself can be discovered and defined simply in its pure presence-at-hand. But when this happens, the Nature which 'stirs and strives', which assails us and enthralls us as landscape, remains hidden. The botanist's plants are not the flowers of the hedgerow; the 'source' which the geographer establishes for a river is not the 'springhead in the dale'.

The work produced refers not only to the "towards-which" of its usability and the "whereof" of which it consists: under simple craft conditions it also has an assignment to the person who is to use it or wear it. The work is cut to his figure; he 'is' there along with it as the work emerges. Even when goods are produced by the dozen, this constitutive assignment is by no means lacking; it is merely indefinite, and points to the random, the average. Thus along with the work, we encounter not only entities ready-to-hand but also entities with Dasein's kind of Being – entities for which, in their concern, the product becomes ready-to-hand; and together with these we encounter the world in which wearers and users live, which is at the same time ours. Any work with which one concerns oneself is ready-to-hand not only in the domestic world of the workshop but also in the *public world*. Along with the public world, the *environing Nature* [*die Umweltnatur*] is discovered and is accessible to everyone. In roads, streets, bridges, buildings, our concern discovers Nature as having some definite direction. A covered railway platform takes account of bad weather; an installation for public lighting takes account of the darkness, or rather of specific changes in the presence or absence of daylight – the 'position of the sun'. In a clock, account is taken of some definite constellation in the world-system. When we look at the clock, we tacitly make use of the 'sun's position', in accordance with which the measurement of time gets regulated in the official astronomical manner. When we make use of the clock-equipment, which is proximally and inconspicuously ready-to-hand, the environing Nature is ready-to-hand along with it. Our concernful absorption in whatever work-world lies closest to us, has a function of discovering; and it is essential to this function that, depending upon the way in which we are absorbed, those entities within-the-world which are brought along [*beigebracht*] in the work and with it (that is to say, in the assignments or references which are constitutive for it) remain discoverable in varying degrees of explicitness and with a varying circumspective penetration.

The kind of Being which belongs to these entities is readiness-to-hand. But this characteristic is not to be understood as merely a way of taking them, as if we were talking such 'aspects' into the 'entities' which we proximally encounter, or as if some world-stuff which is proximally present-at-hand in itself were 'given subjective colouring' in this way. Such an Interpretation would overlook the fact that in this case these entities would have to be understood and discovered beforehand as something purely present-at-hand, and must have priority and take the lead in the sequence of those dealings with the 'world' in which something is discovered and made one's own. But this already runs counter to the ontological meaning of cognition, which we have exhibited as a *founded* mode of Being-in-the-world. To lay bare what is just present-at-hand and no more, cognition must first penetrate *beyond* what is ready-to-hand in our concern. *Readiness-to-hand is the way in which entities as they are 'in themselves' are defined ontologico-categorially.* Yet only by reason of something present-at-hand, 'is there' anything ready-to-hand. Does it follow, however, granting this thesis for the nonce, that readiness-to-hand is ontologically founded upon presence-at-hand?

But even if, as our ontological Interpretation proceeds further, readiness-to-hand should prove itself to be the kind of Being characteristic of those entities which are proximally discovered within-the-world, and even if its primordiality as compared with pure presence-at-hand can be demonstrated, have all these explications been of the slightest help towards understanding the phenomenon of the world ontologically? In Interpreting these entities within-the-world, however, we have always 'presupposed' the world. Even if we join them together, we still do not get anything like the 'world' as their sum. If, then, we start with the Being of these entities, is there any avenue that will lead us to exhibiting the phenomenon of the world?

§ 16 How the worldly character of the environment announces itself in entities within-the-world

The world itself is not an entity within-the-world; and yet it is so determinative for such entities that only in so far as 'there is' a world can they be encountered and show themselves, in their Being, as entities which have been discovered. But in what way 'is there' a world? If Dasein is ontically constituted by Being-in-the-World, and if an understanding of the Being of its Self belongs just as essentially to its Being, no matter how indefinite that understanding may be, then does not

Dasein have an understanding of the world – a pre-ontological understanding, which indeed can and does get along without explicit ontological insights? With those entities which are encountered within-the-world – that is to say, with their character as within-the-world – does not something like the world show itself for concernful Being-in-the-world? Do we not have a pre-phenomenological glimpse of this phenomenon? Do we not always have such a glimpse of it, without having to take it as a theme for ontological Interpretation? Has Dasein itself, in the range of its concernful absorption in equipment ready-to-hand, a possibility of Being in which the worldhood of those entities within-the-world with which it is concerned is, in a certain way, lit up for it, *along with* those entities themselves?

If such possibilities of Being for Dasein can be exhibited within its concernful dealings, then the way lies open for studying the phenomenon which is thus lit up, and for attempting to 'hold it at bay', as it were, and to interrogate it as to those structures which show themselves therein.

To the everydayness of Being-in-the-world there belong certain modes of concern. These permit the entities with which we concern ourselves to be encountered in such a way that the worldly character of what is within-the-world comes to the fore. When we concern ourselves with something, the entities which are most closely ready-to-hand may be met as something unusable, not properly adapted for the use we have decided upon. The tool turns out to be damaged, or the material unsuitable. In each of these cases *equipment* is here, ready-to-hand. We discover its unusability, however, not by looking at it and establishing its properties, but rather by the circumspection of the dealings in which we use it. When its unusability is thus discovered, equipment becomes conspicuous. This *conspicuousness* presents the ready-to-hand equipment as in a certain un-readiness-to-hand. But this implies that what cannot be used just lies there; it shows itself as an equipmental Thing which looks so and so, and which, in its readiness-to-hand as looking that way, has constantly been present-at-hand too. Pure presence-at-hand announces itself in such equipment, but only to withdraw to the readiness-to-hand of something with which one concerns oneself – that is to say, of the sort of thing we find when we put it back into repair. This presence-at-hand of something that cannot be used is still not devoid of all readiness-to-hand whatsoever; equipment which is present-at-hand *in this way* is still not just a Thing which occurs somewhere. The damage to the equipment is still not a mere alteration of a Thing – not a change of properties which just occurs in something present-at-hand.

In our concernful dealings, however, we not only come up against unusable things *within* what is ready-to-hand already: we also find things which are missing – which not only are not 'handy' ["*handlich*"] but are not 'to hand' ["*zur Hand*"] at all. Again, to miss something in this way amounts to coming across something un-ready-to-hand. When we notice what is un-ready-to-hand, that which is ready-to-hand enters the mode of *obtrusiveness*. The more urgently we need what is missing, and the more authentically it is encountered in its un-readiness-to-hand, all the more obtrusive does that which is ready-to-hand become – so much so, indeed, that it seems to lose its character of readiness-to-hand. It reveals itself as something just present-at-hand and no more, which cannot be budged without the thing that is missing. The helpless way in which we stand before it is a deficient mode of concern, and as such it uncovers the Being-just-present-at-hand-and-no-more of something ready-to-hand.

In our dealings with the world of our concern, the un-ready-to-hand can be encountered not only in the sense of that which is unusable or simply missing, but as something un-ready-to-hand which is *not* missing at all and *not* unusable, but which 'stands in the way' of our concern. That to which our concern refuses to turn, that for which it has 'no time', is something *un*-ready-to-hand in the manner of what does not belong here, of what has not as yet been attended to. Anything which is unready-to-hand in this way is disturbing to us, and enables us to see the *obstinacy* of that with which we must concern ourselves in the first instance before we do anything else. With this obstinacy, the presence-at-hand of the ready-to-hand makes itself known in a new way as the Being of that which still lies before us and calls for our attending to it.

The modes of conspicuousness, obtrusiveness, and obstinacy all have the function of bringing to the fore the characteristic of presence-at-hand in what is ready-to-hand. But the ready-to-hand is not thereby just *observed* and stared at as something present-at-hand; the presence-at-hand which makes itself known is still bound up in the readiness-to-hand of equipment. Such equipment still does not veil itself in the guise of mere Things. It becomes 'equipment' in the sense of something which one would like to shove out of the way. But in such a Tendency to shove things aside, the ready-to-hand shows itself as still ready-to-hand in its unswerving presence-at-hand.

Now that we have suggested, however, that the ready-to-hand is thus encountered under modifications in which its presence-at-hand is revealed, how far does this clarify the *phenomenon of the world*? Even in analysing these modifications we have not gone beyond the Being of what is within-the-world, and we have come no closer to the world-phenomenon than before. But though we have not as yet grasped it, we have brought ourselves to a point where we can bring it into view.

In conspicuousness, obtrusiveness, and obstinacy, that which is ready-to-hand loses its readiness-to-hand in a certain way. But in our dealings with what is ready-to-hand, this readiness-to-hand is itself understood, though not thematically. It does not vanish simply, but takes its farewell, as it were, in the conspicuousness of the unusable. Readiness-to-hand still shows itself, and it is precisely here that the worldly character of the ready-to-hand shows itself too.

The structure of the Being of what is ready-to-hand as equipment is determined by references or assignments. In a peculiar and obvious manner, the 'Things' which are closest to us are 'in themselves' ["An sich"]; and they are encountered as 'in themselves' in the concern which makes use of them without noticing them explicitly – the concern which can come up against something unusable. When equipment cannot be used, this implies that the constitutive assignment of the "in-order-to" to a "towards-this" has been disturbed. The assignments themselves are not observed; they are rather 'there' when we concernfully submit ourselves to them [*sich stellen unter sie*]. But *when an assignment has been disturbed* – when something is unusable for some purpose – then the assignment becomes explicit. Even now, of course, it has not become explicit as an ontological structure; but it has become explicit ontically for the circumspection which comes up against the damaging of the tool. When an assignment to some particular "towards-this" has been thus circumspectively aroused, we catch sight of the "towards-this" itself, and along with it everything connected with the work – the whole 'work-shop' – as that wherein concern always dwells. The context of equipment is lit up, not as something never seen before, but as a totality constantly sighted beforehand in circumspection. With this totality, however, the world announces itself.

Similarly, when something ready-to-hand is found missing, though its everyday presence [*Zugegensein*] has been so obvious that we have never taken any notice of it, this makes a *break* in those referential contexts which circumspection discovers. Our circumspection comes up against emptiness, and now sees for the first time *what* the missing article was ready-to-hand *with*, and *what* it was ready-to-hand *for*. The environment announces itself afresh. What is thus lit up is not itself just one thing ready-to-hand among others; still less is it something *present-at-hand* upon which equipment ready-to-hand is somehow founded: it is in the 'there' before anyone has observed or ascertained it. It is itself inaccessible to circumspection, so far as circumspection is always directed towards entities; but in each case it has already been disclosed for circumspection. 'Disclose' and 'disclosedness' will be used as technical terms in the passages that follow, and shall signify 'to lay open' and 'the character of having been laid open.' Thus 'to disclose' never means anything like 'to obtain indirectly by inference'.

That the world does not 'consist' of the ready-to-hand shows itself in the fact (among others) that whenever the world is lit up in the modes of concern which we have been Interpreting, the ready-to-hand becomes deprived of its worldhood so that Being-just-present-at-hand comes to the fore. If, in our everyday concern with the 'environment', it is to be possible for equipment ready-to-hand to be encountered in its 'Being-in-itself' [*in seinem "An-sich-sein"*], then those assignments and referential totalities in which our circumspection 'is absorbed' cannot become a theme for that circumspection any more than they can for grasping things 'thematically' but non-circumspectively. If it is to be possible for the ready-to-hand not to emerge from its inconspicuousness, the world *must not announce itself*. And it is in this that the Being-in-itself of entities which are ready-to-hand has its phenomenal structure constituted.

In such privative expressions as "inconspicuousness", "unobtrusiveness", and "non-obstinacy", what we have in view is a positive phenomenal character of the Being of that which is proximally ready-to-hand. With these negative prefixes we have in view the character of the ready-to-hand – to as "holding itself in"; this is what we have our eye upon in the "Being-in-itself" of something, though 'proximally' we ascribe it to the present-at-hand – to the present-at-hand as that which can be thematically ascertained. As long as we take our orientation primarily and exclusively from the present-at-hand, the 'in-itself' can by no means be ontologically clarified. If, however, this talk about the 'in-itself' has any ontological importance, some interpretation must be called for. This "in-itself" of Being is something which gets invoked with considerable emphasis, mostly in an ontical way, and rightly so from a phenomenal standpoint. But if some *ontological* assertion is supposed to be given when this is *ontically* invoked, its claims are not fulfilled by such a procedure. As the foregoing analysis has already made clear, only on the basis of the phenomenon of the world can the Being-in-itself of entities within-the-world be grasped ontologically.

But if the world can, in a way, be lit up, it must assuredly be disclosed. And it has already been disclosed beforehand whenever what is ready-to-hand within-the-world is accessible for circumspective concern. The world is therefore something 'wherein' Dasein as an entity already *was*, and if in any manner it explicitly comes away from anything, it can never do more than come back to the world.

Being-in-the-world, according to our Interpretation hitherto, amounts to a non-thematic circumspective absorption in references or assignments constitutive for the readiness-to-hand of a totality of equipment. Any concern is already as it is, because of some familiarity with the world. In this familiarity Dasein can lose itself in what it encounters within-the-world and be fascinated with it. What is it that Dasein is familiar with? Why can the worldly character of what is within-the-world be lit up? The presence-at-hand of entities is thrust to the fore by the possible breaks in that referential totality in which circumspection 'operates'; how are we to get a closer understanding of this totality?

These questions are aimed at working out both the phenomenon and the problems of worldhood, and they call for an inquiry into the inter-connections with which certain structures are built up. To answer them we must analyse these structures more concretely.

§ 17 Reference and signs

In our provisional Interpretation of that structure of Being which belongs to the ready-to-hand (to 'equipment'), the phenomenon of reference or assignment became visible; but we merely gave an indication of it, and in so sketchy a form that we at once stressed the necessity of uncovering it with regard to its onto-logical origin. It became plain, moreover, that assignments and referential total-ities could in some sense become constitutive for worldhood itself. Hitherto we have seen the world lit up only in and for certain definite ways in which we con-cern ourselves environmentally with the ready-to-hand, and indeed it has been lit up only *with* the readiness-to-hand of that concern. So the further we proceed in understanding the Being of entities within-the-world, the broader and firmer becomes the phenomenal basis on which the world-phenomenon may be laid bare.

We shall again take as our point of departure the Being of the ready-to-hand, but this time with the purpose of grasping the phenomenon of *reference* or *assignment* itself more precisely. We shall accordingly attempt an ontological analysis of a kind of equipment in which one may come across such 'references' in more senses than one. We come across 'equipment' in *signs*. The word "sign" designates many kinds of things: not only may it stand for different *kinds* of signs, but Being-a-sign-for can itself be formalized as a *universal kind of relation*, so that the sign-structure itself provides an ontological clue for 'characterizing' any entity whatsoever.

But signs, in the first instance, are themselves items of equipment whose specific character as equipment consists in *showing* or *indicating*. We find such signs in signposts, boundary-stones, the ball for the mariner's storm-warning, signals, banners, signs of mourning, and the like. Indicating can be defined as a 'kind' of referring. Referring is, if we take it as formally as possible, a *relating*. But relation does not function as a genus for 'kinds' or 'species' of references which may somehow become differentiated as sign, symbol, expression, or signification. A relation is something quite formal which may be read off directly by way of 'formalization' from any kind of context, whatever its subject-matter or its way of Being.

Every reference is a relation, but not every relation is a reference. Every 'indication' is a reference, but not every referring is an indicating. This implies at the same time that every 'indication' is a relation, but not every relation is an indicating. The formally general character of relation is thus brought to light. If we are to investigate such phenomena as references, signs, or even significations, nothing is to be gained by characterizing them as relations. Indeed we shall eventually have to show that 'relations' themselves, *because of* their formally general character, have their ontological source in a reference.

If the present analysis is to be confined to the Interpretation of the sign as distinct from the phenomenon of reference, then even within this limitation we cannot properly investigate the full multiplicity of possible signs. Among signs there are symptoms [*Anzeichen*], warning signals, signs of things that have happened already [*Rückzeichen*], signs to mark something, signs by which things are recognized; these have different ways of indicating, regardless of what may be serving as such a sign. From such 'signs' we must distinguish traces, residues, commemorative monuments, documents, testimony, symbols, expressions, appearances, significations. These phenomena can easily be formalized because of their formal relational character; we find it especially tempting nowadays to take such a 'relation' as a clue for subjecting every entity to a kind of 'Interpretation' which always 'fits' because at bottom it says nothing, no more than the facile schema of content and form.

As an example of a sign we have chosen one which we shall use again in a later analysis, though in another regard. Motor cars are sometimes fitted up with an adjustable red arrow, whose position indicates the direction the vehicle will take – at an intersection, for instance. The position of the arrow is controlled by the driver. This sign is an item of equipment which is ready-to-hand for the driver in his concern with driving, and not for him alone: those who are not travelling with him – and they in particular – also make use of it, either by giving way on the proper side or by stopping. This sign is ready-to-hand within-the-world in the whole equipment-context of vehicles and traffic regulations. It is equipment for indicating, and as equipment, it is constituted by reference or assignment. It has the character of the "in-order-to", its own definite serviceability; it is for indicating. This indicating which the sign performs can be taken as a kind of 'referring'. But here we must notice that this 'referring' as indicating is not the ontological structure of the sign as equipment.

Instead, 'referring' as indicating is grounded in the Being-structure of equipment, in serviceability for. ... But an entity may have serviceability without thereby becoming a sign. As equipment, a 'hammer' too is constituted by a serviceability, but this does not make it a sign. Indicating, as a 'reference', is a way in which the "towards-which" of a serviceability becomes ontically concrete; it determines an item of equipment as for this "towards-which" [*und bestimmt ein Zeug zu diesem*]. On the other hand, the kind of reference we get in 'serviceability-for', is an ontologico-categorial attribute of equipment *as* equipment. That the "towards-which" of serviceability should acquire its concreteness in indicating, is an accident of its equipment-constitution as such. In this example of a sign, the difference between the reference of serviceability and the reference of indicating becomes visible in a rough and ready fashion. These are so far from coinciding that only when they are united does the concreteness of a definite kind of equipment become possible. Now it is certain that indicating differs in principle from reference as a constitutive state of equipment; it is just as incontestable that the sign in its turn is related in a peculiar and even distinctive way to the kind of Being which belongs to whatever equipmental totality may be ready-to-hand in the environment, and to its worldly character. In our concernful dealings, equipment for indicating [*Zeig-zeug*] gets used in a *very special* way. But simply to establish this Fact is ontologically insufficient. The basis and the meaning of this special status must be clarified.

What do we mean when we say that a sign "indicates"? We can answer this only by determining what kind of dealing is appropriate with equipment for indicating. And we must do this in such a way that the readiness-to-hand of that equipment can be genuinely grasped. What is the appropriate way of having-to-do with signs? Going back to our example of the arrow, we must say that the kind of behaving (Being) which corresponds to the sign we encounter, is either to 'give way' or to 'stand still' *vis-à-vis* the car with the arrow. Giving way, as taking a direction, belongs essentially to Dasein's Being-in-the-world. Dasein is always somehow directed [*ausgerichtet*] and on its way; standing and waiting are only limiting cases of this directional 'on-its-way'. The sign addresses itself to a Being-in-the-world which is specifically 'spatial'. The sign is *not* authentically 'grasped' ["*erfasst*"] if we just stare at it and identify it as an indicator-Thing which occurs. Even if we turn our glance in the direction which the arrow indicates, and look at something present-at-hand in the region indicated, even then the sign is not authentically encountered. Such a sign addresses itself to the circumspection of our concernful dealings, and it does so in such a way that the circumspection which goes along with it, following where it points, brings into an explicit 'survey' whatever aroundness the environment may have at the time. This circumspective survey does not *grasp* the ready-to-hand; what it achieves is rather an orientation within our environment. There is also another way in which we can experience equipment: we may encounter the arrow simply as equipment which belongs to the car. We can do this without discovering what character it specifically has as equipment: what the arrow is to indicate and how it is to do so, may remain completely undetermined; yet what we are encountering is not a mere Thing. The experiencing of a Thing requires a *definiteness* of its own [*ihre eigene Bestimmtheit*], and must be contrasted with coming across a manifold of equipment, which may often be quite indefinite, even when one comes across it as especially close.

Signs of the kind we have described let what is ready-to-hand be encountered; more precisely, they let some context of it become accessible in such a way that our concernful dealings take on an orientation and hold it secure. A sign is not a Thing which stands to another Thing in the relationship of indicating; it is rather *an item of equipment which explicitly raises a totality of equipment into our circumspection so that together with it the worldly character of the ready-to-hand announces itself.* In a symptom or a warning-signal, 'what is coming' 'indicates itself', but not in the sense of something merely occurring, which comes as an addition to what is already present-at-hand; 'what is coming' is the sort of thing which we are ready for, or which we 'weren't ready for' if we have been attending to something else. In signs of something that has happened already, what has come to pass and run its course becomes circumspectively accessible. A sign to mark something indicates what one is 'at' at any time. Signs always indicate primarily 'wherein' one lives, where one's concern dwells, what sort of involvement there is with something.

The peculiar character of signs as equipment becomes especially clear in 'establishing a sign' ["*Zeichenstiftung*"]. This activity is performed in a circumspective foresight [*Vorsicht*] out of which it arises, and which requires that it be possible for one's particular environment to announce itself for circumspection at any time by means of something ready-to-hand, and that this possibility should itself be ready-to-hand. But the Being of what is most closely ready-to-hand within-the-world possesses the character of holding-itself-in and not emerging, which we have described above. Accordingly our circumspective dealings in the environment require some equipment ready-to-hand which in its character as equipment takes over the 'work' of *letting* something ready-to-hand *become conspicuous*. So when such equipment (signs) gets produced, its conspicuousness must be kept in mind. But even when signs are thus conspicuous, one does not let them be present-at-hand at random; they get 'set up' ["*angebracht*"] in a definite way with a view towards easy accessibility.

In establishing a sign, however, one does not necessarily have to produce equipment which is not yet ready-to-hand at all. Signs also arise when one *takes as a sign* [*Zum-Zeichen-nehmen*] something that is ready-to-hand already. In this mode, signs "get established" in a sense which is even more primordial. In indicating, a ready-to-hand equipment totality, and even the environment in general, can be provided with an availability which is circumspectively oriented; and not only this: establishing a sign can, above all, reveal. What gets taken as a sign becomes accessible only through its readiness-to-hand. If, for instance, the south wind 'is accepted' ["*gilt*"] by the farmer as a sign of rain, then this 'acceptance' ["*Geltung*"] – or the 'value' with which the entity is 'invested' – is not a sort of bonus over and above what is already present-at-hand in itself – *viz*, the flow of air in a definite geographical direction. The south wind may be meteorologically accessible as something which just occurs; but it is *never* present-at-hand *proximally* in such a way as this, only occasionally taking over the function of a warning signal. On the contrary, only by the circumspection with which one takes account of things in farming, is the south wind discovered in its Being.

But, one will protest, *that which* gets taken as a sign must first have become accessible in itself and been apprehended *before* the sign gets established. Certainly it must in any case be such that in some way we can come across it. The question simply remains as to *how* entities are discovered in this previous encountering, whether as mere Things which occur, or rather as equipment which has not been understood – as something ready-to-hand with which we have hitherto not known 'how to begin', and which has accordingly kept itself veiled from the purview of circumspection. *And here again, when the equipmental characters of the ready-to-hand are still circumspectively undiscovered, they are not to be Interpreted as bare Thinghood presented for an apprehension of what is just present-at-hand and no more.*

The Being-ready-to-hand of signs in our everyday dealings, and the conspicuousness which belongs to signs and which may be produced for various purposes
and in various ways, do not merely serve to document the inconspicuousness
constitutive for what is most closely ready-to-hand; the sign itself gets its conspicuousness from the inconspicuousness of the equipmental totality, which is
ready-to-hand and 'obvious' in its everydayness. The knot which one ties in a
handkerchief [*der bekannte "Knopf im Taschentuch"*] as a sign to mark something is an example of this. What such a sign is to indicate is always something
with which one has to concern oneself in one's everyday circumspection. Such a
sign can indicate many things, and things of the most various kinds. The wider the
extent to which it can indicate, the narrower its intelligibility and its usefulness.
Not only is it, for the most part, ready-to-hand as a sign only for the person who
'establishes' it, but it can even become inaccessible to him, so that another sign is
needed if the first is to be used circumspectively at all. So when the knot cannot be
used as a sign, it does not lose its sign-character, but it acquires the disturbing
obtrusiveness of something most closely ready-to-hand.

One might be tempted to cite the abundant use of 'signs' in primitive Dasein, as
in fetishism and magic, to illustrate the remarkable role which they play in everyday concern when it comes to our understanding of the world. Certainly the
establishment of signs which underlies this way of using them is not performed
with any theoretical aim or in the course of theoretical speculation. This way of
using them always remains completely within a Being-in-the-world which is
'immediate'. But on closer inspection it becomes plain that to interpret fetishism
and magic by taking our clue from the idea of signs in general, is not enough to
enable us to grasp the kind of 'Being-ready-to-hand' which belongs to entities
encountered in the primitive world. With regard to the sign-phenomenon, the
following Interpretation may be given: for primitive man, the sign coincides with
that which is indicated. Not only can the sign represent this in the sense of serving
as a substitute for what it indicates, but it can do so in such a way that the sign
itself always *is* what it indicates. This remarkable coinciding does not mean, however, that the sign-Thing has already undergone a certain 'Objectification' – that it
has been experienced as a mere Thing and misplaced into the same realm of Being
of the present-at-hand as what it indicates. This 'coinciding' is not an identification of things which have hitherto been isolated from each other: it consists
rather in the fact that the sign has not as yet become free from that of which it is
a sign. Such a use of signs is still absorbed completely in Being-towards what
is indicated, so that a sign as such cannot detach itself at all. This coinciding is
based not on a prior Objectification but on the fact that such Objectification is
completely lacking. This means, however, that signs are not discovered as equipment at all – that ultimately what is 'ready-to-hand' within-the-world just does
not have the kind of Being that belongs to equipment. Perhaps even readiness-to-
hand and equipment have nothing to contribute [*nichts auszurichten*] as ontological clues in Interpreting the primitive world; and certainly the ontology of
Thinghood does even less. But if an understanding of Being is constitutive for
primitive Dasein and for the primitive world in general, then it is all the more
urgent to work out the 'formal' idea of worldhood – or at least the idea of a
phenomenon modifiable in such a way that all ontological assertions to the effect
that in a given phenomenal context something is *not yet* such-and-such or *no*

longer such-and-such, may acquire a *positive* phenomenal meaning in terms of what it is *not*.

The foregoing Interpretation of the sign should merely provide phenomenal support for our characterization of references or assignments. The relation between sign and reference is threefold. 1. Indicating, as a way whereby the "towards-which" of a serviceability can become concrete, is founded upon the equipment-structure as such, upon the "in-order-to" (assignment). 2. The indicating which the sign does is an equipmental character of something ready-to-hand, and as such it belongs to a totality of equipment, to a context of assignments or references. 3. The sign is not only ready-to-hand with other equipment, but in its readiness-to-hand the environment becomes in each case explicitly accessible for circumspection. *A sign is something ontically ready-to-hand, which functions both as this definite equipment and as something indicative of* [*was ... anzeigt*] *the ontological structure of readiness-to-hand, of referential totalities, and of worldhood.* Here is rooted the special status of the sign as something ready-to-hand in that environment with which we concern ourselves circumspectively. Thus the reference or the assignment itself cannot be conceived as a sign if it is to serve ontologically as the foundation upon which signs are based. Reference is not an ontical characteristic of something ready-to-hand, when it is rather that by which readiness-to-hand itself is constituted.

In what sense, then, is reference 'presupposed' ontologically in the ready-to-hand, and to what extent is it, as such an ontological foundation, at the same time constitutive for worldhood in general?

§ 18 Involvement and significance; the worldhood of the world

The ready-to-hand is encountered within-the-world. The Being of this entity, readiness-to-hand, thus stands in some ontological relationship towards the world and towards worldhood. In anything ready-to-hand the world is always 'there'. Whenever we encounter anything, the world has already been previously discovered, though not thematically. But it can also be lit up in certain ways of dealing with our environment. The world is that in terms of which the ready-to-hand is ready-to-hand. How can the world let the ready-to-hand be encountered? Our analysis hitherto has shown that what we encounter within-the-world has, in its very Being, been freed for our concernful circumspection, for taking account. What does this previous freeing amount to, and how is this to be understood as an ontologically distinctive feature of the world? What problems does the question of the worldhood of the world lay before us?

We have indicated that the state which is constitutive for the ready-to-hand as equipment is one of reference or assignment. How can entities with this kind of Being be freed by the world with regard to their Being? Why are these the first entities to be encountered? As definite kinds of references we have mentioned serviceability-for-, detrimentality [*Abträglichkeit*], usability, and the like. The "towards-which" [*das Wozu*] of a serviceability and the "for-which" [*das Wofür*] of a usability prescribed the ways in which such a reference or assignment can become concrete. But the 'indicating' of the sign and the 'hammering' of the hammer are not properties of entities. Indeed, they are not properties at all, if the ontological structure designated by the term 'property' is that of some definite character which it is possible for Things to possess [*einer möglichen Bestimmtheit von Dingen*]. Anything ready-to-hand is, at the worst, appropriate for some purposes and inappropriate for others; and its 'properties' are, as it were, still bound up in these ways in which it is appropriate or inappropriate, just as presence-at-hand, as a possible kind of Being for something ready-to-hand, is bound up in readiness-to-hand. Serviceability too, however, as a constitutive state of equipment (and serviceability is a reference), is not an appropriateness of some entity; it is rather the condition (so far as Being is in question) which makes it possible for the character of such an entity to be defined by its appropriatenesses. But what, then, is "reference" or "assignment" to mean? To say that the Being of the ready-to-hand has the structure of assignment or reference means that it has in itself the character of *having been assigned or referred* [*Verwiesenheit*]. An entity is discovered when it has been assigned or referred to something, and referred as that entity which it is. *With* any such entity there is an involvement which it has *in* something. The character of Being which belongs to the ready-to-hand is just such an *involvement*. If something has an involvement, this implies letting it be involved in something. The relationship of the "with . . . in . . ." shall be indicated by the term "assignment" or "reference".

When an entity within-the-world has already been proximally freed for its Being, that Being is its "involvement". With any such entity as entity, there is some involvement. The fact that it has such an involvement is *ontologically* definitive for the Being of such an entity, and is not an ontical assertion about it. That in which it is involved is the "towards-which" of serviceability, and the "for-which" of usability. With the "towards-which" of serviceability there can again be an involvement: *with* this thing, for instance, which is ready-to-hand, and which we accordingly call a "hammer", there is an involvement in hammering; with hammering, there is an involvement in making something fast; with making something fast, there is an involvement in protection against bad weather; and this protection 'is' for the sake of [*um-willen*] providing shelter for Dasein – that is to say, for the sake of a possibility of Dasein's Being. Whenever something ready-to-hand has an involvement with it, *what* involvement this is, has in each case been outlined in advance in terms of the totality of such involvements. In a workshop, for example, the totality of involvements which is constitutive for the ready-to-hand in its readiness-to-hand, is 'earlier' than any single item of equipment; so too for the farmstead with all its utensils and outlying lands. But the totality of involvements itself goes back ultimately to a "towards-which" in which there is *no* further involvement: this "towards-which" is not an entity with the kind of Being that belongs to what is ready-to-hand within a world; it is rather an entity whose Being is defined as Being-in-the-world, and to whose state of Being, worldhood itself belongs. This primary "towards-which" is not just another "towards-this" as something in which an involvement is possible. The primary 'towards-which' is a "for-the-sake-of-which". But the 'for-the-sake-of' always pertains to the Being of *Dasein*, for which, in its Being, that very Being is essentially an *issue*. We have thus indicated the interconnection by which the structure of an involvement leads to Dasein's very Being as the sole authentic "for-the-sake-of-which"; for the present, however, we shall pursue this no further. 'Letting something be involved' must first be clarified enough to give the phenomenon of worldhood the kind of definiteness which makes it possible to formulate any problems about it.

Ontically, "letting something be involved" signifies that within our factical concern we let something ready-to-hand *be* so-and-so *as* it is already and *in order that* it be such. The way we take this ontical sense of 'letting be' is, in principle, ontological. And therewith we Interpret the meaning of previously freeing what is proximally ready-to-hand within-the-world. Previously letting something 'be' does not mean that we must first bring it into its Being and produce it; it means rather that something which is already an 'entity' must be discovered in its readiness-to-hand, and that we must thus let the entity which has this Being be encountered. This '*a priori*' letting-something-be-involved is the condition for the possibility of encountering anything ready-to-hand, so that Dasein, in its ontical dealings with the entity thus encountered, can thereby let it be involved in the ontical sense. On the other hand, if letting something be involved is understood ontologically, what is then pertinent is the freeing of *everything* ready-to-hand as ready-to-hand, no matter whether, taken ontically, it is involved thereby, or whether it is rather an entity of precisely such a sort that ontically it is *not* involved thereby. Such entities are, proximally and for the most part, those with which we concern ourselves when we do not let them 'be' as we have discovered that they are, but work upon them, make improvements in them, or smash them to pieces.

When we speak of having already let something be involved, so that it has been freed for that involvement, we are using a *perfect* tense *a priori* which characterizes the kind of Being belonging to Dasein itself. Letting an entity be involved, if we understand this ontologically, consists in previously freeing it for [*auf*] its readiness-to-hand within the environment. When we let something be involved, it must be involved in something; and in terms of this "in-which", the "with-which" of this involvement is freed. Our concern encounters it as this thing that is ready-to-hand. To the extent that any *entity* shows itself to concern – that is, to the extent that it is discovered in its Being – it is already something ready-to-hand environmentally; it just is not 'proximally' a 'world-stuff' that is merely present-at-hand.

As the Being of something ready-to-hand, an involvement is itself discovered only on the basis of the prior discovery of a totality of involvements. So in any involvement that has been discovered (that is, in anything ready-to-hand which we encounter), what we have called the "worldly character" of the ready-to-hand has been discovered beforehand. In this totality of involvements which has been discovered beforehand, there lurks an ontological relationship to the world. In letting entities be involved so that they are freed for a totality of involvements, one must have disclosed already that for which [*woraufhin*] they have been freed. But that for which something environmentally ready-to-hand has thus been freed (and indeed in such a manner that it becomes accessible *as* an entity within-the-world first of all), cannot itself be conceived as an entity with this discovered kind of Being. It is essentially not discoverable, if we henceforth reserve "*discoveredness*" as a term for a possibility of Being which every entity *without* the character of Dasein may possess.

But what does it mean to say that that for which entities within-the-world are proximally freed must have been previously disclosed? To Dasein's Being, an understanding of Being belongs. Any understanding [*Verständnis*] has its Being in an act of understanding [*Verstehen*]. If Being-in-the-world is a kind of Being which is essentially befitting to Dasein, then to understand Being-in-the-world belongs to the essential content of its understanding of Being. The previous disclosure of that for which what we encounter within-the-world is subsequently freed, amounts to nothing else than understanding the world – that world towards which Dasein as an entity always comports itself.

Whenever we let there be an involvement with something in something beforehand, our doing so is grounded in our understanding such things as letting something be involved, and such things as the "with-which" and the "in-which" of involvements. Anything of this sort, and anything else that is basic for it, such as the "towards-this" as that in which there is an involvement, or such as the "for-the-sake-of-which" to which every "towards-which" ultimately goes back – all these must be disclosed beforehand with a certain intelligibility [*Verständlichkeit*]. And what is that wherein Dasein as Being-in-the-world understands itself pre-ontologically? In understanding a context of relations such as we have mentioned, Dasein has assigned itself to an "in-order-to" [*Um-zu*], and it has done so in terms of a potentiality-for-Being for the sake of which it itself is – one which it may have seized upon either explicitly or tacitly, and which may be either authentic or inauthentic. This "in-order-to" prescribes a "towards-this" as a possible "in-which" for letting something be involved; and the structure of letting it be involved implies that this is an involvement which something *has* – an involvement which is *with* something. Dasein always assigns itself from a "for-the-sake-of-which" to the "with-which" of an involvement; that is to say, to the extent that it is, it always lets entities be encountered as ready-to-hand. *That wherein [Worin]* Dasein understands itself beforehand in the mode of assigning itself is *that for which [das Woraufhin]* it has let entities be encountered beforehand. *The "wherein" of an act of understanding which assigns or refers itself, is that for which one lets entities be encountered in the kind of Being that belongs to involvements; and this "wherein" is the phenomenon of the world.* And the structure of that to which [woraufhin] Dasein assigns itself is what makes up the *worldhood* of the world.

That wherein Dasein already understands itself in this way is always something with which it is primordially familiar. This familiarity with the world does not necessarily require that the relations which are constitutive for the world as world should be theoretically transparent. However, the possibility of giving these relations an explicit ontologico-existential Interpretation, is grounded in this familiarity with the world; and this familiarity, in turn, is constitutive for Dasein, and goes to make up Dasein's understanding of Being. This possibility is one which can be seized upon explicitly in so far as Dasein has set itself the task of giving a primordial Interpretation for its own Being and for the possibilities of that Being, or indeed for the meaning of Being in general.

Part VII

HANS-GEORG GADAMER
Phenomenology, Hermeneutics and Tradition

HANS-GEORG GADAMER (b. 1900)

Introduction

Hans-Georg Gadamer was born in Marburg in 1900 and enrolled in the University of Breslau in 1918 before moving to Marburg University in 1919 to study philosophy and classics, completing his doctorate on Plato under Paul Natorp and Nicolai Hartmann in 1922. Gadamer travelled to Freiburg to meet Heidegger in 1923, and returned to Marburg to study with him from 1924 to 1928, completing his *Habilitation* in 1928, published as *Plato's Dialectical Ethics* (1931). Gadamer first taught as *Privatdozent* at Marburg, before securing a temporary post in Kiel from 1934 to 1935 in controversial circumstances, as he was replacing a friend, Richard Kroner, a Jewish lecturer who had been dismissed under the new Nazi laws. Gadamer returned to Marburg in 1935, becoming a professor in 1937. In 1938 he moved to Leipzig, where he remained throughout the war. He was appointed Rector there in 1946 to 1947, but soon left for a position in Frankfurt, where he was active in bringing Adorno and others back from exile in the USA. In 1949 Gadamer was appointed Professor in Heidelberg, where he taught until his retirement in 1968. Although Gadamer had published books and articles (mainly on classical Greek philosophy and Hegel), it was his book, *Wahrheit und Methode* (*Truth and Method*, 1960), which brought him to prominence as a philosopher. This book takes the form of a loosely related series of essays on central concepts of the classical tradition, arguing for the general point that we can talk of the truth of art and of cultural products in a genuine sense; not all truth is encapsulated in scientific method. Following his retirement, he has travelled and lectured extensively in the USA and elsewhere, participating in debates with prominent philosophers, such as Habermas, Derrida, Ricoeur and Apel, on the nature and value of hermeneutical philosophy. His *Philosophical Apprenticeships* is a fascinating intellectual autobiography, and his hundredth birthday was commemorated with conferences and publications in 2000. At the time of writing, he continues to reside in Heidelberg.

Schooled in the neo-Kantian tradition at Marburg, Gadamer was captivated by the promise of the phenomenological approach of Husserl and Heidegger. He was also attracted to the hermeneutical studies of Wilhelm Dilthey, specifically his reconstruction of Schleiermacher, and also by the tradition of German idealism, and specifically Hegel's attempts to understand the nature of historical and cultural processes. *Hermeneutics*, the art of interpretation or understanding, specifically the interpretation of the living legacy of Greek philosophy, became his main philosophical focus. Gadamer begins from Heidegger's insight in *Being and Time* (§§32–34) that understanding (*Verstehen*) is *the* central mode of human 'being-in-the-world', a world encountered and inhabited in and through language. Hermeneutics, for

Gadamer, signifies this ongoing, never completable process of understanding in the light of human *finitude* and 'linguisticality' (*Sprachlichkeit*). As Gadamer puts it in *Truth and Method*, "language is the medium of the hermeneutic experience". Given this understanding of hermeneutics, philosophy, for Gadamer, is an ongoing conversation leading towards mutual understanding, where phenomenology, and especially its focus on the *experience* of art, provides the best way to describe the *experience of understanding* itself. For Gadamer, what Husserl termed *the things themselves*, the essences of situations, come to light in speech and specifically in dialogue. The shared understanding that emerges in dialogue goes beyond the intentions of the speakers, such that, as Gadamer says, "a genuine conversation is never the one we wanted to conduct". Gadamer thus emphasises the anti-subjectivist nature of genuine understanding. Mutual understanding occurs through a process of the interpenetration of our approaches, the 'fusion of horizons' (*Horizontsverschmelzung*), whereby our own understanding of the present and of the past are transformed and come to qualify each other in particular ways.

Gadamer's paradigm of genuine cultural understanding is always the experience of art, and he was deeply influenced by Heidegger's 1935 lectures on "The Origin of the Work of Art", to which he wrote an introduction. Gadamer opposes subjectivist approaches to aesthetic experience and supports Heidegger's view that truth is revealed by art. Moreover, art can be understood and interpreted only within the context of a cultural tradition.

Since understanding takes place only in the context of an existing tradition (*Überlieferung*), every act of understanding already presupposes a certain amount, essentially our own presumptions or 'prejudices' (which Gadamer does not understand in a negative sense), an essential aspect of our being-in-the-world. Part of Gadamer's aim, then, involves the rehabilitation of the notion of prejudice, which was so dismissed in the presuppositionless philosophising of Husserl and in the emancipatory rhetoric of the Enlightenment. For Gadamer, all understanding is determined by *prejudice* or 'prejudgement' (*Vorurteil*), and our prejudgements are formed by what Gadamer calls *Wirkungsgeschichte*, 'effective history' or the 'history of effect', the historical working out of the effects of actions which we inevitably inherit and in which we are inescapably involved.

Our reading is an excerpt from Gadamer's *Truth and Method*, where he outlines his theory of hermeneutics in terms of his rehabilitation of the notion of prejudice against the Enlightenment campaign against 'superstition', and emphasises that it is the "tyranny of hidden prejudices that makes us deaf to what speaks to us in tradition". Gadamer argues that all understanding takes place within tradition, and that all our understanding is already affected by history. Indeed it is this consciousness of being affected by history which constitutes the hermeneutic situation. Understanding emerges from the consciousness of the distance between our horizon of understanding and that of the past which we are trying to understand.

Further reading

Gadamer, Hans-Georg. *Dialogue and Dialectic. Eight Hermeneutical Studies on Plato*, trans. P. Christopher Smith. New Haven, CT: Yale University Press, 1980.

Gadamer, Hans-Georg. *Gesammelte Werke* (10 vols). Tübingen: Mohr Siebeck, 1999.

Gadamer, Hans-Georg. *Hegel's Dialectic. Five Hermeneutical Studies*, trans. P. Christopher Smith. New Haven, CT: Yale University Press, 1976.

Gadamer, Hans-Georg. *Heidegger Ways*, trans. J. W. Stanley. Albany, NY: SUNY Press, 1994.

Gadamer, Hans-Georg. *Literature and Philosophy in Dialogue*, trans. R. H. Paslick. Albany, NY: SUNY Press, 1994.

Gadamer, Hans-Georg. *Philosophical Apprenticeships*, trans. Robert R. Sullivan. Cambridge, MA: MIT Press, 1990.

Gadamer, Hans-Georg. *Philosophical Hermeneutics*, trans. and ed. David E. Linge. Berkeley: University of California Press, 1977.

Gadamer, Hans-Georg. *Plato's Dialectical Ethics*, trans. Robert M. Wallace. New Haven, CT: Yale University Press, 1991.

Gadamer, Hans-Georg. *Reason in the Age of Science*, trans. F. G. Lawrence. Cambridge, MA: MIT Press, 1981.

Gadamer, Hans-Georg. *The Idea of the Good in Platonic–Aristotelian Philosophy*. New Haven, CT: Yale University Press, 1986.

Gadamer, Hans-Georg. *The Relevance of the Beautiful and Other Essays*, trans. N. Walker. Cambridge: Cambridge University Press, 1986.

Gadamer, Hans-Georg (ed.) *Truth and Historicity*. The Hague: Nijhoff, 1972.

Gadamer, Hans-Georg. *Truth and Method*. 2nd, Revised Edition, trans. Joel Weinsheimer and Donald G. Marshall. London: Sheed & Ward, 1989.

Betti, E. "Hermeneutics as the General Methodology of the *Geisteswissenschaften*", in J. Bleicher, ed. *Contemporary Hermeneutics*. London: Routledge & Kegan Paul, 1980.

Grondin, Jean. "On the Sources of *Truth and Method*", in *Sources of Hermeneutics*. Albany, NY: SUNY Press, 1995.

Grondin, Jean. *Hans-Georg Gadamer. Eine Biographie*. Tübingen: Mohr Siebeck, 1999.

Hahn, Lewis E. (ed.) *The Philosophy of Hans-Georg Gadamer*. Library of the Living Philosophers. La Salle: Open Court, 1997.

Michelfelder, Diane P. and Richard E. Palmer (eds). *Dialogue and Deconstruction. The Gadamer–Derrida Encounter*. Albany, NY: SUNY Press, 1989.

Misgeld, Dieter and Graeme Nicholson (eds). *Hans-Georg Gadamer on Education, Poetry and History. Applied Hermeneutics*. Albany, NY: SUNY Press, 1992.

Palmer, Richard O. *Hermeneutics. Interpretation Theory in Schleiermacher, Dilthey, Heidegger, and Gadamer*. Evanston: Northwestern University Press, 1969.

Silverman, H. J. (ed.). *Gadamer and Hermeneutics*. London: Routledge, 1991.

Wachterhauser, Brice R. *Hermeneutics and Modern Philosophy*. Albany, NY: SUNY Press, 1986.

Warnke, G. *Gadamer: Hermeneutics, Tradition and Reason*. Cambridge: Polity Press, 1987.

Weinsheimer, J. *Gadamer's Hermeneutics: A Reading of Truth and Method*. New Haven, CT: Yale University Press, 1985.

1

ELEMENTS OF A THEORY OF HERMENEUTIC EXPERIENCE

(A) THE HERMENEUTIC CIRCLE AND THE PROBLEM OF PREJUDICES

(i) Heidegger's disclosure of the fore-structure of understanding

Heidegger entered into the problems of historical hermeneutics and critique only in order to explicate the fore-structure of understanding for the purposes of ontology.[1] Our question, by contrast, is how hermeneutics, once freed from the ontological obstructions of the scientific concept of objectivity, can do justice to the historicity of understanding. Hermeneutics has traditionally understood itself as an art or technique.[2] This is true even of Dilthey's expansion of hermeneutics into an organon of the human sciences. One might wonder whether there is such an art or technique of understanding – we shall come back to the point. But at any rate we can inquire into the consequences for the hermeneutics of the human sciences of the fact that Heidegger derives the circular structure of understanding from the temporality of Dasein. These consequences do not need to be such that a theory is applied to practice so that the latter is performed differently – i.e., in a way that is technically correct. They could also consist in correcting (and refining) the way in which constantly exercised understanding understands itself – a process that would benefit the art of understanding at most only indirectly.

Hence we will once more examine Heidegger's description of the hermeneutical circle in order to make its new fundamental significance fruitful for our purposes. Heidegger writes, "It is not to be reduced to the level of a vicious circle, or even of a circle which is merely tolerated. In the circle is hidden a positive possibility of the most primordial kind of knowing, and we genuinely grasp this possibility only when we have understood that our first, last, and constant task in interpreting is never to allow our fore-having, fore-sight, and fore-conception to be presented to us by fancies and popular conceptions, but rather to make the scientific theme secure by working out these fore-structures in terms of the things themselves".[3]

What Heidegger is working out here is not primarily a prescription for the practice of understanding, but a description of the way interpretive understanding is achieved. The point of Heidegger's hermeneutical reflection is not so much

H.-G. Gadamer, *Truth and Method*, 2nd, Revised Edition, 1989, trans. Joel Weinsheimer and Donald G. Marshall, pp. 265–307. London: Sheed & Ward.

to prove that there is a circle as to show that this circle possesses an ontologically positive significance. The description as such will be obvious to every interpreter who knows what he is about. All correct interpretation must be on guard against arbitrary fancies and the limitations imposed by imperceptible habits of thought, and it must direct its gaze "on the things themselves" (which, in the case of the literary critic, are meaningful texts, which themselves are again concerned with objects). For the interpreter to let himself be guided by the things themselves is obviously not a matter of a single, "conscientious" decision, but is "the first, last, and constant task." For it is necessary to keep one's gaze fixed on the thing throughout all the constant distractions that originate in the interpreter himself. A person who is trying to understand a text is always projecting. He projects a meaning for the text as a whole as soon as some initial meaning emerges in the text. Again, the initial meaning emerges only because he is reading the text with particular expectations in regard to a certain meaning. Working out this fore-projection, which is constantly revised in terms of what emerges as he penetrates into the meaning, is understanding what is there.

This description is, of course, a rough abbreviation of the whole. The process that Heidegger describes is that every revision of the fore-projection is capable of projecting before itself a new projection of meaning; rival projects can emerge side by side until it becomes clearer what the unity of meaning is; interpretation begins with fore-conceptions that are replaced by more suitable ones. This constant process of new projection constitutes the movement of understanding and interpretation. A person who is trying to understand is exposed to distraction from fore-meanings that are not borne out by the things themselves. Working out appropriate projections, anticipatory in nature, to be confirmed "by the things" themselves, is the constant task of understanding. The only "objectivity" here is the confirmation of a fore-meaning in its being worked out. Indeed, what characterizes the arbitrariness of inappropriate fore-meanings if not that they come to nothing in being worked out? But understanding realizes its full potential only when the fore-meanings that it begins with are not arbitrary. Thus it is quite right for the interpreter not to approach the text directly, relying solely on the fore-meaning already available to him, but rather explicitly to examine the legitimacy – i.e., the origin and validity – of the fore-meanings dwelling within him.

This basic requirement must be seen as the radicalization of a procedure that we in fact exercise whenever we understand anything. Every text presents the task of not simply leaving our own linguistic usage unexamined – or in the case of a foreign language the usage that we are familiar with from writers or from daily intercourse. Rather, we regard our task as deriving our understanding of the text from the linguistic usage of the time or of the author. The question is, of course, how this general requirement can be fulfilled. Especially in the field of semantics we are confronted with the problem that our own use of language is unconscious. How do we discover that there is a difference between our own customary usage and that of the text?

I think we must say that generally we do so in the experience of being pulled up short by the text. Either it does not yield any meaning at all or its meaning is not compatible with what we had expected. This is what brings us up short and alerts us to a possible difference in usage. Someone who speaks the same language as I do uses the words in the sense familiar to me – this is a general presupposition that can be questioned only in particular cases. The same thing is true in the case of a foreign language: we all think we have a standard knowledge of it and assume this standard usage when we are reading a text.

What is true of fore-meanings that stem from usage, however, is equally true of the fore-meanings concerning content with which we read texts, and which make up our fore-understanding. Here too we may ask how we can break the spell of our own fore-meanings. There can, of course, be a general expectation that what the text says will fit perfectly with my own meanings and expectations. But what another person tells me, whether in conversation, letter, book, or whatever, is generally supposed to be his own and not my opinion; and this is what I am to take note of without necessarily having to share it. Yet this presupposition is not something that makes understanding easier, but harder, since the fore-meanings that determine my own understanding can go entirely unnoticed. If they give rise to misunderstandings, how can our misunderstandings of a text be perceived at all if there is nothing to contradict them? How can a text be protected against misunderstanding from the start?

If we examine the situation more closely, however, we find that meanings cannot be understood in an arbitrary way. Just as we cannot continually misunderstand the use of a word without its affecting the meaning of the whole, so we cannot stick blindly to our own fore-meaning about the thing if we want to understand the meaning of another. Of course this does not mean that when we listen to someone or read a book we must forget all our fore-meanings concerning the content and all our own ideas. All that is asked is that we remain open to the meaning of the other person or text. But this openness always includes our situating the other meaning in relation to the whole of our own meanings or ourselves in relation to it. Now, the fact is that meanings represent a fluid multiplicity of possibilities (in comparison to the agreement presented by a language and a vocabulary), but within this multiplicity of what can be thought – i.e., of what a reader can find meaningful and hence expect to find – not everything is possible; and if a person fails to hear what the other person is really saying, he will not be able to fit what he has misunderstood into the range of his own various expectations of meaning. Thus there is a criterion here also. *The hermeneutical task becomes of itself a questioning of things* and is always in part so defined. This places hermeneutical work on a firm basis. A person trying to understand something will not resign himself from the start to relying on his own accidental fore-meanings, ignoring as consistently and stubbornly as possible the actual meaning of the text until the latter becomes so persistently audible that it breaks through what the interpreter imagines it to be. Rather, a person trying to understand a text is prepared for it to tell him something. That is why a hermeneutically trained consciousness must be, from the start, sensitive to the text's alterity. But this kind of sensitivity involves neither "neutrality" with respect to content nor the extinction of one's self, but the foregrounding and appropriation of one's own fore-meanings and prejudices. The important thing is to be aware of one's own bias, so that the text can present itself in all its otherness and thus assert its own truth against one's own fore-meanings.

When Heidegger disclosed the fore-structure of understanding in what is considered merely "reading what is there," this was a completely correct phenomenological description. He also exemplified the task that follows from this. In *Being and Time* he gave the general hermeneutical problem a concrete form in the question of being.[4] In order to explain the hermeneutical situation of the question of being in terms of fore-having, fore-sight, and fore-conception, he critically tested his question, directed at metaphysics, on important turning points in the history of metaphysics. Here he was only doing what historical-hermeneutical consciousness requires in every case. Methodologically conscious understanding will be concerned not merely to form anticipatory ideas, but to make them conscious, so as to check them and thus acquire right understanding from the things themselves. This is what Heidegger means when he talks about making our scientific theme "secure" by deriving our fore-having, fore-sight and foreconception from the things themselves.

It is not at all a matter of securing ourselves against the tradition that speaks out of the text then, but, on the contrary, of excluding everything that could hinder us from understanding it in terms of the subject matter. It is the tyranny of hidden prejudices that makes us deaf to what speaks to us in tradition. Heidegger's demonstration that the concept of consciousness in Descartes and of spirit in Hegel is still influenced by Greek substance ontology, which sees being in terms of what is present, undoubtedly surpasses the self-understanding of modern metaphysics, yet not in an arbitrary, willful way, but on the basis of a "fore-having" that in fact makes this tradition intelligible by revealing the ontological premises of the concept of subjectivity. On the other hand, Heidegger discovers in Kant's critique of "dogmatic" metaphysics the idea of a metaphysics of finitude which is a challenge to his own ontological scheme. Thus he "secures" the scientific theme by framing it within the understanding of tradition and so putting it, in a sense, at risk. All of this is a concretization of the historical consciousness involved in understanding.

The recognition that all understanding inevitably involves some prejudice gives the hermeneutical problem its real thrust. In light of this insight it appears that *historicism, despite its critique of rationalism and of natural law philosophy, is based on the modern Enlightenment and unwittingly shares its prejudices.* And there is one prejudice of the Enlightenment that defines its essence: the fundamental prejudice of the Enlightenment is the prejudice against prejudice itself, which denies tradition its power.

The history of ideas shows that not until the Enlightenment does *the concept of prejudice* acquire the negative connotation familiar today. Actually "prejudice" means a judgment that is rendered before all the elements that determine a situation have been finally examined. In German legal terminology a "prejudice" is a provisional legal verdict before the final verdict is reached. For someone involved in a legal dispute, this kind of judgment against him affects his chances adversely. Accordingly, the French préjudice, as well as the Latin praejudicium, means simply "adverse effect," "disadvantage," "harm." But this negative sense is only derivative. The negative consequence depends precisely on the positive validity, the value of the provisional decision as a prejudgment, like that of any precedent.

Thus "prejudice" certainly does not necessarily mean a false judgment, but part of the idea is that it can have either a positive or a negative value. This is clearly due to the influence of the Latin *praejudicium*. There are such things as *préjugés légitimes*. This seems a long way from our current use of the word. The German Vorurteil, like the English "prejudice" and even more than the French *préjugé*, seems to have been limited in its meaning by the Enlightenment critique of religion simply to the sense of an "unfounded judgment."[5] The only thing that gives a judgment dignity is its having a basis, a methodological justification (and not the fact that it may actually be correct). For the Enlightenment the absence of such a basis does not mean that there might be other kinds of certainty, but rather that the judgment has no foundation in the things themselves – i.e., that it is "unfounded." This conclusion follows only in the spirit of rationalism. It is the reason for discrediting prejudices and the reason scientific knowledge claims to exclude them completely.

In adopting this principle, modern science is following the rule of Cartesian doubt, accepting nothing as certain that can in any way be doubted, and adopting the idea of method that follows from this rule. In our introductory observations we have already pointed out how difficult it is to harmonize the historical knowledge that helps to shape our historical consciousness with this ideal and how difficult it is, for that reason, to comprehend its true nature on the basis of the modern conception of method. This is the place to turn those negative statements into positive ones. The concept of "prejudice" is where we can start.

(ii) The discrediting of prejudice by the enlightenment

If we consider the Enlightenment doctrine of prejudice, we find that it makes the following division: we must make a basic distinction between the prejudice due to human authority and that due to overhastiness.[6] This distinction is based on the origin of prejudices in the persons who have them. Either the respect we have for others and their authority leads us into error, or else an overhastiness in ourselves. That authority is a source of prejudices accords with the well-known principle of the Enlightenment that Kant formulated: Have the courage to make use of your *own* understanding.[7] Although this distinction is certainly not limited to the role that prejudices play in understanding texts, its chief application is still in the sphere of hermeneutics, for Enlightenment critique is primarily directed against the religious tradition of Christianity – i.e., the Bible. By treating the Bible as a historical document, biblical criticism endangers its own dogmatic claims. This is the real radicality of the modern Enlightenment compared to all other movements of enlightenment: it must assert itself against the Bible and dogmatic interpretation of it.[8] It is therefore particularly concerned with the hermeneutical problem. It wants to understand tradition correctly – i.e., rationally and without prejudice. But there is a special difficulty about this, since the sheer fact that something is written down gives it special authority. It is not altogether easy to realize that what is written down can be untrue. The written word has the tangible quality of something that can be demonstrated and is like a proof. It requires a special critical effort to free oneself from the prejudice in favor of what is written down and to distinguish here also, no less than in the case of oral assertions, between opinion and truth.[9] In general, the Enlightenment tends to accept no authority and to decide everything before the judgment seat of reason. Thus the written tradition of Scripture, like any other historical document, can claim no absolute validity; the possible truth of the tradition depends on the credibility that reason accords it. It is not tradition but reason that constitutes the ultimate source of all authority. What is written down is not necessarily true. We can know better: this is the maxim with which the modern Enlightenment approaches tradition and which ultimately leads it to undertake historical research. It takes tradition as an object of critique, just as the natural sciences do with the evidence of the senses. This does not necessarily mean that the "prejudice against prejudices" was everywhere taken to the extremes of free thinking and atheism, as in England and France. On the contrary, the German Enlightenment recognized the "true prejudices" of the Christian religion. Since the human intellect is too weak to manage without prejudices, it is at least fortunate to have been educated with true prejudices.

It would be valuable to investigate to what extent this kind of modification and moderation of the Enlightenment[10] prepared the way for the rise of the romantic movement in Germany, as undoubtedly did the critique of the Enlightenment and the revolution by Edmund Burke. But none of this alters the fundamental fact. True prejudices must still finally be justified by rational knowledge, even though the task can never be fully completed.

Thus the criteria of the modern Enlightenment still determine the self-understanding of historicism. They do so not directly, but through a curious refraction caused by romanticism. This can be seen with particular clarity in the fundamental schema of the philosophy of history that romanticism shares with the Enlightenment and that precisely through the romantic reaction to the Enlightenment became an unshakable premise: the schema of the conquest of mythos by logos. What gives this schema its validity is the presupposition of the progressive retreat of magic in the world. It is supposed to represent progress in the history of the mind, and precisely because romanticism disparages this development, it takes over the schema itself as a self-evident truth. It shares the presupposition of the Enlightenment and only reverses its values, seeking to establish the validity of what is old simply on the fact that it is old: the "gothic" Middle Ages, the Christian European community of states, the permanent structure of society, but also the simplicity of peasant life and closeness to nature.

In contrast to the Enlightenment's faith in perfection, which thinks in terms of complete freedom from "superstition" and the prejudices of the past, we now find that olden times – the world of myth, unreflective life, not yet analyzed away by consciousness, in a "society close to nature," the world of Christian chivalry – all these acquire a romantic magic, even a priority over truth. Reversing the Enlightenment's presupposition results in the paradoxical tendency toward restoration – i.e., the tendency to reconstruct the old because it is old, the conscious return to the unconscious, culminating in the recognition of the superior wisdom of the primeval age of myth. But the romantic reversal of the Enlightenment's criteria of value actually perpetuates the abstract contrast between myth and reason. All criticism of the Enlightenment now proceeds via this romantic mirror image of the Enlightenment. Belief in the perfectibility of reason suddenly changes into the perfection of the "mythical" consciousness and finds itself reflected in a paradisiacal primal state before the "fall" of thought.

In fact the presupposition of a mysterious darkness in which there was a mythical collective consciousness that preceded all thought is just as dogmatic and abstract as that of a state of perfect enlightenment or of absolute knowledge. Primeval wisdom is only the counterimage of "primeval stupidity." All mythical consciousness is still knowledge, and if it knows about divine powers, then it has progressed beyond mere trembling before power (if this is to be regarded as the primeval state), but also beyond a collective life contained in magic rituals (as we find in the early Orient). It knows about itself, and in this knowledge it is no longer simply outside itself.[11]

There is the related point that even the contrast between genuine mythical thinking and pseudomythical poetic thinking is a romantic illusion based on a prejudice of the Enlightenment: namely that the poetic act no longer shares the binding quality of myth because it is a creation of the free imagination. It is the old quarrel between the poets and the philosophers in the modern garb appropriate to the age of belief in science. It is now said, not that poets tell lies, but that they are incapable of saying anything true; they have only an aesthetic effect and, through their imaginative creations, they merely seek to stimulate the imagination and vitality of their hearers or readers. [. . .]

The fact that the restorative tendency of romanticism could combine with the fundamental concerns of the Enlightenment to create the historical sciences simply indicates that the same break with the continuity of meaning in tradition lies behind both. If the Enlightenment considers it an established fact that all tradition that reason shows to be impossible (i.e., nonsense) can only be understood historically – i.e., by going back to the past's way of looking at things – then the historical consciousness that emerges in romanticism involves a radicalization of the Enlightenment. For nonsensical tradition, which had been the exception, has become the general rule for historical consciousness. Meaning that is generally accessible through reason is so little believed that the whole of the past – even, ultimately, all the thinking of one's contemporaries – is understood only "historically." Thus the romantic critique of the Enlightenment itself ends in Enlightenment, for it evolves as historical science and draws everything into the orbit of historicism. The basic discreditation of all prejudices, which unites the experimental fervor of the new natural sciences during the Enlightenment, is universalized and radicalized in the historical Enlightenment.

This is the point at which the attempt to critique historical hermeneutics has to start. The overcoming of all prejudices, this global demand of the Enlightenment, will itself prove to be a prejudice, and removing it opens the way to an appropriate understanding of the finitude which dominates not only our humanity but also our historical consciousness.

Does being situated within traditions really mean being subject to prejudices and limited in one's freedom? Is not, rather, all human existence, even the freest, limited and qualified in various ways? If this is true, the idea of an absolute reason is not a possibility for historical humanity. Reason exists for us only in concrete, historical terms – i.e., it is not its own master but remains constantly dependent on the given circumstances in which it operates. This is true not only in the sense in which Kant, under the influence of the skeptical critique of Hume, limited the claims of rationalism to the a priori element in the knowledge of nature; it is still truer of historical consciousness and the possibility of historical knowledge. For that man is concerned here with himself and his own creations (Vico) is only an apparent solution of the problem posed by historical knowledge. Man is alien to himself and his historical fate in a way quite different from the way nature, which knows nothing of him, is alien to him.

The epistemological question must be asked here in a fundamentally different way. We have shown above that Dilthey probably saw this, but he was not able to escape his entanglement in traditional epistemology. Since he started from the awareness of "experiences" (*Erlebnisse*), he was unable to build a bridge to the historical realities, because the great historical realities of society and state always have a predeterminate influence on any "experience." Self-reflection and auto-biography – Dilthey's starting points – are not primary and are therefore not an adequate basis for the heremeneutical problem, because through them history is made private once more. In fact history does not belong to us; we belong to it. Long before we understand ourselves through the process of self-examination, we understand ourselves in a self-evident way in the family, society, and state in which we live. The focus of subjectivity is a distorting mirror. The self-awareness of the individual is only a flickering in the closed circuits of historical life. *That is why the prejudices of the individual, far more than his judgments, constitute the historical reality of his being.*

PREJUDICES AS CONDITIONS OF UNDERSTANDING

The Rehabilitation of Authority and Tradition

Here is the point of departure for the hermeneutical problem. This is why we examined the Enlightenment's discreditation of the concept of "prejudice." What appears to be a limiting prejudice from the viewpoint of the absolute self-construction of reason in fact belongs to historical reality itself. If we want to do justice to man's finite, historical mode of being, it is necessary to fundamentally rehabilitate the concept of prejudice and acknowledge the fact that there are legit-imate prejudices. Thus we can formulate the fundamental epistemological ques-tion for a truly historical hermeneutics as follows: what is the ground of the legitimacy of prejudices? What distinguishes legitimate prejudices from the count-less others which it is the undeniable task of critical reason to overcome?

We can approach this question by taking the Enlightenment's critical theory of prejudices, as set out above, and giving it a positive value. The division of preju-dices into those of "authority" and those of "overhastiness" is obviously based on the fundamental presupposition of the Enlightenment, namely that method-ologically disciplined use of reason can safeguard us from all error. This was Descartes' idea of method. Overhastiness is the source of errors that arise in the use of one's own reason. Authority, however, is responsible for one's not using one's own reason at all. Thus the division is based on a mutually exclusive antith-esis between authority and reason. The false prepossession in favor of what is old, in favor of authorities, is what has to be fought. Thus the Enlightenment attrib-utes to Luther's reforms the fact that "the prejudice of human prestige, especially that of the philosophical [he means Aristotle] and the Roman pope, was greatly weakened."[12] The Reformation, then, gives rise to a flourishing hermeneutics which teaches the right use of reason in understanding traditionary texts. Neither the doctrinal authority of the pope nor the appeal to tradition can obviate the work of hermeneutics, which can safeguard the reasonable meaning of a text against all imposition.

This kind of hermeneutics need not lead to the radical critique of religion that we found, for example, in Spinoza. Rather, the possibility of supernatural truth can remain entirely open. Thus especially in the field of German popular philosophy, the Enlightenment limited the claims of reason and acknowledged the authority of Bible and church. We read in Walch, for example, that he distinguishes between the two classes of prejudice – authority and overhastiness – but considers them two extremes, between which it is necessary to find the right middle path, namely a mediation between reason and biblical authority. Accordingly, he regards prejudices deriving from overhastiness as prejudices in favor of the new, a predisposition to the overhasty rejection of truths simply because they are old and attested by authorities.[13] Thus he disputes the British free thinkers (such as Collins and others) and defends the historical faith against the norm of reason. Here the meaning of prejudice deriving from overhastiness is given a conservative reinterpretation.

There can be no doubt, however, that the real consequence of the Enlightenment is different: namely the subjection of all authority to reason. Accordingly, prejudice from overhastiness is to be understood as Descartes understood it – i.e., as the source of all error in the use of reason. This fits in with the fact that after the victory of the Enlightenment, when hermeneutics was freed from all dogmatic ties, the old division returns in a new guise. Thus Schleiermacher distinguishes between partiality and overhastiness as the causes of misunderstanding.[14] To the lasting prejudices due to partiality he contrasts the momentary ones due to overhastiness, but only the former are of interest to those concerned with scientific method. It no longer even occurs to Schleiermacher that among the prejudices in favor of authorities there might be some that are true – yet this was implied in the concept of authority in the first place. His alteration of the traditional division of prejudices documents the victory of the Enlightenment. Partiality now means only an individual limitation of understanding. "The one-sided preference for what is close to one's own sphere of ideas."

In fact, however, the decisive question is concealed behind the concept of partiality. That the prejudices determining what I think are due to my own partiality is a judgment based on the standpoint of their having been dissolved and enlightened, and it holds only for unjustified prejudices. If, on the other hand, there are justified prejudices productive of knowledge, then we are back to the problem of authority. Hence the radical consequences of the Enlightenment, which are still to be found in Schleiermacher's faith in method, are not tenable.

The Enlightenment's distinction between faith in authority and using one's own reason is, in itself, legitimate. If the prestige of authority displaces one's own judgment, then authority is in fact a source of prejudices. But this does not preclude its being a source of truth, and that is what the Enlightenment failed to see when it denigrated all authority. To be convinced of this, we need only consider one of the greatest forerunners of the European Enlightenment, namely Descartes. Despite the radicalness of his methodological thinking, we know that Descartes excluded morality from the total reconstruction of all truths by reason. This was what he meant by his provisional morality. It seems to me symptomatic that he did not in fact elaborate his definitive morality and that its principles, as far as we can judge from his letters to Elizabeth, contain hardly anything new. It is obviously unthinkable to defer morality until modern science has progressed enough to provide a new basis for it. In fact the denigration of authority is not the only prejudice established by the Enlightenment. It also distorted the very concept of authority. Based on the Enlightenment conception of reason and freedom, the concept of authority could be viewed as diametrically opposed to reason and freedom: to be, in fact, blind obedience. This is the meaning that we find in the language critical of modern dictatorships.

But this is not the essence of authority. Admittedly, it is primarily persons that have authority; but the authority of persons is ultimately based not on the subjection and abdication of reason but on an act of acknowledgement and knowledge – the knowledge, namely, that the other is superior to oneself in judgment and insight and that for this reason his judgment takes precedence – i.e., it has priority over one's own. This is connected with the fact that authority cannot actually be bestowed but is earned, and must be earned if someone is to lay claim to it. It rests on acknowledgment and hence on an act of reason itself which, aware of its own limitations, trusts to the better insight of others. Authority in this sense, properly understood, has nothing to do with blind obedience to commands. Indeed, authority has to do not with obedience but rather with knowledge. It is true that authority implies the capacity to command and be obeyed. But this proceeds only from the authority that a person has. Even the anonymous and impersonal authority of a superior which derives from his office is not ultimately based on this hierarchy, but is what makes it possible. Here also its true basis is an act of freedom and reason that grants the authority of a superior fundamentally because he has a wider view of things or is better informed – i.e., once again, because he knows more.[15] Thus, acknowledging authority is always connected with the idea that what the authority says is not irrational and arbitrary but can, in principle, be discovered to be true. This is the essence of the authority claimed by the teacher, the superior, the expert. The prejudices that they implant are legitimized by the person who presents them. But in this way they become prejudices not just in favor of a person but a content, since they effect the same disposition to believe something that can be brought about in other ways – e.g., by good reasons. Thus the essence of authority belongs in the context of a theory of prejudices free from the extremism of the Enlightenment.

Here we can find support in the romantic criticism of the Enlightenment; for there is one form of authority particularly defended by romanticism, namely tradition. That which has been sanctioned by tradition and custom has an authority that is nameless, and our finite historical being is marked by the fact that the authority of what has been handed down to us – and not just what is clearly grounded – always has power over our attitudes and behavior. All education depends on this, and even though, in the case of education, the educator loses his function when his charge comes of age and sets his own insight and decisions in the place of the authority of the educator, becoming mature does not mean that a person becomes his own master in the sense that he is freed from all tradition. The real force of morals, for example, is based on tradition. They are freely taken over but by no means created by a free insight or grounded on reasons.

This is precisely what we call tradition: the ground of their validity. And in fact it is to romanticism that we owe this correction of the Enlightenment: that tradition has a justification that lies beyond rational grounding and in large measure determines our institutions and attitudes. What makes classical ethics superior to modern moral philosophy is that it grounds the transition from ethics to "politics," the art of right legislation, on the indispensability of tradition.[16] By comparison, the modern Enlightenment is abstract and revolutionary.

The concept of tradition, however, has become no less ambiguous than that of authority, and for the same reason – namely that what determines the romantic understanding of tradition is its abstract opposition to the principle of enlightenment. Romanticism conceives of tradition as an antithesis to the freedom of reason and regards it as something historically given, like nature. And whether one wants to be revolutionary and oppose it or preserve it, tradition is still viewed as the abstract opposite of free self-determination, since its validity does not require any reasons but conditions us without our questioning it. Of course, the romantic critique of the Enlightenment is not an instance of tradition's automatic dominance of tradition, of its persisting unaffected by doubt and criticism. Rather, a particular critical attitude again addresses itself to the truth of tradition and seeks to renew it. We can call it "traditionalism."

It seems to me, however, that there is no such unconditional antithesis between tradition and reason. However problematical the conscious restoration of old or the creation of new traditions may be, the romantic faith in the "growth of tradition," before which all reason must remain silent, is fundamentally like the Enlightenment, and just as prejudiced. The fact is that in tradition there is always an element of freedom and of history itself. Even the most genuine and pure tradition does not persist because of the inertia of what once existed. It needs to be affirmed, embraced, cultivated. It is, essentially, preservation, and it is active in all historical change. But preservation is an act of reason, though an inconspicuous one. For this reason, only innovation and planning appear to be the result of reason. But this is an illusion. Even where life changes violently, as in ages of revolution, far more of the old is preserved in the supposed transformation of everything than anyone knows, and it combines with the new to create a new value. At any rate, preservation is as much a freely chosen action as are revolution and renewal. That is why both the Enlightenment's critique of tradition and the romantic rehabilitation of it lag behind their true historical being.

These thoughts raise the question of whether in the hermeneutics of the human sciences the element of tradition should not be given its full value. Research in the human sciences cannot regard itself as in an absolute antithesis to the way in which we, as historical beings, relate to the past. At any rate, our usual relationship to the past is not characterized by distancing and freeing ourselves from tradition. Rather, we are always situated within traditions, and this is no objectifying process – i.e., we do not conceive of what tradition says as something other, something alien. It is always part of us, a model or exemplar, a kind of cognizance that our later historical judgment would hardly regard as a kind of knowledge but as the most ingenuous affinity with tradition.

Hence in regard to the dominant epistemological methodologism we must ask: has the rise of historical consciousness really divorced our scholarship from this natural relation to the past? Does understanding in the human sciences understand itself correctly when it relegates the whole of its own historicality to the position of prejudices from which we must free ourselves? Or does "unprejudiced scholarship" share more than it realizes with that naive openness and reflection in which traditions live and the past is present?

In any case, understanding in the human sciences shares one fundamental condition with the life of tradition: it lets itself be *addressed* by tradition. Is it not true of the objects that the human sciences investigate, just as for the contents of tradition, that what they are really about can be experienced only when one is addressed by them? However mediated this significance may be, and though it may proceed from a historical interest that appears to bear no relation to the present – even in the extreme case of "objective" historical research – the real fulfillment of the historical task is to determine anew the significance of what is examined. But the significance exists at the beginning of any such research as well as at the end: in choosing the theme to be investigated, awakening the desire to investigate, gaining a new problematic.

At the beginning of all historical hermeneutics, then, *the abstract antithesis between tradition and historical research, between history and the knowledge of it, must be discarded.* The effect (*Wirkung*) of a living tradition and the effect of historical study must constitute a unity of effect, the analysis of which would reveal only a texture of reciprocal effects.[17] Hence we would do well not to regard historical consciousness as something radically new – as it seems at first – but as a new element in what has always constituted the human relation to the past. In other words, we have to recognize the element of tradition in historical research and inquire into its hermeneutic productivity.

That an element of tradition affects the human sciences despite the methodological purity of their procedures, an element that constitutes their real nature and distinguishing mark, is immediately clear if we examine the history of research and note the difference between the human and natural sciences with regard to their history. Of course none of man's finite historical endeavors can completely erase the traces of this finitude. The history of mathematics or of the natural sciences is also a part of the history of the human spirit and reflects its destinies. Nevertheless, it is not just historical naivete when the natural scientist writes the history of his subject in terms of the present state of knowledge. For him errors and wrong turnings are of historical interest only, because the progress of research is the self-evident standard of examination. Thus it is only of secondary interest to see how advances in the natural sciences or in mathematics belong to the moment in history at which they took place. This interest does not affect the epistemic value of discoveries in those fields.

There is, then, no need to deny that elements of tradition can also affect the natural sciences – e.g., particular lines of research are preferred at particular places. But scientific research as such derives the law of its development not from these circumstances but from the law of the object it is investigating, which conceals its methodical efforts.

It is clear that the human sciences cannot be adequately described in terms of this conception of research and progress. Of course it is possible to write a history of the solution of a problem – e.g., the deciphering of barely legible inscriptions – in which the only interest is in ultimately reaching the final result. Were this not so, it would have been impossible for the human sciences to have borrowed the methodology of the natural ones, as happened in the last century. But what the human sciences share with the natural is only a subordinate element of the work done in the human sciences.

This is shown by the fact that the great achievements in the human sciences almost never become outdated. A modern reader can easily make allowances for

325

the fact that, a hundred years ago, less knowledge was available to a historian, and he therefore made judgments that were incorrect in some details. On the whole, he would still rather read Droysen or Mommsen than the latest account of the subject from the pen of a historian living today. What is the criterion here? Obviously the value and importance of research cannot be measured by a criterion based in the subject matter. Rather, the subject matter appears truly significant only when it is properly portrayed for us. Thus we are certainly interested in the subject matter, but it acquires its life only from the light in which it is presented to us. We accept the fact that the subject presents different aspects of itself at different times or from different standpoints. We accept the fact that these aspects do not simply cancel one another out as research proceeds, but are like mutually exclusive conditions that exist by themselves and combine only in us. Our historical consciousness is always filled with a variety of voices in which the echo of the past is heard. Only in the multifariousness of such voices does it exist: this constitutes the nature of the tradition in which we want to share and have a part. Modern historical research itself is not only research, but the handing down of tradition. We do not see it only in terms of progress and verified results; in it we have, as it were, a new experience of history whenever the past resounds in a new voice.

Why is this so? Obviously, in the human sciences we cannot speak of an object of research in the same sense as in the natural sciences, where research penetrates more and more deeply into nature. Rather, in the human sciences the particular research questions concerning tradition that we are interested in pursuing are motivated in a special way by the present and its interests. The theme and object of research are actually constituted by the motivation of the inquiry. Hence historical research is carried along by the historical movement of life itself and cannot be understood teleologically in terms of the object into which it is inquiring. Such an "object in itself" clearly does not exist at all. This is precisely what distinguishes the human sciences from the natural sciences. Whereas the object of the natural sciences can be described idealiter as what would be known in the perfect knowledge of nature, it is senseless to speak of a perfect knowledge of history, and for this reason it is not possible to speak of an "object in itself" toward which its research is directed. [. . .]

(iii) The hermeneutic significance of temporal distance

Let us next consider how hermeneutics goes about its work. What consequences for understanding follow from the fact that belonging to a tradition is a condition of hermeneutics? We recall the hermeneutical rule that we must understand the whole in terms of the detail and the detail in terms of the whole. This principle stems from ancient rhetoric, and modern hermeneutics has transferred it to the art of understanding. It is a circular relationship in both cases. The anticipation of meaning in which the whole is envisaged becomes actual understanding when the parts that are determined by the whole themselves also determine this whole.

We know this from learning ancient languages. We learn that we must "construe" a sentence before we attempt to understand the linguistic meaning of the individual parts of the sentence. But the process of construal is itself already governed by an expectation of meaning that follows from the context of what has gone before. It is of course necessary for this expectation to be adjusted if the text calls for it. This means, then, that the expectation changes and that the text unifies its meaning around another expectation. Thus the movement of understanding is constantly from the whole to the part and back to the whole. Our task is to expand the unity of the understood meaning centrifugally. The harmony of all the details with the whole is the criterion of correct understanding. The failure to achieve this harmony means that understanding has failed.

Schleiermacher elaborated this hermeneutic circle of part and whole in both its objective and its subjective aspects. As the single world belongs in the total context of the sentence, so the single text belongs in the total context of a writer's work, and the latter in the whole of the literary genre or of literature. At the same time, however, the same text, as a manifestation of a creative moment, belongs to the whole of its author's inner life. Full understanding can take place only within this objective and subjective whole. Following this theory, Dilthey speaks of "structure" and of the "centering in a mid-point," which permits one to understand the whole. In this he is applying to the historical world what has always been a principle of all textual interpretation: namely that a text must be understood in its own terms.

The question is, however, whether this is an adequate account of the circular movement of understanding. Here we must return to what we concluded from our analysis of Schleiermacher's hermeneutics. We can set aside Schleiermacher's ideas on subjective interpretation. When we try to understand a text, we do not try to transpose ourselves into the author's mind but, if one wants to use this terminology, we try to transpose ourselves into the perspective within which he has formed his views. But this simply means that we try to understand how what he is saying could be right. If we want to understand, we will try to make his arguments even stronger. This happens even in conversation, and it is a fortiori true of understanding what is written down that we are moving in a dimension of meaning that is intelligible in itself and as such offers no reason for going back to the subjectivity of the author. The task of hermeneutics is to clarify this miracle of understanding, which is not a mysterious communion of souls, but sharing in a common meaning.

But even Schleiermacher's description of the objective side of this circle does not get to the heart of the matter. We have seen that the goal of all attempts to reach an understanding is agreement concerning the subject matter. Hence the task of hermeneutics has always been to establish agreement where there was none or where it had been disturbed in some way. The history of hermeneutics confirms this if, for example, we think of Augustine, who sought to mediate the Gospel with the Old Testament, or early Protestantism, which faced the same problem; or, finally, the Enlightenment, when (almost as if renouncing the possibility of agreement) it was supposed that a text could be "fully understood" only by means of historical interpretation. It is something qualitatively new when romanticism and Schleiermacher universalize historical consciousness by denying that the binding form of the tradition from which they come and in which they are situated provides a solid basis for all hermeneutic endeavor.

One of the immediate predecessors of Schleiermacher, the philologist Friedrich Ast, still had a view of hermeneutical work that was markedly concerned with content, since for him its purpose was to establish harmony between the worlds of classical antiquity and Christianity, between a newly discovered genuine antiquity

and the Christian tradition. This is something new. In contrast to the Enlightenment, this hermeneutics no longer evaluates and rejects tradition according to the
criterion of natural reason. But in its attempt to bring about a meaningful agreement between the two traditions to which it sees itself as belonging, this kind of
hermeneutics is still pursuing the task of all preceding hermeneutics, namely to
bring about agreement *in content*.

In going beyond the "particularity" of this reconciliation of the ancient
classical world and Christianity, Schleiermacher and, following him, nineteenth-
century science conceive the task of hermeneutics in a way that is *formally*
universal. They were able to harmonize it with the natural sciences' ideal of
objectivity, but only by ignoring the concretion of historical consciousness in
hermeneutical theory.

Heidegger's description and existential grounding of the hermeneutic circle, by
contrast, constitute a decisive turning point. Nineteenth-century hermeneutic
theory often discussed the circular structure of understanding, but always within
the framework of a formal relation between part and whole – or its subjective
reflex, the intuitive anticipation of the whole and its subsequent articulation in the
parts. According to this theory, the circular movement of understanding runs
backward and forward along the text, and ceases when the text is perfectly understood. This view of understanding came to its logical culmination in Schleiermacher's theory of the divinatory act, by means of which one places oneself entirely
within the writer's mind and from there resolves all that is strange and alien about
the text. In contrast to this approach, Heidegger describes the circle in such a way
that the understanding of the text remains permanently determined by the anticipatory movement of fore-understanding. The circle of whole and part is not
dissolved in perfect understanding but, on the contrary, is most fully realized.

The circle, then, is not formal in nature. It is neither subjective nor objective,
but describes understanding as the interplay of the movement of tradition and
the movement of the interpreter. The anticipation of meaning that governs our
understanding of a text is not an act of subjectivity, but proceeds from the commonality that binds us to the tradition. But this commonality is constantly being
formed in our relation to tradition. Tradition is not simply a permanent precondition; rather, we produce it ourselves inasmuch as we understand, participate in the
evolution of tradition, and hence further determine it ourselves. Thus the circle of
understanding is not a "methodological" circle, but describes an element of the
ontological structure of understanding.

The circle, which is fundamental to all understanding, has a further hermeneutic implication which I call the "fore-conception of completeness." But this,
too, is obviously a formal condition of all understanding. It states that only what
really constitutes a unity of meaning is intelligible. So when we read a text we
always assume its completeness, and only when this assumption proves mistaken –
i.e., the text is not intelligible – do we begin to suspect the text and try to discover
how it can be remedied. The rules of such textual criticism can be left aside,
for the important thing to note is that applying them properly depends on
understanding the content.

The fore-conception of completeness that guides all our understanding is, then,
always determined by the specific content. Not only does the reader assume
an immanent unity of meaning, but his understanding is likewise guided by the

constant transcendent expectations of meaning that proceed from the relation to the truth of what is being said. Just as the recipient of a letter understands the news that it contains and first sees things with the eyes of the person who wrote the letter – i.e., considers what he writes as true, and is not trying to understand the writer's peculiar opinions as such – so also do we understand traditionary texts on the basis of expectations of meaning drawn from our own prior relation to the subject matter. And just as we believe the news reported by a correspondent because he was present or is better informed, so too are we fundamentally open to the possibility that the writer of a transmitted text is better informed than we are, with our prior opinion. It is only when the attempt to accept what is said as true fails that we try to "understand" the text, psychologically or historically, as another's opinion. The prejudice of completeness, then, implies not only this formal element – that a text should completely express its meaning – but also that what it says should be the complete truth.

Here again we see that understanding means, primarily, to understand the content of what is said, and only secondarily to isolate and understand another's meaning as such. Hence the most basic of all hermeneutic preconditions remains one's own foreunderstanding, which comes from being concerned with the same subject. This is what determines what can be realized as unified meaning and thus determines how the fore-conception of completeness is applied.

Thus the meaning of "belonging" – i.e., the element of tradition in our historical-hermeneutical activity – is fulfilled in the commonality of fundamental, enabling prejudices. Hermeneutics must start from the position that a person seeking to understand something has a bond to the subject matter that comes into language through the traditionary text and has, or acquires, a connection with the tradition from which the text speaks. On the other hand, hermeneutical consciousness is aware that its bond to this subject matter does not consist in some self-evident, unquestioned unanimity, as is the case with the unbroken stream of tradition. Hermeneutic work is based on a polarity of familiarity and strangeness; but this polarity is not to be regarded psychologically, with Schleiermacher, as the range that covers the mystery of individuality, but truly hermeneutically – i.e., in regard to what has been said: the language in which the text addresses us, the story that it tells us. Here too there is a tension. It is in the play between the traditionary text's strangeness and familiarity to us, between being a historically intended, distanciated object and belonging to a tradition. *The true locus of hermeneutics is this in-between.*

Given the intermediate position in which hermeneutics operates, it follows that its work is not to develop a procedure of understanding, but to clarify the conditions in which understanding takes place. But these conditions do not amount to a "procedure" or method which the interpreter must of himself bring to bear on the text; rather, they must be given. The prejudices and fore-meanings that occupy the interpreter's consciousness are not at his free disposal. He cannot separate in advance the productive prejudices that enable understanding from the prejudices that hinder it and lead to misunderstandings.

Rather, this separation must take place in the process of understanding itself, and hence hermeneutics must ask how that happens. But that means it must foreground what has remained entirely peripheral in previous hermeneutics: temporal distance and its significance for understanding.

This point can be clarified by comparing it with the hermeneutic theory of romanticism. We recall that the latter conceived of understanding as the reproduction of an original production. Hence it was possible to say that one should be able to understand an author better than he understood himself. We examined the origin of this statement and its connection with the aesthetics of genius, but must now come back to it, since our present inquiry lends it a new importance.

That subsequent understanding is superior to the original production and hence can be described as superior understanding does not depend so much on the conscious realization that places the interpreter on the same level as the author (as Schleiermacher said) but instead denotes an insuperable difference between the interpreter and the author that is created by historical distance. Every age has to understand a transmitted text in its own way, for the text belongs to the whole tradition whose content interests the age and in which it seeks to understand itself. The real meaning of a text, as it speaks to the interpreter, does not depend on the contingencies of the author and his original audience. It certainly is not identical with them, for it is always co-determined also by the historical situation of the interpreter and hence by the totality of the objective course of history. A writer like Chladenius, who does not yet view understanding in terms of history, is saying the same thing in a naive, ingenuous way when he says that an author does not need to know the real meaning of what he has written; and hence the interpreter can, and must, often understand more than he. But this is of fundamental importance. Not just occasionally but always, the meaning of a text goes beyond its author. That is why understanding is not merely a reproductive but always a productive activity as well. Perhaps it is not correct to refer to this productive element in understanding as "better understanding." For this phrase is, as we have shown, a principle of criticism taken from the Enlightenment and revised on the basis of the aesthetics of genius. Understanding is not, in fact, understanding better, either in the sense of superior knowledge of the subject because of clearer ideas or in the sense of fundamental superiority of conscious over unconscious production. It is enough to say that we understand in a *different* way, *if we understand at all*.

Such a conception of understanding breaks right through the circle drawn by romantic hermeneutics. Since we are now concerned not with individuality and what it thinks but with the truth of what is said, a text is not understood as a mere expression of life but is taken seriously in its claim to truth. That this is what is meant by "understanding" was once self-evident (we need only recall Chladenius). But this dimension of the hermeneutical problem was discredited by historical consciousness and the psychological turn that Schleiermacher gave to hermeneutics, and could only be regained when the aporias of historicism came to light and led finally to the fundamentally new development to which Heidegger, in my view, gave the decisive impetus. For the hermeneutic productivity of temporal distance could be understood only when Heidegger gave understanding an ontological orientation by interpreting it as an "existential" and when he interpreted Dasein's mode of being in terms of time.

Time is no longer primarily a gulf to be bridged because it separates; it is actually the supportive ground of the course of events in which the present is rooted. Hence temporal distance is not something that must be overcome. This was, rather, the naive assumption of historicism, namely that we must transpose ourselves into the spirit of the age, think with its ideas and its thoughts, not with our own, and thus advance toward historical objectivity. In fact the important thing is to recognize temporal distance as a positive and productive condition enabling understanding. It is not a yawning abyss but is filled with the continuity of custom and tradition, in the light of which everything handed down presents itself to us. Here it is not too much to speak of the genuine productivity of the course of events. Everyone is familiar with the curious impotence of our judgment where temporal distance has not given us sure criteria. Thus the judgment of contemporary works of art is desperately uncertain for the scholarly consciousness. Obviously we approach such creations with unverifiable prejudices, presuppositions that have too great an influence over us for us to know about them; these can give contemporary creations an extra resonance that does not correspond to their true content and significance. Only when all their relations to the present time have faded away can their real nature appear, so that the understanding of what is said in them can claim to be authoritative and universal.

In historical studies this experience has led to the idea that objective knowledge can be achieved only if there has been a certain historical distance. It is true that what a thing has to say, its intrinsic content, first appears only after it is divorced from the fleeting circumstances that gave rise to it. The positive conditions of historical understanding include the relative closure of a historical event, which allows us to view it as a whole, and its distance from contemporary opinions concerning its import. The implicit presupposition of historical method, then, is that the permanent significance of something can first be known objectively only when it belongs to a closed context – in other words, when it is dead enough to have only historical interest. Only then does it seem possible to exclude the subjective involvement of the observer. This is, in fact, a paradox, the epistemological counterpart to the old moral problem of whether anyone can be called happy before his death. Just as Aristotle showed how this kind of problem can serve to sharpen the powers of human judgment,[18] so hermeneutical reflection cannot fail to find here a sharpening of the methodological self-consciousness of science. It is true that certain hermeneutic requirements are automatically fulfilled when a historical context has come to be of only historical interest. Certain sources of error are automatically excluded. But it is questionable whether this is the end of the hermeneutical problem. Temporal distance obviously means something other than the extinction of our interest in the object. It lets the true meaning of the object emerge fully. But the discovery of the true meaning of a text or a work of art is never finished; it is in fact an infinite process. Not only are fresh sources of error constantly excluded, so that all kinds of things are filtered out that obscure the true meaning; but new sources of understanding are continually emerging that reveal unsuspected elements of meaning. The temporal distance that performs the filtering process is not fixed, but is itself undergoing constant movement and extension. And along with the negative side of the filtering process brought about by temporal distance there is also the positive side, namely the value it has for understanding. It not only lets local and limited prejudices die away, but allows those that bring about genuine understanding to emerge clearly as such.

Often temporal distance can solve question of critique in hermeneutics, namely how to distinguish the true prejudices, by which we *understand*, from the *false* ones, by which we *misunderstand*. Hence the hermeneutically trained mind will also include historical consciousness. It will make conscious the prejudices governing our own understanding, so that the text, as another's meaning, can be isolated and valued on its own. Foregrounding (*abheben*) a prejudice clearly requires suspending its validity for us. For as long as our mind is influenced by a prejudice, we do not consider it a judgment. How then can we foreground it? It is impossible to make ourselves aware of a prejudice while it is constantly operating unnoticed, but only when it is, so to speak, provoked. The encounter with a traditionary text can provide this provocation. For what leads to understanding must be something that has already asserted itself in its own separate validity. Understanding begins, as we have already said above, when something addresses us. This is the first condition of hermeneutics. We now know what this requires, namely the fundamental suspension of our own prejudices. But all suspension of judgments and hence, a fortiori, of prejudices, has the logical structure of a *question*.

The essence of the *question* is to open up possibilities and keep them open. If a prejudice becomes questionable in view of what another person or a text says to us, this does not mean that it is simply set aside and the text or the other person accepted as valid in its place. Rather, historical objectivism shows its naivete in accepting this disregarding of ourselves as what actually happens. In fact our own prejudice is properly brought into play by being put at risk. Only by being given full play is it able to experience the other's claim to truth and make it possible for him to have full play himself.

The naivete of so-called historicism consists in the fact that it does not undertake this reflection, and in trusting to the fact that its procedure is methodical, it forgets its own historicity. We must here appeal from a badly understood historical thinking to one that can better perform the task of understanding. Real historical thinking must take account of its own historicity. Only then will it cease to chase the phantom of a historical object that is the object of progressive research, and learn to view the object as the counterpart of itself and hence understand both. The true historical object is not an object at all, but the unity of the one and the other, a relationship that constitutes both the reality of history and the reality of historical understanding.[19] A hermeneutics adequate to the subject matter would have to demonstrate the reality and efficacy of history within understanding itself. I shall refer to this as "history of effect." *Understanding is, essentially, a historically effected event.*

(iv) The principle of history of effect (*Wirkungsgeschichte*)

Historical interest is directed not only toward the historical phenomenon and the traditionary work but also, secondarily, toward their effect in history (which also includes the history of research); the history of effect is generally regarded as a mere supplement to historical inquiry, from Hermann Grimm's *Raffael* to Gundolf and beyond – though it has occasioned many valuable insights. To this extent, history of effect is not new. But to require an inquiry into history of effect every time a work of art or an aspect of the tradition is led out of the twilight region between tradition and history so that it can be seen clearly and openly in terms of its own meaning – this is a new demand (addressed not to research, but to its methodological consciousness) that proceeds inevitably from thinking historical consciousness through.

It is not, of course, a hermeneutical requirement in the sense of the traditional conception of hermeneutics. I am not saying that historical inquiry should develop inquiry into the history of effect as a kind of inquiry separate from understanding the work itself. The requirement is of a more theoretical kind. Historical consciousness must become conscious that in the apparent immediacy with which it approaches a work of art or a traditionary text, there is also another kind of inquiry in play, albeit unrecognized and unregulated. If we are trying to understand a historical phenomenon from the historical distance that is characteristic of our hermeneutical situation, we are always already affected by history. It determines in advance both what seems to us worth inquiring about and what will appear as an object of investigation, and we more or less forget half of what is really there – in fact, we miss the whole truth of the phenomenon – when we take its immediate appearance as the whole truth.

In our understanding, which we imagine is so innocent because its results seem so self-evident, the other presents itself so much in terms of our own selves that there is no longer a question of self and other. In relying on its critical method, historical objectivism conceals the fact that historical consciousness is itself situated in the web of historical effects. By means of methodical critique it does away with the arbitrariness of "relevant" appropriations of the past, but it preserves its good conscience by failing to recognize the presuppositions – certainly not arbitrary, but still fundamental – that govern its own understanding, and hence falls short of reaching that truth which, despite the finite nature of our understanding, could be reached. In this respect, historical objectivism resembles statistics, which are such excellent means of propaganda because they let the "facts" speak and hence simulate an objectivity that in reality depends on the legitimacy of the questions asked.

We are not saying, then, that history of effect must be developed as a new independent discipline ancillary to the human sciences, but that we should learn to understand ourselves better and recognize that in all understanding, whether we are expressly aware of it or not, the efficacy of history is at work. When a naive faith in scientific method denies the existence of effective history, there can be an actual deformation of knowledge. We are familiar with this from the history of science, where it appears as the irrefutable proof of something that is obviously false. But on the whole the power of effective history does not depend on its being recognized. This, precisely, is the power of history over finite human consciousness, namely that it prevails even where faith in method leads one to deny one's own historicity. Our need to become conscious of effective history is urgent because it is necessary for scientific consciousness. But this does not mean it can ever be absolutely fulfilled. That we should become completely aware of effective history is just as hybrid a statement as when Hegel speaks of absolute knowledge, in which history would become completely transparent to itself and hence be raised to the level of a concept. Rather, historically effected consciousness (*wirkungsgeschichtliches Bewußtsein*) is an element in the act of understanding itself and, as we shall see, is already effectual in *finding the right questions to ask*.

Consciousness of being affected by history (*wirkungsgeschichtliches Bewußtsein*) is primarily consciousness of the hermeneutical *situation*. To acquire an awareness of a situation is, however, always a task of peculiar difficulty. The very idea of a situation means that we are not standing outside it and hence are unable to have any objective knowledge of it.[20] We always find ourselves within a situation, and throwing light on it is a task that is never entirely finished. This is also true of the hermeneutic situation – i.e., the situation in which we find ourselves with regard to the tradition that we are trying to understand. The illumination of this situation – reflection on effective history – can never be completely achieved; yet the fact that it cannot be completed is due not to a deficiency in reflection but to the essence of the historical being that we are. *To be historically means that knowledge of oneself can never be complete.* All self-knowledge arises from what is historically pregiven, what with Hegel we call "substance," because it underlies all subjective intentions and actions, and hence both prescribes and limits every possibility for understanding any tradition whatsoever in its historical alterity. This almost defines the aim of philosophical hermeneutics: its task is to retrace the path of Hegel's phenomenology of mind until we discover in all that is subjective the substantiality that determines it.

Every finite present has its limitations. We define the concept of "situation" by saying that it represents a standpoint that limits the possibility of vision. Hence essential to the concept of situation is the concept of "*horizon.*" The horizon is the range of vision that includes everything that can be seen from a particular vantage point. Applying this to the thinking mind, we speak of narrowness of horizon, of the possible expansion of horizon, of the opening up of new horizons, and so forth. Since Nietzsche and Husserl, the word has been used in philosophy to characterize the way in which thought is tied to its finite determinancy, and the way one's range of vision is gradually expanded. A person who has no horizon does not see far enough and hence over-values what is nearest to him. On the other hand, "to have a horizon" means not being limited to what is nearby but being able to see beyond it. A person who has an horizon knows the relative significance of everything within this horizon, whether it is near or far, great or small. Similarly, working out the hermeneutical situation means acquiring the right horizon of inquiry for the questions evoked by the encounter with tradition.

In the sphere of historical understanding, too, we speak of horizons, especially when referring to the claim of historical consciousness to see the past in its own terms, not in terms of our contemporary criteria and prejudices but within its own historical horizon. The task of historical understanding also involves acquiring an appropriate historical horizon, so that what we are trying to understand can be seen in its true dimensions. If we fail to transpose ourselves into the historical horizon from which the traditionary text speaks, we will misunderstand the significance of what it has to say to us. To that extent this seems a legitimate hermeneutical requirement: we must place ourselves in the other situation in order to understand it. We may wonder, however, whether this phrase is adequate to describe the understanding that is required of us. The same is true of a conversation that we have with someone simply in order to get to know him – i.e., to discover where he is coming from and his horizon. This is not a true conversation – that is, we are not seeking agreement on some subject – because the specific contents of the conversation are only a means to get to know the horizon of the other person. Examples are oral examinations and certain kinds of conversation between doctor and patient. Historical consciousness is clearly doing something similar when it transposes itself into the situation of the past and thereby claims to have acquired the right historical horizon. In a conversation, when we have discovered the other person's standpoint and horizon, his ideas become intelligible without our necessarily having to agree with him; so also when someone thinks historically, he comes to understand the meaning of what has been handed down without necessarily agreeing with it or seeing himself in it.

In both cases, the person understanding has, as it were, stopped trying to reach an agreement. He himself cannot be reached. By factoring the other person's standpoint into what he is claiming to say, we are making our own standpoint safely unattainable. In considering the origin of historical thinking, we have seen that in fact it makes this ambiguous transition from means to ends – i.e., it makes an end of what is only a means. The text that is understood historically is forced to abandon its claim to be saying something true. We think we understand when we see the past from a historical standpoint – i.e., transpose ourselves into the historical situation and try to reconstruct the historical horizon. In fact, however, we have given up the claim to find in the past any truth that is valid and intelligible for ourselves. Acknowledging the otherness of the other in this way, making him the object of objective knowledge, involves the fundamental suspension of his claim to truth.

However, the question is whether this description really fits the hermeneutical phenomenon. Are there really two different horizons here – the horizon in which the person seeking to understand lives and the historical horizon within which he places himself? Is it a correct description of the art of historical understanding to say that we learn to transpose ourselves into alien horizons? Are there such things as closed horizons, in this sense? We recall Nietzsche's complaint against historicism that it destroyed the horizon bounded by myth in which alone a culture is able to live.[21] Is the horizon of one's own present time ever closed in this way, and can a historical situation be imagined that has this kind of closed horizon?

Or is this a romantic refraction, a kind of Robinson Crusoe dream of historical enlightenment, the fiction of an unattainable island, as artificial as Crusoe himself – i.e., as the alleged primacy of the solus ipse? Just as the individual is never simply an individual because he is always in understanding with others, so too the closed horizon that is supposed to enclose a culture is an abstraction. The historical movement of human life consists in the fact that it is never absolutely bound to any one standpoint, and hence can never have a truly closed horizon. The horizon is, rather, something into which we move and that moves with us. Horizons change for a person who is moving. Thus the horizon of the past, out of which all human life lives and which exists in the form of tradition, is always in motion. The surrounding horizon is not set in motion by historical consciousness. But in it this motion becomes aware of itself.

When our historical consciousness transposes itself into historical horizons, this does not entail passing into alien worlds unconnected in any way with our own; instead, they together constitute the one great horizon that moves from within and that, beyond the frontiers of the present, embraces the historical depths of our self-consciousness. Everything contained in historical consciousness is in fact embraced by a single historical horizon. Our own past and that other past toward which our historical consciousness is directed help to shape this moving horizon out of which human life always lives and which determines it as heritage and tradition.

Understanding tradition undoubtedly requires a historical horizon, then. But it is not the case that we acquire this horizon by transposing ourselves into a historical situation. Rather, we must always already have a horizon in order to be able to transpose ourselves into a situation. For what do we mean by "transposing ourselves"? Certainly not just disregarding ourselves. This is necessary, of course, insofar as we must imagine the other situation. But into this other situation we must bring, precisely, ourselves. Only this is the full meaning of "transposing ourselves." If we put ourselves in someone else's shoes, for example, then we will understand him – i.e., become aware of the otherness, the indissoluble individuality of the other person – by putting *ourselves* in his position.

Transposing ourselves consists neither in the empathy of one individual for another nor in subordinating another person to our own standards; rather, it always involves rising to a higher universality that overcomes not only our own particularity but also that of the other. The concept of "horizon" suggests itself because it expresses the superior breadth of vision that the person who is trying to understand must have. To acquire a horizon means that one learns to look beyond what is close at hand – not in order to look away from it but to see it better, within a larger whole and in truer proportion. To speak, with Nietzsche, of the many changing horizons into which historical consciousness teaches us to place ourselves is not a correct description. If we disregard ourselves in this way, we have no historical horizon. Nietzsche's view that historical study is deleterious to life is not, in fact, directed against historical consciousness as such, but against the self-alienation it undergoes when it regards the method of modern historical science as its own true nature. We have already pointed out that a truly historical consciousness always sees its own present in such a way that it sees itself, as well as the historically other, within the right relationships. It requires a special effort to acquire a historical horizon. We are always affected, in hope and fear, by what is nearest to us, and hence we approach the testimony of the past under its influence. Thus it is constantly necessary to guard against overhastily assimilating the past to our own expectations of meaning. Only then can we listen to tradition in a way that permits it to make its own meaning heard.

We have shown above that this is a process of foregrounding (*abheben*). Let us consider what this idea of foregrounding involves. It is always reciprocal. Whatever is being foregrounded must be foregrounded from something else, which, in turn, must be foregrounded from it. Thus all foregrounding also makes visible that from which something is foregrounded. We have described this above as the way prejudices are brought into play. We started by saying that a hermeneutical situation is determined by the prejudices that we bring with us. They constitute, then, the horizon of a particular present, for they represent that beyond which it is impossible to see. But now it is important to avoid the error of thinking that the horizon of the present consists of a fixed set of opinions and valuations, and that the otherness of the past can be foregrounded from it as from a fixed ground.

In fact the horizon of the present is continually in the process of being formed because we are continually having to test all our prejudices. An important part of this testing occurs in encountering the past and in understanding the tradition from which we come. Hence the horizon of the present cannot be formed without the past. There is no more an isolated horizon of the present in itself than there are historical horizons which have to be acquired. *Rather, understanding is always the fusion of these horizons supposedly existing by themselves.* We are familiar with the power of this kind of fusion chiefly from earlier times and their naivete about themselves and their heritage. In a tradition this process of fusion is continually going on, for there old and new are always combining into something of living value, without either being explicitly foregrounded from the other.

If, however, there is no such thing as these distinct horizons, why do we speak of the fusion of horizons and not simply of the formation of the one horizon, whose bounds are set in the depths of tradition? To ask the question means that we are recognizing that understanding becomes a scholarly task only under special circumstances and that it is necessary to work out these circumstances as a hermeneutical situation. Every encounter with tradition that takes place within historical consciousness involves the experience of a tension between the text and the present. The hermeneutic task consists in not covering up this tension by attempting a naive assimilation of the two but in consciously bringing it out. This is why it is part of the hermeneutic approach to project a historical horizon that is different from the horizon of the present. Historical consciousness is aware of its own otherness and hence foregrounds the horizon of the past from its own. On the other hand, it is itself, as we are trying to show, only something superimposed upon continuing tradition, and hence, it immediately recombines with what it has foregrounded itself from in order to become one with itself again in the unity of the historical horizon that it thus acquires.

Projecting a historical horizon, then, is only one phase in the process of understanding; it does not become solidified into the self-alienation of a past consciousness, but is overtaken by our own present horizon of understanding. In the process of understanding, a real fusing of horizons occurs – which means that as the historical horizon is projected, it is simultaneously superseded. To bring about this fusion in a regulated way is the task of what we called historically effected consciousness. Although this task was obscured by aesthetic-historical positivism following on the heels of romantic hermeneutics, it is, in fact, the central problem of hermeneutics. It is the problem of *application*, which is to be found in all understanding.

Notes

1 Heidegger, *Sein und Zeit*, Tübingen: Max Riemeyer, 1927), § 63, pp. 312 ff., trans. J. Macquarrie & E. Robinson, *Being and Time* (Oxford: Basil Blackwell, 1967), pp. 359 ff.
2 Cf. Schleiermacher's *Hermeneutik*, ed. Heinz Kimmerle in *Abhandlungen der Heidelberger Akademie*, (1959), 2nd *Abhandlung*, which is explicitly committed to the old ideal of an art formulated in rules (p. 127, n.: "I . . . hate it when theory does not go beyond nature and the bases of art, whose object it is").
3 Heidegger, *Sein und Zeit*, op. cit., p. 153; *Being and Time*, English translation, p. 195.
4 *Sein und Zeit*, pp. 312ff., *Being and Time*, pp. 359 ff.
5 Cf. Leo Strauss, *Die Religionskritik Spinozas*, p. 163: "The word 'prejudice' is the most suitable expression for the great aim of the Enlightenment, the desire for free, untrammeled verification; the *Vorurteil* is the unambiguous polemical correlate of the very ambiguous word 'freedom.'"
6 *Praeiudicium auctoritatis et precipitantiae*, which we find as early as Christian Thomasius' *Lectiones de praeiudiciis* (1689/90) and his *Einleitung der Vernunftlehre*, ch. 13, §§ 39–40. Cf. the article in Walch, *Philosophisches Lexikon* (1726), pp. 2794ff.

7 At the beginning of his essay, "What Is Enlightenment?" (1784).

8 The enlightenment of the classical world, the fruit of which was Greek philosophy and its culmination in sophism, was quite different in nature and hence permitted a thinker like Plato to use philosophical myths to convey the religious tradition and the dialectical method of philosophizing. Cf. Erich Frank, *Philosophische Erkenntnis und religiöse Wahrheit*, pp. 31ff., and my review of it in the *Theologische Rundschau*, (1950), pp. 260–66. And see especially Gerhard Krüger, *Einsicht und Leidenschaft* (2nd ed., 1951).

9 A good example of this is the length of time it has taken for the authority of the historical writing of antiquity to be destroyed in historical studies and how slowly the study of archives and the research into sources have established themselves (cf. R. G. Collingwood, *Autobiography* [Oxford, 1939], ch. 11, where he more or less draws a parallel between turning to the study of sources and the Baconian revolution in the study of nature).

10 As we find, for example, in G. F. Meier's *Beiträge zu der Lehre von den Vorurteilen des menschlichen Geschlechts* (1766).

11 Horkheimer and Adorno seem to me right in their analysis of the "dialectic of the Enlightenment" (although I must regard the application of sociological concepts such as "bourgeois" to Odysseus as a failure of historical reflection, if not, indeed, a confusion of Homer with Johann Heinrich Voss [author of the standard German translation of Homer], who had already been criticized by Goethe.

12 Walch, *Philosophisches Lexicon* (1726), p. 1013.

13 Walch, op. cit., pp. 1006ff. under the entry "Freiheit zu gedenken."

14 Schleiermacher, *Werke*, I, part 7, 31.

15 (It seems to me that the tendency to acknowledge authority, as for instance in Karl Jaspers, *Von der Wahrheit*, pp. 766ff., and Gerhard Krüger, *Freiheit und Weltverwaltung*, pp. 231ff., lacks an intelligible basis so long as this proposition is not acknowledged.) The notorious statement, "The party (or the Leader) is always right" is not wrong because it claims that a certain leadership is superior, but because it serves to shield the leadership, by a dictatorial decree, from any criticism that might be true. True authority does not have to be authoritarian. [This issue has meanwhile been much debated, particularly in my exchange with Jürgen Habermas. See *Hermeneutik und Ideologiekritik*, ed. Jürgen Habermas (Frankfurt, 1977) and my lecture at Solothurn, "Über den Zusammenhang von Autorität und kritischer Freiheit," *Schweizer Archiv für Neurologie, Neurochirurgie und Psychiatrie*, 133 (1983), 11–16. Arnold Gehlen especially has worked out the role of institutions.]

16 Cf. Aristotle, *Nichomachean Ethics*, X, 10.

17 I don't agree with Scheler that the preconscious pressure of tradition decreases as historical study proceeds (*Stellung des Menschen im Kosmos*, p. 37). The independence of historical study implied in this view seems to me a liberal fiction of a sort that Scheler is generally able to see through. (Cf. similarly in his *Nachlass*, 1, 228ff., where he affirms his faith in enlightenment through historical study or sociology of knowledge.)

18 *Nicomachean Ethics*, 1, 7.

19 [Here constantly arises the danger of "appropriating" the other person in one's own understanding and thereby failing to recognize his or her otherness.]

20 The structure of the concept of situation has been illuminated chiefly by Karl Jaspers, *Die geistige Situation der Zeit*, and Erich Rothacker.

21 Nietzsche, *Untimely Meditations*, II, at the beginning.

Part VIII

HANNAH ARENDT
Phenomenology of the Public World

HANNAH ARENDT (1906–1975)
Introduction

Hannah Arendt was born into a bourgeois family of assimilated Jews in Königsberg, East Prussia, in 1906. Due to anti-Semitism in school, she largely educated herself at home, developing a particular aptitude for classics. She entered Marburg University in 1924 to study theology with Rudolf Bultmann (1884–1976), but was soon drawn to philosophy through the lectures of Martin Heidegger, recently arrived from Freiburg. Heidegger's radical phenomenological readings of Plato and Aristotle were causing a storm among students. She embarked on an affair with the married Heidegger, but later in 1926, on his advice, transferred to the University of Heidelberg to work with Karl Jaspers, under whose supervision she completed her doctorate in 1929 with a thesis on *Saint Augustine's Concept of Love*. She also attended Husserl's lectures in Freiburg for a semester but was not at all inspired by his attempts to build phenomenology into a systematic philosophy.

Arendt planned a *Habilitation* thesis on the German Jewish writer and salon hostess Rahel Varnhagen (1771–1833), but, due to her political activities against Nazism, she was arrested and forced to flee Germany in 1933. She moved to Paris, where she worked with a Zionist organisation and met other *émigrés*, including Walter Benjamin and Alexandre Koyré, as well as the French philosophers Raymond Aron, Jean Wahl and Jean-Paul Sartre. In Paris she finally managed to complete her study of Rahel Varnhagen in 1938; however, the book, a phenomenological attempt to narrate Varnhagen's life from the inside, was not published until 1957. When the Second World War broke out, Arendt was detained by the French authorities in an internment camp from which she later escaped. Her partner, the communist activist Heinrich Blücher, was also detained, but was released, and the two eventually made their way to America. Arendt brought with her Walter Benjamin's papers, some of which she later edited.

Officially a stateless person, Arendt worked as a freelance political journalist, especially active in the defence of Jewish interests. She held part-time teaching positions at Brooklyn College, Wesleyan University, and later at Chicago, Princeton, and the New School for Social Research in New York, and wrote some famous essays for *The Nation* and the *New Yorker*. She visited Europe in 1949 where she met Heidegger for the first time since 1933, and thereafter they renewed their friendship. In 1961, as correspondent for the *New Yorker*, she attended the trial in Jerusalem of Adolf Eichmann, and her series of articles appeared as *Eichmann in Jerusalem. A Report on the Banality of Evil* (1963).

Arendt died in 1975. Her last book was published posthumously as *The Life of the Mind* in 1978, and her Kant lectures delivered at the New School for Social Research in 1970 appeared as *Lectures on Kant's Political Philosophy* in 1982. Her manuscripts and papers are preserved in the Library of Congress, Washington, DC and there is also an Arendt archive in Germany.

Arendt is now primarily known as a creative and original thinker in the area of politics, particularly regarded for her analyses of the nature of totalitarianism and of the circumstances which give rise to political life. Her major study, *The Origins of Totalitarianism*, was published in 1951, in which she argued that totalitarianism is only possible in modern society where everything is managed and manipulated, and individuals are isolated. However, her most important philosophical work, *The Human Condition. A Study of the Central Dilemmas Facing Modern Man* (1958) offers a broadly phenomenological account of human action in the public realm, drawing heavily on Aristotle and the ideal of the Greek city-state or *polis*, but also questioning the major Western tradition from Plato to Marx which locates human fulfilment in the theoretical life. For Arendt, the traditional emphasis on the theoretical is a betrayal of concrete practical life (*vita activa*). Arendt distinguishes between three levels of human activity that she labels "work", "labour" and "action". *Labour* involves the endlessly repetitive, enclosed world of the peasant, seeking nourishment, clothing, protection from the elements and so on, whereas Arendt understands *work* as the manufacture of goods, which, having an independent and enduring existence from the producers, take on a life of their own, thereby creating the human world of the marketplace. Work, however, leads to reification, as Marx saw, and to the instrumentalisation of the world. *Action*, for Arendt, is understood in an Aristotelian sense, namely as *political action*, *praxis*. For Arendt, the Greek *polis* opened a space where humans could freely interact with one another. It is only in the life of *action*, as opposed to the life of abstract thought, that humans become fully authentic. The realm of action is the realm where it is possible to achieve *arete*, excellence, where individuals seek to immortalise themselves through great deeds. The public space is the realm where individual achievements occur in the space made by a life lived with others, and is to be fundamentally distinguished from the private sphere of the *oikos* (household) and from what Arendt calls "the social", which refers to the modern management of mass society, involving the elimination of difference. Arendt wants to stand against such mass homogenisation of society by defending plurality: "plurality is specifically *the* condition . . . of all political life" (*The Human Condition*). Arendt's strict differentiation between the private and the public has been criticised by political theorists.

Our first reading is Arendt's 1946 essay, "What is Existenz Philosophy?", first published in *Partisan Review*. Here she lays out her criticisms of both Husserl's and Heidegger's approaches to phenomenology as overly systematic. She sees Husserl as expressing the predicament of modernity, namely the divorce between the subject and the world of objects, but as attempting to overcome this divorce through his move into the life of consciousness, whereas she sees Heidegger as intent upon reviving systematic ontology. She sides with her mentor Karl Jaspers, who stresses existential situations which force a kind of reflection that cannot be systematised but which can be effectively communicated as a kind of experience.

Our second reading, "Labor, Work, Action", is a lecture in which Arendt explains her conception of the distinction between different kinds of human activity she labels *labour*, *work* and *action*, categories already elaborated in *The Human Condition*. Arendt is interested in characterising the essence of the active life, conceived of, with a deliberate eye towards Aristotle's discussions in the *Nicomachean Ethics* and *Politics*, as the life of the free, independently minded citizen who deliberates and argues with others (in the plural) upon essential questions and enhances the public space by so doing. This active dialogical engagement in the political life of the state is to be contrasted with the model of contemplation as a withdrawal from active life which later developed during the Christian Middle Ages. On Arendt's account, action is inextricably wedded to speech and words, and hence to the human community. Because of human historicality and the contingency and unreliability of human affairs, actions in Arendt's sense rarely succeed, but what is produced is a web of stories and narratives, where each is called on to explain who he or she is. In the frailty of human affairs, and in the absence of a God or final end, Arendt finds a kind of redemption in the act of promising and forgiving, in the acts of promising to do something new, and releasing people from the prison of what they have done.

Further reading

Arendt, Hannah. *Between Past and Future: Eight Exercises in Political Thought*, 1961. Reprinted New York: Penguin, 1977.

Arendt, Hannah. *Crises of the Republic*. New York: Harcourt Brace Jovanovich, 1972.

Arendt, Hannah. *Eichmann in Jerusalem. A Report on the Banality of Evil*. Second Revised Edition. New York: Penguin, 1964.

Arendt, Hannah. *Essays in Understanding, 1930–1954*, ed. Jerome Kohn. New York: Harcourt Brace Jovanovich, 1994.

Arendt, Hannah. *Lectures on Kant's Political Philosophy*, ed. Ronald Beiner. Chicago, IL: University of Chicago Press, 1982.

Arendt, Hannah. *Love and St. Augustine*, ed. Joanna V. Scott and Judith C. Stark. Chicago, IL: University of Chicago Press, 1996.

Arendt, Hannah. *Men in Dark Times*. New York: Harcourt Brace Jovanovich, 1968.

Arendt, Hannah. *Rahel Varnhagen. The Life of A Jewish Woman*, trans. Richard and Clara Winston, Revised Edition. New York: Harcourt Brace Jovanovich, 1974.

Arendt, Hannah. *The Human Condition. A Study of the Central Dilemmas Facing Modern Man*. Chicago, IL: University of Chicago Press, 1958. (Second Edition Reprint, 1998.)

Arendt, Hannah. *The Life of the Mind. Vol. One: Thinking*. New York: Harcourt Brace & Co, 1971.

Arendt, Hannah. *The Life of the Mind. Vol. Two: Willing*. New York: Harcourt Brace & Co, 1978.

Arendt, Hannah. *The Origins of Totalitarianism*. New York: Harcourt Brace Jovanovich, 1951.

Benhabib, Seyla. *The Reluctant Modernism of Hannah Arendt*. London: Sage, 1996.

Canovan, Margaret. *The Political Thought of Hannah Arendt*. London: Dent, 1979.

Gottsegen, Michael S. *The Political Thought of Hannah Arendt*. Albany: SUNY Press, 1993.

Hill, Melvyn A. (ed.). *Hannah Arendt. The Recovery of the Public World*. New York: St. Martin's Press, 1979.

Hinchman, Lewis P. and Sandra K. Hinchman. Eds. *Hannah Arendt. Critical Essays*. Albany, NY: SUNY Press, 1993.

Honig, Bonnie (ed.). *Feminist Interpretations of Hannah Arendt*. University Park: University of Pennsylvania Press, 1995.

Kateb, George. *Hannah Arendt. Politics, Conscience, Evil*. Totowa, NJ: Rowman and Allanheld, 1984.

Passerin D'Entreves, Maurizio. *The Political Philosophy of Hannah Arendt*. London: Routledge, 1994.

Pitkin, Hannah Fenichel. *The Attack of the Blob: Hannah Arendt's Concept of the Social*. Chicago, IL: University of Chicago Press, 1998.

Taminiaux, Jacques. *The Thracian Maid and the Professional Thinker*, trans. Michael Gendre. Albany, NY: SUNY Press, 1997.

Villa, Dana R. *Arendt and Heidegger. The Fate of the Political*. Princeton, NJ: Princeton University Press, 1996.

Young-Bruehl, Elisabeth. *Hannah Arendt. For Love of the World*. New Haven, CT: Yale University Press, 1982.

1

WHAT IS EXISTENZ PHILOSOPHY?

As distinct from existentialism, a French literary movement of the last decade, Existenz philosophy has at least a century-old history. It began with Schelling in his late period and with Kierkegaard, developed in Nietzsche along a great number of as yet unexhausted possibilities, determined the essential part of Bergson's thought and of the so-called life-philosophy (*Lebensphilosophie*), until finally in postwar Germany, with Scheler, Heidegger, and Jaspers, it reached a consciousness, as yet unsurpassed, of what really is at stake in modern philosophy.

The term "Existenz" indicates, first, nothing more than the being of man, independent of all qualities and capacities that can be psychologically investigated. Thus far, what Heidegger once rightly remarked of "life-philosophy," that the name was about as meaningful as the botany of plants, also holds for Existenz philosophy. Except that there is no accident that the word "Being" is replaced by the word "Existenz." In this terminological change one of the fundamental problems of modern philosophy is, in fact, concealed.

Hegel's philosophy, which with a completeness never attained before, had explained and organized into a weirdly coherent whole all natural and historical phenomena, was truly "the owl of Minerva, that takes flight only in the evening." This system, immediately after Hegel's death, appeared to be the last word in the whole of western philosophy, in so far as western philosophy – despite all its variety and apparent contradictions – since Parmenides had not dared to doubt that: *to gar auto esti noein te kai einai*, being and thought are identical. What came after Hegel was either derivative, or it was a rebellion of the philosophers against philosophy in general, rebellion against or doubt of this identity.

This derivative character is peculiar to all the so-called schools of modern philosophy. They all seek to re-establish the unity of thought and being; whether they aim at this harmony in making matter (the materialists) or mind (the Idealists) dominant, is indifferent; indifferent also whether by playing with the notion of aspects they seek to establish a whole more spinozistic in character.

The phenomenological attempt at reconstruction

Among the derivative philosophical currents of the last hundred years the most modern and interesting are pragmatism and phenomenology. Phenomenology,

Hannah Arendt, *Partisan Review*, 1946, Vol. XIII, pp. 34–56.

above all, has exercised an influence on contemporary philosophy which is neither accidental nor due only to its method. Husserl sought to reestablish the ancient relation between Being and Thought, which had guaranteed man a home in this world, by a detour through the intentional structure of consciousness. Since every act of consciousness has by its very nature an object, I can at least be certain of one thing, namely that I "have" the object of my consciousness. Thereby the question of reality, altogether abstracted from the essence of things, can be "bracketed"; I have all Being as that which I am conscious of and as consciousness I am, in the manner of man, the Being of the world. (The *seen* tree, the tree as object of my consciousness, need not be the "real" tree, it is in any case the real object of my consciousness.)

The modern feeling of homelessness in the world has always ended up with things torn out of their functional context. A proof of this, scarcely to be overlooked, is modern literature and a good part of modern painting. However one may interpret this homelessness sociologically or psychologically, its philosophical basis lies in the fact that though the functional context of the world, in which also I myself am involved, can always justify and explain that there are, for example, tables and chairs generally, nevertheless it can never make me grasp conceptually that *this* table *is*. And it is the existence of *this* table, independent of tables in general, which evokes the philosophical shock.

Phenomenology appeared to master this problem, which is much more than merely theoretical. In its description of consciousness it grasped precisely these isolated things torn out of their functional context as the contents of arbitrary acts of consciousness and appeared to connect these up again with man through the "stream of consciousness." Indeed Husserl maintained that by this detour through consciousness and by starting from a complete grasp of all the factual contents of consciousness (a new *mathesis universalis*), he would be able to rebuild the world which had fallen to pieces. Such a reconstruction of the world from consciousness would equal a second creation, since in this reconstruction its contingent character, which is at the same time its character as reality, would be removed from the world, which would thus no longer appear as something given to man but as something created by him.

In this fundamental claim of phenomenology lies the most properly permanent and most modern attempt to find a new foundation for humanism. Hofmannsthal's famous farewell letter to Stefan George, in which he espouses "the little things" against big words, since precisely in these small things the secret of reality lies hidden, is most intimately bound up with the feeling of life from which phenomenology has arisen. Husserl and Hofmannsthal are equally classicists, if classicism is the attempt – through an imitation, consistent to the end, of the classic, founded upon man's being at home in the world – to evoke magically a home again out of the world which has become alien. Husserl's "to the things themselves" is no less a magic formula than Hofmannsthal's "little things." If one could still achieve something with magic – in an age whose only good is that it has forsworn all magic – then one would surely have to begin with the littlest and apparently most modest things, with homely "little things," with homely words.

It was due to this magical homeliness that Husserl's analysis of consciousness (which Jaspers, since he inclined neither to magic nor to classicism, found unimportant for philosophy) decisively influenced both Heidegger and Scheler in their youth, although Husserl was able to contribute little of its concrete content to Existenz philosophy. Contrary to the widespread opinion that Husserl's influence was only methodologically important, the fact is that he freed modern philosophy, to which he himself did not properly belong, from the fetters of historicism. Following Hegel and under the influence of an extraordinarily intensified interest in history, philosophy threatened to degenerate into speculation as to whether the historical flux exhibited possible laws or not. Here it is not relevant whether such speculations were optimistically or pessimistically colored, whether they sought to reckon progress as unavoidable or decline as predestined. The essential thing was that in both cases Man, in Herder's words, was like the ant that only crawls on the wheel of destiny. Husserl's insistence on "the things themselves," which eliminates such empty speculation and goes on to separate the phenomenally given content of a process from its genesis, had a liberating influence in that Man himself, and not the historical or natural or biological or psychological flux into which he is sucked, could once again become a theme of philosophy.

This separation has become much more important than Husserl's positive philosophy, in which he seeks to make us tranquil about a fact over which modern philosophy cannot become tranquil – that man is compelled to assent to a Being which he has never created and to which he is essentially alien. With the transformation of alien Being into consciousness he seeks to make the world again human, as Hofmannsthal with the magic of little things sought to awaken in us again the old fondness for the world. But what this modern humanism, this good will towards the modest and homely, is always *wrecked* upon is the equally modern *hubris* which lies at its basis and which furtively (in Hofmannsthal) or openly and naively (in Husserl) hopes, in this inconspicuous way, to become what man cannot be, creator of the world and of himself.

In opposition to the arrogant modesty of Husserl the modern philosophy which is underivative seeks along many paths to come to terms with the fact that man is not the creator of the world. Towards this end it searches further and further in the direction where it shows its best inclinations, to place man in the position where Schelling, in a moment of self-misunderstanding, placed God – in the position of "Master of Being."

Kant's demolition of the old world and Schelling's cry for a new one

The word "Existenz" in the modern sense appears, to my knowledge, for the first time in the later Schelling. Schelling knew exactly what he was rebelling against when over against "negative philosophy," against the philosophy of pure thought, he placed "positive philosophy," which proceeds from Existenz, which it has only as the pure "*That.*"

He knew that with this the philosopher said goodbye to the "contemplative life"; knew that it is the I AM, "which has given the signal for the revolution" of pure thought, no longer able "to explain the contingency and actuality of things," is overcome by "final despair." All modern irrationalism, all the modern hostility to mind and reason, has its basis in this despair.

With the knowledge that the What can never explain the That, modern philosophy begins with a dreadful collision against bare reality. The more one empties Reality of all qualities, the more immediately and nakedly appears the one thing that from now on is to be the only interesting one – *That* it is. Hence, this philosophy from its start glorifies contingency, since there Reality falls directly upon Man as altogether incalculable, unthinkable, and unforeseen. Hence the enumeration of the philosophical "extreme situations" (Jaspers), which means the situations in which Man is driven to philosophize, such as death, guilt, fate, chance, since in all these experiences Reality shows itself as something that cannot be evaded, cannot be resolved by thought. In these situations Man arrives at the consciousness that he is dependent – not upon some individual thing and not even upon some general character of Limitation, – but dependent on the fact that he *is*.

Therefore too, since essence obviously has nothing more to do with existence, modern philosophy turns away from the sciences, which investigate the *What* of things. As Kierkegaard would put it, the objective truth of science is indifferent since it is neutral to the question of Existenz, and the subjective truth of the "existing individual" is a paradox, since it can never be objective, never universally valid. Since Being and thought are no longer identical, since through thought I can no longer enter into the proper reality of things, since the nature of things has nothing to do with their reality, then science may be whatever it happens to be – in any case it no longer yields truth for man to possess, no truth that interests man. This turning away from science has often been misunderstood, especially because of Kierkegaard's example, as an attitude stemming from Christianity. To this philosophy, passionately intent upon Reality, it's no concern that, in view of another and truer world, occupation with the things of this world distracts one from salvation of the soul (as *curiositas* or *dispersio*). What this philosophy wishes is *this* world, *this* world completely, which has lost precisely only its character as Reality.

The unity of Being and thought presupposed the pre-established coincidence of essence and existence, that, namely, everything thinkable also exists and every existent, because it is knowable, must also be rational. This unity was destroyed by Kant, the true, if also clandestine, founder of the new philosophy: who has likewise remained till the present time its secret king. Kant's proof of the antinomy-structure of Reason, and his analysis of synthetic propositions which proves that in every proposition in which something is asserted about Reality we go beyond the concept (the *essentia*) of a given thing – had already robbed man of the ancient security in Being. Even Christianity had not attacked this security, but only reinterpreted it within "God's plan of salvation." Now, however, one could be sure neither of the meaning or Being of the Christian world, nor of the always present Being of the ancient Cosmos; and even the traditional definition of truth as *adequatio intellectus et rei* was no longer valid.

Already before Kant's revolutionising of the western conception of Being, Descartes had posed the question of Reality in a very modern sense, although he then gave an answer which was completely bound up with the traditional sense. The question whether Being, in general, *is*, is just as modern as the answer of the *cogito ergo sum* is useless; since this answer proves, as Nietzsche remarked, never the existence of the ego cogitans (the thinking ego), but at most the existence of the cogitare (the act of thought). In other words, the truly living "I" never arises from the I-think, but only an "I" as object of thought. We know this precisely from the time of Kant.

More depends than is commonly supposed in the history of secularization on Kant's destruction of the ancient unity of thought and Being. Kant's refutation of the ontological proof of God destroyed that rational belief in God which rested on the notion that what I can rationally conceive must also be; a notion which is not only older than Christianity, but probably also much more strongly rooted in European man since the Renaissance. This so-called atheising of the world – the knowledge, namely, that we cannot prove God through reason – touches the ancient philosophical concepts at least as much as the Christian religion. In this atheised world man can be interpreted in his "abandonment" or in his "individual autonomy." For every modern philosopher – and not only for Nietzsche – this interpretation becomes a touchstone of his philosophy.

Hegel was for us the last ancient philosopher, since he was the last to sneak past this question successfully. With Schelling modern philosophy begins, since he clearly explains that he is concerned with the individual who "wishes to have a providential God" who "is Master of Being," – whereby Schelling really intends the real man, the "individual freed of everything universal"; since "it is not the universal in man that longs after happiness, but the individual." In this astonishing directness of the individual's claim for happiness (after Kant's contempt for the ancient will to be happy it was not at all so simple to admit it again) there lies more than the desperate wish to return to the security of a Providence. What Kant hadn't understood, when he destroyed the ancient conception of Being, was that he was at the same time putting in question the Reality of everything beyond the individual; that, indeed, he implied what Schelling now directly says: "There exists nothing universal but only the individual, and the universal being exists only if it *is* the *absolute individual*."

With this position, which resulted immediately from Kant, the absolute and rationally conceivable kingdom of Ideas and universal values was at one stroke lopped off; and Man was placed in the middle of a world where he could no longer rely on anything, neither on his Reason, which clearly could not arrive at a knowledge of Being, nor on the Ideals of his Reason, whose existence was not provable, nor on the universal, since this existed only as he himself.

From now on the word "existing" is used always in opposition to that which is only thought of, only contemplated; as the concrete in opposition to the mere abstract; as the individual in contrast to the mere universal. Which means nothing more nor less than that philosophy, which since Plato has thought only in concepts, has now become mistrustful of the concept itself. Henceforth, philosophers never get rid of their bad conscience, so to speak, in the pursuit of philosophy.

Kant's destruction of the ancient conception of Being had as its purpose the establishing of the *autonomy* of man, what he himself called the dignity of man. He is the first philosopher who wishes to understand Man according to his own law, and who frees man from the universal context of Being, in which Man would be a thing among things (even if as *res cogitans* he is opposed to *res extensa*). In Lessing's sense, Man's coming of age is here established in thought, and it is no accident that this philosophic clarification of Man's coming of age coincides with the French Revolution. Kant is truly *the* philosopher of the French Revolution. As it was decisive for the development of the nineteenth century that nothing be quicker demolished than the new revolutionary concept of the *citoyen*, so was it decisive for the development of post-Kantian philosophy that nothing be quicker demolished than this new concept of Man, here for the first time developed in germ. Neither was an accident.

Kant's destruction of the ancient conception of Being accomplished only half the job. He destroyed the old identity of Being and thought and with it the notion of the pre-established harmony between Man and the world. What he did not destroy, but implicitly held on to, was the concept, equally old and intimately associated, of Being as the given, to whose laws Man is in all cases subject. Man could suffer this notion only so long as he had, in the feeling of his security in Being and his belonging to the world, at least the certainty that he could know Being and the course of the World. On it rested the ancient world's and the whole western world's conception of fate up to the nineteenth century (which means till the appearance of the novel); without this pride, tragedy as well as western philosophy would have been impossible. Likewise, Christianity had never denied that Man has an insight into God's plan of salvation; whether this insight be due to his own godlike reason or to God's revelation, is indifferent. In any case, he remained initiated into the secrets of the cosmos and the course of the world.

What holds for Kant's destruction of the ancient notion of Being, holds in stronger measure for his new concept of Man's freedom – a concept in which, oddly enough, the modern lack of freedom is indicated. According to Kant, Man has the possibility of determining his own actions out of the freedom of the good will; these actions themselves, however, fall under the causality of nature, a sphere essentially alien to Man. As soon as human action leaves subjectivity, which is freedom, it enters the objective sphere, which is causality, and loses its character as freedom. Man, free in himself, is hopelessly surrendered to the course of nature alien to him, a fate contrary to him, destructive of his freedom. Herein is expressed the contradictory structure of his human reality, so far as this plays its rôle in the world. While Kant made Man the master and measure of Man, at the same time he lowered him to a slave of Being. Every new philosopher since Schelling has protested against this devaluation. Modern philosophy is still occupied with this reduction of Man, who has just come of age. It is as if Man had never before risen so high and fallen so low.

Since Kant, every philosophy maintains an element of defiance, on the one hand, and an open or concealed concept of fate, on the other hand. Even Marx – who nevertheless, as he himself explained, wished no longer to interpret the world but to change it, and therefore stood on the crest of a new concept of Being and the World, in which Being and the World are no longer recognized as only given, but as a possible product of Man – quickly fled back to the old security when he agreed with Hegel that freedom is insight into necessity. Nietzsche's *amor fati*, Heidegger's Resoluteness, Camus's Defiance which would risk living despite the absurdity of the human condition, which consists in the homelessness of Man in the world, – are nothing else but this effort to save themselves by a return to security. The hero's gesture has not accidentally become *the* pose of philosophy since Nietzsche; it requires heroism to live in the world as Kant left it. Recent philosophers with their modern pose of the hero show only too plainly that they could follow Kant to the end in many directions, but not a step beyond him, if in fact they have not fallen, consistently and desperately, a few steps behind him. For they all, with the one great exception of Jaspers, have given up at some point Kant's basic conception of freedom and dignity. When Schelling desired to "have" the "real Master of Being," he wished again to participate in the movement of the world, from which, since Kant, the free man had been excluded. Schelling flees again to a philosophic God, precisely because he accepts from Kant "the fact of decline," without, however, making use of Kant's extraordinary calmness in simply coming to terms with it. For Kant's tranquillity, which seems so imposing to us, is in the end due only to the fact that he was strongly rooted in the tradition that philosophy is essentially identical with contemplation – a tradition which Kant himself unconsciously destroyed. Schelling's "positive philosophy" seeks refuge in God, in order that he "may oppose the fact of *defection*," in order that he may bring Man – who, as soon as he found freedom, lost his Reality – to a Reality.

The reason why Schelling is usually overlooked in discussions of Existenz philosophy is that no philosopher has taken his path towards the solution of Kant's difficulties concerning subjective freedom and objective necessity. Instead of a "positive philosophy" they sought (with the exception of Nietzsche) to reinterpret Man, in order that he might enter again into this world that robs him of value; his failure was to belong to his Being and not merely to be his fate, his failure was to be due not to a nature hostile to him, because it was completely determined by causal law, but was already to be traced in his own nature. Hence Kant's concepts of human freedom and dignity, as well as of humanity, as the regulative principle of all political action, were abandoned and there arose that distinctive melancholy which, since Kierkegaard, has been the hallmark of all except the most superficial philosophy. It always appeared more attractive to be subjected to "decline" as an inner law of human Existenz, rather than to meet one's fall through the alien, causally organized world. The first of these philosophers is Kierkegaard.

The birth of the self: Kierkegaard

Modern Existenz philosophy begins with Kierkegaard. There are no Existenz philosophers on whom his influence would not be traceable. Kierkegaard himself sets out consciously from a critique of Hegel (and, one might add, the unmentioned influence of Schelling, whose later philosophy he knew from lectures). To the Hegelian system, which pretended to grasp and explain the "whole," he opposed the "single person," the individual man, for whom neither place nor meaning was left in the Whole directed by the World-Mind. In other words, Kierkegaard starts from the forlornness of the individual in the completely explained world. The individual finds himself in permanent contradiction to this explained world, since his "Existenz," namely the pure factual character of his existing in all its contingency (that, precisely, I am *I* and no one else, and that, precisely, I *am* rather than am not), can be neither foreseen by reason nor resolved into something purely thinkable.

But this Existenz, which I am continually but momentarily, and which I cannot grasp by Reason, is the only thing of which I can be unquestionably certain. Thus, man's task is to "become subjective," a consciously existing being, who perpetually realizes the paradoxical implications of his life in the world. All essential questions of philosophy – as, say, the immortality of the soul, human freedom, the unity of the world, which means all the questions whose contradictory structure Kant had shown in his antinomies of pure Reason – are to be grasped only as "subjective truths," not to be known as objective truths. The example of an "existing" philosopher is Socrates with his "If there is immortality." "Was he thus a doubter?" Kierkegaard begins one of the greatest interpretations in all his works which are so rich in interpretations. "Not at all. On this 'if' he stakes his whole life, he dares to die – the Socratic uncertainty was thus the expression of the fact that the eternal truth is related to an existing individual, and hence must remain a paradox to him so long as he exists."

Thus the universal, with which philosophy has so long been occupied in the task of pure knowledge, is to be brought into a real relation with Man. This relation can only be paradoxical insofar as Man is always an individual. In the paradox the individual can grasp the universal, make it the content of his Existenz, and thereby lead that paradoxical life, which Kierkegaard reports about himself. In the paradoxical life Man seeks to realize the contradiction that "the universal is staked as the individual" if it is to become at all real and meaningful for Man. Kierkegaard therefore interprets such a life later in the category of "exception," – an exception, namely, from the universal average everyday human existence; an exception on which man decides only because God has called him to it in order to establish an example of how the paradox of man's life in the world is posed. In the exception man realizes the universal structure of human reality. It is characteristic of all of Existenz philosophy, that by "existential" it fundamentally understands what Kierkegaard had presented in the category of the Exception. The existential attitude turns about the realizing (in opposition to that which is only contemplated) of the most universal structures of life.

The passion to become subjective flares up in Kierkegaard with the realized anxiety before death as the event in which I alone am guaranteed as an individual, separated from average everyday life. The thought of death becomes an action, since in it man makes himself subjective, withdraws from the world and from everyday life with other men. Psychologically, this inner technique of reflection has simply as its basis the supposition that with the thought that I shall no longer be, my interest in what is must also be extinguished. On this presupposition rests not only modern "Inwardness," but also the fanatical resoluteness, which enters likewise in Kierkegaard, to seize earnestly the moment, – since only in the moment is Existenz, namely Reality, guaranteed.

This new earnestness towards life, which recoils from death, did not at all imply necessarily a Yea to life or to the human reality of man as such. In fact, only Nietzsche and, following him, Jaspers, have made such a Yea the groundwork of their philosophy; and this is also the reason why a positive way leads from their philosophical investigations to philosophy. Kierkegaard, and Heidegger after him, have always interpreted death as the peculiar "objection" against the Being of Man, as proof of his nothingness – in which, possibly, Heidegger's analysis of death and the character of human life bound up with it surpasses that of Kierkegaard in cogency and precision. The new French school, especially Camus and Sartre, if they have not thought out Heidegger's results to the end, have at least perceived what the end is, and have consequently arrived at a philosophy, which has scarcely a place for the anxiety before death, since it is so full of nausea towards life, – as it were, overcome by the sheer *That* of Being. "Quelle saleté, quelle saleté," Sartre cries out (in *La Nausée*), as he discovers that he cannot think the Nothing, since everything, absolutely everything "exists," has reality.

It is clear that Kierkegaard's peculiar inner activity, his "becoming subjective," immediately leads us out of philosophy. It goes with philosophy only in so far as philosophic grounds for the philosopher's revolt against philosophy must be found. Similarly, though at the directly opposite pole, lies the case of Marx, who likewise explained philosophically that man can change the world and hence should cease to interpret it. Common to both was the fact that they immediately wished to arrive at activity and did not get the idea of beginning philosophy on a new basis after they had once begun to doubt the prerogatives of contemplation and to despair of the possibility of a purely contemplative knowledge. The result was that Kierkegaard took refuge in psychology in the description of inner activity, Marx in political science in the description of external activity. With the difference, to be sure, that Marx again accepted the certainty of Hegelian philosophy, which his "turning it on its head" changed less than he supposed. It was not so decisive for philosophy that Hegel's principle of mind was replaced by Marx's principle of matter, as that the unity of man and the world was restored in a doctrinaire, purely hypothetical manner – hence, one not convincing to modern man.

Since Kierkegaard held fast to his despair with philosophy, he has become so much the more important for the later development of philosophy. Philosophy has taken over from him all its new concrete contents. These are, essentially, the following: *Death* as guarantee of the *principium individuationis*, since death, as the most common of occurrences, nevertheless strikes me unavoidably alone. *Contingency* as guarantee of reality as only given, which overwhelms and persuades me precisely through its incalculability and irreducibility to thought. *Guilt* as the category of all human activity, which is wrecked not upon the world but upon itself, insofar as I always take responsibilities upon myself which I cannot overlook, and am compelled through my decisions themselves to neglect other activity. Guilt is thus the mode and the manner in which I myself become real, plunge into reality.

In full explicitness these new contents of philosophy appear for the first time in Jaspers' *Psychologie der Weltanschauungen* [*Psychology of Worldviews*] as "Extreme situations" (*Grenzsituationen*), in which Man is placed because of the contradictory structure of his human reality and which give him his proper impulse to philosophize. Jaspers himself seeks to found a new kind of philosophy on the basis of these situations, and he adds to the content he has taken over from Kierkegaard something further, which he now calls struggle, now love, but which later becomes, in his theory of communication, the new form of philosophic intelligence. As opposed to Jaspers, Heidegger seeks with the new content to revive Systematic Philosophy in the completely traditional sense.

The self as all and nothing: Heidegger

Heidegger's attempt, despite and against Kant, to re-establish an ontology led to a far-reaching alteration of the traditional philosophical terminology. For this reason Heidegger always appears on first glance more revolutionary than Jaspers, and this terminological appearance has very much interfered with the correct estimate of his philosophy. He says explicitly that he wishes to found an ontology, and he can have nothing else in mind than to undo the destruction, begun with Kant, of the ancient concept of Being. One cannot escape taking this seriously even if one should arrive at the knowledge that on the basis of this content, which arises from the revolt against philosophy, no ontology in the traditional sense can be re-established.[1] Heidegger has not really established his ontology, since the second volume of *Sein und Zeit* has never appeared. To the question concerning the meaning of Being he has given the provisional answer, in itself unintelligible, that the meaning of Being is temporality. With this he implied, and with his analysis of human reality (i.e., of the Being of Man), which is conditioned by death, he established that the meaning of Being is nothingness. Thus Heidegger's attempt to find a new foundation for metaphysics ends consistently not with the second promised volume, which was to determine the meaning of Being generally on the basis of the analysis of human Being, but with a small brochure *What is Metaphysics?*, in which it is quite consistently shown, despite all tricks and sophistries of speech, that Being in the Heideggerian sense is the Nothing.

The peculiar fascination, which the thought of the Nothing has exercised on modern philosophy, is not simply characteristic of Nihilism. If we look at the problem of the Nothing in our context of a philosophy revolting against philosophy as pure contemplation, then we see it as an effort to become "Master of Being" and thereby to question philosophically in such a manner that we progress immediately to the deed; thus the thought that Being is really the Nothing has a tremendous advantage. Basing himself on this, Man can imagine himself, can relate himself to Being that is given, no less than the Creator before the creation of the world, which, as we know, was created out of nothing. In the characterizing of Being as Nothing there is, finally, the attempt to get away from the definition of Being as the given, and to transform the activities of Man from being godlike to being divine. This is also the real reason why in Heidegger the Nothing suddenly becomes active and begins to "nothing." The Nothing tries, so to speak, to reduce to nothing the given-ness of Being, and to put itself in Being's place. If Being, which I have not created, is the occasion of a nature which I am not and do not know, then perhaps the Nothing is the really free domain of Man. Since I am not a world-creating being, perhaps my nature is to be a world-destroying being. (These conclusions are now quite freely and clearly developed in Camus and Sartre.) This, in any case, is the philosophical basis for modern Nihilism, its origin in the old ontology; the attempt to stretch the new questions and content to the old framework here takes its revenge.

But whatever the point of departure of Heidegger's attempt, its great advantage was that it took up directly the questions which Kant had interrupted and which nobody after him had broached. Amid the ruins of the ancient pre-established harmony of Being and thought, of essence and existence, of the existing being and the What of the existing being conceivable through reason, – Heidegger maintains that he has found a being, in whom essence and existence are immediately identical, and this is Man. His essence is his existence. "The substance of Man is not mind . . . but Existenz." Man has no substance, the important thing is *that* he is; one cannot ask after Man's What as after the What of a thing, but only after his Who. Man as the identity of Existenz and essence appeared to give a new key to the question concerning Being in general. One need only recall that for traditional metaphysics God was the being in whom essence and existence coincided, in whom thought and activity were identical, and who was therefore interpreted as the otherworldly ground for all this world's Being, – in order to understand how seductive this scheme was. It was, in fact, the attempt to make Man directly the "Master of Being."

The Being of Man Heidegger calls Existenz or *Dasein*. Through establishing this terminology, he gets away from using the expression "Man." This is not arbitrary terminology, its purpose is to resolve Man into a series of modes of Being which are phenomenologically demonstrable. Hence he discards all those characteristics of Man which Kant had provisionally sketched as freedom, human dignity, and Reason; and which arise from the spontaneity of Man and hence are not phenomenologically demonstrable, since, being spontaneous, they are more than mere functions of Being, and since in them Man intends more than himself. Heidegger's ontological approach hides a rigid functionalism in which Man appears only as a conglomerate of modes of Being, which is in principle arbitrary, since no concept of Man determines the modes of his Being.

The "Self" has entered in place of Man: "With the expression Self we answer the question concerning the Who of human reality." For human reality (the Being of Man) is singled out by the fact that "in its very Being it is concerned with its Being." This self-reflexive character of human reality can be "existentially" grasped; which is all that remains of Man's power and freedom.

This grasping of one's own Existenz is, according to Heidegger, the act of philosophising itself: "philosophical questioning must be existentially seized as a possibility inherent in the Being of existing human reality." Philosophy is the exceptional existential possibility of human reality – which is, in the end, only a reformulation of Aristotle's *Bios Theoretikos*, of the contemplative life as the highest possibility for man. This is all the more intensified by the fact that in Heidegger's philosophy Man is made a kind of *summum ens*, the "Master of Being," insofar as existence and essence are identical in him. After Man was discovered as the being for whom he had so long taken God, it appears that such a being is also, in fact, powerless, and that there is no "Master of Being." The only things that remain are anarchical modes of Being.

Human reality is thus characterized by the fact not that it simply *is*, but that its very Being is to put its own Being at stake. This fundamental structure is "Care," which lies at the basis of all our everyday carefulness in the world. Carefulness, taking care, has truly a self-reflexive character; it is only apparently directed towards the object with which it is occupied.

The Being, for which human reality is care-ridden, is "Existenz," which, perpetually threatened by death, is condemned in the end to extinction. Human reality stands continuously in relation to Existenz thus menaced; and from this point of view all attitudes are to be understood, and the analysis of Man coherently made. The structures of Man's Existenz, namely the structures of his That, Heidegger calls *existential*, and their structural interrelatedness *existentiality*. The individual possibility of grasping these existential structures and thereby of *existing* in an explicit sense, Heidegger calls *existentiele*. In this concept of the existential, the question, never put to rest since Schelling and Kierkegaard, how the universal can *be*, comes out into the open, together with the answer which had already been given by Kierkegaard.

Seen from the point of view of Nietzsche, who had always nobly tried to make Man a real "Master of Being," Heidegger's philosophy is the first absolutely and uncompromisingly this-worldly philosophy. Man's Being is characterized as Being-in-the-world, and what is at stake for this Being in the world is, finally, nothing else than to maintain himself in the world. Precisely this is not given him; hence the fundamental character of Being-in-the-world is uneasiness in the double meaning of homelessness and fearfulness. In anxiety, which is fundamentally anxiety before death, the not-being-at-home in the world becomes explicit. "Being-in-the-world appears in the existentiel mode of not-being-at-home." This is uneasiness.

Human reality would be truly itself only if it could withdraw from this Being-in-the-world to itself; which it essentially never can do, hence is always essentially a decline, a falling away, from itself. "Human reality always falls away from itself as a real unity – declines into the 'world'." Only in the realization of death, which will take him away from the world, has Man the certainty of being himself.

By bringing back reality to the Self without the detour through Man, the question concerning the meaning of Being has fundamentally been given up, and replaced by the question, obviously more basic to this philosophy, concerning the meaning of the Self. But this question appears, in fact, unanswerable, since a Self taken in its absolute isolation is meaningless; if not isolated, on the other hand, it becomes (sunk to the everyday life of the public individual) no longer a Self. Heidegger arrives at this ideal of the Self as a consequence of his making Man what God was in the earlier ontology. Such a highest being is, in fact, possible only as a unique individual being who knows no equals. What, consequently, appears as "Fall" in Heidegger, are all those modes of human existence which rest on the fact that Man lives together in the world with his fellows. To put it historically, Heidegger's Self is an ideal which has been working mischief in German philosophy and literature since Romanticism. In Heidegger this arrogant passion to will to be a Self has contradicted itself; for never before was it so clear as in his philosophy that this is probably the one being which Man cannot be.

Within the framework of this philosophy the Self "falls" in the following way: as Being-in-the-world Man has not made himself, but has been "thrown" into this his Being. He seeks to escape from the condition of being thrown through the "project" which always anticipates death as his most extreme possibility. But "in the structure of being thrown (*Geworfenheit*) as in the project there lies essentially a Nothingness": Man has not contrived to bring himself to be and he usually does not contrive to escape from being. (Suicide plays no role in Heidegger; Camus, in maintaining "*Il n'y a qu'un problème philosophique vraiment sérieux: c'est le suicide,*" is the first to draw from this position a consequence which is contrary to Heidegger, since the latter does not leave Man even the freedom of suicide.) In other words, the character of Man's Being is essentially determined by what he is *not*, his nothingness. The only thing the Self can do to become a Self is to take upon itself "resolutely" this factual character of its Being, so that in its Existenz it "*is* the void (*nichtig*) ground of its nothingness."

In the "resoluteness" to become what Man on the basis of his nothingness cannot be, namely a Self, Man recognizes that "human reality *as such* is guilty." The Being of Man is such that, perpetually falling to the world, it perpetually hears the "Cry of conscience from the ground of its Being." Existentially, living means therefore: "The Will-to-have-conscience resolves to be guilty."

The most essential characteristic of this Self is its absolute egoism, its radical separation from all its fellows. The anticipation of death as existential was introduced to achieve this; for in death Man realizes the absolute *principium individuationis*. Death alone tears him from the context of his fellows, within which he becomes a public person and is hindered from being a Self. Death may indeed be the end of human reality; at the same time it is the guarantee that nothing matters but myself. With the experience of death as nothingness I have the chance of devoting myself exclusively to being a Self, and once and for all freeing myself from the surrounding world.

In this absolute isolation, the Self emerges as the concept really contrary to Man. If, namely, since Kant the nature of Man consisted in the fact that every individual man represents humanity; and if since the French Revolution and the rationalizing of human law it belonged to the concept of Man that in every single individual humanity can be debased or exalted; then the Self is the concept of Man according to which he can exist independently of humanity and need represent no one but himself – his own nothingness. As the Categorical Imperative in Kant asserted that every action must assume responsibility for all humanity, so the experience of guilty nothingness would precisely eliminate the presence of humanity in every man. The Self as conscience has put itself in place of humanity, and the Being of the Self in place of the Being of Man.

Heidegger has therefore attempted in later lectures to bring in, by way of afterthought, such mythologizing confusions as Folk and Earth as a social foundation for his isolated Selves. It is evident that such conceptions can lead one only out of philosophy into some naturalistic superstition. If it is not part of the concept of Man that he inhabits the world with his fellows, then there remains only a mechanical reconciliation by which the atomised Self is given a substratum essentially discordant with its own concept. This can only serve to organize the Selves engaged in willing themselves into an Over-self, in order to make a transition from the fundamental guilt, grasped through resoluteness, to action.

Indications of human Existenz: Jaspers

From an historical point of view, it would have been more correct to have begun the discussion of contemporary Existenz philosophy with Jaspers. The *Psychologie der Weltanschauungen*, first printed in 1919, is undoubtedly the first book of the new "school." On the other hand, there was not only the external circumstance that Jaspers' big *Philosophie* (in three volumes) appeared some five years after *Sein und Zeit*, but also, more significantly, the fact that Jaspers' philosophy is not really closed and is at the same time more modern. By modern we mean no more than that it immediately yields more clues for contemporary philosophical thinking. There are such clues, naturally, also in Heidegger; but they have the peculiarity that they can lead either only to clues for polemic or to the occasion of a radicalization of Heidegger's project – as in contemporary French philosophy. In other words, either Heidegger has said his last word on the condition of contemporary philosophy or he will have to break with his own philosophy. While

Jaspers belongs without any such break to contemporary philosophy, and will develop and decisively intervene in its discussion.

Jaspers achieved his break with the traditional philosophy in his *Psychologie der Weltanschauungen*, where he represents and relativizes all philosophical systems as mythologizing structures, in which Man, seeking protection, flees before the real questions of his Existenz. A *Weltanschauung* [*worldview*] which pretends to have grasped the meaning of Being, systems as "formulated doctrines of the Whole," are for Jaspers only shells which "drain the experience of extreme situations" and confer a peace of mind which is fundamentally unphilosophical. From these extreme situations he seeks to project a new type of philosophising, in which he invokes Kierkegaard and Nietzsche; this new philosophizing will, above all, teach nothing; it will be, rather, a "perpetual shaking up, a perpetual *appeal* (my italics) to the powers of life in oneself and others." In this manner Jaspers places himself in the revolt, fundamental to the new philosophy, of the philosophers against philosophy. He seeks to dissolve philosophy in philosophizing and to find ways in which philosophical "results" can be so communicated that they lose their character as results.

One of the principal problems of this philosophy becomes therefore the question of communicability generally. Communication is the extraordinary form of philosophic intelligence; at the same time it goes along with philosophizing, in which there is no question of results but of the "Illumination of Existenz." The affinity of this method to the Socratic maieutic is evident; except that what Socrates calls maieutic, Jaspers calls appeal. This difference in stress is again no accident. Jaspers searches, in fact, with the Socratic method, but by removing its pedagogical character. In Jaspers, as in Socrates, there does not exist *the* philosopher, who (since Aristotle) has led an Existenz singled out from other men. Nor with him does the Socratic priority of the questioner exist; for in communication the philosopher moves among his fellows, to whom he appeals as they in turn can appeal to him. Thereby philosophy has left the sphere of the sciences and specializations, the philosopher has deprived himself of every specialized prerogative.

In so far as Jaspers communicates "results," he puts them in the form of "playful metaphysics," in the form of a perpetually experimenting, never fixed representation of definite movements of thought, which have at the same time the character of proposals that men can be brought to work with – namely, to philosophize with.

Existenz is for Jaspers no form of Being, but a form of human freedom and indeed the form in which "Man as possibility of his spontaneity turns against his mere Being-a-result." Man's Being as such and as given is not Existenz, but "Man is in his human reality possible Existenz." Thus the word "Existenz" expresses the meaning that only in so far as Man moves in the freedom that rests upon his own spontaneity and is "directed in communication to the freedom of others," is there Reality for him.

Thus the question concerning the That of reality, which cannot be resolved into thought, acquires a new meaning without losing its character as real. The That of Being as the given – whether as the reality of the world, as the incalculability of one's fellow men, or the fact that I have not created myself – becomes the backdrop against which man's freedom emerges, becomes at the same time the stuff which kindles it. That I cannot resolve the real to the object of thought becomes the triumph of possible freedom. In this context the question concerning the meaning of Being can be so suspended that the answer to it runs: "Being is such that this human reality is possible."

We become aware of Being by a process of thought which proceeds from "the illusory world of the thinkable" to the limits of Reality, which is no longer to be grasped as pure object of thought or pure possibility. This bringing oneself in thought to the limits of the thinkable Jaspers calls *transcending*; and his "playful metaphysics" is an ordered enumeration of such movements of thought which transcend, overstep themselves. The decisive thing for these movements is that Man as "master of his thoughts" is more than anyone of these movements of thought, so that philosophising itself does not become a highest existential mode of Man's Being, but rather a preparation for the reality both of myself and the world. "Brought into suspense by passing beyond all knowledge of the world which would fix Being, philosophizing sounds the appeal to my freedom and creates the space for an unconditioned deed that would invoke transcendence." This "deed" arising out of extreme situations appears in the world through communication with others, who as my fellows and through the appeal to our common reason guaranteed the universal; through activity it carries out the freedom of Man in the world and becomes thereby "a seed, though perishing, of the creation of a world."

In Jaspers, thinking has the function of leading Man to determinate experience, in which thought itself (though not the thinking man) fails. In the foundering of thought (and not of the man) Man, – who is more than thought, because more real and more free – experiences what Jaspers calls "the cipher of transcendence." That transcendence is experienced as a cipher only in foundering, is itself a sign of Existenz, which "is aware not only that as human reality it has not created itself and that as human reality it is helplessly surrendered to inevitable destruction, but also that even as freedom it is not indebted to itself alone." That transcendence is experienced in failure is a sign of the limitation of human Existenz.

Jaspers' "failure" is not to be confused with what Heidegger called "Fall" or "Decline"; which latter Jaspers himself calls "Slipping away" (*Abgleiten*). In Jaspers this latter is described in many ways, is psychologically explicable, but is not (as in Heidegger) a structurally necessary Fall from one's authentic Being as a man. Jaspers holds that in philosophy every ontology claiming it can say what Being really is, is a Slipping-away into the absolutizing of particular categories of Being. The existentiel meaning of such Slipping-away would be that such a philosophy robs Man of a freedom which can persist only so long as Man does not know what Being really is.

Expressed formally, Being is transcendence and as such a "reality without transformation into possibility"; something which I can't represent to myself as not being – which, in principle, I can do for every individual thing that is. Through the fact that my thinking fails on the That of Reality, the "weight of Reality" first becomes felt. In this measure the failure of thought is the condition for Existenz, which as free always seeks to transcend the merely given world; the condition, namely, for the fact that Existenz, encountering this "weight of Reality" inserts itself into it and belongs to it in the only way in which Man can belong to it – in that he chooses it.

In this failure Man experiences the fact that he can neither know nor create Being and that thus he is not God. In this experience he realizes the limitation of his Existenz, the limits of which he tries to trace in philosophizing. In the failing transcendence of all limits he experiences Reality given to him as the cipher of a Being which he himself is not.

The task of philosophy is to free Man from "the illusory world of the pure object of thought" and "let him find his way home to Reality." Philosophic thought can never cancel the fact that Reality cannot be resolved into the thinkable; its job is rather "to aggravate . . . this unthinkability." This is all the more urgent in that the "reality of the thinker precedes his thought" and his real freedom alone decides what he thinks and what not.

The real content of Jaspers' philosophy is not to be summarized in the form of a report, since this content lies essentially in the ways and movements of his philosophizing. In this fashion Jaspers has come to all the fundamental problems of contemporary philosophy, without answering or settling any of them in a conclusive way. He has singled out for modern philosophy the ways it must travel if it is not to get stuck in the blind alley of a positivistic or nihilistic fanaticism.

The most important among these ways appear to be the following: Being as such is not knowable, it is to be experienced only as something "surrounding" us. Thus the very ancient search for an ontology is liquidated – a search which looked for Being in the existant, so to speak, as if for a magical all-pervasive substance, which makes present everything that is, and which appears in language in the little word "is." With the liberation of this world from the ghost of Being and the illusion of being able to understand it, there disappeared the necessity of having to explain it monistically from one principle – namely, from this all-pervasive substance. Instead of which, the "discordance of Being" (where this Being does not mean the Being of ontologies) can be admitted; and the modern feeling of alienation in the world can be taken into account, as well as the modern will to create a human world which can be a home within a world which is no longer a home. It is as if with this concept of Being as that which "surrounds" us in fluid contour there were traced an island, on which Man, unmenaced by the dark Unknowable, that in traditional philosophy pervades every existant like an additional quality – can freely rule and choose.

The limits of this island of human freedom are traced out in the "extreme situations," in which man experiences the limitations which immediately become the conditions of his freedom and the ground of his activity. Proceeding from them, he can "illuminate" his Existenz, trace out what he can and cannot do: and thereby from mere "Being as a result" pass to "Existenz" – which, in Jaspers, is only another, and more explicit, word for being a man.

Existenz itself is never essentially isolated; it exists only in communication and in the knowledge of the Existenz of others. One's fellow men are not (as in Heidegger) an element which, though structurally necessary, nevertheless destroys Existenz; but, on the contrary, Existenz can develop only in the togetherness of men in the common given world. In the concept of communication there lies embedded, though not fully developed, a new concept of humanity as the condition for man's Existenz. In any case, men move together within this "surrounding" Being; and they hunt neither the phantom of the Self nor do they live in the arrogant illusion that they can be Being generally.

Through the essentially human movement of transcendence through thought, and of the failure of thought bound up with this, we at least arrive at the conclusion that Man, as "Master of his thoughts," not only is more than any of his thoughts (and this would probably be the fundamental condition for a new definition of human dignity), but that from the first man's nature is to be more than himself and to will more than himself. With this, Existenz philosophy has left the period of its egoism.

Note

1 Another question worth discussing is whether Heidegger's philosophy has not generally been taken too seriously, simply because it deals with the most serious things. In any case, Heidegger has done everything to warn us that we should take him seriously. As is well known, he entered the Nazi Party in a very sensational way in 1933 – an act which made him stand out pretty much by himself among colleagues of the same calibre. Further, in his capacity as Rector of Freiburg University, he forbade Husserl, his teacher and friend, whose lecture chair he had inherited, to enter the faculty, because Husserl was a Jew. Finally, it has been rumored that he has placed himself at the disposal of the French occupational authorities for the re-education of the German people.

In view of the real comedy of this development, and of the no less real low level of political thought in German universities, one is naturally inclined not to bother with the whole story. On the other hand, there is the point that this whole mode of behavior has exact parallels in German Romanticism, so that one can scarcely believe the coincidence is accidental. Heidegger is, in fact, the last (we hope) romantic – as it were, a tremendously gifted Friedrich Schlegel or Adam Mueller, whose complete irresponsibility was attributed partly to the delusion of genius, partly to desperation.

2

LABOR, WORK, ACTION

For this short hour, I should like to raise an apparently odd question. My question is: What does an active life consist of? What do we do when we are active? In asking this question, I shall assume that the age-old distinction between two ways of life, between a *vita contemplativa* and a *vita activa*, which we encounter in our tradition of philosophical and religious thought up to the threshold of the modern age, is valid, and that when we speak of contemplation and action we speak not only of certain human faculties but of two distinct ways of life. Surely, the question is of some relevance. For even if we don't contest the traditional assumption that contemplation is of a higher order than action, or that all action actually is but a means whose true end is contemplation, we can't doubt – and no one ever doubted – that it is quite possible for human beings to go through life without ever indulging in contemplation, while, on the other hand, no man can remain in the contemplative state throughout his life. Active life, in other words, is not only what most men are engaged in but even what no man can escape altogether. For it is in the nature of the human condition that contemplation remains dependent upon all sorts of activities – it depends upon labor to produce whatever is necessary to keep the human organism alive, it depends upon work to create whatever is needed to house the human body, and it needs action in order to organize the living together of many human beings in such a way that peace, the condition for the quiet of contemplation is assured.

Since I started with our tradition, I just described the three chief articulations of active life in a traditional way, that is, as serving the ends of contemplation. It is only natural that active life has always been described by those who themselves followed the contemplative way of life. Hence, the *vita activa* was always defined from the viewpoint of contemplation; compared with the absolute quiet of contemplation, all sorts of human activity appeared to be similar insofar as they were characterized by un-quiet, by something negative: by *a-skholia* or by *nec-octium*, non-leisure or absence of the conditions which make contemplation possible. Compared with this attitude of quiet, all distinctions and articulations within the *vita activa* disappear. Seen from the viewpoint of contemplation, it does not matter what disturbs the necessary quiet so long as it is disturbed.

Traditionally therefore the *vita activa* received its meaning from the *vita*

H. Arendt, *Amor Mundi. Explorations in the Faith and Thought of Hannah Arendt*, 1987, ed. James W. Bernauer, pp. 29–42. Dordrecht: Nijhoff.

contemplativa; a very restricted dignity was bestowed upon it because it served the needs and wants of contemplation in a living body. Christianity with its belief in a hereafter, whose joys announce themselves in the delights of contemplation, conferred a religious sanction upon the abasement of the *vita activa* while, on the other hand, the command to love your neighbor acted as a counterweight against this estimation unknown to antiquity. But the determination of the order itself, according to which contemplation was the highest of the human faculties, was Greek, and not Christian in origin; it coincided with the discovery of contemplation as the philosopher's way of life which as such was found superior to the political way of life of the citizen in the polis. The point of the matter, which I can only mention here in passing, is that Christianity, contrary to what has frequently been assumed, did not elevate active life to a higher position, did not save it from its being derivative, and did not, at least not theoretically, look upon it as something which has its meaning and end within itself. And a change in this hierarchical order was indeed impossible so long as truth was the one comprehensive principle to establish an order among the human faculties, a truth moreover, which was understood as revelation, as something essentially given to man, as distinguished from truth being either the result of some mental activity – thought or reasoning – or as that knowledge which I acquire through making.

Hence, the question arises: Why was the *vita activa*, with all its distinction and articulations, not discovered after the modern break with tradition and the eventual reversal of its hierarchical order, the "re-evaluation of all values" through Marx and Nietzsche? And the answer, though in actual analysis quite complicated, may be summed up briefly here: It lies in the very nature of the famous turning upside-down of philosophic systems or hierarchies of values that the conceptual framework itself is left intact. This is especially true for Marx who was convinced that turning Hegel upside down was enough to find the truth – i.e. the truth of the Hegelian system, which is the discovery of the dialectical nature of history.

Let me shortly explain how this identity shows itself in our context. When I enumerated the chief human activities: Labor–Work–Action, it was obvious that action occupied the highest position. Insofar as action relates to the political sphere of human life, this estimation agrees with the pre-philosophic, pre-Platonic current opinion of Greek polis life. The introduction of contemplation as the highest point of the hierarchy had the result that this order was in fact rearranged, though not always in explicit theory. (Lip service to the old hierarchy was frequently paid when it had already been reversed in the actual teaching of the philosophers.) Seen from the viewpoint of contemplation, the highest activity was not action but work; the rise of the activity of the craftsman in the scale of estimations makes its first dramatic appearance in the Platonic dialogues. Labor, to be sure, remained at the bottom but political activity as something necessary for the life of contemplation was now recognized only to the extent that it could be pursued in the same way as the activity of the craftsman. Only if seen in the image of a working activity, could political action be trusted to produce lasting results. And such lasting results meant peace, the peace needed for contemplation: No change.

If you now look upon the reversal in the modern age, you are immediately aware that its most important feature in this respect is its glorification of labor, surely the last thing any member of one of the classical communities, be it Rome or Greece, would have thought of as worthy of this position. However, the moment you go deeper into this matter you will see that not labor as such occupied this position (Adam Smith, Locke, Marx are unanimous in their contempt for menial tasks, unskilled labor which helps only to consume), but *productive* labor. Again the standard of lasting results is the actual yardstick. Thus Marx, surely the greatest of the labor philosophers, was constantly trying to re-interpret labor in the image of the working activity – again at the expense of political activity. To be sure, things had changed. Political activity was no longer seen as the laying down of immutable laws which would *make* a commonwealth, have as its end-result a reliable product, looking exactly as it had been blueprinted by the maker – as though laws or constitutions were things of the same nature as the table fabricated by the carpenter according to the blueprint he had in mind before he started to make it. Political activity was now supposed to "make history" – a phrase that occurred for the first time in Vico – and not a commonwealth, and this history had, as we all know, its end-product, the classless society which would be the end of the historical process just as the table is indeed the end of the fabrication process. In other words, since on the theoretical level, no more was done by the great re-evaluators of the old values than to turn things upside-down, the old hierarchy within the *vita activa* was hardly disturbed; the old modes of thinking prevailed, and the only relevant distinction between the new and the old was that this order, whose origin and meaningfulness lay in the actual experience of contemplation, became highly questionable. For the actual event which characterizes the modern age in this respect was that contemplation itself had become meaningless.

With this event we shall not deal here. Instead, accepting the oldest, pre-philosophical hierarchy, I propose to look into these activities themselves. And the first thing of which you might have become aware by now is my distinction between labor and work which probably sounded somewhat unusual to you. I draw it from a rather casual remark in Locke who speaks of "the labor of our body and the work of our hands." (Laborers, in Aristotelic language, are those who "with their bodies administer to the needs of life.") The phenomenal evidence in favor of this distinction is too striking to be ignored, and yet it is a fact that, apart from a few scattered remarks and important testimony of social and institutional history, there is hardly anything to support it.

Against this scarcity of evidence stands the simple obstinate fact that every European language, ancient or modern, contains two etymologically unrelated words for what we have come to think of as the same activity: Thus, the Greek distinguished between *ponein* and *ergazesthai*, the Latin between *laborare* and *facere* or *fabricari*, the French between *travailler* and *ouvrer*, the German between *arbeiten* and *werken*. In all these cases, the equivalents for labor have an unequivocal connotation of bodily experiences, of toil and trouble, and in most cases they are significantly also used for the pangs of birth. The last to use this original connection was Marx, who defined labor as the "reproduction of individual life" and begetting, the production of "foreign life," as the production of the species.

If we leave aside all theories, especially the modern labor theories after Marx, and follow solely the etymological and historical evidence, it is obvious that labor is an activity which corresponds to the biological processes of the body, that it is, as the young Marx said, the metabolism between man and nature or the human mode of this metabolism which we share with all living organisms. By laboring, men produce the vital necessities that must be fed into the life process of the human body. And since this life process, though it leads us from birth to death in a rectilinear progress of decay, is in itself circular, the laboring activity itself must follow the cycle of life, the circular movement of our bodily functions, which means that the laboring activity never comes to an end as long as life lasts; it is endlessly repetitive. Unlike working, whose end has come when the object is finished, ready to be added to the common world of things and objects, laboring always moves in the same circle prescribed by the living organism, and the end of its toil and trouble comes only with the end, i.e., the death of the individual organism.

Labor, in other words, produces consumer goods, and laboring and consuming are but two stages of the ever-recurring cycle of biological life. These two stages of the life process follow each other so closely that they almost constitute one and the same movement, which is hardly ended when it must be started all over again. Labor, unlike all other human activities, stands under the sign of necessity, the "necessity of subsisting" as Locke used to say, or the "eternal necessity imposed by nature" in the words of Marx. Hence, the actual goal of the revolution in Marx is not merely the emancipation of the laboring or working classes, but the emancipation of man from labor. For "the realm of freedom begins only where labor determined through want" and the immediacy of "physical needs" ends. And this emancipation, as we know now, to the extent that it is possible at all, occurs not by political emancipation – the equality of all classes of the citizenry – but through technology. I said: To the extent that it is possible, and I meant by this qualification that consumption, as a stage of the cyclical movement of the living organism is in a way also laborious.

Goods for consumption, the immediate result of the laboring process, are the least durable of tangible things. They are, as Locke pointed out, "of short duration, such as – if they are not consumed – will decay and perish by themselves." After a brief stay in the world, they return into the natural process that yielded them either through absorption into the life process of the human animal or through decay; in their man-made shape they disappear more quickly than any other part of the world. They are the least worldly and, at the same time, the most natural and the most necessary of all things. Although they are man-made, they come and go, are produced and consumed, in accordance with the ever-recurrent cyclical movement of nature. Hence, they cannot be "heaped up" and "stored away", as would have been necessary if they were to serve Locke's main purpose, to establish the validity of private property on the rights men have to own their own body.

But while labor in the sense of producing anything lasting – something outlasting the activity itself and even the life-span of the producer – is quite "unproductive" and futile, it is highy productive in another sense. Man's labor power is such that he produces more consumer goods than is necessary for the survival of himself and his family. This, as it were, natural abundance of the laboring process has enabled men to enslave or exploit their fellowmen, thus liberating themselves from life's burden; and while this liberation of the few has always been achieved through the use of force by a ruling class, it would never have been possible without this inherent fertility of human labor itself. Yet even this specifically human "productivity" is part and parcel of nature, it partakes of the superabundance we see everywhere in nature's household. It is but another mode of "Be ye fruitful and multiply" in which it is as though the voice of nature herself speaks to us.

Since labor corresponds to the condition of life itself, it partakes not only in life's toil and trouble but also in the sheer bliss with which we can experience our being alive. The "blessing or the joy of labor," which plays so great a part in modern labor theories, is no empty notion. Man, the author of the human artifice, which we call world in distinction to nature, and men, who are always involved with each other through action and speech, are by no means merely natural beings. But insofar as we too are just living creatures, laboring is the only way we can also remain and swing contentedly in nature's prescribed cycle, toiling and resting laboring and consuming, with the same happy and purposeless regularity with which day and night, life and death follow each other. The reward of toil and trouble, though it does not leave anything behind itself, is even more real, less futile than any other form of happiness. It lies in nature's fertility, in the quiet confidence that he who in "toil and trouble" has done his part, remains a part of nature in the future of his children and his children's children. The Old Testament, which, unlike classical antiquity, held life to be sacred and therefore neither death nor labor to be an evil (certainly not an argument against life), shows in the stories of the patriarchs how unconcerned about death they were and how death came to them in the familiar shape of night and quiet and eternal rest "in a good old age and full of years."

The blessing of life as a whole, inherent in labor, can never be found in work and should not be mistaken for the inevitably brief spell of joy that follows accomplishment and attends achievement. The blessing of labor is that effort and gratification follow each other as closely as producing and consuming, so that happiness is a concomitant of the process itself. There is no lasting happiness and contentment for human beings outside the prescribed cycle of painful exhaustion and pleasurable regeneration. Whatever throws this cycle out of balance – misery where exhaustion is followed by wretchedness or an entirely effortless life where boredom takes the place of exhaustion and where the mills of necessity, or consumption and digestion grind an impotent human body mercilessly to death – ruins the elemental happiness that comes from being alive. An element of laboring is present in all human activities, even the highest, insofar as they are undertaken as "routine" jobs by which we make our living and keep ourselves alive. Their very repetitiveness, which more often than not we feel to be a burden that exhausts us, is what provides that minimum of animal contentment for which the great and meaningful spells of joy that are rare and never last, can never be a substitute, and without which the longer lasting though equally rare spells of real grief and sorrow could hardly be borne.

The work of our hands, as distinguished from the labor of our bodies, fabricates the sheer unending variety of things whose sum total constitutes the human artifice, the world we live in. They are not consumer goods but use-objects, and their proper use does not cause them to disappear. They give the world the stability and solidity without which it could not be relied upon to house the unstable and mortal creature that is man.

To be sure, the durability of the world of things is not absolute; we do not consume things but use them up, and if we don't, they will simply decay, return into the overall natural process from which they were drawn and against which they were erected by us. If left to itself or expelled from the human world, the chair will again become wood, and the wood will decay and return to the soil from which the tree sprang before it was cut down to become the material upon which to work and with which to build. However, while usage is bound to use up these objects, this end is not planned before, it was not the goal for which it was made, as the "destruction" or immediate consumption of the bread is its inherent end; what usage wears out is durability. In other words, destruction, though unavoidable, is incidental to use but inherent in consumption. What distinguishes the most flimsy pair of shoes from mere consumer goods is that they do not spoil if I don't wear them, they are objects and therefore possess a certain "objective" independence of their own, however modest. Used or unused they will remain in the world for a certain while unless they are wantonly destroyed.

It is this durability that gives the things of the world their relative independence from men who produced and use them, their "objectivity" that makes them withstand, "stand against" and endure at least for a time the voracious needs and wants of their living users. From this viewpoint, the things of the world have the function of stabilizing human life, and their objectivity lies in the fact that men, their everchanging nature notwithstanding, can retrieve their identity by being related to the enduring sameness of objects, the same chair today and tomorrow, the same house formerly from birth to death. Against the subjectivity of men stands the objectivity of the man-made artifice, not the indifference of nature. Only because we have erected a world of objects from what nature gives us and have built this artificial environment into nature, thus protecting us from her, can we look upon nature as something "objective". Without a world between men and nature, there would be eternal movement, but no objectivity.

Durability and objectivity are the result of fabrication, the work of *homo faber*. It consists of reification. Solidity, inherent in even the most fragile things, comes ultimately from matter which is transformed into material. Material is already a product of human hands that have removed it from its natural location, either killing a life process, as in the case of the tree which provides wood, or interrupting one of nature's slower processes, as in the case of iron, stone, or marble torn out of the womb of the earth. This element of violation and violence is present in all fabrication, and man as the creator of the human artifice has always been a destroyer of nature. The experience of this violence is the most elemental experience of human strength, and by the same token the very opposite of the painful, exhausting effort experienced in sheer labor. This is no longer the earning of one's bread "in the sweat of his brow," in which man may indeed be the lord and master of all living creatures but still remains the servant of nature, his own natural needs, and of the earth. *Homo faber* becomes lord and master of nature herself insofar as he violates and partly destroys what was given to him.

The process of making is itself entirely determined by the categories of means and end. The fabricated thing is an end product in the twofold sense that the production process comes to an end in it and that it is only a means to produce this end. Unlike the laboring activity, where labor and consumption are only two stages of an identical process – the life process of the individual or of society – fabrication and usage are two altogether different processes. The end of the fabrication process has come when the thing is finished, and this process need not be repeated. The impulse toward repetition comes from the craftsman's need to earn his means of subsistence, that is, from the element of labor inherent in his work. It also may come from the demand for multiplication on the market. In either case, the process is repeated for reasons outside itself, unlike the compulsory repetition inherent in laboring, where one must eat in order to labor and must labor in order to eat. Multiplication should not be confused with repetition, although it may be felt by the individual craftsman as mere repetition which a machine can better and more productively achieve. Multiplication actually multiplies things, whereas repetition merely follows the recurrent cycle of life in which its products disappear almost as fast as they have appeared.

To have a definite beginning and a definite predictable end is the mark of fabrication, which through this characteristic alone distinguishes itself from all other human activities. Labor, caught in the cyclical movement of the biological process, has neither a beginning nor an end properly speaking – only pauses, intervals between exhaustion and regeneration. Action, though it may have a definite beginning, never, as we shall see, has a predictable end. This great reliability of work is reflected in that the fabrication process, unlike action, is not irreversible: every thing produced by human hands can be destroyed by them, and no use object is so urgently needed in the life process that its maker cannot survive and afford its destruction. Man, the fabricator of the human artifice, his own world, is indeed a lord and master, not only because he has set himself up as the master of all nature, but because he is master of himself and his doings. This is true neither of laboring, where men remain subject to the necessity of their life, nor of acting, where they remain in dependence upon their fellow men. Alone with his image of the future product, *homo faber* is free to produce, and again facing alone the work of his hands, he is free to destroy.

I said before that all fabrication processes are determined by the category of means and end. This shows itself most clearly in the enormous role which tools and instruments play in it. From the standpoint of *homo faber*, man is indeed, as Benjamin Franklin said, a "tool-maker". To be sure, tools and implements are also used in the laboring process, as every housewife proudly owning all the gadgets of a modern kitchen knows; but these implements have a different character and function when used for laboring; they serve to lighten the burden and mechanize the labor of the laborer, they are, as it were, anthropocentric, whereas the tools of fabrication are designed and invented for the fabrication of things, their fitness and precision are dictated by "objective" aims rather than subjective needs and wants. Moreover, every fabrication process produces things that last considerably longer than the process which brought them into existence, whereas in a laboring process, bringing forth these goods of "short duration," the tools and instruments it uses are the only things which survive the laboring process itself. They are the use-things for laboring, and as such not the result of the laboring activity itself. What dominates the laboring with one's body, and incidentally all work processes performed in the mode of laboring, is neither the purposeful effort nor the product itself, but the motion of the process and the rhythm it imposes upon the laborers. Labor implements are drawn into this rhythm where body and tool swing in the same repetitive movement – until in the use of machines, which are best suited to the performance of laboring because of their movement, it is no longer the body's movement that determines the movement of the implement, but the machine's movement that enforces the movements of the body, while, in a more advanced state, it replace it altogether. It seems to me highly characteristic that the much discussed question of whether man should be "adjusted" to the machine or the machines should be adjusted to the nature of man never arose with respect to mere tools or instruments. And the reason is that all tools of workmanship remain the servants of the hand, whereas machines indeed demand that the laborer should serve them, adjust the natural rhythm of his body to their mechanical movement. In other words, even the most refined tool remains a servant unable to guide or to replace the hand; even the most primitive machine guides and ideally replaces the body's labor.

The most fundamental experience we have with instrumentality arises out of the fabrication process. Here it is indeed true that the end justifies the means; it does more, it produces and organizes them. The end justifies the violence done to nature to win the material, as the wood justifies killing the tree, and the table justifies destroying the wood. In the same way, the end product organizes the work process itself, decides about the needed specialists, the measure of co-operation, the number of assistants or cooperators. Hence, everything and everybody is judged here in terms of suitability and usefulness for the desired end product, and nothing else.

Strangely enough, the validity of the means–end category is not exhausted with the finished product for which everything and everybody becomes a means. Though the object is an end with respect to the means by which it was produced and the actual end of the making process, it never becomes, so to speak, an end in itself, at least not as long as it remains an object for use. It immediately takes its place in another means-end chain by virtue of its very usefulness; as a mere use-object it becomes a means for, let us say, comfortable living, or as an exchange object, that is, insofar [as] a definite value has been bestowed upon the material used for fabrication, it becomes a means for obtaining other objects. In other words, in a strictly utilitarian world, all ends are bound to be of short duration; they are transformed into means for some further ends. Once the end is attained, it ceases to be an end, it becomes an object among objects which at any moment can be transformed into means to pursue further ends. The perplexity of utilitarianism, the philosophy, as it were, of *homo faber*, is that it gets caught in the unending chain of means and ends without ever arriving at some principle which could justify the category, that is, utility itself.

The usual way out of this dilemma is to make the user, man himself, the ultimate end to stop the unending chain of ends and means. That man is an end in himself and should never be used as a means to pursue other ends, no matter how elevated these might be, is well-known to us from the moral philosophy of Kant, and there is no doubt that Kant wanted first of all to relegate the means–end category and its philosophy of utilitarianism to its proper place and prevent it from ruling the relations between man and man instead of the relationship between men and things. However, even Kant's intrinsically paradoxical formula fails to solve the perplexities of *homo faber*. By elevating man the user into the

369

position of an ultimate end, he degrades even more forcefully all other "ends" to mere means. If man the user is the highest end, "the measure of all things," then not only nature, treated by fabrication as the almost "worthless material" upon which to work and to bestow "value" (as Locke said), but the "valuable" things themselves have become mere means, losing thereby their own intrinsic worth. Or to put it another way, the most worldly of all activities loses its original objective meaning, it becomes a means to fulfill subjective needs; in and by itself, it is no longer meaningful, no matter how useful it may be.

From the viewpoint of fabrication the finished product is as much an end in itself, an independent durable entity with an existence of its own, as man is an end in himself in Kant's moral philosophy. Of course, the issue at stake here is not instrumentality as such, the use of means to achieve an end, but rather the generalization of the fabrication experience in which usefulness and utility are established as the ultimate standards for the world as well as for the life of acting men moving in it. *Homo faber*, we can say, has transgressed the limits of his activity when, under the disguise of utilitarianism, he proposes that instrumentality rule the realm of the finished world as exclusively as it rules the activity through which all things contained in it come into being. This generalization will always be the specific temptation of *homo faber* although, in the final analysis, it will be his own undoing: he will be left with meaninglessness in the midst of usefulness; utilitarianism never can find the answer to the question Lessing once put to the utilitarian philosophers of his time: "And what, if you please, is the use of use?"

In the sphere of fabrication itself, there is only one kind of objects to which the unending chain of means and ends does not apply, and this is the work of art, the most useless and, at the same time, the most durable thing human hands can produce. Its very characteristic is its remoteness from the whole context of ordinary usage, so that in case a former use object, say a piece of furniture of a by-gone age, is considered by a later generation to be a "masterpiece," it is put into a museum and thus carefully removed from any possible usage. Just as the purpose of a chair is actualized when it is sat upon, the inherent purpose of a work of art – whether the artist knows it or not, whether the purpose is achieved or not – is to attain permanence throughout the ages. Nowhere else does the sheer durability of the man-made world appear in such purity and clarity, nowhere else therefore does this thing-world reveal itself so spectacularly as the non-mortal home for mortal beings. And though the actual source of inspiration of these permanent things is thought, this does not prevent their being things. The thought process no more produces anything tangible than the sheer ability to use objects produces them. It is the reification that occurs in writing something down, painting an image, composing a piece of music, etc. which actually *makes* the thought a reality; and in order to produce these thought things, which we usually call art works, the same workmanship is required that through the primordial instrument of human hands builds the other, less durable and more useful things of the human artifice.

The man-made world of things becomes a home for mortal men, whose stability will endure and outlast the ever-changing movement of their lives and deeds, only insomuch as it transcends both the sheer functionalism of consumer-goods and the sheer utility of use objects. Life in its non-biological sense, the span of time each man is given between birth and death, manifests itself in action and speech, to which we now must turn our attention. With word and deed we insert ourselves into the human world, and this insertion is like a second birth, in which we confirm and take upon ourselves the naked fact of our original physical appearance. Since through birth we entered Being, we share with all other entities the quality of Otherness, an important aspect of plurality that makes [sic] that we can define only by distinction, that we are unable to say what anything *is* without distinguishing it from something else. In addition to this we share with all living organisms that kind of distinguishing trait which makes it an individual entity. However only man can *express* otherness and individuality, only he can distinguish himself and communicate *himself*, and not merely something – thirst or hunger, affection or hostility or fear. In man, otherness and distinctness become uniqueness, and what man inserts with word and deed into the company of his own kind is uniqueness. This insertion is not forced upon us through necessity like labor and it is not prompted by wants and desires like work. It is unconditioned; its impulse springs from the beginning that came into the world when we were born and to which we respond by beginning something new on our own initiative. To act, in its most general sense, means to take an initiative, to begin, as the Greek word: *arkhein* indicates, or to set something into motion, which is the original meaning of the Latin *agere*.

All human activities are conditioned by the fact of human plurality, that not One man, but men in the plural inhabit the earth and in one way or another live together. But only action and speech relate specifically to this fact that to live always means to live among men, among those who are my equals. Hence, when I insert myself into the world, it is a world where others are already present. Action and speech are so closely related because the primordial and specifically human act must always also answer the question asked of every newcomer: "Who are you?" The disclosure of "who somebody is" is implicit in the fact that speechless action somehow does not exist, or if it exists [it] is irrelevant; without speech, action loses the actor, and the doer of deeds is possible only to the extent that he is at the same time the speaker of words, who identifies himself as the actor and announces what he is doing, what he has done, or what he intends to do. It is exactly as Dante once said – and more succinctly than I could (*De Monarchia*, 1, 13) –: "For in every action what is primarily intended by the doer . . . is the disclosure of his own image. Hence it comes about that every doer, in so far as he does, takes delight in doing; since everything that is desires its own being, and since in action the being of the doer is somehow intensified, delight necessarily follows . . . Thus nothing acts unless by acting it makes patent its latent self." To be sure, this disclosure of "who" always remains hidden from the person himself – like the *daimon* in Greek religion who accompanies man throughout his life, always looking over his shoulder from behind and thus visible only to those he encounters. Still, though unknown to the person, action is intensely personal. Action without a name, a "who" attached to it, is meaningless whereas an art work retains its relevance whether or not we know the master's name. Let me remind you of the monuments to the Unknown Soldier after World War I. They bear testimony to the need for finding a "who", an indentifiable somebody, whom four years of mass slaughter should have revealed. The unwillingness to resign oneself to the brutal fact that the agent of the war was actually Nobody inspired the erection of the monuments to the unknown ones – that is to all those whom

371

the war had failed to make known, robbing them thereby, not of their achievement, but of their human dignity.

Wherever men live together, there exists a web of human relationships which is, as it were, woven by the deeds and words of innumerable persons, by the living as well as by the dead. Every deed and every new beginning falls into an already existing web, where it nevertheless somehow starts a new process that will affect many others even beyond those with whom the agent comes into direct contact. It is because of this already existing web of human relationships with its conflicting wills and intentions, that action almost never achieves its purpose. And it is also because of this medium and the attending quality of unpredictability that action always produces stories, with or without intention, as naturally as fabrication produces tangible things. These stories may then be recorded in documents and monuments, they may be told in poetry and historiography, and worked into all kinds of material. They themselves, however, are of an entirely different nature than these reifications. They tell us more about their subjects, the "hero" in each story, than any product of human hands ever tells us about the master who produced it, and yet they are not products properly speaking. Although everybody starts his own story, at least his own life-story, nobody is the author or producer of it. And yet, it is precisely in these stories that the actual meaning of a human life finally reveals itself. That every individual life between birth and death can eventually be told as a story with beginning and end is the prepolitical and prehistorical condition of history, the great story without beginning and end. But the reason why each human life tells its story and why history ultimately becomes the storybook of mankind, with many actors and speakers and yet without any recognizable author, is that both are the outcome of action. The real story in which we are engaged as long as we live has no visible or invisible maker because it is not *made*.

The absence of a maker in this realm accounts for the extraordinary frailty and unreliability of strictly human affairs. Since we always act into a web of relationships, the consequences of each deed are boundless, every action touches off not only a reaction but a chain reaction, every process is the cause of unpredictable new processes. This boundlessness is inescapable; it could not be cured by restricting one's acting to a limited graspable framework or circumstances or by feeding all pertinent material into giant computers. The smallest act in the most limited circumstances bears the seed of the same boundlessness and unpredictability; one deed, one gesture, one word may suffice to change every constellation. In acting, in contradistinction to working, it is indeed true that we can really never know what we are doing.

There stands however in stark contrast to this frailty and unreliability of human affairs another character of human action which seems to make it even more dangerous than we are entitled to assume anyhow. And this is the simple fact that, though we don't know what we are doing when we are acting, we have no possibility ever to undo what we have done. Action processes are not only unpredictable, they are also irreversible; there is no author or maker who can undo, destroy, what he has done if he does not like it or when the consequences prove to be disastrous. This peculiar resiliency of action, apparently in opposition to the frailty of its results, would be altogether unbearable if this capability had not some remedy within its own range.

The possible redemption from the predicament of irreversibility is the faculty of forgiving, and the remedy for unpredictability is contained in the faculty to make and keep promises. The two remedies belong together: forgiving relates to the past and serves to undo its deeds, while binding oneself through promises serves to set up in the ocean of future uncertainty islands of security without which not even continuity, let alone durability of any kind, would ever be possible in the relationships between men. Without being forgiven, released from the consequences of what we have done, our capacity to act would, as it were, be confined to one single deed from which we could never recover; we would remain the victims of its consequences forever, not unlike the sorcerer's apprentice who lacked the magic formula to break the spell. Without being bound to the fulfilment of promises, we would never be able to achieve that amount of identity and continuity which together produce the "person" about whom a story can be told; each of us would be condemned to wander helplessly and without direction in the darkness of his own lonely heart, caught in its ever changing moods, contradictions, and equivocalities. (This subjective identity, achieved through binding oneself in promises, must be distinguished from the "objective", i.e. object-related, identity that arises out of being confronted with the sameness of the world which I mentioned in the discussion of work.) In this respect; forgiving and making promises are like control mechanisms built into the very faculty to start new and unending processes.

Without action, without the capacity to start something new and thus articulate the new beginning that comes into the world with the birth of each human being, the life of man, spent between birth and death, would indeed be doomed beyond salvation. The life span itself, running toward death would inevitably carry everything human to ruin and destruction. Action, with all its uncertainties, is like an ever-present reminder that men, though they must die, are not born in order to die but in order to begin something new. *Initium ut esset homo creatus est* – "that there be a beginning man was created," said Augustine. With the creation of man, the principle of beginning came into the world – which, of course, is only another way of saying that with the creation of man, the principle of freedom appeared on earth.

Part IX

JEAN-PAUL SARTRE
Transcendence and Freedom

JEAN-PAUL SARTRE (1905–1980)

Introduction

Jean-Paul Sartre was born in Thiviers, France in 1905. He lost his father the following year, and his mother moved the family to Paris in 1911. He was educated first at home by his grandfather Charles Schweitzer and then in the Lycées Henri IV and Louis-le-Grand, gaining admission to the Ecole Normale Supérieure in 1924. Here Sartre began his lifelong relationship with another philosophy student, Simone de Beauvoir. Inspired by a discussion with Raymond Aron about phenomenology, he obtained funding in 1933 to go to the French Institute in Berlin to read phenomenology. Some of his most important works have their genesis in these studies, including *The Transcendence of the Ego* (1936), *The Psychology of Imagination* (1940), and *Being and Nothingness* (1943), his greatest book. Sartre soon abandoned teaching to become a professional writer, and quickly gained recognition as a dramatist and writer, eventually being awarded the Nobel Prize for literature in 1964 (he declined the award for political reasons). To this day *Nausea* (1938) remains his best-known philosophical novel. In 1944 he founded the important political and literary journal, *Les Temps Modernes*, with de Beauvoir and Merleau-Ponty and other French intellectuals. His unfinished two-volume *Critique of Dialectical Reason* (1960, 1985) shows both his commitment to Marxism and his brilliant originality as a political thinker. His literary output was prodigious, with studies of Baudelaire and others, and he remained active politically on the left until a few years before his death in Paris in 1980.

The archetype of the politically engaged intellectual, Sartre is certainly the best-known, even the most notorious, phenomenological philosopher, being particularly associated with existentialism, especially following his 1945 lecture "Existentialism is a Humanism". His central concerns include human freedom and responsibility and the psychology of human action, themes already raised in their own way by Husserl and Heidegger. Husserl understood the transcendental attitude of reflection as a radical exercise in freedom and self-responsibility, while Heidegger took up the idea of responsibility for the meaning of existence in his account of authentic Dasein. For Sartre, however, freedom and responsibility are not so much capacities of human existence as ongoing and unavoidable actualities, such that we are 'condemned to be free'.

Our first reading is a short article Sartre published in 1939 on Husserl's concept of intentionality. Sartre is critical of the focus in French philosophy of his day on epistemology, whereas Husserl recognises that our contact with things is not limited to knowledge, and furthermore, the picture of knowledge in modern epistemology as a kind of 'digestion' of the object distorts the true nature of the intentional relation, which is a kind of explosion or bursting out of consciousness on to the world. Husserl gives primacy to the transcendence of things in the world. As Sartre puts it: "Husserl has restored to things their horror and their charm."

Our second reading is an abridgement of *The Transcendence of the Ego*, written shortly after Sartre's discovery of phenomenology. Drawing on Husserl's account of the role of the ego in intentional experiences in the *Investigations* and *Ideas I*, Sartre argues that the ego is neither formally nor materially inside consciousness; rather it is outside, an object in the world like the ego of another. Put another way, it is transcendent, neither immanent nor transcendental. Although Kant had contended that transcendental consciousness is the set of logical conditions required for empirical consciousness, he should not have described the former as an 'I think', since on Sartre's account it is a pre-personal transcendental field. The 'I think' pertains to the personal and empirical ego which pure consciousness makes possible. Husserl had already recognised this in the Fifth Logical Investigation, though he lapsed into a more Kantian account of a transcendental I from *Ideas I* on. This is somewhat ironic on Sartre's account, since, taken in themselves, Husserl's later analyses have no need of such an I.

The fact that an ego or I is an object does not entail that it must inhabit consciousness. If I read a book or see a chair, it is not the case that 'I have consciousness' of the book's characters or the chair. Instead, Sartre argues, there is only consciousness of the characters or the chair. There is no I in this unreflected consciousness; the I only appears as an object through reflected consciousness. Yet its givenness is not apodictic or indubitable, since by saying 'I' one affirms more than can be known from one's living present or memory. Nor is it adequate, since the I is presented as an opaque reality whose content has to be unfolded. It appears veiled and indistinct through consciousness, like a pebble beneath running waters. The I none the less has a concrete existence, different from mathematical truths and meanings and spatio-temporal beings, but no less real.

The ego is constituted as a unity of states, actions and qualities. If I hate someone, this state appears in and through experiences of anger or repugnance, but it is not identifiable with any one of them, since it continues when I am absorbed otherwise and no consciousness reveals it. Hatred is a transcendent object, and each experience of anger or repulsiveness is one of its aspects or appearances. However, I may be mistaken about states – it may turn out that these experiences are in fact aspects of jealousy rather than hatred. Actions too are objects. This is seen in playing a piano or driving a car, which are obviously in the world, but is also the case with actions like reasoning or making a hypotheses, which can be reflexively exhibited as transcendencies realised over time. Finally, there are qualities or psychic dispositions. If there are enough experiences of a state, it may be laid down as a disposition that is in turn actualised in further states. The disposition exists objectively as a potentiality or virtuality.

Above all, the ego is not to be seen in terms of Husserl's concept of an X-pole, a pole which on Sartre's interpretation would support and be indifferent to psychic phenomena, a sort of skeletal owner that would remain if we stripped them all away. The ego is nothing outside the concrete totality of states and actions and qualities it supports. It is the synthetic, transcendent totality of the latter, marked or coloured by each one of them. This conception of the ego, claims Sartre, is the liberation and purification of the Transcendental Field. The latter is a nothing, since all physical and psychical objects are outside it, and everything, since it is consciousness of all these objects. This impersonal, spontaneous consciousness can frighten us with its absolute and tireless upsurge. The ego or I, by contrast, is out in the world with its states and actions and qualities. Peter and Paul may apprehend Peter's state of love in different ways, but if Paul's apprehension is less intimate or clear, it is no less intuitional. The transcendent I participates in the vicissitudes of a world which it has not created, and here its values must be located. I and world are contemporaneous objects for impersonal consciousness, and by virtue of it they are connected.

Our final reading is an abridgement of "Bad Faith", a chapter from *Being and Nothingness*. In this work, which he characterises as an analysis of self-deception, Sartre qualifies his earlier conception of a pre-personal transcendental field. While consciousness still precedes the empirical ego as existence to essence, it can now become marked by ego-qualities which are objectifiable and examinable. As objectifiable, however, such qualities do not destroy the translucency of consciousness. Borrowing Hegelian and Husserlian terms, Sartre argues that consciousness cannot be determined or constrained like a physical thing or 'in-itself' (*en-soi*) prey to causal forces. The human reality of consciousness is 'for-itself' (*pour-soi*), a free existence which constantly chooses to accept or reject its current situation. Sartre describes the refusal to own up to this fundamental freedom as bad faith (*mauvaise foi*).

When it refuses to either embrace or reject a particular situation (i.e. to negate the situation's meaning if not always its physical reality), consciousness turns its negation towards itself. It affects itself with bad faith. Sartre regards bad faith as a lie to oneself of which one is aware. The person lying and the person lied to are one and the same in the unity of a single project. It might be objected that I cannot be in bad faith if I know I am lying to myself, but the awareness of which Sartre speaks is more usually implicit and pre-reflexive, an evanescent rather than an explicit phenomenon. This being said, an alternative explanation of bad faith may be suggested by psychoanalysis – the ego's deceiver is an unconscious, censorious id. Psychoanalysis substitutes for bad faith the idea of a lie without a liar. But for Sartre, this breaking in two of the ego cannot explain how such a censor could discern the lie to be hidden without knowing it, and indeed without knowing that this is what must be repressed. Yet to refute finally the psychoanalytic interpretation, it is necessary to show that concrete patterns of bad faith themselves appear in the translucency of consciousness.

Embarking on phenomenological description, Sartre considers a woman who consents to go out with a man who has made his sexual intentions very clear. She knows that sooner or later she must choose to accept or reject him, but postpones that decision. Wishing to be attractive and yet respected at the same time, she disarms his remarks as to her attractiveness of their sexual background. When he puts his hand on hers, furthermore, she leaves it where it is and affects not to notice, talking about other matters – to accept it noticeably would be to commit herself, while to push it away would be to break the charm of the hour. She disarms his action of its meaning by pretending that it is an in-itself event, a bare physical occurrence of no significance. This woman is in bad faith, knowing well the decision to be made when she uses these various procedures. She maintains herself like a passive and unresponsive object, wilfully obscuring the transcendence that is her free existence.

For Sartre, we make ourselves what we are as players of a game. The waiter we see in the café moves a little too precisely, his posture a little too eager and his manner a little too solicitous. If we watch for a while we can explain his overall comportment; he is playing at *being* a waiter in a café. He plays at his condition so as to realise it, and so too do the grocer and tailor and auctioneer. They endeavour to persuade their clientele that they are nothing but their respective occupation. Each represents the relevant role for himself or herself and others, while not being identical with that role. It might of course be objected that these roles eventually become someone's own being, so that someone is sincerely and genuinely what one appears to be. In Sartre's paradoxical formulation one is never what one is, or bad faith would be impossible. Sincerity is an ideal that cannot be achieved totally. The champion of sincerity might demand that a gay man who feels guilty should confess or come out, that he openly be what he is. But over and above the fact that no one is identical to their orientation, the man who acknowledges being gay is not the man who existed prior to this, so the champion of sincerity is asking the man to be what he is so as to no longer be what he is.

The strongest objection to the notion of bad faith, according to Sartre, is that it is faith. If belief is adherence to an object when it is not given, or is given indistinctly, then bad faith is a belief. Bad faith apprehends evidence against it, but is resigned in advance to not being persuaded by this evidence or transformed into good faith; bad faith is itself in bad faith. There is no question here of a reflexive, voluntary decision, for bad faith involves a sort of passivity, like putting oneself to sleep. It does involve, none the less, a pre-reflexive awareness of its structure. If this consciousness refuses to be convinced by contrary evidence, it is not thereby convinced completely of and by itself. To believe is to know that one believes without self-evident intuitions. With bad faith, therefore, one never wholly believes what one believes.

Further reading

Sartre, Jean-Paul. *Anti-Semite and Jew*, trans. George J. Becker. New York: Schocken Books, 1965.

Sartre, Jean-Paul. *Baudelaire*, trans. M. Turnell. London: Hamish Hamilton, 1964.

Sartre, Jean-Paul. *Being and Nothingness. An Essay on Phenomenological Ontology*, trans. Hazel Barnes. London: Routledge, 1995.

Sartre, Jean-Paul. *Critique of Dialectical Reason. Volume 1. Theory of Practical Ensembles*, trans. Alan Sheridan-Smith. London: New Left Books, 1976.

Sartre, Jean-Paul. *Critique of Dialectical Reason. Volume 2. Intelligibility of History*, ed. Arlette Elkiaim-Sartre, trans. Quintin Hoare. London: Verso, 1991.

Sartre, Jean-Paul. *Nausea*, trans. Robert Baldick. Harmondsworth: Penguin, 1965.

Sartre, Jean-Paul. *Notebooks for an Ethics*, trans. David Pellauer. Chicago, IL: University of Chicago Press, 1992.

Sartre, Jean-Paul. *Saint Genet. Actor and Martyr*, trans. Bernard Frechtman. New York: Braziller, 1963.

Sartre, Jean-Paul. *Sketch for a Theory of the Emotions*. London: Methuen, 1971

Sartre, Jean-Paul. *The Psychology of Imagination*, trans. Bernard Frechtman. London: Methuen, 1972.

Sartre, Jean-Paul. *The Transcendence of the Ego*, trans. Forrest Williams and Robert Kirkpatrick. New York: Farrar, Straus and Giroux, 1957.

Sartre, Jean-Paul. *The War Diaries*, trans. Quintin Hoare. London: Verso, 1984.

Caws, Peter. *Sartre*. London: Routledge & Kegan Paul, 1979.

Danto, Arthur C. *Sartre*. London: Fontana & Collins, 1975.

Howells, Christina (ed.). *The Cambridge Companion to Sartre*. Cambridge: Cambridge University Press, 1992.

McCulloch, Gregory. *Using Sartre: An Analytic Introduction to Early Sartrean Themes*. London: Routledge, 1994.

Priest, Stephen (ed.). *Jean-Paul Sartre. Basic Writings*. London: Routledge, 2001.

Schilpp, P. A. (ed.). *The Philosophy of Jean-Paul Sartre*. La Salle, IL: Open Court, 1981.

Wider, Kathleen V. *The Bodily Nature of Consciousness: Sartre and Contemporary Philosophy of Mind*. Ithaca, NY: Cornell University Press, 1997.

1

INTENTIONALITY:
A FUNDAMENTAL IDEA OF
HUSSERL'S PHENOMENOLOGY[1]

"He devoured her with his eyes." This expression and many other signs point to the illusion common to both realism and idealism: to know is to eat. After a hundred years of academicism, French philosophy remains at that point. We have all read Brunschvicg, Lalande, and Meyerson. We have all believed that the spidery mind trapped things in its web, covered them with a white spit and slowly swallowed them, reducing them to its own substance. What is a table, a rock, a house? A certain assemblage of "contents of consciousness", a class of such contents. O digestive philosophy! Yet nothing seemed more obvious: is not the table the actual content of my perception? Is not my perception the present state of my consciousness? Nutrition, assimilation! Assimilation, Lalande said, of things to ideas, of ideas by ideas, of minds by minds. The corpulent skeletons of the world were picked clean by these diligent diastases: assimilation, unification, identification. The simplest and plainest among us vainly looked for something solid, something not just mental, but would encounter everywhere only a soft and very genteel mist: themselves.

Against the digestive philosophy of empirico-criticism, of neo-Kantianism, against all "psychologism", Husserl persistently affirmed that one cannot dissolve things in consciousness. You see this tree, to be sure. But you see it just where it is: at the side of the road, in the midst of the dust, alone and writhing in the heat, eight miles from the Mediterranean coast. It could not enter into your consciousness, for it is not of the same nature as consciousness. One is perhaps reminded of Bergson and the first chapter of *Matter and Memory*. But Husserl is not a realist: this tree on its bit of parched earth is not an absolute which would subsequently enter into communication with us. Consciousness and the world are given at one stroke: essentially external to consciousness, the world is nevertheless essentially relative to consciousness. Husserl sees consciousness as an irreducible fact which no physical image can account for. Except perhaps the quick, obscure image of a burst. To know is to "burst toward", to tear oneself out of the moist gastric intimacy, veering out there beyond oneself, out there near the tree and yet beyond it, for the tree escapes me and repulses me, and I can no more lose myself in the tree than it can dissolve itself in me. I'm beyond it: it's beyond me.

J.-P. Sartre, "Intentionality: A Fundamental Idea of Husserl's Phenomenology", trans. Joseph P. Fell, *Journal of the British Society for Phenomenology*, 1970, Vol. 1, No. 2, pp. 4–5.

Do you recognize in this description your own circumstances and your own impressions? You certainly knew that the tree was not you, that you could not make it enter your dark stomach and that knowledge could not, without dishonesty, be compared to possession. All at once consciousness is purified, it is clear as a strong wind. There is nothing in it but a movement of fleeing itself, a sliding beyond itself. If, impossible though it be, you could enter "into" a consciousness you would be seized by a whirlwind and thrown back outside, in the thick of the dust near the tree, for consciousness has no "inside". It is just this being beyond itself, this absolute flight, this refusal to be a substance which makes it a consciousness.

Imagine for a moment a connected series of bursts which tear us out of ourselves, which do not even allow to an "ourselves" the leisure of composing ourselves behind them, but which instead throw us beyond them into the dry dust of the world, on to the plain earth, amidst things. Imagine us thus rejected and abandoned by our own nature in an indifferent, hostile, and restive world – you will then grasp the profound meaning of the discovery which Husserl expresses in his famous phrase. "All consciousness is consciousness *of* something". No more is it necessary to dispose of the effeminate philosophy of immanence, where everything happens by compromise, by protoplasmic transformations, by a tepid cellular chemistry. The philosophy of transcendence throws us on to the highway, in the midst of dangers, under a dazzling light.

Being, says Heidegger, is being-in-the-world. One must understand this "being-in" as movement. To be is to fly out into the world, to spring from the nothingness of the world and of consciousness in order suddenly to burst out as consciousness-in-the-world. When consciousness tries to recoup itself, to coincide with itself once and for all, closeted off all warm and cosy, it destroys itself. This necessity for consciousness to exist as consciousness of something other than itself Husserl calls "intentionality".

I have spoken primarily of knowledge to make myself better understood: the French philosophy that has moulded us understands little besides epistemology. But for Husserl and the phenomenologists our consciousness of things is by no means limited to knowledge of them. Knowledge, or pure "representation", is only one of the possible forms of my consciousness "of" this tree; I can also love it, fear it, hate it, and this surpassing of consciousness by itself that is called "intentionality" finds itself again in fear, hatred, and love. Hating another is just a way of bursting forth toward him; it is finding oneself suddenly confronted by a stranger in whom one lives, in whom one suffers from the very first, the objective quality "hateful".

So it is that all at once hatred, love, fear, sympathy – all these famous "subjective" reactions which were floating in the malodorous brine of the mind – are pulled out. They are merely ways of discovering the world. It is things which abruptly unveil themselves to us as hateful, sympathetic, horrible, lovable. Being dreadful is a *property* of this Japanese mask, an inexhaustible and irreducible property which constitutes its very nature – and not the sum of our subjective reactions to a piece of sculptured wood.

Husserl has restored to things their horror and their charm. He has restored to us the world of artists and prophets: frightening, hostile, dangerous, with its havens of mercy and love. He has cleared the way for a new treatise on the passions which would be inspired by this simple truth, so utterly ignored by the refined among us: if we love a woman, it is because she is lovable. We are delivered from Proust. We are likewise delivered from the "internal life": in vain would we seek the caresses and fondlings of our intimate selves, like Amiel[2] or like a child who kisses his own shoulder, since everything is finally outside, everything, even ourselves. Outside, in the world, among others. It is not in some hiding-place that we will discover ourselves: it is on the road, in the town, in the midst of the crowd, a thing among things, a man among men.

January 1939.

Notes

This essay first appeared in *Nouvelle Revue Française*, LII, January 1939. [Tr.]

1 Translation by Joseph P. Fell of "Une Idée fondamentale de la phénoménologie de Husserl: l'intentionnalité", in *Situations I* (Paris: Gallimard, 1947). This essay first appeared in *Nouvelle Revue Française*, LII, January 1939. [Tr.] We are indebted to Editions Gallimard, to whom the copyright belongs, for permission to print this translation.
2 Henri Frederic Amiel (1821–1881). Swiss philosopher and author of *Journal intime*. [Tr.]

2

THE TRANSCENDENCE
OF THE EGO

For most philosophers the ego is an "inhabitant" of consciousness. Some affirm its formal presence at the heart of *Erlebnisse*, as an empty principle of unification. Others – psychologists for the most part – claim to discover its material presence, as the center of desires and acts, in each moment of our psychic life. We should like to show here that the ego is neither formally nor materially *in* consciousness: it is outside, *in the world*. It is a being of the world, like the ego of another.

i The I and the me

A. The theory of the formal presence of the I

It must be conceded to Kant that "the I Think *must be able* to accompany all our representations." But need we then conclude that an *I in fact* inhabits all our states of consciousness and actually effects the supreme synthesis of our experience? This inference would appear to distort the Kantian view. The Critical problem being one of validity, Kant says nothing concerning the actual existence of the *I Think*. On the contrary, he seems to have seen perfectly well that there are moments of consciousness without the *I*, for he says "*must be able* to accompany." The problem, indeed, is to determine the conditions for the possibility of experience. One of these conditions is that I can always regard my perception or thought as *mine*: nothing more. But there is in contemporary philosophy a dangerous tendency [. . .] which consists of making into a reality the conditions, determined by Criticism, for the possibility of experience. This is the tendency which leads certain writers to ask, for example, what "transcendental consciousness" can *be*. [. . .] For Kant, transcendental consciousness is nothing but the set of conditions which are necessary for the existence of an empirical consciousness. Consequently, *to make into a reality* the transcendental *I*, to make of it the inseparable companion of each of our "consciousnesses,"[1] is to pass on *fact*, not on validity, and to take a point of view radically different from that of Kant. [. . .]

If we reject all the more or less forced interpretations of the *I Think* offered by the post-Kantians, and nevertheless wish to solve the problem of the existence *in fact* of the *I* in consciousness, we meet on our path the phenomenology of

J.-P. Sartre, *The Transcendence of the Ego*, 1972, trans. Forrest Williams and Robert Kirkpatrick, pp. 31–106. New York: Farrar, Straus & Giroux.

Husserl. Phenomenology is a scientific, not a Critical, study of consciousness. Its essential way of proceeding is by intuition.[2] Intuition, according to Husserl, puts us in the presence of *the thing*. We must recognize, therefore, that phenomenology is a science of *fact*, and that the problems it poses are problems *of fact*;[3] which can be seen, moreover, from Husserl's designation of phenomenology as a *descriptive* science. Problems concerning the relations of the *I* to consciousness are therefore existential problems. Husserl, too, discovers the transcendental consciousness of Kant, and grasps it by the ἐποχή.[4] But this consciousness is no longer a set of logical conditions. It is a fact which is absolute. Nor is this transcendental consciousness a hypostatization of validity, an unconscious which floats between the real and the ideal. It is a real consciousness accessible to each of us as soon as the "reduction" is performed. And it is indeed this transcendental consciousness which constitutes our empirical consciousness, our consciousness "in the world," our consciousness with its psychic and psycho-physical *me*.

For our part, we readily acknowledge the existence of a constituting consciousness. We find admirable all of Husserl's descriptions in which he shows transcendental consciousness constituting the world by imprisoning itself in empirical consciousness. Like Husserl, we are persuaded that our psychic and psychophysical *me* is a transcendent object which must fall before the ἐποχή. But we raise the following question: is not this psychic and psycho-physical *me* enough? Need one double it with a transcendental *I*, a structure of absolute consciousness?

The consequences of a reply are obvious. If the reply is negative, the consequences are:

First, the transcendental field becomes impersonal; or, if you like, "prepersonal," *without an I.*

Second, the *I* appears only at the level of humanity and is only one aspect of the *me*, the active aspect.

Third, the *I Think* can accompany our representations because it appears on a foundation of unity which it did not help to create; rather, this prior unity makes the *I Think* possible.

Fourth, one may well ask if personality (even the abstract personality of an *I*) is a necessary accompaniment of a consciousness, and if one cannot conceive of absolutely impersonal consciousness.

To this question, Husserl has given his reply. After having determined (in *Logische Untersuchungen*[5]) that the *me* is a synthetic and transcendent production of consciousness, he reverted in *Ideen zu einer reinen Phänomenologie und phänomenologischen Philosophie*[6] to the classic position of a transcendental *I*. This *I* would be, so to speak, behind each consciousnesses, a necessary structure of consciousness whose rays (*Ichstrahlen*) would light upon each phenomenon presenting itself in the field of attention. Thus transcendental consciousness becomes thoroughly personal. Was this notion necessary? Is it compatible with the definition of consciousness given by Husserl?[7]

It is ordinarily thought that the existence of a transcendental *I* may be justified by the need that consciousness has for unity and individuality. It is because all my perceptions and all my thoughts refer themselves back to this permanent seat that my consciousness is unified. It is because I can say *my* consciousness, and because Peter and Paul can also speak of *their* consciousnesses, that these consciousnesses distinguish themselves from each other. The *I* is the producer of inwardness.

386

Now, it is certain that phenomenology does not need to appeal to any such unifying and individualizing *I*. Indeed, consciousness is defined by intentionality. By intentionality consciousness transcends itself. It unifies itself by escaping from itself. The unity of a thousand active consciousnesses by which I have added, do add, and shall add two and two to make four, is the transcendent object "two and two make four." Without the permanence of this eternal truth a real unity would be impossible to conceive, and there would be irreducible operations as often as there were operative consciousnesses. It is possible that those believing "two and two make four" to be the *content* of my representation may be obliged to appeal to a transcendental and subjective principle of unification, which will then be the *I*. But it is precisely Husserl who has no need of such a principle. The object is transcendent to the consciousnesses which grasp it, and it is in the object that the unity of the consciousnesses is found.

It will be said that a principle of unity *within duration* is nonetheless needed if the continual flux of consciousness is to be capable of positing transcendent objects outside the flux. Consciousnesses must be perpetual syntheses of past consciousnesses and present consciousness. This is correct. But it is characteristic that Husserl, who studied this subjective unification of consciousnesses in *Vorlesungen zur Phänomenologie des inneren Zeitbewusstseins*,[8] never had recourse to a synthetic power of the *I*. It is consciousness which unifies itself, concretely, by a play of "transversal" intentionalities which are concrete and real retentions of past consciousnesses. Thus consciousness refers perpetually to itself. Whoever says "a consciousness" says "the whole of consciousness," and this singular property belongs to consciousness itself, aside from whatever relations it may have to the *I*. In *Cartesianische Meditationen*,[9] Husserl seems to have preserved intact this conception of consciousness unifying itself in time.

Furthermore, the individuality of consciousness evidently stems from the nature of consciousness. Consciousness (like Spinoza's substance) can be limited only by itself. Thus, it constitutes a synthetic and individual totality entirely isolated from other totalities of the same type, and the *I* can evidently be only an *expression* (rather than a condition) of this incommunicability and inwardness of consciousnesses. Consequently we may reply without hesitation: the phenomenological conception of consciousness renders the unifying and individualizing role of the *I* totally useless. It is consciousness, on the contrary, which makes possible the unity and the personality of my *I*. The transcendental *I*, therefore, has no *raison d'être*.

But, in addition, this superfluous *I* would be a hindrance. If it existed it would tear consciousness from itself; it would divide consciousness; it would slide into every consciousness like an opaque blade. The transcendental *I* is the death of consciousness. Indeed, the existence of consciousness is an absolute because consciousness is consciousness of itself. This is to say that the type of existence of consciousness is to be consciousness of itself. And consciousness is aware of itself *in so far as it is consciousness of a transcendent object*. All is therefore clear and lucid in consciousness: the object with its characteristic opacity is before consciousness, but consciousness is purely and simply consciousness of being consciousness of that object. This is the law of its existence.

We should add that this consciousness of consciousness – except in the case of reflective consciousness which we shall dwell on later – is not *positional*, which is to say that consciousness is not for itself its own object. Its object is by nature outside of it, and that is why consciousness *posits* and *grasps* the object in the same act. Consciousness knows itself only as absolute inwardness. We shall call such a consciousness: consciousness in the first degree, or *unreflected* consciousness.

Now we ask: is there room for an *I* in such a consciousness? The reply is clear: evidently not. Indeed, such an *I* is not the object (since by hypothesis the *I* is inner); nor is it an *I of consciousness*, since it is something for consciousness. It is not a translucent quality of consciousness, but would be in some way an inhabitant. In fact, however formal, however abstract one may suppose it to be, the *I*, with its personality, would be a sort of center of opacity. It would be to the concrete and psycho-physical *me* what a point is to three dimensions: it would be an infinitely contracted *me*. Thus, if one introduces this opacity into consciousness, one thereby destroys the fruitful definition cited earlier. One congeals consciousness, one darkens it. Consciousness is then no longer a spontaneity; it bears within itself the germ of opaqueness. But in addition we would be forced to abandon that original and profound view which makes of consciousnesses a *non-substantial* absolute. A pure consciousness is an absolute quite simply because it is consciousness of itself. It remains therefore a "phenomenon" in the very special sense in which "to be" and "to appear" are one. It is all lightness, all translucence. This it is which differentiates the *Cogito* of Husserl from the Cartesian *Cogito*. But if the *I* were a necessary structure of consciousness, this opaque *I* would at once be raised to the rank of an absolute. We would then be in the presence of a monad. And this, indeed, is unfortunately the orientation of the new thought of Husserl (see *Cartesianische Meditationen*[10]). Consciousness is loaded down; consciousness has lost that character which rendered it the absolute existent *by virtue of non-existence*. It is heavy and *ponderable*. All the results of phenomenology begin to crumble if the *I* is not, by the same title as the world, a relative existent: that is to say, an object *for* consciousness.

B. The cogito *as reflective consciousness*

The Kantian *I Think* is a condition of possibility. The *Cogito* of Descartes and of Husserl is an apprehension of fact. We have heard of the "factual necessity"[11] of the *Cogito*, and this phrase seems to me most apt. Also, it is undeniable that the *Cogito* is personal. In the *I Think* there is an *I* who thinks. We attain here the *I* in its purity, and it is indeed from the *Cogito* that an "Egology" must take its point of departure. The fact that can serve for a start is, then, this one: each time we apprehend our thought, whether by an immediate intuition or by an intuition based on memory, we apprehend an *I* which is the *I* of the apprehended thought, and which is given, in addition, as transcending this thought and all other possible thoughts. If, for example, I want to remember a certain landscape perceived yesterday from the train, it is possible for me to bring back the memory of that landscape as such. But I can also recollect that *I* was seeing that landscape. This is what Husserl calls, in *Vorlesungen zur Phänomenologie des inneren Zeitbewusstseins*,[12] the possibility of *reflecting in memory*. In other words, I can always perform any recollection whatsoever in the personal mode, and at once the *I* appears. Such is the *factual* guarantee of the Kantian claim *concerning validity*. Thus it seems that there is not one of my consciousnesses which I do not apprehend as provided with an *I*.

But it must be remembered that all the writers who have described the *Cogito* have dealt with it as a reflective operation, that is to say, as an operation of the second degree. Such a *Cogito* is performed by a consciousness *directed upon consciousness*, a consciousness which takes consciousness as an object. Let us agree: the certitude of the *Cogito* is absolute, for, as Husserl said, there is an indissoluble unity of the reflecting consciousness and the reflected consciousness (to the point that the reflecting consciousness could not exist without the reflected consciousness). But the fact remains that we are in the presence of a synthesis of two consciousnesses, one of which is consciousness *of* the other. Thus the essential principle of phenomenology, "all consciousness is consciousness *of* something,"[13] is preserved. Now, my reflecting consciousness does not take itself for an object when I effect the *Cogito*. What it affirms concerns the reflected consciousness. Insofar as my reflecting consciousness is consciousness of itself, it is *non-positional* consciousness. It becomes positional only by directing itself upon the reflected consciousness which itself was not a positional consciousness of itself before being reflected. Thus the consciousness which says *I Think* is precisely not the consciousness which thinks. Or rather it is not *its own* thought which it posits by this thetic act. We are then justified in asking ourselves if the *I* which thinks is common to the two superimposed consciousnesses, or if it is not rather the *I* of the reflected consciousness. All reflecting consciousness is, indeed, in itself unreflected, and a new act of the third degree is necessary in order to posit it. Moreover, there is no infinite regress here, since a consciousness has no need at all of a reflecting consciousness in order to be conscious of itself. It simply does not posit itself as an object.

But is it not precisely the reflective act which gives birth to the *me* in the reflected consciousness? Thus would be explained how every thought apprehended by intuition possesses an *I*, without falling into the difficulties noted in the preceding section. Husserl would be the first to acknowledge that an unreflected thought undergoes a radical modification in becoming reflected. But need one confine this modification to a loss of "naïveté"? Would not the appearance of the *I* be what is essential in this change?

One must evidently revert to a concrete experience, which may seem impossible, since by definition such an experience is reflective, that is to say, supplied with an *I*. But every unreflected consciousness, being non-thetic consciousness of itself, leaves a non-thetic memory that one can consult. To do so it suffices to try to reconstitute the complete moment in which this unreflected consciousness appeared (which by definition is always possible). For example, I was absorbed just now in my reading. I am going to try to remember the circumstances of my reading, my attitude, the lines that I was reading. I am thus going to revive not only these external details but a certain depth of unreflected consciousness, since the objects could only have been perceived *by* that consciousness and since they remain relative to it. That consciousness must not be posited as object of a reflection. On the contrary, I must direct my attention to the revived objects, but *without losing sight of the unreflected consciousness*, by joining in a sort of conspiracy with it and by drawing up an inventory of its content in a non-positional manner. There is no doubt about the result: while I was reading, there was consciousness *of* the book, *of* the heroes of the novel, but the *I* was not inhabiting this consciousness. It was only consciousness of the object and non-positional consciousness of itself. I can now make these a-thetically apprehended results the object of a thesis and declare: there was no *I* in the unreflected consciousness. [. . .]

Let us also note that the *I Think* does not appear to reflection as the reflected consciousness: it is given *through* reflected consciousness. To be sure, it is apprehended by intuition and is an object grasped with evidence. But we know what a service Husserl has rendered to philosophy by distinguishing diverse kinds of evidence. Well, it is only too certain that the *I* of the *I Think* is an object grasped with neither apodictic nor adequate evidence.[14] The evidence is not apodictic, since by saying *I* we affirm far more than we know. It is not adequate, for the *I* is presented as an opaque reality whose content would have to be unfolded. To be sure, the *I* manifests itself as the source of consciousness. But that alone should make us pause. Indeed, for this very reason the *I* appears veiled, indistinct through consciousness, like a pebble at the bottom of the water. For this very reason the *I* is deceptive from the start, since we know that nothing but consciousness can be the source of consciousness.

In addition, if the *I* is a part of consciousness, there would then be *two I's*: the *I* of the reflective consciousness and the *I* of the reflected consciousness. Fink, the disciple of Husserl, is even acquainted with a third *I*, disengaged by the ἐποχή, the *I* of transcendental consciousness. Hence the problem of the three *I*'s, whose difficulties Fink agreeably mentions.[15] For us, this problem is quite simply insoluble. For it is inadmissible that any communication could be established between the reflective *I* and the reflected *I* if they are real elements of consciousness; above all, it is inadmissible that they may finally achieve identity in one unique *I*.

By way of conclusion to this analysis, it seems to me that one can make the following statements:

First, the *I* is an *existent*. It has a concrete type of existence, undoubtedly different from the existence of mathematical truths, of meanings, or of spatio-temporal beings, but no less real. The *I* gives itself as transcendent.

Second, the *I* proffers itself to an intuition of a special kind[16] which apprehends it, always inadequately, behind the reflected consciousness.

Third, the *I* never appears except on the occasion of a reflective act. In this case, the complex structure of consciousness is as follows: there is an unreflected act of reflection, without an *I*, which is directed on a reflected consciousness. The latter becomes the object of the reflecting consciousness without ceasing to affirm its own object (a chair, a mathematical truth, etc.). At the same time, a new object appears which is the occasion for an affirmation by reflective consciousness, and which is consequently not on the same level as the unreflected consciousness (because the latter consciousness is an absolute which has no need of reflective consciousness in order to exist), nor on the same level as the object of the reflected consciousness (chair, etc.). This transcendent object of the reflective act is the *I*.

Fourth, the transcendent *I* must fall before the stroke of phenomenological reduction. The *Cogito* affirms too much. The certain content of the pseudo-"Cogito" is not "*I have* consciousness of this chair," but "There is consciousness of this chair." This content is sufficient to constitute an infinite and absolute field of investigation for phenomenology.

C. The theory of the material presence of the me

For Kant and for Husserl the *I* is a formal structure of consciousness. We have tried to show that an *I* is never purely formal, that it is always, even when conceived abstractly, an infinite contraction of the material *me*. But before going further we need to free ourselves of a purely psychological theory which for psychological reasons affirms the material presence of the *me* in all our consciousness. This is the theory of the "self-love" moralists. According to them, the love of self – and consequently the *me* – lies concealed within all emotions in a thousand different forms. In a very general way, the *me*, as a function of this love that it bears for itself, would desire *for itself* all the objects it desires. The essential structure of each of my acts would be a *reference to myself*. The "return to me" would be constitutive of all consciousnesses. [. . .]

Now the interest of this thesis, it seems to us, is that it puts in bold relief a very frequent error among psychologists. The error consists in confusing the essential structure of reflective acts with the essential structure of unreflected acts. It is overlooked that two forms of existence are always possible for a consciousness. Then, each time the observed consciousnesses are given as unreflected, one superimposes on them a structure, belonging to reflection, which one doggedly alleges to be unconscious.

I pity Peter, and I go to his assistance. For my consciousness only one thing exists at that moment: Peter-having-to-be-helped. This quality of "having-to-be-helped" lies in Peter. It acts on me like a force. Aristotle said it: the desirable is that which moves the desiring. At this level, the desire is given to consciousness as centrifugal (it transcends itself; it is thetic consciousness of "having-to-be" and non-thetic consciousness of itself) and as impersonal (there is no *me*: I am in the presence of Peter's suffering just as I am in the presence of the color of this inkstand; there is an objective world of things and of actions, done or to be done, and the actions come to adhere as qualities to the things which call for them).

Now, this first moment of desire – supposing that it has not completely escaped the self-love theorists – is not considered a complete and autonomous moment. They have imagined another state behind it which remains in a half-light: for example, I help Peter in order to put an end to the disagreeable state into which the sight of his sufferings has put me. But this disagreeable state can be known as such, and one can try to suppress it only following an act of reflection. A distaste on the unreflected level, in fact, transcends itself in the same way that the unreflected consciousness of pity transcends itself. It is the intuitive apprehension of a disagreeable quality of an object. And to the extent that the distaste is accompanied by a desire, it does not desire to suppress *itself*, but to suppress the unpleasant object. It is therefore no use to place behind the unreflected pitying consciousness an unpleasant state which is to be made the underlying cause of the pitying act: for unless this consciousness of unpleasantness turns back on itself in order to posit itself as an unpleasant state, we will remain indefinitely in the impersonal and unreflected. Thus, without even realizing it, the self-love theorists suppose that the reflected is first, original, and concealed in the unconscious. There is scarcely need to bring to light the absurdity of such a hypothesis. Even if the unconscious exists, who could be led to believe that it contains spontaneities of a reflected sort? Is it not the definition of the reflected that it be posited by a consciousness? But, in addition, how can it be held that the reflected is first in relation to the unreflected? Undoubtedly, one can conceive that in certain cases a consciousness may appear immediately as reflected. But even then the unreflected has the ontological priority over the reflected because the unreflected conscious-ness does not need to be reflected in order to exist, and because reflection presup-poses the intervention of a second-degree consciousness.

We arrive then at the following conclusion: unreflected consciousness must be considered autonomous. It is a totality which needs no completing at all, and we must acknowledge with no qualifications that the character of unreflected desire is to transcend itself by apprehending on the subject the quality of desirability. Everything happens as if we lived in a world whose objects, in addition to their qualities of warmth, odor, shape, etc., had the qualities of repulsive, attractive, delightful, useful, etc., and as if these qualities were forces having a certain power over us. In the case of reflection, and only in that case, affectivity is posited for itself, as desire, fear, etc. Only in the case of reflection can I think "*I* hate Peter," "*I* pity Paul," etc.

Contrary to what has been held, therefore, it is on the reflected level that the ego-life has its place, and on the unreflected level that the impersonal life has its place (which naturally does not mean that all reflected life is necessarily egoistic, or that all unreflected life is necessarily altruistic). [. . .]

Thus a purely psychological examination of "intra-mundane" consciousness leads us to the same conclusions as our phenomenological study: *the me must not be sought in the states of unreflected consciousness, nor behind* them. The *me* appears only with the reflective act, and as a noematic correlate[17] of a reflective intention. We begin to get a glimpse of the fact that the *I* and the *me* are only one. We are going to try to show that this ego, of which *I* and *me* are but two aspects, constitutes the ideal and indirect (noematic) unity of the infinite series of our reflected consciousness.

The *I* is the ego as the unity of actions. The *me* is the ego as the unity of states and of qualities. The distinction that one makes between these two aspects of one and the same reality seems to us simply functional, not to say grammatical.

ii The constitution of the ego

The ego is not directly the unity of reflected consciousness. There exists an *imma-nent* unity of these consciousnesses: the flux of consciousness constituting itself as the unity of itself.[18] And there exists a *transcendent* unity: states and actions. The ego is the unity of states and of actions – optionally, of qualities. It is the unity of transcendent unities, and itself transcendent. It is a transcendent pole of synthetic unity, like the object-pole of the unreflected attitude, except that this pole appears solely in the world of reflection.

We shall examine successively the constitution of *states*, of *actions*, and of *qualities*, and the appearance of the *me* as the pole of these transcendences.

A. States as transcendent unities of consciousness

The *state* appears to reflective consciousness. The state is given to it, and is the object of a concrete intuition. If I hate Peter, my hatred of Peter is a state that I can apprehend by reflection. This state is *present* to the gaze of reflective consciousness. It is *real*.

Is it therefore necessary to conclude that the state is immanent and certain? Surely not. We must not make of reflection a mysterious and infallible power, nor believe that everything reflection attains is indubitable *because* attained by reflection. Reflection has limits, both limits of validity and limits in fact. It is a consciousness which posits a consciousness. Everything that it affirms regarding this consciousness is certain and adequate. But if other objects appear to it through this consciousness, there is no reason that these objects should participate in the characteristics of consciousness. Let us consider a reflective experience of hatred. I see Peter, I feel a sort of profound convulsion of repugnance and anger at the sight of him (I am already on the reflective level): the convulsion is consciousness. I cannot be mistaken when I say: I feel at this moment a violent repugnance for Peter. But is this experience of repugnance hatred? Obviously not. Moreover, it is not given as such. In reality, I have hated Peter a long time and I think that I shall hate him always. An instantaneous consciousness of repugnance could not, then, be my hatred. If I limited it to what it is, to something instantaneous, I could not even speak of hatred anymore. I would say: "I feel a repugnance for Peter at this moment," and thus I would not implicate the future. But precisely by this refusal to implicate the future, I would cease to hate.

Now my hatred appears to me at the same time as my experience of repugnance. But it appears *through* this experience. It is given precisely as not being limited to this experience. My hatred was given *in* and *by* each movement of disgust, of repugnance, and of anger, but at the same time it *is not* any of them. My hatred escapes from each of them by affirming its permanence. It affirms that it had already appeared when I thought about Peter with so much fury yesterday, and that it will appear tomorrow. It effects by itself, moreover, a distinction between *to be* and *to appear*, since it gives itself as continuing *to be* even when I am absorbed in other occupations and no consciousness reveals it. This is enough, it would seem, to enable us to affirm that hatred is not *of* consciousness. It overflows the instantaneousness of consciousness, and it does not bow to the absolute law of consciousness for which no distinction is possible between appearance and being. Hatred, then, is a transcendent object. Each *Erlebnis* reveals it as a whole, but at the same time the *Erlebnis* is a profile, a projection (an *Abschattung*). Hatred is credit for an infinity of angry or repulsed consciousness in the past and in the future. It is the transcendent unity of this infinity of consciousness. Thus, to say "I hate" or "I love" on the occasion of a particular consciousness of attraction or repugnance is to effect a veritable passage to infinity, rather analogous to that which we effect when we perceive *an* inkstand, or *the blue* of the blotter.

No more is needed in order for the rights of reflection to be singularly limited. It is certain that Peter is repugnant to me. But it is and always will remain doubtful that I hate him. Indeed, this affirmation infinitely exceeds the power of reflection. Naturally, one need not therefore conclude that hatred is a mere hypothesis, an empty concept: it is indeed a real object which I am apprehending through the

Erlebnis. But this object is outside consciousness, and the very nature of its existence implies its "dubitability." Reflection too has its certain domain and its doubtful domain, a sphere of adequate evidence and a sphere of inadequate evidence. Pure reflection (which, however, is not necessarily phenomenological reflection) keeps to the given without setting up claims for the future. This can be seen when someone, after having said in anger, "I detest you," catches himself and says, "It is not true, I do not detest you, I said that in anger." We see here two reflections: the one, impure and conniving, which effects then and there a passage to the infinite, and which through the *Erlebnis* abruptly constitutes hatred as its transcendent object; the other, pure, merely descriptive, which disarms the unreflected consciousness by granting its instantaneousness. These two reflections apprehend the same, certain data, but the one affirms *more* than it knows, directing itself through the reflected consciousness upon an object situated outside consciousness.

As soon as one leaves the domain of pure or impure reflection and meditates on the results of reflection, one is tempted to confuse the transcendent meaning of the *Erlebnis* with its character as immanent. This confusion leads the psychologist to two types of error. Because I am often mistaken about my emotions – because, for example, I come to believe I love when I hate – I may conclude that introspection is deceptive. In this case I definitively separate my *state* from its appearances. I hold that a symbolical interpretation of all appearances (considered as symbols) is necessary in order to determine the emotion, and I assume a relation of causality between the emotion and its appearances. Now the unconscious re-emerges. Or else, because I know on the contrary that my introspection is sound, that I cannot doubt my consciousness of repugnance so long as I have it, I think I am entitled to transfer this certitude to the emotion. I thus conclude that my hatred can shut itself up in the immanence and adequation of an instantaneous consciousness.

Hatred is a *state*. And by this term I have tried to express the character of passivity which is constitutive of hatred. Undoubtedly it will be said that hatred is a force, an irresistible drive, etc. But an electric current or the fall of water are also forces to be reckoned with: does this diminish one whit the passivity and inertia of their nature? Is it any less the case that they receive their energy *from the outside*? The passivity of a spatio-temporal thing is constituted by virtue of its existential relativity. A relative existence can only be passive, since the least activity would free it from the relative and would constitute it as absolute. In the same way, hatred is *inert*, since it is existence relative to reflective consciousness. And, naturally, in speaking of the inertia of hatred we mean to say nothing if not that hatred appears so to consciousness. In fact, do we not say, "My hatred was reawakened," "His hatred was combated by the violent desire to . . . ," etc.? [. . .]

B. The constitution of actions

We shall not attempt to establish the distinction between *active* consciousness and simply spontaneous consciousness. Moreover, it seems to us that this is one of the most difficult problems of phenomenology. We would simply like to remark that concerted action is first of all (whatever the nature of the active consciousness may be) a transcendent. That is obvious for actions like "playing the piano," "driving a car," "writing," because these actions are "taken" in the world of things. But purely psychical actions like doubting, reasoning, meditating, making a hypothesis, these too must be conceived as transcendences. What deceives us here is that action is not only the noematic[19] unity of a stream of consciousnesses: it is also a concrete realization. But we must not forget that action requires time to be accomplished. It has articulations; it has moments. To these moments correspond concrete, active consciousnesses, and the reflection which is directed on the consciousnesses apprehends the total action in an intuition which exhibits it as the transcendent unity of the active consciousnesses. In this sense, one can say that the spontaneous doubt which invades me when I glimpse an object in the shadows is a *consciousness*, but the methodological doubt of Descartes is an action, that is to say, a transcendent object of reflective consciousness. Here one sees the danger: when Descartes says, "I doubt therefore I am," is this a matter of the spontaneous doubt that reflective consciousness apprehends in its instantaneousness, or is this precisely a matter of the enterprise of doubting? This ambiguity, we have seen, may be the origin of serious errors.

C. Qualities as optional unities of states

The ego, we shall see, is directly the transcendent unity of states and of actions. Nevertheless there can exist an intermediary between actions and states: the quality. When we have experienced hatred several times toward different persons, or tenacious resentments, or protracted angers, we unify these diverse manifestations by intending a psychic disposition for producing them. This psychic disposition (I am very spiteful, I am capable of hating violently, I am ill-tempered) is naturally more and other than a mere contrivance. It is a transcendent object. It represents the substratum of the states, as the states represent the substratum of the *Erlebnisse*. But its relation with the emotions is not a relation of emanation. Emanation only connects consciousnesses to psychic passivities. The relation of the quality to the state (or to the action) is a relation of actualization. The quality is given as a potentiality, a virtuality, which, under the influence[20] of diverse factors, can pass into actuality. Its actuality is precisely the state (or the action). We see the essential difference between the quality and the state. The state is a noematic unity of spontaneities. The quality is a unity of objective passivities. In the absence of any consciousness of hatred, hatred is given as actually existing. On the contrary, in the absence of any feeling of spite, the corresponding quality remains a potentiality. Potentiality is not mere possibility: it presents itself as something which really exists, but its mode of existence is potency. Naturally, faults, virtues, tastes, talents, tendencies, instincts, etc., are of this type. These unifications are always possible. The influence of preconceived ideas and of social factors is here preponderant. Concomitantly, such unifications are never indispensable, because states and actions can find directly in the ego the unity that they demand.

D. The constitution of the ego as the pole of actions, states, and qualities

We have been learning to distinguish "the psychic" from consciousness. The psychic is the transcendent object of reflective consciousness.[21] It is also the object of the science called "psychology." The ego appears to reflection as a transcendent object effecting the permanent synthesis of the psychic. The ego is *on the side of* the psychic. Let us note here that the ego that we are considering is psychic, not psycho-physical. It is not by abstraction that we separate these two aspects of the ego. The psycho-physical *me* is a synthetic enrichment of the psychic ego, which can very well (and without reduction of any sort) exist in a free state. It is certain, for example, that when we say "I am undecided," we do not directly refer to the psycho-physical *me*.

It would be tempting to constitute the ego as a "subject-pole" like that "object-pole" which Husserl places at the center of the noematic nucleus. This object-pole is an X which supports determinations:

> *Predicates, however, are predicates of "something." This something also belongs to the nucleus in question and obviously cannot be separated from the nucleus. It is the central point of unity of which we were speaking earlier. It is the point of attachment for predicates, their support. But in no respect is it a unity of the predicates in the sense of some complex, in the sense of some linkage of predicates. It is necessarily to be distinguished from predicates, even if one cannot set it beside them, nor separate it from them; just as they are* its *predicates, unthinkable without it and yet distinguishable from it.*[22]

By that Husserl means to indicate that he considers things as syntheses which are at least ideally analyzable. Undoubtedly, this tree, this table are synthetic complexes and each quality is tied to every other. But each is tied to each *in so far as each quality belongs to the same object, X*. What is logically first are unilateral relations by which each quality belongs (directly or indirectly) to this X like a predicate to a subject. It follows that an analysis is always possible.

This notion is most debatable, but this is not the place to examine it. What matters to us is that an indissoluble synthetic totality which could support itself would have no need of a supporting X, provided of course that it were really and concretely unanalyzable. If we take a melody, for example, it is useless to presuppose an X which would serve as a support for the different notes. The unity here comes from the absolute indissolubility of the elements which cannot be conceived as separated, save by abstraction. The subject of the predicate here will be the concrete totality, and the predicate will be a quality abstractly separated from the totality, a quality which has its full meaning only if one connects it again to the totality.[23]

For these very reasons we shall not permit ourselves to see the ego as a sort of X-pole which would be the support of psychic phenomena. Such an X would, by definition, be indifferent to the psychic qualities it would support. But the ego, as we shall see, is never indifferent to its states; it is "compromised" by them. Now, to be exact, a support can be thus compromised by what it supports only in case it is a concrete totality which supports and contains its own qualities. The ego is nothing outside of the concrete totality of states and actions it supports. Undoubtedly it is transcendent to all the states which it unifies, but not as an abstract X whose mission is only to unify: rather, it is the infinite totality of states and of actions which is never reducible to *an* action or to *a* state. If we were to seek for unreflected consciousness an analogue of what the ego is for consciousness of the second degree, we rather believe that it would be necessary to think of the *World*, conceived as the infinite synthetic totality of all things. Sometimes we do, in fact, apprehend the World beyond our immediate surroundings as a vast concrete existence. In this case, the things which surround us appear only as the extreme point of this World which surpasses them and envelops them. The ego is to psychical objects what the World is to things. But the appearance of the World in the background of things is rather rare; special circumstances, described very well by Heidegger in *Sein und Zeit*,[24] are necessary for it to "reveal" itself. The ego, on the contrary, always appears at the horizon of states. Each state, each action is given as incapable of being separated from the ego without abstraction. And if judgment separates the *I* from its state (as in the phrase: *I* am in love), this can be only in order to bind them at once. The movement of separation would end in an empty and false meaning if it were not given as incomplete, and if it did not complete itself by a movement of synthesis.

This transcendent totality participates in the questionable character of all transcendence. This is to say that everything given to us by our intuitions of the ego is always given as capable of being contradicted by subsequent intuitions. For example, I can see clearly that I am ill-tempered, jealous, etc., and nevertheless I may be mistaken. In other words, I may deceive myself in thinking that I have *such* a me. The error, moreover, is not committed on the level of judgment, but already on the level of pre-judgmental evidence.[25] This questionable character of my ego – or even the intuitional error that I commit – does not signify that I have a *true me* which I am unaware of, but only that the intended ego has in itself the character of dubitability (in certain cases, the character of falsehood). The metaphysical hypothesis according to which my ego would not be composed of elements having existed in reality (ten years ago or a second ago), but would only be constituted of false memories, is not excluded. The power of the *malin génie* extends so far.

But if it is in the nature of the ego to be a dubitable object, it does not follow that the ego is *hypothetical*. In fact, the ego is the spontaneous, transcendent unification of our states and our actions. In this capacity, it is no hypothesis. I do not say to myself, "Perhaps I have an ego," as I may say to myself, "Perhaps I hate Peter." I do not seek here a unifying *meaning* of my states. When I unify my consciousnesses under the title "hatred," I add a certain meaning to them, I qualify them. But when I incorporate my states in the concrete totality *me*, I add nothing to them. In reality, the relation of the ego to the qualities, states, and actions is neither a relation of emanation (like the relation of consciousness to emotion), nor a relation of actualization (like the relation of the quality to the state). It is a relation on the order of poetic production (in the sense of ποιεῖν), or if you like, a relation of creation.

Everyone, by consulting the results of his intuition, can observe that the ego is given as producing its states. We undertake here a description of this transcendent ego such as it reveals itself in intuition.

We begin therefore with this undeniable fact: each new state is fastened directly (or indirectly, by the quality) to the ego, as to its origin. This mode of creation is indeed a creation *ex nihilo*, in the sense that the state is not given as having formerly been in the *me*.

Even if hatred is given as the actualization of a certain power of spite or hatred, it remains something new in relation to the power it actualizes. Thus the unifying act of reflection fastens each new state, in a very special way, to the concrete totality, *me*. Reflection is not confined to apprehending the new state as attaching to this totality, as fusing with it: reflection intends a relation which traverses time backwards and which gives the *me* as the source of the state. The same is true, naturally, for actions in relation to the *I*. As for qualities, although *qualifying* the *me*, they are not given as something by virtue of which the *me* exists (as is the case, for example, for an aggregate: each stone, each brick exists through itself, and their aggregate exists by virtue of each of them). But, on the contrary, the ego maintains its qualities through a genuine, continuous creation. Nevertheless, we do not finally apprehend the ego as a pure creative source beside the qualities. It does not seem to us that we could find a skeletal pole if we took away, one after the other, all the qualities. If the ego appears as beyond each quality, or even as beyond all qualities, this is because the ego is opaque like an object: we would have to undertake an infinite plundering in order to take away all its powers. And, at the end of this plundering, nothing would remain; the ego would have vanished. The ego is the creator of its states and sustains its qualities in existence by a sort of preserving spontaneity. [. . .]

The ego is "compromised" by what it produces. Here a relation reverses itself: the action or the state returns upon the ego to qualify it. This leads us again to the relation of "participation." Each new state produced by the ego colors and tinges the ego slightly the moment the ego produces it. The ego is in some way spellbound by this action, it "participates" with it. It was not the crime of Raskolnikoff which was incorporated into his ego. Or rather, to be exact, it was the crime, but in a condensed form, in the form of a "killing bruise."[26] Thus everything that the ego produces affects it. We must add: *and only* what it produces. One might object that the *me* can be transformed by external events (catastrophe, mourning, trickery, change in social environment, etc.). But this is so only insofar as external events are for the *me* the occasion of states or actions. Everything happens as if the ego were protected by its phantom-like spontaneity from any direct contact with the outside, as if it could communicate with the World only by the intermediary of states or actions. We see the reason for this isolation: quite simply, the ego is an object which appears only to reflection, and which is thereby radically cut off from the World. The ego does not live on the same level.

Just as the ego is an irrational synthesis of activity and passivity, it is a synthesis of interiority and transcendence. It is, in a sense, more "internal to" consciousness than are states. This is precisely the interiority of the reflected consciousness, contemplated by the reflective consciousness. But one could easily suppose this to mean that reflection makes interiority into an object by *contemplation*. Yet what do we mean by "interiority"? Simply that to be and to be aware of itself are one and the same thing for consciousness. This may be expressed in different ways: I may say, for example, that for consciousness appearance is the absolute to the extent that it is appearance; or, again, that consciousness is a being whose essence involves its existence. These diverse formulations permit us to conclude that one *lives* interiority (that one "*exists inward*"), but that one does not contemplate it, since interiority would itself be beyond contemplation, as its condition.

It would be no use to object that reflection posits the reflected consciousness and thereby its interiority. The case is a special one: reflection and reflected are only one, as Husserl has very well shown, and the interiority of the one fuses with that of the other. To posit interiority before oneself, however, is necessarily to give it the load of an object. This transpires as if interiority closed upon itself and proffered us only its outside; as if one had to "circle about" it in order to understand it. And this is just how the ego gives itself to reflection: as an interiority closed upon itself. It is inward *for itself, not for consciousness*. Naturally, we are dealing with a contradictory composite: for an absolute interiority never has an outside. It can be conceived only by itself, and that is why we cannot apprehend the consciousnesses of others (for that reason only, and not because bodies separate us).

In reality, this degraded and irrational interiority may be analyzed into two very special structures: *intimacy* and *indistinctness*. In relation to consciousness, the ego is given as intimate. Everything happens as though the ego were *of* consciousness, with only this particular and essential difference: that the ego is opaque to consciousness. And this opaqueness is apprehended as *indistinctness*. Indistinctness, which under different forms is frequently utilized in philosophy, is interiority seen from the outside; or, if one prefers, indistinctness is the degraded projection of interiority. [. . .]

Finally, what radically prevents the acquisition of real cognitions of the ego is the very special way in which it is given to reflective consciousness. The ego never appears, in fact, except when one is not looking at it. The reflective gaze must be fixed on the *Erlebnis*, insofar as it emanates from the state. Then, behind the state, at the horizon, the ego appears. It is, therefore, never seen except "out of the corner of the eye." As soon as I turn my gaze toward it and try to reach it without passing through the *Erlebnis* and the state, it vanishes. This is because in trying to apprehend the ego for itself and as a direct object of my consciousness, I fall back onto the unreflected level, and the ego disappears along with the reflective act. Whence that vexing sense of uncertainty, which many philosophers express by putting the *I* on this side of the state of consciousness and affirming that consciousness must return upon itself in order to perceive the *I* which is behind it. That is not it: rather, the ego is *by nature* fugitive.

It is certain, however, that the *I* does appear on the unreflected level. If someone asks me "What are you doing?" and I reply, all preoccupied, "I am trying to hang this picture," or "I am repairing the rear tire," these statements do not transport us to the level of reflection. I utter them without ceasing to work, without ceasing to envisage actions only as done or to be done – not insofar as I am doing them. But this "I" which is here in question nevertheless is no mere syntactical form. It has a meaning; it is quite simply an empty concept which is destined to remain empty. Just as I can think of a chair in the absence of any chair merely by a concept, I can in the same way think of the *I* in the absence of the *I*. This is what a consideration of states such as "What are you doing this afternoon?" "I am going to the office," or "I have met my friend Peter," or "I must write him," etc., makes obvious. But the *I*, by falling from the reflective level to the unreflected level, does not simply empty itself. It degrades itself: it loses its *intimacy*. The concept could never be filled by the data of intuition, for now it aims at something other than those data. The *I* that we find here is in some way the support of actions that "I" do, or have to do, in the world insofar as these actions are qualities of the world and not unities of consciousnesses. For example, the wood *has to* be broken into small pieces for the fire to catch. It *has to:* this is a quality of the wood and an objective relation of the wood to the fire which *has to* be lighted. Now *I* am breaking the wood, that is to say, the action is realized in the world, and the objective and empty support of this action is the *I-concept*. This is why the body and bodily images can consummate the total degradation of the concrete *I* of reflection to the "*I*-concept" by functioning for the "*I*-concept" as its illusory fulfillment. I say: "'I' break the wood and I see and feel the object, 'body,' engaged in breaking the wood." The body there serves as a visible and tangible symbol for the *I*. We see, then, the series of refractions and degradations with which an "egology" would be concerned:

Reflective level
{
Reflected consciousness: immanence, interiority.
Intuited ego: transcendence, intimacy (the domain of the psychical).
}

Unreflected level
{
I-concept (optional): a transcendent which is empty, without "intimacy."
Body as the illusory fulfillment of the *I*-concept (the domain of the psycho-physical).
}

E. The I *and consciousness in the* cogito

One might ask why the *I* appears on the occasion of the *Cogito*, since the *Cogito*, correctly performed, is an apprehension of a pure consciousness, without any constitution of states or actions. To tell the truth, the *I* is not necessary here, since it is never a direct unity of consciousnesses. One can even suppose a consciousness performing a pure reflective act which delivers consciousness to itself as a non-personal spontaneity. Only we must realize that phenomenological reduction is never perfect. Here intervene a host of psychological motivations. When Descartes performs the *Cogito*, he performs it in conjunction with methodological doubt, with the ambition of "advancing science," etc., which are *actions* and *states*. Thus the Cartesian method, doubt, etc., are by nature given as undertakings of an *I*. It is quite natural that the *Cogito*, which appears at the end of these undertakings, and *which is given as logically bound to methodological doubt*, sees an *I* appear on its horizon. This *I* is a form of ideal connection, a way of affirming that the *Cogito* is indeed of the same form as doubt. In a word, the *Cogito* is impure. It is a spontaneous consciousness, no doubt, but it remains synthetically tied to consciousnesses of states and actions. The proof is that the *Cogito* is given at once as the logical result of doubt and as that which puts an end to doubt. A reflective apprehension of spontaneous consciousness as non-personal spontaneity would have to be accomplished *without any antecedent motivation*. This is always possible in principle, but remains very improbable or, at least, extremely rare in our human condition. At any rate, as we have said above, the *I* which appears on the horizon of the *I Think* is not given as the producer of conscious spontaneity. Consciousness produces itself facing the *I* and goes toward it, goes to rejoin it. That is all one can say.

Conclusions

In conclusion, we would like simply to offer the three following remarks:

1. The conception of the ego which we propose seems to us to effect the liberation of the Transcendental Field, and at the same time its purification.

The Transcendental Field, purified of all egological structure, recovers its primary transparency. In a sense, it is a *nothing*, since all physical, psycho-physical, and psychic objects, all truths, all values are outside it; since my *me* has itself ceased to be any part of it. But this nothing is *all* since it is *consciousness of* all these objects. There is no longer an "inner life" in the sense in which Brunschvicg opposes "inner life" and "spiritual life," because there is no longer anything which is an *object* and which can at the same time partake of the intimacy of consciousness. Doubts, remorse, the so-called "mental crises of consciousness," etc. – in short, all the content of intimate diaries – become sheer *performance*. And perhaps we could derive here some sound precepts of moral discretion. But, in addition, we must bear in mind that from this point of view my emotions and my states, my ego itself, cease to be my exclusive property. To be precise: up to now a radical distinction has been made between the objectivity of a spatio-temporal thing or of an external truth, and the subjectivity of psychical "states." It seemed as if the subject had a privileged status with respect to his own states. When two men, according to this conception, talk about the same chair, they really are talking about the *same* thing. This chair which one takes hold of and lifts is *the same* as the chair which the other sees. There is not merely a correspondence of images; there is only one object. But it seemed that when Paul tried to understand a psychical state of Peter, he could not *reach* this state, the intuitive apprehension of which belonged only to Peter. He could only envisage an equivalent, could only create empty concepts which tried in vain to reach a reality by essence removed from intuition. Psychological understanding occurred by analogy. Phenomenology has come to teach us that *states* are objects, that an emotion as such (a love or a hatred) is a transcendent object and cannot shrink into the interior unity of a "consciousness." Consequently, if Paul and Peter both speak of Peter's love, for example, it is no longer true that the one speaks blindly and by analogy of that which the other apprehends in full. They speak of the same thing. Doubtless they apprehend it by different procedures, but these procedures may be equally intuitional.[27] And Peter's emotion is no more *certain* for Peter than for Paul. For both of them, it belongs to the category of objects which can be called into question. But the whole of this profound and novel conception is compromised if the *me* of Peter, that *me* which hates or which loves, remains an essential structure of consciousness. The emotion, after all, remains attached to the *me*. This emotion "sticks to" the *me*. If one draws the *me* into consciousness, one draws the emotion along with it. To us, it seemed, on the contrary, that the *me* was a transcendent object, like the *state*, and that because of this fact it was accessible to two sorts of intuition: an intuitive apprehension by the consciousness *of which it is the me*, and an intuitive apprehension less clear, but no less intuitive, by other consciousnesses. In a word, Peter's *me* is accessible to my intuition as well as to Peter's intuition, and in both cases it is the object of inadequate evidence. If that is the case, then there is no longer anything "impenetrable" about Peter; unless it is his very consciousness. But his consciousness is *radically* impenetrable. We mean that it is not only refractory to intuition, but to thought.[28] I cannot *conceive* Peter's consciousness without making an object of it (since I do not conceive it as being *my consciousness*). I cannot conceive it because I would have to think of it as pure interiority and as transcendence *at the same time*, which is impossible. A consciousness cannot conceive of a consciousness other than itself. Thus we can distinguish, thanks to our conception of the *me*, a sphere accessible to psychology, in which the method of external observation and the introspective method have the same rights and can mutually assist each other, and a pure transcendental sphere accessible to phenomenology alone.

This transcendental sphere is a sphere of *absolute* existence, that is to say, a sphere of pure spontaneities which are never objects and which determine their own existence. The *me* being an object, it is evident that I shall never be able to say: *my* consciousness, that is, the consciousness of my *me* (save in a purely designative sense, as one says for example: the day of *my* baptism). The ego is not the owner of consciousness; it is the object of consciousness. To be sure, we constitute spontaneously our states and actions as productions of the ego. But our states and actions are also objects. We never have a direct intuition of the spontaneity of an instantaneous consciousness as produced by the ego. That would be impossible. It is only on the level of meanings and psychological hypotheses that we can conceive such production – and this error is possible only because on this level the ego and the consciousness are indicated *emptily*.[29] In this sense, if one understands the *I Think* so as to make of thought a production of the *I*, one has already constituted thought as passivity and as *state*, that is to say, as object. One has left the level of pure reflection, in which the ego undoubtedly appears, but appears *on the horizon* of a spontaneity. The reflective attitude is correctly expressed in this famous sentence by Rimbaud (in the letter of the seer): "I is *an other*." The context proves that he simply meant that the spontaneity of consciousness could not emanate from the *I*, the spontaneity *goes toward* the *I*, rejoins the *I*, lets the *I* be glimpsed beneath its limpid density, but is itself given above all as *individuated* and *impersonal* spontaneity. [. . .]

We may therefore formulate our thesis: transcendental consciousness is an impersonal spontaneity. It determines its existence at each instant, without our being able to conceive anything *before* it. Thus each instant of our conscious life reveals to us a creation *ex nihilo*. Not a new *arrangement*, but a new existence. There is something distressing for each of us, to catch in the act this tireless creation of existence of which *we* are not the creators. At this level man has the impression of ceaselessly escaping from himself, of overflowing himself, of being surprised by riches which are always unexpected. And once more it is an unconscious from which he demands an account of this surpassing of the *me* by consciousness. Indeed, the *me* can do nothing to this spontaneity, for *will is an object which constitutes itself for and by this spontaneity*. The will directs itself upon states, upon emotions, or upon things, but it never turns back upon consciousness. We are well aware of this in the occasional cases in which we try *to will* a consciousness (I *will* fall asleep, I *will* no longer think about that, etc.). In these various cases, it is *by essence* necessary that the will be maintained and preserved *by that consciousness which is radically opposed* to the consciousness it wants to give rise to (if I *will* to fall asleep, I stay awake; if I *will* not to think about this or that, I think about it *precisely on that account*). It seems to us that this monstrous spontaneity is at the origin of numerous psychasthenic ailments. Consciousness is frightened by its own spontaneity because it senses this spontaneity as *beyond* freedom. This is clearly seen in an example from Janet. A young bride was in terror, when her husband left her alone, of sitting at the window and summoning the passers-by like a prostitute. Nothing in her education, in her past, nor in her character could serve as an explanation of such a fear. It seems to us simply that a negligible circumstance (reading, conversation, etc.) had determined in her what one might call "a vertigo of possibility." She found herself monstrously free, and this vertiginous freedom appeared to her *at the opportunity* for this action which she was afraid of doing. But this vertigo is comprehensible only if consciousness suddenly appeared to itself as infinitely overflowing in its possibilities the *I* which ordinarily serves as its unity.

Perhaps, in reality, the essential function of the ego is not so much theoretical as practical. We have noticed, indeed, that it does not bind up the unity of phenomena; that it is limited to reflecting an *ideal* unity, whereas the real and concrete unity has long been effected. But perhaps the essential role of the ego is to mask from consciousness its very spontaneity. A phenomenological description of spontaneity would show, indeed, that spontaneity renders impossible any distinction between action and passion, or any conception of an autonomy of the will. These notions have meaning only on a level where all activity is given as emanating from a passivity which it transcends; in short, on a level at which man considers himself as at once subject and object. But it is an essential necessity that one not be able to distinguish between voluntary spontaneity and involuntary spontaneity.

Everything happens, therefore, as if consciousness constituted the ego as a false representation of itself, as if consciousness hypnotized itself before this ego which it has constituted, absorbing itself in the ego as if to make the ego its guardian and its law. It is thanks to the ego, indeed, that a distinction can be made between the possible and the real, between appearance and being, between the willed and the undergone.

But it can happen that consciousness suddenly produces itself on the pure reflective level. Perhaps not without the ego, yet as escaping from the ego on all sides, as dominating the ego and maintaining the ego outside the consciousness by a continued creation. On this level, there is no distinction between the possible and the real, since the appearance is the absolute. There are no more barriers, no more limits, nothing to hide consciousness from itself. Then consciousness, noting what could be called the fatality of its spontaneity, is suddenly anguished: it is this dread, absolute and without remedy, this fear of itself, which seems to us constitutive of pure consciousness, and which holds the key to the psychasthenic ailment we spoke of. If the *I* of the *I Think* is the primary structure of consciousness, this dread is impossible. If, on the contrary, our point of view is adopted, not only do we have a coherent explanation of this ailment, but we have, moreover, a permanent motive for carrying out the phenomenological reduction. As we know, in his article in *Kantstudien*[30] Fink admits, not without some melancholy, that as long as one remains in the "natural" attitude, there is *no reason*, no "motive" for exercising the ἐποχή. In fact, this natural attitude is perfectly coherent. There one will find none of those contradictions which, according to Plato, lead the philosopher to effect a philosophical conversion. Thus, the ἐποχή appears in the phenomenology of Husserl as a miracle. Husserl himself, in *Cartesianische Meditationen*,[31] made an extremely vague allusion to certain psychological motives which would lead to undertaking reduction. But these motives hardly seem sufficient. Moreover, reduction seems capable of being performed only at the end of lengthy study. It appears, then, as a *knowledgeable* operation, which confers on it a sort of gratuitousness. On the other hand, if "the natural attitude" appears wholly as an effort made by consciousness to escape from itself by projecting itself into the *me* and becoming absorbed there, and if this effort is never completely rewarded, and if a simple act of reflection suffices in order for conscious spontaneity to tear itself abruptly away from the *I* and be given as independent, then the ἐποχή is no longer a miracle, an intellectual method, an erudite procedure: it is an anxiety which is imposed on us and which we cannot avoid: it is both a pure event of transcendental origin and an ever possible accident of our daily life.

2. This conception of the ego seems to us the only possible refutation of solipsism. The refutation that Husserl presents in *Formale und transzendentale Logik*[32] and in *Cartesianische Meditationen*[33] does not seem to us capable of unsettling a determined and intelligent solipsist. As long as the *I* remains a structure of consciousness, it will always remain possible to oppose consciousness, with its *I*, to all other existents. Finally, then, it is really the *me* who must produce the world. Small matter if certain layers of this world necessitate by their very nature a relation to others. This relation can be a mere quality of the world that I create and in no way obliges me to accept the real existence of other *I*'s.

But if the *I* becomes a transcendent, it participates in all the vicissitudes of the world. It is no absolute; it has not created the universe; it falls like other existences at the stroke of the ἐποχή; and solipsism becomes unthinkable from the moment that the *I* no longer has a privileged status. Instead of expressing itself in effect as "I alone exist as absolute," it must assert that "absolute consciousness alone exists as absolute," which is obviously a truism. My *I*, in effect, is *no more certain for consciousness than the I of other men*. It is only more intimate.

3. The theorists of the extreme Left have sometimes reproached phenomenology for being an idealism and for drowning reality in the stream of ideas. But if idealism is the philosophy without evil of Brunschvicg, if it is a philosophy in which the effort of spiritual assimilation never meets external resistances, in which suffering, hunger, and war are diluted in a slow process of the unification of ideas, nothing is more unjust than to call phenomenologists "idealists." On the contrary, for centuries we have not felt in philosophy so realistic a current. The phenomenologists have plunged man back into the world; they have given full measure to man's agonies and sufferings, and also to his rebellions. Unfortunately, as long as the *I* remains a structure of absolute consciousness, one will still be able to reproach phenomenology for being an escapist doctrine, for again pulling a part of man out of the world and, in that way, turning our attention from the real problems. It seems to us that this reproach no longer has any justification if one makes the *me* an existent, strictly contemporaneous with the world, whose existence has the same essential characteristics as the world. It has always seemed to me that a working hypothesis as fruitful as historical materialism never needed for a foundation the absurdity which is metaphysical materialism. In fact, it is not necessary that the object precede the subject for spiritual pseudo-values to vanish

and for ethics to find its bases in reality. It is enough that the *me* be contemporaneous with the World, and that the subject-object duality, which is purely logical, definitively disappear from philosophical preoccupations. The World has not created the *me*: the *me* has not created the World. These are two objects for absolute, impersonal consciousness, and it is by virtue of this consciousness that they are connected. This absolute consciousness, when it is purified of the *I*, no longer has anything of the *subject*. It is no longer a collection of representations. It is quite simply a first condition and an absolute source of existence. And the relation of interdependence established by this absolute consciousness between the *me* and the World is sufficient for the *me* to appear as "endangered" before the World, for the *me* (indirectly and through the intermediary of states) to draw the whole of its content from the World. No more is needed in the way of a philosophical foundation for an ethics and a politics which are absolutely positive.

Notes

1 I shall use here the term "consciousness" ["*conscience*"] to translate the German word *Bewusstsein*, which signifies both the whole of consciousness – the monad – and each moment of this consciousness. The expression "state of consciousness" seems to me inaccurate owing to the passivity which it introduces into consciousness. [AUTHOR.]

2 No single term is more central to phenomenology and more alien to current trends in British and American philosophy than the term "intuition." Its exposition would merit an essay longer than this translation. The interested reader is referred to the classic discussions by Edmund Husserl in "Ideen zur einer reinen Phänomenologie und Phänomenologischen Philosophie – Volume I," published in *Jahrbuch für Philosophie und phänomenologische Forschung*, I (1922), pp. 1–323 (henceforth abbreviated *Ideas I*). An English translation to which the reader may refer by Section numbers is published under the title *Ideas* (New York: Macmillan, 1931). The most relevant passages are in Secs. 1–4, 7, and 18–24.

Perhaps the essential point to be retained in connection with this phenomenologically oriented essay by Sartre is that for the phenomenologist the primary mode of evidence is intuitive. An intuition (summarily explained) is an act of consciousness by which the object under investigation is *confronted*, rather than merely indicated *in absentia*. Thus, it is one thing merely to indicate the Eiffel Tower (merely "to have it in mind," as we say), and another thing to confront the indicated object by an act of imagination or perception. The indicative act is "empty"; the intuitive act of imagination or perception is "filled out." Once this distinction has been made, it would seem difficult to disagree with the phenomenologist that every cognitive inquiry must ultimately base its claims upon acts of intuition, even if supplementary modes of evidence (e.g., inductive reasoning regarding the external world which is confronted by perceptual intuition) must be invoked to develop the inquiry. For an object must be present, confronted, to be investigated, however far from such original confrontation the investigation may wander as it proceeds. In the physical sciences, the reliance in the last analysis upon perceptual evidence is patent. In phenomenology, the subject matter under investigation is consciousness. The method is intuitive, then, in the sense that consciousness must regard itself to determine just what consciousness is, what consciousness does and does not include. In the present essay, of course, the issue is whether consciousness is or is not inhabited by an "I" or ego operating within or behind consciousness. When Sartre writes in the present passage, therefore, that phenomenology is a "scientific" rather than a "Critical" study of consciousness because phenomenology proceeds by "intuition," he means that as in any descriptive science the first requirement is to *look at* the subject matter, in contrast to Kantian philosophy, which might be said to begin with the nature of science and to construct subsequently an account of consciousness by inference.

Owing to the impracticality of a detailed account in this place of the phenomenological concept of intuition, it may be helpful to note briefly some familiar senses of
"intuition" which would be quite out of place. First, intuitive knowledge has no traffic
with mystical insight. The "filling out" of a previously empty consciousness of an object
represents a logically distinct kind of consciousness, not some flow of feeling. Second,
intuitive knowledge is not an identification with the object in the Bergsonian sense. Third,
intuitive knowledge is not limited to the familiar type of intuition of the external world
which we call "sense-perception." Intuition may be directed to consciousness itself (i.e.,
introspectively). Intuition may be directed to a highly complex object, i.e., a "state of
affairs," previously set forth for consciousness by a process of judgment. For example, I
may confront by an act of intuition the state of affairs "that this knife is to the right of the
plate." Fourth, as may be evident from the last example, intuition is possible at any level
of abstraction (e.g., I may confront in intuition the genus Red). Fifth, almost invariably to
intuit an object or state of affairs is not to know its existence (e.g., to imagine the Eiffel
Tower and to perceive the Eiffel Tower are both intuitive confrontations of the object).
The exception concerns reflective intuition of the specious present. Sixth, to intuit an
object is not necessarily to know everything about it, viz., the inadequacy of sense-
perception, which is always an apprehension of the object "in profile." (Cf. below, n. 17,
on the alleged inadequacy of intuition of the ego.) Thus, the notion of intuition in
phenomenology does not necessarily imply the notion of certain knowledge. Yet the
primary mode of evidence in any cognitive inquiry must be intuitive, according to the
phenomenologist, for to learn, one must at the very least confront some of the objects in
question, e.g., physical things, psychological states, number, principles of logic. [TRS.]

3 Husserl would say, "a science of essences." But, for the point of view we adopt, it
amounts to the same. [AUTHOR.] In a study of consciousness by consciousness, *what*
present consciousness is (its essence) and *that* it is (the fact that it exists) obviously make
up only one question. Consequently, Sartre speaks indifferently of an "essential" and a
"factual" inquiry. This would not appear to be orthodox Husserlian phenomenology
(viz., *Ideas I*, Introduction). [TRS.]

4 The *epoché* (ἐποχή) is an act of withdrawal from the usual assertiveness of consciousness
regarding what does and does not exist in the world. The effect of this withdrawal is to
reveal the world as a correlate of consciousness. The term "reduction" employed in the
same paragraph has the same meaning. (Cf. *Ideas I*, Secs. 31–34.) [TRS.]

5 Halle, 1900–1901 (5th Investigation, Sec. 4). See also, Marvin Farber, *The Foundation of
Phenomenology* (Cambridge, 1943), pp. 337–338. [TRS.]

6 Cf. *Ideen I*, Sec. 57. [TRS.]

7 Two paragraphs below Sartre asserts that "consciousness is defined by intentionality."
Five paragraphs after that assertion, reference is made once more to "the fruitful definition cited earlier." Strictly speaking, Husserl never concerned himself with a final
definition, but certainly he regarded intentionality as essential to consciousness, i.e.,
consciousness is necessarily consciousness *of something*. (Cf. *Ideen I*, Sec. 84.) [TRS.]

8 Published in *Jahrbuch für Philosophie und phänomenologische Forschung*, IX (1928),
pp. 367–498. [TRS.]

9 Published in *Husserliana*, I (1950), pp. 1–183. A French translation by G. Peiffer and
E. Levinas is published under the title *Méditations Cartésiennes* (Paris, J. Vrin, 1947).
trans. J. Caines, Cartesian Meditation (The Hague: Nighoff, 1960). For the discussion of
temporal unifications, see esp. Secs. 18 and 37. [TRS.]

10 Cf. *op. cit.*, "Meditation V." [TRS.]

11 The phrase is quoted from *Ideen I*, Sec. 46. In the *Cogito*, the fact that the *Cogito* is
taking place is necessarily so. [TRS.]

12 Cf. *op. cit.* [TRS.]

13 Cf. *Ideas I*, Sec. 84. [TRS.]

14 The "I" is grasped "with evidence" in reflection in the sense that the "I" is intuitively
apprehended (cf. above, n. 2). Evidence is "adequate" when the object in question is
grasped in its entirety (e.g., perceptual intuition is always inadequate evidence). Evidence is "apodictic" when the object or state of affairs in question is apprehended as
being necessarily thus-and-so (e.g., that color is extended may be known apodictically).
Sartre points out that the "I" with which reflective intuition is confronted is grasped
neither adequately nor apodictically. [TRS.]

15 Cf. Eugen Fink, "Die phänomenologische Philosophie Edmund Husserls in der gegenwärtigen Kritik. Mit einem Vorwort von Edmund Husserl," *Kantstudien*, XXXVIII (1933), pp. 356 ff., 381ff. [TRS.]

16 It will be recalled (see above, n. 2) that there are no mystical or magical connotations to this "special kind" of "intuition." In reflection, consciousness can intuit the "I" in a "special" manner in the sense that confronting this transcendent object is not the same as, say, confronting a physical thing by an act of perceptual intuition. [TRS.]

17 The term "noematic correlate" (or "noema") is employed in phenomenology to refer to the terminus of an intention as given for consciousness (e.g., this book as the object of consciousness). The noematic correlate does not necessarily exist in fact. The "noesis" is the apprehension which is directed upon the noema. (Cf. *Ideen I*, Secs. 85 *et seq.*) [TRS.]

18 Cf. *Vorlesungen zur Phänomenologie des inneren Zeitbewusstseins, op. cit., passim*. [AUTHOR.]

19 Regarding the term "noematic" here and elsewhere, cf. n. 17, above. [TRS.]

20 The French text contains the phrase *sans l'influence*, which we have read as a misprint for *sous l'influence*. [TRS.]

21 But it can also be aimed at and reached through perception of behavior. We hope to explain in some other place the deep-seated identity of *all* psychological methods. [AUTHOR.]

22 *Ideas I*, Sec. 131, p. 270. [AUTHOR.]

23 We may add that Husserl was well acquainted with this type of synthetic totality, to which he devoted a remarkable study in *Logische Untersuchungen* [*op. cit.*], vol. II, pt. 1, Investigation No. 3. [AUTHOR.] Cf. Marvin Farber, *op cit.*, ch. X, pp. 283–312. [TRS.]

24 *Zein und Zeit* (Halle, Niemeyer, 1929), vol. I, pp. 364–366, and *passim. Being and Time*, trans. J. Macquarrie and J. Robinson, (NY: Harper & Row, 1962), pp. 415–418. [TRS.]

25 Since the fundamental source of evidence is intuition (see above, n. 2), evidential experiences prior to explicit judgment are possible. [TRS.]

26 The pun on "meurtrissure" is virtually untranslatable. It expresses with ingenuity the sense in which the murderous deed of Raskolnikov (*le meurtre*) affects in kind his murderous ego in the form of a bruise to the ego (*une meurtrissure*). [TRS.]

27 This is only to say that Peter and Paul may both directly confront by an act of consciousness the public object which is the ego of Peter. (Cf. above, n. 2, on "intuition.") [TRS.]

28 The difficulty regarding another consciousness, in other words, is not like the difficulty regarding the other side of the moon, which can be thought (but never intuited, because it so happens we always see the same face). From no *conceivable* vantage-point could we be confronted by another consciousness. [TRS.]

29 When we see the words "this book," in all likelihood we will indicate this book emptily; we will "merely have it in mind." Were we to *imagine* this book, however, or actually *look at* the book, we would have "filled out" our consciousness of it; we would have confronted the object by an act of intuition. (Cf. above, n. 2.) The belief that the ego can produce consciousness remains possible only so long as one does not attempt to verify it intuitively, by "looking to see" if it is so. [TRS.]

30 Cf. Eugen Fink, *loc. cit.*, pp. 346–351. [TRS.]

31 Cf. *op. cit.*, Sec. 1. [TRS.]

32 Halle, Niemeyer, 1929, pp. 205–215, *Being and Time*, pp. 249–258 [TRS.]

33 Cf. *op. cit.*, "Meditation V." [TRS.]

3

BAD FAITH

I Bad faith and falsehood

The human being is not only the being by whom *négatités* are disclosed in the world; he is also the one who can take negative attitudes with respect to himself. [. . .] But it is out of the question to discuss the attitude of self-negation in its universality. The kinds of behavior which can be ranked under this heading are too diverse; we risk retaining only the abstract form of them. It is best to choose and to examine one determined attitude which is essential to human reality and which is such that consciousness instead of directing its negation outward turns it toward itself. This attitude, it seems to me, is *bad faith* (*mauvaise foi*).

Frequently this is identified with falsehood. We say indifferently of a person that he shows signs of bad faith or that he lies to himself. We shall willingly grant that bad faith is a lie to oneself, on condition that we distinguish the lie to oneself from lying in general. Lying is a negative attitude, we will agree to that. But this negation does not bear on consciousness itself; it aims only at the transcendent. The essence of the lie implies in fact that the liar actually is in complete possession of the truth which he is hiding. A man does not lie about what he is ignorant of; he does not lie when he spreads an error of which he himself is the dupe; he does not lie when he is mistaken. The ideal description of the liar would be a cynical consciousness, affirming truth within himself, denying it in his words, and denying that negation as such. [. . .]

The situation can not be the same for bad faith if this, as we have said, is indeed a lie to oneself. To be sure, the one who practices bad faith is hiding a displeasing truth or presenting as truth a pleasing untruth. Bad faith then has in appearance the structure of falsehood. Only what changes everything is the fact that in bad faith it is from myself that I am hiding the truth. Thus the duality of the deceiver and the deceived does not exist here. Bad faith on the contrary implies in essence the unity of a *single* consciousness. This does not mean that it can not be conditioned by the *Mit-sein* like all other phenomena of human reality, but the *Mit-sein* can call forth bad faith only by presenting itself as a *situation* which bad faith permits surpassing; bad faith does not come from outside to human reality. One does not undergo his bad faith; one is not infected with it; it is not a state. But consciousness affects itself with bad faith. There must be an original intention and a project of bad faith; this project implies a comprehension of bad faith as

J.-P. Sartre, *Being and Nothingness*, 1995, trans. Hazel Barnes, pp. 47–69. London: Routledge.

such and a pre-reflective apprehension (of) consciousness as affecting itself with bad faith. It follows first that the one to whom the lie is told and the one who lies are one and the same person, which means that I must know in my capacity as deceiver the truth which is hidden from me in my capacity as the one deceived. Better yet I must know the truth very exactly in *order* to conceal it more carefully – and this not at two different moments, which at a pinch would allow us to reestablish a semblance of duality – but in the unitary structure of a single project. How then can the lie subsist if the duality which conditions it is suppressed?

To this difficulty is added another which is derived from the total translucency of consciousness. That which affects itself with bad faith must be conscious (of) its bad faith since the being of consciousness is consciousness of being. It appears then that I must be in good faith, at least to the extent that I am conscious of my bad faith. But then this whole psychic system is annihilated. We must agree in fact that if I deliberately and cynically attempt to lie to myself, I fail completely in this undertaking; the lie falls back and collapses beneath my look; it is ruined *from behind* by the very consciousness of lying to myself which pitilessly constitutes itself well within my project as its very condition. We have here an *evanescent* phenomenon which exists only in and through its own differentiation. To be sure, these phenomena are frequent and we shall see that there is in fact an "evanescence" of bad faith, which, it is evident, vacillates continually between good faith and cynicism: Even though the existence of bad faith is very precarious, and though it belongs to the kind of psychic structures which we might call "metastable,"[1] it presents nonetheless an autonomous and durable form. It can even be the normal aspect of life for a very great number of people. A person can *live* in bad faith, which does not mean that he does not have abrupt awakenings to cynicism or to good faith, but which implies a constant and particular style of life. Our embarrassment then appears extreme since we can neither reject nor comprehend bad faith.

To escape from these difficulties people gladly have recourse to the unconscious. In the psychoanalytical interpretation, for example, they use the hypothesis of a censor, conceived as a line of demarcation with customs, passport division, currency control, *etc.*, to reestablish the duality of the deceiver and the deceived. Here instinct or, if you prefer, original drives and complexes of drives constituted by our individual history, make up *reality*. It is neither true nor *false* since it does not exist for itself. It simply is, exactly like this table, which is neither true nor false in *itself* but simply *real*. As for the conscious symbols of the instinct, this interpretation takes them not for appearances but for real psychic facts. Fear, forgetting, dreams exist really in the capacity of concrete facts of consciousness in the same way as the words and the attitudes of the liar are concrete, really existing patterns of behavior. The subject has the same relation to these phenomena as the deceived to the behavior of the deceiver. He establishes them in their reality and must interpret them. There is a truth in the activities of the deceiver; if the deceived could reattach them to the situation where the deceiver establishes himself and to his project of the lie, they would become integral parts of truth, by virtue of being lying conduct. Similarly there is a truth in the symbolic acts; it is what the psychoanalyst discovers when he reattaches them to the historical situation of the patient, to the unconscious complexes which they express, to the blocking of the censor. Thus the subject deceives himself about the meaning of his conduct, he apprehends it in its concrete existence but not in its truth, simply because he cannot derive it from an original situation and from a psychic constitution which remain alien to him.

By the distinction between the "id" and the "ego," Freud has cut the psychic whole into two. I am the ego but I am *not* the id. I hold no privileged position in relation to my unconscious psyche. I am my own psychic phenomena in so far as I establish them in their conscious reality. For example I am the impulse to steal this or that book from this bookstall. I am an integral part of the impulse; I bring it to light and I determine myself hand-in-hand with it to commit the theft. But I *am* not those psychic facts, in so far as I receive them passively and am obliged to resort to hypotheses about their origin and their true meaning, just as the scholar makes conjectures about the nature and essence of an external phenomenon. This theft, for example, which I interpret as an immediate impulse determined by the rarity, the interest, or the price of the volume which I am going to steal – it is in truth a process derived from self-punishment, which is attached more or less directly to an Oedipus complex.

Thus psychoanalysis substitutes for the notion of bad faith, the idea of a lie without a liar; it allows me to understand how it is possible for me to be lied to without lying to myself since it places me in the same relation to myself that the Other is in respect to me; it replaces the duality of the deceiver and the deceived, the essential condition of the lie, by that of the "id" and the "ego." It introduces into my subjectivity the deepest intersubjective structure of the *Mit-sein*. Can this explanation satisfy us?

Considered more closely the psychoanalytic theory is not as simple as it first appears. It is not accurate to hold that the "id" is presented as a thing in relation to the hypothesis of the psychoanalyst, for a thing is indifferent to the conjectures which we make concerning it, while the "id" on the contrary is sensitive to them when we approach the truth. Freud in fact reports resistance when at the end of the first period the doctor is approaching the truth. This resistance is objective behavior apprehended from without; the patient shows defiance, refuses to speak, gives fantastic accounts of his dreams, sometimes even removes himself completely from the psychoanalytic treatment. It is a fair question to ask what part of himself can thus resist. It can not be the "Ego," envisaged as a psychic totality of the facts of consciousness; this could not suspect that the psychiatrist is approaching the end since the ego's relation to the *meaning* of its own reactions is exactly like that of the psychiatrist himself. At the very most it is possible for the ego to appreciate objectively the degree of probability in the hypotheses set forth, as a witness of the psychoanalysis might be able to do, according to the number of subjective facts which they explain. Furthermore, this probability would appear to the ego to border on certainty, which he could not take offence at since most of the time it is he who by a conscious decision is in pursuit of the psychoanalytic therapy. Are we to say that the patient is disturbed by the daily revelations which the psychoanalyst makes to him and that he seeks to remove himself, at the same time pretending in his own eyes to wish to continue the treatment? In this case it is no longer possible to resort to the unconscious to explain bad faith; it is there in full consciousness, with all its contradictions. But this is not the way that the psychoanalyst means to explain this resistance; for him it is secret and deep, it comes from afar; it has its roots in the very thing which the psychoanalyst is trying to make clear.

Furthermore it is equally impossible to explain the resistance as emanating from the complex which the psychoanalyst wishes to bring to light. The complex as such is rather the collaborator of the psychoanalyst since it aims at expressing itself in clear consciousness, since it plays tricks on the censor and seeks to elude it. The only level on which we can locate the refusal of the subject is that of the censor. It alone can comprehend the questions or the revelations of the psycho-analyst as approaching more or less near to the real drives which it strives to repress – it alone because it alone *knows* what it is repressing.

If we reject the language and the materialistic mythology of psychoanalysis, we perceive that the censor in order to apply its activity with discernment must know what it is repressing. In fact if we abandon all the metaphors representing the repression as the impact of blind forces, we are compelled to admit that the censor must choose and in order to choose must be aware of so doing. How could it happen otherwise that the censor allows lawful sexual impulses to pass through, that it permits needs (hunger, thirst, sleep) to be expressed in clear consciousness? And how are we to explain that it can relax its surveillance, that it can even be deceived by the disguises of the instinct? But it is not sufficient that it discern the condemned drives; it must also apprehend them *as to be repressed*, which implies in it at the very least an awareness of its activity. In a word, how could the censor discern the impulses needing to be repressed without being conscious of discern-ing them? How can we conceive of a knowledge which is ignorant of itself? To know is to know that one knows, said Alain. Let us say rather: All knowing is consciousness of knowing. Thus the resistance of the patient implies on the level of the censor an awareness of the thing repressed as such, a comprehension of the end toward which the questions of the psychoanalyst are leading, and an act of synthetic connection by which it compares the *truth* of the repressed complex to the psychoanalytic hypothesis which aims at it. These various operations in their turn imply that the censor is conscious (of) itself. But what type of self-consciousness can the censor have? It must be the consciousness (of) being con-scious of the drive to be repressed, but precisely *in order not be conscious of it*. What does this mean if not that the censor is in bad faith? [. . .]

How can the repressed drive "disguise itself" if it does not include (1) the consciousness of being repressed, (2) the consciousness of having been pushed back because it is what it is, (3) a project of disguise? No mechanistic theory of condensation or of transference can explain these modifications by which the drive itself is affected, for the description of the process of disguise implies a veiled appeal to finality. And similarly how are we to account for the pleasure or the anguish which accompanies the symbolic and conscious satisfaction of the drive if consciousness does not include – beyond the censor – an obscure com-prehension of the end to be attained as simultaneously desired and forbidden. By rejecting the conscious unity of the psyche, Freud is obliged to imply everywhere a magic unity linking distant phenomena across obstacles, just as sympathetic magic unites the spellbound person and the wax image fashioned in his likeness. The unconscious drive (*Trieb*) through magic is endowed with the character "repressed" or "condemned," which completely pervades it, colors it, and magic-ally provokes its symbolism. Similarly the conscious phenomenon is entirely colored by its symbolic meaning although it can not apprehend this meaning by itself in clear consciousness. [. . .]

Thus on the one hand the explanation by means of the unconscious, due to the fact that it breaks the psychic unity, can not account for the facts which at first sight it appeared to explain. And on the other hand, there exists an infinity of types of behavior in bad faith which explicitly reject this kind of explanation because their essence implies that they can appear only in the translucency of consciousness. We find that the problem which we had attempted to resolve is still untouched.

II Patterns of bad faith

If we wish to get out of this difficulty, we should examine more closely the patterns of bad faith and attempt a description of them. This description will permit us perhaps to fix more exactly the conditions for the possibility of bad faith; that is, to reply to the question we raised at the outset: "What must be the being of man if he is to be capable of bad faith?"

Take the example of a woman who has consented to go out with a particular man for the first time. She knows very well the intentions which the man who is speaking to her cherishes regarding her. She knows also that it will be necessary sooner or later for her to make a decision. But she does not want to realize the urgency; she concerns herself only with what is respectful and discreet in the attitude of her companion. She does not apprehend this conduct as an attempt to achieve what we call "the first approach;" that is, she does not want to see possibilities of temporal development which his conduct presents. She restricts this behavior to what is in the present; she does not wish to read in the phrases which he addresses to her anything other than their explicit meaning. If he says to her, "I find you so attractive!" she disarms this phrase of its sexual background; she attaches to the conversation and to the behavior of the speaker, the immediate meanings, which she imagines as objective qualities. The man who is speaking to her appears to her sincere and respectful as the table is round or square, as the wall coloring is blue or gray. The qualities thus attached to the person she is listening to are in this way fixed in a permanence like that of things, which is no other than the projection of the strict present of the qualities into the temporal flux. This is because she does not quite know what she wants. She is profoundly aware of the desire which she inspires, but the desire cruel and naked would humiliate and horrify her. Yet she would find no charm in a respect which would be only respect. In order to satisfy her, there must be a feeling which is addressed wholly to her *personality* – i.e., to her full freedom – and which would be a recognition of her freedom. But at the same time this feeling must be wholly desire; that is, it must address itself to her body as object. This time then she refuses to apprehend the desire for what it is; she does not even give it a name; she recognizes it only to the extent that it transcends itself toward admiration, esteem, respect and that it is wholly absorbed in the more refined forms which it produces, to the extent of no longer figuring anymore as a sort of warmth and density. But then suppose he takes her hand. This act of her companion risks changing the situation by calling for an immediate decision. To leave the hand there is to consent in herself to flirt, to engage herself. To withdraw it is to break the troubled and unstable harmony which gives the hour its charm. The aim is to postpone the moment of decision as long as possible. We know what happens next; the young woman leaves her hand there, but she *does not notice* that she is leaving it. She does not notice because it happens by chance that she is at this moment all intellect. She draws her companion up to the most lofty regions of sentimental speculation; she speaks of Life, of her life, she shows herself in her essential aspect – a personality, a consciousness. And during this time the divorce of the body from the soul is accomplished; the hand rests inert between the warm hands of her companion – neither consenting nor resisting – a thing.

We shall say that this woman is in bad faith. But we see immediately that she uses various procedures in order to maintain herself in this bad faith. She has disarmed the actions of her companion by reducing them to being only what they are; that is, to existing in the mode of the in-itself. But she permits herself to enjoy his desire, to the extent that she will apprehend it as not being what it is, will recognize its transcendence. Finally while sensing profoundly the presence of her own body – to the degree of being disturbed perhaps – she realizes herself as *not being* her own body, and she contemplates it as though from above as a passive object to which events can *happen* but which can neither provoke them nor avoid them because all its possibilities are outside of it. What unity do we find in these various aspects of bad faith? It is a certain art of forming contradictory concepts which unite in themselves both an idea and the negation of that idea. The basic concept which is thus engendered, utilizes the double property of the human being, who is at once a *facticity* and a *transcendence*. These two aspects of human reality are and ought to be capable of a valid coordination. But bad faith does not wish either to coordinate them nor to surmount them in a synthesis. Bad faith seeks to affirm their identity while preserving their differences. It must affirm facticity as *being* transcendence and transcendence as *being* facticity, in such a way that at the instant when a person apprehends the one, he can find himself abruptly faced with the other. [. . .] The young coquette maintains transcendence to the extent that the respect, the esteem manifested by the actions of her admirer are already on the plane of the transcendent. But she arrests this transcendence, she glues it down with all the facticity of the present; respect is nothing other than respect, it is an arrested surpassing which no longer surpasses itself toward anything.

But although this *metastable* concept of "transcendence-facticity" is one of the most basic instruments of bad faith, it is not the only one of its kind. We can equally well use another kind of duplicity derived from human reality which we will express roughly by saying that its being-for-itself implies complementarily a being-for-others. Upon any one of my conducts it is always possible to converge two looks, mine and that of the Other. The conduct will not present exactly the same structure in each case. But as we shall see later, as each look perceives it, there is between these two aspects of my being, no difference between appearance and being – as if I were to my self the truth of myself and as if the Other possessed only a deformed image of me. The equal dignity of being, possessed by my being-for-others and by my being-for-myself permits a perpetually disintegrating synthesis and a perpetual game of escape from the for-itself to the for-others and from the for-others to the for-itself. We have seen also the use which our young lady made of our being-in-the-midst-of-the-world – *i.e.*, of our inert presence as a passive object among other objects – in order to relieve herself suddenly from the functions of her being-in-the-world – that is, from the being which causes there to be a world by projecting itself beyond the world toward its own possibilities. Let us note finally the confusing syntheses which play on the nihilating ambiguity of these temporal ekstases, affirming at once that I am what I have been (the man who deliberately *arrests himself* at one period in his life and refuses to take into consideration the later changes) and that I am not what I have been (the man who in the face of reproaches or rancor dissociates himself from his past by insisting on his freedom and on his perpetual re-creation). In all these concepts, which have only a transitive role in the reasoning and which are eliminated from the conclusion, (like hypochondriacs in the calculations of physicians), we find again the same structure. We have to deal with human reality as a being which is what it is not and which is not what it is.

But what exactly is necessary in order for these concepts of disintegration to be able to receive even a pretence of existence, in order for them to be able to appear for an instant to consciousness, even in a process of evanescence? A quick examination of the idea of sincerity, the antithesis of bad faith, will be very instructive in this connection. Actually sincerity presents itself as a demand and consequently is not a *state*. Now what is the ideal to be attained in this case? It is necessary that a man be *for himself* only what he *is*. But is this not precisely the definition of the in-itself – or if you prefer – the principle of identity?

If man is what he is, bad faith is for ever impossible and candor ceases to be his ideal and becomes instead his being. But is man what he is? And more generally, how can he be what he is when he exists as consciousness of being? If candor or sincerity is a universal value, it is evident that the maxim "one must be what one is" does not serve solely as a regulating principle for judgments and concepts by which I express what I am. It posits not merely an ideal of knowing but an ideal of *being*; it proposes for us an absolute equivalence of being with itself as a prototype of being. In this sense it is necessary that we make *ourselves* what we are. But what are we then if we have the constant obligation to make ourselves what we are, if our mode of being is having the obligation to be what we are?

Let us consider this waiter in the café. His movement is quick and forward, a little too precise, a little too rapid. He comes toward the patrons with a step a little too quick. He bends forward a little too eagerly; his voice, his eyes express an interest a little too solicitous for the order of the customer. Finally there he returns, trying to imitate in his walk the inflexible stiffness of some kind of automaton while carrying his tray with the recklessness of a tight-rope-walker by putting it in a perpetually unstable, perpetually broken equilibrium which he perpetually reestablishes by a light movement of the arm and hand. All his behavior seems to us a game. He applies himself to chaining his movements as if they were mechanisms, the one regulating the other; his gestures and even his voice seem to be mechanisms; he gives himself the quickness and pitiless rapidity of things. He is playing, he is amusing himself. But what is he playing? We need not watch long before we can explain it: he is playing *at being* a waiter in a café. There is nothing there to surprise us. The game is a kind of marking out and investigation. The child plays with his body in order to explore it, to take inventory of it; the waiter in the café plays with his condition in order to *realize* it. This obligation is not different from that which is imposed on all tradesmen. Their condition is wholly one of ceremony. The public demands of them that they realize it as a ceremony; there is the dance of the grocer, of the tailor, of the auctioneer, by which they endeavour to persuade their clientele that they are nothing but a grocer, an auctioneer, a tailor. A grocer who dreams is offensive to the buyer, because such a grocer is not wholly a grocer. Society demands that he limit himself to his function as a grocer, just as the soldier at attention makes himself into a soldier-thing with a direct regard which does not see at all, which is no longer meant to see, since it is the rule and not the interest of the moment which determines the point he must fix his eyes on (the sight "fixed at ten paces"). There are indeed many precautions to imprison a man in what he is, as if we lived in perpetual fear that he might escape from it, that he might break away and suddenly elude his condition.

In a parallel situation, from within, the waiter in the café can not be immediately a café waiter in the sense that this inkwell *is* an inkwell, or the glass is a glass. It is by no means that he can not form reflective judgments or concepts concerning his condition. He knows well what it "means:" the obligation of getting up at five o'clock, of sweeping the floor of the shop before the restaurant opens, of starting the coffee pot going, etc. He knows the rights which it allows: the right to the tips, the right to belong to a union, etc. But all these concepts, all these judgments refer to the transcendent. It is a matter of abstract possibilities, of rights and duties conferred on a "person possessing rights." And it is precisely this person *who I have to be* (if I am the waiter in question) and who I am not. It is not that I do not wish to be this person or that I want this person to be different. But rather there is no common measure between his being and mine. It is a "representation" for others and for myself, which means that I can be he only in *representation*. But if I represent myself as him, I am not he; I am separated from him as the object from the subject, separated *by nothing*, but this nothing isolates me from him. I can not be he, I can only play *at being* him; that is, imagine to myself that I am he. And thereby I affect him with nothingness. In vain do I fulfill the functions of a café waiter. I can be he only in the neutralized mode, as the actor is Hamlet, by mechanically making the *typical gestures* of my state and by aiming at myself as an imaginary café waiter through those gestures taken as an "analogue."[2] What I attempt to realize is a being-in-itself of the café waiter, as if it were not just in my power to confer their value and their urgency upon my duties and the rights of my position, as if it were not my free choice to get up each morning at five o'clock or to remain in bed, even though it meant getting fired. As if from the very fact that I sustain this role in existence I did not transcend it on every side, as if I did not constitute myself as one *beyond* my condition. Yet there is no doubt that I *am* in a sense a café waiter – otherwise could I not just as well call myself a diplomat or a reporter? But if I am one, this can not be in the mode of being in-itself. I am a waiter in the mode of *being what I am not*. [. . .]

Someone may say that my consciousness at least *is*, whatever may be the object or the state of which it makes itself consciousness. But how do we distinguish my consciousness (of) being sad from sadness? Is it not all one? It is true in a way that my consciousness *is*, if one means by this that for another it is a part of the totality of being on which judgments can be brought to bear. But it should be noted, as Husserl clearly understood, that my consciousness appears originally to the Other as an absence. It is the object always present as the *meaning* of all my attitudes and all my conduct – and always absent, for it gives itself to the intuition

415

of another as a perpetual question – still better, as a perpetual freedom. When Pierre looks at me, I know of course that he is looking at me. His eyes, things in the world, are fixed on my body, a thing in the world – that is the objective fact of which I can say: it *is*. But it is also a fact *in the world*. The meaning of this look is not a fact in the world, and this is what makes me uncomfortable. Although I make smiles, promises, threats, nothing can get hold of the approbation, the free judgment which I seek; I know that it is always beyond. I sense it in my very attitude, which is no longer like that of the worker toward the things he uses as instruments. My reactions, to the extent that I project myself toward the Other, are no longer for myself but are rather mere *presentations*; they await being constituted as graceful or uncouth, sincere or insincere, etc., by an apprehension which is always beyond my efforts to provoke, an apprehension which will be provoked by my efforts only if of itself it lends them force (that is, only in so far as it causes itself to be provoked from the outside), *which is its own mediator with the transcendent*. Thus the objective fact of the being-in-itself of the consciousness of the Other is posited in order to disappear in negativity and in freedom: consciousness of the Other is as not-being; its being-in-itself "here and now" is not-to-be.

Consciousness of the Other is what it is not.

Furthermore the being of my own consciousness does not appear to me as the consciousness of the Other. It *is* because it makes itself, since its being is consciousness of being. But this means that making sustains being; consciousness has to be its own being, it is never sustained by being; it sustains being in the heart of subjectivity, which means once again that it is inhabited by being but that it is not being: *consciousness is not what it is.*

Under these conditions what can be the significance of the ideal of sincerity except as a task impossible to achieve, of which the very meaning is in contradiction with the structure of my consciousness. To be sincere, we said, is to be what one is. That supposes that I am not originally what I am. But here naturally Kant's "You ought, therefore you can" is implicitly understood. I can *become* sincere; this is what my duty and my effort to achieve sincerity imply. But we definitely establish that the original structure of "not being what one is" renders impossible in advance all movement toward being in itself or "being what one is." And this impossibility is not hidden from consciousness; on the contrary, it is the very stuff of consciousness; it is the embarrasing constraint which we constantly experience; it is our very incapacity to recognize ourselves, to constitute ourselves as being what we are. It is this necessity which means that, as soon as we posit ourselves as a certain being, by a legitimate judgment, based on inner experience or correctly deduced from a *priori* or empirical premises, then by that very positing we surpass this being – and that not toward another being but toward emptiness, toward *nothing*. [. . .]

Let us take an example: A homosexual frequently has an intolerable feeling of guilt, and his whole existence is determined in relation to this feeling. One will readily foresee that he is in bad faith. In fact it frequently happens that this man, while recognizing his homosexual inclination, while avowing each and every particular misdeed which he has committed, refuses with all his strength to consider himself "*a paederast*." His case is always "different," peculiar; there enters into it something of a game, of chance, of bad luck; the mistakes are all in the past; they are explained by a certain conception of the beautiful which women can not satisfy; we should see in them the results of a restless search, rather than the manifestations of a deeply rooted tendency, *etc., etc*. Here is assuredly a man in bad faith who borders on the comic since, acknowledging all the facts which are imputed to him, he refuses to draw from them the conclusion which they impose. His friend, who is his most severe critic, becomes irritated with this duplicity. The critic asks only one thing – and perhaps then he will show himself indulgent: that the guilty one recognize himself as guilty, that the homosexual declare frankly – whether humbly or boastfully matters little – "I am a paederast." We ask here: Who is in bad faith? The homosexual or the champion of sincerity?

The homosexual recognizes his faults, but he struggles with all his strength against the crushing view that his mistakes constitute for him a *destiny*. He does not wish to let himself be considered as a thing. He has an obscure but strong feeling that an homosexual is not an homosexual as this table is a table or as this red-haired man is red-haired. It seems to him that he has escaped from each mistake as soon as he has posited it and recognized it; he even feels that the psychic duration by itself cleanses him from each misdeed, constitutes for him an undetermined future, causes him to be born anew. Is he wrong? Does he not recognize in himself the peculiar, irreducible character of human reality? His attitude includes then an undeniable comprehension of truth. But at the same time he needs this perpetual rebirth, this constant escape in order to live; he must constantly put himself beyond reach in order to avoid the terrible judgment of collectivity. Thus he plays on the word *being*. He would be right actually if he understood the phrase, "I am not a paederast" in the sense of "I am not what I am." That is, if he declared to himself, "To the extent that a pattern of conduct is defined as the conduct of a paederast and to the extent that I have adopted this conduct, I am a paederast. But to the extent that human reality can not be finally defined by patterns of conduct, I am not one." But instead he slides surreptitiously towards a different connotation of the word "being." He understands "not being" in the sense of "not-being-in-itself." He lays claim to "not being a paederast" in the sense in which this table *is not* an inkwell. He is in bad faith.

But the champion of sincerity is not ignorant of the transcendence of human reality, and he knows how at need to appeal to it for his own advantage. He makes use of it even and brings it up in the present argument. Does he not wish, first in the name of sincerity, then of freedom, that the homosexual reflect on himself and acknowledge himself as an homosexual? Does he not let the other understand that such a confession will win indulgence for him? What does this mean if not that the man who will acknowledge himself as an homosexual will no longer be *the same* as the homosexual whom he acknowledges being and that he will escape into the region of freedom and of good will? The critic asks the man then to be what he is in order no longer to be what he is. It is the profound meaning of the saying, "A sin confessed is half pardoned." The critic demands of the guilty one that he constitute himself as a thing, precisely in order no longer to treat him as a thing. [. . .]

Very well, someone will say, but our man is abusing sincerity, playing one side against the other. We should not look for sincerity in the relation of the *Mit-sein* but rather where it is pure – in the relations of a person with himself. But who can not see that objective sincerity is constituted in the same way? Who can not see that the sincere man constitutes himself as a thing in order to escape the condition of a thing by the same act of sincerity? The man who confesses that he is evil has exchanged his disturbing "freedom-for-evil" for an inanimate character of evil; he *is* evil, he clings to himself, he *is* what he *is*. But by the same stroke, he escapes from that *thing*, since it is he who contemplates it, since it depends on him to maintain it under his glance or to let it collapse in an infinity of particular acts. He derives a *merit* from his sincerity, and the deserving man is not the evil man as he is evil but as he is beyond his evilness. At the same time the evil is disarmed since it is nothing, save on the plane of determinism, and since in confessing it, I posit my freedom in respect to it; my future is virgin; everything is allowed to me.

Thus the essential structure of sincerity does not differ from that of bad *faith* since the sincere man constitutes himself as what he is *in order not to be it*. This explains the truth recognized by all that one can fall into bad faith through being sincere. [. . .]

Sincerity does not assign to me a mode of being or a particular quality, but in relation to that quality it aims at making me pass from one mode of being to another mode of being. This second mode of being, the ideal of sincerity, I am prevented by nature from attaining; and at the very moment when I struggle to attain it, I have a vague prejudicative comprehension that I shall not attain it. But all the same, in order for me to be able to conceive an intention in bad faith, I must have such a nature that within my being I escape from my being. If I were sad or cowardly in the way in which this inkwell is an inkwell, the possibility of bad faith could not even be conceived. Not only should I be unable to escape from my being; I could not even imagine that I could escape from it. But if bad faith is possible by virtue of a simple project, it is because so far as my being is concerned, there is no difference between being and non-being if I am cut off from my project.

Bad faith is possible only because sincerity is conscious of missing its goal inevitably, due to its very nature. I can try to apprehend myself as "*not being cowardly*," when I *am so*, only on condition that the "being cowardly" is itself "in question" at the very moment when it exists, on condition that it is itself *one* question, that at the very moment when I wish to apprehend it, it escapes me on all sides and annihilates itself. [. . .]

But bad faith is not restricted to denying the qualities which I posses, to not seeing the being which I am. It attempts also to constitute myself as being what I am not. It apprehends me positively as courageous when I am not so. And that is possible, once again, only if I am what I am not; that is, if non-being in me does not have being even as non-being. Of course necessarily I *am not* courageous; otherwise bad faith would not be *bad* faith. But in addition my effort in bad faith must include the ontological comprehension that even in my usual being what I *am*, I am not it really and that there is no such difference between the being of "being-sad," for example – which I am in the mode of not being what I am – and the "non-being" of not-being-courageous which I wish to hide from myself. Moreover it is particularly requisite that the very negation of being should be itself the object of a perpetual nihilation, that the very meaning of "non-being" be perpetually in question in human reality. If I *were not* courageous in the way in which this inkwell is not a table; that is, if I were isolated in my cowardice, propped firmly against it, incapable of putting it in relation to its opposite, if I were not capable of *determining* myself as cowardly – that is, to deny courage to myself and thereby to escape my cowardice in the very moment that I posit it – if it were not on principle *impossible* for me to coincide with my *not-being-courageous* as well as with my being-courageous – then any project of bad faith would be prohibited me. Thus in order for bad faith to be possible, sincerity itself must be in bad faith. The condition of the possibility for bad faith is that human reality, in its most immediate being, in the intrastructure of the pre-reflective *cogito*, must be what it is not and not be what it is.

III The "faith" of bad faith

We have indicated for the moment only those conditions which render bad faith conceivable, the structures of being which permit us to form concepts of bad faith. We can not limit ourselves to these considerations; we have not yet distinguished bad faith from falsehood. The two-faced concepts which we have described would without a doubt be utilized by a liar to discountenance his questioner, although their two-faced quality being established on the being of man and not on some empirical circumstance, can and ought to be evident to all. The true problem of bad faith stems evidently from the fact that bad faith is *faith*. It can not be either a cynical lie or certainty – if certainty is the intuitive possession of the object. But if we take belief as meaning the adherence of being to its object when the object is not given or is given indistinctly, then bad faith is belief; and the essential problem of bad faith is a problem of belief.

How can we believe by bad faith in the concepts which we forge expressly to persuade ourselves? We must note in fact that the project of bad faith must be itself in bad faith. I am not only in bad faith at the end of my effort when I have constructed my two-faced concepts and when I have persuaded myself. In truth, I have not persuaded myself; to the extent that I could be so persuaded, I have always been so. And at the very moment when I was disposed to put myself in bad faith, I of necessity was in bad faith with respect to this same disposition. For me to have represented it to myself as bad faith would have been cynicism; to believe it sincerely innocent would have been in good faith. The decision to be in bad faith does not dare to speak its name; it believes itself and does not believe itself in bad faith; it believes itself and does not believe itself in good faith. It is this which from the upsurge of bad faith, determines the later attitude and, as it were, the *Weltanschauung* of bad faith.

Bad faith does not hold the norms and criteria of truth as they are accepted by the critical thought of good faith. What it decides first, in fact, is the nature of truth. With bad faith a truth appears, a method of thinking, a type of being which is like that of objects; the ontological characteristic of the world of bad faith with which the subject suddenly surrounds himself is this: that here being is what it is not, and is not what it is. Consequently a peculiar type of evidence appears; *non-persuasive* evidence. Bad faith apprehends evidence but it is resigned in advance to not being fulfilled by this evidence, to not being persuaded and transformed into good faith. It makes itself humble and modest; it is not ignorant, it says, that faith is decision and that after each intuition, it must decide and *will what it is*. Thus bad faith in its primitive project and in its coming into the world decides on the exact nature of its requirements. It stands forth in the firm resolution *not to demand too much*, to count itself satisfied when it is barely persuaded, to force

419

itself in decisions to adhere to uncertain truths. This original project of bad faith is a decision in bad faith on the nature of faith. Let us understand clearly that there is no question of a reflective, voluntary decision, but of a spontaneous determination of our being. One *puts oneself* in bad faith as one goes to sleep and one is in bad faith as one dreams. Once this mode of being has been realized, it is as difficult to get out of it as to wake oneself up; bad faith is a type of being in the world, like waking or dreaming, which by itself tends to perpetuate itself, although its structure is of the *metastable* type. But bad faith is conscious of its structure, and it has taken precautions by deciding that the metastable structure is the structure of being and that non-persuasion is the structure of all convictions. It follows that if bad faith is faith and if it includes in its original project its own negation (it determines itself to be not quite convinced in order to convince itself that I am what I am not), then to start with, a faith which wishes itself to be not quite convinced must be possible. What are the conditions for the possibility of such a faith?

I believe that my friend Pierre feels friendship for me. I believe it in *good faith*. I believe it but I do not have for it any self-evident intuition, for the nature of the object does not lend itself to intuition. I *believe it*; that is, I allow myself to give in to all impulses to trust it; I decide to believe in it, and to maintain myself in this decision; I conduct myself, finally, as if I were certain of it – and all this in the synthetic unity of one and the same attitude [. . .] But the nature of consciousness is such that in it the mediate and the immediate are one and the same being. To believe is to know that one believes, and to know that one believes is no longer to believe. Thus to believe is not to believe any longer because that is only to believe – this in the unity of one and the same non-thetic self-consciousness. To be sure, we have here forced the description of the phenomenon by designating it with the word to *know*; non-thetic consciousness is not to *know*. But it is in its very translucency at the origin of all knowing. Thus the non-thetic consciousness (of) believing is destructive of belief. But at the same time the very law of the pre-reflective *cogito* implies that the being of believing ought to be the consciousness of believing.

Thus belief is a being which questions its own being, which can realize itself only in its destruction, which can manifest itself to itself only by denying itself. It is a being for which to be is to appear and to appear is to deny itself. To believe is not-to-believe. We see the reason for it; the being of consciousness is to exist by itself, then to make itself be and thereby to pass beyond itself. In this sense consciousness is perpetually escaping itself, belief becomes non-belief, the immediate becomes mediation, the absolute becomes relative, and the relative becomes absolute. The ideal of good faith (to believe what one believes) is, like that of sincerity (to be what one is), an ideal of being-in-itself. Every belief is a belief that falls short; one never wholly believes what one believes. Consequently the primitive project of bad faith is only the utilization of this self-destruction of the fact of consciousness.

Notes

1 Sartre's own word, meaning subject to sudden changes or transitions. [Tr.]
2 Cf. *L'Imaginaire*. Conclusion.

Part X

MAURICE MERLEAU-PONTY
Embodied Perception

MAURICE MERLEAU-PONTY
(1908–1961)
Introduction

Maurice Merleau-Ponty was born in Rochefort-sur-Mer, France in 1908. Following his father's death in 1913, the family moved to Paris, where he attended the Lycées Janson-de-Sailly and Louis-le-Grand, before entering the Ecole Normale Supérieure in 1926, where he was taught by Léon Brunschvicg and Georges Gurwitsch. He may have been present at Husserl's Paris Lectures in 1929, and he attended Alexandre Kojève's lectures on Hegel in the following decade. He became a friend of Sartre, helping him to launch and edit *Les Temps Modernes*, though he broke with him after the war over the question of Sartre's support for Stalinism and for the Gulag. Merleau-Ponty wrote two theses for his doctorate: *The Structure of Behaviour* (published 1942), a critique of behaviourism and vitalism in psychology, and his *magnum opus*, *Phenomenology of Perception* (1945). He lectured at the University of Lyons from 1945, becoming Professor in 1948, and, in 1952, was elected to the Chair of Philosophy at the Collège de France. In May 1961, at the height of his career, Merleau-Ponty died suddenly at his desk. He wrote extensively on politics and art as well as on phenomenology, and his essay collections include *Signs* (1960) and *Sense and Non-sense*. He left several manuscripts including *The Visible and the Invisible*, published posthumously in 1964.

Merleau-Ponty is the thinker who, more than any other, applies the method of phenomenological description to the human existent to reveal it precisely as a carnal being or 'body-subject' (*corps-sujet*). He was influenced, not just by the manuscripts of Husserl's *Ideas II* and *The Crisis of European Sciences*, which he read in the Husserl Archive, but also by Bergson, Scheler, Heidegger, Gestalt psychology (via Gurwitsch) and contemporary developments in physiology, and of course by Sartre's discussion of the body in *Being and Nothingness*. In his earlier work especially, Merleau-Ponty develops the implications of Husserl's insight that the human organism is primarily an active living body (*Leib*), and should not be taken as a passive, spatially extended machine. A physicalist conception of the body as an 'in-itself' automaton is as much an abstraction as the notion of a disembodied Cartesian ego that would somehow exist 'for-itself'. Mind–body dualism is rejected in favour of an existent who lives 'in between' these extremes, and for whom nature and culture are primordially intertwined.

Our first reading is an abridgement of "The Body as Object and Mechanistic Physiology", from *Phenomenology of Perception*. Here Merleau-Ponty outlines his theory of the body-subject. He notes that physiologists are abandoning the idea, common to traditional empiricism and intellectualism (his term for idealism), that the living body is an assemblage of parts whose relations to external objects and to each other involve efficient or mechanical causality. The then-current physiology had recognised the lack of one-to-one correspondences between stimuli and reflexes. The living body apprehends the stimuli it receives as elements of an objective situation, tracing out an external object as a significant whole or global unity without waiting to build it up point by point. It always gives its stimuli a shape, so its reflexes should be called 'responses to situations' rather than 'reactions to stimuli'.

A global unity also marks our inner sense of ourselves. In purposeful experiences, I experience my whole arm in turning a handle, my whole leg in walking; bodily parts are felt as unified. For example, in the case of the phantom limb, an amputated limb is felt, not just as a pain, but in its original, comprehensive unity. Merleau-Ponty also considers cases of anosognosia, where limbs that are paralysed but still sensitive are ignored by acting subjects, who deny any disability in practice. This examination of pathological cases involves an adaptation of the phenomenological reduction. Husserl 'bracketed' the natural world of naïve realism to make it strange, to throw into relief the cognitional structures which the subject brings to bear on it. In analogous fashion, Merleau-Ponty looks at cases where the perceiving and acting body has broken down to illuminate the taken-for-granted corporeal performances of an ordinary body-subject.

The ordinary subject makes global sense of his or her stimuli and body parts through a certain outlook. I understand my environment and living body through a complex of projects to which I am committed. Such a projective outlook is pre-objective in every case, incapable of being seen as a voluntary act. The pathological cases show that it is a middle term between the psychic and the physiological. With anosognosia, the subject is not simply ignorant of a paralysed limb. He or she leaves the limb out of account so that the handicap will not be consciously felt, which supposes an implicit knowledge of it – the deficiency can only be evaded by knowing where there is a risk of encountering it. As an obstacle, it is made virtually absent. The subject with a phantom limb does not take it as an obstacle to projects, but as their complement. It is not intellectually represented as actually present, but implicitly taken as virtually present, treated in practice as a real limb at his or her disposal. Someone who has recently lost a leg may therefore leap out of bed and attempt to walk, only then noticing the loss of the limb in a cruel and acute manner.

On this account, my body becomes unperceived in my projective turn to the world. This is because it comprises two layers – it is both a *habitual* and a *present* body. In the past my living body acquired certain skills (e.g. of walking or opening doors or tying shoelaces). Such a set of skills or habits is put at the disposal of my present body, orienting it towards certain situations in certain ways – the habitual body constitutes a horizon of capacities for the present body. Precisely because these bodily skills are available and ingrained as habits, they do not intrude on me – I take them for granted. As a child I encountered a tap as something which could be 'manipulatable for me', and had to learn to turn it. When this became a habit I forgot about my body and focused on the tap, not as manipulatable for me, but as 'manipulatable in itself'. The body at my disposal became 'almost impersonal' or 'anonymous'. Hence the painful experience of handicap when a habitual expectation is suddenly frustrated.

For Merleau-Ponty, the habitual character of the body brings out the temporality of incarnate being, the fact of a past at the disposal of a present which is understood in futural or projective terms. It also brings out 'organic repression'. Psychoanalysis shows that a certain complex or fixation can come from a traumatic event which was repressed. What was a personal and datable event lives on in hidden form and affects present experience. In an analogous way my bodily skills become 'sedimented', laid down as anonymous but available. There is a ceaseless sublimation of the biological and natural into the personal and cultural, with this fusion of body and soul leaving the present open to novel projects and activities where the new is built upon the old. This is why I am not usually swallowed up by my present context and can readily go beyond it. The body is both a temporal and an anonymous unity, an internal fusion of the physical and mental lying at the disposal of my projects.

Our second reading comprises the main text of "The Primacy of Perception", an address given by Merleau-Ponty to the Société française de philosophie in 1946, which neatly summarises the major theses of *Phenomenology of Perception* and also serves as a clue to a number of the themes developed in his later work. He argues that things in the world are not given through a Kantian-type intellectual synthesis, but through a practical or perceptual one. Objects are really there for me, and their invisible aspects have reality precisely because I can move around so as to bring them into view and touch them. There is a paradox of immanence and transcendence in all perception – the object perceived cannot be completely foreign to the perceiver, and at the same time contains more than is ever given at any one time and standpoint. Intellectual analysis is always preceded by lived experience; things do not originally impose themselves as true for every intellect, but as real for any subject standing where I am.

Merleau-Ponty is adamant that the affirmation of a pre-reflective realm of lived experience is not a negation of the value of reflection. The latter, however, should not pretend to be ignorant of its origins, nor pretend that experience can be purged of all vagueness and ambiguity at the scientific level. Unconditioned exactitude is not so much the accomplishment of scientific knowledge as the goal to which it approximates. Both perception and thought have a past and future horizon, with our ideas expressing not only the truth, but our capacity to attain it at that moment. All experience is a process of gradual clarification and rectification through a dialogue with itself and others. What saves us is the possibility of new development – we can think through our errors, locating them in a widening domain of truth. On this account, the only solid *cogito* is one which reveals, not a subject transparent to itself and constitutive of everything else, but a particular thought engaged with objects it seeks to clarify, a thought in act which feels rather than sees itself and can only be certain of itself on this basis.

It is the great insight of Gestalt psychology, continues Merleau-Ponty, to have shown that structure and meaning are as visible in objectively observable behaviour as in the self-experience of the *cogito*, provided we do not confuse objectivity with what is measurable. Psychology and philosophy are not two kinds of knowledge, but two different degrees of clarification of the same knowledge, with questions becoming more formalised at the philosophical level. This is not to give psychology too big a place; rather it is to recognise that reason cannot be placed above the vicissitudes of history. For the same reason, philosophy should learn from sociology, ethnography, history and psychiatry, and not elevate itself by disavowing acquired knowledge.

Above all, philosophy must not disavow the primacy of perception, which teaches us the true conditions of objectivity itself and summons us to the tasks of knowledge and action. In the primacy of perception we find the remedy to scepticism and pessimism, even if the bodily situations disclosed through it are not absolutely reassuring, since they can be damaged and destroyed by sickness or accident. For Merleau-Ponty, there is no destruction of the absolute or of rationality in this account, but only of an absolute or a rationality sundered from experience.

Further reading

Merleau-Ponty, M. *Phenomenology of Perception*, trans. Colin Smith. London: Routledge & Kegan Paul, 1962.

Merleau-Ponty, M. *Sense and Nonsense*, trans. H. Dreyfus. Evanston, IL: Northwestern University Press, 1964.

Merleau-Ponty, M. *Signs*, trans. R. McCleary. Evanston, IL: Northwestern University Press, 1964.

Merleau-Ponty, M. *The Primacy of Perception*, ed. James Edie. Evanston, IL: Northwestern University Press, 1964.

Merleau-Ponty, M. *The Prose of the World*, ed. Claude Lefort, trans. J. O'Neill. Evanston, IL: Northwestern University Press, 1973.

Merleau-Ponty, M. *The Structure of Behavior*, trans. A. L. Fisher. Boston, MA: Beacon Press, 1963.

Merleau-Ponty, M. *The Visible and the Invisible. Followed by Working Notes*, trans. Alphonso Lingis. Evanston, IL: Northwestern University Press, 1968.

Merleau-Ponty, M. *Themes from the Lectures at the Collège de France 1952–1960*, trans. J. O'Neill. Evanston, IL: Northwestern University Press, 1970.

Bannan, J. F. *The Philosophy of Merleau-Ponty*. New York: Harcourt, Brace and World, 1967.

Dillon, M. C. *Merleau-Ponty's Ontology*. Evanston, IL: Northwestern University Press, 1997.

Hoeller, Keith (ed.). *Merleau-Ponty and Psychology*. Atlantic Highlands, NJ: Humanities Press, 1993.

Kwant, Remi. *The Phenomenological Philosophy of Merleau-Ponty*. Pittsburgh: Duquesne University Press, 1963.

Madison, Gary. *The Phenomenology of Merleau-Ponty*. Athens, OH: Ohio University Press, 1981.

Priest, Stephen. *Merleau-Ponty*. London: Routledge, 1998.

Schmidt, James. *Maurice Merleau-Ponty: Between Phenomenology and Structuralism*. London: Routledge, 1987.

1

THE BODY AS OBJECT AND MECHANISTIC PHYSIOLOGY

The definition of the object is, as we have seen, that it exists *partes extra partes*, and that consequently it acknowledges between its parts, or between itself and other objects only external and mechanical relationships, whether in the narrow sense of motion received and transmitted, or in the wider sense of the relation of function to variable. Where it was desired to insert the organism in the universe of objects and close that universe through it, it was necessary to translate the functioning of the body into the language of the *in-itself* and discover, beneath behaviour, the linear dependence of stimulus and receptor, receptor and *Empfinder*. It was of course realized that in the circuit of behaviour new particular forms emerge, and the theory of specific nervous energy, for example, certainly endowed the organism with the power of transforming the physical world. But in fact it attributed to the nervous systems the occult power of creating the different structures of our experience, and whereas sight, touch and hearing are so many ways of gaining access to the object, these structures found themselves transformed into compact qualities derived from the local distinction between the organs used. Thus the relationship between stimulus and perception could remain clear and objective, and the psycho-physical event was of the same kind as the causal relations obtaining "in the world". Modern physiology no longer has recourse to these pretences. It no longer links the different qualities of one and the same sense, and the data of different senses, to distinct material instruments. [. . .]

[. . .] [T]he "sensible quality", the spatial limits set to the percept, and even the presence or absence of a perception, are not *de facto* effects of the situation outside the organism, but represent the way in which it meets stimulation and is related to it. An excitation is not perceived when it strikes a sensory organ which is not "attuned" to it. The function of the organism in receiving stimuli is, so to speak, to "conceive" a certain form of excitation. The "psychophysical event" is therefore no longer of the type of "worldly" causality, the brain becomes the seat of a process of "patterning" which intervenes even before the cortical stage, and which, from the moment the nervous system comes into play, confuses the relations of stimulus to organism. The excitation is seized and reorganized by transversal functions which make it *resemble* the perception which it is *about to*

M. Merleau-Ponty, *Phenomemology of Perception*, 1962, trans. Colin Smith, pp. 73–89. London: Routledge.

arouse. I cannot envisage this form which is traced out in the nervous system, this exhibiting of a structure, as a set of processes in the third person, as the transmission of movement or as the determination of one variable by another. I cannot acquire detached knowledge of it. In so far as I guess what it may be, it is by abandoning the body as an object, *partes extra partes*, and by going back to the body which I experience at this moment, in the manner, for example, in which my hand moves round the object it touches, anticipating the stimuli and itself tracing out the form which I am about to perceive. I cannot understand the function of the living body except by enacting it myself, and except in so far as I am a body which rises towards the world.

Thus exteroceptivity demands that stimuli be given a shape; the consciousness of the body invades the body, the soul spreads over all its parts, and behaviour overspills its central sector. But one might reply that this "bodily experience" is itself a "representation", a "psychic fact", and that as such it is at the end of a chain of physical and physiological events which alone can be ascribed to the "real body". Is not my body, exactly as are external bodies, an object which acts on receptors and finally gives rise to the consciousness of the body? Is there not an "interoceptivity" just as there is an "exteroceptivity"? Cannot I find in the body message wires sent by the internal organs to the brain, which are installed by nature to provide the soul with the opportunity of feeling its body? The consciousness of the body, and the soul, are thus repressed. The body becomes the highly polished machine which the ambiguous notion of behaviour nearly made us forget. For example, if, in the case of a man who has lost a leg, a stimulus is applied, instead of to the leg, to the path from the stump to the brain, the subject will feel a phantom leg, because the soul is immediately linked to the brain and to it alone.

What has modern physiology to say about this? Anaesthesia with cocaine does not do away with the phantom limb, and there are cases of phantom limbs without amputation as a result of brain injury. Finally the imaginary limb is often found to retain the position in which the real arm was at the moment of injury: a man wounded in battle can still feel in his phantom arm the shell splinters that lacerated his real one. Is it then necessary to abandon the "peripheral theory" in favour of a "central theory"? But a central theory would get us no further if it added no more to the peripheral conditions of the imaginary limb than cerebral symptoms. For a collection of cerebral symptoms could not represent the relationships in consciousness which enter into the phenomenon. It depends indeed on "psychic" determinants. An emotion or circumstance, which recalls those in which the wound was received, creates a phantom limb in subjects who had none. It happens that the imaginary arm is enormous after the operation, but that it subsequently shrinks and is absorbed into the stump "as the patient consents to accept his mutilation". The phenomenon of the phantom limb is here elucidated by that of anosognosia,[1] which clearly demands a psychological explanation. Subjects who systematically ignore their paralysed right hand, and hold out their left hand when asked for their right, refer to their paralysed arm as "a long, cold snake", which rules out any hypothesis of real anaesthesia and suggests one in terms of the refusal to recognize their deficiency. Must we then conclude that the phantom limb is a memory, a volition or a belief, and, failing any physiological explanation, must we provide a psychological explanation for it? But no psychological explanation can overlook the fact that the severance of the nerves to the brain abolishes the phantom limb.

What has to be understood, then, is how the psychic determining factors and the physiological conditions gear into each other: it is not clear how the imaginary limb, if dependent on physiological conditions and therefore the result of a third person causality, can *in another context* arise out of the personal history of the patient, his memories, emotions and volitions. For in order that the two sets of conditions might together bring about the phenomenon, as two components bring about a resultant, they would need an identical point of application or a common ground, and it is difficult to see what ground could be common to "physiological facts" which are in space and "psychic facts" which are nowhere: or even to objective processes like nervous influxes which belong to the realm of the *in-itself*, and *cogitationes* such as acceptance and refusal, awareness of the past, and emotion, which are of the order of the *for-itself*. A hybrid theory of the phantom limb which found a place for both sets of conditions may, then, be valid as a statement of the known facts; but it is fundamentally obscure. The phantom limb is not the mere outcome of objective causality; no more is it a *cogitatio*. It could be a mixture of the two only if we could find a means of linking the "psychic" and the "physiological", the "for-itself" and the "in-itself", to each other to form an articulate whole, and to contrive some meeting-point for them: if the third person processes and the personal acts could be integrated into a common middle term. [. . .]

[R]eflexes themselves are never blind processes: they adjust themselves to a "direction" of the situation, and express our orientation towards a "behavioural setting" just as much as the action of the "geographical setting" upon us. They trace out from a distance the structure of the object without waiting for its point by point stimulation. It is this global presence of the situation which gives a meaning to the partial stimuli and causes them to acquire importance, value or existence for the organism. The reflex does not arise from objective stimuli, but moves back towards them, and invests them with a meaning which they do not possess taken singly as psychological agents, but only when taken as a situation. It causes them to exist as a situation, it stands in a "cognitive" relation to them, which means that it shows them up as that which it is destined to confront. The reflex, in so far as it opens itself to the meaning of a situation, and perception; in so far as it does not first of all posit an object of knowledge and is an intention of our whole being, are modalities of a *preobjective view* which is what we call being-in-the-world. Prior to stimuli and sensory contents, we must recognize a kind of inner diaphragm which determines, infinitely more than they do, what our reflexes and perceptions will be able to aim at in the world, the area of our possible operations, the scope of our life. Some subjects can come near to blindness without changing their "world": they can be seen colliding with objects everywhere, but they are not aware of no longer being open to visual qualities, and the structure of their conduct remains unmodified. Other patients, on the other hand, lose their world as soon as its contents are removed; they abandon their habitual way of life even before it has become impossible, making themselves into premature invalids and breaking their vital contact with the world before losing sensory contact with it. There is, then, a certain consistency in our "world", relatively independent of stimuli, which refuses to allow us to treat being-in-the-world as a collection of reflexes – a certain energy in the pulsation of existence, relatively independent of our voluntary thoughts, which prevents us from treating it as an *act* of consciousness. It is because it is a preobjective view that being-in-the-world can be distinguished from every third person process, from every modality of the *res extensa*, as from every *cogitatio*, from every first person form of knowledge – and that it can effect the union of the "psychic" and the "physiological".

Let us return now to the problem with which we began. Anosognosia and the phantom limb lend themselves neither to a physiological nor to a psychological explanation, nor yet to a mixture of the two, though they can be related to the two sets of conditions. A physiological explanation would account for anosognosia and the phantom limb as the straightforward suppression or equally straightforward persistence of "interoceptive" stimulations. According to this hypothesis, anosognosia is the absence of a fragment of representation which ought to be given, since the corresponding limb is there; the phantom limb is the presence of part of the representation of the body which should not be given, since the corresponding limb is not there. If one now gives a psychological account of the phenomena, the phantom limb becomes a memory, a positive judgement or a perception, while anosognosia becomes a bit of forgetfulness, a negative judgement or a failure to perceive. In the first case the phantom limb is the actual presence of a representation, anosognosia the actual absence of a representation. In the second case the phantom limb is the representation of an actual presence, whereas anosognosia is the representation of an actual absence. In both cases we are imprisoned in the categories of the objective world, in which there is no middle term between presence and absence. In reality the anosognosic is not simply ignorant of the existence of his paralysed limb: he can evade his deficiency only because he knows where he risks encountering it, just as the subject, in psychoanalysis, knows what he does not want to face, otherwise he would not be able to avoid it so successfully. We do not understand the absence or death of a friend until the time comes when we expect a reply from him and when we realize that we shall never again receive one; so at first we avoid asking in order not to have to notice this silence; we turn aside from those areas of our life in which we might meet this nothingness, but this very fact necessitates that we intuit them. In the same way the anosognosic leaves his paralysed arm out of account in order not to have to feel his handicap, but this means that he has a preconscious knowledge of it. It is true that in the case of the phantom limb the subject appears to be unaware of the mutilation and relies on his imaginary limb as he would on a real one, since he tries to walk with his phantom leg and is not discouraged even by a fall. But he can describe quite well, in spite of this, the peculiarities of the phantom leg, for example its curious motility, and if he treats it in practice as a real limb, this is because, like the normal subject, he has no need, when he wants to set off walking, of a clear and articulate perception of his body: it is enough for him to have it "at his disposal" as an undivided power, and to sense the phantom limb as vaguely involved in it. The consciousness of the phantom limb remains, then, itself unclear. The man with one leg feels the missing limb in the same way as I feel keenly the existence of a friend who is, nevertheless, not before my eyes; he has not lost it because he continues to allow for it, just as Proust can recognize the death of his grandmother, yet without losing her, as long as he can keep her on the horizon of his life. The phantom arm is not a representation of the arm, but the ambivalent presence of an arm. The refusal of mutilation in the case of the phantom limb, or the refusal of disablement in anosognosia are not deliberate decisions, and do not take place at the level of positing consciousness which takes up its position explicitly after considering various possibilities. The will to have a sound body or the rejection of an infirm one are not formulated for themselves; and the awareness of the amputated arm as present or of the disabled arm as absent is not of the kind: "I think that . . ."

This phenomenon, distorted equally by physiological and psychological explanations, is, however, understood in the perspective of being-in-the-world. What it is in us which refuses mutilation and disablement is an *I* committed to a certain physical and inter-human world, who continues to tend towards his world despite handicaps and amputations and who, to this extent, does not recognize them *de jure*. The refusal of the deficiency is only the obverse of our inherence in a world, the implicit negation of what runs counter to the natural momentum which throws us into our tasks, our cares, our situation, our familiar horizons. To have a phantom arm is to remain open to all the actions of which the arm alone is capable; it is to retain the practical field which one enjoyed before mutilation. The body is the vehicle of being in the world, and having a body is, for a living creature, to be intervolved in a definite environment, to identify oneself with certain projects and be continually committed to them. In the self-evidence of this complete world in which manipulatable objects still figure, in the force of their movement which still flows towards him, and in which is still present the project of writing or playing the piano, the cripple still finds the guarantee of his wholeness. But in concealing his deficiency from him, the world cannot fail simultaneously to reveal it to him: for if it is true that I am conscious of my body *via* the world, that it is the unperceived term in the centre of the world towards which all objects turn their face, it is true for the same reason that my body is the pivot of the world: I know that objects have several facets because I could make a tour of inspection of them, and in that sense I am conscious of the world through the medium of my body. It is precisely when my customary world arouses in me habitual intentions that I can no longer, if I have lost a limb, be effectively drawn into it, and the utilizable objects, precisely in so far as they present themselves as utilizable, appeal to a hand which I no longer have. Thus are delimited, in the totality of my body, regions of silence. The patient therefore realizes his disability precisely in so far as he is ignorant of it, and is ignorant of it precisely to the extent that he knows of it. This paradox is that of all being in the world: when I move towards a world I bury my perceptual and practical intentions in objects which ultimately appear prior to and external to those intentions, and which nevertheless exist for me only in so far as they arouse in me thoughts or volitions. In the case under consideration, the ambiguity of knowledge amounts to this: our body comprises as it were two distinct layers, that of the customary body and that of the body at this moment. In the first appear manipulatory movements which have disappeared from the second, and the problem how I can have the sensation of still possessing a limb which I no longer have amounts to finding out how the habitual body can act as guarantee for the body at this moment. How can I perceive objects as manipulatable when I can no longer manipulate them? The manipulatable must have ceased to be what I am now manipulating, and become what *one* can manipulate; it must have ceased to be a thing *manipulatable for me*

431

and become a thing *manipulatable in itself*. Correspondingly, my body must be apprehended not only in an experience which is instantaneous, peculiar to itself and complete in itself, but also in some general aspect and in the light of an impersonal being.

In that way the phenomenon of the phantom limb is absorbed into that of repression, which we shall find throwing some light on it. For repression, to which psycho-analysis refers, consists in the subject's entering upon a certain course of action – a love affair, a career, a piece of work – in his encountering on this course some barrier, and, since he has the strength neither to surmount the obstacle nor to abandon the enterprise, he remains imprisoned in the attempt and uses up his strength indefinitely renewing it in spirit. Time in its passage does not carry away with it these impossible projects; it does not close up on traumatic experience; the subject remains open to the same impossible future, if not in his explicit thoughts, at any rate in his actual being. [. . .] All repression is, then, the transition from first person existence to a sort of abstraction of that existence, which lives on a former experience, or rather on the memory of having had the memory, and so on, until finally only the essential form remains. Now as an advent of the impersonal, repression is a universal phenomenon, revealing our condition as incarnate beings by relating it to the temporal structure of being in the world. To the extent that I have "sense organs", a "body", and "psychic functions" comparable with other men's, each of the moments of my experience ceases to be an integrated and strictly unique totality, in which details exist only in virtue of the whole; I become the meeting point of a host of "causalities". In so far as I inhabit a "physical world", in which consistent "stimuli" and typical situations recur – and not merely the historical world in which situations are never exactly comparable – my life is made up of rhythms which have not their *reason* in what I have chosen to be, but their *condition* in the humdrum setting which is mine. Thus there appears round our personal existence a margin of *almost* impersonal existence, which can be practically taken for granted, and which I rely on to keep me alive; round the human world which each of us has made for himself is a world in general terms to which one must first of all belong in order to be able to enclose oneself in the particular context of a love or an ambition. Just as we speak of repression in the limited sense when I retain through time one of the momentary worlds through which I have lived, and make it the formative element of my whole life – so it can be said that my organism, as a prepersonal cleaving to the general form of the world, as an anonymous and general existence, plays, beneath my personal life, the part of an *inborn complex*. It is not some kind of inert thing; it too has something of the momentum of existence. It may even happen when I am in danger that my human situation abolishes my biological one, that my body lends itself without reserve to action. But these moments can be no more than moments, and for most of the time personal existence represses the organism without being able either to go beyond it or to renounce itself; without, in other words, being able either to reduce the organism to its existential self, or itself to the organism. [. . .] It can now be said that, *a fortiori*, the specific past, which our body is, can be recaptured and taken up by an individual life only because that life has never transcended it, but secretly nourishes it, devoting thereto part of its strength, because its present is still that past. This can be seen in cases of illness in which bodily events become the events of the day. What enables us to centre our existence is also what prevents us from centring it completely, and the anonymity of our body is inseparably both freedom and servitude. Thus, to sum up, the ambiguity of being in the world is translated by that of the body, and this is understood through that of time.

We shall return later to the question of time. Let it merely be noted for the moment that starting with this central phenomenon the relationships between the "psychic" and the "physiological" become conceivable. Why can the memories recalled to the one-armed man cause the phantom arm to appear? The phantom arm is not a recollection, it is a quasi-present and the patient feels it now, folded over his chest, with no hint of its belonging to the past. Nor can we suppose that the image of an arm, wandering through consciousness, has joined itself to the stump: for then it would not be a "phantom", but a renascent perception. The phantom arm must be that same arm, lacerated by shell splinters, its visible substance burned or rotted somewhere, which appears to haunt the present body without being absorbed into it. The imaginary arm is, then, like repressed experience, a former present which cannot decide to recede into the past. The memories called up before the patient induce in him a phantom limb, not as an image in associationism summons up another image, but because any memory reopens time lost to us and invites us to recapture the situation evoked. Intellectual memory, in Proust's sense, limits itself to a description of the past, a past as idea, from which it extracts "characteristics" or communicable meaning rather than discovering a structure. But it would not be memory if the object which it constructs were not still held by a few intentional threads to the horizon of the lived-through past, and to that past itself as we should rediscover it if we were to delve beyond these horizons and reopen time. In the same way, if we put back emotion into being in the world, we can understand how it can be the origin of the phantom limb. To feel emotion is to be involved in a situation which one is not managing to face and from which, nevertheless, one does not want to escape. Rather than admit failure or retrace one's steps, the subject, caught in this existential dilemma, breaks in pieces the objective world which stands in his way and seeks symbolical satisfaction in magic acts. The ruin of the objective world, abandonment of true action, flight into a self-contained realm are conditions favouring the illusion of those who have lost a limb in that it too presupposes the erasure of reality. In so far as memory and emotion can call up the phantom limb, this is not comparable to the action of one *cogitatio* which necessitates another *cogitatio*, or that of one condition bringing about its consequence. It is not that an ideal causality here superimposes itself on a physiological one, it is that an existential attitude motivates another and that memory, emotion and phantom limb are equivalents in the context of being in the world.

Now why does the severing of the afferent nerves banish the phantom limb? In the perspective of being in the world this fact means that the impulses arriving from the stump keep the amputated limb in the circuit of existence. They establish and maintain its place, prevent it from being abolished, and cause it still to count in the organism. They keep empty an area which the subject's history fills, they enable the latter to build up the phantom, as structural disturbances allow the content of psychosis to form into delirium. From our point of view, a sensorimotor circuit is, within our comprehensive being in the world, a relatively autonomous current of existence. Not that it always brings to our total being a separable contribution, but because under certain circumstances it is possible to bring to light constant responses to stimuli which are themselves constant. The question is, therefore, how the refusal of the deficiency, which is a total attitude of our existence, needs for its expression such a highly specialized modality as a sensori-motor circuit, and why our being in the world, which provides all our reflexes with their meaning, and which is thus their basis, nevertheless delivers itself over to them and is finally based upon them. Indeed, as we have shown elsewhere, sensori-motor circuits are all the more clearly marked as one is concerned with more integrated existences, and the reflex in its pure state is to be found only in man, who has not only a setting (*Umwelt*), but also a world (*Welt*).

From the existential point of view, these two facts, which scientific induction contents itself with setting side by side, are linked internally and are understood in the light of one and the same idea. If man is not to be embedded in the matrix of that syncretic setting in which animals lead their lives in a sort of *ek-stase*, if he is to be aware of a world as the common reason for all settings and the theatre of all patterns of behaviour, then between himself and what elicits his action a distance must be set, and, as Malebranche put it, forms of stimulation from outside must henceforth impinge on him "respectfully"; each momentary situation must cease to be, for him, the totality of being, each particular response must no longer fill his whole field of action. Furthermore, the elaboration of these responses, instead of occurring at the centre of his existence, must take place on the periphery and finally the responses themselves must no longer demand that on each occasion some special position be taken up, but they must be outlined once and for all in their generality. Thus it is by giving up part of his spontaneity, by becoming involved in the world through stable organs and pre-established circuits that man can acquire the mental and practical space which will theoretically free him from his environment and allow him to *see* it. And provided that even the realization of an objective world is set in the realm of existence, we shall no longer find any contradiction between it and bodily conditioning: it is an inner necessity for the most integrated existence to provide itself with an habitual body. What allows us to link to each other the "physiological" and the "psychic", is the fact that, when reintegrated into existence, they are no longer distinguishable respectively as the order of the *in-itself*, and that of the *for-itself*, and that they are both directed towards an intentional pole or towards a world. Probably the two histories never quite coincide: one is commonplace and cyclic, the other may be open and unusual, and it would be necessary to keep the term "history" for the second order of phenomena if history were a succession of events which not only have a meaning, but furnish themselves with it. However, failing a true revolution which breaks up historical categories so far valid, the figure in history does not create his part completely: faced with typical situations he takes typical decisions and Nicholas II, repeating the very words of Louis XVI, plays the already written part of established power in face of a new power. His decisions translate the *a priori* of a threatened prince as our reflexes translate a specific *a priori*. These stereotypes, moreover, are not a destiny, and just as clothing, jewellery and love transfigure the biological needs from which they arise, in the same way within the cultural world the historical *a priori* is constant only for a given phase and provided that the balance of *forces* allows the same *forms* to remain. So history is neither a perpetual novelty, nor a perpetual repetition, but the *unique* movement which creates stable forms and breaks them up. The organism and its monotonous dialectical processes are therefore not alien to history and as it were inassimilable to it. Man taken as a concrete being is not a psyche joined to an organism, but the movement to and fro of existence which at one time allows itself to take corporeal form and at others moves towards personal acts. Psychological motives and bodily occasions may overlap because there is not a single impulse in a living body which is entirely fortuitous in relation to psychic intentions, not a single mental act which has not found at least its germ or its general outline in physiological tendencies. It is never a question of the incomprehensible meeting of two causalities, nor of a collision between the order of causes and that of ends. But by an imperceptible twist an organic process issues into human behaviour, an instinctive act changes direction and becomes a sentiment, or conversely a human act becomes torpid and is continued absent-mindedly in the form of a reflex. [. . .]

Thus, to the question which we were asking, modern physiology gives a very clear reply: the psycho-physical event can no longer be conceived after the model of Cartesian physiology and as the juxtaposition of a process in itself and a *cogitatio*. The union of soul and body is not an amalgamation between two mutually external terms, subject and object, brought about by arbitrary decree. It is enacted at every instant in the movement of existence.

Note

1 Failure or refusal on the patient's part to recognize the existence of a disease or disability [Tr.].

2

THE PRIMACY OF PERCEPTION
AND ITS PHILOSOPHICAL
CONSEQUENCES[1]

Preliminary summary of the argument

1 Perception as an original modality of consciousness

The unprejudiced study of perception by psychologists has finally revealed that the perceived world is not a sum of objects (in the sense in which the sciences use this word), that our relation to the world is not that of a thinker to an object of thought, and finally that the unity of the perceived thing, as perceived by several consciousnesses, is not comparable to the unity of a proposition [*théorème*], as understood by several thinkers, any more than perceived existence is comparable to ideal existence.

As a result we cannot apply the classical distinction of form and matter to perception, nor can we conceive the perceiving subject as a consciousness which "interprets," "deciphers," or "orders" a sensible matter according to an ideal law which it possesses. Matter is "pregnant" with its form, which is to say that in the final analysis every perception takes place within a certain horizon and ultimately in the "world." We experience a perception and its horizon "in action" [*pratique-ment*] rather than by "posing" them or explicitly "knowing" them. Finally the quasi-organic relation of the perceiving subject and the world involves, in principle, the contradiction of immanence and transcendence.

2 The generalization of these results

Do these results have any value beyond that of psychological description? They would not if we could superimpose on the perceived world a world of ideas. But in reality the ideas to which we recur are valid only for a period of our lives or for a period in the history of our culture. Evidence is never apodictic, nor is thought timeless, though there is some progress in objectification and thought is always valid for more than an instant. The certainty of ideas is not the foundation of the certainty of perception but is, rather, based on it – in that it is perceptual experience which gives us the passage from one moment to the next and thus realizes the unity of time. In this sense all consciousness is perceptual, even the consciousness of ourselves.

M. Merleau-Ponty, *The Primacy of Perception and Other Essays*, 1964, ed. and trans. James M. Edie, pp. 12–27. Evanston, IL: Northwestern University Press.

3 Conclusions

The perceived world is the always presupposed foundation of all rationality, all value and all existence. This thesis does not destroy either rationality or the absolute. It only tries to bring them down to earth.

[. . .] Report of the session

M. Merleau-Ponty. The point of departure for these remarks is that the perceived world comprises relations and, in a general way, a type of organization which has not been recognized by classical psychology and philosophy.

If we consider an object which we perceive but one of whose sides we do not see, or if we consider objects which are not within our visual field at this moment – i.e., what is happening behind our back or what is happening in America or at the South Pole – how should we describe the existence of these absent objects or the nonvisible parts of present objects?

Should we say, as psychologists have often done, that I *represent* to myself the sides of this lamp which are not seen? If I say these sides are representations, I imply that they are not grasped as actually existing; because what is represented is not here before us, I do not actually perceive it. It is only a possible. But since the unseen sides of this lamp are not imaginary, but only hidden from view (to see them it suffices to move the lamp a little bit), I cannot say that they are representations.

Should I say that the unseen sides are somehow anticipated by me, as perceptions which would be produced necessarily if I moved, given the structure of the object? If, for example, I look at a cube, knowing the structure of the cube as it is defined in geometry, I can anticipate the perceptions which this cube will give me while I move around it. Under this hypothesis I would know the unseen side as the necessary consequence of a certain law of the development of my perception. But if I turn to perception itself, I cannot interpret it in this way because this analysis can be formulated as follows: It is *true* that the lamp has a back, that the cube has another side. But this formula, "It is true," does not correspond to what is given to me in perception. Perception does not give me truths like geometry but presences.

I grasp the unseen side as present, and I do not affirm that the back of the lamp exists in the same sense that I say the solution of a problem exists. The hidden side is present in its own way. It is in my vicinity.

Thus I should not say that the unseen sides of objects are simply possible perceptions, nor that they are the necessary conclusions of a kind of analysis or geometrical reasoning. It is not through an intellectual synthesis which would freely posit the total object that I am led from what is given to what is not actually given; that I am given, together with the visible sides of the object, the nonvisible sides as well. It is, rather, a kind of practical synthesis: I can touch the lamp, and not only the side turned toward me but also the other side; I have only to extend my hand to hold it.

The classical analysis of perception reduces all our experience to the single level of what, for good reasons, is judged to be true. But when, on the contrary, I consider the whole setting [*l'entourage*] of my perception, it reveals another modality which is neither the ideal and necessary being of geometry nor the simple sensory event, the "*percipi*," and this is precisely what remains to be studied now.

But these remarks on the setting [*entourage*] of what is perceived enable us better to see the perceived itself. I perceive before me a road or a house, and I perceive them as having a certain dimension: the road may be a country road or a national highway; the house may be a shanty or a manor. These identifications presuppose that I recognize the true size of the object, quite different from that which appears to me from the point at which I am standing. It is frequently said that I restore the true size on the basis of the apparent size by analysis and conjecture. This is inexact for the very convincing reason that the apparent size of which we are speaking is not perceived by me. It is a remarkable fact that the uninstructed have no awareness of perspective and that it took a long time and much reflection for men to become aware of a perspectival deformation of objects. Thus there is no deciphering, no mediate inference from the sign to what is signified, because the alleged signs are not given to me separately from what they signify.

In the same way it is not true that I deduce the true color of an object on the basis of the color of the setting or of the lighting, which most of the time is not perceived. At this hour, since daylight is still coming through the windows, we perceive the yellowness of the artificial light, and it alters the color of objects. But when daylight disappears this yellowish color will no longer be perceived, and we will see the objects more or less in their true colors. The true color thus is not deduced, taking account of the lighting, because it appears precisely when daylight disappears.

If these remarks are true, what is the result? And how should we understand this "I perceive" which we are attempting to grasp?

We observe at once that it is impossible, as has often been said, to decompose a perception, to make it into a collection of sensations, because in it the whole is prior to the parts – and this whole is not an ideal whole. The meaning which I ultimately discover is not of the conceptual order. If it were a concept, the question would be how I can recognize it in the sense data, and it would be necessary for me to interpose between the concept and the sense data certain intermediaries, and then other intermediaries between these intermediaries, and so on. It is necessary that meaning and signs, the form and matter of perception, be related from the beginning and that, as we say, the matter of perception be "pregnant with its form."

In other words, the synthesis which constitutes the unity of the perceived objects and which gives meaning to the perceptual data is not an intellectual synthesis. Let us say with Husserl that it is a "synthesis of transition" [*synthèse de transition*][2] – I anticipate the unseen side of the lamp because I can touch it – or a "horizonal synthesis" [*synthèse d'horizon*] – the unseen side is given to me as "visible from another standpoint," at once given but only immanently. What prohibits me from treating my perception as an intellectual act is that an intellectual act would grasp the object either as possible or as necessary. But in perception it is "real"; it is given as the infinite sum of an indefinite series of perspectival views in each of which the object is given but in none of which is it given exhaustively. It is not accidental for the object to be given to me in a "deformed" way, from the point of view [*place*] which I occupy. That is the price of its being "real." The perceptual synthesis thus must be accomplished by the subject, which can both delimit certain perspectival aspects in the object, the only ones actually given, and at the same time go beyond them. This subject, which takes a point of view, is my body as the field of perception and action [*pratique*] – in so far as my gestures have a certain reach and circumscribe as my domain the whole group of objects familiar to me. Perception is here understood as a reference to a whole which can be grasped, in principle, only through certain of its parts or aspects. The perceived thing is not an ideal unity in the possession of the intellect, like a geometrical notion, for example; it is rather a totality open to a horizon of an indefinite number of perspectival views which blend with one another according to a given style, which defines the object in question.

Perception is thus paradoxical. The perceived thing itself is paradoxical; it exists only in so far as someone can perceive it. I cannot even for an instant imagine an object in itself. As Berkeley said, if I attempt to imagine some place in the world which has never been seen, the very fact that I imagine it makes me present at that place. I thus cannot conceive a perceptible place in which I am not myself present. But even the places in which I find myself are never completely given to me; the things which I see are things for me only under the condition that they always recede beyond their immediately given aspects. Thus there is a paradox of immanence and transcendence in perception. Immanence, because the perceived object cannot be foreign to him who perceives; transcendence, because it always contains something more than what is actually given. And these two elements of perception are not, properly speaking, contradictory. For if we reflect on this notion of perspective, if we reproduce the perceptual experience in our thought, we see that the kind of evidence proper to the perceived, the appearance of "something," requires both this presence and this absence.

Finally, the world itself, which (to give a first, rough definition) is the totality of perceptible things and the thing of all things, must be understood not as an object in the sense the mathematician or the physicist give to this word – that is, a kind of unified law which would cover all the partial phenomena or as a fundamental relation verifiable in all – but as the universal style of all possible perceptions. We must make this notion of the world, which guides the whole transcendental deduction of Kant, though Kant does not tell us its provenance, more explicit. "If a world is to be possible," he says sometimes, as if he were thinking before the origin of the world, as if he were assisting at its genesis and could pose its *a priori* conditions. In fact, as Kant himself said profoundly, we can only think the world because we have already experienced it; it is through this experience that we have the idea of being, and it is through this experience that the words "rational" and "real" receive a meaning simultaneously.

If I now consider not the problem of knowing how it is that there are things for me or how it is that I have a unified, unique, and developing perceptual experience of them, but rather the problem of knowing how my experience is related to the experience which others have of the same objects, perception will again appear as the paradoxical phenomenon which renders being accessible to us.

If I consider my perceptions as simple sensations, they are private; they are mine alone. If I treat them as acts of the intellect, if perception is an inspection of the mind, and the perceived object an idea, then you and I are talking about the same world, and we have *the right* to communicate among ourselves because the world has become an ideal existence and is the same for all of us – just like the Pythagorean theorem. But neither of these two formulas accounts for our experience. If a friend and I are standing before a landscape, and if I attempt to show my friend something which I see and which he does not yet see, we cannot account for the situation by saying that I see something in my own world and that I attempt, by sending verbal messages, to give rise to an analogous perception in the world of my friend. There are not two numerically distinct worlds plus a mediating language which alone would bring us together. There is – and I know it very well if I become impatient with him – a kind of demand that what I see be seen by him also. And at the same time this communication is required by the very thing which I am looking at, by the reflections of sunlight upon it, by its color, by its sensible evidence. The thing imposes itself not as true for every intellect, but as real for every subject who is standing where I am.

I will never know how you see red, and you will never know how I see it; but this separation of consciousnesses is recognized only after a failure of communication, and our first movement is to believe in an undivided being between us. There is no reason to treat this primordial communication as an illusion, as the sensationalists do, because even then it would become inexplicable. And there is no reason to base it on our common participation in the same intellectual consciousness because this would suppress the undeniable plurality of consciousnesses. It is thus necessary that, in the perception of another, I find myself in relation with another "myself," who is, in principle, open to the same truths as I am, in relation to the same being that I am. And this perception is realized. From the depths of my subjectivity I see another subjectivity invested with equal rights appear, because the behavior of the other takes place within my perceptual field. I understand this behavior, the words of another; I espouse his thought because this other, born in the midst of my phenomena, appropriates them and treats them in accord with typical behaviors which I myself have experienced. Just as my body, as the system of all my holds on the world, founds the unity of the objects which I perceive, in the same way the body of the other – as the bearer of symbolic behaviors and of the behavior of true reality – tears itself away from being one of my phenomena, offers me the task of a true communication, and confers on my objects the new dimension of intersubjective being or, in other words, of objectivity. Such are, in a quick résumé, the elements of a description of the perceived world.

Some of our colleagues who were so kind as to send me their observations in writing grant me that all this is valid as a psychological inventory. But, they add, there remains the world of which we say "It is true" – that is to say, the world of knowledge, the verified world, the world of science. Psychological description concerns only a small section of our experience, and there is no reason, according to them, to give such descriptions any universal value. They do not touch being itself but only the psychological peculiarities of perception. These descriptions, they add, are all the less admissible as being in any way definitive because they are contradicted by the perceived world. How can we admit ultimate contradictions? Perceptual experience is contradictory because it is confused. It is necessary to think it. When we think it, its contradictions disappear under the light of the intellect. Finally, one correspondent tells me that we are invited to return to the perceived world as we experience it. That is to say that there is no need to reflect or to think and that perception knows better than we what it is doing. How can this disavowal of reflection be philosophy?

It is true that we arrive at contradictions when we describe the perceived world. And it is also true that if there were such a thing as a non-contradictory thought, it would exclude the world of perception as a simple appearance. But the question is precisely to know whether there is such a thing as logically coherent thought or thought in the pure state. This is the question Kant asked himself and the objection which I have just sketched is a pre-Kantian objection. One of Kant's discoveries, whose consequences we have not yet fully grasped, is that all our experience of the world is throughout a tissue of concepts which lead to irreducible contradictions if we attempt to take them in an absolute sense or transfer them into pure being, and that they nevertheless found the structure of all our phenomena, of everything which *is* for us. It would take too long to show (and besides it is well known) that Kantian philosophy itself failed to utilize this principle fully and that both its investigation of experience and its critique of dogmatism remained incomplete. I wish only to point out that the accusation of contradiction is not decisive, *if the acknowledged contradiction appears as the very condition of consciousness*. It is in this sense that Plato and Kant, to mention only them, accepted the contradiction of which Zeno and Hume wanted no part. There is a vain form of contradiction which consists in affirming two theses which exclude one another at the same time and under the same aspect. And there are philosophies which show contradictions present at the very heart of time and of all relationships. There is the sterile non-contradiction of formal logic and the justified contradictions of transcendental logic. The objection with which we are concerned would be admissible only if we could put a system of eternal truths in the place of the perceived world, freed from its contradictions.

We willingly admit that we cannot rest satisfied with the description of the perceived world as we have sketched it up to now and that it appears as a psychological curiosity if we leave aside the idea of the true world, the world as thought by the understanding. This leads us, therefore, to the second point which I propose to examine: what is the relation between intellectual consciousness and perceptual consciousness?

Before taking this up, let us say a word about the other objection which was addressed to us: you go back to the unreflected [*irréfléchi*]; therefore you renounce reflection. It is true that we discover the unreflected. But the unreflected we go back to is not that which is prior to philosophy or prior to reflection. It is the unreflected which is understood and conquered by reflection. Left to itself, perception forgets itself and is ignorant of its own accomplishments. Far from thinking that philosophy is a useless repetition of life I think, on the contrary, that without reflection life would probably dissipate itself in ignorance of itself or in chaos. But this does not mean that reflection should be carried away with itself or pretend to be ignorant of its origins. By fleeing difficulties it would only fail in its task.

Should we now generalize and say that what is true of perception is also true in the order of the intellect and that in a general way all our experience, all our knowledge, has the same fundamental structures, the same synthesis of transition, the same kind of horizons which we have found in perceptual experience?

No doubt the absolute truth or evidence of scientific knowledge would be opposed to this idea. But it seems to me that the acquisitions of the philosophy of the sciences confirm the primacy of perception. Does not the work of the French school at the beginning of this century, and the work of Brunschvicg, show that scientific knowledge cannot be closed in on itself, that it is always an approximate knowledge, and that it consists in clarifying a pre-scientific world the analysis of which will never be finished? Physico-mathematical relations take on a physical sense only to the extent that we at the same time represent to ourselves the sensible things to which these relations ultimately apply. Brunschvicg reproached positivism for its dogmatic illusion that the law is truer than the fact. The law, he adds, is conceived exclusively to make the fact intelligible. The perceived happening can never be reabsorbed in the complex of transparent relations which the intellect constructs because of the happening. But if this is the case, philosophy is not only consciousness of these relations; it is also consciousness of the obscure element and of the "non-relational foundation" on which these relations are based. Otherwise it would shirk its task of universal clarification. When I think the Pythagorean theorem and recognize it as true, it is clear that this truth is not for this moment only. Nevertheless later progress in knowledge will show that it is not yet a final, unconditioned evidence and that, if the Pythagorean theorem and the Euclidean system once appeared as final, unconditioned evidences, that is itself the mark of a certain cultural epoch. Later developments would not annul the Pythagorean theorem but would put it back in its place as a partial, and also an abstract, truth. Thus here also we do not have a timeless truth but rather the recovery of one time by another time, just as, on the level of perception, our certainty about perceiving a given thing does not guarantee that our experience will not be contradicted, or dispense us from a fuller experience of that thing. Naturally it is necessary to establish here a difference between ideal truth and perceived truth. I do not propose to undertake this immense task just now. I am only trying to show the organic tie, so to speak, between perception and intellection. Now it is incontestable that I dominate the stream of my conscious states and even that I am unaware of their temporal succession. At the moment when I am thinking or considering an idea, I am not divided into the instants of my life. But it is also incontestable that this domination of time, which is the work of thought, is always somewhat deceiving. Can I seriously say that I will always hold the ideas I do at present – and mean it? Do I not know that in six months, in a year, even if I use more or less the same formulas to express my thoughts, they will have changed their meaning slightly? Do I not know that there is a life of ideas, as there is a meaning of everything I experience, and that every one of my most convincing thoughts will need additions and then will be, not destroyed, but at least integrated into a new unity? This is the only conception of knowledge that is scientific and not mythological.

Thus perception and thought have this much in common – that both of them have a future horizon and a past horizon and that they appear to themselves as temporal, even though they do not move at the same speed nor in the same time. We must say that at each moment our ideas express not only the truth but also our capacity to attain it at that given moment. Skepticism begins if we conclude from this that our ideas are always false. But this can only happen with reference to some idol of absolute knowledge. We must say, on the contrary, that our ideas, however limited they may be at a given moment – since they always express our contact with being and with culture – are capable of being true provided we keep them open to the field of nature and culture which they must express. And this possibility is always open to us, just because we are temporal. The idea of going straight to the essence of things is an inconsistent idea if one thinks about it. What is given is a route, an experience which gradually clarifies itself, which gradually rectifies itself and proceeds by dialogue with itself and with others. Thus what we tear away from the dispersion of instants is not an already-made reason; it is, as has always been said, a natural light, our openness to *something*. What saves us is the possibility of a new development, and our power of making even what is false, true – by thinking through our errors and replacing them within the domain of truth.

But finally, it will be objected that I grasp myself in pure reflexion, completely outside perception, and that I grasp myself not now as a perceiving subject, tied by its body to a system of things, but as a thinking subject, radically free with respect to things and with respect to the body. How is such an experience of self, of the *cogito*, possible in our perspective, and what meaning does it have?

There is a first way of understanding the *cogito*: it consists in saying that when I grasp myself I am limited to noting, so to speak, a psychic fact, "I think." This is an instantaneous constatation, and under the condition that the experience has no duration I adhere immediately to what I think and consequently cannot doubt it. This is the *cogito* of the psychologists. It is of this instantaneous *cogito* that Descartes was thinking when he said that I am certain that I exist during the whole time that I am thinking of it. Such certitude is limited to my existence and to my pure and completely naked thought. As soon as I make it specific with any particular thought, I fail, because, as Descartes explains, every particular thought uses premises not actually given. Thus the first truth, understood in this way, is the only truth. Or rather it cannot even be formulated as truth; it is experienced in the instant and in silence. The *cogito* understood in this way – in the skeptical way – does not account for our idea of truth.

There is a second way of understanding the *cogito*: as the grasping not only of the fact that I think but also of the objects which this thought intends, and as evidence not only of a private existence but also of the things which it thinks, at least as it thinks them. In this perspective the *cogito* is neither more certain than the *cogitatum*, nor does it have a different kind of certainty. Both are possessed of ideal evidence. Descartes sometimes presented the *cogito* in this way – as, for example, in the *Regulae* when he placed one's own existence (*se esse*) among the most simple evidences. This supposes that the subject is perfectly transparent for itself, like an essence, and is incompatible with the idea of the hyperbolic doubt which even reaches to essences.

But there is a third meaning of the *cogito*, the only solid one: the act of doubting in which I put in question all possible objects of my experience. This act grasps itself in its own operation [*à l'oeuvre*] and thus cannot doubt itself. The very fact of doubting obturates doubt. The certitude I have of myself is here a veritable perception: I grasp myself, not as a constituting subject which is transparent to itself, and which constitutes the totality of every possible object of thought and experience, but as a particular thought, as a thought engaged with certain objects, as a thought in act; and it is in this sense that I am certain of

443

myself. Thought is given to itself; I somehow find myself thinking and I become aware of it. In this sense I am certain that I am thinking this or that as well as being certain that I am simply thinking. Thus I can get outside the psychological *cogito* – without, however, taking myself to be a universal thinker. I am not simply a constituted happening; I am not a universal thinker [*naturant*].[3] I am a thought which recaptures itself as already possessing an ideal of truth (which it cannot at each moment wholly account for) and which is the horizon of its operations. This thought, which *feels* itself rather than *sees* itself, which searches after clarity rather than possesses it, and which creates truth rather than finds it, is described in a formerly celebrated text of Lagneau. Should we submit to life or create it, he asked. And he answered: "Once again this question does not pertain to the domain of the intellect; we are free and, in this sense, skepticism is true. But to answer negatively is to make the world and the self unintelligible; it is to decree chaos and above all to establish it in the self. But chaos is nothing. To be or not to be, the self and everything else, we must choose" (*Cours sur l'existence de Dieu*). I find here, in an author who spent his whole life reflecting on Descartes, Spinoza, and Kant, the idea – sometimes considered barbarous – of a thought which remembers it began in time and then sovereignly recaptures itself and in which fact, reason, and freedom coincide.

Finally, let us ask what happens, from such a point of view, to rationality and experience, whether there can be any absolute affirmation already implied in experience.

The fact that my experiences hold together and that I experience the concordance of my own experiences with those of others is in no way compromised by what we have just said. On the contrary, this fact is put in relief, against skepticism. Something appears to me, as to anyone else, and these phenomena, which set the boundaries of everything thinkable or conceivable for us, are certain as phenomena. There is meaning. But rationality is neither a total nor an immediate guarantee. It is somehow open, which is to say that it is menaced.

Doubtless this thesis is open to two types of criticism, one from the psychological side and the other from the philosophical side.

The very psychologists who have described the perceived world as I did above, the Gestalt psychologists, have never drawn the philosophical conclusions of their description. In that respect they remain within the classical framework. Ultimately they consider the structures of the perceived world as the simple result of certain physical and physiological processes which take place in the nervous system and completely determine the *Gestalten* and the experience of the *Gestalten*. The organism and consciousness itself are only functions of external physical variables. Ultimately the real world is the physical world as science conceives it, and it engenders our consciousness itself.

But the question is whether Gestalt theory, after the work it has done in calling attention to the phenomena of the perceived world, can fall back on the classical notion of reality and objectivity and incorporate the world of the *Gestalten* within this classical conception of reality. Without doubt one of the most important acquisitions of this theory has been its overcoming of the classical alternatives between objective psychology and introspective psychology. Gestalt psychology went beyond this alternative by showing that the object of psychology is the structure of behavior, accessible both from within and from without. In his book on the chimpanzees, Köhler applied this idea and showed that in order to describe the behavior of a chimpanzee it is necessary, in characterizing this behavior, to bring in notions such as the "melodic line" of behavior. These are anthropomorphic notions, but they can be utilized objectively because it is possible to agree on interpreting "melodic" and "non-melodic" behaviors in terms of "good solutions" and "bad solutions." The science of psychology thus is not something constructed outside the human world; it is, in fact, a property of the human world to make the distinction between the true and the false, the objective and the fictional. When, later on, Gestalt psychology tried to explain itself – in spite of its own discoveries – in terms of a scientist or positivistic ontology, it was at the price of an internal contradiction which we have to reject.

Coming back to the perceived world as we have described it above, and basing our conception of reality on the phenomena, we do not in any way sacrifice objectivity to the interior life, as Bergson has been accused of doing. As Gestalt psychology has shown, structure, *Gestalt*, meaning are no less visible in objectively observable behavior than in the experience of ourselves – provided, of course, that objectivity is not confused with what is measurable. Is one truly objective with respect to man when he thinks he can take him as an object which can be explained as an intersection of processes and causalities? Is it not more objective to attempt to constitute a true science of human life based on the description of typical behaviors? Is it objective to apply tests to man which deal only with abstract aptitudes, or to attempt to grasp the situation of man as he is present to the world and to others by means of still more tests?

Psychology as a science has nothing to fear from a return to the perceived world, nor from a philosophy which draws out the consequences of this return. Far from hurting psychology, this attitude, on the contrary, clarifies the philosophical meaning of its discoveries. For there are not two truths; there is not an inductive psychology and an intuitive philosophy. Psychological induction is never more than the methodological means of bringing to light a certain typical behavior, and if induction includes intuition, conversely intuition does not occur in empty space. It exercises itself on the facts, on the material, on the phenomena brought to light by scientific research. There are not two kinds of knowledge, but two different degrees of clarification of the same knowledge. Psychology and philosophy are nourished by the same phenomena; it is only that the problems become more formalized at the philosophical level.

But the philosophers might say here that we are giving psychology too big a place, that we are compromising rationality by founding it on the texture of experience, as it is manifested in perceptual experience. But either the demand for an absolute rationality is only a wish, a personal preference which should not be confused with philosophy, or this point of view, to the extent that it is well-founded, satisfies it as well as, or even better than, any other. When philosophers wish to place reason above the vicissitudes of history they cannot purely and simply forget what psychology, sociology, ethnography, history, and psychiatry have taught us about the conditioning of human behavior. It would be a very romantic way of showing one's love for reason to base its reign on the disavowal of acquired knowledge. What can be validly demanded is that man never be submitted to the fate of an external nature or history and stripped of his consciousness. Now my philosophy satisfies this demand. In speaking of the primacy of perception, I have never, of course, meant to say (this would be a return to the theses of empiricism) that science, reflection, and philosophy are only transformed sensations or that values are deferred and calculated pleasures. By these words, the "primacy of perception," we mean that the experience of perception is our presence at the moment when things, truths, values are constituted for us; that perception is a nascent *logos*; that it teaches us, outside all dogmatism, the true conditions of objectivity itself; that it summons us to the tasks of knowledge and action. It is not a question of reducing human knowledge to sensation, but of assisting at the birth of this knowledge, to make it as sensible as the sensible, to recover the consciousness of rationality. This experience of rationality is lost when we take it for granted as self-evident, but is, on the contrary, rediscovered when it is made to appear against the background of non-human nature.

The work[4] which was the occasion for this paper is still, in this respect, only a preliminary study, since it hardly speaks of culture or of history. On the basis of perception – taken as a privileged realm of experience, since the perceived object is by definition present and living – this book attempts to define a method for getting closer to present and living reality, and which must then be applied to the relation of man to man in language, in knowledge, in society and religion, as it was applied in this work to man's relation to perceptible reality and with respect to man's relation to others on the level of perceptual experience. We call this level of experience "primordial" – not to assert that everything else derives from it by transformations and evolution (we have expressly said that man perceives in a way different from any animal) but rather that it reveals to us the permanent data of the problem which culture attempts to resolve. If we have not tied the subject to the determinism of an external nature and have only replaced it in the bed of the perceptible, which it transforms without ever quitting it, much less will we submit the subject to some impersonal history. History is other people; it is the interrelationships we establish with them, outside of which the realm of the ideal appears as an alibi.

This leads us . . . to draw certain conclusions from what has preceded as concerns the realm of the practical. If we admit that our life is inherent to the perceived world and the human world, even while it re-creates it and contributes to its making, then morality cannot consist in the private adherence to a system of values. Principles are mystifications unless they are put into practice; it is necessary that they animate our relations with others. Thus we cannot remain indifferent to the aspect in which our acts appear to others, and the question is posed whether intention suffices as moral justification. It is clear that the approval of such or such a group proves nothing, since, in looking for it, we choose our own judges – which comes down to saying that we are not yet thinking for ourselves. It is the very demand of rationality which imposes on us the need to act in such a way that our action cannot be considered by others as an act of aggression but, on the contrary, as generously meeting the other in the very particularity of a given situation. Now from the very moment when we start bringing the consequences of our actions for others into morality (and how can we avoid doing so if the universality of the act is to be anything more than a word?), it appears possible that our relations with others are involved in immorality, if perchance our perspectives are irreconcilable – if, for instance, the legitimate interests of one nation are incompatible with those of another. Nothing guarantees us that morality is possible, as Kant said in a passage which has not yet been fully understood. But even less is there any fatal assurance that morality is impossible. We observe it in an experience which is the perception of others, and, by sketching here the dangerous consequences which this position entails, we are very much aware of its difficulties – some of which we might wish to avoid. Just as the perception of a thing opens me up to being, by realizing the paradoxical synthesis of an infinity of perceptual aspects, in the same way the perception of the other founds morality by realizing the paradox of an *alter ego*, of a common situation, by placing my perspectives and my incommunicable solitude in the visual field of another and of all the others. Here as everywhere else the primacy of perception – the realization, at the very heart of our most personal experience, of a fecund contradiction which submits this experience to the regard of others – is the remedy to skepticism and pessimism. If we admit that sensibility is enclosed within itself, and if we do not seek communication with the truth and with others except on the level of a disembodied reason, then there is not much to hope for. Nothing is more pessimistic or skeptical than the famous text in which Pascal, asking himself what it is to love, remarks that one does not love a woman for her beauty, which is perishable, or for her mind, which she can lose, and then suddenly concludes: "One never loves anybody; one loves only qualities." Pascal is proceeding like the skeptic who asks *if* the world exists, remarks that the table is only a sum of sensations, the chair another sum of sensations, and finally concludes: one never sees anything; one sees only sensations.

If, on the contrary, as the primacy of perception requires, we call what we perceive "the world," and what we love "the person," there is a type of doubt concerning man, and a type of spite, which become impossible. Certainly, the world which we thus find is not absolutely reassuring. We weigh the hardihood of the love which promises beyond what it knows, which claims to be eternal when a sickness, perhaps an accident, will destroy it. . . . But it is *true*, at the moment of this promise, that our love extends beyond *qualities*, beyond the body, beyond time, even though we could not love without qualities, bodies, and time. In order to safeguard the ideal unity of love, Pascal breaks human life into fragments at will and reduces the person to a discontinuous series of states. The absolute which he looks for beyond our experience is implied in it. Just as I grasp time through my present and by being present, I perceive others through my individual life, in the tension of an experience which transcends itself.

There is thus no destruction of the absolute or of rationality here, only of the absolute and the rationality separated from experience. To tell the truth, Christianity consists in replacing the separated absolute by the absolute in men. Nietzsche's idea that God is dead is already contained in the Christian idea of the death of God. God ceases to be an external object in order to mingle in human life, and this life is not simply a return to a non-temporal conclusion. God needs human history. As Malebranche said, the world is unfinished. My viewpoint differs from the Christian viewpoint to the extent that the Christian believes in another side of things where the *"renversement du pour au contre"* takes place. In my view this "reversal" takes place before our eyes. And perhaps some Christians would agree that the other side of things must already be visible in the environment in which we live. By advancing this thesis of the primacy of perception, I have less the feeling that I am proposing something completely new than the feeling of drawing out the conclusions of the work of my predecessors.

. . .

Discussion

M. Bréhier. Your paper contains not only the exposition of your ideas but also a discussion of them. You have spoken on two different points: a theory of perception and a certain philosophy. . . . I will speak to the second point, which I find the more interesting.

On the first point you have made a number of remarks of great interest. You have shown that the problem of perception should not be posed in the manner in which it is usually posed, by first presupposing objects, then a man who enters this region of objects from without, and then the relations between this man and these objects. Merleau-Ponty recognizes neither these objects nor this man, and he restricts himself to perception. And I believe he has said some very interesting things on this point, with which I am in full agreement.

But there is in M. Merleau-Ponty a philosopher, and with this philosopher we can certainly find many points of disagreement. M. Merleau-Ponty changes and inverts the ordinary meaning of what we call philosophy.

Philosophy was born of the difficulties encountered in ordinary perception [*perception vulgaire*]. It was from ordinary perception and by getting away from it that men began to philosophize. The first philosophers and Plato, our common ancestor, philosophized in this way. Far from wanting to return to an immediate perception, to a lived perception, he took his point of departure in the insufficiencies of this lived perception in order to arrive at a conception of the intelligible world which was coherent, which satisfied reason, which supposed another faculty of knowing other than perception itself.

You take up this Platonic idealism and follow a specifically reverse direction. You attempt to reintegrate it in perception, and I believe that all your difficulties lie here. These are difficulties which you yourself have indicated.

The first is a relativism which you attempt not to excuse but to explain in a manner which would satisfy the demands of our scientific and intellectual life. But I believe your explanation is insufficient, and the question I would pose is this: is not your relativism purely and simply a Protagorism? When you speak of the perception of the other, this other does not even exist, according to you, except in relation to us and in his relations with us. This is not the other as I perceive him immediately; it certainly is not an ethical other; it is not this person who suffices to himself. It is someone I posit outside myself at the same time I posit objects. Now this is very serious; the other is posited by us in the world just like other things.

But even this is not the principal difficulty. It is a question of whether philosophy consists in engaging oneself in the world, in engaging oneself in things – not to the point of identifying oneself with them, but to the point of following all their sinuosities – or of whether philosophy does not consist precisely in following a route directly contrary to this engagement.

In my view philosophy always supposes an inversion of this kind. Suppose philosophers had been phenomenologists from antiquity. I ask you this question: would our science exist now? Could you have constructed your science if Anaximenes and Anaximander had not said: this perception, we do not believe in it; the true reality is air, or fire, or (as the Pythagoreans said) number. If instead of positing these realities they had already been phenomenologists, do you think they could have created philosophy?

M. Merleau-Ponty. This hypothesis is itself impossible. Phenomenology could never have come about before all the other philosophical efforts of the rationalist tradition, nor prior to the construction of science. It measures the distance between our experience and this science. How could it ignore it? How could it precede it? Second, there have not always been phenomenologists, but there have always been skeptics who have always been accorded a place in the history of philosophy. If there had been only the Greek skeptics, or only Montaigne, or only Hume, could science have progressed? It seems to me that your objection is even more valid with respect to them.

M. Bréhier. I do not think so. Montaigne criticized reason in a manner which helped science progress.

M. Merleau-Ponty. The will to apply reason to what is taken as irrational is a progress for reason.

M. Bréhier. You do not have the right to incorporate Montaigne and Hume in your viewpoint. They followed a route completely different from yours.

M. Merleau-Ponty. Hume is one of the authors Husserl read the most. For my part, I read Montaigne and Hume very sympathetically, though I find them too timid in the return to the positive after their skeptical criticisms. The whole question is to know whether by recognizing the difficulties in the exercise of reason one is working for or against reason. You have said that Plato tried to quit perception for ideas. One could also say that he placed the movement of life in the ideas, as they are in the world – and he did it by breaking through the logic of identity, by showing that ideas transform themselves into their contraries.

M. Bréhier. To combat the rationalists you have to attribute to them a notion of reason which they do not hold.

M. Merleau-Ponty. Then I am in agreement with them.

M. Bréhier. Then your position in fact forces you to agree with them.

I would say that in the very formulation of your doctrine you destroy it. If I am exaggerating a little, I ask your pardon. In order to formulate your doctrine of perception you are obliged to say that man perceives objects, and consequently you must speak of man and objects separately. There results a fatal contradiction, which you indicate under the name of the contradiction of immanence and transcendence. But this contradiction comes from the fact that, once you formulate your doctrine, you necessarily posit an object exterior to man. Thus your doctrine, in order not to be contradictory, must remain unformulated, only lived. But is a doctrine which is only lived still a philosophical doctrine?

M. Merleau-Ponty. Assuredly a life is not a philosophy. I thought I had indicated in passing that description is not the return to immediate experience; one never returns to immediate experience. It is only a question of whether we are to try to understand it. I believe that to attempt to express immediate experience is not to betray reason but, on the contrary, to work toward its aggrandizement.

M. Bréhier. It is to betray immediate experience.

M. Merleau-Ponty. It is to begin the effort of expression and of what is expressed; it is to accept the condition of a beginning reflection. What is encouraging in this effort is that there is no pure and absolutely unexpressed life in man; the unreflected [*irréfléchi*] comes into existence for us only through reflection. To enter into these contradictions, as you have just said, seems to me to be a part of the critical inventory of our lives as philosophers.

M. Bréhier. I see your ideas as being better expressed in literature and in painting than in philosophy. Your philosophy results in a novel. This is not a defect, but I truly believe that it results in that immediate suggestion of realities which we associate with the writings of novelists. . . .

M. Merleau-Ponty. I would like to answer briefly one of M. Bréhier's earlier remarks – namely, that it is "serious" to posit the other in his relations with us and to posit him in the world. I think that you mean to say "ethically dangerous." It was never my intention to posit the other except as an ethical subject, and I am sure I have not excluded the other as an ethical subject.

M. Bréhier. It is a consequence of your theory.

M. Merleau-Ponty. It is a consequence which you draw.

M. Bréhier. Yes.

M. Merleau-Ponty. From the simple fact that I make of morality a problem, you conclude that I deny it. But the question is posed for all of us. How do we know there is someone there before us unless we look? What do we see, first of all, but corporeal appearances? How do these automata . . . become men for me? It is not the phenomenological method which creates this problem – though it does, in my view, allow us better to solve it. When Brunschvicg said that the "I" is achieved by reciprocity and it is necessary that I become able to think the other as reciprocable with me, he meant that morality is not something given but something to be created. I do not see how anyone could posit the other without the self; it is an impossibility for my experience.

M. Bréhier. The other is "reciprocable to me" by reason of a universal norm. Where is your norm?

M. Merleau-Ponty. If it is permissible to answer one question by another, I would ask: where is yours? We are all situated in an experience of the self and of others which we attempt to dominate by thought, but without ever being able to flatter ourselves that we have completely achieved this. Even when I believe I am thinking universally, if the other refuses to agree with me, I experience this universality as only a private universality (as I am verifying once more at this moment). Apart from a pure heteronomy accepted by both sides (but I do not think you meant "norm" in the sense of "heteronomy") there is no given universality; there is only a presumptive universality. We are back at the old problem: how do we reach the universal? It is a problem which has always existed in philosophy, though it has never been posed in such a radical manner as it is today because two centuries after Descartes philosophers, in spite of their professions of atheism, are still thinking on the basis of Cartesian theology. Thus these problems seem to me more or less traditional. If I have given a different impression to those who have heard this paper, it is only a question of terminology.

M. Lenoir . . . I was impressed with the resolutely realistic attitude which you have adopted. I find no fault with this. The aftermaths of all the great social upheavals have presented a similar phenomenon. In 1920 we saw the important Anglo-American movement of neorealism; a plethora of different philosophical systems arose in the same year in the United States. There was a similar development in an even more troubled epoch, at the time Victor Cousin dictated the laws of traditional philosophy and when he attempted to lay down the fundamental attitudes of mind which determine the main lines of the various philosophical systems: materialism, idealism, skepticism, mysticism. And here you give us, with your realism, a kind of materialism in reverse. But if you apply it to the problems of perception, it is vitiated, and I agree with M. Bréhier. Your analysis is somehow paralyzed by terminological difficulties. We use, in the realm of psychology, groups of associated words which have connotations that do not go together, that do not correspond to one another. Thus alongside the real problems which are suggested by this terminology there arise false problems or deviations from the true problems. But I think that the French tradition has attempted to overcome this danger of terminology. Auguste Comte himself indicated the way out. He attempted to get away from the tendency common to ideologists, "psychologists," and phrenologists. For this psychological orientation he substituted a fundamental notion of contemporary physics – energy. The notion of energy was his starting point. He showed how all the encyclopedic divisions which attempt to classify the human attitudes called behavior should be abandoned. He returned to the classical attitude, that of Descartes, who distinguished reflexion, meditation, and contemplation. Comte appealed only to secondary aspects. But he insisted on *synergie*, on the contrast between impression and impulsion – that is to say, between the aspects which come from without and those which come from within. You also have alluded to this.

The difficulties that arose for philosophy after Comte, which accepted the data of voluntarism and Renouvier, came from an attempt to effect an exchange analogous to the exchange in physics between the notion of matter and the notion of energy. Perception is dematerialized into true hallucinations in Taine, into the immediate data of consciousness in Bergson, into mystical experience in Lévy-Bruhl. However, William James attempted to materialize sensation by turning to the work of the artist. Perception, which has been so impoverished that it is now reduced to nothing but a motor schema of present existence, can only recover its fullness and its meaning in esthetic activity.

M. Merleau-Ponty. I deliberately avoided the use of the word "realism," since this would involve us in all sorts of historical explanations of the kind you have gone into, and I see no advantage in using this term. It only prolongs the discussion without clarifying it. For my part, I would prefer to answer a concrete question rather than a question bearing on the interrelations of historical doctrines.

M. Lupasco. What I have to say concerns mathematical experience. Euclidean geometry, which is the geometry of the perceived world, has been shown to be only an ideal geometry, and the physical universe, whose geometry is Riemannian, and whose internal structure is of a more and more abstract mathematical complexity, escapes more and more from the psychology of perception.

M. Merleau-Ponty. There is a misunderstanding, doubtless through my fault. I did not mean to say that mathematical thought was a reflection, or a double, of perceptual experience. I meant to say that mathematical thought has the same fundamental structures; it is not absolute. Even when we believe we are dealing with eternal truths, mathematical thought is still tied to history.

M. Lupasco. It is conceived independently; it has its own history. It is, rather, mathematics which commands and modifies perception, to the extent that it commands and modifies the physical world and even history. Generally speaking, I do not see what would become of the mathematical world in a universe in which everything is perception.

M. Bauer. Perhaps my language will appear naïve, but it seems to me impossible to base a theory of knowledge on perception. Perception is almost as far removed from the primitive data of our senses as science itself. It seems to me that there is a discontinuity between perception and scientific knowledge; the former is an instinctive and rudimentary scientific knowledge. When we perceive a table, or a lamp on this table, we already interpret our visual sensations to a large extent. We associate them with other possible sensations, tactile or visual – for example, of the underside of the table, its solidity, or of the other side of the lamp. We thus make a synthesis; we enunciate an invariable connection between certain actual sensations and other virtual sensations. Science does nothing more than extend and make this process of synthesis more and more precise.

From this point of view we can say that the most abstract sciences, geometry, and even arithmetic or algebra, are colored by sensations. It seems to me at any rate that when I affirm, as a physicist, that "the sky is blue because there are molecules of air which diffuse the light of the sun," the workings of my mind are about the same as when I say "I perceive a lamp" at the moment when I see a green shade covering a brightly lighted spot. Only, in this latter case, the sense of my affirmation is more easily understood and its experimental verification more immediate.

M. Merleau-Ponty. This answers M. Lupasco's question. I would only add that it is necessary to distinguish perception from the construction of a mathematical theory; it is necessary to create a theory of language and of presumptively "exact" science.

I did not mean to say that culture consists in perceiving. There is a whole cultural world which constitutes a second level above perceptual experience. Perception is rather the fundamental basis which cannot be ignored.

M. Salzi . . . The primacy of perception can have three meanings, and I think M. Merleau-Ponty moves from one sense to the other.

The first would be that of the primacy of psychology. The primacy of perception would follow necessarily from the notion of consciousness in which it is comprised. I believe that this is already an error in psychology. When a small baby is hungry, its consciousness of hunger is the consciousness of a lack. At the beginning, in the psychology of the infant, there is no distinction between the consciousness of a lack and consciousness of an object or of a subject. There is no duality; there is consciousness of a lack without there being either object or subject. This is one objection to this conception of the primacy of perception.

The second meaning could be that perception, as intuition or the basic contact with the real, is the exclusive source of truth. But it seems to me that, no matter how brilliant present-day science may be, we cannot erase metaphysical intuition any more than we can do away with mystical intuition or, perhaps even less, psychological intuition.

The third meaning would involve saying that this is not a question of fact but of principle [*de droit*], that, whatever the development of the human intellect through history may have been, we know henceforth, through the triumphs of contemporary science – and M. Merleau-Ponty seems to incline in this direction – that all our hypotheses must be supported by contact with perceptual experience.

And here I would oppose this sense of the primacy of perception. For contemporary science has little by little removed its postulates and its implications from perception. It denounces the postulates and implications derived from perception as inexact and says they must be replaced by other postulates which have nothing to do with perception – thus, for instance, the discontinuity of the quantum of energy, or we could mention the recent analysis of infra-atomic particles. The perceptual space – this space and time which since the time of Kant have served as the basis of perception – disappears, and consequently the physicist no longer has any concern at all with perception. Thus the world of the scientists would seem to escape the fetters of perception to a greater and greater degree. . . .

M. Merleau-Ponty. I have never claimed that perception (for example, the seeing of colors or forms), in so far as it gives us access to the most immediate properties of objects, has a monopoly on truth. What I mean to say is that we find in perception a mode of access to the object which is rediscovered at every level, and in speaking of the perception of the other I insisted that the word "perception" includes the whole experience which gives the thing itself. Consequently I do not detract anything from the more complex forms of knowledge; I only show how they refer to this fundamental experience as the basic experience which they must render more determinate and explicit. Thus it has never entered my mind to do away with science, as you say. It is rather a question of understanding the scope and the meaning of science. It is the problem of Poincaré in his book *La Valeur de la science*; when he put this title on his work no one thought that he was denying science. To be more specific, do you think that natural science gives you a total explanation of man – I say "total" – or do you not think there is something more?

M. Salzi. Without any doubt. I have, therefore, misunderstood the sense of the "primacy of perception."

M. Merleau-Ponty. If we reflect on our objects of thought and science, they ultimately send us back to the perceived world, which is the terrain of their final application. However, I did not mean to say that the perceived world, in the sense of the world of colors and forms, is the totality of our universe. There is the ideal or cultural world. I have not diminished its original character; I have only tried to say that it is somehow created *à ras de terre*.

It seems to me that these objections could be made to any philosopher who recognizes that philosophy has an original role distinct from that of science. The scientists have often said to philosophers, "Your work is otiose; you reflect on science but you do not understand it at all. This disqualifies you." And it is certain that by asserting that there *is* philosophy we thereby take something away from the scientist; we take away his monopoly on truth. But this is the only way in which I would limit the role of science.

As to mystical experience, I do not do away with that either. It is only a question of knowing just what it proves. Is it the effective passage to the absolute, or is it only an illusion? I recall a course by Brunschvicg which was entitled *Les Techniques du passage à l'absolu*. Brunschvicg studied the various methods, all of which he considered fallacious, by which men attempt to reach the absolute.

When I ask myself whether mystical experience means exactly what it thinks it means, I am posing a question to myself which everyone should pose. If, in order to be fair with respect to the fact of mystical experience, it is necessary to grant in advance that it is what it claims to be, if every question is an offense, then we must give up the quest for truth altogether.

I have expressed myself poorly if I have given the impression that I meant to do away with everything. On the contrary, I find everything interesting and, in a certain way, *true* – on the sole condition that we take things as they are presented in our fully elucidated experience. M. Bréhier asked me just now, "Do you posit the other as an absolute value?" I answered, "Yes, in so far as a man can do so." But when I was in the army, I had to call for an artillery barrage or an air attack, and at that moment I was not recognizing an absolute value in the enemy soldiers who were the objects of these attacks. I can in such a case promise to hold generous feelings toward the enemy; I cannot promise not to harm him. When I say I love someone at this moment, can I be sure that in this love I have reached the substance of the person, a substance which will absolutely never change? Can I guarantee that what I know of this person and what makes me love her, will be verified throughout her whole life? Perception anticipates, goes ahead of itself. I would ask nothing better than to see more clearly, but it seems to me that no one sees more clearly. I can promise here and now to adopt a certain mode of behavior; I cannot promise my future feelings. Thus it is necessary to confide in the generosity of life – which enabled Montaigne to write in the last book of his *Essais: "J'ai plus tenu que promis ni dû."*

Mme Roire. Is there a scale of values in all these experiences, and what is it? For example, are mystical experiences or the mathematical sciences at the top? Is there a scale of values with respect to the primacy of perception? How are the other forms of experience to be situated?

M. Merleau-Ponty. Assuredly for me there is a scale. This does not mean, however, that what is at the bottom is to be suppressed. It seems to me, for instance, that if we make it our goal to reach the concrete, then in certain respects we must put art above science because it achieves an expression of the concrete man which science does not attempt. But the hierarchies of which you are speaking suppose a point of view; from one point of view you get one hierarchy and from another point of view you get another hierarchy. Our research must be concentric rather than hierarchized.

Mme Prenant . . . First of all, in this scale of values which has just been mentioned, does M. Merleau-Ponty place a higher value on the sun of the astronomer or on the sun of the peasant? . . . Does he consider the scientific theory as absolutely opposed to perception? And yet does not what he has said of the asymptotic character of scientific truth in Brunschvicg establish a certain continuity between ordinary perception and scientific perception? Are these diverse theories of perception opposed to one another, and should not M. Bauer's question be repeated?

My second question is related to the first: . . . Do I not possess a way of thinking which shows me that the sun of the astronomer is superior to the sun of the peasant?

M. Merleau-Ponty. I am in complete agreement with this and for two reasons. Recall the famous phrase from Hegel: "The earth is not the physical center of the world, but it is the metaphysical center." The originality of man in the world is manifested by the fact that he has acquired the more exact knowledge of the world of science. It is strictly necessary that we teach everybody about the world and the sun of the astronomer. There is no question of discrediting science. Philosophical awareness is possible only on the basis of science. It is only when one has conceived the world of the natural sciences in all their rigor that one can see appear, by contrast, man in his freedom. What is more, having passed a certain point in its development, science itself ceases to hypostatize itself; it leads us back to the structures of the perceived world and somehow recovers them. For example, the convergence between the phenomenological notion of space and the notion of space in the theory of relativity has been pointed out. Philosophy has nothing to fear from a mature science, nor has science anything to fear from philosophy.

Mme Prenant. By the same token, history is a concrete study.

M. Merleau-Ponty. Certainly. For my part, I would not separate history from philosophy. That is what I meant to say when I said that we could not imagine philosophers being phenomenologists from the beginning.

Mme Prenant. One could say that geodesy is also a science of the concrete.

M. Merleau-Ponty. Why not? But human geography much more so. As to the asymptotic character of scientific truths, what I meant to say was that, for a long time and in some respects, science seems to have tried to give us an image of the universe as immobile. It seemed to lack any conception of processes. To that extent, we can consider it to have been incomplete and partial.

. . .

M. Césari. I only wish to ask M. Merleau-Ponty for a simple clarification. He seems to affirm that there is a certain continuity between science and perception. We can admit this point of view, which is that of Brunschvicg and which could be that of M. Bachelard, to the extent that new experiences can bring about an evolution within the realm of ideas. But M. Merleau-Ponty has insisted in an exaggerated fashion on the instability of the realm of ideas. But that is a question of degree; what confuses me is something else. I do not see how the phenomenological study of perception can serve the progress of science in any way. It seems to me that there is a discontinuity between perception as you describe it – that is, lived perception – and the perception on which the scientist bases himself in order to construct certain theories. It seems to me that there is a contradiction in your arguments. You say, "The study of perception, carried out by psychologists without presuppositions, reveals that the perceived world is not a sum of objects in the sense in which the sciences understand this word." Perfect. We are in complete agreement. It is a fact that perception at the level of lived experience does not describe objects in the way science does. But this being the case, what purpose does it serve for us to appeal to this purely lived experience to construct scientific experience, which, as M. Bachelard has said, must get away from immediate experience? Science will not be constructed unless we abandon the sensations and perceptions of ordinary experience, unless we define facts as technical effects – like the Compton-effect, for example.

Under these conditions, I do not see how phenomenology can be of any use to science.

M. Merleau-Ponty. The first thing to be said is that I do not know whether the phenomenological attitude is of any use to the other sciences, but it certainly is of use to psychology.

M. Césari. I agree as to psychology, but to evaluate the role of reason in science itself is another matter. You have compared phenomenological experience with that of Brunschvicg, who speaks of a highly elaborated experience which has nothing to do with lived experience.

M. Merleau-Ponty. Lived experience is of immediate interest only to those who are interested in man. I have never hoped that my work would be of much interest to the physicist as physicist. But your complaint could as well be addressed to all works of philosophy.

M. Césari. I am not making a complaint. I consider your point of view very interesting as it concerns the psychology of perception, but in its relation to scientific thought, I do not see its relevance except, once again, for psychology.

There is a second question which I would like to pose. You said at one point in your paper that "matter is pregnant with its form," and at that point you follow Gestalt theory. And in this theory there is an explanation of the genesis of perception (isomorphism). You have, on the contrary, compared your point of view to that of Bergson as it is given at the beginning of *Matière et mémoire*. But I have been unable to understand whether, according to you, the problem of the relation of the stimulus to perception really poses itself, since it is a question which interests science, while the existential viewpoint obliges you to consider the man-world complex as indissoluble, as giving perception immediately. I separate myself from the world when I ask about the relation between sensation and perception.

Since in your paper you uphold the view that there is no discontinuity between the existential and the scientific viewpoints, at some point the question of the relation between the stimulus and perception will perhaps pose itself, no doubt in a paradoxical manner. Exactly what solution do you give for this problem? For Bergson it was a question of possible reactions of the body to the world.

M. Merleau-Ponty. I have said that the point of view of the scientist with respect to perception – a stimulus *en soi* which produces a perception – is, like all forms of naive realism, absolutely insufficient. Philosophically I do not believe that this image of perception is ultimately defensible. But it seems to me indispensable for science to continue its own proper study of perception. For the time comes when, precisely because we attempt to apply the procedures of scientific thought to perception, we see clearly why perception is not a phenomenon of the order of physical causality. We observe a response of the organism which "interprets" the stimuli and gives them a certain configuration. To me it seems impossible to hold that this configuration is produced by the stimuli. It comes from the organism and from the behavior of the organism in their presence.

It seems to me valuable, even for psychology and philosophy, that science attempt to apply its usual procedures even if, and precisely if, this attempt ends in failure.

M. Césari. Doubtless these explanations are satisfactory. The only question which remains is that of the relation between the motivating rationalism of science and the phenomenology of perception.

M. Merleau-Ponty. I refuse to recognize a dilemma here.

M. Hyppolite. I would say simply that I do not see the necessary connection between the two parts of your paper – between the description of perception, which presupposes no ontology, and the philosophical conclusions which you draw, which do presuppose an ontology, namely, an ontology of meaning. In the first part of your paper you show that perception has a meaning, and in the second part you arrive at the very being of this meaning, which constitutes the unity of man. And the two parts do not seem to me to be completely interdependent. Your description of perception does not necessarily involve the philosophical conclusions of the second part of your paper. Would you accept such a separation?

M. Merleau-Ponty. Obviously not. If I have spoken of two things it is because they have some relation to one another.

M. Hyppolite. Does the description of perception require the philosophical conclusion on "the being of meaning" which you have developed after it?

M. Merleau-Ponty. Yes. Only I have not, of course, said everything which it would be necessary to say on this subject. For example, I have not spoken of time or its role as foundation and basis.

M. Hyppolite. This problem of "the being of meaning," with the implied unity of the relative and the absolute, which is finality – this recovered unity leads me to a question which is perhaps more precise: it does not seem to me that you have made clear the drama which reflexion causes in the pre-reflexive life – that is to say, the new form of life which is created by the projection of an eternal norm by means of reflexion. The fact of reflexion, joining itself to the pre-reflexive life, leads to a going-beyond, to a transcendence – formal perhaps, illusory perhaps, but without which reflexion could not occur.

Mme Prenant. The Drama of the evil genius.

M. Hyppolite. Perhaps. Do you agree that this reflexion gives us a new sense of transcendence?

M. Merleau-Ponty. Certainly there is much to be added to what I have said. On the basis of what I have said, one might think that I hold that man lives only in the realm of the real. But we also live in the imaginary, also in the world of ideality. Thus it is necessary to develop a theory of imaginary existence and of ideal existence. I have already indicated in the course of this discussion that by placing perception at the center of consciousness I do not claim that consciousness is enclosed in the observation of a natural datum. I meant to say that even when we transform our lives in the creation of a culture – and reflexion is an acquisition of this culture – we do not suppress our ties to time and space; in fact, we utilize them. Reciprocally one could say that in a completely explicated human perception we would find all the originalities of human life. Human perception is directed to the world; animal perception is directed to an environment, as Scheler said. The same creative capacity which is at work in imagination and in ideation is present, in germ, in the first human perception (and I have obviously been incomplete on this point). But the essential difference between my point of view and that of a philosophy of the understanding is that, in my view, even though consciousness is able to detach itself from things to see itself, human consciousness never possesses itself in complete detachment and does not recover itself at the level of culture except by recapitulating the expressive, discrete, and contingent operations by means of which philosophical questioning itself has become possible.

M. Hyppolite. My question does not only concern the incomplete character of your exposition. It is to know whether human reflexion, contrary to every other form of life, does not pose problems not only of this or that meaning but of meaning in general, and whether this introduction of a reflexion on "the very being of all meaning" does not imply a new problem and a new form of life.

M. Merleau-Ponty. I am in complete agreement with that.

M. Hyppolite. Still it does not seem to me that the solution you give is a satisfying one, because man is led to pose to himself the question of a "being of all meaning," the problem of an "absolute being of all meaning."

In other words, there is in human reflexion a kind of total reflexion,

M. Merleau-Ponty. In my paper, taking up a saying from Rimbaud, I said that there is a center of consciousness by which "we are not in the world." But this absolute emptiness is observable only at the moment when it is filled by experience. We do not ever see it, so to speak, except marginally. It is perceptible only on the ground of the world. In short, you are simply saying that I have no religious philosophy. I think it is proper to man to think God, which is not the same thing as to say that God exists.

M. Hyppolite. You said that God was dead.

M. Merleau-Ponty. I said that to say God is dead, as the Nietzscheans do, or to speak of the death of God, like the Christians do, is to tie God to man, and that in this sense the Christians themselves are obliged to tie eternity to time.

M. Hyppolite. You attempted to do a kind of ontology of the problem, which I have the right to call ambiguous, when you spoke of the death of God.

M. Merleau-Ponty. One is always ambiguous when one tries to understand others. What is ambiguous is the human condition. But this discussion is becoming too rapid; it is necessary to go over all this.

M. Hyppolite. Therefore you are not engaged by your description of perception, and you admit it.

M. Merleau-Ponty. I do not admit it at all. In a sense perception is everything because there is not one of our ideas or one of our reflexions which does not carry a date, whose objective reality exhausts its formal reality, or which transcends time.

M. Beaufret. What I have to say will not add much to what Hyppolite has already said. I wish only to emphasize that many of the objections which have been addressed to Merleau-Ponty seem to me unjustified. I believe that they come down simply to objecting to his perspective itself, which is that of phenomenology. To say that Merleau-Ponty stops at a phenomenology without any means of going beyond it is to fail to understand that the phenomenon itself, in the phenomenological sense of the term, goes beyond the realm of the empirical. The phenomenon in this sense is not empirical but rather that which manifests itself really, that which we can really experience, in opposition to what would be only the construction of concepts. Phenomenology is not a falling back into phenomenalism but the maintenance of contact with "the thing itself." If phenomenology rejects "intellectualist" explanations of perception, it is not to open the door to the irrational but to close it to verbalism. Nothing appears to me less pernicious than the *Phenomenology of Perception.* The only reproach I would make to the author is not that he has gone "too far," but rather that he has not been sufficiently radical. The phenomenological descriptions which he uses in fact maintain the vocabulary of idealism. In this they are in accord with Husserlian descriptions. But the whole problem is precisely to know whether phenomenology, fully developed, does not require the abandonment of subjectivity and the vocabulary of subjective idealism as, beginning with Husserl, Heidegger has done.

M. Parodi. We may have to leave one another without treating the principal question – namely, to come to a precise understanding of your theory of perception. In general, what do you think of the classical doctrine of perception which you seem to reject? I would like to see the positive part of your thesis recalled before we end this session. If perception is only a construction composed of materials borrowed from memory and based on immediate sensations, how do you explain the process?

M. Merleau-Ponty. Naturally there is a development of perception; naturally it is not achieved all at once. What I have attempted to say here presupposes (perhaps too much) the reading of the book which I devoted to this question. On the other hand, it seemed neither possible nor desirable for me to repeat it here.

M. Parodi. Could you tell us what is your most important contribution on this question of fact? You began with very clear examples: we think we perceive things which we really only see in part, or more or less. What, according to you, is the essential element in this operation?

M. Merleau-Ponty. To perceive is to render oneself present to something through the body. All the while the thing keeps its place within the horizon of the world, and the structurization consists in putting each detail in the perceptual horizons which belong to it. But such formulas are just so many enigmas unless we relate them to the concrete developments which they summarize.

M. Parodi. I would be tempted to say that the body is much more essential for sensation than it is for perception.

M. Merleau-Ponty. Can they be distinguished?

Notes

1 This address to the *Société française de philosophie* was given shortly after the publication of Merleau-Ponty's major work, the *Phenomenology of Perception*, and it represents his attempt to summarize and defend the central thesis of that work. The following translation gives the complete text of Merleau-Ponty's address and the discussion which followed it, with the exception of a few incidental remarks unrelated to the substance of the discussion. These minimal omissions are indicated by the insertion of suspension points in the text. The discussion took place on November 23, 1946, and was published in the *Bulletin de la société française de philosophie* vol. 49 (December, 1947), pp. 119–53. [*Trans.*]
2 The more usual term in Husserl is "passive synthesis," which designates the "synthesis" of perceptual consciousness as opposed to the "active synthesis" of imagination and categorial thought. [*Trans.*]
3 The reference is to Spinoza's *natura naturans*. [*Trans.*]
4 The *Phenomenology of Perception*. [*Trans.*]

Part XI

SIMONE DE BEAUVOIR
Phenomenology and Feminism

SIMONE DE BEAUVOIR (1908–1986)

Introduction

Born in Paris in 1908 into a bourgeois family of declining circumstances, Simone de Beauvoir studied philosophy at the Sorbonne, completing her *agrégation* at the Ecole Normale Supérieure, where she met Sartre, Merleau-Ponty, Maurice de Gandillac, Raymond Aron and other young philosophers. Her thesis on Leibniz, written in 1929, was supervised by Léon Brunschwicg. She first met Sartre in 1929 when he was studying for his repeat examinations, and from then on they remained intimately associated. They married but maintained their freedom to engage in other relationships. Beauvoir taught philosophy first at a lycée in Marseilles, then in Rouen, and finally in Paris. She was with Sartre when together they learned of phenomenology from their friend Raymond Aron, who had just returned from Germany. During the Vichy period, she continued to teach (signing a form attesting to her non-Jewish background), until forced to resign because of her relationship with a student, Natalie Sorokine. For money, she took part in broadcasts on the Vichy state radio, Radiodiffusion Nationale, regarded as an act of collaboration by the French resistance. In 1943 she published a novel, *L'Invitée* (*She Came to Stay*), an account of the strain on a couple's relationship caused by the long-term stay of a young woman. In 1944 she decided to commit herself to writing full time and quickly became a distinguished novelist and commentator in her own right. Her best-known novel, *The Mandarins* (1954), won the Goncourt Prize. With Sartre and Merleau-Ponty, she was one of the founding members of *Les Temps Modernes*, which first appeared in 1945. Sartre and de Beauvoir travelled extensively, and she wrote accounts of her travels, for example, *The Long March* (1957), an account of her trip to China. She engaged in political protests and supported radical causes throughout her life, being particularly concerned with anti-colonialism (e.g. Algeria) and with issues concerning women's rights (e.g. the availability of abortion). Her many intense friendships and relationships (including friendships with Albert Camus and Merleau-Ponty, and affairs with Natalie Sorokine, the American novelist Nelson Algren, Claude Lanzmann and others) are detailed in her voluminous correspondence and journals. She wrote several volumes of autobiographical reflections (six volumes were published in her lifetime) documenting her intellectual development against the backdrop of the intellectual atmosphere in France at that time. One of these, *The Force of Age* (1960), details her relation with Sartre. *Une Mort très douce* (*A Very Easy Death*, 1964), a reflection of her mother's death, and *La Vieillesse* (*Old Age*, 1970), a critique of society's treatment of the elderly, are recognised as important studies of the phenomenon of ageing. One of her last works, *La Cérémonie des adieux* (*Adieux: A Farewell to Sartre*, 1981) documented in rather explicit terms her care of the ageing and increasingly debilitated Sartre until his death in 1980.

While still at the Sorbonne, de Beauvoir kept a diary in which she formulated her early philosophical ideas, including the approach to philosophy through literature. However, she always wanted to be a writer rather than a philosopher, and, like Sartre, was uninterested in pursuing an academic career. As soon as she could afford it, she gave up her teaching to write full time. Her work therefore does not seek to be explicitly philosophical in any formal or technical manner. Nevertheless, she did make a significant contribution to philosophy, notably in her analyses of concrete ethical issues regarding freedom, relations with others, the nature of gender and sexuality, old age, embodiment, and interpersonal relationships generally. Her approach is to emphasise the uniqueness of individual situations, and she resists generalisation and universalisation in moral matters, emphasising the importance of safeguarding freedom. She wrote an early philosophical essay *Pyrrhus et Cinéas* (1944), a dialogue intended to complement Sartre's *Being and Nothingness* (1943), in which she addresses an existential dilemma concerning the exercise of freedom within situation. Her treatise, *Pour une morale de l'ambiguïté* (*The Ethics of Ambiguity*, 1947), attempts to complete the project of Sartre's *Being and Nothingness* by supplying it with an ethics, broadening Sartre's existentialism by emphasising the importance of living with others whose projects are in conflict with one's own exercise of freedom. As with Sartre, she focuses on issues of bad faith and self-deception. De Beauvoir is best known, however, for her sociological and philosophical study, *Le Deuxième Sexe* (*The Second Sex* 1949), which provided an important stimulus to the re-emergence of feminism in the second half of the twentieth century. Here she argued against the myth of the 'eternal feminine' and against biological determinism, and for the view that women are not born but made. De Beauvoir argues that women have been objectified and treated as 'the other'. *The Second Sex* draws on then-current biology, social and economic history, and sociology, to argue that there are no typically 'masculine' or 'feminine' traits, but rather that these are products of culture (for example, it was fashionable for men to cry in the eighteenth century but not in the mid-twentieth century). Women are currently in a state which is defined as 'immanence', enclosed in their allocated roles as mothers and so on, but must learn to transcend their biological givenness (without at the same time denying it or falsifying it) to attain the same freedom and autonomy which men already possess. *The Second Sex* quickly gained notoriety in France when the Catholic novelist François Mauriac denounced it as scandalous. The work had a huge impact on the feminist movement in America and in France, and de Beauvoir's assumption, that women are somehow made 'immanent' by their biology and must transcend it, has led to the accusation that she in fact accepts a certain essentialism, which is in tension with her overt claims concerning the social construction of gender.

In her writings de Beauvoir rarely explicitly discusses phenomenology or invokes its terminology or techniques. Nevertheless, her existential descriptions do show some phenomenological tendencies. Her initial interest in Husserl was awoken by Raymond Aron, and she began reading Heidegger in 1939 and Hegel in the 1940s. She even translated part of Husserl's lectures on time consciousness for Sartre. She was an early critic of Levinas, and reviewed Merleau-Ponty's *Phenomenology of Perception*. For her, phenomenology seeks to overcome the division between subject and object, and aims to provide a true description of concrete human situations. She later wrote a strong denunciation of Merleau-Ponty's attack on Sartre.

Our reading is drawn from Book One, Part One, of *The Second Sex* (1949), entitled "Destiny". Here de Beauvoir is analysing traditional approaches to woman that define her in terms of her biology which is also construed as her destiny. She both rejects the view that biological accounts of sexual differentiation provide any basis for regarding differences of gender as 'necessary' or 'natural', and all attempts to specify the nature of gender a priori, and instead asserts: "we can hope to grasp the significance of sexuality only by studying it in its concrete manifestations." Since de Beauvoir takes the view that living processes aim at certain ends, women are to be understood as 'projects' in Sartre's sense and aim to transcend the current situation. De Beauvoir then elaborates on this theme, arguing that woman is not to be defined in terms of the relative strengths or weaknesses of her body. She claims to be following phenomenology (Heidegger, Sartre and Merleau-Ponty) in reading the body not as a thing but as a 'situation'. Biology must be considered to be a science that abstracts from concrete human existence. The body does not define what woman is, as much as her free actions and her situation. This leads her to ask the question why woman has always been treated as 'the other'. She admires psychoanalysis as recognising the importance of meaning in relation to acts of the body, and for its recognition of the pervasiveness of sexuality in life, but she goes on to criticise it for not interrogating the basic meaning of many of its assumptions and for its rigid determinism which does not recognise the role of choice. De Beauvoir recognises the complexity of one's self-understanding of sexuality insofar as one has internalised the understanding of society at that time.

Our second reading is drawn from the chapter on "Woman's Situation and Character" towards the end of *The Second Sex* (Book Two, Part Five). Her analysis here aims to show that many typical traits traditionally ascribed to women are in fact products of her role in the situation that has been given to her. As she says, "Many of the faults for which women are reproached – mediocrity, laziness, frivolity, servility – simply express the fact that their horizon is closed." Much of her discussion here analyses the patterns of thinking and behaviour that become manifest when someone is placed in a restricted, servile and essentially powerless situation, specifically, for women, that means an attention to the world and to the details and refinements of daily living, and at the same time an attachment to mystical transcendence beyond the world. Of course, all de Beauvoir's claims and interpretations in these passages may be contested, but her mode of approach to the phenomena of concrete human existence offers an example of the kind of speculative reasoning involved in the existential direction taken by phenomenological philosophy in France.

Further reading

De Beauvoir, Simone. *Adieux: A Farewell to Sartre*, trans. Patrick O'Brian. New York: Pantheon, 1984.

De Beauvoir, Simone. *Coming of Age*, trans. Patrick O'Brian. New York: Putnam, 1972.

De Beauvoir, Simone. *Force of Circumstance*, trans. Richard Howard. New York: Putnam, 1965.

De Beauvoir, Simone. "*La Phénoménologie de la perception* de Maurice Merleau-Ponty", *Les Temps Modernes* 1 (November 1945), pp. 363–367.

De Beauvoir, Simone. *Letters to Sartre*, ed. Sylvie Le Bon de Beauvoir, trans. and ed. Quintin Hoare. New York: Little, Brown, 1992.

De Beauvoir, Simone. *Memoires of a Dutiful Daughter*, trans. James Kirkup. Cleveland, OH: World Publishing, 1959.

De Beauvoir, Simone. *The Ethics of Ambiguity*, trans. Bernard Frechtman. New York: Philosophical Library, 1958.

De Beauvoir, Simone. *The Prime of Life*, trans. Peter Green. Cleveland, OH: World Publishing, 1962.

De Beauvoir, Simone. *The Second Sex*, trans. H. M. Parshley. London: Picador, 1988.

Bennett, Joy, and Gabriella Hochmann. *Simone de Beauvoir: An Annotated Bibliography*. New York: Garland, 1988.

Bergoffen, Debra. *The Philosophy of Simone de Beauvoir: Gendered Phenomenologies, Erotic Generosities*. Albany, NY: State University of New York Press, 1997.

Fullbrook, Kate and Edward. *Simone de Beauvoir. A Critical Introduction*. Cambridge: Polity Press, 1998.

Howarth, Marianne. *After the Second Sex: Conversations with Simone de Beauvoir*. New York: Pantheon, 1984.

Simons, Margaret A. (ed.). *Feminist Interpretations of Simone de Beauvoir*. University Park: The Pennsylvania State University, 1995.

Vintges, Karen. *Philosophy as Passion: The Thinking of Simone de Beauvoir*, trans. A. Lavelle. Bloomington: Indiana University Press, 1996.

1

DESTINY

The data of biology

It has been frequently maintained that in physiology alone must be so
answers to these questions: Are the chances for individual success the san
two sexes? Which plays the more important role in the species? But it n
noted that the first of these problems is quite different in the case of wom
compared with other females; for animal species are fixed and it is possi\
define them in static terms – by merely collecting observations it can be dec
whether the mare is as fast as the stallion, or whether male chimpanzees e
their mates in intelligence tests – whereas the human species is for ever in a st
of change, for ever becoming.

   Certain materialist savants have approached the problem in a purely static fash
ion; influenced by the theory of psychophysiological parallelism, they sought to
work out mathematical comparisons between the male and female organism –
and they imagined that these measurements registered directly the functional capacities of the two sexes. For example, these students have engaged in elaborately
trifling discussions regarding the absolute and relative weight of the brain in man
and woman – with inconclusive results, after all corrections have been made. But
what destroys much of the interest of these careful researches is the fact that it has
not been possible to establish any relation whatever between the weight of the
brain and the level of intelligence. And one would similarly be at a loss to present
a psychic interpretation of the chemical formulae designating the male and female
hormones.

   As for the present study, I categorically reject the notion of psychophysiological
parallelism, for it is a doctrine whose foundations have long since been thoroughly
undermined. If I mention it at all, it is because it still haunts many minds in spite
of its philosophical and scientific bankruptcy. I reject also any comparative system that assumes the existence of a *natural* hierarchy or scale of values – for
example, an evolutionary hierarchy. It is vain to ask if the female body is or is not
more infantile than that of the male, if it is more or less similar to that of the apes,
and so on. All these dissertations which mingle a vague naturalism with a still
more vague ethics or aesthetics are pure verbiage. It is only in a human perspective that we can compare the female and the male of the human species. But
man is defined as a being who is not fixed, who makes himself what he is. As

S. de Beauvoir, *The Second Sex*, 1988, trans. and ed. H. M. Parshley, pp. 65–91. London: Picador.

467

rleau-Ponty very justly puts it, man is not a natural species: he is a historical a. Woman is not a completed reality, but rather a becoming, and it is in her coming that she should be compared with man; that is to say, her possibilities ould be defined. What gives rise to much of the debate is the tendency to reduce er to what she has been, to what she is today, in raising the question of her apabilities; for the fact is that capabilities are clearly manifested only when they have been realized – but the fact is also that when we have to do with a being whose nature is transcendent action, we can never close the books.

Nevertheless it will be said that if the body is not a *thing*, it is a situation, as viewed in the perspective I am adopting – that of Heidegger, Sartre, and Merleau-Ponty: it is the instrument of our grasp upon the world, a limiting factor for our projects. Woman is weaker than man, she has less muscular strength, fewer red blood corpuscles, less lung capacity, she runs more slowly, can lift less heavy weights, can compete with man in hardly any sport; she cannot stand up to him in a fight. To all this weakness must be added the instability, the lack of control, and the fragility already discussed: these are facts. Her grasp on the world is thus more restricted; she has less firmness and less steadiness available for projects that in general she is less capable of carrying out. In other words, her individual life is less rich than man's.

Certainly these facts cannot be denied – but in themselves they have no significance. Once we adopt the human perspective, interpreting the body on a basis of existence, biology becomes an abstract science; whenever the physiological fact (for instance, muscular inferiority) takes on meaning, this meaning is at once seen as dependent on a whole context; the "weakness" is revealed as such only in the light of the ends man proposes, the instruments he has available, and the laws he establishes. If he does not wish to seize the world, then the idea of a *grasp* on things has no sense; when in this seizure the full employment of bodily power is not required, above the available minimum, then differences in strength are annulled; wherever violence is contrary to custom, muscular force cannot be a basis for domination. In brief, the concept of *weakness* can be defined only with reference to existentialist, economic, and moral considerations. It has been said that the human species is anti-natural, a statement that is hardly exact, since man cannot deny facts; but he establishes their truth by the way in which he deals with them; nature has reality for him only to the extent that it is involved in his activity – his own nature not excepted. As with her grasp on the world, it is again impossible to measure in the abstract the burden imposed on woman by her reproductive function. The bearing of maternity upon the individual life, regulated naturally in animals by the oestrus cycle and the seasons, is not definitely prescribed in woman – society alone is the arbiter. The bondage of woman to the species is more or less rigorous according to the number of births demanded by society and the degree of hygienic care provided for pregnancy and childbirth. Thus, while it is true that in the higher animals the individual existence is asserted more imperiously by the male than by the female, in the human species individual "possibilities" depend upon the economic and social situation.

But in any case it does not always happen that the male's individual privileges give him a position of superiority within the species, for in maternity the female acquires a kind of autonomy of her own. Sometimes, as in the baboons studied by Zuckermann,[1] the male does dominate; but in many species the two members

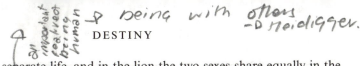

all important looking human → *being with others* —D Heidigger.

of the pair lead a separate life, and in the lion the two sexes share equally in the duties of the den. Here again the human situation cannot be reduced to any other; it is not as single individuals that human beings are to be defined in the first place; men and women have never stood opposed to each other in single combat; the couple is an original *Mitsein,* a basic combination; and as such it always appears as a permanent or temporary element in a large collectivity.

Within such a society, which is more necessary to the species, male or female? At the level of the gametes, at the level of the biological functions of coition and pregnancy, the male principle creates to maintain, the female principle maintains to create, as we have seen; but what are the various aspects of this division of labour in different forms of social life? In sessile species, attached to other organisms or to substrata, in those furnished by nature with abundant sustenance obtainable without effort, the role of the male is limited to fecundation; where it is necessary to seek, to hunt, to fight in order to provide the food needed by the young, the male in many cases co-operates in their support. This co-operation becomes absolutely indispensable in a species where the offspring remain unable to take care of themselves for a long time after weaning; here the male's assistance becomes extremely important, for the lives he has begotten cannot be maintained without him. A single male can fecundate a number of females each year; but it requires a male for every female to assure the survival of the offspring after they are born, to defend them against enemies, to wrest from nature the wherewithal to satisfy their needs. In human history the equilibrium between the forces of production and of reproduction is brought about by different means under different economic conditions, and these conditions govern the relations of male and female to offspring and in consequence to each other. But here we are leaving the realm of biology; by its light alone we could never decide the primacy of one sex or the other in regard to the perpetuation of the species. *rise above – go beyond.*

But in truth a society is not a species, for it is in a society that the species attains the status of existence – transcending itself towards the world and towards the future. Its ways and customs cannot be deduced from biology, for the individuals that compose the society are never abandoned to the dictates of their nature; they are subject rather to that second nature which is custom and in which are reflected the desires and the fears that express their essential nature. It is not merely as a body, but rather as a body subject to taboos, to laws, that the subject is conscious of himself and attains fulfillment – it is with reference to certain values that he evaluates himself. And, once again, it is not upon physiology that values can be based; rather, the facts of biology take on the values that the existent bestows upon them. If the respect or the fear inspired by woman prevents the use of violence towards her, then the muscular superiority of the male is no source of power. If custom decrees – as in certain Indian tribes – that the young girls are to choose their husbands, or if the father dictates the marriage choice, then the sexual aggressiveness of the male gives him no power of initiative, no advantage. The close bond between mother and child will be for her a source of dignity or indignity according to the value placed upon the child – which is highly variable – and this very bond, as we have seen, will be recognized or not according to the presumptions of the society concerned.

Thus we must view the facts of biology in the light of an ontological, economic, social, and psychological context. The enslavement of the female to the species and the limitations of her various powers are extremely important facts; the body of woman is one of the essential elements in her situation in the world. But that body is not enough to define her as woman; there is no true living reality except as manifested by the conscious individual through activities and in the bosom of a society. Biology is not enough to give an answer to the question that is before us: why is woman the *Other*? Our task is to discover how the nature of woman has been affected throughout the course of history; we are concerned to find out what humanity has made of the human female.

The psychoanalytic point of view

The tremendous advance accomplished by psychoanalysis over psychophysiology lies in the view that no factor becomes involved in the psychic life without having taken on human significance; it is not the body-object described by biologists that actually exists, but the body as lived in by the subject. Woman is a female to the extent that she feels herself as such. There are biologically essential features that are not a part of her real, experienced situation: thus the structure of the egg is not reflected in it, but on the contrary an organ of no great biological importance, like the clitoris, plays in it a part of the first rank. It is not nature that defines woman; it is she who defines herself by dealing with nature on her own account in her emotional life.

An entire system has been built up in this perspective, which I do not intend to criticize as a whole, merely examining its contribution to the study of woman. It is not an easy matter to discuss psychoanalysis *per se*. Like all religions – Christianity and Marxism, for example – it displays an embarrassing flexibility on a basis of rigid concepts. Words are sometimes used in their most literal sense, the term *phallus*, for example, designating quite exactly that fleshy projection which marks the male; again, they are indefinitely expanded and take on symbolic meaning, the phallus now expressing the virile character and situation *in toto*. If you attack the letter of his doctrine, the psychoanalyst protests that you misunderstand its spirit; if you applaud its spirit, he at once wishes to confine you to the letter. The doctrine is of no importance, says one, psychoanalysis is a method; but the success of the method strengthens the doctrinaire in his faith. After all, where is one to find the true lineaments of psychoanalysis if not among the psychoanalysts? But there are heretics among these, just as there are among Christians and Marxists; and more than one psychoanalyst has declared that "the worst enemies of psychoanalysis are the psychoanalysts". In spite of a scholastic precision that often becomes pedantic, many obscurities remain to be dissipated. As Sartre and Merleau-Ponty have observed, the proposition "Sexuality is co-extensive with existence" can be understood in two very different ways; it can mean that every experience of the existent has a sexual significance, or that every sexual phenomenon has an existential import. It is possible to reconcile these statements, but too often one merely slips from one to the other. Furthermore, as soon as the "sexual" is distinguished from the "genital", the idea of sexuality becomes none too clear. According to Dalbiez, "the sexual with Freud is the intrinsic aptitude for releasing the genital". But nothing is more obscure than the idea of "aptitude" – that is, of possibility – for only realization gives indubitable proof of what is possible. Not being a philosopher, Freud has refused to justify his system philosophically; and his disciples maintain that on this account he is exempt from all metaphysical attack. There are metaphysical assumptions behind all his dicta, however, and to use his language is to adopt a philosophy. It is just such confusions that call for criticism, while making criticism difficult.

Freud never showed much concern with the destiny of woman; it is clear that he simply adapted his account from that of the destiny of man, with slight modifications. Earlier the sexologist Marañon had stated that "As specific energy, we may say that the libido is a force of virile character. We will say as much of the orgasm". According to him, women who attain orgasm are "viriloid" women; the sexual impulse is "in one direction" and woman is only half way along the road. Freud never goes to such an extreme; he admits that woman's sexuality is evolved as fully as man's; but he hardly studies it in particular. He writes: "The libido is constantly and regularly male in essence, whether it appears in man or in woman." He declines to regard the feminine libido as having its own original nature, and therefore it will necessarily seem to him like a complex deviation from the human libido in general. This develops at first, he thinks, identically in the two sexes – each infant passes first through an oral phase that fixates it upon the maternal breast, and then through an anal phase; finally it reaches the genital phase, at which point the sexes become differentiated.

Freud further brought to light a fact the importance of which had not been fully appreciated: namely, that masculine erotism is definitely located in the penis, whereas in woman there are two distinct erotic systems: one the clitoral, which develops in childhood, the other vaginal, which develops only after puberty. When the boy reaches the genital phase, his evolution is completed, though he must pass from the auto-erotic inclination, in which pleasure is subjective, to the hetero-erotic inclination, in which pleasure is bound up with an object, normally woman. This transition is made at the time of puberty through a narcissistic phase. But the penis will remain, as in childhood, the specific organ of erotism. Woman's libido, also passing through a narcissistic phase, will become objective, normally towards man; but the process will be much more complex, because woman must pass from clitoral pleasure to vaginal. There is only one genital stage for man, but there are two for woman; she runs a much greater risk of not reaching the end of her sexual evolution, of remaining at the infantile stage and thus of developing neuroses.

While still in the auto-erotic stage, the child becomes more or less strongly attached to an object. The boy becomes fixed on his mother and desires to identify himself with his father; this presumption terrifies him and he dreads mutilation at the hands of his father in punishment for it. Thus the castration complex springs from the Oedipus complex. Then aggressiveness towards the father develops, but at the same time the child interiorizes the father's authority; thus the superego is built up in the child and censures his incestuous tendencies. These are repressed, the complex is liquidated, and the son is freed from his fear of his father, whom he has now installed in his own psyche under the guise of moral precepts.[2] The super-ego is more powerful in proportion as the Oedipus complex has been more marked and more rigorously resisted.

Freud at first described the little girl's history in a completely corresponding fashion, later calling the feminine form of the process the Electra complex; but it is clear that he defined it less in itself than upon the basis of his masculine pattern.

He recognized a very important difference between the two, however: the little girl at first has a mother fixation, but the boy is at no time sexually attracted to the father. This fixation of the girl represents a survival of the oral phase. Then the child identifies herself with the father; but towards the age of five she discovers the anatomical difference between the sexes, and she reacts to the absence of the penis by acquiring a castration complex – she imagines that she has been mutilated and is pained at the thought. Having then to renounce her virile pretensions, she identifies herself with her mother and seeks to seduce the father. The castration complex and the Electra complex thus reinforce each other. Her feeling of frustration is the keener since, loving her father, she wishes in vain to be like him; and, inversely, her regret strengthens her love, for she is able to compensate for her inferiority through the affection she inspires in her father. The little girl entertains a feeling of rivalry and hostility towards her mother. Then the super-ego is built up also in her, and the incestuous tendencies are repressed; but her super-ego is not so strong, for the Electra complex is less sharply defined than the Oedipus because the first fixation was upon the mother, and since the father is himself the object of the love that he condemns, his prohibitions are weaker than in the case of his son-rival. It can be seen that like her genital development the whole sexual drama is more complex for the girl than for her brothers. In consequence she may be led to react to the castration complex by denying her femininity, by continuing obstinately to covet a penis and to identify herself with her father. This attitude will cause her to remain in the clitoral phase, to become frigid, or to turn towards homosexuality.

The two essential objections that may be raised against this view derive from the fact that Freud based it upon a masculine model. He assumes that woman feels that she is a mutilated man. But the idea of mutilation implies comparison and evaluation. Many psychoanalysts today admit that the young girl may regret not having a penis without believing, however, that it has been removed from her body; and even this regret is not general. It could not arise from a simple anatomical comparison; many little girls, in fact, are late in discovering the masculine construction, and if they do, it is only by sight. The little boy obtains from his penis a living experience that makes it an object of pride to him, but this pride does not necessarily imply a corresponding humiliation for his sisters, since they know the masculine organ in its outward aspect only – this outgrowth, this weak little rod of flesh can in itself inspire them only with indifference, or even disgust. The little girl's covetousness, when it exists, results from a previous evaluation of virility. Freud takes this for granted, when it should be accounted for.[3] On the other hand, the concept of the Electra complex is very vague, because it is not supported by a basic description of the feminine libido. Even in boys the occurrence of a definitely genital Oedipus complex is by no means general; but, apart from very few exceptions, it cannot be admitted that the father is a source of genital excitation for his young daughter. One of the great problems of feminine eroticism is that clitoral pleasure is localized; and it is only towards puberty that a number of erogenous zones develop in various parts of the body, along with the growth of vaginal sensation. To say, then, that in a child of ten the kisses and caresses of her father have an "intrinsic aptitude" for arousing clitoral pleasure is to assert something that in most cases is nonsense. If it is admitted that the Electra complex has only a very diffuse emotional character, then the whole question of emotion is raised, and Freudianism does not help us in defining emotion as distinguished from sexuality. What deifies the father is by no means the feminine libido (nor is the mother deified by the desire she arouses in the son); on the contrary, the fact that the feminine desire (in the daughter) is directed towards a sovereign being gives it a special character. It does not determine the nature of its object; rather it is affected by the latter. The sovereignty of the father is a fact of social origin, which Freud fails to account for; in fact, he states that it is impossible to say what authority decided, at a certain moment in history, that the father should take precedence over the mother – a decision that, according to Freud, was progressive, but due to causes unknown. "It could not have been patriarchal authority, since it is just this authority which progress conferred upon the father", as he puts it in his last work.[4]

Adler took issue with Freud because he saw the deficiency of a system that undertook to explain human life upon the basis of sexuality alone; he holds that sexuality should be integrated with the total personality. With Freud all human behaviour seems to be the outcome of desire – that is, of the search for pleasure – but for Adler man appears to be aiming at certain goals; for the sexual urge he substitutes motives, purposes, projects. He gives so large a place to the intelligence that often the sexual has in his eyes only a symbolic value. According to his system, the human drama can be reduced to three elemental factors: in every individual there is a will to *power*, which, however, is accompanied by an *inferiority complex*; the resulting conflict leads the individual to employ a thousand ruses in a *flight from reality* – a reality with which he fears he may not be able to cope; the subject thus withdraws to some degree from the society of which he is apprehensive and hence becomes afflicted with the neuroses that involve disturbance of the social attitude. In woman the inferiority complex takes the form of a shamed rejection of her femininity. It is not the lack of the penis that causes this complex, but rather woman's total situation; if the little girl feels penis envy it is only as the symbol of privileges enjoyed by boys. The place the father holds in the family, the universal predominance of males, her own education – everything confirms her in her belief in masculine superiority. Later on, when she takes part in sexual relations, she finds a new humiliation in the coital posture that places woman underneath the man. She reacts through the "masculine protest": either she endeavours to masculinize herself, or she makes use of her feminine weapons to wage war upon the male. Through maternity she may be able to find an equivalent of the penis in her child. But this supposes that she begins by wholly accepting her role as woman and that she assumes her inferiority. She is divided against herself much more profoundly than is the male.

I shall not enlarge here upon the theoretical differences that separate Adler and Freud nor upon the possibilities of a reconciliation; but this may be said: neither the explanation based upon the sexual urge nor that based upon motive is sufficient, for every urge poses a motive, but the motive is apprehended only through the urge – a synthesis of Adlerianism and Freudianism would therefore seem possible of realization. In fact, Adler retains the idea of psychic causation as an integral part of his system when he introduces the concepts of goal and of finality, and he is somewhat in accord with Freud in regard to the relation between drives and mechanism: the physicist always recognizes determinism when he is concerned with conflict or a force of attraction. The axiomatic proposition held in common by all psychoanalysts is this: the human story is to be explained by the interplay of determinate elements. And all the psychoanalysts allot the same destiny to woman. Her drama is epitomized in the conflict between her "viriloid" and her "feminine" tendencies, the first expressed through the clitoral system, the second in vaginal erotism. As a child she identifies herself with her father; then she becomes possessed with a feeling of inferiority with reference to the male and is faced with a dilemma: either to assert her independence and become virilized – which, with the underlying complex of inferiority, induces a state of tension that threatens neurosis – or to find happy fulfilment in amorous submission, a solution that is facilitated by her love for the sovereign father. He it is whom she really seeks in lover or husband, and thus her sexual love is mingled with the desire to be dominated. She will find her recompense in maternity, since that will afford her a new kind of independence. This drama would seem to be endowed with an energy, a dynamism, of its own; it steadily pursues its course through any and all distorting incidents, and every woman is passively swept along in it.

The psychoanalysts have had no trouble in finding empirical confirmation for their theories. As we know, it was possible for a long time to explain the position of the planets on the Ptolemaic system by adding to it sufficiently subtle complications; and by superposing an inverse Oedipus complex upon the Oedipus complex, by disclosing desire in all anxiety, success has been achieved in integrating with the Freudian system the very facts that appear to contradict its validity. It is possible to make out a form only against a background, and the way in which the form is apprehended brings out the background behind it in positive detail; thus, if one is determined to describe a special case in a Freudian perspective, one will encounter the Freudian schema behind it. But when a doctrine demands the indefinite and arbitrary multiplication of secondary explanations, when observation brings to light as many exceptions as instances conformable to rule, it is better to give up the old rigid framework. Indeed, every psychoanalyst today is busily engaged after his fashion in making the Freudian concepts less rigid and in attempting compromises. For example, a contemporary psychoanalyst[5] writes as follows: "Wherever there is a complex, there are by definition a number of components ... The complex consists in the association of these disparate elements and not in the representation of one among them by the others." But the concept of a simple association of elements is unacceptable, for the psychic life is not a mosaic, it is a single whole in every one of its aspects and we must respect that unity. This is possible only by our recovering through the disparate facts the original purposiveness of existence. If we do not go back to this source, man appears to be the battleground of compulsions and prohibitions that alike are devoid of meaning and incidental.

All psychoanalysts systematically reject the idea of *choice* and the correlated concept of value, and therein lies the intrinsic weakness of the system. Having dissociated compulsions and prohibitions from the free choice of the existent, Freud fails to give us an explanation of their origin – he takes them for granted. He endeavoured to replace the idea of value with that of authority; but he admits in *Moses and Monotheism* that he has no way of accounting for this authority. Incest, for example, is forbidden because the father has forbidden it – but why did he forbid it? It is a mystery. The super-ego interiorizes, introjects commands and prohibitions emanating from an arbitrary tyranny, and the instinctive drives are there, we know not why: these two realities are unrelated because morality is envisaged as foreign to sexuality. The human unity appears to be disrupted, there is no thoroughfare from the individual to society; to reunite them Freud was forced to invent strange fictions, as in *Totem and Taboo*. Adler saw clearly that the castration complex could be explained only in social context; he grappled with the problem of valuation, but he did not reach the source in the individual of the values recognized by society, and he did not grasp the fact that values are involved in sexuality itself, which led him to misjudge its importance.

Sexuality most certainly plays a considerable role in human life; it can be said to pervade life throughout. We have already learned from physiology that the living activity of the testes and the ovaries is integrated with that of the body in general. The existent is a sexual, a sexuate body, and in his relations with other existents who are also sexuate bodies, sexuality is in consequence always involved. But if body and sexuality are concrete expressions of existence, it is with reference to this that their significance can be discovered. Lacking this perspective, psychoanalysis takes for granted unexplained facts. For instance, we are told that the little girl is *ashamed* of urinating in a squatting position with her bottom uncovered – but whence comes this shame? And likewise, before asking whether the male is proud of having a penis or whether his pride is expressed in his penis, it is necessary to know what pride is and how the aspirations of the subject can be incarnated in an object. There is no need of taking sexuality as an irreducible datum, for there is in the existent a more original "quest of being", of which sexuality is only one of the aspects. Sartre demonstrates this truth in *L'Être et le néant*, as does Bachelard in his works on Earth, Air, and Water. The psychoanalysts hold that the primary truth regarding man is his relation with his own body and with the bodies of his fellows in the group; but man has a primordial interest in the substance of the natural world which surrounds him and which he tries to discover in work, in play, and in all the experiences of the "dynamic imagination". Man aspires to be at one concretely with the whole world, apprehended in all possible ways. To work the earth, to dig a hole, are activities as original as the embrace, as coition, and they deceive themselves who see here no more than sexual symbols. The hole, the ooze, the gash, hardness, integrity are primary realities; and the interest they have for man is not dictated by the libido, but rather the libido will be coloured by the manner in which he becomes aware of them. It is not because it symbolizes feminine virginity that integrity fascinates man; but it is his admiration for integrity that renders virginity precious. Work, war, play, art signify ways of being concerned with the world which cannot be reduced to any others; they disclose qualities that interfere with those which sexuality reveals. It is at once in their light and in the light of these erotic experiences that the individual exercises his power of choice. But only an ontological point of view, a comprehension of being in general, permits us to restore the unity of this choice.

It is this concept of choice, indeed, that psychoanalysis most vehemently rejects in the name of determinism and the "collective unconscious"; and it is this unconscious that is supposed to supply man with prefabricated imagery and a universal symbolism. Thus it would explain the observed analogies of dreams, of purposeless actions, of visions of delirium, of allegories, and of human destinies. To speak of liberty would be to deny oneself the possibility of explaining these disturbing conformities. But the idea of liberty is not incompatible with the existence of certain constants. If the psychoanalytic method is frequently rewarding in spite of the errors in its theory, that is because there are in every individual case certain factors of undeniable generality: situations and behaviour patterns constantly recur, and the moment of decision flashes from a cloud of generality and repetition. "Anatomy is destiny", said Freud; and this phrase is echoed by that of Merleau-Ponty: "The body is generality." Existence is all one, bridging the gaps between individual existents; it makes itself manifest in analogous organisms, and therefore constant factors will be found in the bonds between the ontological and the sexual. At a given epoch of history the techniques, the economic and social structure of a society, will reveal to all its members an identical world, and there a constant relation of sexuality to social patterns will exist; analogous individuals, placed in analogous conditions, will see analogous points of significance in the given circumstances. This analogy does not establish a rigorous universality, but it accounts for the fact that general types may be recognized in individual case histories.

The symbol does not seem to me to be an allegory elaborated by a mysterious unconscious; it is rather the perception of a certain significance through the analogue of the significant object. Symbolic significance is manifested in the same way to numerous individuals, because of the identical existential situation connecting all the individual existents, and the identical set of artificial conditions that all must confront. Symbolism did not come down from heaven nor rise up from subterranean depths – it has been elaborated, like language, by that human reality which is at once *Mitsein* and separation; and this explains why individual invention also has its place, as in practice psychoanalysis has to admit, regardless of doctrine. Our perspective allows us, for example, to understand the value widely accorded to the penis.[6] It is impossible to account for it without taking our departure from an existential fact: the tendency of the subject towards *alienation*. The anxiety that his liberty induces in the subject leads him to search for himself in things, which is a kind of flight from himself. This tendency is so fundamental that immediately after weaning, when he is separated from the Whole, the infant is compelled to lay hold upon his alienated existence in mirrors and in the gaze of his parents. Primitive people are alienated in mana, in the totem; civilized people in their individual souls, in their egos, their names, their property, their work. Here is to be found the primary temptation to inauthenticity, to failure to be genuinely oneself. The penis is singularly adapted for playing this role of "double" for the little boy – it is for him at once a foreign object and himself; it is a plaything, a doll, and yet his own flesh; relatives and nurse-girls behave towards it as if it were a little person. It is easy to see, then, how it becomes for the child "an *alter ego* ordinarily more artful, more intelligent, and more clever than the individual".[7] The penis is regarded by the subject as at once himself and other than himself, because the functions of urination and later of erection are processes midway between the voluntary and involuntary, and because it is a capricious and as it were a foreign source of pleasure that is felt subjectively. The individual's specific transcendence takes concrete form in the penis and it is a source of pride. Because the phallus is thus set apart, man can bring into integration with his subjective individuality the life that overflows from it. It is easy to see, then, that the length of the penis, the force of the urinary jet, the strength of erection and ejaculation become for him the measure of his own worth.[8]

Thus the incarnation of transcendence in the phallus is a constant; and since it is also a constant for the child to feel himself transcended – that is to say, frustrated in his own transcendence by the father – we therefore continually come upon the Freudian idea of the "castration complex". Not having that *alter ego*, the little girl is not alienated in a material thing and cannot retrieve her integrity. On this account she is led to make an object of her whole self, to set up herself as the Other. Whether she knows that she is or is not comparable with boys is secondary; the important point is that, even if she is unaware of it, the absence of the penis prevents her from being conscious of herself as a sexual being. From this flow many consequences. But the constants I have referred to do not for all that establish a fixed destiny – the phallus assumes such worth as it does because it symbolizes a dominance that is exercised in other domains. If woman should succeed in establishing herself as subject, she would invent equivalents of the phallus; in fact, the doll, incarnating the promise of the baby that is to come in the future, can become a possession more precious than the penis.[9] There are matrilineal societies in which the women keep in their possession the *masks* in which the group finds alienation; in such societies the penis loses much of its glory. The fact is that a true human privilege is based upon the anatomical privilege only in virtue of the total situation. Psychoanalysis can establish its truths only in the historical context.

Woman can be defined by her consciousness of her own femininity no more satisfactorily than by saying that she is a female, for she acquires this consciousness under circumstances dependent upon the society of which she is a member. Interiorizing the unconscious and the whole psychic life, the very language of psychoanalysis suggests that the drama of the individual unfolds within him – such words as *complex, tendency*, and so on make that implication. But a life is a relation to the world, and the individual defines himself by making his own choices through the world about him. We must therefore turn towards the world to find answers for the questions we are concerned with. In particular psychoanalysis fails to explain why woman is the *Other*. For Freud himself admits that the prestige of the penis is explained by the sovereignty of the father, and, as we have seen, he confesses that he is ignorant regarding the origin of male supremacy.

We therefore decline to accept the method of psychoanalysis, without rejecting *en bloc* the contributions of the science or denying the fertility of some of its insights. In the first place, we do not limit ourselves to regarding sexuality as something given. The insufficiency of this view is shown by the poverty of the resulting descriptions of the feminine libido; as I have already said, the psychoanalysts have never studied it directly, but only in taking the male libido as their point of departure. They seem to ignore the fundamental ambivalence of the attraction exerted on the female by the male. Freudians and Adlerians explain the anxiety felt by the female confronted by the masculine sex as being the inversion of a frustrated desire. Stekel saw more clearly that an original reaction was concerned, but he accounts for it in a superficial manner. Woman, he says, would fear defloration, penetration, pregnancy, and pain, and such fear would restrain her desire – but this explanation is too rational. Instead of holding that her desire is disguised in anxiety or is contested by fear, we should regard as an original fact this blending of urgency and apprehension which is female desire: it is the indissoluble synthesis of attraction and repulsion that characterizes it. We may note that many female animals avoid copulation even as they are soliciting it, and we are tempted to accuse them of coquetry or hypocrisy; but it is absurd to pretend to explain primitive behaviour patterns by asserting their similarity to complex modes of conduct. On the contrary, the former are in truth at the source of the attitudes that in woman are called coquetry and hypocrisy. The notion of a "passive libido" is baffling, since the libido has been defined, on the basis of the male, as a drive, an energy; but one would do no better to hold the opinion that a light could be at once yellow and blue – what is needed is the intuition of green. We would more fully encompass reality if instead of defining the libido in vague terms of "energy" we brought the significance of sexuality into relation with that of other human attitudes – taking, capturing, eating, making, submitting, and so forth; for it is one of the various modes of apprehending an object. We should study also the qualities of the erotic object as it presents itself not only in the sexual act but also to observation in general. Such an investigation extends beyond the frame of psychoanalysis, which assumes eroticism as irreducible.

 Furthermore, I shall pose the problem of feminine destiny quite otherwise: I shall place woman in a world of values and give her behaviour a dimension of liberty. I believe that she has the power to choose between the assertion of her transcendence and her alienation as object; she is not the plaything of contradictory drives; she devises solutions of diverse values in the ethical scale. Replacing value with authority, choice with drive, psychoanalysis offers an *Ersatz*, a substitute for morality – the concept of normality. This concept is certainly most useful in therapeutics, but it has spread through psychoanalysis in general to a disquieting extent. The descriptive schema is proposed as a law; and most assuredly a mechanistic psychology cannot accept the notion of moral invention; it can in strictness render an account of the less and never of the more; in strictness it can admit of checks, never of creations. If a subject does not show in his totality the development considered as normal, it will be said that his development has been arrested, and this arrest will be interpreted as a lack, a negation, but never as a positive decision. This it is, among other things, that makes the psychoanalysis of great men so shocking: we are told that such and such a transference, this or that sublimation, has not taken place in them; it is not suggested that perhaps they have refused to undergo the process, perhaps for good reasons of their own; it is not thought desirable to regard their behaviour as possibly motivated by purposes freely envisaged; the individual is always explained through ties with his past and not in respect to a future towards which he projects his aims. Thus the psychoanalysts never give us more than an inauthentic picture, and for the inauthentic there can hardly be found any other criterion than normality. Their statement of the feminine destiny is absolutely to the point in this connection. In the sense in which the psychoanalysts understand the term, "to identify oneself" with the mother or with the father is to *alienate oneself* in a model, it is to prefer a foreign image to the spontaneous manifestation of one's own existence, it is to play at being. Woman is shown to us as enticed by two modes of alienation. Evidently to play at being a man will be for her a source of frustration; but to play at being a woman is also a delusion: to be a woman would mean to be the object, the *Other* – and the Other nevertheless remains subject in the midst of her resignation.

The true problem for woman is to reject these flights from reality and seek self-fulfilment in transcendence. The thing to do, then, is to see what possibilities are opened up for her through what are called the virile and the feminine attitudes. When a child takes the road indicated by one or the other of its parents, it may be because the child freely takes up their projects; its behaviour may be the result of a choice motivated by ends and aims. Even with Adler the will to power is only an absurd kind of energy; he denominates as "masculine protest" every project involving transcendence. When a little girl climbs trees it is, according to Adler, just to show her equality with boys; it does not occur to him that she likes to climb trees. For the mother her child is something other than an "equivalent of the penis". To paint, to write, to engage in politics – these are not merely "sublimations"; here we have aims that are willed for their own sakes. To deny it is to falsify all human history.

The reader will note a certain parallelism between this account and that of the psychoanalysts. The fact is that from the male point of view – which is adopted by both male and female psychoanalysts – behaviour involving alienation is regarded as feminine, that in which the subject asserts his transcendence as virile. Donaldson, a historian of woman, remarked that the definitions: "man is a male human being, woman is a female human being", have been asymmetrically distorted; and it is among the psychoanalysts in particular that man is defined as a human being and woman as a female – whenever she behaves as a human being she is said to imitate the male. The psychoanalyst describes the female child, the young girl, as incited to identification with the mother and the father, torn between "viriloid" and "feminine" tendencies; whereas I conceive her as hesitating between the role of *object, Other* which is offered her, and the assertion of her liberty. Thus it is that we shall agree on a certain number of facts, especially when we take up the avenues of inauthentic flight open to women. But we accord them by no means the same significance as does the Freudian or the Adlerian. For us woman is defined as a human being in quest of values in a world of values, a world of which it is indispensable to know the economic and social structure. We shall study woman in an existential perspective with due regard to her total situation.

The point of view of historical materialism

The theory of historical materialism has brought to light some most important truths. Humanity is not an animal species, it is a historical reality. Human society is an antiphysis – in a sense it is against nature; it does not passively submit to the presence of nature but rather takes over the control of nature on its own behalf. This arrogation is not an inward, subjective operation; it is accomplished objectively in practical action.

Thus woman could not be considered simply as a sexual organism, for among the biological traits, only those have importance that take on concrete value in action. Woman's awareness of herself is not defined exclusively by her sexuality: it reflects a situation that depends upon the economic organization of society, which in turn indicates what stage of technical evolution mankind has attained. As we have seen, the two essential traits that characterize woman, biologically speaking, are the following: her grasp upon the world is less extended than man's, and she is more closely enslaved to the species.

But these facts take on quite different values according to the economic and social context. In human history grasp upon the world has never been defined by the naked body: the hand, with its opposable thumb, already anticipates the instrument that multiplies its power; from the most ancient records of prehistory, we see man always as armed. In times when heavy clubs were brandished and wild beasts held at bay, woman's physical weakness did constitute a glaring inferiority: if the instrument required strength slightly beyond that at woman's disposal, it was enough to make her appear utterly powerless. But, on the contrary, technique may annul the muscular inequality of man and woman: abundance makes for superiority only in the perspective of a need, and to have too much is no better than to have enough. Thus the control of many modern machines requires only a part of the masculine resources, and if the minimum demanded is not above the female's capacity, she becomes, as far as this work is concerned, man's equal. Today, of course, vast displays of energy can be controlled by pressing a button. As for the burdens of maternity, they assume widely varying importance according to the customs of the country: they are crushing if the woman is obliged to undergo frequent pregnancies and if she is compelled to nurse and raise the children without assistance; but if she procreates voluntarily and if society comes to her aid during pregnancy and is concerned with child welfare, the burdens of maternity are light and can be easily offset by suitable adjustments in working conditions.

Engels retraces the history of woman according to this perspective in *The Origin of the Family, Private Property, and the State*, showing that this history depended essentially on that of techniques. In the Stone Age, when the land belonged in common to all members of the clan, the rudimentary character of the primitive spade and hoe limited the possibilities of agriculture, so that woman's strength was adequate for gardening. In this primitive division of labour, the two sexes constituted in a way two classes, and there was equality between these classes. While man hunts and fishes, woman remains in the home; but the tasks of domesticity include productive labour – making pottery, weaving, gardening – and in consequence woman plays a large part in economic life. Through the discovery of copper, tin, bronze, and iron, and with the appearance of the plough, agriculture enlarges its scope, and intensive labour is called for in clearing woodland and cultivating the fields. Then man has recourse to the labour of other men, whom he reduces to slavery. Private property appears: master of slaves and of the earth, man becomes the proprietor also of woman. This was "the great historical defeat of the feminine sex". It is to be explained by the upsetting of the old division of labour which occurred in consequence of the invention of new tools. "The same cause which had assured to woman the prime authority in the house – namely, her restriction to domestic duties – this same cause now assured the domination there of the man; for woman's housework henceforth sank into insignificance in comparison with man's productive labour – the latter was everything, the former a trifling auxiliary." Then maternal authority gave place to paternal authority, property being inherited from father to son and no longer from woman to her clan. Here we see the emergence of the patriarchal family founded upon private property. In this type of family woman is subjugated. Man in his sovereignty indulges himself in sexual caprices, among others – he fornicates with slaves or courtesans or he practises polygamy. Wherever the local customs make reciprocity at all possible, the wife takes revenge through infidelity – marriage finds its natural fulfilment in adultery. This is woman's sole defence against the domestic slavery in which she is bound; and it is this economic oppression that gives rise to the social oppression to which she is subjected. Equality cannot be re-established until the two sexes enjoy equal rights in law; but this enfranchisement requires participation in general industry by the whole female sex. "Woman can be emancipated only when she can take part on a large social scale in production and is engaged in domestic work only to an insignificant degree. And this has become possible only in the big industry of modern times, which not only admits of female labour on a grand scale but even formally demands it . . ."

Thus the fate of woman and that of socialism are intimately bound up together, as is shown also in Bebel's great work on woman. "Woman and the proletariat," he says, "are both downtrodden." Both are to be set free through the economic development consequent upon the social upheaval brought about by machinery. The problem of woman is reduced to the problem of her capacity for labour. Puissant at the time when techniques were suited to her capabilities, dethroned when she was no longer in a position to exploit them, woman regains in the modern world her equality with man. It is the resistance of the ancient capitalistic paternalism that in most countries prevents the concrete realization of this equality; it will be realized on the day when this resistance is broken, as is the fact already in the Soviet Union, according to Soviet propaganda. And when the socialist society is established throughout the world, there will no longer be men and women, but only workers on a footing of equality.

Although this chain of thought as outlined by Engels marks an advance upon those we have been examining, we find it disappointing – the most important problems are slurred over. The turning-point of all history is the passage from the régime of community ownership to that of private property, and it is in no wise indicated how this could have come about. Engels himself declares in *The Origin of the Family* that "at present we know nothing about it"; not only is he ignorant of the historical details: he does not even suggest any interpretation. Similarly, it is not clear that the institution of private property must necessarily have involved the enslavement of women. Historical materialism takes for granted facts that call for explanation: Engels assumes without discussion the bond of *interest* which ties man to property; but where does this interest, the source of social institutions, have its own source? Thus Engels's account remains superficial, and the truths that he does reveal are seemingly contingent, incidental. The fact is that we cannot plumb their meaning without going beyond the limits of historical materialism. It cannot provide solutions for the problems we have raised, because these concern the whole man and not that abstraction: *Homo oeconomicus*.

It would seem clear, for example, that the very concept of personal possession can be comprehensible only with reference to the original condition of the existent. For it to appear, there must have been at first an inclination in the subject to think of himself as basically individual, to assert the autonomy and separateness of his existence. We can see that this affirmation would have remained subjective, inward, without validity as long as the individual lacked the practical means for carrying it out objectively. Without adequate tools, he did not sense at first any power over the world, he felt lost in nature and in the group, passive, threatened, the plaything of obscure forces; he dared think of himself only as identified with the clan: the totem, mana, the earth were group realities. The discovery of bronze enabled man, in the experience of hard and productive labour, to discover himself as creator; dominating nature, he was no longer afraid of it, and in the fact of obstacles overcome he found courage to see himself as an autonomous active force, to achieve self-fulfilment as an individual.[10] But this accomplishment would never have been attained had not man originally willed it so; the lesson of work is not inscribed upon a passive subject: the subject shapes and masters himself in shaping and mastering the land.

On the other hand, the affirmation of the subject's individuality is not enough to explain property: each conscious individual through challenge, struggle, and single combat can endeavour to raise himself to sovereignty. For the challenge to have taken the form of *potlatch* or ceremonial exchange of gifts – that is, of an economic rivalry – and from this point on for first the chief and then the members of the clan to have laid claim to private property, required that there should be in man another original tendency. As we have seen in the preceding chapter, the existent succeeds in finding himself only in estrangement, in alienation; he seeks through the world to find himself in some shape, other than himself, which he makes his own. The clan encounters its own alienated existence in the totem, the mana, the terrain it occupies; and when the individual becomes distinguished from the community, he requires a personal incarnation. The mana becomes individualized in the chief, then in each individual; and at the same time each person tries to appropriate a piece of land, implements, crops. Man finds himself in these goods which are his because he has previously lost himself in them; and it is therefore understandable that he places upon them a value no less fundamental than upon his very life. Thus it is that man's *interest* in his property becomes an intelligible relation. But we see that this cannot be explained through the tool alone: we must grasp in its entirety the attitude of man wielding the tool, an attitude that implies an ontological substructure, a foundation in the nature of his being.

On the same grounds it is impossible to *deduce* the oppression of woman from the institution of private property. Here again the inadequacy of Engels's point of view is obvious. He saw clearly that woman's muscular weakness became a real point of inferiority only in its relation to the bronze and iron tool; but he did not see that the limitations of her capacity for labour constituted in themselves a concrete disadvantage only in a certain perspective. It is because man is a being of transcendence and ambition that he projects new urgencies through every new tool: when he had invented bronze implements, he was no longer content with gardens – he wanted to clear and cultivate vast fields. And it was not from the bronze itself that this desire welled up. Woman's incapacity brought about her ruin because man regarded her in the perspective of his project for enrichment and expansion. And this project is still not enough to explain why she was oppressed; for the division of labour between the sexes could have meant a friendly association. If the original relation between a man and his fellows was exclusively a relation of friendship, we could not account for any type of enslavement; but no, this phenomenon is a result of the imperialism of the human consciousness, seeking always to exercise its sovereignty in objective fashion. If the human consciousness had not included the original category of the Other and an original aspiration to dominate the Other, the invention of the bronze tool could not have caused the oppression of woman.

No more does Engels account for the peculiar nature of this oppression. He tried to reduce the antagonism of the sexes to class conflict, but he was half-hearted in the attempt; the thesis is simply untenable. It is true that division of labour according to sex and the consequent oppression bring to mind in some ways the division of society by classes, but it is impossible to confuse the two. For one thing, there is no biological basis for the separation of classes. Again, the slave in his toil is conscious of himself as opposed to his master; and the proletariat has always put its condition to the test in revolt, thereby going back to essentials and constituting a threat to its exploiters. And what it has aimed at is its own disappearance as a class. I have pointed out in the Introduction how different woman's situation is, particularly on account of the community of life and interests which entails her solidarity with man, and also because he finds in her an accomplice; no desire for revolution dwells within her, nor any thought of her own disappearance as a sex – all she asks is that certain sequels of sexual differentiation be abolished.

What is still more serious, woman cannot in good faith be regarded simply as a worker; for her reproductive function is as important as her productive capacity, no less in the social economy than in the individual life. In some periods, indeed, it is more useful to produce offspring than to plough the soil. Engels slighted the problem, simply remarking that the socialist community would abolish the family – certainly an abstract solution. We know how often and how radically Soviet Russia has had to change its policy on the family according to the varying relation between the immediate needs of production and those of re-population. But for that matter, to do away with the family is not necessarily to emancipate woman. Such examples as Sparta and the Nazi régime prove that she can be none the less oppressed by the males, for all her direct attachment to the State.

A truly socialist ethics, concerned to uphold justice without suppressing liberty and to impose duties upon individuals without abolishing individuality, will find most embarrassing the problems posed by the condition of woman. It is impossible simply to equate gestation with a *task*, a piece of work, or with a *service*, such as military service. Woman's life is more seriously broken in upon by a demand for children than by regulation of the citizen's employment – no state has ever ventured to establish obligatory copulation. In the sexual act and in maternity not only time and strength but also essential values are involved for woman. Rationalist materialism tries in vain to disregard this dramatic aspect of sexuality; for it is impossible to bring the sexual instinct under a code of regulations. Indeed, as Freud said, it is not sure that it does not bear within itself a denial of its own satisfaction. What is certain is that it does not permit of integration with the social, because there is in eroticism a revolt of the instant against time, of the individual against the universal. In proposing to direct and exploit it, there is risk of killing it, for it is impossible to deal at will with living spontaneity as one deals at will with inert matter; and no more can it be obtained by force, as a privilege may be.

There is no way of directly compelling woman to bring forth: all that can be done is to put her in a situation where maternity is for her the sole outcome – the law or the mores enjoin marriage, birth control and abortion are prohibited, divorce is forbidden. These ancient patriarchal restraints are just what Soviet Russia has brought back today; Russia has revived the paternalistic concepts of marriage. And in doing so, she has been induced to ask woman once more to make of herself an erotic object: in a recent pronouncement female Soviet citizens were requested to pay careful attention to their garb, to use make-up, to employ the arts of coquetry in holding their husbands and fanning the flame of desire. As this case shows clearly, it is impossible to regard woman simply as a productive force: she is for man a sexual partner, a reproducer, an erotic object – an Other through whom he seeks himself. In vain have the totalitarian or authoritative régimes with one accord prohibited psychoanalysis and declared that individual, personal drama is out of order for citizens loyally integrated with the community; the erotic experience remains one in which generality is always regained by an individuality. And for a democratic socialism in which classes are abolished but not individuals, the question of individual destiny would keep all its importance – and hence sexual differentiation would keep all its importance. The sexual relation that joins woman to man is not the same as that which he bears to her; and the bond that unites her to the child is *sui generis*, unique. She was not created by the bronze tool alone; and the machine alone will not abolish her. To claim for her every right, every chance to be an all-round human being does not mean that we should be blind to her peculiar situation. And in order to comprehend that situation we must look beyond the historical materialism that perceives in man and woman no more than economic units.

So it is that we reject for the same reasons both the sexual monism of Freud and the economic monism of Engels. A psychoanalyst will interpret all social claims of woman as phenomena of the "masculine protest"; for the Marxist, on the contrary, her sexuality only expresses her economic situation in more or less complex, roundabout fashion. But the categories of "clitorid" and "vaginal", like the categories of "bourgeois" or "proletarian", are equally inadequate to encompass a concrete woman. Underlying all individual drama, as it underlies the economic history of mankind, there is an existentialist foundation that alone enables us to understand in its unity that particular form of being which we call a human life. The virtue of Freudianism derives from the fact that the existent is a body: what he experiences as a body confronted by other bodies expresses his existential situation concretely. Similarly, what is true in the Marxian thesis is that the ontological aspirations – the projects for becoming – of the existent take concrete form according to the material possibilities offered, especially those opened up by technological advances. But unless they are integrated into the totality of human reality, sexuality and technology alone can explain nothing. That is why in Freud the prohibitions of the super-ego and the drives of the ego appear to be contingent, and why in Engels's account of the history of the family the most important developments seem to arise according to the caprices of mysterious fortune. In our attempt to discover woman we shall not reject certain contributions of biology, of psychoanalysis, and of historical materialism; but we shall hold that the body, the sexual life, and the resources of technology exist concretely for man only in so far as he grasps them in the total perspective of his existence. The value of muscular strength, of the phallus, of the tool can be defined only in a world of values; it is determined by the basic project through which the existent seeks transcendence.

Notes

1 *The Social Life of Monkeys and Apes* (1932).
2 "The super-ego or conscience is a precipitate of all the prohibitions and inhibitions that were originally inculcated into us by our parents, especially by the father." (Brill, *Freud's Contribution to Psychiatry* [W. W. Norton & Co., 1944], p. 153.) – TR.
3 This discussion will be resumed at much greater length in Book Two, chap. 1.
4 Freud, *Moses and Monotheism*, translated by Katherine Jones (Alfred A. Knopf, 1939).
5 Baudouin, *L'Âme enfantine et la psychanalyse*.
6 We shall return to this subject at greater length in Book Two, chap. 1.
7 Alice Balint, *La Vie intime de l'enfant*, p. 101.
8 I have been told of peasant children amusing themselves in excremental competition; the one who produced the most copious and solid faeces enjoyed a prestige unmatched by any other form of success, whether in games or even in fighting. The faecal mass here plays the same part as the penis – there is alienation in both cases.

  [Pride in this peculiar type of eminence is by no means confined to European peasant children; it has been observed in young Americans and is doubtless well-nigh universal. – TR.]
9 We shall return to these ideas in the second part; I note them here only as a matter of method.
10 Gaston Bachelard in *La Terre et les rêveries de la volonté* makes among others a suggestive study of the blacksmith. He shows how man, through the hammer and the anvil, asserts himself and his individuality. "The blacksmith's instant is an instant at once well marked off and magnified. It promotes the worker to the mastery of time, through the forcefulness of an instant" (p. 142); and farther on: "The man at the forge accepts the challenge of the universe arrayed against him."

2

WOMAN'S SITUATION AND CHARACTER

We can now understand why there should be so many common features in the indictments drawn up against woman, from the Greeks to our own times. Her condition has remained the same through superficial changes, and it is this condition that determines what is called the "character" of woman: she "revels in immanence", she is contrary, she is prudent and petty, she has no sense of fact or accuracy, she lacks morality, she is contemptibly utilitarian, she is false, theatrical, self-seeking, and so on. There is an element of truth in all this. But we must only note that the varieties of behaviour reported are not dictated to woman by her hormones nor predetermined in the structure of the female brain: they are shaped as in a mould by her situation. In this perspective we shall endeavour to make a comprehensive survey of woman's situation. This will involve a certain amount of repetition, but it will enable us to apprehend the eternal feminine in the totality of her economic, social, and historical conditioning.

Sometimes the "feminine world" is contrasted with the masculine universe, but we must insist again that women have never constituted a closed and independent society; they form an integral part of the group, which is governed by males and in which they have a subordinate place. They are united only in a mechanical solidarity from the mere fact of their similarity, but they lack that organic solidarity on which every unified community is based; they are always compelled – at the time of the mysteries of Eleusis as today in clubs, salons, social-service institutes – to band together in order to establish a counter-service, but they always set it up within the frame of the masculine universe. Hence the paradox of their situation: they belong at one and the same time to the male world and to a sphere in which that world is challenged; shut up in their world, surrounded by the other, they can settle down nowhere in peace. Their docility must always be matched by a refusal, their refusal by an acceptance, in this respect their attitude approaches that of the young girl, but it is more difficult to maintain, because for the adult woman it is not merely a matter of dreaming her life through symbols, but of living it out in actuality.

Woman herself recognizes that the world is masculine on the whole; those who fashioned it, ruled it, and still dominate it today are men. As for her, she does not consider herself responsible for it; it is understood that she is inferior and dependent; she has not learned the lessons of violence, she has never stood forth as

S. de Beauvoir, *The Second Sex*, 1988, trans. and ed. H. M. Parshley, pp. 608–39. London: Picador.

subject before the other members of the group. Shut up in her flesh, her home, she sees herself as passive before these gods with human faces who set goals and establish values. In this sense there is truth in the saying that makes her the "eternal child". Workers, black slaves, colonial natives, have also been called grown-up children – as long as they were not feared; that meant that they were to accept without argument the verities and the laws laid down for them by other men. The lot of woman is a respectful obedience. She has no grasp, even in thought, on the reality around her. It is opaque to her eyes.

And it is true that she lacks the technical training that would permit her to dominate matter. As for her, it is not matter she comes to grips with, but life; and life cannot be mastered through the use of tools: one can only submit to its secret laws. The world does not seem to woman "an assemblage of implements" intermediate between her will and her goals, as Heidegger defines it; it is on the contrary something obstinately resistant, unconquerable; it is dominated by fatality and shot through with mysterious caprices. This mystery of a bloody strawberry that inside the mother is transformed into a human being is one no mathematics can express in an equation, no machine can hasten or delay; she feels the strength of a continuity that the most ingenious instruments are unable to divide or to multiply; she feels it in her body, swayed by the lunar rhythm and first ripened, then corrupted, by the years. Each day the kitchen also teaches her patience and passivity; here is alchemy; one must obey the fire, the water, wait for the sugar to melt, for the dough to rise, and also for the wash to dry, for the fruits to ripen on the shelf. Household activities come close to being technical operations, but they are too rudimentary, too monotonous, to prove to a woman the laws of mechanical causation. Besides, even here things are capricious; there are materials that will stand washing and others that will not, spots that can be removed and others that persist, objects that break all by themselves, dusts that spring up like plants.

Woman's mentality perpetuates that of agricultural civilizations which worshipped the magic powers of the land: she believes in magic. Her passive eroticism makes desire seem to her not will and aggression but an attraction akin to that which causes the divining rod to dip; the mere presence of her flesh swells and erects the male's sex; why should not hidden water make the hazel rod quiver? She feels that she is surrounded by waves, radiations, mystic fluids; she believes in telepathy, astrology, radiotherapy, mesmerism, theosophy, table-tipping, clairvoyants, faith healers; her religion is full of primitive superstition: wax candles, answered prayers; she believes the saints incarnate the ancient spirits of nature: this one protects travellers, that one women in labour, this other finds lost articles; and, of course, no prodigy can surprise her. Her attitude will be one of conjuration and prayer; to obtain a certain result, she will perform certain well-tested rites.

It is easy to see why woman clings to routine; time has for her no element of novelty, it is not a creative flow; because she is doomed to repetition, she sees in the future only a duplication of the past. If one knows the word and the formula, duration allies itself with the powers of fecundity – but this is itself subject to the rhythm of the months, the seasons; the cycle of each pregnancy, each flowering, exactly reproduces the one that preceded. In this play of cyclical phenomena the sole effect of time is a slow deterioration; it wears out furniture and clothes as it ruins the face; the reproductive powers are gradually destroyed by the passing of years. Thus woman puts no trust in this relentless force for destruction.

Not only is she ignorant of what constitutes a true action, capable of changing the face of the world, but she is lost in the midst of the world as if she were at the heart of an immense, vague nebula. She is not familiar with the use of masculine logic. Stendhal remarked that she could handle it as adroitly as a man if driven to it by necessity. But it is an instrument that she hardly has occasion to use. A syllogism is of no help in making a successful mayonnaise, nor in quieting a child in tears; masculine reasoning is quite inadequate to the reality with which she deals. And in the world of men, her thought, not flowing into any project, since she *does* nothing, is indistinguishable from day-dreaming. She has no sense of factual truth, for lack of effectiveness; she never comes to grips with anything but words and mental pictures, and that is why the most contradictory assertions give her no uneasiness; she takes little trouble to elucidate the mysteries of a sphere that is in every way beyond her reach. She is content, for her purposes, with extremely vague conceptions, confusing parties, opinions, places, people, events; her head is filled with a strange jumble.

But, after all, to see things clearly is not her business, for she has been taught to accept masculine authority. So she gives up criticizing, investigating, judging for herself, and leaves all this to the superior caste. Therefore the masculine world seems to her a transcendent reality, an absolute. "Men make the gods," says Frazer, "women worship them." Men cannot kneel with complete conviction before the idols they have made; but when women encounter these mighty statues along the roads, they think they are not made with hands, and obediently bow down.[1] In particular they like to have Order and Right embodied in a leader. In every Olympus there is a supreme god; the magic male essence must be concentrated in an archetype of which father, husband, lovers, are only faint reflections. It is rather satirical to say that their worship of this grand totem is of sexual nature; but it is true that in this worship they will fully satisfy their childhood dream of bowing the knee in resignation. In France generals like Boulanger, Pétain, and de Gaulle[2] have always had the support of the women; and one recalls with what fluttering pens the lady journalists on the Communist paper *L'Humanité* formerly celebrated Tito and his splendid uniform. The general, the dictator – eagle-eyed, square-jawed – is the heavenly father demanded by all serious right-thinkers, the absolute guarantor of all values. Women's ineffectiveness and ignorance are what give rise to the respect accorded by them to heroes and to the laws of the masculine world; they accept them not through sound judgement but by an act of faith – and faith gets its fanatical power from the fact that it is not knowledge: it is blind, impassioned, obstinate, stupid; what it declares, it declares unconditionally, against reason, against history, against all denial.

This obstinate reverence can take one of two forms according to circumstances: it may be either the content of the law, or merely its empty form that woman passionately adheres to. If she belongs to the privileged *élite* that benefits from the established social order, she wants it to be unshakable and she is notably uncompromising in this desire. Man knows that he can develop different institutions, another ethic, a new legal code; aware of his ability to transcend what is, he regards history as a becoming. The most conservative man knows that some evolution is inevitable and realizes that he must adapt his action and his thinking to

488

it; but as woman takes no part in history, she fails to understand its necessities; she is suspiciously doubtful of the future and wants to arrest the flow of time. If the idols set up by her father, her brothers, her husband, are being torn down, she can offer no way of repopulating the heavens; she rushes wildly to the defence of the old gods.

During the American War of Secession no Southerners were more passionate in upholding slavery than the women. In England during the Boer War, in France during the Commune, it was the women who were most belligerently inflamed. They seek to compensate for their inactivity by the intensity of the sentiments they exhibit. With victory won, they rush like hyenas upon the fallen foe; in defeat, they bitterly reject any efforts at conciliation. Their ideas being merely attitudes, they support quite unconcernedly the most outdated causes: they can be legitimists in 1914, czarists in 1953. A man will sometimes smilingly encourage them, for it amuses him to see their fanatical reflections of ideas he expresses in more measured terms; but he may also find it irritating to have his ideas take on such a stupid, stubborn, aspect.

Woman assumes this indomitable attitude only in strongly integrated civilizations and social classes. More generally, she respects the law simply because it is the law, since her faith is blind; if the law changes, it retains its spell. In woman's eyes, might makes right because the rights she recognizes in men depend upon their power. Hence it is that when a society breaks down, women are the first to throw themselves at the feet of the conqueror. On the whole, they accept what is. One of their distinguishing traits is resignation. When the ruins of Pompeii were dug up, it was noticed that the incinerated bodies of the men were fixed in attitudes of rebellion, defying the heavens or trying to escape, while those of the women, bent double, were bowed down with their faces towards the earth. Women feel they are powerless against things: volcanoes, police, patrons, men. "Women are born to suffer," they say; "it's life – nothing can be done about it."

This resignation inspires the patience often admired in women. They can stand physical pain much better than men; they are capable of stoical courage when circumstances demand it; lacking the male's aggressive audacity, many women distinguish themselves by their calm tenacity in passive resistance. They face crises, poverty, misfortune, more energetically than their husbands; respecting duration, which no haste can overcome, they do not ration their time. When they apply their quiet persistence to an enterprise, they are sometimes startlingly successful. "Never underestimate the power of a woman." In a generous woman resignation takes the form of forbearance: she puts up with everything, she condemns no one, because she holds that neither people nor things can be other than they are. A proud woman can make a lofty virtue of resignation, as did the stoical Mme de Charrière. But it also engenders a sterile prudence; women are always trying to conserve, to adapt, to arrange, rather than to destroy and build anew; they prefer compromise and adjustment to revolution.

In the nineteenth century, women were one of the greatest obstacles in the way of the effort to free the workers: for one Flora Tristan, one Louise Michel, how many timid housewives begged their husbands not to take any chances! They were not only afraid of strikes, unemployment, and poverty: they feared that revolt might be a mistake. It is easy to understand that, if they must suffer, they preferred what was familiar to adventuring, for they could achieve a meagre welfare more easily at home than in the streets.

Women's fate is bound up with that of perishable things; in losing them they lose all. Only a free subject, asserting himself as above and beyond duration of things, can check all decay; this supreme recourse has been denied to woman. The real reason why she does not believe in a liberation is that she has never put the powers of liberty to a test; the world seems to her to be ruled by an obscure destiny against which it is presumptuous to rise in protest. She has not herself marked out those dangerous roads she is asked to follow, and so it is natural enough for her not to plunge into them with enthusiasm.[3] Let the future be opened to her and she will no longer cling desperately to the past. When women are called upon for concrete action, when they recognize their interest in the designated goals, they are as bold and courageous as men.[4]

Many of the faults for which women are reproached – mediocrity, laziness, frivolity, servility – simply express the fact that their horizon is closed. It is said that woman is sensual, she wallows in immanence; but she has first been shut up in it. The harem slave feels no morbid passion for rose preserves and perfumed baths: she has to kill time. When woman suffocates in a dull gynaeceum – brothel or middle-class home – she is bound to take refuge in comfort and well-being; besides that, if she eagerly seeks sexual pleasure, it is very often because she is deprived of it. Sexually unsatisfied, doomed to male crudeness, "condemned to masculine ugliness", she finds consolation in creamy sauces, heady wines, velvets, the caress of water, of sunshine, of a woman friend, of a young lover. If she seems to man so "physical" a creature, it is because her situation leads her to attach extreme importance to her animal nature. The call of the flesh is no louder in her than in the male, but she catches its least murmurs and amplifies them. Sexual pleasure, like rending pain, represents the stunning triumph of the immediate; in the violence of the instant, the future and the universe are denied; what lies outside the carnal flame is nothing; for the brief moment of this apotheosis, woman is no longer mutilated and frustrated. But, once again, she values these triumphs of immanence only because immanence is her lot.

Her frivolity has the same cause as her "sordid materialism"; she considers little things important for lack of any access to great things, and, furthermore, the futilities that fill her days are often of the most serious practical concern to her. She owes her charm and her opportunities to her dress and her beauty. She often appears to be lazy, indolent; but the occupations available to her are as empty as the pure passage of time. If she is a chatterer, a scribbler, it is to divert her idle hours: for impossible action, she substitutes words. The truth is that when a woman is engaged in an enterprise worthy of a human being, she is quite able to show herself as active, efficient, taciturn – and as ascetic – as a man.

She is accused of being servile; she is always ready, it is said, to lie down at her master's feet and kiss the hand that strikes her, and it is true that she is generally lacking in real pride. The counsel dispensed in columns of "advice to the love-lorn", to deceived wives and abandoned lovers, is full of the spirit of abject submission. Woman wears herself out in haughty scenes, and in the end gathers up the crumbs that the male cares to toss to her. But what can be done without masculine support by a woman for whom man is at once the sole means and the sole reason for living? She is bound to suffer every humiliation; a slave cannot

490

have the sense of human dignity; it is enough if a slave gets out of it with a whole skin.

And finally, if woman is earthy, commonplace, basely utilitarian, it is because she is compelled to devote her existence to cooking and washing diapers – no way to acquire a sense of grandeur! It is her duty to assure the monotonous repetition of life in all its mindless factuality. It is natural for woman to repeat, to begin again without even inventing, for time to seem to her to go round and round without ever leading anywhere. She is occupied without ever *doing* anything, and thus she identifies herself with what she *has*. This dependence on things, a consequence of the dependence in which men keep her, explains her frugality, her avarice. Her life is not directed towards ends: she is absorbed in producing or caring for things that are never more than means, such as food, clothing, and shelter. These things are inessential intermediaries between animal life and free existence. The sole value that appertains to the inessential means is utility; it is at the level of utility that the housekeeper lives, and she does not flatter herself that she is anything more than a person useful to her kindred.

But no existent can be satisfied with an inessential role, for that immediately makes means into ends – as may be observed, for example, in politicians – and the value of the means comes to seem an absolute value. Thus utility reigns in the housekeeper's heaven, above truth, beauty, liberty; and it is in this perspective that she envisages the entire universe. This is why she adopts the Aristotelian morality of the golden mean – that is, of mediocrity. How could one expect her to show audacity, ardour, disinterestedness, grandeur? These qualities appear only when a free being strikes forward through an open future, emerging far beyond all given actuality. Woman is shut up in a kitchen or in a boudoir, and astonishment is expressed that her horizon is limited. Her wings are clipped, and it is found deplorable that she cannot fly. Let but the future be opened to her, and she will no longer be compelled to linger in the present.

The same inconsistency is displayed when, after being enclosed within the limits of her ego or her household, she is reproached for her narcissism, her egotism, with all their train: vanity, touchiness, malice, and so on. She is deprived of all possibility of concrete communication with others; she does not experience either the appeal or the benefits of solidarity, since she is consecrated entirely to her own family, in isolation. She could hardly be expected, then, to transcend herself towards the general welfare. She stays obstinately within the one realm that is familiar to her, where she can control things and in the midst of which she enjoys a precarious sovereignty.

Lock the doors and close the shutters as she will, however, woman fails to find complete security in her home. It is surrounded by that masculine universe which she respects from afar, without daring to venture into it. And precisely because she is incapable of grasping it through technical skill, sound logic, and definite knowledge, she feels, like the child and the savage, that she is surrounded by dangerous mysteries. She projects her magical conception of reality into that male world; the course of events seems to her to be inevitable, and yet anything can happen; she does not clearly distinguish between the possible and the impossible and is ready to believe anything, no matter what. She listens to and spreads rumours and starts panics. Even when things are quiet, she feels anxious; lying half asleep at night, her rest is disturbed by the nightmare shapes that reality assumes; and thus for woman condemned to passivity, the inscrutable future is haunted by phantoms of war, revolution, famine, poverty; being unable to act, she worries. Her husband, her son, when undertaking an enterprise or facing an emergency, run their own risks; their plans, the regulations they follow, indicate a sure road through obscurity. But woman flounders in confusion and darkness; she gets used to it because she does nothing; in her imagination all possibilities have equal reality: the train may be derailed, the operation may go wrong, the business may fail. What she is endeavouring to exercise in her gloomy ruminations is the spectre of her own powerlessness.

Her anxiety is the expression of her distrust of the world as given; if it seems threatening, ready to collapse, this is because she is unhappy in it. For most of the time she is not resigned to being resigned; she knows very well that she suffers as she does against her will: she is a woman without having been consulted in the matter. She dares not revolt; she submits unwillingly; her attitude is one of constant reproach. All those in whom women confide – doctors, priests, social workers – know that the usual tone is one of complaint. Among friends, woman groans over her own troubles, and they all complain in chorus about the injustice of fate, the world, and men in general.

A free individual blames only himself for his failures, he assumes responsibility for them; but everything happens to woman through the agency of others, and therefore these others are responsible for her woes. Her mad despair spurns all remedies; it does not help matters to propose solutions to a woman bent on complaining: she finds none acceptable. She insists on living in her situation precisely as she does – that is, in a state of impotent rage. If some change is proposed she throws up her hands: "That's the last straw!" She knows that her trouble goes deeper than is indicated by the pretexts she advances for it, and she is aware that it will take more than some expedient to deliver her from it. She holds the entire world responsible because it has been made without her, and against her; she has been protesting against her condition since her adolescence, ever since her childhood. She has been promised compensations, she has been assured that if she would place her fortune in man's hands, it would be returned a hundredfold – and she feels she has been swindled. She puts the whole masculine universe under indictment. Resentment is the reverse side of dependence: when one gives all, one never receives enough in return.

Woman is obliged also, however, to regard the male universe with some respect; she would feel in danger without a roof over her head, if she were in total opposition; so she adopts the Manichaeist position – the clear separation of good and evil – which is also suggested by her experience as a housekeeper. The individual who acts considers himself, like others, as responsible for both evil and good, he knows that it is for him to define ends, to bring them to success; he becomes aware, in action, of the ambiguousness of all solutions; justice and injustice, gains and losses, are inextricably mixed. But anyone who is passive is out of the game and declines to pose ethical problems even in thought: the good *should* be realized, and if it is not, there must be some wrong-doing for which those to blame must be punished. Like the child, woman conceives good and evil in simple images, as co-existing, discrete entities; this Manichaeism of hers sets her mind at rest by doing away with the anxiety of making difficult choices. To decide between an evil and a lesser evil, between a present good and a greater good to come, to have to define for herself what is defeat and what is victory – all this involves terrible risks. For the Manichaeist, the good wheat is clearly distinct from the tares, and one has merely to remove the tares; dust stands self-condemned and cleanliness is complete absence of dirt; to clean house is to remove dirt and rubbish.

Thus woman thinks that "it is all the Jews' fault", or the Freemasons' or the Bolsheviks', or the government's; she is always *against* someone or something. They do not always know just where the evil principle may lie, but what they expect of a "good government" is to sweep it out as they sweep dust out of the house.

But these hopes are always for the uncertain future; in the mean time evil continues to corrode the good; and since she cannot get her hands on the Jews, the Freemasons, the Bolsheviks, the woman looks about for someone responsible against whom her indignation can find concrete expression. Her husband is the favourite victim. He embodies the masculine universe, through him male society has taken charge of her and swindled her. He bears the weight of the world, and if things go wrong, it is his fault. When he comes in at night, she complains to him about the children, the shopkeepers, the cost of living, her rheumatism, the wea-ther – and wants him to feel to blame. She often entertains special grievances against him; but he is guilty in the first place of being a man. He may very well have maladies and cares of his own – "that's different" – but he holds a privilege which she constantly feels as an injustice. It is a remarkable thing that the hostility she feels towards her husband or lover attaches her to him instead of alienating her from him. A man who has begun to detest wife or mistress tries to get away from her; but woman wants to have the man she hates close at hand so she can make him pay. Recrimination is not a way to get rid of her ills but to wallow in them; the wife's supreme consolation is to pose as a martyr. Life, men, have conquered her: she will turn defeat itself into victory. This explains why she will cheerfully abandon herself to frantic tears and scenes, as in her childhood.

Certainly woman's aptitude for facile tears comes largely from the fact that her life is built upon a foundation of impotent revolt; it is also doubtless true that physiologically she has less nervous control than man and that her education has taught her to let herself go more readily. This effect of education, or custom, is indeed evident, since in the past men like Benjamin Constant and Diderot, for instance, used to pour out floods of tears, and then men ceased weeping when it became unfashionable for them. But, above all, the fact is that woman is always prepared to take an attitude of frustration towards the world because she has never frankly accepted it. A man does accept the world; not even misfortune will change his attitude, he will face it, he will not let himself "give up"; whereas it takes only a little trouble to remind a woman of the hostility of the universe and the injustice of her lot. Then she hastily retires to her surest refuge: herself. These warm traces on her cheeks, these reddened eyes, what are they but the visible presence of her grief-stricken soul? Cool to her skin, scarcely salty on her tongue, tears are also a gentle if bitter caress; her face burns under the merciful flow. Tears are at once plaint and consolation, fever and cooling appeasement. Tears are woman's supreme alibi; sudden as a squall, loosed by fits and starts, typhoon, April shower, they make woman into a plaintive fountain, a stormy sky. Her eyes are blinded, misty; unseeing, they melt in rain; sightless, she returns to the passivity of natural things. One wants her conquered, but she founders in her defeat; she sinks like a stone, she drowns, she eludes the man who is contemplating her, powerless as before a cataract. He considers this performance unfair; but she considers the struggle unfair from the start, because no other effective weapon has been put in her hands. She is resorting once more to a magic conjuration. And the fact that her sobs infuriate the male is one more reason for sobbing.

Whenever tears are insufficient to express her revolt, she will make scenes of such incoherent violence as to abash a man still more. In some circles a husband may strike his wife actual blows; in others he declines to use violence precisely because he is the stronger and his fist is an effective weapon. But a woman, like a child, indulges in symbolic outbursts: she can throw herself on a man, beating and scratching, but it is only a gesture. Yet above all she is engaged in expressing, through the pantomime of the nervous crisis, the insubordination she is unable to carry out in actuality. There are other than physiological reasons for her susceptibility to convulsive manifestations: a convulsion is an interiorization of energy which, when directed outward into the environment, fails to act there on any object; it is an aimless discharge of all the negative forces set up by the situation. The mother rarely has nervous crises with her young children, because she can punish them, strike them; it is rather with her grown son, her husband, or her lover, over whom she has no real power, that woman gives way to her furious tantrums. Mme Tolstoy's hysterical scenes are significant; no doubt she did very wrong in never trying to understand her husband, and in the light of her diary she seems ungenerous, insensitive, and insincere, far from an engaging figure. But whether she was right or wrong in no way changes the horror of her situation. All her life she did nothing but bear up, amid constant reproaches, under marital embraces, maternities, solitude, and the mode of life imposed by her husband. When new decrees of Tolstoy's heightened the conflict, she was unarmed against his inimical will, which she opposed with all her powerless will; she burst out in theatrics of refusal – feigned suicides, feigned flights, feigned maladies, and the like – which were disagreeable to those about her and wearing for herself. It is hard to see that any other outcome was possible for her, since she had no positive reason to conceal her feelings of revolt, and no effective way of expressing them.

There is a way out that is open to the woman who has reached the end of her resistance – it is suicide. But it seems less often resorted to by women than by men. Here the statistics are very ambiguous.[5] Successful suicides are much more common in men than in women, but attempts to end their lives are commoner in the latter. This may be so because women are more likely to be satisfied with play-acting: they *pretend* self-destruction more often than they really *want* it. It is also, in part, because the usual brutal methods are repellent: women almost never use cold steel or firearms. They are much more likely to drown themselves, like Ophelia, attesting the affinity of woman with water, where, in the still darkness, it seems that life might find passive dissolution. In general we see here again the ambiguity I have already signalized: what woman detests she does not honestly try to renounce. She plays at breaking off but in the end remains with the man who is the cause of her woes; she pretends to quit the life which hurts her, but it is relatively rare for her to succeed in killing herself. She has no taste for definitive solutions. She protests against man, against life, against her situation, but she does not make good her escape from them.

There are many aspects of feminine behaviour that should be interpreted as forms of protest. We have seen that a woman often deceives her husband through defiance and not for pleasure; and she may be purposely careless and extravagant because he is methodical and economical. Misogynists who accuse woman of always being late think she lacks a sense of punctuality; but as we have seen, the fact is that she can adjust herself very well to the demands of time. When she is late, she has deliberately planned to be. Some coquettish women think they stimulate the man's desire in this way and make their presence the more highly appreciated; but in making the man wait a few minutes, the woman is above all protesting against that long wait: her life.

In a sense her whole existence is waiting, since she is confined in the limbo of immanence and contingence, and since her justification is always in the hands of others. She awaits the homage, the approval of men, she awaits love, she awaits the gratitude and praise of her husband or her lover. She awaits her support, which comes from man; whether she keeps the cheque-book or merely gets a weekly or monthly allowance from her husband, it is necessary for him to have drawn his pay or obtained that rise if she is to be able to pay the grocer or buy a new dress. She waits for man to put in an appearance, since her economic dependence places her at his disposal; she is only one element in masculine life while man is her whole existence. The husband has his occupations outside the home, and the wife has to put up with his absence all day long; the lover – passionate as he may be – is the one who decides on their meetings and separations in accordance with his obligations. In bed, she awaits the male's desire, she awaits – sometimes anxiously – her own pleasure.

All she can do is arrive later at the rendezvous her lover has set, not be ready at the time designated by her husband; in that way she asserts the importance of her own occupations, she insists on her independence; and for the moment she becomes the essential subject to whose will the other passively submits. But these are timid attempts at revenge; however persistent she may be in keeping men waiting, she will never compensate for the interminable hours she has spent in watching and hoping, in awaiting the good pleasure of the male.

Woman is bound in a general way to contest foot by foot the rule of man, though recognizing his over-all supremacy and worshipping his idols. Hence that famous "contrariness" for which she has often been reproached. Having no independent domain, she cannot oppose positive truths and values of her own to those asserted and upheld by males; she can only deny them. Her negation is more or less thorough-going, according to the way respect and resentment are proportioned in her nature. But in fact she knows all the faults in the masculine system, and she has no hesitation in exposing them.

Women have no grasp on the world of men because their experience does not teach them to use logic and technique; inversely, masculine apparatus loses its power at the frontiers of the feminine realm. There is a whole region of human experience which the male deliberately chooses to ignore because he fails to *think* it: this experience woman *lives*. The engineer, so precise when he is laying out his diagrams, behaves at home like a minor god: a word, and behold, his meal is served, his shirts ironed, his children quieted; procreation is an act as swift as the wave of Moses' wand; he sees nothing astounding in these miracles. The concept of the miracle is different from the idea of magic: it presents, in the midst of a world of rational causation, the radical discontinuity of an event without cause, against which the weapons of thought are shattered; whereas magical phenomena are unified by hidden forces the continuity of which can be accepted – without being understood – by a docile mind. The newborn child is miraculous to the paternal minor god, magical for the mother who has experienced its coming to term within her womb. The experience of the man is intelligible but interrupted by blanks; that of the woman is, within its own limits, mysterious and obscure but complete. This obscurity makes her weighty; in his relations with her, the male seems light: he has the lightness of dictators, generals, judges, bureaucrats, codes of law, and abstract principles. This is doubtless what a housekeeper meant when she said, shrugging her shoulders: "Men, they don't think!" Women say, also: "Men, they don't know, they don't know life." To the myth of the praying mantis, women contrast the symbol of the frivolous and obtrusive drone bee.

It is understandable, in this perspective, that woman takes exception to masculine logic. Not only is it inapplicable to her experience, but in his hands, as she knows, masculine reasoning becomes an underhand form of force; men's undebatable pronouncements are intended to confuse her. The intention is to put her in a dilemma: either you agree or you do not. Out of respect for the whole system of accepted principles she should agree; if she refuses, she rejects the entire system. But she cannot venture to go so far; the lacks the means to reconstruct society in different form. Still, she does not accept it as it is. Half way between revolt and slavery, she resigns herself reluctantly to masculine authority. On each occasion he has to force her to accept the consequences of her half-hearted yielding. Man pursues that chimera, a companion half slave, half free: in yielding to him, he would have her yield to the convincingness of an argument, but she knows that he has himself chosen the premises on which his rigorous deductions depend. As long as she avoids questioning them, he will easily reduce her to silence; nevertheless he will not convince her, for she senses his arbitrariness. And so, annoyed, he will accuse her of being obstinate and illogical; but she refuses to play the game because she knows the dice are loaded.

Woman does not entertain the positive belief that the truth is something *other* than men claim; she recognizes, rather, that there *is not* any fixed truth. It is not only the changing nature of life that makes her suspicious of the principle of constant identity, nor is it the magic phenomena with which she is surrounded that destroy the notion of causality. It is at the heart of the masculine world itself, it is in herself as belonging to this world that she comes upon the ambiguity of all principle, of all value, of everything that exists. She knows that masculine morality, as it concerns her, is a vast hoax. Man pompously thunders forth his code of virtue and honour; but in secret he invites her to disobey it, and he even counts on this disobedience; without it, all that splendid façade behind which he takes cover would collapse.

Man gladly accepts as his authority Hegel's idea according to which the citizen acquires his ethical dignity in transcending himself towards the universal, but as a private individual he has a right to desire and pleasure. His relations with woman, then, lie in a contingent region, where morality no longer applies, where conduct is a matter of indifference. With other men he has relations in which values are involved; he is a free agent confronting other free agents under laws fully recognized by all; but with woman – she was invented for this purpose – he casts off the responsibility of existence, he abandons himself to the mirage of his *en-soi*, or fixed, lower nature, he puts himself on the plane of inauthenticity. He shows himself tyrannical, sadistic, violent, or puerile, masochistic, querulous; he tries to satisfy his obsessions and whims; he is "at ease", he "relaxes", in view of the rights acquired in his public life.

His wife is often astonished at the contrast between the lofty tone of his public utterances and behaviour, and "his persevering inventions in the dark". He preaches the higher birth rate, but he is skilful at begetting no more children than suits his convenience. He lauds chaste and faithful wives, but he asks his neighbour's wife to commit adultery. We have seen how hypocritically men decree that abortion is criminal, when each year in France a million women are put by men in a position to need abortion; often enough the husband or lover demands this solution; often, too, they assume tacitly that it will be adopted if necessary. They count openly on the woman's willingness to make herself guilty of a crime: her "immorality" is necessary to the harmony of the moral society respected by men.

The most flagrant example of this duplicity is the male's attitude towards prostitution, for it is his demand that creates the supply. I have noted with what disgusted scepticism prostitutes regard the respectable gentlemen who condemn vice in general but view their own personal whims with indulgence; yet they regard the girls who live off their bodies as perverted and debauched, not the males who use them. An anecdote will serve to illustrate this state of mind. At the turn of the century the police found two little girls of twelve and thirteen in a brothel; testifying at the trial, the girls referred to their clients, who were men of importance, and one of the girls was about to give a name. The judge stopped her at once: "*You must not befoul the name of a respectable man!*" A gentleman decorated by the Legion of Honour is still a respectable man when deflowering a little girl; he has his weaknesses, as who does not? Whereas the little girl who has no aspirations towards the ethical realm of the universal – who is not a magistrate, or a general, or a great Frenchman, nothing but a little girl – stakes her moral value in the contingent realm of sexuality: she is perverse, corrupted, vicious, fit only for the reformatory.

In many cases man, without besmirching his lofty image, can perpetrate with woman's connivance actions that for her are infamous. She does not understand these subtleties very well; what she does comprehend is that man does not act according to the principles he professes and asks her to disobey them; he does not wish what he says he wishes. So she does not give him what she pretends to give him. She is to be a chaste and faithful wife – and on the sly she will yield to his desires; she is to be an admirable mother – but she will carefully practise birth control and will have an abortion if necessary. Man disapproves of her officially – it's the rule of the game – but he is secretly grateful for her "easy virtue", for her sterility.

Woman plays the part of those secret agents who are left to the firing squad if they get caught, and are loaded with rewards if they succeed; it is for her to shoulder all man's immorality: not the prostitute only, but all women who serve as sewer to the shining, wholesome edifice where respectable people have their abode. When, thereupon, to these women one speaks of dignity, honour, loyalty, of all the lofty masculine virtues, it is not astonishing if they decline to "go along". They laugh in derision particularly when the virtuous males have just reproached them for not being disinterested, for play-acting, for lying.[6] They well know that no other way out is open to them. Man, too, is not "disinterested" regarding money and success, but he has the means for attaining them in his work. Woman has been assigned the role of parasite – and every parasite is an exploiter. Woman has need of the male in order to gain human dignity, to eat, to enjoy life, to procreate; it is through the service of sex that she gets these benefits; because she is confined to that function, she is wholly an instrumentality of exploitation.

As for lying, except in the case of prostitution, there is no question of a frank business deal between her and her protector. Man even demands play-acting: he wants her to be the *Other*; but all existents remain subjects, try as they will to deny themselves. Man wants woman to be object: she *makes* herself object; at the very moment when she does that, she is exercising a free activity. Therein is her original treason; the most docile, the most passive, is still a conscious being; and sometimes the fact that in giving herself to him she looks at him and judges him is enough to make him feel duped; she is supposed to be only something offered, no more than prey. He also demands, however, that this "thing" give herself over to him of her own free will: in bed he asks her to feel pleasure; in the home she must sincerely recognize his superiority and his merits. She is, then, to feign independence at the moment of obedience, although at other moments she actively plays the comedy of being passive. She lies to hold the man who provides her daily bread; there are scenes and tears, transports of love, crises of nerves – all false – and she lies also to escape from the tyranny she accepts through self-interest. He encourages her in make-believe that flatters his lordliness and his vanity; and she uses against him in return her powers of dissimulation. Thus she gains revenge that is doubly sweet, for in deceiving him she satisfies her own desires and enjoys the pleasure of treating him with derision. The wife and the courtesan lie when they feign transports they do not feel; afterwards, with lovers or woman friends, they make fun of the naïve vanity of their dupes. "They not only bungle things, but they expect us to wear ourselves out showing pleasure," they say resentfully.

Such conversations are very like those of domestics talking over their employers critically in the servants' quarters. Woman has the same faults because she is a victim of the same paternalistic oppression; she has the same cynicism because she sees man from top to toe, as a valet sees his master. But it is clear that none of woman's traits manifest an originally perverted essence or will: they reflect a situation. "There is dissimulation everywhere under a coercive régime," says Fourier. "Prohibition and contraband are inseparable in love as in trade." And men know that woman's faults indicate her situation so well that, anxious to maintain the hierarchy of sexes, they encourage in their companions the very traits that merit their contempt. No doubt the husband or lover is irritated by the faults of the particular woman he lives with, and yet when they extol the charms of femininity in general, they believe it to be inseparable from its defects. If woman is not faithless, futile, cowardly, indolent, she loses her seductiveness.

In Ibsen's *A Doll's House*, Helmer explains how strong, just, understanding, indulgent, a man feels when he pardons frail woman her childish faults. And similarly the husbands in Bernstein's plays are moved to tears – with the collusion of the author – over the thieving, malicious, adulterous wife; bending over her solicitously, they display in contrast their own virile goodness. American racists and French colonials, as we have seen, similarly want the black man to be thievish, lazy, lying: this proves his unworthiness; it puts right on the side of the oppressors; if he insists on being honest and loyal, he is regarded as a "bad actor". Woman's faults, then, are magnified the more in that she will not try to combat them but, on the contrary, will make an ornament of them.

Not accepting logical principles and moral imperatives, sceptical about the laws of nature, woman lacks the sense of the universal; to her the world seems a confused conglomeration of special cases. This explains why she believes more readily in the tittle-tattle of a neighbour than in a scientific explanation. No doubt she respects the printed book, but she respectfully skims the pages of type without getting at the meaning; on the contrary, the anecdote told by some unknown in a queue or drawing-room at once takes on an overwhelming authority. Within her sphere all is magic; outside, all is mystery. She is unfamiliar with the criterion of plausibility; only immediate experience carries conviction – her own experience, or that of others if stated emphatically enough. As for her own self, she feels she is a special case because she is isolated in her home and hence does not come into active contact with other women; she is always expecting that destiny and men will make an exception in her favour. She believes in her intuitions much more firmly than in universally valid reasoning; she readily admits that they come from God or from some vague world-spirit; regarding some misfortune or accident she calmly thinks: "That will not happen to me." Regarding benefits, on the other hand, she imagines that "an exception will be made in my case": she rather expects special favours. The shopkeeper will give her a discount, the policeman will let her through without a pass; she has been taught to overestimate the value of her smile, and no one has told her that all women smile. It is not that she thinks herself more extraordinary than her neighbour; she does not make the comparison. And for the same reason experience rarely shows her how wrong she is: she meets with one failure after another, but she does not sum them up in a valid conclusion.

This shows why women do not succeed in building up a solid counter-universe whence they can challenge the males; now and then they rail at men in general, they tell what happens in the bedroom or at childbirth, they exchange horoscopes and beauty secrets. But they lack the conviction necessary to build this grievance-world their resentment calls for; their attitude towards man is too ambivalent. Doubtless he is a child, a necessitous and vulnerable body, he is a simpleton, a bothersome drone, a mean tyrant, a vain egotist; but he is also the liberating hero, the divinity who bestows values. His desire is gross appetite, his embrace a degrading duty; yet his fire and virile force seem like demiurgic power. When a woman says ecstatically: "He is a man!" she evokes at once the sexual vigour and the social effectiveness of the man she admires. In both he displays the same creative superiority; she does not conceive of his being a great artist, a great man of business, a general, a leader, without being a potent lover, and thus his social successes always have a sexual attractiveness; inversely, she is quick to see genius in the man who satisfies her desires.

We must add that in this she is returning to one of the masculine myths. For Lawrence, as for many others, the phallus represents both living energy and human transcendence. Thus woman can see in the pleasures of the couch a communion with the spirit of the world. In mystical worship of man she is lost and also finds herself again in her glory. The contradiction is easily explained, thanks to the variety of sexually potent individuals. Some of them – whose ineffectual contingence she knows in everyday life – are the embodiment of human paltriness; in others man's grandeur reaches its summit. But woman can even countenance the confusing of these two figures in one. "If I become famous," writes a young girl in love with a man she considers superior, "R. will surely marry me, for his vanity will be flattered; he would swell with pride, out walking with me on his arm." Yet she admired him madly. In a woman's eyes the same person may very well be stingy, mean, vain, ridiculous, and a god; after all, the gods have their weaknesses. An individual who is loved as a free being, in his humanity, is regarded with that critical, demanding severity which is the other side of genuine esteem; whereas a woman submissively kneeling before her male can very well pride herself on knowing how to "manage", to "handle" him; she complaisantly flatters his "weak side" without his losing prestige. This is proof that she does not care for his individual personality as it finds expression in actual activity; she is bowing down blindly before the generalized essence in which her idol shares. Virility is a sacred aura, a given, set value that makes itself felt in spite of the pettinesses of the individual who carries it; he does not count; on the contrary, the woman, jealous of his privileged status, finds pleasure in assuming a malicious superiority over him in various respects.

The ambiguity of woman's feelings towards man is found again in her general attitude towards herself and the world. The domain in which she is confined is surrounded by the masculine universe, but it is haunted by obscure forces of which men are themselves the play-things; if she allies herself with these magical forces, she will come to power in her turn. Society enslaves Nature; but Nature dominates it. The Spirit flames out beyond Life; but it ceases to burn when life no longer supports it. Woman is justified by this equivocation in finding more verity in a garden than in a city, in a malady than in an idea, in a birth than in a revolution; she endeavours to re-establish that reign of the earth, of the Mother, dreamed by Bachofen,[7] in order to become again the essential in face of the inessential. But as she, also, is an existent having transcendence, she can give value to that domain where she is confined only by transfiguring it: she lends it a transcendent dimension. Man lives in a consistent universe that is a reality conceivable in thought. Woman is at grips with a magical reality that defies thought, and she escapes from it through thoughts without real content. Instead of taking up her existence, she contemplates in the clouds the pure Idea of her destiny; instead of acting, she sets up her own image in the realm of imagination: that is, instead of reasoning, she dreams. Hence the fact that while being "physical", she is also artificial, and while being earthy, she makes herself ethereal. Her life is passed in washing pots and pans, and it is a glittering novel; man's vassal, she thinks she is his idol; carnally humiliated, she is all for Love. Because she is condemned to know only the factual contingence of life, she makes herself priestess of the Ideal.

This ambivalence is evident in the way woman regards her body. It is a burden: worn away in service to the species, bleeding each month, proliferating passively, it is not for her a pure instrument for getting a grip on the world but an opaque physical presence; it is no certain source of pleasure and it creates lacerating pains; it contains menaces: woman feels endangered by her "insides". It is a "hysteric" body, on account of the close connection of the endocrine secretions with the nervous and sympathetic systems that control the muscles and the viscera. Her body displays reactions for which the woman denies responsibility; in sobs, vomiting, convulsions, it escapes her control, it betrays her; it is her most intimate verity, but it is a shameful verity that she keeps hidden. And yet it is also her glorious double; she is dazzled in beholding it in the mirror; it is promised happiness, work of art, living statue; she shapes it, adorns it, puts it on show. When she smiles at herself in the glass, she forgets her carnal contingence; in the embrace of love, in maternity, her image is destroyed. But often, as she muses on herself, she is astonished to be at one and the same time that heroine and that flesh.

Nature similarly presents a double face to her, supplying the kitchen and stimulating mystical effusions. When she became a housekeeper and a mother, woman renounced her free roaming of field and wood, she preferred the quiet cultivation of her kitchen garden, she tamed the flowers and put them in vases: yet she is still entranced with moonlight and sunset. In the terrestrial fauna and flora she sees food and ornament before all; but in them a sap circulates which is nobility and magic. Life is not merely immanence and repetition: it has also a dazzling face of light; in flowery meadows it is revealed as Beauty. Attuned to nature by the fertility of her womb, woman is also swept by its animating breeze, which is spirit. And to the extent that she remains unsatisfied and, like the young girl, feels unfulfilled and unlimited, her soul, too, will be lost to sight down roads stretching endlessly on, towards unbounded horizons. Enslaved as she is to her husband, her children, her home, it is ecstasy to find herself alone, sovereign on the hillsides; she is no longer mother, wife, housekeeper, but a human being; she contemplates the passive world, and she remembers that she is wholly a conscious being, an irreducible free individual. Before the mystery of water and the leap of mountain peaks, the male's supremacy fades away. Walking through the heather, dipping her hand in the stream, she is living not for others, but for herself. Any woman who has preserved her independence through all her servitudes will ardently love her own freedom in Nature. Others will find there only pretexts for refined raptures; and they will hesitate at twilight between the danger of catching cold and an ecstasy of the soul.

This double allegiance to the carnal world and to a world of "poetry" defines the metaphysics, the wisdom, to which woman more or less explicitly adheres. She endeavours to combine life and transcendence, which is to say that she rejects Cartesianism, with its formal logic, and all related doctrines. She is at home in a naturalism like that of the Stoics or the Neoplatonists of the sixteenth century. It is not surprising that women, headed by Marguerite of Navarre, should accept a philosophy at once so material and so spiritual. Socially Manichaeistic, as we have seen, woman has a profound need to be ontologically optimistic – she must believe that the nature of things tends on the whole to be good. The moralities of action do not suit her, for she is not allowed to act; she is therefore subject to the given: and the given, then, must be the Good; but a good which, like that of Spinoza, is recognized by reasoning, or, like that of Leibniz, by calculation, cannot concern her.

She craves a good that is a living Harmony in the midst of which she is placed simply by virtue of being alive. The concept of harmony is one of the keys to the feminine universe; it implies a stationary perfection, the immediate justification of each element depending on the whole and on its passive participation in the totality. In a harmonious world woman thus attains what man will seek through action: she meshes with the world, she is necessary to it, she cooperates in the triumph of the Good. The moments that women regard as revelations are those in which they discover their accord with a static and self-sufficient reality: those luminous moments of happiness which Virginia Woolf (in *Mrs Dalloway* and *To the Lighthouse*) and Katherine Mansfield (throughout her work) bestow upon their heroines by way of supreme recompense. The joy that lies in the free surge of liberty is reserved for man; that which woman knows is a quiet sense of smiling plenitude. It is understandable that a mere state of tranquillity can take high value in her eyes, since woman normally lives in the tension of denial, resentment, exaction; and she cannot be reproached for enjoying a fine afternoon or a cool evening. But it is a delusion to seek the hidden soul of the world here. The Good cannot be considered something that *is*: the world is not harmony, and no individual has an essential place in it.

There is a justification, a supreme compensation, which society is ever wont to bestow upon woman: that is, religion. There must be a religion for woman as there must be one for the common people, and for exactly the same reasons. When a sex or a class is condemned to immanence, it is necessary to offer it the mirage of some form of transcendence. Man enjoys the great advantage of having a God endorse the codes he writes; and since man exercises a sovereign authority over woman, it is especially fortunate that this authority has been vested in him by the Supreme Being. For the Jews, Mohammedans, and Christians, among others, man is master by divine right; the fear of God, therefore, will repress any impulse towards revolt in the downtrodden female. One can bank on her credulity. Woman takes an attitude of respect and faith towards the masculine universe: God in His heaven seems to her hardly less remote than a cabinet minister, and the mystery of creation is approached by that of the electric powerhouse. But if woman quite willingly embraces religion, it is above all because it fills a profound need.

In modern civilization, which – even for woman – has a share in promoting freedom, religion seems much less an instrument of constraint than an instrument of deception. Woman is asked in the name of God not so much to accept her inferiority as to believe that, thanks to Him, she is the equal of the lordly male; even the temptation to revolt is suppressed by the claim that the injustice is over-come. Woman is no longer denied transcendence, since she is to consecrate her immanence to God; the worth of souls is to be weighed only in heaven and not according to their accomplishments on earth. As Dostoyevsky says, here below it is just a matter of different occupations: shining shoes or building a bridge, all alike is vanity; above and beyond social discriminations, the equality of the sexes is restored. This is why the little girl and the adolescent are much more fervent devotees than their brothers; the eye of God, which transcends the boy's tran-scendence, humiliates him: under this mighty guardianship he will remain a child for ever; it is a more radical castration than that threatened by his father's exist-ence. But the "eternal child", if female, finds her salvation in this eye that trans-forms her into a sister of the angels. It cancels the advantage of the penis. A sincere faith is a great help to the little girl in avoiding an inferiority complex: she is neither male nor female, but God's creature.

Hence it is that we find a quite masculine firmness in many of the great female saints: St Bridget, St Catherine of Siena, arrogantly claim to lord it over the world; they recognize no masculine authority whatever. Catherine very severely directed even her spiritual directors; Joan of Arc and St Theresa went their appointed ways with an intrepidity unsurpassed by any man. The Church sees to it that God never authorizes women to escape male guardianship; she has put exclusively in man's hands such powerful weapons as denial of absolution and excommunication; obstinately true to her visions, Joan of Arc was burned at the stake.

Although subordinated to the law of men by the will of God Himself, woman none the less finds in Him a mighty refuge from them. Masculine logic is confuted by holy mysteries; men's pride becomes a sin, their agitation for this and that is more than absurd, it is blame-worthy: why remodel this world which God Himself created? The passivity enforced upon woman is sanctified. Telling her beads by the fire, she knows she is nearer heaven than is her husband gadding about to political meetings. There is no need to do anything to save her soul, it is enough to *live* in obedience. The synthesis of life and spirit is accomplished: a mother not only engenders the flesh, she produces a soul for God; and this is a greater work than penetrating the futile secrets of the atom. With the heavenly Father's connivance, woman can boldly lay claim to the glory of her femininity in defiance of man.

Thus God not alone restores the feminine sex in general to its place of dignity; but each woman will find in the heavenly absent One a special support. As a human person she has little influence, but once she acts in the name of divine inspiration, her wishes become sacred. Mme Guyon[8] says she learned, in connection with a nun's illness, "what it is to command by the Word and to obey by the same Word"; thus the devotee disguises her authority in humble obedience. When she is bringing up her children, governing a convent, organizing a charitable society, she is only a humble tool in supernatural hands; she cannot be disobeyed without offending God Himself. Men, to be sure, do not disdain this support; but it is not too reliable when they are dealing with other men, who can claim it equally well: the conflict is so arranged as to reach a decision on the human level. Woman invokes the divine will to justify her authority absolutely in the eyes of those naturally subordinated to her already and to justify it in her own eyes. If she finds this co-operation of real use, it is because she is occupied above all by her relations with herself – even when these relations affect others; for the supreme Silence can have the force of law in these wholly inward debates alone.

The fact is that woman makes religion a pretext for satisfying her own desires. Is she frigid, masochistic, sadistic? She finds holiness in renouncing the flesh, in playing the martyr, in crushing every living impulse around her. By mutilating, annihilating herself, she rises several degrees in the hierarchy of the elect; when she martyrizes husband and children, denying them all worldly happiness, she is preparing for them a choice place in paradise. According to her pious biographer, Margaret of Cortona maltreated the offspring of her fault "to punish herself for having sinned"; she fed him only after feeding all the vagrant beggars. As we have seen, hatred of the unwanted child is common: it is a godsend – literally – to be able to give way to it with righteous anger. For her part, the woman of easy virtue easily arranges things with God; the assurance of obtaining absolution for her sins tomorrow often helps the pious woman conquer her scruples today.

Whether she has chosen asceticism or sensuality, pride or humility, the concern she feels for her salvation leads her to yield to that pleasure which she prefers to all others; namely, being occupied with herself. She listens to her heartbeats, she notes the thrills of her flesh, justified by the presence of God's grace within her as is the pregnant woman by that of her fruit. Not only does she scrutinize herself with fond vigilance, but she reports on herself to her confessor; in former times she could even savour the ecstasy of public confession. They tell of that same Margaret of Cortona that, *to punish herself for a moment of vanity*, she stood on her terrace and began to cry out like a woman in labour: "Arise, people of Cortona, arise with candles and lanterns and come out to hear the sinner!" She rehearsed all her sins, proclaiming her woe to the stars. By this vociferous humility she satisfied that need for exhibitionism often exemplified in narcissistic women. Religion sanctions woman's self-love; it gives her the guide, father, lover, divine guardian she longs for nostalgically; it feeds her day-dreams; it fills her empty hours. But, above all, it confirms the social order, it justifies her resignation, by giving her the hope of a better future in a sexless heaven. This is why women today are still a powerful trump in the hand of the Church; it is why the Church is notably hostile to all measures likely to help in woman's emancipation. There must be religion for women; and there must be women, "true women", to perpetuate religion.

It is evident that woman's "character" – her convictions, her values, her wisdom, her morality, her tastes, her behaviour – are to be explained by her situation. The fact that transcendence is denied her keeps her as a rule from attaining the loftiest human attitudes: heroism, revolt, disinterestedness, imagination, creation; but even among the males they are none too common. There are many men who, like women, are restricted to the sphere of the intermediary and instrumental, of the inessential means. The worker escapes from it through political action expressing a will to revolution; but the men of the classes called precisely "middle" implant themselves in that sphere deliberately. Destined like women to the repetition of daily tasks, identified with ready-made values, respectful of public opinion, and seeking on earth nothing but a vague comfort, the employee, the merchant, the office worker, are in no way superior to their accompanying females. Cooking, washing, managing her house, bringing up children, woman shows more initiative and independence than the man working under orders. All day long he must obey his superiors, wear a white collar, and keep up his social standing; she can dawdle around the house in a wrapper, sing, laugh with her neighbours; she does as she pleases, takes little risks, tries to succeed in getting certain results. She lives less than her husband in an atmosphere of conventional concern for appearances.

The office universe which, among other things, Kafka has described, this universe of formalities, of absurd gestures, of purposeless behaviour, is essentially masculine. Woman gets her teeth more deeply into reality; for when the office worker has drawn up his figures, or translated boxes of sardines into money, he has nothing in his hands but abstractions. The baby fed and in his cradle, clean linen, the cooking, constitute more tangible assets; yet just because, in the concrete pursuit of these aims, she feels their contingence – and accordingly her own – it often happens that woman does not identify herself with them, and she still has something left of herself. Man's enterprises are at once projects and evasions: he lets himself be smothered by his career and his "front"; he often becomes self-important, serious. Being against man's logic and morality, woman does not fall into these traps, which Stendhal found much to his taste in her; she does not take refuge in her pride from the ambiguity of her position; she does not hide behind the mask of human dignity; she reveals her undisciplined thoughts, her emotions, her spontaneous reactions, more frankly. Thus her conversation is much less tiresome than her husband's whenever she speaks for herself and not as her lord and master's loyal "better half". He discusses what are called general ideas – that is to say, words, formulas, to be found in the columns of his paper or in technical books – she reveals a limited but concrete experience.

The well-known "feminine sensitivity" derives somewhat from myth, somewhat from make-believe; but it is also a fact that woman is more attentive than man to herself and to the world. She lives sexually in a crude masculine climate and in compensation has a liking for "nice things", which can give rise to finical affectation, but also to real delicacy. Because her sphere is limited, the objectives she does attain seem precious; not regarding them as bound up with either concepts or projects, she simply puts their splendour on display. Her wish to escape is expressed in her love of festivity: she is enchanted by the useless charm of a bouquet of flowers, a cake, a well-set table; she enjoys turning her empty leisure into a bountiful offering. Loving laughter, song, adornments, and knick-knacks, she is prepared to accept all that throbs around her: the spectacle of the street, of the sky; an invitation, an evening out, open new horizons to her. Man often declines to take part in these pleasures; when he comes into the house, the gay voices are silenced, the women of the family assume the bored and proper air he expects of them.

From the depths of her solitude, her isolation, woman gains her sense of the personal bearing of her life. The past, death, the passage of time – of these she has a more intimate experience than does man; she feels deep interest in the adventures of her heart, of her flesh, of her mind, because she knows that this is all she has on earth. And more, from the fact that she is passive, she experiences more passionately, more movingly, the reality in which she is submerged than does the individual absorbed in an ambition or a profession; she has the leisure and the inclination to abandon herself to her emotions, to study her sensations and unravel their meaning. When her imagination is not lost in empty dreams, she becomes all sympathy: she tries to understand others as individuals and to identify them with herself; with her husband or lover she is capable of making this identification complete: she makes his projects and cares hers in a way he cannot imitate.

She bestows this anxious attention upon the whole world; it seems an enigma to her, and each person, each object, can be an answer; she questions them eagerly. When she grows old, her disappointed expectation is transformed into irony and an often spicy cynicism; she declines to be fooled by man's mystifications, seeing the contingent, absurd, unnecessary inverse of the imposing structure built by the males. Her dependence forbids detachment, but from the well of her imposed self-sacrifice she sometimes draws up real generosity. She forgets herself in favour of her husband, her lover, her child; she ceases to think of herself; she is pure gift, pure offering. Being poorly adapted to man's society, she is often forced to invent her mode of behaviour on the spur of the moment; she is not fully satisfied with ready-made forms and clichés; with the best will in the world, she has a sense of misgiving about them which is nearer to authenticity than is the self-important assurance of her husband.

But she will have these advantages over the male only on condition that she rejects the deceptions he offers. In the upper classes women are eager accomplices of their masters because they stand to profit from the benefits provided. We have seen that the women of the upper middle classes and the aristocracy have always defended their class interests even more obstinately than have their husbands, not hesitating radically to sacrifice their independence as human beings. They repress all thought, all critical judgement, all spontaneous impulses; they parrot accepted opinions, they confuse with the ideal whatever the masculine code imposes on them; all genuineness is dead in their hearts and even in their faces. The housekeeper regains some independence in her work, gaining a concrete if limited experience from it; but a woman whose work is done by servants has no grip on the world; she lives in dreams and abstractions, in a vacuum. She does not understand the bearing of the ideas she professes; the words she uses in discussion have lost all their meaning. The financier, the captain of industry, sometimes even the military leader, know toil and care, they assume risks; they buy their privileges in an unfair market, but at least they pay for them in person. But their wives give nothing, do nothing, in exchange for all they get; on this account they believe in their indefeasible rights with so much the blinder faith. Their vain arrogance, their radical incapability, their obstinate ignorance, make them the most useless nonentities ever produced by the human species.

It is as absurd, then, to speak of "woman" in general as of the "eternal" man. And we understand why all comparisons are idle which purport to show that woman is superior, inferior, or equal to man, for their situations are profoundly different. If we compare these situations rather than the people in them, we see clearly that man's is far preferable; that is to say, he has many more opportunities to exercise his freedom in the world. The inevitable result is that masculine accomplishment is far superior to that of women, who are practically forbidden to *do* anything. Moreover, to compare the use which, within their limitations, men and women make of their liberty is *a priori* a meaningless attempt, since precisely what they do is use it freely. Under various forms, the snares of bad faith and the deceptions of over-seriousness – temptations not to be genuine – await the one sex as much as the other; inner liberty is complete in both. But simply from the fact that liberty in woman is still abstract and empty, she can exercise it only in revolt, which is the only road open to those who have no opportunity of doing anything constructive. They must reject the limitations of their situation and seek to open the road of the future. Resignedness is only abdication and flight, there is no other way out for woman than to work for her liberation.

This liberation must be collective, and it requires first of all that the economic evolution of woman's condition be accomplished. There have been, however, and there are many women trying to achieve individual salvation by solitary effort. They are attempting to justify their existence in the midst of their immanence – that is, to realize transcendence in immanence. It is this ultimate effort – sometimes ridiculous, often pathetic – of imprisoned woman to transform her prison into a heaven of glory, her servitude into sovereign liberty, that we shall observe in the narcissist, in the woman in love, in the mystic.

Notes

1 See Sartre's play *Les Mains sales*. "Hoederer: They need props, you understand, they are given ready-made ideas, then they believe in them as they do in God. We're the ones who make these ideas and we know how they are cooked up; we are never quite sure of being right."

2 "When the general passed through, the public consisted largely of women and children." (Newspaper report of his visit to Savoy.)

3 Compare the passage in *The Journals of André Gide*, vol. I, p. 301, translated by Justin O'Brien: "Creusa or Lot's wife; one tarries and the other looks back, which is a worse way of tarrying . . . There is no greater cry of passion than this:

And Phaedra having braved the Labyrinth with you
Would have been found with you or lost with you.

But passion blinds her; after a few steps, to tell the truth, she would have sat down, or else would have wanted to go back – or even would have made him carry her."

(The lines quoted are from the *Phèdre* of Racine. The Creusa referred to above was the first wife of Aeneas and mother of Ascanius. As related in Virgil's *Aeneid*, when Troy was taken and burned, they became separated in the confusion, Aeneas escaping and Creusa remaining in the city, to be rescued by Cybele, whose priestess she became. Lot's wife looked back at burning Sodom and was punished by being turned into a pillar of salt. [Tr.])

4 The attitude of proletarian women has changed in just this way after a century; as a particular example, during the recent strikes in mines of northern France, they gave proof of as much passion and energy as the men, demonstrating and fighting beside them.

5 See Halbwachs, *Les Causes du suicide*.

6 "All with that little air of delicacy and touch-me-not prudery, assumed in a long past of slavery, with no other means of salvation and support than that air of unintentional seductiveness biding its time." (Jules Laforgue.)

7 See reference in H. Deutsch, *Psychology of Women*, vol. I, p. 281. [Tr.]

8 French mystic of the early eighteenth century, who taught that the pure love of God is sufficient for salvation. [Tr.]

Part XII

EMMANUEL LEVINAS
The Primacy of the Other

EMMANUEL LEVINAS (1906–1995)

Introduction

Emmanuel Levinas was born in Kaunas, Lithuania in 1906. In 1923 he went to the University of Strasbourg in France to study classics, psychology and sociology, although he eventually concentrated on philosophy, focusing in particular on Bergson and Husserl. In 1928 he spent two semesters at the University of Freiburg, attending the seminars, first of Husserl, and subsequently of Heidegger. He completed his doctorate in Strasbourg in 1929. Levinas' first published book was *The Theory of Intuition in Husserl's Phenomenology* (1930). He co-translated Husserl's *Cartesian Meditations* a year later. As a French officer he was interned by the Germans during the Second World War but lost most of his family in the Holocaust. After the war he was appointed Director of *L'Ecole Normale Israélite Orientale*. He published *Existence and Existents* and *Time and the Other* in 1947, and *Discovering Existence with Husserl and Heidegger* in 1949. *Totality and Infinity* (1961) and *Otherwise than Being or Beyond Essence* (1974) are generally regarded as his greatest works. Also worthy of mention are *Ethics and Infinity* (1982) and his various lectures and commentaries on the Talmud, some of which are translated in *Nine Talmudic Readings* (1996). Levinas became Professor of Philosophy at Poitiers (1963), Paris-Nanterre (1967) and the Sorbonne (1973). He died in 1995.

Levinas was largely responsible for introducing phenomenology to French philosophy students of the 1930s. Husserl and Heidegger were constant influences on his thought, as was his fellow Jewish thinker Franz Rosenzweig. Levinas greatly admired Husserl's account of intuition, in which value is not confined to the sphere of judgements, but already present in concrete experience. At the same time he accepted Heidegger's critique of the former's transcendental idealism and theoreticism. Inspired by Rosenzweig, however, Levinas went on to reject what he regarded as Heidegger's totalising philosophy of being. The consistent thread in Levinas' work is that the Western ontological tradition up to and including Heidegger has more often than not sought to reduce the Other – where this term indicates the other person – to the same. Put more precisely, it has tried to comprehensively represent and account for Otherness through the totalising sameness of impersonal concepts and categories. For Levinas, by contrast, I encounter the Other as absolute and singular transcendence outside myself and outside all possible forms of representation and explanation. This transcendence is in his view the ground of ethics, of a fundamental and indeclinable responsibility for the Other person that precedes every ontology.

Levinas' middle and late prose is not notable for its clarity, with its elliptical, paradoxical character ensuing from his wish to avoid a rationalistic or representational terminology. Our first selection is one of his best known, and comprises the greater part of "Ethics and the Face", taken from the third section of *Totality and Infinity*. In the preceding section of this work, Levinas had contended that the human being lives initially at a level of sensibility. Here it is a centre of sensations, some of which it naturally prefers because they satisfy its needs. The satisfaction of a need is characterised chiefly by enjoyment. The human being enjoys the food and drink that it incorporates and the multifarious things that it appropriates so as to sustain and enhance its being. At the level of sensibility and enjoyment, things are there to be consumed – that is, absorbed or encompassed – by a centripetal, egoistic self. They are reducible to the sameness or homogeneity of a self-concerned individual.

"Ethics and the Face" opens with the claim that the face of the Other cannot be enveloped or encompassed like a thing. Levinas foregrounds the phenomenon of the human face because it is a unique locus of expressivity. To experience the face is to experience, not an object represented or constituted by myself and my needs, but an irreducible alterity who faces me and whose eyes look into mine. It is to be referred to a source of meanings outside the self and its own resources. Husserl had already suggested that the 'I', when taken transcendentally, is not just one more worldly being, but a unique, unrepeatable and indeclinable existent who opens up and on to the world and who escapes naturalistic categories and third-person explanations. Levinas inverts this position; the intimation of infinite transcendence or unrepeatable uniqueness is to be found, not through self-reflection following on the reduction, but precisely through the experience of the Other's face. The face of the Other is in the world, a thing among things, and yet its very expressivity breaks through or interrupts its mundane, phenomenal form. It is the epiphany of infinite transcendence, of an alterity that cannot be accounted for within the sameness of a self or genus or species.

It is the infinity given by the face, on Levinas' account, which alone maintains the non-spatial exteriority of the Other with respect to the same. And if the Other resists my constitutive grasp by overflowing my thought by that which exceeds its capacity, this resistance is presaged, he goes on to state, by the nudity or openness of his or her eyes, completely defenceless as they are of themselves alone. Devoid of qualitatively or quantifiably determinable force, resistance is nothing but an ethical injunction to not commit murder, to be responsible for the Other wherever possible. It is only the Other that one can wish to kill, since he or she is the sole existent absolutely independent of me, the sole existent with a transcendence beyond sensibility that is susceptible, not to thing-like domination, but to total annihilation. The face can indeed threaten eventual conflict, yet this is not its first epiphany – the struggle which one may have with the Other presupposes the transcendence of expression.

Levinas holds that language has its origin in the face-to-face encounter with the Other. It is not the mediation of the linguistic sign that forms signification, but the significance of the face that makes the sign-function possible. To put it another way, language does not commence as the translation of an interior and pre-existent thought into a string of signs. It is instead a response to the unforeseen expressiveness of the Other who faces and addresses me. Husserl's mistake, according to Levinas, was to make the Other who communicates into the product of my thoughts; I first constitute the Other in the independence of subjective, transcendental consciousness. Only such a prefabricated being can then come to address me. For Levinas, by contrast, humanity is already present in the Other's eyes and in his or her speech, and it is only in the responsibility evoked by it that I can discern my own human selfhood.

The subjectivist bias which is to be found in some of Husserl's work is traced by Levinas back to Descartes. But Levinas' account takes a surprising turn from here; he finds an openness to the Other – and by the same token a respect for Descartes' own Otherness – in the very heart of the latter's *cogito*. Although the Second Meditation takes consciousness to be certain of itself by itself, the Third Meditation traces the clear conditions of this certitude back to the existence of God. The divine Other furnishes me with an idea of infinity by means of which I can recognise the finitude of my own thought, for the idea of infinity is not itself an infinite idea. Descartes realises that the infinity of God cannot be thematised or made into an object. In this way he discovers a relation to a total alterity that is irreducible to interiority.

Our second selection, "Beyond Intentionality", first published in 1983, was specially composed for a collection of essays in which contemporary French philosophers set out their work in summary. Levinas elaborates some of the recurring themes in his thought, among them the claims that philosophical questions of being and meaning are opened up, not by our knowledge of the world, but in our response to the Other. For Husserl and his predecessors, the bestowal of meaning is taken as the thematisation of a particular presence; sense is bestowed on something as it becomes present to me. Perceptual presence is completed when the object is taken in hand and manipulated for my purposes. In its fullest sense, intentionality is both a pointing at something and a possessing of it. Here is found the non-metaphorical origin of the idea of truth as a conceptual grasp of things or adequation of thought and Being.

In this approach, being and meaning are equated with presence, and presence is whatever is amenable to the synthesising power of the subject; not only things but the past and future are made present as presences that were and will be, since all of them are thought together in the ideal, living present of awareness. Because the being that is external to thought is itself bound together by synthesising thought, adds Levinas, we end up with an idealism whereby the exteriority found in immanent experience is itself constituted immanently. Intentionality thus points reductively to the immanence of all exteriority. The self that grounds these representations, furthermore, is common to every person, and could just as well exist as a single consciousness.

Levinas seeks to indicate the possibility of an otherness that is irreducible to presence and anterior to any past that consciousness synthetically constitutes as a bygone present, a present upon which sense once was (and is again) bestowed centrifugally. Such an otherness is discernible, once more, in the encounter with the face. The Other's face is proximate to me because in its strangeness it immediately cuts across the distance separating our bodies. Proximity is a relation of the Same and the Other that cannot be synchronised with my own temporality. Here I can find a meaning that is beyond my intentional acts precisely in disrupting them; the ineffaceable strangeness and vulnerability of the face summons and surprises me by invoking my responsibility before any attempt to grasp it cognitively. Such a provocative proximity in the Other's resistance to the constituting self the later Levinas stresses increasingly.

The way in which the Other as stranger thrusts himself or herself upon me and invokes my responsibility is seen by Levinas as the way in which a God who would love the stranger and question me might enter the scene. In this connection he cites an old Jewish commentary on Genesis 18. Abraham asks the Eternal who has appeared not to leave but to wait for him, since it is important for him to welcome three passers-by into his tent. On Levinas' reading, the commentary suggests that there is more revelation of God in helping the travellers than in direct communication with Him – we cannot appreciate God beyond human beings so much as through them. God is a transcendent signification tied intimately to responsibility for the other person, not a presence that is reachable by philosophical argumentation.

Further reading

Levinas, Emmanuel. *Discovering Existence with Husserl*, trans. Richard Cohen and Michael Smith. Evanston, IL: Northwestern University Press, 1998.

Levinas, Emmanuel. *Ethics and Infinity*, trans. Richard Cohen. Pittsburgh, PA: Duquesne University Press, 1985.

Levinas, Emmanuel. *Otherwise than Being or Beyond Essence*, trans. Alphonso Lingis. The Hague: Martinus Nijhoff, 1981.

Levinas, Emmanuel. *The Theory of Intuition in Husserl's Phenomenology*, trans. André Orianne. Evanston, IL: Northwestern University Press, 1973.

Levinas, Emmanuel. *Time and the Other*, trans. Richard Cohen. Pittsburgh, PA: Duquesne University Press, 1987.

Levinas, Emmanuel. *Totality and Infinity. An Essay on Exteriority*, trans. Alphonso Lingis. Pittsburgh, PA: Duquesne University Press, 1969.

Bernasconi, Robert, and Critchley, Simon. Eds. *Re-Reading Levinas*. London: Athlone Press, 1991.

Davis, Colin. *Levinas: An Introduction*. Cambridge: Polity Press, 1996.

Gibbs, R. *Correlations in Rosenzweig and Levinas*. Princeton, NJ: Princeton University Press, 1992.

Llewelyn, John. *Emmanuel Levinas: The Genealogy of Ethics*. London: Routledge, 1995.

Peperzak, Adriaan. *To the Other: An Introduction to the Philosophy of Emmanuel Levinas*. West Lafayette, IN: Purdue University Press, 1993.

Wyschogrod, Edith. *Emmanuel Levinas: The Problem of Ethical Metaphysics*. The Hague: Martinus Nijhoff, 1974.

1

ETHICS AND THE FACE

1 Infinity and the face

Inasmuch as the access to beings concerns vision, it dominates those beings, exercises a power over them. A thing is *given*, offers itself to me. In gaining access to it I maintain myself within the same.

The face is present in its refusal to be contained. In this sense it cannot be comprehended, that is, encompassed. It is neither seen nor touched – for in visual or tactile sensation the identity of the I envelops the alterity of the object, which becomes precisely a content.

The Other is not other with a relative alterity as are, in a comparison, even ultimate species, which mutually exclude one another but still have their place within the community of a genus – excluding one another by their definition, but calling for one another by this exclusion, across the community of their genus. The alterity of the Other does not depend on any quality that would distinguish him from me, for a distinction of this nature would precisely imply between us that community of genus which already nullifies alterity.

And yet the Other does not purely and simply negate the I; total negation, of which murder is the temptation and the attempt, refers to an antecedent relation. The relation between the Other and me, which dawns forth in his expression, issues neither in number nor in concept. The Other remains infinitely transcendent, infinitely foreign; his face in which his epiphany is produced and which appeals to me breaks with the world that can be common to us, whose virtualities are inscribed in our *nature* and developed by our existence. Speech proceeds from absolute difference. Or, more exactly, an absolute difference is not produced in a process of specification descending from genus to species, in which the order of logical relations runs up against the given, which is not reducible to relations. The difference thus encountered remains bound up with the logical hierarchy it contrasts with, and appears against the ground of the common genus.

Absolute difference, inconceivable in terms of formal logic, is established only by language. Language accomplishes a relation between terms that breaks up the unity of a genus. The terms, the interlocutors, absolve themselves from the relation, or remain absolute within relationship. Language is perhaps to be defined as the very power to break the continuity of being or of history.

E. Levinas, *Totality and Infinity*, 1969, trans. Alfonso Lingis, pp. 194–212. Pittsburgh, PA: Duquesne University Press.

The incomprehensible nature of the presence of the Other, which we spoke of above, is not to be described negatively. Better than comprehension, *discourse* relates with what remains essentially transcendent. For the moment we must attend to the formal work of language, which consists in presenting the transcendent; a more profound signification will emerge shortly. Language is a relation between separated terms. To the one the other can indeed present himself as a theme, but his presence is not reabsorbed in his status as a theme. The word that bears on the Other as a theme seems to contain the Other. But already it is said to the Other who, as interlocutor, has quit the theme that encompassed him, and upsurges inevitably behind the said. Words are said, be it only by the silence kept, whose weight acknowledge this evasion of the Other. The knowledge that absorbs the Other is forthwith situated within the discourse I address to him. Speaking, rather than "letting be," solicits the Other. Speech cuts across vision. In knowledge or vision the object seen can indeed determine an act, but it is an act that in some way appropriates the "seen" to itself, integrates it into a world by endowing it with a signification, and, in the last analysis, constitutes it. In discourse the divergence that inevitably opens between the Other as my theme and the Other as my interlocutor, emancipated from the theme that seemed a moment to hold him, forthwith contests the meaning I ascribe to my interlocutor. The formal structure of language thereby announces the ethical inviolability of the Other and, without any odor of the "numinous," his "holiness."

The fact that the face maintains a relation with me by discourse does not range him in the same; he remains absolute within the relation. The solipsist dialectic of consciousness always suspicious of being in captivity in the same breaks off. For the ethical relationship which subtends discourse is not a species of consciousness whose ray emanates from the I; it puts the I in question. This putting in question emanates from the other.

The presence of a being not entering into, but overflowing, the sphere of the same determines its "status" as infinite. This overflowing is to be distinguished from the image of liquid overflowing a vessel, because this overflowing presence is effectuated as a position *in face of* the same. The facing position, opposition par excellence, can be only as a moral summons. This movement proceeds from the other. The idea of infinity, the infinitely more contained in the less, is concretely produced in the form of a relation with the face. And the idea of infinity alone maintains the exteriority of the other with respect to the same, despite this relation. Thus a structure analogous to the ontological argument is here produced: the exteriority of a being is inscribed in its essence. But what is produced here is not a reasoning, but the epiphany that occurs as a face. The metaphysical desire for the absolutely other which animates intellectualism (or the radical empiricism that confides in the teaching of exteriority) deploys its *energy* in the vision of the face [vision du visage], or in the idea of infinity. The idea of infinity exceeds my powers (not quantitatively, but, we will see later, by calling them into question); it does not come from our a priori depths – it is consequently experience par excellence.

The Kantian notion of infinity figures as an ideal of reason, the projection of its exigencies in a beyond, the ideal completion of what is given incomplete – but without the incomplete being confronted with a privileged *experience* of infinity, without it drawing the limits of its finitude from such a confrontation. The finite is here no longer conceived by relation to the infinite; quite the contrary, the infinite presupposes the finite, which it amplifies infinitely (although this passage to the limit or this projection implicates in an unacknowledged form the idea of infinity, with all the consequences Descartes drew from it, and which are presupposed in this idea of projection). The Kantian finitude is described positively by sensibility, as the Heideggerian finitude by the being for death. This infinity referring to the finite marks the most anti-Cartesian point of Kantian philosophy as, later, of Heideggerian philosophy.

Hegel returns to Descartes in maintaining the positivity of the infinite, but excluding all multiplicity from it; he posits the infinite as the exclusion of every "other" that might maintain a relation with the infinite and thereby limit it. The infinite can only encompass all relations. Like the god of Aristotle it refers only to itself, though now at the term of a history. The relation of a particular with infinity would be equivalent to the entry of this particular into the sovereignty of a State. It becomes infinite in negating its own finitude. But this outcome does not succeed in smothering the protestation of the private individual, the apology of the separated being (though it be called empirical and animal), of the individual who experiences as a tyranny the State willed by his reason, but in whose impersonal destiny he no longer recognizes his reason. We recognize in the finitude to which the Hegelian infinite is opposed, and which it encompasses, the finitude of man before the elements, the finitude of man invaded by the *there is*, at each instant traversed by faceless gods against whom labor is pursued in order to realize the security in which the "other" of the elements would be revealed as the same. But the other absolutely other – the Other – does not limit the freedom of the same; calling it to responsibility, it founds it and justifies it. The relation with the other as face heals allergy. It is desire, teaching received, and the pacific opposition of discourse. In returning to the Cartesian notion of infinity, the "idea of infinity" put in the separated being by the infinite, we retain its positivity, its anteriority to every finite thought and every thought of the finite, its exteriority with regard to the finite; here there was the possibility of separated being. The idea of infinity, the overflowing of finite thought by its content, effectuates the relation of thought with what exceeds its capacity, with what at each moment it learns without suffering shock. This is the situation we call welcome of the face. The idea of infinity is produced in the *opposition* of conversation, in sociality. The relation with the face, with the other absolutely other which I can not contain, the other in this sense infinite, is nonetheless my Idea, a commerce. But the relation is maintained without violence, in peace with this absolute alterity. The "resistance" of the other does not do violence to me, does not act negatively; it has a positive structure: ethical. The first revelation of the other, presupposed in all the other relations with him, does not consist in grasping him in his negative resistance and in circumventing him by ruse. I do not struggle with a faceless god, but I respond to his expression, to his revelation.

2 Ethics and the face

The face resists possession, resists my powers. In its epiphany, in expression, the sensible, still graspable, turns into total resistance to the grasp. This mutation can occur only by the opening of a new dimension. For the resistance to the grasp is not produced as an insurmountable resistance, like the hardness of the rock against which the effort of the hand comes to naught, like the remoteness of a star in the immensity of space. The expression the face introduces into the world does not defy the feebleness of my powers, but my ability for power.[1] The face, still a thing among things, breaks through the form that nevertheless delimits it. This means concretely: the face speaks to me and thereby invites me to a relation incommensurate with a power exercised, be it enjoyment or knowledge.

And yet this new dimension opens in the sensible appearance of the face. The permanent openness of the contours of its form in expression imprisons this openness which breaks up form in a caricature. The face at the limit of holiness and caricature is thus still in a sense exposed to powers. In a sense only: the depth that opens in this sensibility modifies the very nature of power, which henceforth can no longer take, but can kill. Murder still aims at a sensible datum, and yet it finds itself before a datum whose being can not be *suspended* by an appropriation. It finds itself before a datum absolutely non-neutralizable. The "negation" effected by appropriation and usage remained always partial. The grasp that contests the independence of the thing preserves it "for me." Neither the destruction of things, nor the hunt, nor the extermination of living beings aims at the face, which is not of the world. They still belong to labor, have a finality, and answer to a need. Murder alone lays claim to total negation. Negation by labor and usage, like negation by representation, effect a grasp or a comprehension, rest on or aim at affirmation; they can. To kill is not to dominate but to annihilate; it is to renounce comprehension absolutely. Murder exercises a power over what escapes power. It is still a power, for the face expresses itself in the sensible, but already impotency, because the face rends the sensible. The alterity that is expressed in the face provides the unique "matter" possible for total negation. I can wish to kill only an existent absolutely independent, which exceeds my powers infinitely, and therefore does not oppose them but paralyzes the very power of power. The Other is the sole being I can wish to kill.

But how does this disproportion between infinity and my powers differ from that which separates a very great obstacle from a force applied to it? It would be pointless to insist on the banality of murder, which reveals the quasi-null resistance of the obstacle. This most banal incident of human history corresponds to an exceptional possibility – since it claims the total negation of a being. It does not concern the force that this being may possess as a part of the world. The Other who can sovereignly say *no* to me is exposed to the point of the sword or the revolver's bullet, and the whole unshakeable firmness of his "for itself" with that intransigent *no* he opposes is obliterated because the sword or the bullet has touched the ventricles or auricles of his heart. In the contexture of the world he is a quasi-nothing. But he can oppose to me a struggle, that is, oppose to the force that strikes him not a force of resistance, but the very *unforeseeableness* of his reaction. He thus opposes to me not a greater force, an energy assessable and consequently presenting itself as though it were part of a whole, but the very transcendence of his being by relation to that whole; not some superlative of power, but precisely the infinity of his transcendence. This infinity, stronger than murder, already resists us in his face, is his face, is the primordial *expression*, is the first word: "you shall not commit murder." The infinite paralyses power by its infinite resistance to murder, which, firm and insurmountable, gleams in the face of the Other, in the total nudity of his defenceless eyes, in the nudity of the absolute openness of the Transcendent. There is here a relation not with a very great resistance, but with something absolutely *other*: the resistance of what has no resistance – the ethical resistance. The epiphany of the face brings forth the possibility of gauging the infinity of the temptation to murder, not only as a temptation to total destruction, but also as the purely ethical impossibility of this temptation and attempt. If the resistance to murder were not ethical but real, we would have a *perception* of it, with all that reverts to the subjective in perception. We would remain within the idealism of a *consciousness* of struggle, and not in relationship with the Other, a relationship that can turn into struggle, but already overflows the consciousness of struggle. The epiphany of the face is ethical. The struggle this face can threaten *presupposes* the transcendence of expression. The face threatens the eventuality of a struggle, but this threat does not exhaust the epiphany of infinity, does not formulate its first word. War presupposes peace, the antecedent and non-allergic presence of the Other; it does not represent the first event of the encounter.

The impossibility of killing does not have a simply negative and formal signification; the relation with infinity, the idea of infinity in us, conditions it positively. Infinity presents itself as a face in the ethical resistance that paralyses my powers and from the depths of defenceless eyes rises firm and absolute in its nudity and destitution. The comprehension of this destitution and this hunger establishes the very proximity of the other. But thus the epiphany of infinity is expression and discourse. The primordial essence of expression and discourse does not reside in the information they would supply concerning an interior and hidden world. In expression a being presents itself; the being that manifests itself attends its manifestation and consequently appeals to me. This attendance is not the *neutrality* [*le neutre*] of an image, but a solicitation that concerns me by its destitution and its Height. To speak to me is at each moment to surmount what is necessarily plastic in manifestation. To manifest oneself as a face is to *impose oneself* above and beyond the manifested and purely phenomenal form, to present oneself in a mode irreducible to manifestation, the very straightforwardness of the face to face, without the intermediary of any image, in one's nudity, that is, in one's destitution and hunger. In *Desire* are conjoined the movements unto the Height and unto the Humility of the Other.

Expression does not radiate as a splendor that spreads unbeknown to the radiating being – which is perhaps the definition of beauty. To manifest oneself in attending one's own manifestation is to invoke the interlocutor and expose oneself to his response and his questioning. Expression does not impose itself as a true representation or as an action. The being offered in true representation remains a possibility of appearance. The world which invades me when I engage myself in it is powerless against the "free thought" that suspends that engagement, or even refuses it interiorly, being capable of living hidden. The being that expresses itself imposes itself, but does so precisely by appealing to me with its destitution and nudity – its hunger – without my being able to be deaf to that appeal. Thus in expression the being that imposes itself does not limit but promotes my freedom, by arousing my goodness. The order of responsibility, where the gravity of ineluctable being freezes all laughter, is also the order where freedom is ineluctably invoked. It is thus the irremissible weight of being that gives

519

rise to my freedom. The ineluctable has no longer the inhumanity of the fateful, but the severe seriousness of goodness.

This bond between expression and responsibility, this ethical condition or essence of language, this function of language prior to all disclosure of being and its cold splendor, permits us to extract language from subjection to a preexistent thought, where it would have but the servile function of translating that preexistent thought on the outside, or of universalizing its interior movements. The presentation of the face is not true, for the true refers to the non-true, its eternal contemporary, and ineluctably meets with the smile and silence of the skeptic. The presentation of being in the face does not leave any logical place for its contradictory. Thus I cannot evade by silence the discourse which the epiphany that occurs as a face opens, as Thrasymachus, irritated, tries to do, in the first book of the *Republic* (moreover without succeeding). "To leave men without food is a fault that no circumstance attenuates; the distinction between the voluntary and the involuntary does not apply here," says Rabbi Yochanan.[2] Before the hunger of men responsibility is measured only "objectively"; it is irrecusable. The face opens the primordial discourse whose first word is obligation, which no "interiority" permits avoiding. It is that discourse that obliges the entering into discourse, the commencement of discourse rationalism prays for, a "force" that convinces even "the people who do not wish to listen"[3] and thus founds the true universality of reason.

Preexisting the disclosure of being in general taken as basis of knowledge and as meaning of being is the relation with the existent that expresses himself; preexisting the plane of ontology is the ethical plane.

3 Reason and the face

Expression is not produced as the manifestation of an intelligible form that would connect terms to one another so as to establish, across distance, the assemblage of parts in a totality, in which the terms joined up already derive their meaning from the situation created by their community, which, in its turn, owes its meaning to the terms combined. This "circle of understanding" is not the primordial event of the logic of being. Expression precedes these coordinating effects visible to a third party.

The event proper to expression consists in bearing witness to oneself, and guaranteeing this witness. This attestation of oneself is possible only as a face, that is, as speech. It produces the commencement of intelligibility, initiality itself, principality, royal sovereignty, which commands unconditionally. The principle is possible only as command. A search for the influence that expression would have undergone or an unconscious source from which it would emanate would presuppose an inquiry that would refer to new testimonies, and consequently to an original sincerity of an expression.

Language as an exchange of ideas about the world, with the mental reservations it involves, across the vicissitudes of sincerity and deceit it delineates, presupposes the originality of the face without which, reduced to an action among actions whose meaning would require an infinite psychoanalysis or sociology, it could not commence. If at the bottom of speech there did not subsist this originality of expression, this break with every influence, this dominant position of the speaker foreign to all compromise and all contamination, this straightforwardness of the face to face, speech would not surpass the plane of activity, of which it is evidently not a species – even though language can be integrated into a system of acts and serve as an instrument. But language is possible only when speaking precisely renounces this function of being action and returns to its essence of being expression.

Expression does not consist in *giving* us the Other's interiority. The Other who expresses himself precisely does not *give* himself, and accordingly retains the freedom to lie. But deceit and veracity already presuppose the absolute authenticity of the face – the privileged case of a presentation of being foreign to the alternative of truth and non-truth, circumventing the ambiguity of the true and the false which every truth risks – an ambiguity, moreover, in which all values move. The presentation of being in the face does not have the status of a value. What we call the face is precisely this exceptional presentation of self by self, incommensurable with the presentation of realities simply given, always suspect of some swindle, always possibly dreamt up. To seek truth I have already established a relationship with a face which can guarantee itself, whose epiphany itself is somehow a word of honor. Every language as an exchange of verbal signs refers already to this primordial word of honor. The verbal sign is placed where someone signifies something to someone else. It therefore already presupposes an authentification of the signifier.

The ethical relation, the face to face, also cuts across every relation one could call mystical, where events other than that of the presentation of the original being come to overwhelm or sublimate the pure sincerity of this presentation, where intoxicating equivocations come to enrich the primordial univocity of expression, where discourse becomes incantation as prayer becomes rite and liturgy, where the interlocutors find themselves playing a role in a drama that has begun outside of them. Here resides the rational character of the ethical relation and of language. No fear, no trembling could alter the straightforwardness of this relationship, which preserves the discontinuity of relationship, resists fusion, and where the response does not evade the question. To poetic activity – where influences arise unbeknown to us out of this nonetheless conscious activity, to envelop it and beguile it as a rhythm, and where action is borne along by the very work it has given rise to, where in a dionysiac mode the artist (according to Nietzsche's expression) becomes a work of art – is opposed the language that at each instant dispels the charm of rhythm and prevents the initiative from becoming a role. Discourse is rupture and commencement, breaking of rhythm which enraptures and transports the interlocutors – prose.

The face in which the other – the absolutely other – presents himself does not negate the same, does not do violence to it as do opinion or authority or the thaumaturgic supernatural. It remains commensurate with him who welcomes; it remains terrestrial. This presentation is preeminently nonviolence, for instead of offending my freedom it calls it to responsibility and founds it. As nonviolence it nonetheless maintains the plurality of the same and the other. It is peace. The relation with the other – the absolutely other – who has no frontier with the same is not exposed to the allergy that afflicts the same in a totality, upon which the Hegelian dialectic rests. The other is not for reason a scandal which launches it into dialectical movement, but the first rational teaching, the condition for all teaching. The alleged scandal of alterity presupposes the tranquil identity of the same, a freedom sure of itself which is exercised without scruples, and to whom the foreigner brings only constraint and limitation. This flawless identity freed from all participation, independent in the I, can nonetheless lose its tranquillity if the other, rather than countering it by upsurging on the same plane as it, speaks to it, that is, shows himself in expression, in the face, and comes from on high. Freedom then is inhibited, not as countered by a resistance, but as arbitrary, guilty, and timid; but in its guilt it rises to responsibility. Contingency, that is, the irrational, appears to it not outside of itself in the other, but within itself. It is not limitation by the other that constitutes contingency, but egoism, as unjustified of itself. The relation with the Other as a relation with his transcendence – the relation with the Other who puts into question the brutal spontaneity of one's immanent destiny – introduces into me what was not in me. But this "action" upon my freedom precisely puts an end to violence and contingency, and, in this sense also, founds Reason. To affirm that the passage of a content from one mind to the other is produced without violence only if the truth taught by the master is from all eternity in the student is to extrapolate maieutics beyond its legitimate usage. The idea of infinity in me, implying a content overflowing the container, breaks with the prejudice of maieutics without breaking with rationalism, since the idea of infinity, far from violating the mind, conditions nonviolence itself, that is, establishes ethics. The other is not for reason a scandal that puts it in dialectical movement, but the first teaching. A being *receiving* the idea of Infinity, *receiving* since it cannot derive it from itself, is a being taught in a non-maieutic fashion, a being whose very existing consists in this incessant reception of teaching, in this incessant overflowing of self (which is time). To think is to have the idea of infinity, or to be taught. Rational thought refers to this teaching. Even if we confine ourselves to the formal structure of logical thought, which starts from a definition, infinity, relative to which concepts are delimited, can not be defined in its turn. It accordingly refers to a "knowledge" of a new structure. We seek to fix it as a relation with the face and to show the ethical essence of this relation. The face is the evidence that makes evidence possible – like the divine veracity that sustains Cartesian rationalism.

4 Discourse founds signification

Language thus conditions the functioning of rational thought: it gives it a commencement in being, a primary identity of signification in the face of him who speaks, that is, who presents himself by ceaselessly undoing the equivocation of his own image, his verbal signs. Language conditions thought – not language in its physical materiality, but language as an attitude of the same with regard to the Other irreducible to the representation of the Other, irreducible to an intention of thought, irreducible to a consciousness of . . . , since relating to what no consciousness can contain, relating to the infinity of the Other. Language is not enacted within a consciousness; it comes to me from the Other and reverberates in consciousness by putting it in question. This event is irreducible to consciousness, where everything comes about from within – even the strangeness of suffering. To regard language as an attitude of the mind does not amount to disincarnating it, but is precisely to account for its incarnate essence, its difference from the constitutive, egological nature of the transcendental thought of idealism. The originality of discourse with respect to constitutive intentionality, to pure consciousness, destroys the concept of immanence: the idea of infinity in consciousness is an overflowing of a consciousness whose incarnation offers new powers to a soul no long paralytic – powers of welcome, of gift, of full hands, of hospitality. But to take incarnation as a primary fact of language, without indicating the ontological structure it accomplishes, would be to assimilate language to activity, to that prolongation of thought in corporeity, the *I think* in the *I can*, which has indeed served as a prototype for the category of the lived body [corps propre] or incarnate thought, which dominates one part of contemporary philosophy. The thesis we present here separates radically language and activity, expression and labor, in spite of all the practical side of language, whose importance we may not underestimate.

Until very recently the fundamental function of discourse in the upsurge of reason was not recognized. The function of words was understood in their dependence on reason: words reflected thought. Nominalism was the first to seek in words another function: that of an *instrument* of reason. A symbolic function of the word symbolizing the non-thinkable rather than signifying thought contents, this symbolism amounted to association with a certain number of conscious, intuitive data, an association that would be self-sufficient and would not require thought. The theory had no other purpose than to explain a divergence between thought, incapable of aiming at a general object, and language, which does seem to refer to general objects. Husserl's critique, completely subordinating words to reason, showed this divergency to be only apparent. The word is a window; if it forms a screen it must be rejected. With Heidegger Husserl's esperantist words take on the color and weight of a historical reality. But they remain bound to the process of comprehension.

The mistrust of verbalism leads to the incontestable primacy of rational thought over all the *operations* of expression that insert a thought into a particular language as into a system of signs, or bind it to a system of language presiding over the choice of these signs. Modern investigations in the philosophy of language have made familiar the idea of an underlying solidarity of thought with speech. Merleau-Ponty, among others, and better than others, showed that disincarnate thought thinking speech before speaking it, thought constituting the world of speech, adding a world of speech to the world antecedently constituted out of significations in an always transcendental operation, was a myth. Already thought consists in foraging in the system of signs, in the particular tongue of a people or civilization, and receiving signification from this very operation. It ventures forth at random, inasmuch as it does not start with an antecedent representation, or with those significations, or with phrases to be articulated. Hence one might say thought operates in the "I can" of the body. It operates in it before representing this body to itself or constituting it. Signification surprises the very thought that thought it.

But why is language, the recourse to the system of signs, necessary for thought? Why does the object, and even the perceived object, need a name in order to become a signification? What is it to have a meaning? Signification, though received from this incarnate language, nonetheless remains, throughout this conception, an "intentional object." The structure of constitutive consciousness recovers all its rights after the mediation of the body that speaks or writes. Does not the surplus of signification over representation consist in a new mode of being presented (new with respect to constitutive intentionality), whose secret the analysis of "body intentionality" does not exhaust? Does the mediation of the sign constitute the signification because it would introduce into an objective and static representation the "movement" of symbolic relation? But then language would again be suspected of taking us away from "the thing themselves." . . .

It is the contrary that must be affirmed; it is not the mediation of the sign that forms signification, but signification (whose primordial event is the face to face) that makes the sign function possible. The primordial essence of language is to be sought not in the corporeal operation that discloses it to me and to others and, in the recourse to language, builds up a thought, but in the presentation of meaning. This does not bring us back to a transcendental consciousness constituting objects, against which the theory of language we have just evoked protests with such just rigor. For significations do not present themselves to theory, that is, to the constitutive freedom of a transcendental consciousness; *the being of signification consists in putting into question in an ethical relation constitutive freedom itself*. Meaning is the face of the Other, and all recourse to words takes place already within the primordial face to face of language. Every recourse to words presupposes the comprehension of the primary signification, but this comprehension, before being interpreted as a "consciousness of," is society and obligation. Signification is the Infinite, but infinity does not present itself to a transcendental thought, nor even to meaningful activity, but presents itself in the Other; the Other faces me and puts me in question and *obliges* me by his essence qua infinity. That "something" we call signification arises in being with language because the essence of language is the relation with the Other. This relation is not added to the interior monologue – be it Merleau-Ponty's "corporeal intentionality" – like an address added to the fabricated object one puts in the mailbox; the welcoming of the being that appears in the face, the ethical event of sociality, already commands inward discourse. And the epiphany that is produced as a face is not constituted as are all other beings, precisely because it "reveals" infinity. Signification is infinity, that is, the Other. The intelligible is not a concept, but an intelligence. Signification precedes *Sinngebung*, and rather than justifying idealism, marks its limit.

In a sense signification is to perception what the symbol is to the object symbolized. The symbol marks the inadequateness of what is given in consciousness with regard to the being it symbolizes, a consciousness needy and hungry for the being it lacks, for the being announced in the very precision with which its absence is lived, a potency that evinces the act. Signification resembles it, as an overflowing of the intention that envisages by the being envisaged. But here the inexhaustible surplus of infinity overflows the actuality of consciousness. The shimmer of infinity, the face, can no longer be stated in terms of consciousness, in metaphors referring to light and the sensible. It is the ethical exigency of the face, which puts into question the consciousness that welcomes it. The consciousness of obligation is no longer a consciousness, since it tears consciousness up from its center, submitting it to the Other.

If the face to face founds language, if the face brings the first signification, establishes signification itself in being, then language does not only serve reason, but is reason. Reason in the sense of an impersonal legality does not permit us to account for discourse, for it absorbs the plurality of the interlocutors. Reason, being unique, cannot speak to another reason. A reason immanent in an individual consciousness is, to be sure, conceivable, in the way of naturalism, as a system of laws that regulate the nature of this consciousness, individuated like all natural beings but in addition individuated also as oneself. The concordance between consciousnesses would then be explained by the resemblance of beings constituted in the same fashion. Language would be reduced to a system of signs awakening, from one consciousness to the other, like thoughts. In that case one must disregard the intentionality of rational thought, which opens upon a universal order, and run all the risks of naturalist psychologism, against which the arguments of the first volume of the *Logische Untersuchungen* are ever valid.

Retreating from these consequences, and in order to conform oneself more to the "phenomenon," one can call reason the internal coherence of an ideal order realized in being in the measure that the individual consciousness, in which it is learnt or set up, would renounce its particularity as an individual and an ipseity, and either withdraw unto a noumenal sphere, from which it would exercise intemporally its role as absolute subject in the I think, or be reabsorbed in the universal order of the State, which at first it seemed to foresee or constitute. In both cases the role of language would be to dissolve the ipseity of individual consciousness, fundamentally antagonistic to reason, either to transform it into an "I think" which no longer speaks, or to make it disappear into its own discourse, whereupon, having entered into the State, it could only undergo the judgment of history, rather than remain me, that is, judge that history.

In such a rationalism there is no longer any society, that is, no longer any relation whose terms absolve themselves from the relation.

The Hegelians may attribute to human animality the consciousness of tyranny the individual feels before impersonal law, but they have yet to make understandable how a rational animal is possible, how the particularity of oneself can be affected by the simple universality of an idea, how an egoism can abdicate?

If, on the contrary, reason lives in language, if the first rationality gleams forth in the opposition of the face to face, if the first intelligible, the first signification, is the infinity of the intelligence that presents itself (that is, speaks to me) in the face, if reason is defined by signification rather than signification being defined by the impersonal structures of reason, if society precedes the apparition of these impersonal structures, if universality reigns as the presence of humanity in the eyes that look at me, if, finally, we recall that this look appeals to my responsibility and consecrates my freedom as responsibility and gift of self – then the pluralism of society could not disappear in the elevation to reason, but would be its condition. It is not the impersonal in me that Reason would establish, but an I myself capable of society, an I that has arisen in enjoyment as separated, but whose separation would itself be necessary for infinity *to be* – for its infinitude is accomplished as the "facing."

5 Language and objectivity

A meaningful world is a world in which there is the Other through whom the world of my enjoyment becomes a theme having a signification. Things acquire a rational signification, and not only one of simple usage, because an other is associated with my relations with them. In designating a thing I designate it to the Other. The act of designating modifies my relation of enjoyment and possession with things, places the things in the perspective of the Other. Utilizing a sign is therefore not limited to substituting an indirect relation for the direct relation with a thing, but permits me to render the things offerable, detach them from my own usage, alierate them, render them exterior. The word that designates things attests their apportionment between me and the others. The objectivity of the object does not follow from a suspension of usage and enjoyment, in which I possess things without assuming them. Objectivity results from language, which permits the putting into question of possession. This disengagement has a positive meaning: the entry of the thing into the sphere of the other. The thing becomes a theme. To thematize is to offer the world to the Other in speech. "Distance" with regard to the object thus exceeds its spatial signification.

This objectivity is correlative not of some trait in an isolated subject, but of his relation with the Other. Objectification is produced in the very work of language, where the subject is detached from the things possessed as though it hovered over its own existence, as though it were detached from it, as though the existence it exists had not yet completely reached it. This distance is more radical than every distance in the world. The subject must find itself "at a distance" from its own being, even with regard to that taking distance that is inherent in the home, by which it is still in being. For negation remains within the totality, even when it bears upon the totality of the world. In order that objective distance be hollowed out, it is necessary that while in being the subject be not yet in being, that in a certain sense it be not yet born – that it not be in nature. If the subject capable of objectivity *is* not yet completely, this "not yet," this state of potency relative to act, does not denote a less than being, but denotes time. Consciousness of the object – thematization – rests on distance with regard to oneself, which can only be time; or, if one prefers, it rests on self-consciousness, if we recognize the "distance from self to self" in self-consciousness to be "time." However, time can designate a "not yet" that nevertheless would not be a "lesser being" – it can remain distant both from being and from death – only as the inexhaustible future of infinity, that is, as what is produced in the very relationship of language. In designating what it possesses to the other, in speaking, the subject hovers over its own existence. But it is from the welcoming of the infinity of the other that it receives the freedom with regard to itself that this dispossession requires. It detains it finally from the Desire which does not arise from a lack or a limitation but from a surplus, from the idea of Infinity.

Language makes possible the objectivity of objects and their thematization. Already Husserl affirmed that the objectivity of thought consists in being valid for everyone. To know objectively would therefore be to constitute my thought in such a way that it already contained a reference to the thought of the others. What I communicate therefore is already constituted in function of others. In speaking I do not transmit to the Other what is objective for me: the objective becomes objective only through communication. But in Husserl the Other who makes this communication possible is first constituted for a monadic thought. The basis of objectivity is constituted in a purely subjective process. In positing the relation with the Other as ethical, one surmounts a difficulty that would be inevitable if, contrary to Descartes, philosophy started from a *cogito* that would posit itself absolutely independently of the Other.

For the Cartesian *cogito* is discovered, at the end of the Third Meditation, to be supported on the certitude of the divine existence qua infinite, by relation to which the finitude of the *cogito*, or the doubt, is posited and conceivable. This finitude could not be determined without recourse to the infinite, as is the case in the moderns, for whom finitude is, for example, determined on the basis of the mortality of the subject. The Cartesian subject is given a point of view exterior to itself from which it can apprehend itself. If, in a first movement, Descartes takes a consciousness to be indubitable of itself by itself, in a second movement – the reflection on reflection – he recognizes conditions for this certitude. This certitude is due to the clarity and distinctness of the *cogito*, but certitude itself is sought because of the presence of infinity in this finite thought, which without this presence would be ignorant of its own finitude: "... *manifeste intelligo plus realitatis esse in substantia infinita quam in finita, ac proinde priorem quodammodo in me esse perceptionem infiniti quam finiti, hoc est Dei quam mei ipsius. Qua enim ratione intelligerem me dubitare me cupere, hoc est aliquid mihi deesse, et me non esse omnino perfectum si nulla idea entis perfectionis in me esset, ex cujus comparatione defectus meos cognoscerem?*"[4]

Is the position of thought in the midst of the infinite that created it and has given it the idea of infinity discovered by a reasoning or an intuition that can posit only themes? The infinite can not be thematized, and the distinction between reasoning and intuition does not apply to the access to infinity. Is not the relation with infinity, in the twofold structure of infinity present to the finite, but present outside of the finite, foreign to theory? We have seen in it the ethical relation. If Husserl sees in the *cogito* a subjectivity without any support outside of itself, this *cogito* constitutes the idea of infinity itself and gives it to itself as an object. The non-constitution of infinity in Descartes leaves a door open; the reference of the finite *cogito* to the infinity of God does not consist in a simple thematization of God. I of myself account for every object; I contain them. The idea of infinity is not for me an object. The ontological argument lies in the mutation of this "object" into being, into independence with regard to me; God is the other. If to think consists in referring to an object, we must suppose that the thought of infinity is not a thought. What is it positively? Descartes does not raise the question. It is in any case evident that the intuition of infinity retains a rationalist meaning, and will not become any sort of invasion of God across an inward emotion. Descartes, better than an idealist or a realist, discovers a relation with a total alterity irreducible to interiority, which nevertheless does not do violence to interiority – a receptivity without passivity, a relation between freedoms.

The last paragraph of the Third Meditation brings us to a relation with infinity in thought which overflows thought and becomes a personal relation. Contemplation turns into admiration, adoration, and joy. It is a question no longer of an "infinite object" still known and thematized, but of a majesty: "*placet hic aliquamdiu in ipsius Dei contemplatione immorari, eius attributa apud me expendere et immensi huius luminis pulchritudinem quantum caligantis ingenii mei acies ferre poterit, intueri, admirari, adorare. Ut enim in hac sola divinae majestatis contemplatione summan alterius vitae felicitatem consistere fide credimus, ita etiam jam ex eadem licet multo minus perfecta, maximum cujus in hac vita capaces simus voluptatem percipi posse experimur.*"[5]

To us this paragraph appears to be not a stylistic ornament or a prudent hommage to religion, but the expression of this transformation of the idea of infinity conveyed by knowledge into Majesty approached as a face.

Notes

1 "Mon pouvoir de pouvoir."
2 Treatise *Synhedrin*, 104 b.
3 Plato, *Republic*, 327 b.
4 Ed. Tannery, T. VII, pp. 45–6. ["... there is manifestly more reality in the infinite substance than in the finite substance, and my awareness of the infinite must therefore be in some way prior to my awareness of the finite, that is to say, my awareness of God must be prior to that of myself. For how could I know that I doubt and desire, i.e., know that something is lacking to me and that I am not wholly perfect, save by having in me the idea of a being more perfect than myself, by comparison with which I may recognize my deficiencies." Eng. trans. by Norman Kemp Smith, *Descartes, Philosophical Writings* (New York, 1958), p. 205.]
5 "... It seems to me right to linger for a while on the contemplation of this all-perfect God, to ponder at leisure His marvelous attributes, to intuit, to admire, to adore, the incomparable beauty of this inexhaustible light, so far at least as the powers of my mind may permit, dazzled as they are by what they are endeavoring to see. For just as by faith we believe that the supreme felicity of the life to come consists in the contemplation of the Divine majesty, so do we now experience that a similar meditation, though one so much less perfect, can enable us to enjoy the highest contentment of which we are capable in this present life." *Ibid.*, p. 211.

2

BEYOND INTENTIONALITY

1. Does thought have meaning only through knowledge of the world – through the presence of the world and in virtue of our presence to the world – even when this presence is given in the horizons of past and future, temporal modes which are themselves also dimensions of re-*presentation* in which *presence* is after all recovered? Or, does not sense, in senseful thought, possess – perhaps prior to presence or to re-presentable presence, and to a greater extent than these – a meaning which is already *determined* and through which the very notion of sense comes to the mind before it is specified in terms of the formal structure of reference as it refers to a world unveiled, to a system, to an aim? Is not meaning *par excellence* that which would provide a justification for Being itself, that meaning the search for which is reflected in the now daily words of people who say they are concerned with the "meaning of life"? Does Being provide its own reason for existing as the alpha and omega of intelligibility, first philosophy and eschatology? Does it not, on the contrary, carry on with its task of being, while still calling for a justification (as a question preceding every other question)? Is not the *for-the-other* (*pour-l'autre*) – which, in the guise of humanity, manages to disrupt the "easy conscience" of the *conatus*, of the animal persistence of beings in Being, concerned solely for their own space and for the time of their own life – is not the *for-the-other* the opening of this question and the formulation of this meaning, *par excellence*? These problems make up the dominant theme of this essay.

It starts from certain standpoints found in Husserlian phenomenology, inasmuch as this is the conclusion to which one of the characteristic traditions of philosophy leads, according to which knowledge of entities and of their presence is the "natural place" of the senseful and is equivalent to spirituality or to the psychic life of thought itself.

2. For Husserl – and for the whole venerable philosophical tradition which he completes or of which, at least, he makes certain presuppositions explicit – the "bestowal of sense" (*Sinngebung*) is produced in a thought, understood as thought of . . . as thought of *this* or *that*; the this or that are taken as present to our thoughts (*cogitationes*) inasmuch as they are thought (*cogitatum*) to the point at which we are unable to determine or to recognize in reflection any thoughts

E. Levinas, "Beyond Intentionality", in Alan Montefiori (ed.), *Philosophy in France Today*, 1983, trans. Kathleen McLaughlin, pp. 100–15. Cambridge: Cambridge University Press.

without naming the *this* or *that* of which they are the thoughts. "Meaning-bestowing" thought is constructed as the thematization (whether implicit or explicit) of *this* or *that*, more precisely, as knowledge. The very breath of the spirit in thought is held to constitute *knowledge*. This is what is expressed when it is said that meaning-bestowing con-sciousness (con*science*) is intentional, organized as the *noesis* of a *noema* where the noema is *concrete* in the intention of the noesis. By means of the *this* or *that*, which are ineliminable from the description of the *bestowal of sense*, a notion such as the *presence* of *something* appears with the emergence of sense itself. Presence of something: *Seinsinn*, the sense of Being, according to Husserl, which in Heidegger – descending through all the harmonics of the history of philosophy – becomes the Being of beings.

The "bestowal of sense", constructed as knowledge, is understood in Husserl as a "wanting-to-arrive-in-one-way-or-another-at-this-or-that", and reflection upon this thought as showing *what* thought *wants to get at* and *how it wants to get there*. Intentionality is thus an intention of the soul, a spontaneity, a *willing*, and the sense bestowed itself, in some way, what is *willed*: the way in which beings or their Being manifest themselves to thought in knowledge corresponds to the way in which consciousness "wills" this manifestation through its own resolve or through the intention that animates this knowledge. Cognitive intention is thus a free act. The soul is "affected", yet not passively, as it takes hold of itself again by taking responsibility for what is given in accordance with its own intention. It raises itself. Husserl speaks of a teleology of transcendental consciousness. In this way, thought thinking of Being, from which it distinguishes itself, is an internal process, a staying-in-itself: immanence. Here, in virtue of the "bestowal of sense", there is a deep correspondence between Being and thought. There is nothing beyond the scope of intention in this sense: what is willed does not play games with the willing nor does it take the latter by surprise. Nothing enters thought "without declaring itself", nothing is "smuggled in". Everything stands within the openness of the soul: presence is candour itself. The intentional distance – between Being and thought – constitutes also an extreme accessibility of being. Astonishment, the disproportion between the *cogitatio* and the *cogitatum* where truth is to be sought, subsides in the truth once it is found. Presence, the production of Being or its manifestation, is *given*, is a mode of being-given (*Gegebenheit*). Husserl describes this as filling a void, as satisfaction. He who himself lays stress on the role of human incarnation in the perception of what is given, and on the "lived body" (*Leib*) as the organ of consciousness – since we must move around about things in order to grasp them, turning our head, adjusting our eyes and using our ears – will certainly authorize us to insist on the primary role played by the hand: Being is *bestowed* and this bestowal is to be understood in the literal sense of the word. The Bestowal is completed by the *hand that takes* (*la main qui prend*). It is therefore in this taking of possession (*mainmise*) that presence is "presence proper", presence "in flesh and blood" and not only "in images": presence is produced as a *hand-holding-now* (*maintenant*). It is in the taking-in-hand that the "thing itself" matches what the intention of thought willed and aimed at. The hand verifies the eye, for in it are performed the acts of grasping and assuming as one's own, which are irreducible to tactile sensation. This taking possession is not a simple sensing, it is a putting to the test. Before acting, as Heidegger would have it, as handling and use of tools, it is an appropriation. This is more fully and entirely presence, one would be tempted to say, than the presence given in thematization. It is precisely because of the way it allows itself to be grasped, to be appropriated – the way in which presence lets itself be given (*Gegebenheit*) – that presence is presence of a content, a content involving sensible qualities. This content can, of course, be classified in terms of generic identities and, in any case, in terms of the formal identity of *something* (*etwas überhaupt*), of a something which can be indicated and identified by an *index* as a determinable point within all which is present and gathered together: quiddity and identity of a thing, a solid, a term, a being. It is, no doubt, inseparable from a world out of which it is torn when it is first picked out and grasped, and yet such an act of separation is presupposed in every relation to or between things or beings. We may even go so far as to wonder whether the distinction between *Being* and *beings* is not an essential duality of presence, of that *Gegebenheit* which is sketched out in manifestation. Hands and fingers! The incarnation of consciousness, then, would be not a sorry accident befalling thought, cast down from the empyrean heights into a mere body, but rather the essential circumstance of truth.

To truth itself then, and not only to its use and abuse in a technological world, there belongs a primary technical success, that of the index which points at something and of the hand which grasps it. Perception is an apprehension and the concept, *Begriff*, a comprehending. The adequation of thought and Being at every level of reality *concretely* implies the entire infrastructure of sensible truth, the inevitable ground of all ideal truth. The reference of the categorial and of the general to what is given directly (*schlicht gegeben*) is one of the basic intuitions of Husserl's *Logical Investigations*. Early on, Husserl outlines the thesis put forward in his *Formal and Transcendental Logic* according to which formal ontology refers back to a material ontology and, hence, to sensible perception. He also sets out the thesis, which recurs throughout his entire work, that every notion is to be carried back, while fully respecting the characteristics peculiar to its own level, to a restitution of the elementary conditions of its transcendental genesis. The idea of truth as a *grasp* on things must necessarily have a non-metaphorical sense somewhere. In things, which support and prefigure every superstructure, *to be* signifies *to be given* and *to be rediscoverable*, to be some *thing*, and hence an entity. For every theme which finds its focus in "some one thing", the concept of this "some one thing", though logically empty as the concept of *etwas überhaupt*, never fails concretely to refer to whatever it is that the hand grasps and holds – content and quiddity – and to what the finger points at – this or that. Positing and positivity which are confirmed in the theses – the positional acts – of conceptual thought.

Presence – and Being conceived of as presence on the basis of knowledge – is therefore openness itself and givenness (*Gegebenheit*). Nothing turns up to contradict the intention of thought, nothing emerges from hiding to foil it; there is no chance of an ambush, planned and set up in the darkness or in the mystery of a past or a future refractory to presence. The past is but a present that once was. It remains on a par with the presence of the present, with that manifestation which is perhaps only its emphatic perseverance. It re-presents itself. If the past were to have meaning without being the modification of a present in which it may have commenced, if it were to signify anarchically – this would undoubtedly indicate the rupture of immanence. Immanence connotes this gathering together of the diversity of time in the presence of representation. This ability of the diverse not to reject synchrony, but rather to allow its very diversity to be brought under the unity of a genus or a form – is a logically necessary condition for synchronization or for the results of synchronization. In the present – in the completed present, in the present of ideality – everything allows itself to be thought together. Temporal alteration itself, examined in the sensible realm which fills time and which endures in or thanks to it, may be interpreted on the basis of the metaphor of a flow (made up of drops distinct from and yet resembling each other *par excellence*, "like two drops of water"). Temporal otherness (*altérité*) is thus to be conceived of as inseparable from the qualitative difference of the contents or of spatial intervals, distinct yet equal, discernible yet traversed in a uniform movement. This is a homogeneity, which constitutes a predisposition to synthesis. The past is representable, retained or remembered or reconstructed in an historical narrative; the future, is "pro-tension", anticipated, presupposed by hypothesis.

The temporalization of time – temporal flow – would still be intentional, its diachrony could be synthesized in the representation of qualitative contents bound to time. One might, however, wonder to what extent the properly diachronic difference may not pass unrecognized within that which appears as indissociable from the contents and which makes us think of time as if it were composed of instants – atoms of presence or entities – designatable as terms which pass before us. This is but the differentiation of the *Same* (*le Même*) lending itself to synthesis, that is, to the synchrony which may be held to justify or to give rise to the psyche as re-presentation: memory and anticipation.

In this psyche, capable of apprehending presence, the subject or the self would be, precisely, the agent or the common ground of re-presentation, the possibility of gathering together that which is dispersed. Thus, Brentano was able to maintain that psychic life consists in re-presentation or is supported by re-presentation in all its various forms – theoretical, affective, axiological and active. Similarly, Husserl maintained to the very end that there was a logical stratum in all intentionality, even the non-theoretical sort. *Spirit was held to be presence and relation to being*. Nothing concerning it was alien to truth, to the appearance of Being.

In truth, thought thus moves out of itself towards Being, without thereby ceasing to remain in its own proper sphere (*chez elle*), always equal to itself, never losing its measure, never exceeding it. Thought *satis*fies itself in Being, which as a first move it begins by distinguishing from itself; it *satis*fies itself in adequation. The knowledge in which thought displays itself is a thought thinking "to satiety", always within its own limits. Language, no doubt, suggests a relation *between* thinkers over and beyond this represented content, always identical to itself and thus immanent. However, the rationalism implicit in knowledge interprets this otherness as the mutual rediscovery of interlocutors within the *Same*, a Same of which they are the untoward dispersion. In language, diverse subjects can enter each into the thought of another and so coincide in reason. Reason on this view is the true inner life. The questions and answers which make up an "exchange of ideas" could just as well be held within a *single* consciousness. The relation between thinkers would have no special meaning of its own and would count only as a transmission of signs, thanks to which a multiplicity was reunited around one and the same thought; the multiplicity of consciousnesses in relation with one another should be seen as nothing but the deficiency of a prior or final unity.

Would not the proximity of one consciousness to another take on the sense of a failure of coincidence between them? Language would thus be entirely subordinated to thought, even if in its immanent functioning, the latter would have to have recourse to verbal signs in order to understand – to encompass – and to combine ideas and to preserve what had been acquired.

The rigorous correlation between what is manifested and the *modes* of consciousness enables Husserl to affirm both that consciousness bestows sense and that Being commands the modalities of consciousness which reach it, that Being controls what appears as phenomenon. This final phrase receives an idealist interpretation: Being is immanent in thought and thought does not transcend itself in knowledge. Whether knowledge be sensible, conceptual or even purely symbolical, the transcendent or the absolute, claiming, as it does, to be unaffected by any relation, can in fact bear no transcendental sense without immediately losing it: the very fact of its presence to knowledge signifies the loss of transcendence and of absoluteness. In the final analysis, presence excludes all transcendence. The intentionality of consciousness lies precisely in the fact that the sense of the sensible comes from appearance, that the very perseverance of a being in its Being is manifestation, and that Being as appearing is thus encompassed, equalled and, in some way, *carried* by thought. It is not through some degree of intensity or firmness which would remain unmatchable or unmatched in relation to the principle of noetic identification – nor through the axiological modalities which the Being as posited may be held to possess – that transcendence or absoluteness might be capable of preserving a sense which would remain unaffected even by its presence in manifestation. The energy of manifestation – that is, the noetic identification required for *appearance* – is held to have all the intensity or all the firmness required to persist in Being; of this persistence, manifestation would simply constitute the state of ultimate emphasis. Understood properly, the notion of intentionality signifies at once that Being commands the modes of access to Being and that Being is in accordance with the intention of consciousness. Intentionality signifies an exteriority in immanence and the immanence of all exteriority.

However, does intentionality exhaust all the ways in which thought is meaningful?

3. Does thought have meaning only through consciousness of the world? Or is not the potential surplus of the world itself, over and beyond all *presence*, to be sought in an immemorial past – that is, irreducible to a bygone present – in the trace left by this past which, perhaps, marks it out as a part of creation, a mark we should not be too quick to reduce to the condition of a causal effect and which, in any case, presupposes an otherness representable neither in terms of the correlations of knowledge nor in terms of the synchrony of re-presentation. It is precisely a possible approach to this otherness which this study attempts to describe – a study which, by uncovering in Being, above and beyond its ontological contingency, its putting into "moral question" and its call for a justification, would involve it in the ethical intrigue of otherness.

Is not the significance of thought nothing other than thematization, and so, re-presentation, and, thus, the bringing together of temporal diversity and dispersal? Is thought from the very outset braced towards the adequation of truth, towards the grasp of what is given as phenomenon in its ideal identity as "something"?

Would not thought then be senseful only in the face of pure presence, fulfilled presence, which, in the eternal realm of ideality, no longer "passes by" or "passes on" as in time? Is all *other*ness (*alt*érité) only qualitative, a diversity that allows itself to be collected under genera and forms and brought back to the Same, in the same way as would be permitted by a time that lent itself to synchronization through the re-presentations of knowledge?

A deeper reflection on what is specifically human may, however, lead us to doubt the appropriateness of this line of thought. The self identifies itself independently of any particular characteristic quality which might distinguish one self from another and in which it would recognize itself. As "pure selves", different selves are, precisely, indistinguishable. The otherness of the indiscernible cannot be reduced to a mere difference of "content". So the relation of one self to another is not the bringing together of beings in a world like that found in re-presentation or in the synchronization produced by way of knowledge. Otherness in the case of "indiscernibles" does not refer them back to a common genus nor to a time that might be synchronizable in representations through memory or history. Would these indiscernibles, then, be impossible to gather together and so simply remain separated? *Unless, of course, their gathering together be something quite different from synthesis, that is, unless it be proximity, face-to-face and society.* Face-to-face: the notion of the face that imposes itself here is not that of a datum empirically added onto the prior notion of a plurality of selves, of psyches or of interiorities to be totted up to form a total. It is the face which commands a gathering – or a proximity – quite different from that involved in the synthesis which unites phenomena into a world. It commands a thinking that is more ancient and more aware than knowledge or experience. I can, no doubt, have an experience of another person, but without, precisely, discerning in him his indiscernible difference. Thought alert to the face of the other is the thought of an irreducible difference, a difference which is not a thematization and which disturbs the equilibrium of the impassible soul of knowing. The alertness should not be directly interpreted as intentionality, as a *noesis* matching – whether the intention be fulfilled or remain empty – its *noema* and simultaneous with it. An irreducible otherness is strong enough to "resist" this synchronization of the noetico-noematic correlation and to signify what is immemorial and infinite, balking at presence and at representation, balking at immanence where otherness would fall away, even if re-presentations were to be limited to nostalgia or to a symbolism. As we have just stated: I can, no doubt, have an experience of another and "observe" his face, and yet the knowledge gained in this way would be, if not actually misleading, nevertheless truncated as if the relationship with another were lost in the knowledge, which, here, can occur only through "appresentation" and "empathy" (*Einfühlung*), to use Husserl's expressions. For Husserl, indeed, the sense of the *other* is still meaningful in knowledge, which itself can be preceded by nothing else. Truncated knowledge. Indeed, in "appresentation", I constitute the other on the basis of the perceived behaviour of a body analogous to the one I inhabit. However, this "knowledge" of another self lacks any direct mode of access to this life, lacks the means to pierce the secret of his inner life and his personal identity, the *forever-indirect* knowledge of the unknowable. What is at issue is, in fact, an otherness that cannot be reduced to the grafting of a specific and characteristic difference onto a fundamental identity, itself common to a diversity that is already synchronous, or synchronizable, a diversity thus assured of the common formal ground, the ultimate homogeneity necessary for every relation involving knowledge – but a common ground upon which the other would have lost his radical and indiscernible otherness and be brought back to the level of things in the world.

What we take to be the secret of the other man in appresentation is precisely the hidden side of a meaning other than knowledge: awakening to the other man in his identity, an identity indiscernible for knowledge, thought in which the proximity of one's fellow is a source of meaning, "commerce" with *the other* which cannot be reduced to experience, the *approach* of the other, of the first comer.

This proximity of the unknown lies in the meaningfulness of the face, which from the outset carries meaning over and beyond that of the surface plasticities which cover it with their presence in perception. Before any particular expression – and under every particular expression – there lies an extreme rectitude; a point-blank rectitude, perhaps the ethical source and "latent birth" of geometrical straightness, the straightness of the arrow's flight or of the projectile that kills. This is the extreme uprightness of that which does not appear simply in the context of an ensemble gathered beneath the sun and within the shadows of a horizon; in other words, that which strictly speaking does not appear, is not a phenomenon. In speaking of this uprightness – stretched by its exposition to . . . to the point of nudity, destitution, without defence or recourse to any possible digression – we have said elsewhere that the face of the other man is for me at one and the same time a temptation to kill and the "thou shalt not kill" by which I am already accused or suspected, but which also already *summons me*. It is a concrete expression of mortality: the break up of plastic forms, a nakedness starker than any other in the uprightness of an exposition to the invisibility of death, to the mystery of death, to the never to be resolved alternative between Being and not Being. But this involves, certainly, even more: an alternative between this alternative and a third possibility, one that is excluded and unthinkable, but due precisely to which death is a mystery extending *beyond* the unknown. A beyond excluded both from knowledge and from ignorance and yet giving rise to the question in which just what is problematic in the question is to be found – the question *par excellence* in virtue of the uprightness of the face, but a question in which *I am summoned* as well. The face itself constitutes the fact that *someone summons me* and demands my presence. Ethical proximity begins here: in my response to this summons. This response cannot be conceived of as the communication of information; it is the response of responsibility for the other man. In the approach to others *indebtedness* takes the place of the grasp or the comprehension of knowledge.

Beyond surface plasticities. Not in any sense an experience of the beyond, not the knowledge of another presence, which, if it were to be attributed to the beyond, would be quite absurd, reducing this beyond to a mere continuation of intentionality, extending into a mythological other-world. Instead, a "beyond" that is the break-up of presence, and, consequently, of synchronizable time. A relation between non-synthetizables, between non-synchronizables, a relation of the Same to the Other: ethical thinking or human fraternity. The singular character of this fraternal thinking among all the relations based upon presence and upon the synchronizable time of re-presentation and of the world is shown in the strange lucidity whereby two men born of the same maternal womb may suddenly recognize themselves as sufficiently foreign each to the other for the brother to be no longer his brother's keeper. Fraternity is precisely the relation across the abyss that is itself unbridgeable by mere knowledge of human otherness, and which, as responsibility, is neither a diminished knowledge nor a consequence of knowledge. I am responsible for others whether or not we share a common present. I am responsible for others above and beyond anything I may or may not have done in their regard, beyond anything that may or may not concern my own acts. It is as if, in virtue of this fraternity, my relation to the other no longer went back to a prior intimacy of what had once been *mine*, what I had once appropriated, to what Heidegger as early as Paragraph 9 of *Sein und Zeit* calls *Jemeinigkeit*, a concept that in his thought dominates the entire theory of authenticity, of *Eigentlichkeit*. Rather, it is as if my very self were constituted only through a relation to others, a relation that was gratuitous with respect to accounting for what may be mine and what another's. Responsible without being culpable, I am as if open to an accusation which the alibi of my otherness cannot excuse. A brother despite my strangeness! Fraternity, accusation and my responsibility come before any contemporaneousness, any freedom in myself, out of an immemorial-non-representable-past, before any beginning to be found in myself, before any present. I respond to a question more ancient than "my consciousness", a question that my consciousness could not have perceived yet which commits me, in accordance with the strange schema evident in a creature that must have been able to respond to the *fiat* of Genesis, before ever having been of the world and in the world, before having been capable of hearing. Diachrony as relation: non-relation which is relation. Non-relation in that diachrony is the multiplicity of the unassemblable which could never be counted together, whereas the terms of a relation share at least a common time and can be thought of simultaneously. Non-relation, too, because no preposition could ever convey the orientation of time without betraying it; relation whose unique figure is the very diachrony of time itself; and consequently, non-relation which is relation.

Proximity of the other man, meaningful in a different way from that through which appresentation draws its knowledge; yet meaningful also in a different way from that of the representations and direct experience that another man has of himself. Is it certain, however, that the ultimate and peculiar sense of man lies in what is exhibited, in what is manifested or in manifestation, in unveiled truth or in the noesis of knowledge? This is what the opening lines of our study left open: what is *sense*? Is it certain that man has no sense beyond, precisely, what man can be and what he can show himself to be? Does not this sense reside, rather, in his secretness as "first comer", in his strangeness as other, inasmuch as it is precisely this strangeness which underlies the way in which he thrusts himself upon my responsibility, the way in which he places me under his command? Does the sense of another man lie in his manifestation? Is the way in which the stranger thrusts himself upon me not the very manner in which a God who loved the stranger and who put me into question by summoning me would "enter on the scene"?

The meaning of this ineffaceable strangeness of the other within my responsibility for him or this "difference between indiscernibles" lacking any common genus – myself and the other – coincides with a non-indifference in myself with regard to the other. Is this not the very meaning of the face, of the primordial speaking that *summons me*, questions me, stirs me, provokes my response or my responsibility, which – before any knowledge I may have of myself, before any reflexive presence of myself to myself, and beyond my perseverance in Being and my repose in myself – would be the *for-the-other*, whereby the psychic life of humanity would be brought down to earth, and to a break with Heideggerian *Jemeinigkeit*?

The face "signifies" beyond, neither as an index nor as a symbol, but precisely and irreducibly as a face that *summons me*. It signifies *to-God* (*à-Dieu*), not as a sign, but as the questioning of myself, as if I were being summoned or called, that is to say, awakened or cited as myself. In this summons, the *question* harkens back to its primordial, underived meaning. It finds it, evidently, not in its original state as a modality or as a moment of the doxic apophantic modality, such as doubt, probability, or pure possibility which remain immanent in thought. Although we are accustomed to the leading role of the question in the theoretical realm, the question, unlike knowledge, is not indifferent as to its expression; the latter is determined by factors outside the semantic content of knowledge, since already by virtue of its very meaning the question breaks out of the immanence of thought. Its problematical character is itself a summons and a call to others. It marks the point at which language in some sense tears thought open, and thought, which in intentionality is still "transcendence in immanence", moves towards others. However, when it comes to the question of death, the question *par excellence*, I am summoned as though in the egoism of my *conatus* I were thereby to leave the other man alone to face the hazard of the death that puts him into question. My being put into question and my relationship-to-God (*à-Dieu*) seem to point up a certain foreignness of the *esse* where Being would take on a meaning in virtue of my responsibility for the other.

These interrogations and these conditionals do not, of course, constitute a return to the great psychoanalytic thesis according to which the analyst sees more accurately into the other man than he himself sees in his spontaneous and reflective consciousness. In this case, it is a question neither of seeing nor of knowing. We are asking rather whether man's humanity is to be defined solely by what he is or whether, in the face which *summons me*, a different – and more ancient – meaning than the ontological one is not taking shape and awakening a thinking other than knowledge, a thinking which constitutes probably the very pulsation of the Self. The sense of the human is not to be measured by presence, not even by self-presence. The meaning of proximity exceeds the limits of ontology, of the human essence, and of the world. It signifies by way of transcendence and the relationship-to-God-in-me (*l'à-Dieu-en-moi*) which is the putting of myself into question. The face signifies in the fact of summoning, of *summoning me* – in its nudity or its destitution, in everything that is precarious in questioning, in all the hazards of mortality – to the unresolved alternative between Being and Nothingness, a questioning which, *ipso facto, summons me*.

The Infinite in its absolute difference withholds itself from presence in me; the Infinite does not come to meet me in a contemporaneousness like that in which noesis and noema meet simultaneously together, nor in the way in which interlocutors responding to one another may meet. The Infinite is not indifferent to me. It is in calling me to other men that transcendence concerns me. In this unique intrigue of transcendence, the non-absence of the Infinite is neither presence, nor re-presentation. Instead, the idea of the infinite is to be found in my responsibility for the Other.

Thought of the unencompassable, thought of the transcendent, thought of an otherness that refuses to admit of presence and simultaneity. Yet this refusal is not pure negation, it isolates one in the solitude of an inalienable responsibility, it is a refusal by way of responsibilities conferred. This negation constitutes the finiteness of the finite precisely in terms of responsibility, but a responsibility which is also the interweaving of the Infinite with the finite: the *In* of Infinite signifies at one and the same time, the *not* of the Infinite, the transcendence of the finite, and the overflow of the Infinite *in* the finite.

The transcendence of the movement towards God (*à-Dieu*) moves as if across a gap that no genus, not even an empty form, can ever span and both this transcendence and the relation to the Absolute or to the Infinite have an ethical significance, that is to say that their meaning is to be found in the proximity of the other man, he who is a stranger and who may be naked, destitute and undesirable; but also in his face, that undesirable face which *summons me*, which concerns me, which puts me into question – none of this should be taken as a "new proof of the existence of God", a problem that, most likely, has a sense only within the world. All this describes only the circumstance in which the very meaning of the word "God" comes to mind, even more imperiously than a presence, a circumstance in which this word signifies neither Being, nor persistence in Being, in which it signifies no "other" world – nothing could be further from a world! – and yet, in which, precisely, these negations do not slip back into negative theology.

The singular signification of God is tied to responsibility for the other man. We should like to recall in this connection an apologue recounted in old Jewish texts concerning a well-known biblical passage at the beginning of chapter 18 of Genesis, where Abraham is visited by three angels. The first verse of this biblical text, in the Hebraic version, opens with a verb that expressly signifies Revelation: "Revealed Himself to him, did the Lord, in the plains of Mamre, while he was sitting at the entrance to his tent during the heat of the day." And the Doctors of Israel have commented on this in the form of a parable: the Lord revealed Himself to Abraham while he was sitting at the entrance to his tent, watching for passers-by tired by the heat and whom he wanted to invite into the shade of his lodging. Second verse: "As he raised his eyes and looked, he saw three persons standing before him. And seeing them, he ran to them from the doorway of his tent and prostrated himself on the ground." If these three figures who – we later learn – are angels, but who in the eyes of Abraham, following the obvious sense of the text, can only be three passers-by worn out by the journey and by the desert dust, if these three travellers to be welcomed are taken to represent what is meant by the revelation of God spoken of in the first verse, this would already be not at all a bad interpretation as an illustration of the idea of a God inseparable from the face of the other man, and from the *summons* that this face signifies. But there is a third verse: "And he said, Lord, if I have found grace in your eyes, do not pass by this way before your servant." Addressing his invitation to the three travellers, Abraham pronounces the word "Adonaï", which means Lord, in the singular. Whom is he addressing? There are three travellers. The Jewish commentator first looks for the natural sense of this vocative that can indeed be understood in the singular: Abraham is supposed to be addressing the most important or the oldest among the three men in order to invite, through him, the entire group, of which the oldest is probably the leader. The term "Adonaï" by which he addresses him is, of course, used to invoke God, but it can perfectly well carry a profane sense and concern a man. This is a textual meaning that is quite acceptable. But here is the sense that the passage calls for – the parabolic sense – of this singularity and of this singular: verse three should follow verse one, and verse two become verse three. "The Lord revealed Himself to him in the plains of Mamre, while he was seated at the entrance to his tent during the heat of the day. And he said, Adonaï, if I find grace in your eyes do not pass by this way before your servant. As he raised his eyes and looked, he saw three persons standing before him; he ran to them from the doorway of his tent and prostrated himself on the ground." In this version, Abraham asks the Eternal who is appearing to him not to leave but to wait for him, for it is important to him to run out to the travellers whom he wants to welcome under his tent. Was Abraham thereby lacking in respect to the Eternal who was revealing Himself to him or might it have been of greater urgency to greet the travellers than to listen to the Revelation? Or might there have been more revelation of God in greeting the travellers than in the *tête-à-tête* with the Eternal?

The singular epiphany of God in the face of three men wandering in the desert! One can, of course, separate out of this or isolate from it the idea of God. One can think it or know it while forgetting the circumstances. Religions and theologies thrive on this abstraction just as mystics do on this isolation. But so do wars of religion.

Part XIII

JACQUES DERRIDA
Phenomenology and Deconstruction

JACQUES DERRIDA (b. 1930)

Introduction

Jacques Derrida was born in Algeria in 1930. As a secondary school student in Algiers, his interest in philosophy was first aroused through hearing a radio broadcast by Albert Camus, and he decided to study in France. In 1949 he moved to Paris to study at the Lycée Louis-le-Grand (Alma Mater to both Sartre and Merleau-Ponty). In 1952 he entered the Ecole Normale Supérieure, where he befriended Louis Althusser, and attended the lectures of Michel Foucault and Jean Hyppolite (later his research director). Derrida's first book, *Edmund Husserl's Origin of Geometry: An Introduction* (1962), was a translation of Husserl with a long commentary, but it was only in 1967 that Derrida came to prominence with the publication of three books: *Speech and Phenomena*, *Writing and Difference*, and *Of Grammatology*. A prolific author, subsequent publications include *Margins of Philosophy* (1972) and *Of Spirit: Heidegger and the Question* (1987). Derrida has taught at the Ecole Normale, the Sorbonne, Yale and Johns Hopkins. More recently he has been Director of Studies at the Ecole des Haute Etudes en Sciences Sociales, Paris, and Visiting Professor of Humanities at the University of California, Irvine.

Although he is usually associated with the post-structuralist wave of recent French philosophy, Derrida claims to receive his orientation from phenomenology, in particular his readings of Husserl and Heidegger. Derrida is best known for his 'deconstructive' readings of philosophical and literary texts. Derrida began his deconstructive itinerary with lengthy interpretations of the writings of Husserl, his earliest and most constant influence. Underlying these treatments is the claim that, despite their critical acumen, many authors have come to privilege the notion of perfect presence: that is, the notion that certain things or ideas may be given immediately and fully (or 'adequately'). They have done this by implicitly denigrating or leaving out of account those conditions of possibility of presence and givenness that preclude not just immediacy, but also the attainment of adequacy. Derrida's readings seek to show how all such attempts at exclusion 'deconstruct' or come undone from within. Neither linguistic terms nor concepts nor conscious episodes are self-subsistent, for in each case their constitution supposes a differential structure involving other terms and concepts and episodes, including those which the relevant authors sought to exclude.

Our first reading consists of the close of Chapter 4 and the whole of Chapter 5 ("Signs and the Blink of an Eye") of *Speech and Phenomena* (1967). In this book Derrida maintains that certain essential (and problematical) distinctions proposed by Husserl in *Logical Investigations* remain operative throughout his later works. Chief amongst these is the distinction between indications and expressions introduced in the First Investigation. An indication is a sign, a sound or mark pointing to or representing a thing or state of affairs, but possessing no meaning of itself alone. To be more than an empty signifier it has to be animated by an intention so as to become an expression. Expressions differ from indications in being inherently meaningful, in being the expressions of intentions. They are what they are through the conscious acts attaching to them. According to Husserl, expressions are always interwoven with indications in communicative speech, but there is one field where the communicative function is not required, namely the field of inner experience or 'solitary mental life'. One's conscious acts in silent soliloquy do not indicate anything to oneself with signs or use any linguistic expressions, since the conscious acts in question are themselves experienced at the very same moment in the 'blink' or glance of an eye (*Augenblick*).

In our selection, Derrida begins by observing that this notion of the uselessness of signs in inner life hinges on the thesis that consciousness can be punctually present to itself in the temporal present, a thesis that Husserl always seeks to save. However, Derrida proceeds to note that the idea of a punctual instant of self-presence is ultimately undercut by Husserl himself in *The Phenomenology of Internal Time-Consciousness*, where the latter recognised that the present of self-presence is not simple, but a self-relation that is 'constituted in a primordial and irreducible synthesis'. On examination, every moment of awareness turns out to be an extended 'living present' with a threefold intentional structure. It involves a primal impression of an intuitive content as 'now-present', together with a retention or primary memory of a previous content as 'just-lapsed' or 'just-past', and a protention or primary expectation of a future content as 'about-to-be'. In a living present of self-awareness the retended content becomes thematised as the object of a reflective gaze.

Derrida argues that Husserl tries to conserve the self-identity of the now by making the primal impression the source point of the living present, the anchor around which the other intentional forms cluster. Yet this primordiality of the 'now' is only an apparent one, in Derrida's view, for retention and protention are essentially and indispensably involved in its possibility. It might still be held that indications or signs are redundant on this description, given that the retention required for the constitution of the self-present now is itself a perception or presentation of the just-past. Derrida's reply is that retention should in fact be regarded as the non-perceptual re-presentation of something which was present – the just-past within the living present points to or indicates a primal impression instead of giving it in original form. This strikes at the root of the thesis of the uselessness of signs in the self-relation. Self-presence is never a hermetically sealed interior, since its very possibility supposes a trace, the indication of a bygone moment in the flow of inner time. Derrida introduces '*différance*' to denote the 'movement' by which otherness and non-presence are always already insinuated inside actual presence and perpetually defer putatively perfect presence. He concludes by suggesting that *différance* is involved in signification in general.

Our second reading is an abridgement of the famous paper 'Différance', given to the Société française de philosophie in January 1968. Here Derrida assembles the different ways he uses the term, which is not a word or concept *per se*, but rather what he understands in quasi-Hegelian language as a 'differentiating relation'. Consciousness has already been shown to require a certain *différance* or play of differences and deferrals. In this second piece Derrida takes up the suggestion that *différance* is a condition of every concept and linguistic term. Influenced by Saussure, he describes it as the movement according to which any code or system of signs in general is 'constituted' as a weaving of differences. The identity of a word as sound or written mark depends on its being distinguished from other such aural or visual images. Put another way, its identity is a product of differences, ensuing from its place within a system of differential relationships. In the ordinary course of events we do not focus on this or that play of differences, for they are not themselves objects of appearance (we hear different syllables, for example, but not the intervening difference itself). Derrida writes *différance* with an 'a' to foreground this play, to try and make a condition of linguistic phenomena into one more phenomenon. He draws on the fact that in the French pronunciation alone, the 'e' spelling in the final syllable of *différence* cannot be heard, just as in writing alone the 'a' pronunciation is missed. Only in the irreducible commerce between speech and writing can this difference be revealed.

Derrida is careful to stress that *différance* is nothing by itself, neither an agent nor a patient. Its character is largely signified by the grammatical form of the middle voice in certain natural languages, for it is a relation that enables a system and is itself enabled in the same process, being equiprimordial with that system. He describes the structure of *différance* in terms of 'spacing' and 'temporisation'. An interval must separate every present element in a system from what it is not in order for that element to be present in the first place. In consciousness the present requires a retention separated from it in time. In written language a word currently apprehended requires other words separated from it in space. This structure is also entitled 'arche-writing', since it allows for the ordinary graphic writing that is one of its instantiations.

In *Speech and Phenomena* Derrida had written of a retentional trace as the representation of a primal impression. In "Différance", however, he claims that to talk of the present as an originary synthesis of marks or traces of retentions and protentions is to use a phenomenological and transcendental language that is ultimately inadequate. The trace insinuated into the present by *différance* is taken to refer, not only to a lapsed present, but, in Merleau-Ponty's phrase, to 'a past that was never present', a realm of unconsciousness that is forever 'delayed', incapable of being accessed by reflection in a dialectical process of recovery. According to Derrida, the association of *différance* with unconsciousness brings us to the point of greatest obscurity, prefigured in the work of Nietzsche and Freud. In allowing for presence, *différance* introduces otherness. Yet in so doing, it involves something which was never present at any juncture, thereby exceeding the simple metaphysical opposition of presence and absence.

In the final pages of the essay, Derrida turns his attention to the later Heidegger, who discerns in the Western tradition of metaphysics a primordial forgetfulness of the 'ontological difference' between Being and beings. Derrida wishes to return to Heidegger's thesis its power to provoke, suggesting that thinking through the indefinite play of *différance* can illuminate the radical consequences of the former. Precisely because there never was a simple ontological difference to be obscured, we cannot look back to a single 'Truth' of 'Being' that could be captured by a unique word of proper name. Not a monolithic genus for objectification, Being is both concealed and revealed by *différance*, speaking throughout all our languages.

Further reading

Derrida, Jacques. *Edmund Husserl's Origin of Geometry: An Introduction*, trans. John P. Leavey Jnr. Lincoln: University of Nebraska Press, 1978.

Derrida, Jacques. *Margins of Philosophy*, trans. Alan Bass. Brighton: Harvester Press, 1982.

Derrida, Jacques. *Of Grammatology*, trans, Gayatri C. Spivak. Baltimore, MD: Johns Hopkins University Press, 1998.

Derrida, Jacques. *Of Spirit: Heidegger and the Question*, trans. G. Bennington and R. Bowlby. Chicago, IL: Chicago University Press, 1990.

Derrida, Jacques. *Speech and Phenomena and Other Essays on Husserl's Theory of Signs*, trans. David Allison. Evanston, IL: Northwestern University Press, 1973.

Derrida, Jacques. *Writing and Difference*, trans. Alan Bass. London: Routledge & Kegan Paul, 1978.

Critchley, Simon. *The Ethics of Deconstruction: Derrida and Levinas*. Oxford: Blackwell, 1992.

Evans, Joseph Claude. *Strategies of Deconstruction: Derrida and the Myth of the Voice*. Minneapolis, MS: University of Minnesota Press, 1991.

Glendinning, Simon (ed.). *Arguing with Derrida. Ratio* Special Issue. Oxford: Blackwell, 2000.

Hobson, Marian. *Jacques Derrida: Opening Lines*. London: Routledge, 1998.

Howells, Christina. *Derrida: Deconstruction from Phenomenology to Ethics*. Cambridge: Polity Press, 1998.

Norris, Christopher. *Derrida*. London: Fontana & Collins, 1987.

Wood, David, and Bernasconi, Robert (eds). *Derrida and Différance*. Evanston, IL: Northwestern University Press, 1988.

1

SIGNS AND THE BLINK OF AN EYE

[C]onsciousness is the self-presence of the living, the *Erleben*, of experience. Experience thus understood is simple and is in its essence free of illusion, since it relates only to itself in an absolute proximity. The illusion of speaking to oneself would float on the surface of experience as an empty, peripheral, and secondary consciousness. Language and its representation is added on to a consciousness that is simple and simply present to itself, or in any event to an experience which could reflect its own presence in silence.

As Husserl will say in *Ideas* [*Pertaining to a Pure Phenomenology and to a Phenomenological Philosophy*] *I*, § 111,

> every experience generally (every really living one, so to speak) is an experience according to the mode of "being present." It belongs to its very essence that it should be able to reflect upon that same essence in which it is necessarily characterized as *being* certain and present (p. 310, modified).

Signs would be foreign to this self-presence, which is the ground of presence in general. It is because signs are foreign to the self-presence of the living present that they may be called foreign to presence in general in (what is currently styled) intuition or perception.

If the representation of indicative speech in the monologue is false, it is because it is useless; this is the ultimate basis of the argumentation in this section (§ 8) of the First Investigation. If the subject indicates nothing to himself, it is because he cannot do so, and he cannot do so because there is no need of it. Since lived experience is immediately self-present in the mode of certitude and absolute necessity, the manifestation of the self to the self through the delegation or representation of an indicative sign is impossible because it is superfluous. It would be, in every sense of the term, *without reason* – thus without cause. Without cause because without purpose: *zwecklos*, Husserl says.

This *Zwecklosigkeit* of inward communication is the non-alterity, the nondifference in the identity of presence as self-presence. Of course this concept of *presence* not only involves the enigma of a being appearing in absolute proximity to oneself; it also designates the temporal essence of this proximity – which does not

J. Derrida, *Speech and Phenomena and Other Essays on Husserl's Theory of Signs*, 1973, trans. David B. Allison, pp. 58–69. Evanston, IL: Northwestern University Press.

serve to dispel the enigma. The self-presence of experience must be produced in the present taken as a now. And this is just what Husserl says: if "mental acts" are not announced to themselves through the intermediary of a "*Kundgabe*," if they do not have to be informed about themselves through the intermediary of indications, it is because they are "lived by us in the same instant" (*im selben Augenblick*). The present of self-presence would be as indivisible as the *blink of an eye*. [. . .] The force of this demonstration presupposes the instant as a point, the identity of experience instantaneously present to itself. Self-presence must be produced in the undivided unity of a temporal present so as to have nothing to reveal to itself by the agency of signs. Such a perception or intuition of self by self in presence would not only be the case where "signification" in general could not occur, but also would assure the general possibility of a primordial perception or intuition, i.e., of *nonsignification* as the "principle of principles." Later, whenever Husserl wants to stress the sense of primordial intuition, he will recall that it is the experience of the absence and uselessness of signs.[1]

The demonstration we are now concerned with was elaborated before his lectures on *The Phenomenology of Internal Time-Consciousness*;[2] for reasons that are as much historical as systematic, the temporality of experience is not a theme of the *Logical Investigations*. At this point, however, we cannot avoid noting that a certain concept of the "now," of the present as punctuality of the instant, discretely but decisively sanctions the whole system of "essential distinctions." If the punctuality of the instant is a myth, a spatial or mechanical metaphor, an inherited metaphysical concept, or all that at once, and if the present of self-presence is not *simple*, if it is constituted in a primordial and irreducible synthesis, then the whole of Husserl's argumentation is threatened in its very principle.

We cannot here go closely into the admirable analysis of *The Phenomenology of Internal Time-Consciousness*, which Heidegger, in *Sein und Zeit*, calls the first in the history of philosophy to break with a concept of time inherited from Aristotle's *Physics*, determined according to the basic notions of the "now," the "point," the "limit," and the "circle." Let us, however, assemble some references from the lectures that are relevant for our own point of view.

1. Whether or not it is a metaphysical presupposition, the concept of *punctuality*, of the *now* as *stigmē*, still plays a major role in *The Phenomenology of Internal Time-Consciousness*. Undoubtedly, no now can be isolated as a pure instant, a pure punctuality. Not only does Husserl recognize this ("it belongs to the essence of lived experiences that they must be extended in this fashion, that a punctual phase can never be for itself" [*ITC*, § 19; p. 70], but his whole description is incomparably well adapted to the original modifications of this irreducible spreading-out. This spread is nonetheless thought and described on the basis of the self-identity of the now as point, as a "source-point." In phenomenology, the idea of primordial presence and in general of "beginning," "absolute beginning" or *principium*,[3] always refers back to this "source-point." Although the flow of time is "not severable into parts which could be by themselves nor divisible into phases, points of the continuity, which could be by themselves," the "modes of running-off of an immanent temporal Object have a beginning, that is to say, a source-point. This is the mode of running-off with which the immanent Object begins to be. It is characterized as now" (*ITC*, § 10; pp. 48–49).

Despite all the complexity of its structures, temporality has a nondisplaceable center, an eye or living core, the punctuality of the real now. The "now-apprehension is, as it were, the nucleus of a comet's tail of retentions" (*ibid.*, § 11; p. 52) and "a punctual phase is actually present as now at any given moment, while the others are connected as a retentional train" (*ibid.*, § 16; p. 61). "The actual *now* is necessarily something punctual (*ein Punktuelles*) and remains so, *a form that persists through continuous change of matter*" (*Ideas I*, § 81; p. 237, modified).

It is to this self-same identity of the actual now that Husserl refers in the "*im selben Augenblick*" we began with. Moreover, within philosophy there is no possible objection concerning this privilege of the present-now; it defines the very element of philosophical thought, it is *evidence* itself, conscious thought itself, it governs every possible concept of truth and sense. No sooner do we question this privilege than we begin to get at the core of consciousness itself from a region that lies elsewhere than philosophy, a procedure that would remove every possible *security* and *ground* from discourse. In the last analysis, what is at stake is indeed the privilege of the actual present, the now. This conflict, necessarily unlike any other, is between philosophy, which is always a philosophy of presence, and a meditation on nonpresence – which is not perforce its contrary, or necessarily a meditation on a negative absence, or a theory of nonpresence *qua* unconsciousness.

The dominance of the now not only is integral to the system of the founding contrast established by metaphysics, that between *form* (or *eidos* or idea) and *matter* as a contrast between *act* and *potency* ("the actual *now* is necessarily something punctual and remains so, *a form that persists through continuous change of matter*") (*Ideas I*, § 81; p. 237); it also assures the tradition that carries over the Greek metaphysics of presence into the "modern" metaphysics of presence understood as self-consciousness, the metaphysics of the idea as representation (*Vorstellung*). It therefore designates the locus of a problem in which phenomenology confronts every position centered on nonconsciousness that can approach what is ultimately at stake, what is at bottom decisive: the concept of time. It is no accident that *The Phenomenology of Internal Time-Consciousness* both confirms the dominance of the present and rejects the "after-event" of the becoming conscious of an "unconscious content" which is the structure of temporality implied throughout Freud's texts.[4] Husserl writes to this effect:

> It is certainly an absurdity to speak of a content of which we are "unconscious," one of which we are conscious only later (*nachträglich*). Consciousness (*Bewusstsein*) is necessarily a being-conscious (*bewusstsein*) in each of its phases. Just as the retentional phase was conscious of the preceding one without making it an object, so also are we conscious of the primal datum – namely, in the specific form of the "now" – without its being objective; . . . retention of a content of which we are not conscious is impossible; . . . if every "content" necessarily and in itself is "unconscious" then the question of an additional dator consciousness becomes senseless. (*ITC*, Appendix IX; pp. 162–63, modified).

2. Despite this motif of the punctual now as "primal form" (*Urform*) of consciousness (*Ideas I*), the body of the description in *The Phenomenology of Internal*

Time-Consciousness and elsewhere prohibits our speaking of a simple self-identity of the present. In this way not only is what could be called the metaphysical assurance par excellence shaken, but, closer to our concerns, the *"im selben Augenblick"* argument in the *Investigations* is undermined.

In its critical as well as descriptive work, *The Phenomenology of Internal Time-Consciousness* demonstrates and confirms throughout the irreducibility of re-presentation (*Vergegenwärtigung, Repräsentation*) to presentative perception (*Gegenwärtigen, Präsentieren*), secondary and reproductive memory to retention, imagination to the primordial impression, the re-produced now to the perceived or retained actual now, etc. Without being able, here, to follow the rigorous development of this text (and without its being necessary to question its demonstrative worth), we can still examine its foundation of evidence and the *context* of these distinctions, which relates the terms distinguished to one another and constitutes the very possibility of their *comparison*.

One then sees quickly that the presence of the perceived present can appear as such only inasmuch as it is *continuously compounded* with a nonpresence and nonperception, with primary memory and expectation (retention and protention). These nonperceptions are neither added to, nor do they *occasionally* accompany, the actually perceived now; they are essentially and indispensably involved in its possibility. Husserl admittedly says that retention is still a perception. But this is the absolutely unique case – Husserl never recognized any other – of a perceiving in which the perceived is not a present but a past existing as a modification of the present:

> ... If we call perception *the act in which all "origination"* lies, which *constitutes originarily*, then *primary remembrance is perception.* For only in *primary remembrance do we see what is past*; only in it is the past constituted, i.e., *not in a representative but in a presentative way.* (*ITC*, § 17, p. 64).

Thus, in retention, the presentation that enables us to see gives a nonpresent, a past and unreal present. We might suspect, then, that if Husserl nonetheless calls it perception, this is because he holds to establishing a radical discontinuity between retention and reproduction, between perception and imagination, etc., and not between perception and retention. This is the *nervus demonstrandi* of his critique of Brentano. Husserl resolutely maintains that there is "no mention here of a continuous accommodation of perception to its opposite" (*ibid.*).

And yet, did not the preceding section quite explicitly entertain this very possibility?

> If we now relate what has been said about perception to the *differences of the givenness* with which temporal Objects make their appearance, then the *antithesis of perception* is *primary remembrance*, which appears here, and *primary expectation* (retention and protention), whereby *perception and non-perception continually* pass over into one another. (*ITC*, § 16; p. 62)

Further he writes:

> In an ideal sense, then, perception (impression) would be the phase of consciousness which constitutes the pure now, and memory every other phase of the continuity. But this is just an ideal limit, something abstract which can be nothing for itself. Moreover, it is also true that even this ideal now is not something *toto caelo* different from the not-now but continually accommodates itself thereto. The continual transition from perception to primary remembrance conforms to this accommodation. (*ITC*, § 16; p. 63)

As soon as we admit this continuity of the now and the not-now, perception and nonperception, in the zone of primordiality common to primordial impression and primordial retention, we admit the other into the self-identity of the *Augenblick*; nonpresence and nonevidence are admitted into the *blink of the instant*. There is a duration to the blink, and it closes the eye. This alterity is in fact the condition for presence, presentation, and thus for *Vorstellung* in general; it precedes all the dissociations that could be produced in presence, in *Vorstellung*. The difference between retention and reproduction, between primary and secondary memory, is not the radical difference Husserl wanted between perception and nonperception; it is rather a difference between two modifications of nonperception. Whatever the phenomenological difference between these two modifications may be, and despite the immense problems it poses and the necessity of taking them into account, it only serves to separate two ways of relating to the irreducible nonpresence of another now. Once again, this relation to nonpresence neither befalls, surrounds, nor conceals the presence of the primordial impression; rather it makes possible its ever renewed upsurge and virginity. However, it radically destroys any possibility of a simple self-identity. And this holds in depth for the constituting flux itself:

> If . . . we now consider the *constitutive* phenomena, we find a *flux*, and every phase of this flux is a *continuity of shading*. However, in principle, no phase of this flux is to be broadened out to a continuous succession; therefore, the flux should not be thought to be so transformed that this phase is extended in identity with itself (*ITC*, § 35; p. 99; italics added).

The fact that nonpresence and otherness are internal to presence strikes at the very root of the argument for the uselessness of signs in the self-relation.

3. Doubtless Husserl would refuse to assimilate the necessity of retention and the necessity of signs, for it is only the latter which (like the image) belong to the genus of representation and symbolism. Moreover, Husserl cannot give up this rigorous distinction without bringing into question the axiomatic *principium* of phenomenology itself. The force with which he maintains that retention and protention belong to the sphere of the primordial, provided it be understood "in the broad sense," and the insistence with which he contrasts the absolute validity of primary memory with the relative validity of secondary memory,[5] clearly indicate both his intent and his uneasiness. His uneasiness stems from the fact that he is trying to retain two apparently irreconcilable possibilities: (*a*) The living now is constituted as the absolute perceptual source only in a state of continuity with

retention taken as nonperception. Fidelity to experience and to "the things themselves" forbids that it be otherwise. (*b*) The source of certitude in general is the primordial character of the living now; it is necessary therefore to keep retention in the sphere of primordial certitude and to shift the frontier between the primordial and the nonprimordial. The frontier must pass not between the pure present and the nonpresent, i.e , between the actuality and inactuality of a living now, but rather between two forms of the re-turn or re-stitution of the present: re-tention and re-presentation.

Without reducing the abyss which may indeed separate retention from re-presentation, without hiding the fact that the problem of their relationship is none other than that of the history of "life" and of life's becoming conscious, we should be able to say *a priori* that their common root – the possibility of re-petition in its most general form, that is, the constitution of a trace in the most universal sense – is a possibility which not only must inhabit the pure actuality of the now but must constitute it through the very movement of difference it introduces. Such a trace is – if we can employ this language without immediately contradicting it or crossing it out as we proceed – more "primordial" than what is phenomenologically primordial. For the ideality of the form (*Form*) of presence itself implies that it be infinitely re-peatable, that its re-turn, as a return of the same, is necessary *ad infinitum* and is inscribed in presence itself. It implies that the re-turn is the return of a present which will be retained in a *finite* movement or retention and that primordial truth, in the phenomenological sense of the term, is only to be found rooted in the finitude of this retention. It is furthermore implied that the relation with infinity can be instituted only in the opening of the form of presence upon ideality, as the possibility of a re-turn *ad infinitum*. How can it be explained that the possibility of reflection and re-presentation belongs by essence to every experience, without this nonself-identity of the presence called primordial? How could it be explained that this possibility belongs, like a pure and ideal freedom, to the essence of consciousness? Husserl ceaselessly emphasizes that it does, in speaking of reflection, especially in *Ideas I*,[6] and in speaking of re-presentation, already in *The Phenomenology of Internal Time-Consciousness*.[7] In all these directions, the presence of the present is thought of as arising from the bending-back of a return, from the movement of repetition, and not the reverse. Does not the fact that this bending-back is irreducible in presence or in self-presence, that this trace or difference is always older than presence and procures for it its openness, prevent us from speaking about a simple self-identity "*im selben Augenblick*"? Does this not compromise the usage Husserl wants to make of the concept of "solitary mental life," and consequently of the rigorous separation of indication from expression? Do indication and the several concepts on whose basis we have thus far tried to think it through (the concepts of existence, nature, mediation, the empirical, etc.) not have an ineradicable origin in the movement of transcendental temporalization? By the same token, does not everything that is announced already in this reduction to "solitary mental life" (the transcendental reduction in all its stages, and notably the reduction to the monadic sphere of "ownness" – *Eigenheit* – etc.) appear to be stricken in its very possibility by what we are calling time? But what we are calling time must be given a different name – for "time" has always designated a movement conceived in terms of the present, and can mean nothing else. Is not the concept of pure solitude – of the monad in the phenomenological sense – *undermined* by its own origin, by the very condition of its self-presence, that is, by "time," to be conceived anew on the basis now of difference within auto-affection, on the basis of identifying identity and nonidentity within the "sameness" of the *im selben Augenblick*? Husserl himself evoked the analogy between the relation with the *alter ego*, constituted within the absolute monad of the ego, and the relation with the other present, the past present, as constituted in the absolute actuality of the living present (*Cartesian Meditations*, § 52).

Does not this "dialectic" – in every sense of the term and before any speculative subsumption of this concept – open up living to difference, and constitute, in the pure immanence of experience, the *divergence* involved in indicative communication and even in signification in general? And we mean the divergence of indicative communication *and signification in general*, for Husserl not only intends to exclude indication from "solitary mental life"; he will consider language in general, the element of logos, in its expressive form itself, as a secondary event, superadded to a primordial and pre-expressive stratum of sense. Expressive language itself would be something supervenient upon the absolute silence of self-relationship.

Notes

1 For example, the whole of the Sixth Investigation continually points out that between intuitive acts and contents, on the one hand, and significative acts and contents, on the other, the phenomenological difference is "irreducible" (see, especially, § 26). And yet the possibility of a "mixture" is admitted there – which provokes questions. The whole of *The Phenomenology of Internal Time-Consciousness* is based upon the radical discontinuity between intuitive presentation and the symbolic representation "which not only represents the object voidly but also represents it 'by means of' signs or images" (Edmund Husserl, *Vorlesungen zur Phänomenologie des inneren Zeitbewusstseins* [Halle: Max Niemeyer, 1929]; English translation by James S. Churchill, *The Phenomenology of Internal Time-Consciousness* [Bloomington: Indiana University Press, 1964], Appendix II; p. 134). [Hereafter abbreviated, in references, as *ITC*. – Translator.] In *Ideas I* we read that "between *perception* on the one hand and the *symbolic representation by means of images or signs* on the other, there exists an insurmountable eidetic difference." "We collapse into nonsense when, as is ordinarily done, we completely mix up these modes of presentation with their essentially different constructions" (trans. W. R. Boyce Gibson, *Ideas. General Introduction to Pure Phenomenology* (London/New York: George Allen & Unwin; Humanitis Pr., 1931), § 43, pp. 136–37 [hereafter '*Ideas I*'] pp. 136–37). And what Husserl says about the perception of sensible corporeal things also holds for perception in general, namely, that, by being given in person in presence, it is a "sign for itself" (*Ideas I*, § 52; p. 161). Is being a sign of itself (*index sui*) the same as not being a sign? It is in this sense that, "in the very instant" it is perceived, experience is a sign of itself, present to itself without the indicative detour.

2 *ITC*, § 19; p. 70.

3 It is perhaps opportune here to reread the definition of the "principle of principles." "But enough of such topsy-turvy theories! No theory we can conceive can mislead us in regard to the *principle of all principles: that every primordial dator Intuition is a source of authority (Rechtsquelle) for knowledge*, that *whatever presents itself in 'intuition' in primordial form* (as it were in its bodily reality), *is simply to be accepted as it gives itself out to be*, though *only within the limits in which it then presents itself*. Let our insight grasp this fact that the theory itself in its turn could not derive its truth except from primordial data. Every statement which does nothing more than give expression to such data through

merely unfolding their meaning and adjusting it accurately is thus really, as we have put it in the introductory words of this chapter, an *absolute beginning*, called in a genuine sense to provide foundations, a *principium*" (*Ideas I*, § 24; p. 92).

4 Cf., on this subject, our essay "Freud et la scène de l'écriture" in *L'Ecriture et la différence* (Paris: Seuil, 1967), pp. 293–340.

5 Cf., for example, among many analogous texts, Appendix III to *The Phenomenology of Internal Time-Consciousness*. "Accordingly, we have as essential modes of time-consciousness: (1) 'sensation' as actual presentation and essentially entwined (*verflochtene*) with it but also capable of autonomy, retention, and protention (originary spheres in the broader sense); (2) positing presentification (memory), co-presentification, and re-presentification (expectation); (3) phantasy-presentification as pure phantasy, in which all the same modes occur in phantasy-consciousness" (p. 142). Here again, it will be observed, the core of the problem assumes the form of an interweaving (*Verflechtung*) of threads whose essences phenomenology carefully unravels.

This extension of the primordial sphere is what permits us to distinguish between the absolute certainty attached to retention and the relative certainty dependent upon secondary memory or recall (*Wiedererinnerung*) in the form of re-presentation. Speaking of perceptions as primal experiences (*Urerlebnisse*), Husserl writes in *Ideas I*: "For closer inspection reveals in their concreteness only *one*, but that always a continuously flowing *absolute primordial phase*, that of the living *now*. . . . Thus, for instance, we grasp the *absolute right* of immanent *perceiving* reflexion, i.e., of immanent perception *simpliciter*, and indeed in respect of that which it brings in its flow to real primordial givenness; likewise the *absolute right of immanent retention*, in respect of that in it of which we are conscious as 'still' living and having 'just' happened, but of course no further than the content of what is thus characterized reaches. . . . We likewise grasp the *relative* right of immanent recollection" (*Ideas I*, § 78; pp. 221–22).

6 Particularly in § 77, where the problem of the difference and relations between reflection and representation is posed, for example, in secondary memory.

7 Cf., for example, § 42: "But to every present and presenting consciousness there corresponds the ideal possibility of an exactly matching presentification of this consciousness" (p. 115).

2

DIFFERANCE

The verb "to differ" [*différer*] seems to differ from itself. On the one hand, it indicates difference as distinction, inequality, or discernibility; on the other, it expresses the interposition of delay, the interval of a *spacing* and *temporalizing* that puts off until "later" what is presently denied, the possible that is presently impossible. Sometimes the *different* and sometimes the *deferred* correspond [in French] to the verb "to differ." This correlation, however, is not simply one between act and object, cause and effect, or primordial and derived.

In the one case "to differ" signifies nonidentity; in the other case it signifies the order of the *same*. Yet there must be a common, although entirely differant[1] [*différante*], root within the sphere that relates the two movements of differing to one another. We provisionally give the name *differance* to this *sameness* which is not *identical:* by the silent writing of its *a*, it has the desired advantage of referring to differing, *both* as spacing/temporalizing and as the movement that structures every dissociation.

As distinct from difference, *differance* thus points out the irreducibility of temporalizing (which is also temporalization – in transcendental language which is no longer adequate here, this would be called the constitution of primordial temporality – just as the term "spacing" also includes the constitution of primordial spatiality). Differance is not simply active (any more than it is a subjective accomplishment); it rather indicates the middle voice, it precedes and sets up the opposition between passivity and activity. With its *a*, differance more properly refers to what in classical language would be called the origin or production of differences and the differences between differences, the *play* [*jeu*] of differences. Its locus and operation will therefore be seen wherever speech appeals to difference.

Differance is neither a *word* nor a *concept*. In it, however, we shall see the juncture – rather than the summation – of what has been most decisively inscribed in the thought of what is conveniently called our "epoch": the difference of forces in Nietzsche, Saussure's principle of semiological difference, differing as the possibility of [neurone] facilitation,[2] impression and delayed effect in Freud, difference as the irreducibility of the trace of the other in Levinas, and the ontic-ontological difference in Heidegger.

Reflection on this last determination of difference will lead us to consider

J. Derrida, *Speech and Phenomena and Other Essays on Husserl's Theory of Signs*, 1973, trans. David B. Allison, pp. 129–60. Evanston, IL: Northwestern University Press.

differance as the *strategic* note or connection – relatively or provisionally *privileged* – which indicates the closure of presence, together with the closure of the conceptual order and denomination, a closure that is effected in the functioning of traces.

I SHALL SPEAK, THEN, OF A LETTER – the first one, if we are to believe the alphabet and most of the speculations that have concerned themselves with it.

I shall speak then of the letter *a*, this first letter which it seemed necessary to introduce now and then in writing the word "difference." This seemed necessary in the course of writing about writing, and of writing within a writing. [. . .] Now, in point of fact, it happens that this graphic difference (the *a* instead of the *e*), this marked difference between two apparently vocalic notations, between vowels, remains purely graphic: it is written or read, but it is not heard. It cannot be heard, and we shall see in what respects it is also beyond the order of understanding. It is put forward by a silent mark, by a tacit monument, or, one might even say, by a pyramid – keeping in mind not only the capital form of the printed letter but also that passage from Hegel's *Encyclopaedia* where he compares the body of the sign to an Egyptian pyramid. The *a* of differance, therefore, is not heard; it remains silent, secret, and discreet, like a tomb.[3] [. . .]

Doubtless this pyramidal silence of the graphic difference between the *e* and the *a* can function only within the system of phonetic writing and within a language or grammar historically tied to phonetic writing and to the whole culture which is inseparable from it. But I will say that it is just this – this silence that functions only within what is called phonetic writing – that points out or reminds us in a very opportune way that, contrary to an enormous prejudice, there is no phonetic writing. There is no purely and strictly phonetic writing. What is called phonetic writing can only function – in principle and *de jure*, and not due to some factual and technical inadequacy – by incorporating nonphonetic "signs" (punctuation, spacing, etc.); but when we examine their structure and necessity, we will quickly see that they are ill described by the concept of signs. Saussure had only to remind us that the play of difference was the functional condition, the condition of possibility, for every sign; and it is itself silent. The difference between two phonemes, which enables them to exist and to operate, is inaudible. The inaudible opens the two present phonemes to hearing, as they present themselves. If, then, there is no purely phonetic writing, it is because there is no purely phonetic phone. The difference that brings out phonemes and lets them be heard and understood [*entendre*] itself remains inaudible.

It will perhaps be objected that, for the same reasons, the graphic difference itself sinks into darkness, that it never constitutes the fullness of a sensible term, but draws out an invisible connection, the mark of an inapparent relation between two spectacles. That is no doubt true. Indeed, since from this point of view the difference between the *e* and the *a* marked in "differance" eludes vision and hearing, this happily suggests that we must here let ourselves be referred to an order that no longer refers to sensibility. But we are not referred to intelligibility either, to an ideality not fortuitously associated with the objectivity of *theōrein* or understanding. We must be referred to an order, then, that resists philosophy's founding opposition between the sensible and the intelligible. The order that resists this opposition, that resists it because it sustains it, is designated in a movement of differance (with an *a*) between two differences or between two letters. This differ-ance belongs neither to the voice nor to writing in the ordinary sense, and it takes place, like the strange space that will assemble us here for the course of an hour, *between* speech and writing and beyond the tranquil familiarity that binds us to one and to the other, reassuring us sometimes in the illusion that they are two separate things. [. . .]

Although "differance" is neither a word nor a concept, let us nonetheless attempt a simple and approximative semantic analysis which will bring us in view of what is at stake [*en vue de l'enjeu*].

We do know that the verb "to differ" [*différer*] (the Latin verb *differre*) has two seemingly quite distinct meanings; in the *Littré* dictionary, for example, they are the subject of two separate articles. In this sense, the Latin *differre* is not the simple translation of the Greek *diapherein*; this fact will not be without con-sequence for us in tying our discussion to a particular language, one that passes for being less philosophical, less primordially philosophical, than the other. For the distribution of sense in the Greek *diapherein* does not carry one of the two themes of the Latin *differre*, namely, the action of postponing until later, of tak-ing into account, the taking-account of time and forces in an operation that implies an economic reckoning, a detour, a respite, a delay, a reserve, a representa-tion – all the concepts that I will sum up here in a word I have never used but which could be added to this series: *temporalizing*. "To differ" in this sense is to temporalize, to resort, consciously or unconsciously, to the temporal and tempo-ralizing mediation of a detour that suspends the accomplishment or fulfillment of "desire" or "will," or carries desire or will out in a way that annuls or tempers their effect. We shall see, later, in what respects this temporalizing is also a tempo-ralization and spacing, is space's becoming-temporal and time's becoming-spatial, is "primordial constitution" of space and time, as metaphysics or transcendental phenomenology would call it in the language that is here criticized and displaced.

The other sense of "to differ" [*différer*] is the most common and most identifi-able, the sense of not being identical, of being other, of being discernible, etc. And in "differents," whether referring to the alterity of dissimilarity or the alterity of allergy or of polemics, it is necessary that interval, distance, *spacing* occur among the different elements and occur actively, dynamically, and with a certain perseverence in repetition.

But the word "difference" (with an *e*) could never refer to differing as temporal-izing or to difference as *polemos*. It is this loss of sense that the word differance (with an *a*) will have to schematically compensate for. Differance can refer to the whole complex of its meanings at once, for it is immediately and irreducibly multivalent, something which will be important for the discourse I am trying to develop. It refers to this whole complex of meanings not only when it is supported by a language or interpretive context (like any signification), but it already does so somehow of itself. Or at least it does so more easily by itself than does any other word: here the *a* comes more immediately from the present participle [*différant*] and brings us closer to the action of "differing" that is in progress, even before it has produced the effect that is constituted as different or resulted in difference (with an *e*). Within a conceptual system and in terms of classical requirements, differance could be said to designate the productive and primordial constituting causality, the process of scission and division whose differings and differences would be the constituted products or effects. But while bringing us closer to the infinitive and active core of differing, "differance" with an *a* neutralizes what the infinitive denotes as simply active, in the same way that "parlance" does not signify the simple fact of speaking, of speaking to or being spoken to. Nor is resonance the act of resonating. Here in the usage of our language we must consider that the ending -*ance* is undecided between active and passive. And we shall see why what is designated by "differance" is neither simply active nor simply passive, that it announces or rather recalls something like the middle voice, that it speaks of an operation which is not an operation, which cannot be thought of either as a passion or as an action of a subject upon an object, as starting from an agent or from a patient, or on the basis of, or in view of, any of these *terms*. But philosophy has perhaps commenced by distributing the middle voice, expressing a certain intransitiveness, into the active and the passive voice, and has itself been constituted in this repression.

How are differance as temporalizing and differance as spacing conjoined?

Let us begin with the problem of signs and writing – since we are already in the midst of it. We ordinarily say that a sign is put in place of the thing itself, the present thing – "thing" holding here for the sense as well as the referent. Signs represent the present in its absence; they take the place of the present. When we cannot take hold of or show the thing, let us say the present, the being-present, when the present does not present itself, then we signify, we go through the detour of signs. We take up or give signs; we make signs. The sign would thus be a deferred presence. Whether it is a question of verbal or written signs, monetary signs, electoral delegates, or political representatives, the movement of signs defers the moment of encountering the thing itself, the moment at which we could lay hold of it, consume or expend it, touch it, see it, have a present intuition of it. What I am describing here is the structure of signs as classically determined, in order to define – through a commonplace characterization of its traits – signification as the differance of temporalizing. Now this classical determination presupposes that the sign (which defers presence) is conceivable only *on the basis of* the presence that it defers and *in view of* the deferred presence one intends to reappropriate. Following this classical semiology, the substitution of the sign for the thing itself is both *secondary* and *provisional*: it is second in order after an original and lost presence, a presence from which the sign would be derived. It is provisional with respect to this final and missing presence, in view of which the sign would serve as a movement of mediation.

In attempting to examine these secondary and provisional aspects of the substitute, we shall no doubt catch sight of something like a primordial differance. Yet we could no longer even call it primordial or final, inasmuch as the characteristics of origin, beginning, *telos, eschaton*, etc., have always denoted presence – *ousia, parousia*, etc. To question the secondary and provisional character of the sign, to oppose it to a "primordial" differance, would thus have the following consequences:

1. Differance can no longer be understood according to the concept of "sign," which has always been taken to mean the representation of a presence and has been constituted in a system (of thought or language) determined on the basis of and in view of presence.

2. In this way we question the authority of presence or its simple symmetrical contrary, absence or lack. We thus interrogate the limit that has always constrained us, that always constrains us – we who inhabit a language and a system of thought – to form the sense of being in general as presence or absence, in the categories of being or beingness (*ousia*). [. . .]

But first of all, let us remain with the semiological aspects of the problem to see how differance as temporalizing is conjoined with differance as spacing. Most of the semiological or linguistic research currently dominating the field of thought (whether due to the results of its own investigations or due to its role as a generally recognized regulative model) traces its genealogy, rightly or wrongly, to Saussure as its common founder. It was Saussure who first of all set forth the *arbitrariness of signs* and the *differential character* of signs as principles of general semiology and particularly of linguistics. And, as we know, these two themes – the arbitrary and the differential – are in his view inseparable. Arbitrariness can occur only because the system of signs is constituted by the differences between the terms, and not by their fullness. The elements of signification function not by virtue of the compact force of their cores but by the network of oppositions that distinguish them and relate them to one another. "Arbitrary and differential" says Saussure "are two correlative qualities."

As the condition for signification, this principle of difference affects the *whole sign*, that is, both the signified and the signifying aspects. The signified aspect is the concept, the ideal sense. The signifying aspect is what Saussure calls the material or physical (e.g., acoustical) "image." We do not here have to enter into all the problems these definitions pose. Let us only cite Saussure where it interests us:

> The conceptual side of value is made up solely of relations and differences with respect to the other terms of language, and the same can be said of its material side. . . . Everything that has been said up to this point boils down to this: in language there are only differences. Even more important: a difference generally implies positive terms between which the difference is set up; but in language there are only differences *without positive terms*. Whether we take the signified or the signifier, language has neither ideas nor sounds that existed before the linguistic system, but only conceptual and phonic differences that have issued from the system. The idea or phonic substance that a sign contains is of less importance than the other signs that surround it.[4]

The first consequence to be drawn from this is that the signified concept is never present in itself, in an adequate presence that would refer only to itself. Every concept is necessarily and essentially inscribed in a chain or a system, within which it refers to another and to other concepts, by the systematic play of differences. Such a play, then – differance – is no longer simply a concept, but the possibility of conceptuality, of the conceptual system and process in general. For the same reason, differance, which is not a concept, is not a mere word; that is, it is not what we represent to ourselves as the calm and present self-referential unity of a concept and sound [*phone*]. We shall later discuss the consequences of this for the notion of a word.

The difference that Saussure speaks about, therefore, is neither itself a concept nor one word among others. We can say this *a fortiori* for differance. Thus we are brought to make the relation between the one and the other explicit.

Within a language, within the *system* of language, there are only differences. A taxonomic operation can accordingly undertake its systematic, statistical, and classificatory inventory. But, on the one hand, these differences *play a role* in language, in speech as well, and in the exchange between language and speech. On the other hand, these differences are themselves *effects*. They have not fallen from the sky ready made; they are no more inscribed in a *topos noētos* than they are prescribed in the wax of the brain. If the word "history" did not carry with it the theme of a final repression of differance, we could say that differences alone could be "historical" through and through and from the start.

What we note as *differance* will thus be the movement of play that "produces" (and not by something that is simply an activity) these differences, these effects of difference. This does not mean that the differance which produces differences is before them in a simple and in itself unmodified and indifferent present. Differance is the nonfull, nonsimple "origin"; it is the structured and differing origin of differences.

Since language (which Saussure says is a classification) has not fallen from the sky, it is clear that the differences have been produced; they are the effects produced, but effects that do not have as their cause a subject or substance, a thing in general, or a being that is somewhere present and itself escapes the play of difference. If such a presence were implied (quite classically) in the general concept of cause, we would therefore have to talk about an effect without a cause, something that would very quickly lead to no longer talking about effects. I have tried to indicate a way out of the closure imposed by this system, namely, by means of the "trace." No more an effect than a cause, the "trace" cannot of itself, taken outside its context, suffice to bring about the required transgression.

As there is no presence before the semiological difference or outside it, we can extend what Saussure writes about language to signs in general: "Language is necessary in order for speech to be intelligible and to produce all of its effects; but the latter is necessary in order for language to be established; historically, the fact of speech always comes first."[5]

Retaining at least the schema, if not the content, of the demand formulated by Saussure, we shall designate by the term *differance* the movement by which language, or any code, any system of reference in general, becomes "historically" constituted as a fabric of differences. Here, the terms "constituted," "produced," "created," "movement," "historically," etc., with all they imply, are not to be understood only in terms of the language of metaphysics, from which they are taken. It would have to be shown why the concepts of production, like those of constitution and history, remain accessories in this respect to what is here being questioned; this, however, would draw us too far away today, toward the theory of the representation of the "circle" in which we seem to be enclosed. I only use these terms here, like many other concepts, out of strategic convenience and in order to prepare the deconstruction of the system they form at the point which is now most decisive. In any event, we will have understood, by virtue of the very circle we appear to be caught up in, that differance, as it is written here, is no more static than genetic, no more structural than historical. Nor is it any less so. And it is completely to miss the point of this orthographical impropriety to want to object to it on the basis of the oldest of metaphysical oppositions – for example, by opposing some generative point of view to a structuralist-taxonomic point of view, or conversely. These oppositions do not pertain in the least to differance; and this, no doubt, is what makes thinking about it difficult and uncomfortable.

If we now consider the chain to which "differance" gets subjected, according to the context, to a certain number of nonsynonymic substitutions, one will ask why we resorted to such concepts as "reserve," "protowriting," "prototrace," "spacing," indeed to "supplement" or *pharmakon*," and, before long, to "hymen," etc.[6]

Let us begin again. Differance is what makes the movement of signification possible only if each element that is said to be "present," appearing on the stage of presence, is related to something other than itself but retains the mark of a past element and already lets itself be hollowed out by the mark of its relation to a future element. This trace relates no less to what is called the future than to what is called the past, and it constitutes what is called the present by this very relation to what it is not, to what it absolutely is not; that is, not even to a past or future considered as a modified present. In order for it to be, an interval must separate it from what it is not; but the interval that constitutes it in the present must also, and by the same token, divide the present in itself, thus dividing, along with the present, everything that can be conceived on its basis, that is, every being – in particular, for our metaphysical language, the substance or subject. Constituting itself, dynamically dividing itself, this interval is what could be called *spacing*; time's becoming-spatial or space's becoming-temporal (*temporalizing*). And it is this constitution of the present as a "primordial" and irreducibly nonsimple, and, therefore, in the strict sense nonprimordial, synthesis of traces, retentions, and protentions (to reproduce here, analogically and provisionally, a phenomenological and transcendental language that will presently be revealed as inadequate) that I propose to call protowriting, prototrace, or differance. The latter (is) (both) spacing (and) temporalizing.[7]

Given this (active) movement of the (production of) differance without origin, could we not, quite simply and without any neographism, call it *differentiation*? Among other confusions, such a word would suggest some organic unity, some primordial and homogeneous unity, that would eventually come to be divided up and take on difference as an event. Above all, formed on the verb "to differentiate," this word would annual the economic signification of detour, temporalizing delay, "deferring." I owe a remark in passing to a recent reading of one of Koyré's texts entitled "Hegel at Jena."[8] In that text, Koyré cites long passages from the Jena *Logic* in German and gives his own translation. On two occasions in Hegel's text he encounters the expression "*differente Beziehung*." This word (*different*), whose root is Latin, is extremely rare in German and also, I believe, in Hegel, who instead uses *verschieden* or *ungleich*, calling difference *Unterschied* and qualitative variety *Verschiedenheit*. In the Jena *Logic*, he uses the word *different* precisely at the point where he deals with time and the present. Before coming to Koyré's valuable remark, here are some passages from Hegel, as rendered by Koyré:

> The infinite, in this simplicity is – as a moment opposed to the self-identical – the negative. In its moments, while the infinite presents the

totality to (itself) and in itself, (it is) excluding in general, the point or limit; but in this, its own (action of) negating, it relates itself immediately to the other and negates itself. The limit or moment of the present (*der Gegenwart*), the absolute "this" of time or the now, is an absolutely negative simplicity, absolutely excluding all multiplicity from itself, and by this very fact is absolutely determined; it is not an extended whole or *quantum* within itself (and) which would in itself also have an undetermined aspect or qualitative variety, which of itself would be related, indifferently (*gleichgültig*) or externally to another, but on the contrary, this is an absolutely different relation of the simple.[9]

And Koyré specifies in a striking note: "Different relation: *differente Beziehung*. We could say: differentiating relation." And on the following page, from another text of Hegel, we can read: "*Diese Beziehung ist Gegenwart, als eine differente Beziehung*" (This relation is [the] present, as a different relation). There is another note by Koyré: "The term '*different*' is taken here in an active sense."

Writing "differing" or "differance" (with an *a*) would have had the utility of making it possible to translate Hegel on precisely this point with no further qualifications – and it is a quite decisive point in his text. The translation would be, as it always should be, the transformation of one language by another. Naturally, I maintain that the word "differance" can be used in other ways, too; first of all, because it denotes not only the activity of primordial difference but also the temporalizing detour of deferring. It has, however, an even more important usage. Despite the very profound affinities that differance thus written has with Hegelian speech (as it should be read), it can, at a certain point, not exactly break with it, but rather work a sort of displacement with regard to it. A definite rupture with Hegelian language would make no sense, nor would it be at all likely; but this displacement is both infinitesimal and radical. I have tried to indicate the extent of this displacement elsewhere; it would be difficult to talk about it with any brevity at this point.

Differences are thus "produced" – differed – by differance. But *what* differs, or *who* differs? In other words, *what is* differance? With this question we attain another stage and another source of the problem.

What differs? Who differs? What is differance?

If we answered these questions even before examining them as questions, even before going back over them and questioning their form (even what seems to be most natural and necessary about them), we would fall below the level we have now reached. For if we accepted the form of the question in its own sense and syntax ("What?," "What is?," "Who is?"), we would have to admit that differance is derived, supervenient, controlled, and ordered from the starting point of a being-present, one capable of being something, a force, a state, or power in the world, to which we could give all kinds of names: a *what*, or being-present as a *subject*, a *who*. In the latter case, notably, we would implicitly admit that the being-present (for example, as a self-present being or consciousness) would eventually result in differing: in delaying or in diverting the fulfillment of a "need" or "desire," or in differing from itself. But in none of these cases would such a being-present be "constituted" by this differance.

Now if we once again refer to the semiological difference, what was it that

Saussure in particular reminded us of? That "language [which consists only of differences] is not a function of the speaking subject." This implies that the subject (self-identical or even conscious of self-identity, self-conscious) is inscribed in the language, that he is a "function" of the language. He becomes a *speaking* subject only by conforming his speech – even in the aforesaid "creation," even in the aforesaid "transgression" – to the system of linguistic prescriptions taken as the system of differences, or at least to the general law of differance, by conforming to that law of language which Saussure calls "language without speech." "Language is necessary for the spoken word to be intelligible and so that it can produce all of its effects."[10]

If, by hypothesis, we maintain the strict opposition between speech and language, then differance will be not only the play of differences within the language but the relation of speech to language, the detour by which I must also pass in order to speak, the silent token I must give, which holds just as well for linguistics in the strict sense as it does for general semiology; it dictates all the relations between usage and the formal schema, between the message and the particular code, etc. Elsewhere I have tried to suggest that this differance within language, and in the relation between speech and language, forbids the essential dissociation between speech and writing that Saussure, in keeping with tradition, wanted to draw at another level of his presentation. The use of language or the employment of any code which implies a play of forms – with no determined or invariable substratum – also presupposes a retention and protention of differences, a spacing and temporalizing, a play of traces. This play must be a sort of inscription prior to writing, a protowriting without a present origin, without an *archē*. From this comes the systematic crossing-out of the *archē* and the transformation of general semiology into a grammatology, the latter performing a critical work upon everything within semiology – right down to its matrical concept of signs – that retains any metaphysical presuppositions incompatible with the theme of differance.

We might be tempted by an objection: to be sure, the subject becomes a *speaking* subject only by dealing with the system of linguistic differences; or again, he becomes a *signifying* subject (generally by speech or other signs) only by entering into the system of differences. In this sense, certainly, the speaking or signifying subject would not be self-present, insofar as he speaks or signifies, except for the play of linguistic or semiological differance. But can we not conceive of a presence and self-presence of the subject before speech or its signs, a subject's self-presence in a silent and intuitive consciousness?

Such a question therefore supposes that prior to signs and outside them, and excluding every trace and difference, something such as consciousness is possible. It supposes, moreover, that, even before the distribution of its signs in space and in the world, consciousness can gather itself up in its own presence. What then is consciousness? What does "consciousness" mean? Most often in the very form of "meaning" ["*vouloir-dire*"], consciousness in all its modifications is conceivable only as self-presence, a self-perception of presence. And what holds for consciousness also holds here for what is called subjective existence in general. Just as the category of subject is not and never has been conceivable without reference to presence as *hypokeimenon* or *ousia*, etc., so the subject as consciousness has never been able to be evinced otherwise than as self-presence. The privilege accorded to consciousness thus means a privilege accorded to the present; and even if the transcendental temporality of consciousness is described in depth, as Husserl described it, the power of synthesis and of the incessant gathering-up of traces is always accorded to the "living present."

This privilege is the ether of metaphysics, the very element of our thought insofar as it is caught up in the language of metaphysics. We can only de-limit such a closure today by evoking this import of presence, which Heidegger has shown to be the onto-theological determination of being. Therefore, in evoking this import of presence, by an examination which would have to be of a quite peculiar nature, we question the absolute privilege of this form or epoch of presence in general, that is, consciousness as meaning [*vouloir-dire*] in self-presence.

We thus come to posit presence – and, in particular, consciousness, the being-next-to-itself of consciousness – no longer as the absolutely matrical form of being but as a "determination" and an "effect." Presence is a determination and effect within a system which is no longer that of presence but that of differance; it no more allows the opposition between activity and passivity than that between cause and effect or in-determination and determination, etc. This system is of such a kind that even to designate consciousness as an effect or determination – for strategic reasons, reasons that can be more or less clearly considered and systematically ascertained – is to continue to operate according to the vocabulary of that very thing to be de-limited.

Before being so radically and expressly Heideggerian, this was also Nietzsche's and Freud's move, both of whom, as we know, and often in a very similar way, questioned the self-assured certitude of consciousness. And is it not remarkable that both of them did this by starting out with the theme of differance?

This theme appears almost literally in their work, at the most crucial places. I shall not expand on this here; I shall only recall that for Nietzsche "the important main activity is unconscious" and that consciousness is the effect of forces whose essence, ways, and modalities are not peculiar to it. Now force itself is never present; it is only a play of differences and quantities. There would be no force in general without the difference between forces; and here the difference in quantity counts more than the content of quantity, more than the absolute magnitude itself. [. . .]

We shall therefore call differance this "active" (in movement) discord of the different forces and of the differences between forces which Nietzsche opposes to the entire system of metaphysical grammar, wherever that system controls culture, philosophy, and science.

It is historically significant that this diaphoristics, understood as an energetics or an economy of forces, set up to question the primacy of presence qua consciousness, is also the major theme of Freud's thought; in his work we find another diaphoristics, both in the form of a theory of ciphers or traces and an energetics. The questioning of the authority of consciousness is first and always differential.

The two apparently different meanings of differance are tied together in Freudian theory: differing [*le différer*] as discernibility, distinction, deviation, diastem, *spacing*; and deferring [*le différer*] as detour, delay, relay, reserve, *temporalizing*. I shall recall only that:

1. The concept of trace (*Spur*), of facilitation (*Bahnung*), of forces of

facilitation are, as early as the composition of the *Entwurf*, inseparable from the concept of difference. The origin of memory and of the psyche as a memory in general (conscious or unconscious) can only be described by taking into account the difference between the facilitation thresholds, as Freud says explicitly. There is no facilitation [*Bahnung*] without difference and no difference without a trace.

2. All the differences involved in the production of unconscious traces and in the process of inscription (*Niederschrift*) can also be interpreted as moments of differance, in the sense of "placing on reserve." Following a schema that continually guides Freud's thinking, the movement of the trace is described as an effort of life to protect itself *by deferring* the dangerous investment, by constituting a reserve (*Vorrat*). And all the conceptual oppositions that furrow Freudian thought relate each concept to the other like movements of a detour, within the economy of differance. The one is only the other deferred, the one differing from the other. The one is the other in differance, the one is the differance from the other. Every apparently rigorous and irreducible opposition (for example, that between the secondary and primary) is thus said to be, at one time or another, a "theoretical fiction." In this way again, for example (but such an example covers everything or communicates with everything), the difference between the pleasure principle and the reality principle is only differance as detour (*Aufschieben, Aufschub*). In *Beyond the Pleasure Principle*, Freud writes:

> Under the influence of the ego's instincts of self-preservation, the pleasure principle is replaced by the reality principle. This latter principle does not abandon the intention of ultimately obtaining pleasure, but it nevertheless demands and carries into effect the postponement of satisfaction, the abandonment of a number of possibilities of gaining satisfaction and the temporary toleration of unpleasure as a step on the long indirect road (*Aufschub*) to pleasure.[11]

Here we touch on the point of greatest obscurity, on the very enigma of differance, on how the concept we have of it is divided by a strange separation. We must not hasten to make a decision too quickly. How can we conceive of differance as a systematic detour which, within the element of the same, always aims at either finding again the pleasure or the presence that had been deferred by (conscious or unconscious) calculation, and, *at the same time*, how can we, on the other hand, conceive of differance as the relation to an impossible presence, as an expenditure without reserve, as an irreparable loss of presence, an irreversible wearing-down of energy, or indeed as a death instinct and a relation to the absolutely other that apparently breaks up any economy? [. . .]

The economic character of differance in no way implies that the deferred presence can always be recovered, that it simply amounts to an investment that only temporarily and without loss delays the presentation of presence, that is, the perception of gain or the gain of perception. Contrary to the metaphysical, dialectical, and "Hegelian" interpretation of the economic movement of differance, we must admit a game where whoever loses wins and where one wins and loses each time. If the diverted presentation continues to be somehow definitively and irreducibly withheld, this is not because a particular present remains hidden or absent, but because differance holds us in a relation with what exceeds (though we necessarily fail to recognize this) the alternative of presence or absence. A certain alterity – Freud gives it a metaphysical name, the unconscious – is definitively taken away from every process of presentation in which we would demand for it to be shown forth in person. In this context and under this heading, the unconscious is not, as we know, a hidden, virtual, and potential self-presence. It is differed – which no doubt means that it is woven out of differences, but also that it sends out, that it delegates, representatives or proxies; but there is no chance that the mandating subject "exists" somewhere, that it is present or is "itself," and still less chance that it will become conscious. In this sense, contrary to the terms of an old debate, strongly symptomatic of the metaphysical investments it has always assumed, the "unconscious" can no more be classed as a "thing" than as anything else; it is no more of a thing than an implicit or masked consciousness. This radical alterity, removed from every possible mode of presence, is character- ized by irreducible aftereffects, by delayed effects. In order to describe them, in order to read the traces of the "unconscious" traces (there are no "conscious" traces), the language of presence or absence, the metaphysical speech of phenomenology, is in principle inadequate.

The structure of delay (*retardement: Nachträglichkeit*) that Freud talks about indeed prohibits our taking temporalization (temporalizing) to be a simple dia- lectical complication of the present; rather, this is the style of transcendental phenomenology. It describes the living present as a primordial and incessant syn- thesis that is constantly led back upon itself, back upon its assembled and assembling self, by retentional traces and protentional openings. With the alterity of the "unconscious," we have to deal not with the horizons of modified presents – past or future – but with a "past" that has never been nor will ever be present, whose "future" will never be produced or reproduced in the form of presence. The concept of trace is therefore incommensurate with that of retention, that of the becoming-past of what had been present. The trace cannot be conceived – nor, therefore, can differance – on the basis of either the present or the presence of the present.

A past that has never been present: with this formula Emmanuel Levinas desig- nates (in ways that are, to be sure, not those of psychoanalysis) the trace and the engima of absolute alterity, that is, the Other [*autrui*]. At least within these limits, and from this point of view, the thought of differance implies the whole critique of classical ontology undertaken by Levinas. And the concept of trace, like that of differance, forms – across these different traces and through these differences between traces, as understood by Nietzsche, Freud, and Levinas (these "authors' names" serve only as indications) – the network that sums up and permeates our "epoch" as the de-limitation of ontology (of presence).

The ontology of presence is the ontology of beings and beingness. Everywhere, the dominance of beings is solicited by differance – in the sense that *sollicitare* means, in old Latin, to shake all over, to make the whole tremble. What is ques- tioned by the thought of differance, therefore, is the determination of being in presence, or in beingness. Such a question could not arise and be understood without the difference between Being and beings opening up somewhere. The first consequence of this is that differance is not. It is not a being-present, however excellent, unique, principal, or transcendent one makes it. It commands nothing, rules over nothing, and nowhere does it exercise any authority. It is not marked by a capital letter. Not only is there no realm of differance, but differance is even the subversion of every realm. This is obviously what makes it threatening and necessarily dreaded by everything in us that desires a realm, the past or future presence of a realm. And it is always in the name of a realm that, believing one sees it ascend to the capital letter, one can reproach it for wanting to rule.

Does this mean, then, that differance finds its place within the spread of the ontic-ontological difference, as it is conceived, as the "epoch" conceives itself within it, and particularly "across" the Heideggerian meditation, which cannot be gotten around?

There is no simple answer to such a question.

In one particular respect, differance is, to be sure, but the historical and epochal *deployment* of Being or of the ontological difference. The *a* of differance marks the *movement* of this deployment.

And yet, is not the thought that conceives the *sense* or *truth* of Being, the determination of differance as ontic-ontological difference – difference conceived within the horizon of the question of *Being* – still an intrametaphysical effect of differance? Perhaps the deployment of differance is not only the truth or the epochality of Being. Perhaps we must try to think this *unheard-of* thought, this silent tracing, namely, that the history of Being (the thought of which is committed to the Greco-Western logos), as it is itself produced across the ontological difference, is only one epoch of the *diapherein*. Then we could no longer even call it an "epoch," for the concept of epochality belongs within history understood as the history of Being. Being has always made "sense," has always been conceived or spoken of as such, only by dissimulating itself in beings; thus, in a particular and very strange way, differance (is) "older" than the ontological difference or the truth of Being. In this age it can be called the play of traces. It is a trace that no longer belongs to the horizon of Being but one whose sense of Being is borne and bound by this play; it is a play of traces or differance that has no sense and is not, a play that does not belong. There is no support to be found and no depth to be had for this bottomless chessboard where being is set in play.

It is perhaps in this way that the Heraclitean play of the *hen diapheron heautōi*, of the one differing from itself, of what is in difference with itself, already becomes lost as a trace in determining the *diapherein* as ontological difference.

To think through the ontological difference doubtless remains a difficult task, a task whose statement has remained nearly inaudible. And to prepare ourselves for venturing beyond our own logos, that is, for a difference so violent that it refuses to be stopped and examined as the epochality of Being and ontological difference, is neither to give up this passage through the truth of Being, nor is it in any way to "criticize," "contest," or fail to recognize the incessant necessity for it. On the contrary, we must stay within the difficulty of this passage; we must repeat this passage in a rigorous reading of metaphysics, wherever metaphysics serves as the norm of Western speech, and not only in the texts of "the history of philosophy." Here we must allow the trace of whatever goes beyond the truth of Being to appear/disappear in its fully rigorous way. It is a trace of something that can never present itself; it is itself a trace that can never be presented, that is, can never appear and manifest itself as such in its phenomenon. It is a trace that lies beyond what profoundly ties fundamental ontology to phenomenology. Like differance, the trace is never presented as such. In presenting itself it becomes effaced; in being sounded it dies away, like the writing of the *a*, inscribing its pyramid in differance.

We can always reveal the precursive and secretive traces of this movement in metaphysical speech, especially in the contemporary talk about the closure of ontology, i.e., through the various attempts we have looked at (Nietzsche, Freud, Levinas) – and particularly in Heidegger's work.

The latter provokes us to question the essence of the present, the presence of the present.

What is the present? What is it to conceive the present in its presence?

Let us consider, for example, the 1946 text entitled "Der Spruch des Anaximander." Heidegger there recalls that the forgetting of Being forgets about the difference between Being and beings:

> But the point of Being (*die Sache des Seins*) is to be the Being of beings. The linguistic form of this enigmatic and multivalent genitive designates a genesis (*Genesis*), a provenance (*Herkunft*) of the present from presence (*des Anwesenden aus dem Anwesen*). But with the unfolding of these two, the essence (*Wesen*) of this provenance remains hidden (*verborgen*). Not only is the essence of this provenance not thought out, but neither is the simple relation between presence and present (*Anwesen und Anwesenden*). Since the dawn, it seems that presence and being-present are each separately something. Imperceptibly, presence becomes itself a present.... The essence of presence (*Das Wesen des Anwesens*), and thus the difference between presence and present, is forgotten. *The forgetting of Being is the forgetting of the difference between Being and beings.*[12]

In recalling the difference between Being and beings (the ontological difference) as the difference between presence and present, Heidegger puts forward a proposition, indeed, a group of propositions; it is not our intention here to idly or hastily "criticize" them but rather to convey them with all their provocative force.

Let us then proceed slowly. What Heidegger wants to point out is that the difference between Being and beings, forgotten by metaphysics, has disappeared without leaving a trace. The very trace of difference has sunk from sight. If we admit that differance (is) (itself) something other than presence and absence, if it *traces*, then we are dealing with the forgetting of the difference (between Being and beings), and we now have to talk about a disappearance of the trace's trace. This is certainly what this passage from "Der Spruch des Anaximander" seems to imply:

> The forgetting of Being is a part of the very essence of Being, and is concealed by it. The forgetting belongs so essentially to the destination of Being that the dawn of this destination begins precisely as an unconcealment of the *present* in its *presence*. This means: the history of Being begins by the forgetting of Being, in that Being retains its essence, its difference from beings. Difference is wanting; it remains forgotten. Only what is differentiated – the present and presence (*das Anwesende und das Anwesen*) – becomes uncovered, but not *insofar as* it is differentiated. On the contrary, the matinal trace (*die frühe Spur*) of difference effaces itself

from the moment that presence appears as a being-present (*das Anwesen wie ein Anwesendes erscheint*) and finds its provenance in a supreme (being)-present (*in einem höchsten Anwesenden*).[13]

The trace is not a presence but is rather the simulacrum of a presence that dislocates, displaces, and refers beyond itself. The trace has, properly speaking, no place, for effacement belongs to the very structure of the trace. Effacement must always be able to overtake the trace; otherwise it would not be a trace but an indestructible and monumental substance. In addition, and from the start, effacement constitutes it as a trace – effacement establishes the trace in a change of place and makes it disappear in its appearing, makes it issue forth from itself in its very position. The effacing of this early trace (*die frühe Spur*) of difference is therefore "the same" as its tracing within the text of metaphysics. This metaphysical text must have retained a mark of what it lost or put in reserve, set aside. In the language of metaphysics the paradox of such a structure is the inversion of the metaphysical concept which produces the following effect: the present becomes the sign of signs, the trace of traces. It is no longer what every reference refers to in the last instance; it becomes a function in a generalized referential structure. It is a trace, and a trace of the effacement of a trace.

In this way the metaphysical text is *understood*; it is still readable, and remains to be read. It proposes *both* the monument and the mirage of the trace, the trace as simultaneously traced and effaced, simultaneously alive and dead, alive as always to simulate even life in its preserved inscription; it is a pyramid.

Thus we think through, without contradiction, or at least without granting any pertinence to such contradiction, what is perceptible and imperceptible about the trace. The "matinal trace" of difference is lost in an irretrievable invisibility, and yet even its loss is covered, preserved, regarded, and retarded. This happens in a text, in the form of presence.

Having spoken about the effacement of the matinal trace, Heidegger can thus, in this contradiction without contradiction, consign or countersign the sealing of the trace. We read on a little further:

> The difference between Being and beings, however, can in turn be experienced as something forgotten only if it is already discovered with the presence of the present (*mit dem Anwesen des Anwesenden*) and if it is thus sealed in a trace (*so eine Spur geprägt hat*) that remains preserved (*gewahrt bleibt*) in the language which Being appropriates.[14]

Further on still, while meditating upon Anaximander's τὸ χρεών, translated as *Brauch* (sustaining use), Heidegger writes the following:

> Dispensing accord and deference (*Fug und Ruch verfügend*), our sustaining use frees the present (*das Anwesende*) in its sojourn and sets it free every time for its sojourn. But by the same token the present is equally seen to be exposed to the constant danger of hardening in the insistence (*in das blosse Beharren verhärtet*) out of its sojourning duration. In this way sustaining use (*Brauch*) remains itself and at the same time an abandonment (*Aushändigung*: handing-over) of presence (*des Anwesens*) *in den*

Un-fug, to discord (disjointedness). Sustaining use joins together the dis- (*Der Brauch fügt das Un-*).[15]

And it is at the point where Heidegger determines *sustaining use as trace* that the question must be asked: can we, and how far can we, think of this trace and the *dis-* of differance as *Wesen des Seins*? Doesn't the *dis-* of differance refer us beyond the history of Being, beyond our language as well, and beyond everything that can be named by it? Doesn't it call for – in the language of being – the necessarily violent transformation of this language by an entirely different language?

Let us be more precise here. In order to dislodge the "trace" from its cover (and whoever believes that one tracks down some *thing*? – one tracks down tracks), let us continue reading this passage:

> The translation of τὸ χρεών by "sustaining use" (*Brauch*) does not derive from cogitations of an etymologico-lexical nature. The choice of the word "sustaining use" derives from an antecedent *trans*lation (*Über*setzen) of the thought that attempts to conceive difference in the deployment of Being (*im Wesen des Seins*) toward the historical beginning of the forgetting of Being. The word "sustaining use" is dictated to thought in the apprehension (*Erfahrung*) of the forgetting of Being. *Tò χρεών* properly names a trace (*Spur*) of what remains to be conceived in the word "sustaining use," a trace that quickly disappears (*alsbald verschwindet*) into the history of Being, in its world-historical unfolding as Western metaphysics.[16]

How do we conceive of the outside of a text? How, for example, do we conceive of what stands opposed to the text of Western metaphysics? To be sure, the "trace that quickly disappears into the history of Being, ... as Western metaphysics," escapes all the determinations, all the names it might receive in the metaphysical text. The trace is sheltered and thus dissimulated in these names; it does not appear in the text as the trace "itself." But this is because the trace itself could never itself appear as such. Heidegger also says that difference can never appear *as such*: "Lichtung des Unterschiedes kann deshalb auch nicht bedeuten, dass der Unterschied als der Unterschied erscheint." There is no essence of differance; not only can it not allow itself to be taken up into the *as such* of its name or its appearing, but it threatens the authority of the *as such* in general, the thing's presence in its essence. That there is no essence of differance at this point also implies that there is neither Being nor truth to the play of writing, *insofar* as it involves differance.

For us, differance remains a metaphysical name; and all the names that it receives from our language are still, so far as they are names, metaphysical. This is particularly so when they speak of determining differance as the difference between presence and present (*Anwesen/Anwesend*), but already and especially so when, in the most general way, they speak of determining differance as the difference between Being and beings.

"Older" than Being itself, our language has no name for such a differance. But we "already know" that if it is unnamable, this is not simply provisional; it is not because our language has still not found or received this *name*, or because we would have to look for it in another language, outside the finite system of our language. It is because there is no *name* for this, not even essence or Being – not even the name "differance," which is not a name, which is not a pure nominal unity, and continually breaks up in a chain of different substitutions.

"There is no name for this": we read this as a truism. What is unnamable here is not some ineffable being that cannot be approached by a name; like God, for example. What is unnamable is the play that brings about the nominal effects, the relatively unitary or atomic structures we call names, or chains of substitutions for names. In these, for example, the nominal effect of "differance" is itself involved, carried off, and reinscribed, just as the false beginning or end of a game is still part of the game, a function of the system.

There will be no unique name, not even the name of Being. It must be conceived without *nostalgia*; that is, it must be conceived outside the myth of the purely maternal or paternal language belonging to the lost fatherland of thought. On the contrary, we must *affirm* it – in the sense that Nietzsche brings affirmation into play – with a certain laughter and with a certain dance.

After this laughter and dance, after this affirmation that is foreign to any dialectic, the question arises as to the other side of nostalgia, which I will call Heideggerian *hope*. I am not unaware that this term may be somewhat shocking. I venture it all the same, without excluding any of its implications, and shall relate it to what seems to me to be retained of metaphysics in "Der Spruch des Anaximander," namely, the quest for the proper word and the unique name. In talking about the "first word of Being" (*das frühe Wort des Seins: τὸ χρεών*), Heidegger writes,

> The relation to the present, unfolding its order in the very essence of pre*sence*, is unique (*ist eine einzige*). It is pre-eminently incomparable to any other relation; it belongs to the uniqueness of Being itself (*Sie gehört zur Einzigkeit des Seins selbst*). Thus, in order to name what is deployed in Being (*das Wesende des Seins*), language will have to find a single word, the unique word (*ein einziges, das einzige Wort*). There we see how hazardous is every word of thought (every thoughtful word: *denkendes Wort*) that addresses itself to Being (*das dem Sein zugesprochen wird*). What is hazarded here, however, is not something impossible, because Being speaks through every language; everywhere and always.[17]

Such is the question: the marriage between speech and Being in the unique word, in the finally proper name. Such is the question that enters into the affirmation put into play by differance. The question bears (upon) each of the words in this sentence: "Being/ speaks/ through every language;/ everywhere and always/."

Notes

This essay appeared originally in the *Bulletin de la Société française de philosophie*, LXII, No. 3 (July–September, 1968), 73–101. Derrida's remarks were delivered as a lecture at a meeting of the Société at the Sorbonne, in the Amphithéâtre Michelet, on January 27, 1968, with Jean Wahl presiding. Professor Wahl's introductory and closing remarks have not been translated. The essay was reprinted in *Théorie d'ensemble*, a collection of essays by Derrida and others, published by Editions Seuil in 1968. It is reproduced here by permission of Editions Seuil.

1 The reader should bear in mind that "difference," or difference with an *a*, incorporates two significations: "to differ" and "to defer." [Tr.]

2 For the term "facilitation" (*frayage*) in Freud, cf. "Project for a Scientific Psychology I" in *The Complete Psychological Works of Sigmund Freud*, 24 vols. (New York and London: Macmillan, 1964), 1,300, note 4 by the translator, James Strachey: "The word 'facilitation' as a rendering of the German '*Bahnung*' seems to have been introduced by Sherrington a few years after the *Project* was written. The German word, however, was already in use." The sense that Derrida draws upon here is stronger in the French or German; that is, the opening-up or clearing-out of a pathway. In the context of the "Project for a Scientific Psychology I," facilitation denotes the conduction capability that results from a difference in resistance levels in the memory and perception circuits of the nervous system. Thus, lowering the resistance threshold of a contact barrier serves to "open up" a nerve pathway and "facilitates" the excitatory process for the circuit. Cf. also J. Derrida, *L'Ecriture et la différence*, Chap. VII, "Freud et la scène de l'écriture" (Paris: Seuil, 1967), esp. pp. 297–305. trans. Alan Bass, *Writing and Difference* (London: Routledge & Kegan Paul, 1978). [Tr.]

3 On "pyramid" and "tomb" see J. Derrida, "Le Puits et la pyramide" in *Hegel et la pensée moderne* (Paris: Presses Universitaires de France, 1970), esp. pp. 44–45. [Tr.]

4 Ferdinand de Saussure, *Cours de linguistique générale*, ed. C. Bally and A. Sechehaye (Paris: Payot, 1916); English translation by Wade Baskin, *Course in General Linguistics* (New York: Philosophical Library, 1959), pp. 117–18, 120.

5 *Course in General Linguistics*, p. 18.

6 On "supplement" see J. Derrida, *Speech and Phenomena* (Evanston, IL: Northwestern University Press, 1973), Chap. 7, pp. 88–104. Cf. also Derrida, *De la grammatologie* (Paris: Editions de Minuit, 1967). On "*pharmakon*" see Derrida, "La Pharmacie de Platon," *Tel Quel*, No. 32 (Winter, 1967), pp. 17–59; No. 33 (Spring, 1968), pp. 4–48. On "hymen" see Derrida, "La Double Séance," *Tel Quel*, No. 41 (Spring, 1970), pp. 3–43; No. 42 (Summer, 1970), pp. 3–45. "La Pharmacie de Platon" and "La Double Séance" have been reprinted in a later text of Derrida, *La Dissémination* (Paris: Editions du Seuil, 1972), trans. Barbara Johnson, *Dissemination* (Chicago, IL: University of Chicago Press, 1981). [Tr.]

7 Derrida often brackets or "crosses out" certain key terms taken from metaphysics and logic, and in doing this, he follows Heidegger's usage in *Zur Seinsfrage*. The terms in question no longer have their full meaning, they no longer have the status of a purely signified content of expression – no longer, that is, after the deconstruction of metaphysics. Generated out of the play of differance, they still retain a vestigial trace of sense, however, a trace that cannot simply be gotten around (*incontournable*). An extensive discussion of all this is to be found in *De la grammatologie*, pp. 31–40. [Tr.]

8 Alexandre Koyré, "Hegel à Iéna," *Revue d'histoire et de philosophie religieuse*, XIV (1934), 420–58; reprinted in Koyré, *Etudes d'histoire de la pensée philosophique* (Paris: Armand Colin, 1961), pp. 135–73.

9 Koyré, *Etudes d'histoire*, pp. 153–54. The quotation from Hegel (my translation) comes from "Jenenser Logik, Metaphysik, und Naturphilosophie," *Sämtliche Werke* (Leipzig: F. Meiner, 1925), XVIII, 202. Koyré reproduces the original German text on pp. 153–54, note 2. [Tr.]

10 De Saussure, *Course in General Linguistics*, p. 37.

11 Freud, *Complete Psychological Works*, XVIII, 10.

12 Martin Heidegger, *Holzwege* (Frankfurt: V. Klostermann, 1957), pp. 335–36. All translations of quotations from *Holzwege* are mine. [Tr.]

13 *Ibid.*, p. 336.

14 *Ibid.*

15 *Ibid.*, pp. 339–40.

16 *Ibid.*, p. 340.

17 *Ibid.*, pp. 337–38.

Part XIV

PAUL RICOEUR
Phenomenology as Interpretation

PAUL RICOEUR (b. 1913)

Introduction

Paul Ricoeur was born in Valence, France, in 1913. Following a Master's degree at the University of Rennes, he enrolled in the Sorbonne in 1934, where he concentrated on the philosophy of Gabriel Marcel, but also began to read Husserl and Heidegger. As a prisoner of war in Germany, he continued to study Husserl along with Karl Jaspers. After the war he completed studies of Marcel and Jaspers, and then went on to publish *Husserl: An Analysis of his Phenomenology* in 1950. In the same year he brought out the first volume of his philosophy of the will, *Freedom and Nature: The Voluntary and the Involuntary*. The second volume, published in two parts – *Fallible Man* and *The Symbolism of Evil* – appeared a decade later. Other important publications include *Freud and Philosophy: An Essay on Interpretation* (1965), *The Conflict of Interpretations* (1969), *The Rule of Metaphor* (1975), his three-volume study *Time and Narrative* (1984–87) and *Oneself as Another* (1990). Ricoeur became Professor of the History of Philosophy at Strasbourg in 1948, and Professor of Philosophy at the Sorbonne in 1957. He has also held chairs at Paris-Nanterre and Louvain. Since 1973 he has served as Director of the *Centre d'etudes phénoménologiques et herméneutiques* in Paris, and has been a part-time Professor at the University of Chicago.

Ricoeur worked on a phenomenology of attention before the outbreak of the Second World War and subsequently on Husserl's *Ideas* I, but his creative engagement with phenomenology really originated with his philosophy of the will, which at first comprised a descriptive and eidetic investigation of affectivity and volition. By the time of *The Symbolism of Evil*, however, he concluded that phenomenology must involve a hermeneutical investigation of – or 'detour' through – the symbolic domain of language and other forms of culture. This is because he saw the symbol as giving rise to thought, being much more than the expression of an intentional life that would supposedly lie behind and beneath it. Ricoeur went on to note that symbols are given radically conflictual readings from differing ideological standpoints. Always culturally situated, a hermeneutical phenomenology cannot finally resolve such conflicts. Its task is rather to uncover and delineate the theoretical framework of each interpretive standpoint and to distil its positive insights out of its absolutist claims. In his terminology, a methodology of suspicion is to be coupled with one of affirmation.

Our reading is the unabridged article "Phenomenology and Hermeneutics", first published in Volume One of *Phänomenologische Forschungen* in 1975. In Ricoeur's own words, it reflects the changes of method implied by his evolution from an eidetic phenomenology to an explicitly hermeneutic one. The article also shows precisely those points on which he diverges from the transcendental phenomenology of Husserl. The point of departure is a critique of the principal theses in the Foreword to *Ideas I*, which together with *Cartesian Meditations* is the most extreme expression of Husserlian idealism. Ricoeur's purpose is in fact threefold: to demonstrate that hermeneutics does not destroy phenomenology, but rather its idealistic interpretation, that hermeneutics is itself built on the basis of phenomenology, which remains the unsurpassable presupposition of the former, and finally, that phenomenology is incapable of constituting itself without a hermeneutical presupposition.

Beginning with a critical examination of the theses of Husserlian idealism, Ricoeur remarks that the latter's ideal of scientificity or of an ultimate foundation is couched in terms of a theoretical subject–object relation. Yet both the ideal and the relation find their limits in the ontological condition of understanding, best expressed as 'belonging', a notion Heidegger elaborated in his account of 'being-in-the-world'. The term expresses the primacy of care over the theoretical gaze, and the horizonal character of that to which we are bound; that more original being-involved in the world which precedes reflection.

Husserl locates his ultimate foundation in intuition, confirming the priority of intentional fulfilment as against deduction or speculative construction. Again invoking Heidegger, Ricoeur counters that if intuition involves horizonal structures of prior understanding, then the interpretative explication or laying down of such understanding cannot go beyond it to the presuppositionless grasp of a pre-given being. Yet the vastness of the field of such understanding does point to the correlative vastness of the field of possible interpretation. The universality of interpretation may be readily attested to in conversation. Words in ordinary language have a semantic potential which is not exhausted by particular use but determined by context. Interpretation is the process by which interlocutors determine such contextual values.

The 'short' intersubjective relations in conversations are intertwined with the 'long' intersubjective relations of traditions. Traditions are established and reproduced by monuments and written texts, which survive beyond the here and now (as Husserl recognised), and also invite irreducibly multiple readings. This is the hermeneutic circle between the understanding initiated by the reader and the meanings offered by the text. The condition of the circle is the structure relating explication to the understanding preceding and supporting it. The development of understanding in interpretation is opposed to the project of a final foundation – it places us in the middle of a conversation that has already begun and which we cannot terminate finally. The ideal of an intuitive foundation is of a passage from interpretation to full vision, but for hermeneutics, interpretation is an open process that no single vision can conclude.

Husserl sees subjectivity as the locus of his ultimate foundation, holding that self-knowledge is not presumptive, not given in profiles like objects. But if ideological structures intrude into communication, and if self-knowledge is communication internalised, then such knowledge can be as doubtful as knowledge of the object. Hermeneutics is therefore required to incorporate the critique of ideology into self-understanding. Furthermore, the primacy of subjectivity may be questioned by focusing on what Gadamer calls the matter of the text, the 'being-in-the-world' it opens up, rather than on the intentions of the author. To appropriate this matter, I must distance myself critically from my own world. Against Husserl's notion of ultimate self-responsibility, therefore, Ricoeur proposes a primal responsiveness to meanings that lie outside of myself – I exchange the me, master of myself, for the self, disciple of the text.

Ricoeur embarks on his second task – that of showing that hermeneutics is itself built on phenomenology – by noting that a questioning of any being is also a questioning of its *meaning*. Phenomenology applied the *epoché* to lived experience to reveal its meaning; hermeneutics emulates this with its moment of distanciation from historically transmitted tradition. Husserl's major discovery was that the logical notion of signification is carved out of a wider notion of meaning that is co-extensive with the concept of intentionality. Hence we can explicate the 'meaning' of perception, will, imagination and so on. The intentional model came to be increasingly displaced towards the perceptual plane, where our signifying relation with things originates. In *Ideas I*, noematic constitution precedes the linguistic level where the functions of naming and predication, syntactic liaison and so on are articulated. When hermeneutics subordinates linguistic experience to pre-predicative aesthetic and historical experience, it continues the movement initiated on the perceptual plane. This kinship is all the closer in that Husserl himself began to develop the phenomenology of perception towards a hermeneutics of historical experience, most notably in the *Crisis*.

Ricoeur's final task is to show that phenomenology cannot constitute itself without a hermeneutical presupposition. In *Logical Investigations*, states Ricoeur, Husserl clearly has recourse to *Auslegung*, to explication or interpretation. Indexical expressions (which Husserl had termed 'essentially occasional expressions'), including demonstratives and personal pronouns, have their meanings tied up with the particular occasions in which they are framed and uttered, and we must examine the latter to determine their meanings. Husserl thus anticipates Ricoeur's earlier point, namely that interpretation already intervenes at the level of ordinary language. Husserl also treats of 'objective' expressions, which are univocal in principle but do not always reveal their univocity immediately. In some cases their meanings seem to shade unbrokenly into one another, and we need recourse to illustrative intuitions to elucidate their differences – interpretive work intervenes once more. Husserl argues that the understanding of words is in fact akin to the sense-conferring interpretation that is already at work in perception, an understanding which allows us to intend an intuitive given, not merely as a singular thing, but as the instantiation of a species or universal. In this way, according to Ricoeur, the theory of intuition is inverted step by step into a theory of interpretation.

There is also recourse to *Auslegung* in the Fifth *Cartesian Meditation*, a work concerned with the meaning, not of expressions, but of experience in general. The meaning of the world is reduced to the sense-giving acts of my solitary transcendental ego, and Husserl is left with the difficulty of doing justice to my experience of the *alter ego*, whose experiences are original in being those of someone else. The problem is to constitute the other *in me* precisely as *other*, to adequately describe the other's transcendence within a project of subjective immanence. For Ricoeur, the notions of 'analogical apprehension' and 'pairing' (apprehending an analogy between my 'inner states' and 'outer expressions' and those of the other on the basis of our paired bodies) identify the difficulty rather than resolve it, since they suggest that the other has to be reached derivatively from within my own domain.

Ricoeur contends that a less dichotomous reading of the Fifth *Meditation* is possible once we recognise that *Auslegung* is involved in Husserl's reduction of my ego to the sphere of 'ownness' or bodily belonging. The point is that the latter is never a given from which I progress to another given, but the product of an abstraction from everything 'foreign' (including the experience of the other) that already lay *within* my own original experience. The experiences of my ownness and of otherness are equiprimordial, and it is only through interpretive explication that they are sundered. In Husserl's own words, phenomenology does not 'create' but only 'finds'; it is an explication of a preceding experiential evidence and an evidence of explication. It is in this sense that it can be realised only as hermeneutics.

Further reading

Ricoeur, Paul. *Freedom and Nature: The Voluntary and the Involuntary*, trans. E. V. Kohák. Evanston, IL: Northwestern University Press, 1966.

Ricoeur, Paul. *Hermeneutics and the Human Sciences*, trans. J. B. Thompson. Cambridge: Cambridge University Press, 1981.

Ricoeur, Paul. *Husserl: An Analysis of His Phenomenology*, trans. E. G. Ballard and L. Embree. Evanston, IL: Northwestern University Press, 1967.

Ricoeur, Paul. *Oneself as Another*, trans. Kathleen Blamey. Chicago, IL: University of Chicago Press, 1992.

Ricoeur, Paul. *The Conflict of Interpretations: Essays in Hermeneutics*, trans. Don Ihde. Evanston, IL: Northwestern University Press, 1974.

Ricoeur, Paul. *The Rule of Metaphor*. Toronto: University of Toronto Press, 1977.

Ricoeur, Paul. *Time and Narrative*, Volumes 1, 2, 3, trans. K. McLoughlin and D. Pellauer. Chicago, IL: University of Chicago Press, 1984–87.

Clark, Stephen. *Paul Ricoeur*. London: Routledge, 1990.

Hahn, L. E. (ed.). *The Philosophy of Paul Ricoeur*. Chicago, IL: Open Court, 1995.

Ihde, Don. *Hermeneutic Phenomenology: The Philosophy of Paul Ricoeur*. Evanston, IL: Northwestern University Press, 1971.

Kearney, Richard (ed.). *Paul Ricoeur: The Hermeneutics of Action*. London: Sage, 1996.

Reagan, Charles (ed.). *Studies in the Philosophy of Paul Ricoeur*. Athens, OH: Ohio University Press, 1979.

Van Leeuwen, T. M. *The Surplus of Meaning: Ontology and Eschatology in the Philosophy of Paul Ricoeur*. Amsterdam: Rodopi, 1981.

1

PHENOMENOLOGY AND HERMENEUTICS

This study does not aim to be a contribution to the history of phenomenology, to its archaeology, but rather an inquiry into the destiny of phenomenology today. And if I have chosen the general theory of interpretation or hermeneutics as a touchstone, that does not mean either that I would replace an historical monograph by a chapter on the comparative history of modern philosophy. For with hermeneutics as well, I do not wish to proceed as an historian, even as an historian of the present day. Whatever may be the dependence of the following meditation on Heidegger and above all on Gadamer, what is at stake is the possibility of continuing to do philosophy with them and after them – without forgetting Husserl. Thus my essay will seek to be a debate about the ways in which philosophy can still be pursued.[1]

I propose the following two theses for discussion. *First thesis*: what hermeneutics has ruined is not phenomenology but one of its interpretations, namely its *idealistic* interpretation by Husserl himself; accordingly, I shall speak henceforth of Husserlian idealism. I shall take the "Nachwort" to the *Ideen*[2] as a reference and a guide, submitting its principal theses to the hermeneutical critique. The first part of the essay will thus be purely and simply *antithetical*.

Second thesis: beyond the simple opposition there exists, between phenomenology and hermeneutics, a mutual belonging which it is important to make explicit. This belonging can be recognised from either position. On the one hand, hermeneutics is erected on the basis of phenomenology and thus preserves something of the philosophy from which it nevertheless differs: *phenomenology remains the unsurpassable presupposition of hermeneutics.* On the other hand, phenomenology cannot constitute itself without a *hermeneutical presupposition*. The hermeneutical condition of phenomenology is linked to the role of *Auslegung* [explication] in the fulfilment of its philosophical project.

I The hermeneutical critique of Husserlian idealism

The first part of this essay seeks to disclose the gap, if not the gulf, which separates the project of hermeneutics from all idealistic expressions of phenomenology. The antithetical position of the two philosophical projects will alone be

P. Ricoeur, *Hermeneutics and the Human Sciences*, 1981, ed. and trans. John B. Thompson, pp. 101–28. Cambridge: Cambridge University Press.

developed. We shall nevertheless reserve the possibility that phenomenology as such is not wholly exhausted by one of its interpretations, even that of Husserl himself. It is, in my view, Husserlian idealism which succumbs to the hermeneutical critique.

1 The schematic theses of Husserlian idealism

For the purposes of a necessarily schematic discussion, I have taken the 1930 "Nachwort" to the *Ideen* as a typical document of Husserlian idealism. It constitutes, together with the *Cartesian Meditations*, the most advanced expression of this idealism. I have extracted from it the following theses, which I shall subsequently submit to the critique of hermeneutics.

(a) The ideal of scientificity proclaimed by phenomenology is not in continuity with the sciences, their axioms and their foundational enterprise: the "ultimate justification" which constitutes phenomenology is of a different order (*Hua* v 138ff., 159ff.).

This thesis, which expresses phenomenology's claim to radicality, is asserted in a polemical style; it is the thesis of a combatant philosophy which always has an enemy in view, whether that enemy be objectivism, naturalism, vitalistic philosophy, or anthropology. Phenomenology begins with a radical move that cannot be framed in a demonstrative argument, for whence would it be deduced? Hence the self-assertive style of the claim to radicality, which is attested to only by the denial of what could deny it. The expression *aus letzter Begründung* [ultimate grounding] is most typical in this respect. It recalls the Platonic tradition of the anhypothetical as well as the Kantian tradition of the autonomy of the critical act; it also marks, in the sense of *Rückfrage* [questioning back] (*Hua* v 139), a certain continuity with the questions of principle that the sciences ask of themselves. And yet the process of returning to the foundations is absolutely discontinuous with regard to any foundation internal to a science: for a science of foundations, "there can be no more obscure and problematic concepts, nor any paradoxes" (*Hua* v 160). That does not mean there have not been *several* "ways" answering to this unique Idea; the idea of foundation is rather that which secures the equivalence and convergence of the ways (logical, Cartesian, psychological, historico-teleological, etc.). There are "real beginnings", or rather "paths towards the beginning", elicited by "the absolute absence of presuppositions". It is thus fruitless to inquire into the motivation for such a radical beginning; there is no reason internal to a domain for raising the question of origin. It is in this sense that justification is a *Selbst-Begründung* [self-grounding].

(b) The foundation in principle is of the order of intuition; to found is to see. The "Nachwort" thereby confirms the priority, asserted by the sixth *Logical Investigation*, of intentional fulfilment as opposed to any philosophy of deduction or construction (*Hua* v 141ff., 143ff.).

The key concept in this respect is that of an *Erfahrungsfeld* [field of experience]. The strangeness of phenomenology lies entirely therein: from the outset, the principle is a "field" and the first truth an "experience". In contrast to all "speculative constructions", every question of principle is resolved through vision. I just spoke of strangeness: for is it not astonishing that in spite of (and thanks to) the critique of empiricism, experience in the strict empirical sense is surpassed only in an "experience"? This synonymy of *Erfahrung* signifies that phenomenology is not situated elsewhere, in another world, but rather is concerned with natural experience itself, insofar as the latter is unaware of its meaning. Consequently, however much the emphasis may be placed on the *a priori* character, on the reduction to the *eidos*, on the role of imaginative variations, and even on the notion of "possibility", it is still and always the character of experience which is underlined (one has only to consider the expression "intuitive possibilities"; *Hua* v 142).

(c) The place of plenary intuition is subjectivity. All transcendence is doubtful; immanence alone is indubitable.

This is the central thesis of Husserlian idealism. All transcendence is doubtful because it proceeds by *Abschattungen*, by "sketches" or "profiles"; because the convergence of these *Abschattungen* is always presumptive; because the presumption can be disappointed by some discordance; and finally, because consciousness can form the hyperbolic hypothesis of a radical discordance of appearances, which is the very hypothesis of the "destruction of the world". Immanence is not doubtful, because it is not given by "profiles" and hence involves nothing presumptive, allowing only the coincidence of reflection with what "has just" been experienced.

(d) The subjectivity thus promoted to the rank of the transcendental is not empirical consciousness, the object of psychology. Nevertheless, phenomenology and phenomenological psychology are parallel and constitute a "doublet" which constantly leads to the confusion of the two disciplines, one transcendental and the other empirical. Only the reduction distinguishes and separates them.

Here phenomenology must struggle against a misunderstanding which constantly reappears and which phenomenology itself provokes. For the phenomenological "field of experience" has a structural analogy with non-reduced experience; the reason for this isomorphism lies in the very nature of intentionality (Brentano had discovered intentionality without being aware of the reduction, and the fifth *Logical Investigation* still defined it in terms that are as compatible with intentional psychology as with phenomenology). Moreover, the reduction proceeds "from the natural attitude"; transcendental phenomenology thus presupposes, in a certain way, that which it surpasses and which it reiterates as *the same*, although *in another attitude*. So the difference does not consist in descriptive features but in ontological indices, in *Seinsgeltung* [validity of being]; validity *als Reales* must be "lost",[3] psychological realism must be shattered. Now that would be no small task, if phenomenology is not to be understood as the necessity of losing the world, the body and nature, thereby enclosing itself within an acosmic realm. The paradox is that it is only through this loss that the world is revealed as "pregiven", the body as "existing", and nature as "being" [*étant*]. So the reduction does not take place between me and the world, between the soul and the body, between the spirit and nature, but through the pregiven, the existing and the being, which cease to be self-evident and to be assumed in the blind and opaque *Seinsglaube* [belief in being], becoming instead *meaning: meaning* of the pregiven, *meaning* of the existing, *meaning* of the being. Thus the phenomenological radicality, which severs the transcendental subjectivity from the empirical self, is the same as that radicality which transforms the *Seinsglaube* into the noematic correlate of the noesis. A noetics or no-ology is therefore distinct from a psychology. Their "content" (*Gehalt*) is the same; but the phenomenological is the psychological "reduced". Therein lies the principle of the "parallelism", or better of the "correspondence", between the two. Therein lies also the principle of their difference: for a "conversion" – *the* philosophical conversion – separates them.

(e) The awareness which sustains the work of reflection develops its own ethical implications: reflection is thus the immediately self-responsible act.

The ethical nuance, which the expression *aus letzter Selbstverantwortung* [ultimate self-responsibility] (*Hua* v 139) seems to introduce into the foundational thematic, is not the practical complement of an enterprise which as such would be purely epistemological: the inversion by which reflection tears itself away from the natural attitude is at the same time – in the same breath, so to speak – epistemological and ethical. The philosophical conversion is the supremely autonomous act. What we have called the ethical nuance is thus immediately implied in the foundational act, insofar as the latter can only be self-positing. It is in this sense that it is ultimately self-responsible.

The self-assertive character of the foundation constitutes the philosophical subject as responsible subject. This is the philosophising subject as such.

2 Hermeneutics against Husserlian idealism

It is possible to oppose hermeneutics, thesis by thesis, not perhaps to phenomenology as a whole and as such, but to Husserlian idealism. This "antithetical" approach is the necessary path to the establishment of a genuinely "dialectical" relation between the two.

(a) The ideal of scientificity, construed by Husserlian idealism as ultimate justification, encounters its fundamental limit in the ontological condition of understanding.

This ontological condition can be expressed as finitude. This is not, however, the concept that I shall regard as primary; for it designates, in negative terms, an entirely positive condition which would be better expressed by the concept of belonging. The latter directly designates the unsurpassable condition of any enterprise of justification and foundation, namely that it is always preceded by a relation which supports it. Is this a relation to an object? That is precisely what it is not. The aspect of Husserlian idealism which hermeneutics questions first is the way in which the immense and unsurpassable discovery of intentionality is couched in a conceptuality which weakens its scope, namely the conceptuality of the subject–object relation. It is the latter which gives rise to the necessity of searching for something that unifies the meaning of the object and the necessity of founding this unity in a constituting subjectivity. The first declaration of hermeneutics is to say that the problematic of objectivity presupposes a prior relation of inclusion which encompasses the allegedly autonomous subject and the allegedly adverse object. This inclusive or encompassing relation is what I call belonging. The ontological priority of belonging implies that the question of foundation can no longer simply coincide with that of ultimate justification. Of course, Husserl is the first to underline the discontinuity, instituted by the *epoché*, between the transcendental enterprise of foundation and the internal work, proper to each science, whereby it seeks to elaborate its own grounds. Moreover, he always distinguishes the demand for justification raised by transcendental phenomenology from the pre-established model of the *mathesis universalis*. In this way, as we shall see later, he lays down the phenomenological conditions of hermeneutics. But hermeneutics seeks precisely to radicalise the Husserlian thesis of the discontinuity between transcendental foundation and epistemological grounding.

For hermeneutics, the problem of ultimate foundation still belongs to the sphere of objectifying thought, so long as the ideal of scientificity is not questioned as such. The radicality of such questioning leads from the idea of scientificity back to the ontological condition of belonging, whereby he who questions shares in the very thing about which he questions.

It is the relation of belonging which is subsequently apprehended as the finitude of knowledge. The negative nuance conveyed by the very word "finitude" is introduced into the totally positive relation of belonging – *which is the hermeneutical experience itself* – only because subjectivity has already raised its claim to be the ultimate ground. This claim, this immoderate pretension, this *hybris* makes the relation of belonging appear by contrast as finitude.

Belonging is expressed by Heidegger in the language of being-in-the-world. The two notions are equivalent. The term "being-in-the-world" expresses better the primacy of care over the gaze, and the horizonal character of that to which we are bound. It is indeed being-in-the-world which precedes reflection. At the same time, the term attests to the priority of the ontological category of the *Dasein* which we are over the epistemological and psychological category of the subject which posits itself. Despite the density of meaning in the expression "being-in-the-world", I prefer, following Gadamer, to use the notion of belonging, which immediately raises the problem of the subject–object relation and prepares the way for the subsequent introduction of the concept of distanciation.

(b) The Husserlian demand for the return to intuition is countered by the necessity for all understanding to be mediated by an interpretation.

There is no doubt that this principle is borrowed from the epistemology of the historical sciences. As such, it belongs to the epistemological field delimited by Schleiermacher and Dilthey. However, if interpretation were only an historico-hermeneutical concept, it would remain as regional as the human sciences themselves. But the usage of interpretation in the historico-hermeneutic sciences is only the anchoring point for a universal concept of interpretation which has the same extension as that of understanding and, in the end, as that of belonging. Hence it goes beyond the mere methodology of exegesis and philology, designating the work of explication which adheres to all hermeneutical experience. According to the remark of Heidegger in *Being and Time*, the *Auslegung* is the "development of understanding" in terms of the structure of the "as" (*Als*).[4] In thereby effecting the mediation of the "as", "explication does not transform understanding into something else, but makes it become itself" (*SZ* 148; *BT* 188).

The dependence of interpretation on understanding explains why explication as well always precedes reflection and comes before any constitution of the object by a sovereign subject. This antecedence is expressed at the level of explication by the "structure of anticipation", which prevents explication from ever being a presuppositionless grasp of a pregiven being [*étant*]; explication precedes its object in the mode of the *Vor-habe*, the *Vor-sicht*, the *Vor-Griff*, the *Vor-Meinung* (*SZ* 150; *BT* 191). I shall not comment here on these well-known expressions of Heidegger. What is important to emphasise is that it is not possible to implement the structure of the "as" without also implementing the structure of anticipation. The notion of "meaning" obeys this double condition of the *Als* and the *Vor-*: "Meaning, which is structured by fore-having, fore-sight and fore-conception, forms for any project the horizon in terms of which something can be understood as something" (*SZ* 151; *BT* 193). Thus the field of interpretation is as vast as that of understanding, which covers all projection of meaning in a situation.

The universality of interpretation is attested to in several ways. The most ordinary application is the use of natural languages in the conversational situation. In contrast to well-formed languages, constructed according to the exigencies of mathematical logic and in which all basic terms are defined in an axiomatic way, the use of natural languages rests on the polysemic value of words. The latter contain a semantic potential which is not exhausted by any particular use, but which must be constantly sifted and determined by the context. It is with this selective function of context that interpretation, in the most primitive sense of the word, is connected. Interpretation is the process by which, in the interplay of question and answer, the interlocutors collectively determine the contextual values which structure their conversation. So before any *Kunstlehre*, which would establish exegesis and philology as an autonomous discipline, there is a spontaneous process of interpretation which is part of the most primitive exercise of understanding in any given situation.

But conversation rests upon a relation which is too limited to cover the whole field of explication. Conversation, i.e. ultimately the dialogical relation, is contained within the limits of a *vis-à-vis* which is a *face-à-face*. The historical connection which encompasses it is singularly more complex. The "short" intersubjective relation is intertwined, in the interior of the historical connection, with various "long" intersubjective relations, mediated by diverse social institutions, social roles and collectivities (groups, classes, nations, cultural traditions, etc.). The long intersubjective relations are sustained by an historical tradition, of which dialogue is only a segment. Explication therefore extends much further than dialogue, coinciding with the broadest historical connection.[5]

Mediation by the text, that is, by expressions fixed in writing but also by all the documents and monuments which have a fundamental feature in common with writing, is connected with the use of explication on the scale of the transmission of historical tradition. This common feature, which constitutes the text as a text, is that the meaning contained therein is rendered *autonomous* with respect to the intention of the author, the initial situation of discourse and the original addressee. Intention, situation and original addressee constitute the *Sitz-im-Leben* [site-in-life] of the text. The possibility of multiple interpretations is opened up by a text which is thus freed from its *Sitz-im-Leben*. Beyond the polysemy of words in a conversation is the polysemy of a text which invites multiple readings. This is the moment of interpretation in the technical sense of *textual exegesis*. It is also the moment of the hermeneutical circle between the understanding initiated by the reader and the proposals of meaning offered by the text. The most fundamental condition of the hermeneutical circle lies in the structure of pre-understanding which relates all explication to the understanding which precedes and supports it.

In what sense is the development of all understanding in interpretation opposed to the Husserlian project of *ultimate* foundation? Essentially in the sense that all interpretation places the interpreter *in medias res* and never at the beginning or the end. We suddenly arrive, as it were, in the middle of a conversation which has already begun and in which we try to orientate ourselves in order to be able to contribute to it. Now the ideal of an intuitive foundation is the ideal of an interpretation which, at a certain point, would pass into full vision. This is what Gadamer calls the hypothesis of "total mediation". Only a total mediation would be equivalent to an intuition which is both first and final. Idealist phenomenology can therefore sustain its pretension to ultimate foundation only by adopting, in an intuitive rather than a speculative mode, the Hegelian claim to absolute knowledge. But the key hypothesis of hermeneutic philosophy is that interpretation is an open process which no single vision can conclude.

(c) That the place of ultimate foundation is subjectivity, that all transcendence is doubtful and only immanence indubitable – this in turn becomes eminently doubtful, from the moment that the *cogito* as well seems susceptible to the radical critique which phenomenology otherwise applies to all appearances.

The ruses of self-consciousness are more subtle than those of the thing. Recall the doubt which, in Heidegger's work, accompanies the question "who is *Dasein*?"

> Is it then obvious *a priori* that access to Dasein must be gained only by mere reflective awareness of the "I" of actions? What if this kind of "giving-itself" on the part of Dasein should lead our existential analytic astray and do so, indeed, in a manner grounded in the Being of Dasein itself? Perhaps when Dasein addresses itself in the way which is closest to itself, it always says "I am this entity", and in the long run says this loudest when it is "not" this entity. What if the aforementioned approach, starting with the givenness of the "I" to Dasein itself, and with a rather patient self-interpretation of Dasein, should lead the existential analytic, as it were, into a pitfall? If that which is accessible by mere "giving" can be determined, there is presumably an ontological horizon for determining it; but what if this horizon should remain in principle undetermined? (*SZ* 115; *BT* 151)

Here, as elsewhere, I shall not adhere to the letter of Heidegger's philosophy but shall develop it for my own purposes. It is in the *critique of ideology*, as much as and perhaps more than in psychoanalysis, that I would look for documentation of the doubt contained in Heidegger's question "who is *Dasein*?". The critique of ideology and psychoanalysis provide us today with the means to complement the critique of the object by a critique of the subject. In Husserl's work, the critique of the object is co-extensive with *Dingkonstitution* [constitution of the thing]; it rests, as we have said, on the presumptive character of schematic synthesis. But Husserl believed that self-knowledge could not be presumptive, because it does not proceed by "sketches" or "profiles". Self-knowledge can, however, be presumptive for other reasons. Insofar as self-knowledge is a dialogue of the soul with itself, and insofar as the dialogue can be systematically distorted by violence and by the intrusion of structures of domination into those of communication, self-knowledge as internalised communication can be as doubtful as knowledge of the object, although for different and quite specific reasons.

Could it be said that, through the reduction, the *ego meditans* of phenomenology escapes from the distortions of empirical self-knowledge? This would be to forget that the Husserlian *ego* is not the Kantian *I think*, whose individuality is at least problematic if not devoid of sense. It is because the *ego* can be and must be reduced to the "sphere of belonging" – in a different sense, to be sure, of the word "belonging", which means no longer belonging to the world but belonging to one-self – that it is necessary to found the objectivity of nature and the objectivity of historical communities on intersubjectivity and not on an impersonal subject. Consequently, the distortions of communication directly concern the constitution of the intersubjective network in which a common nature and common historical entities can be formed, entities such as the "personalities of a higher order" discussed in paragraph 58 of the *Cartesian Meditations*. Egology must take the fundamental distortions of communication into account, in the same way as it considers the illusions of perception in the constitution of the thing.

It seems to me that only a hermeneutics of communication can assume the task of incorporating the critique of ideology into self-understanding.[6] It can do this in two complementary ways. On the one hand, it can demonstrate the insurmountable character of the ideological phenomenon through its meditation on the role of "pre-understanding" in the apprehension of any cultural object. Hermeneutics has simply to raise this notion of understanding, initially applied to the exegesis of texts, to the level of a general theory of prejudices, which would be coextensive with the historical connection itself. Just as mis-understanding is a fundamental structure of exegesis (Schleiermacher), so too prejudice is a funda-mental structure of communication in its social and institutional forms. On the other hand, hermeneutics can demonstrate the necessity of a critique of ideology, even if, in virtue of the very structure of pre-understanding, this critique can never be total. Critique rests on the moment of *distanciation* which belongs to the historical connection as such.

The concept of distanciation is the dialectical counterpart of the notion of belonging, in the sense that we belong to an historical tradition through a relation of distance which oscillates between remoteness and proximity. To interpret is to render near what is far (temporally, geographically, culturally, spiritually). In this respect, mediation by the text is the model of a distanciation which would not be simply alienating, like the *Verfremdung* which Gadamer combats throughout his work (*WM* 11, 80, 156, 364ff.; *TM* 15, 75, 145, 348ff.), but which would be genu-inely creative. The text is, *par excellence*, the basis for communication in and through distance.

If that is so, then hermeneutics has the means to account for both the insurmountable character of the ideological phenomenon, and the possibility of beginning, without ever being able to finish, a critique of ideology. Hermeneutics can do this because, in contrast to phenomenological idealism, the subject of which it speaks is always open to the efficacy of history (to make an allusion to Gadamer's famous notion of *wirkungsgeschichtliches Bewusstsein* (*WM* 284; *TM* 267). Since distanciation is a moment of belonging, the critique of ideology can be incorporated, as an objective and explanatory segment, in the project of enlarging and restoring communication and self-understanding. The extension of understanding through textual exegesis and its constant rectification through the critique of ideology are properly part of the process of *Auslegung*. Textual exegesis and critique of ideology are the two privileged routes along which understanding is developed into interpretation and thus becomes itself.

(d) A radical way of placing the primacy of subjectivity in question is to take the theory of the text as the hermeneutical axis. Insofar as the meaning of a text is rendered autonomous with respect to the subjective intention of its author, the essential question is not to recover, behind the text, the lost intention, but to unfold, in front of the text, the "world" which it opens up and discloses.

In other words, the hermeneutical task is to discern the "matter" of the text (Gadamer) and not the psychology of the author. The matter of the text is to its structure as, in the proposition, the reference is to the sense (Frege). Just as, in the proposition, we are not content with the sense which is its ideal object but inquire further into its reference, that is, into its claim to truth, so too with the text we cannot stop at the immanent structure, at the internal system of dependencies arising from the crossing of the "codes" which the text employs; we wish moreover to explicate the world which the text projects. In saying that, I am not unaware that an important category of texts which we call *literature* – namely, narrative fiction, drama, poetry – appears to abolish all reference to everyday reality, to the point where language seems destined to supreme dignity, as if glorifying itself at the expense of the referential function of ordinary discourse. But it is precisely insofar as fictional discourse "suspends" its first order referential function that it releases a second order reference, where the world is manifested no longer as the totality of manipulable objects but as the horizon of our life and our project, in short as *Lebenswelt* [life-world], as being-in-the-world. It is this referential dimension, attaining its full development only with works of fiction and poetry, which raises the fundamental hermeneutical problem. Hermeneutics can be defined no longer as an inquiry into the psychological intentions which are hidden beneath the text, but rather as the explication of the being-in-the-world displayed by the text. What is to be interpreted in the text is a proposed world which I could inhabit and in which I could project my ownmost possibilities. Recalling the principle of distanciation mentioned above, it could be said that the fictional or poetic text not only places the meaning of the text at a *distance* from the intention of the author, but also places the reference of the text at a *distance* from the *world* articulated by everyday language. Reality is, in this way, metamorphosed by means of what I shall call the "imaginative variations" which literature carries out on the real.

What is the consequence for Husserlian idealism of the hermeneutical focus on the matter of the text? Essentially this: the phenomenology which arose with the discovery of the universal character of intentionality has not remained faithful to its own discovery, namely that the meaning of consciousness lies outside of itself. The idealist theory of the constitution of meaning in consciousness has thus culminated in the hypostasis of subjectivity. The price of this hypostasis is indicated by the above-mentioned difficulties in the "parallelism" between phenomenology and psychology. Such difficulties attest that phenomenology is always in danger of reducing itself to a transcendental subjectivism. The radical way of putting an end to this constantly recurring confusion is to shift the axis of interpretation from the problem of subjectivity to that of the world. That is what the theory of the text attempts to do, by subordinating the question of the author's intention to that of the matter of the text.

(e) In opposition to the idealist thesis of the ultimate self-responsibility of the mediating subject, hermeneutics proposes to make subjectivity the final, and not the first, category of a theory of understanding. Subjectivity must be lost as radical origin, if it is to be recovered in a more modest role.

Here again, the theory of the text is a good guide. For it shows that the act of subjectivity is not so much what initiates understanding as what terminates it. This terminal act can be characterised as appropriation (*Zueignung*) (*SZ* 150; *BT* 191). It does not purport, as in Romantic hermeneutics, to rejoin the original subjectivity which would support the meaning of the text. Rather it *responds* to the matter of the text, and hence to the proposals of meaning which the text unfolds. It is thus the counterpart of the distanciation which establishes the autonomy of the text with respect to its author, its situation and its original addressee. It is also the counterpart of that other distanciation by which a new being-in-the-world, projected by the text, is freed from the false evidences of everyday reality. Appropriation is the *response* to this double distanciation which is linked to the matter of the text, as regards its sense and as regards its reference. Thus appropriation can be integrated into the theory of interpretation without surreptitiously reintroducing the primacy of subjectivity which the four preceding theses have destroyed.

That appropriation does not imply the secret return of the sovereign subject can be attested to in the following way: if it remains true that hermeneutics terminates in self-understanding, then the subjectivism of this proposition must be rectified by saying that to understand *one-self* is to understand oneself *in front of the text*. Consequently, what is appropriation from one point of view is disappropriation from another. To appropriate is to make what was alien become one's own. What is appropriated is indeed the matter of the text. But the matter of the text becomes my own only if I disappropriate myself, in order to let the matter of the text be. So I exchange the *me, master* of itself, for the *self, disciple* of the text.

The process could also be expressed as a *distanciation of self from itself* within the interior of appropriation. This distanciation implements all the strategies of suspicion, among which the critique of ideology is a principal modality. Distanciation, in all its forms and figures, constitutes *par excellence* the critical moment in understanding.

This final and radical form of distanciation is the ruin of the *ego*'s pretension to constitute itself as ultimate origin. The *ego* must assume for itself the "imaginative variations" by which it could *respond* to the "imaginative variations" on reality that literature and poetry, more than any other form of discourse, engender. It is this style of "response to . . ." that hermeneutics opposes to the idealism of *ultimate self-responsibility*.

II Towards a hermeneutic phenomenology

The hermeneutical critique of Husserlian idealism is, in my view, only the negative side of a positive research programme which I shall place under the provisional and exploratory title of *hermeneutic phenomenology*. The present essay does not claim to work out – "to do" – this hermeneutic phenomenology. It seeks only to show its possibility by establishing, on the one hand, that beyond the critique of Husserlian idealism, phenomenology remains the unsurpassable presupposition of hermeneutics; and on the other hand, that phenomenology cannot carry out its programme of *constitution* without constituting itself in the *interpretation* of the experience of the *ego*.

1 The phenomenological presupposition of hermeneutics

(a) The most fundamental phenomenological presupposition of a philosophy of interpretation is that every question concerning any sort of "being" [*étant*] is a question about the meaning of that "being".

Thus, in the first few pages of *Being and Time*, we read that the forgotten question is the question of the *meaning* of being. In that respect, the ontological question is a phenomenological question. It is a hermeneutical problem only insofar as the meaning is concealed, not of course in itself, but by everything which forbids access to it. However, in order to become a hermeneutical problem – a problem about concealed meaning – the central question of phenomenology must be recognised as a question about meaning. Thereby the phenomenological attitude is already placed above the naturalistic-objectivistic attitude. *The choice in favour of meaning is thus the most general presupposition of any hermeneutics.*

It may be objected that hermeneutics is older than phenomenology. Even before the word "hermeneutics" was restored to dignity by the eighteenth century, there existed a biblical exegesis and a classical philology, both of which had already "stood up for meaning". That is indeed true; but hermeneutics becomes a philosophy of interpretation – and not simply a methodology of exegesis and philology – only if, going back to the conditions of possibility of exegesis and philology, going beyond even a general theory of the text, it addresses itself to the lingual condition – the *Sprachlichkeit* – of all experience (*WM* 367ff.; *TM* 345ff.).

This lingual condition has its own presupposition in a general theory of "meaning". It must be supposed that experience, in all its fullness (such as Hegel conceived it, as may be seen in Heidegger's famous text on "Hegel's concept of experience")[7] has an expressibility in principle. Experience can be said, it demands to be said. To bring it to language is not to change it into something else, but, in articulating and developing it, to make it become itself.

Such is the presupposition of "meaning" which exegesis and philology employ at the level of a certain category of texts, those which have contributed to our historical tradition. Exegesis and philology may well be historically prior to phenomenological awareness, but the latter precedes them in the order of foundation.

It is difficult, admittedly, to formulate this presupposition in a non-idealist language. The break between the phenomenological attitude and the naturalistic attitude – or as we said, the choice in favour of meaning – seems to amount to nothing more than an opting for the consciousness "in" which meaning occurs. Is it not by "suspending" all *Seinsglaube* that the dimension of meaning is attained? Is not the *epoché* of being-in-itself therefore presupposed by the choice in favour of meaning? Is not every philosophy of meaning idealist?

These implications, it seems to me, are not at all compelling, neither in fact nor in principle. They are not compelling in fact – I mean from a plainly historical point of view; for if we return from Husserl's *Ideas* and *Cartesian Meditations* to his *Logical Investigations*, we rediscover a state of phenomenology where the notions of expression and meaning, of consciousness and intentionality, of intellectual intuition, are elaborated without the "reduction" being introduced in its idealist sense. On the contrary, the thesis of intentionality explicitly states that if all meaning is for a consciousness, then no consciousness is self-consciousness before being consciousness *of* something *towards which* it surpasses itself, or as Sartre said in a remarkable article,[8] of something towards which it "explodes". That consciousness is outside of itself, that it is *towards meaning* before meaning is for it and, above all, before consciousness is *for itself:* is this not what the central discovery of phenomenology implies? Thus to return to the non-idealist sense of the reduction is to remain faithful to the major discovery of the *Logical Investigations*, namely that the logical notion of signification – such as Frege, for example, had introduced – is carved out of a broader notion of meaning which is coextensive with the concept of intentionality. Hence the right to speak of the "meaning" of perception, the "meaning" of imagination, the "meaning" of the will and so on. This subordination of the logical notion of signification to the universal notion of meaning, under the guidance of the concept of intentionality, in no way implies that a transcendental subjectivity has sovereign mastery of the meaning towards which it orients itself. On the contrary, phenomenology could be drawn in the opposite direction, namely towards the thesis of the priority of meaning over self-consciousness.

(b) Hermeneutics comes back to phenomenology in another way, namely by its recourse to distanciation at the very heart of the experience of belonging. Hermeneutical distanciation is not unrelated to the phenomenological *epoché*, that is, to an *epoché* interpreted in a non-idealist sense as an aspect of the intentional movement of consciousness towards meaning. For all consciousness of meaning involves a moment of distanciation, a distancing from "lived experience" as purely and simply adhered to. Phenomenology begins when, not content to "live" or "relive", we interrupt lived experience in order to signify it. Thus the *epoché* and the meaning-intention [*visée de sens*] are closely linked.

This relation is easy to discern in the case of language. The linguistic sign can *stand for* something only if it is *not* the thing. In this respect, the sign possesses a specific negativity, Everything happens as if, in order to enter the symbolic universe, the speaking subject must have at his disposal an "empty space" from which the use of signs can begin. The *epoché* is the virtual event, the imaginary act which inaugurates the whole game by which we exchange signs for things and signs for other signs. Phenomenology is like the explicit revival of this virtual event which it raises to the dignity of the act, the philosophical gesture. It renders thematic what was only operative, and thereby makes meaning appear as meaning.

Hermeneutics extends this philosophical gesture into its own domain, which is that of the historical and, more generally, the human sciences. The "lived experience" which it is concerned to bring to language and raise to meaning is the historical connection, mediated by the transmission of written documents, works, institutions and monuments which render present the historical past. What we have called "belonging" is nothing other than the adherence to this historical lived experience, what Hegel called the "substance" of moral life. The "lived experience" of phenomenology corresponds, on the side of hermeneutics, to consciousness exposed to historical efficacy. Hence hermeneutical distanciation is to belonging as, in phenomenology, the *epoché* is to lived experience. Hermeneutics similarly begins when, not content to belong to transmitted tradition, we interrupt the relation of belonging in order to signify it.

This parallel is of considerable importance if indeed hermeneutics must incorporate a critical moment, a moment of suspicion, from which the critique of ideology, psychoanalysis, etc., can proceed. The critical moment can be integrated with the relation of belonging only if distanciation is consubstantial with belonging. Phenomenology shows that this is possible when it elevates to a philosophical decision the virtual act of instituting the "empty space" which enables a subject to signify his lived experience and his belonging to an historical tradition.

(c) Hermeneutics also shares with phenomenology the thesis of the derivative character of linguistic meaning.

It is easy, in this respect, to return to the phenomenological roots of some well-known hermeneutical theses. Beginning with the most recent theses, those of Gadamer, it can be seen that the secondary character of the problematic of language is reflected in the very composition of *Truth and Method*. Even if it is true that all experience has a "lingual dimension" and that this *Sprachlichkeit* imprints and pervades all experience, nevertheless it is not with *Sprachlichkeit* that hermeneutic philosophy must begin. It is necessary to say first what comes to language. Hence hermeneutic philosophy begins with the experience of art, which is not necessarily linguistic. Moreover it accentuates, in this experience, the more ontological aspects of the experience of *play* – in the playful [*ludique*] as well as the theatrical sense of the word (*WM* 97ff.; *TM* 91ff.). For it is in the participation of players in a game that we find the first experience of belonging susceptible of being examined by the philosopher. And it is in the game that the constitution of the function of exhibition or presentation (*Darstellung*) can be seen, a function which doubtlessly summons the linguistic medium, but which in principle precedes and supports it. Nor is discourse dominant in the second group of experiences interpreted in *Truth and Method*. Consciousness of being exposed to the effects of history, which precludes a total reflection on prejudices and precedes any objectification of the past by the historian, is not reducible to the properly lingual aspects of the transmission of the past. Texts, documents and monuments represent only one mediation among others, however exemplary it may be for the reasons mentioned above. The interplay of distance and proximity, constitutive of the historical connection, is what comes to language rather than what language produces.

This way of subordinating *Sprachlichkeit* to the experience which comes to language is perfectly faithful to Heidegger's gesture in *Being and Time*. Recall how the Analytic of *Dasein* subordinates the level of the assertion (*Aussage*), which is also that of logical signification, of signification in the strict sense (*Bedeutung*), to the level of discourse (*Rede*); and the latter, according to Heidegger, is "equiprimordial" with state-of-mind (*Befindlichkeit*) and *understanding* (*Verstehen*) (*SZ* sec. 34). The logical order is thus preceded by a "saying" which is interwoven with a "finding oneself" and an "understanding". The level of assertion can therefore claim no autonomy; it refers back to the existential structures constitutive of being-in-the-world.

The reference of the linguistic order back to the structure of experience (which comes to language in the assertion) constitutes, in my view, the most important phenomenological presupposition of hermeneutics.

Since the period of the *Logical Investigations*, a development can be discerned which enables logical signification to be situated within a general theory of intentionality. This development implied the displacement of the intentional model from the logical plane towards the perceptive plane, where our first signifying relation with things is formed. At the same time, phenomenology drew back from the predicative and apophantic level of signification – the level of the *Logical Investigations* – to the properly pre-predicative level, where noematic analysis precedes linguistic inquiry. Thus, in *Ideen* I, Husserl goes so far as to say that the layer of expression is an essentially "unproductive" layer (*Hua* III sec. 124); and indeed, the analysis of noetic-noematic correlations can be carried very far without linguistic articulation being considered as such. The strategic level proper to phenomenology is therefore the *noema*, with its modifications (presence, memory, fantasy, etc.), its modes of belief (certitude, doubt, supposition, etc.), and its degrees of actuality and potentiality. The constitution of the *complete noema* precedes the properly linguistic plane upon which the functions of denomination, predication, syntactic liaison and so on come to be articulated.

This way of subordinating the linguistic plane to the pre-linguistic level of noematic analysis is, it seems to me, exemplary for hermeneutics. When the latter subordinates lingual experience to the whole of our aesthetic and historical experience, it continues, on the level of the human sciences, the movement initiated by Husserl on the plane of perceptive experience.

(d) The kinship between the pre-predicative of phenomenology and that of hermeneutics is all the closer in that Husserlian phenomenology itself began to develop the phenomenology of perception in the direction of a hermeneutics of historical experience.

It is well known how, on the one hand, Husserl continued to develop the properly *temporal* implications of perceptual experience. He was thus led, by his own analyses, towards the historicity of human experience as a whole. In particular, it became increasingly evident that the presumptive, inadequate, unfinished character which perceptual experience acquires from its temporal structure could be applied step by step to the whole of historical experience. A new model of truth could thus be elicited from the phenomenology of perception and transposed into the domain of the historical-hermeneutic sciences. Such is the consequence that Merleau-Ponty drew from Husserlian phenomenology.

On the other hand, perceptual experience appeared more and more like an artificially isolated segment of a relation to the "life-world", itself directly endowed with historical and cultural features. Here I shall not emphasise this philosophy of the *Lebenswelt* which characterised the period of the *Crisis*, and which was contemporaneous with Heidegger's Analytic of *Dasein*. It will suffice to say that the return from a nature objectified and mathematicised by Galilean and Newtonian science to the *Lebenswelt* is the very same principle of return which hermeneutics seeks to implement elsewhere, on the plane of the human sciences; for hermeneutics similarly wishes to withdraw from the objectifications and explanations of historical science and sociology to the artistic, historical and lingual experience which precedes and supports these objectifications and explanations. The return to the *Lebenswelt* can more effectively play this paradigmatic role for hermeneutics if the *Lebenswelt* is not confused with some sort of ineffable immediacy and is not identified with the vital and emotional envelope of human experience, but rather is construed as designating the reservoir of meaning, the surplus of sense in living experience, which renders the objectifying and explanatory attitude possible.

These last remarks have already brought us to the point where phenomenology can be the presupposition of hermeneutics only insofar as phenomenology, in turn, incorporates a hermeneutical presupposition.

2 The hermeneutical presupposition of phenomenology

By hermeneutical presupposition, I mean essentially the necessity for phenomenology to conceive of its method as an *Auslegung*, an exegesis, an explication, an interpretation. The demonstration of this necessity will be all the more striking if we address ourselves, not to the texts of the cycle of the *Crisis*, but to the texts of the "logical" and "idealist" periods.

(a) *The recourse to "Auslegung" in the "Logical Investigations"*. The moment of *Auslegung* in the first *Logical Investigation* is contemporaneous with the effort to bring the "signification conferring acts" to intuition.[9] The investigation begins with a very firm declaration against the interference of images in the understanding of an expression (in the logical sense of the word). To understand an expression, says Husserl, is something other than to recover the images related to it. Images can "accompany" and "illustrate" intellection, but they do not constitute it and they always fall short of it. This radicalism of intellection without images is well known: it is all the more interesting to locate the weaknesses in it.

We shall leave aside the case of fluctuating meanings which Husserl examines at a later stage (*LU* II/1 77ff.; *LI* I 312ff.). It would provide, however, an important contribution to our inquiry into the hermeneutical presuppositions of phenomenology. In the first series of fluctuating meanings, Husserl places the occasional meanings such as personal pronouns, demonstratives, descriptions introduced by the definite article, etc. These meanings can be determined and actualised only in the light of a context. In order to understand an expression of this type, "it is essential to orientate actual meaning to the occasion, the speaker and the situation. Only by looking to the actual circumstances of utterance can one definite meaning out of all this mutually connected class be constituted for the hearer" (*LU* II/1 81; *LI* I 315). It is true that Husserl does not speak here of interpretation, but conceives the actual determination of occasional meanings as an instance of the intersection between the indicative function (*LU* II/1 83; *LI* I 316) and the signification function. But the functioning of such meanings coincides, almost to the word, with what appeared above as the first intervention of interpretation at the level of ordinary language, in relation to the polysemy of words and the use of contexts in conversation. Nevertheless, it will be more demonstrative for our purpose to indicate the place of interpretation in the treatment of non-occasional meanings to which, Husserl claims, all forms of meaning return.

The elucidation of meanings which have no occasional aspects appeals, in the most striking way, to *Auslegung*. For these meanings, in principle univocal, do not immediately reveal their univocity. They must, in Husserl's terms, be submitted to the work of elucidation (*Aufklärung*). Now this elucidation cannot be completed unless it is sustained by a minimum of intentional fulfilment, that is, unless some "corresponding" intuition is given (*LU* II/1 71; *LI* I 306). This is the case for meanings which overlap with one another; and here Husserl surprises himself. He introduces the analysis in the form of a question: "One might here ask: If the meaning of expressions functioning purely symbolically lies in an act-character which distinguishes the understanding grasp of a verbal sign from the grasp of a sign stripped of meaning, why is it that we have recourse to intuition when we want to establish differences of meaning, to expose ambiguities, or to limit shifts in our signification-intention [*intention de signification*]?" (*LU* II/1 70; *LI* I 306). Thus arises the problem of an expression "clarified by intuition" (*LU* II/1 71; *LI* I 307). Suddenly the boundary between fluctuating expressions and fixed expressions becomes blurred:

> To recognize differences of meaning, such as that between "moth" and "elephant", requires no special procedures. But where meanings shade unbrokenly into one another, and unnoticed shifts blur boundaries needed for firm judgement, recourse to intuition constitutes the normal process of elucidation. Where the signification-intention of an expression is fulfilled by divergent intuitions which do not fall under the same concept, the sharp difference in the direction of fulfilment shows up the cleavage of signification-intentions. (*LU* II/1 71–2; *LI* I 307)

Thus elucidation (or clarification) requires that meaning be submitted to a genuine form of work, in which representations in imagination [*présentifications*] play a role much less contingent than that of the mere "accompaniments" which alone are allowed, in principle, by Husserl's theory of signification.

It may be said that such elucidation is a long way from what hermeneutics calls interpretation; and of course, Husserl's examples are taken from domains far removed from the historical-hermeneutic sciences. But the *rapprochement* is all the more striking when, in the course of an analysis in the *Logical Investigations*, the concept of *Deutung* – which is indeed interpretation – suddenly appears. This expression appears precisely in order to characterise a phase in the work of the elucidation or clarification of logical meanings. Paragraph 23 of the first *Logical Investigation*, entitled "Apperception (*Auffassung*) as connected with expression and with intuitive presentation", begins with the following remark: "The apperception of understanding, in which the meaning of a word becomes effective, is akin, in so far as *any* apperception is in a sense an understanding and an interpretation (*Deutung*), to the divergently carried out 'objectifying apperceptions' in which, by way of an experienced sense-complex, the intuitive presentation (perception, imagination, reproduction, etc.) of an object (e.g. an external thing) arises" (*LU* II/1 74; *LI* I 309). Thus a kinship is suggested at the very place where we have noted a radical difference. The kinship bears precisely upon the interpretation which is already at work in simple perception and which distinguishes the latter from the mere *data* of sensation. The kinship consists in the signifying activity which allows both the logical operation and the perceptual operation to be called *Auffassung*. It seems that the task of clarification can have recourse to a "corresponding" intuition (mentioned in paragraph 21) only by virtue of this kinship between the two types of *Auffassung*.

A kinship of the same order explains Husserl's use of the term *Vorstellung* – "representation" – to encompass both the consciousness of generality and the consciousness of singularity, which the second *Logical Investigation* is concerned to distinguish; the two forms of consciousness refer respectively to "specific representations" and "singular representations" (*LU* II/2 131, 157; *LI* I 357, 379). For in both cases we are dealing with a *meinen* by which something is "placed before us" ("it is further clear that the universal, as often as we speak of it, is a thing thought by us") (*LU* II/2 124; *LI* I 352). Hence Husserl does not side with Frege, who severs the links between *Sinn* and *Vorstellung*, keeping the first denomination for logic and sending the second back to psychology. Husserl continues to use the term *Vorstellung* to describe the intended meaning of the specific as well as that of the individual.

Above all, grasping the generic and grasping the individual share a common core, which is the interpreted sensation: "Sensations, animated by interpretations, present objective determinations in corresponding percepts of things, but they are not themselves these objective determinations. The apparent object, as it appears in the appearance, transcends this appearance as a phenomenon" (*LU* II/2 129; *LI* I 356). Far from being able to maintain a clear distinction between the intended meaning of the specific and that of the individual, Husserl posits what he calls "a common phenomenal aspect" at the origin of this bifurcation.

> There is, of course, a certain common phenomenal aspect in each case. In each case the same concrete thing makes its appearance, and to the extent that it does so, the same sense-contents are given and interpreted in an identical manner, i.e. the same course of actually given sense- and image-contents serves as a basis for the same "conception" or "interpretation", in which the appearance of the *object* with the *properties* presented by those contents is constituted for us. But the same appearance sustains different acts in the two cases. (*LU* II/2 131; *LI* I 339)

That explains why the same intuitive given may be "on one occasion directly meant as *that thing there*, on another occasion as *sustaining* a universal" (*LU* II/2 131; *LI* I 357). "One and the same sensuous intuition can on one occasion serve as a basis for all these modes of conceiving" (*LU* II/2 131; *LI* I 357). This interpretative core assures the "representative" commonality of the two intended meanings and the transition from one "apprehension" to the other. Thus perception "represents" because it is already the seat of a work of interpretation; and it is because it represents that it can, in spite of its singularity, serve as a "support" for specific representations.

Such is the first way in which phenomenology encounters the concept of interpretation. The concept is embedded in the process whereby phenomenology maintains the ideal of logicity, of univocity, which presides over the theory of signification in the *Logical Investigations*. Husserl states this ideal in the following terms:

> Clearly, in fact, to say that each subjective expression could be replaced by an objective expression, is no more than to assert the *unbounded range of objective reason*. Everything that is, can be known in itself. Its being is a being definite in content, and documented in such and such "truths in themselves" . . . (W)hat is objectively quite definite, must permit objective determination, and what permits objective determination, must, ideally

speaking, permit expression through wholly determinate word-meanings. To being-in-itself correspond truths-in-themselves, and, to these last, fixed, unambiguous assertions. (*LU* II/1 90; *LI* I 321–2)

Hence fixed meanings and the contents of stable expressions must be substituted for fluctuating meanings and subjective expressions. The task is dictated by the ideal of univocity and governed by the axiom of the *unbounded range of objective reason*. It is precisely the execution of the task of clarification which successively reveals, first, the split between essentially *occasional* meanings and univocal meanings; then the function of *accompaniment* fulfilled by illustrative intuitions; and finally the role of *support* played by perceptual interpretations. Step by step, the inversion of the theory of intuition into the theory of interpretation begins.

(b) *The recourse to "Auslegung" in the "Cartesian Meditations"*. These hermeneutical beginnings could not be developed any further by the *Logical Investigations*, in virtue of the logical orientation assumed by the phenomenology of this period. We were thus able to speak of these beginnings only as a residue revealed by the very demand for univocity.

It is quite different with the *Cartesian Meditations*, wherein phenomenology seeks to give an account not simply of the ideal meaning of well-formed expressions, but of the meaning of experience *as a whole*. So if *Auslegung* must play some part in this account, it will no longer be a limited one (limited, that is, to the extent that sense experience must be interpreted in order to serve as a basis for the apprehension of the "generic"); rather, *Auslegung* will enter into problems of constitution *in their totality*.

That is indeed what happens. The concept of *Auslegung* – as has not, perhaps, been sufficiently recognised – intervenes in a decisive manner at the moment when the problematic reaches its most critical point. That is the point at which the egology is set up as the ultimate tribunal of meaning: "the objective world which exists for me (*für mich*), which has existed and will exist for me, this objective world with all of its objects draws from me (*aus mir selbst*) all its meaning and all the validity of being which it has for me".[10] The inclusion of all *Seinsgeltung* "in" the *ego*, which is expressed in the reduction of the *für mich* to the *aus mir*, is finally achieved in the fourth *Cartesian Meditation*. This achievement is at once its culmination and its crisis.

Its culmination: in the sense that only the identification of phenomenology with egology secures the complete reduction of world-meaning to my *ego*. Egology alone satisfies the demand that objects are *for* me only if they draw *from* me all their meaning and all their validity of being.

Its crisis: in the sense that the status of the *alter ego* and, through it, of the very otherness of the world becomes entirely problematic.

Precisely at this point of culmination and crisis, the motif of *Auslegung* intervenes. In paragraph 33 we read: "Since the monadically concrete ego includes also the whole of actual and potential conscious life, it is clear that the problem of *explicating (Auslegung) this monadic ego phenomenologically* (the problem of his constitution for himself) must include *all constitutional problems without exception*. Consequently the phenomenology of this *self-constitution* coincides with phenomenology as a whole" (*Hua* I 102–3; *CM* 68).

What does Husserl mean here by *Auslegung*, and what does he expect from it? To answer these questions, let us pass from the fourth to the fifth *Meditation*, situating ourselves at the heart of the paradox which would remain insoluble without recourse to *Auslegung*. Then, retracing our steps, we shall attempt to understand the strategic role of this concept in the transition from the fourth to the fifth *Meditation*.

The apparently insoluble paradox is this: on the one hand, the reduction of all meaning to the intentional life of the concrete *ego* implies that the other is constituted "in me" and "from me"; on the other hand, phenomenology must account for the originality of the other's experience, precisely insofar as it is the experience of someone other than me. The whole of the fifth *Meditation* is dominated by the tension between these two demands: to constitute the other *in me*, to constitute it as *other*. This formidable paradox was latent in the other four *Meditations*: already the "thing" tore itself away from my life as something other than me, as my *vis-à-vis*, even if it was only an intentional synthesis, a presumed unity. However, the latent tension between the reductive and descriptive demands becomes an open conflict when the other is no longer a thing but another self, a self other than me. For although, absolutely speaking, the only subject is me, the other is not given simply as a psychophysical object, situated in nature; it is also a subject of experience in the same way as I am, and as such it perceives me as belonging to the world of its experience. Moreover, it is on the basis of this intersubjectivity that a "common" nature and a "common" cultural world are constituted. In this respect, the reduction to the sphere of belonging – a veritable reduction within a reduction – can be understood as the conquest of the paradox *qua* paradox: "In this quite particular intentionality, there is constituted a new existential meaning that goes beyond (*überschreitet*) the being of my monadic *ego*; there is constituted an *ego*, not as 'I myself', but as mirrored (*spiegelnden*) in my own *ego*, in my monad" (*Hua* I 125; *CM* 94). Such is the paradox whereby another existence breaks away from my existence at the very moment when I posit the latter as unique.

The paradox is in no way mitigated by recourse to the notions of "analogical apprehension" and "pairing" (*Paarung*), so long as the role of *Auslegung* introduced by the fourth *Meditation* is not perceived. For to say that the other is "appresented" and never properly "presented" seems to be a way of identifying the difficulty rather than resolving it. To say that analogical apprehension is not reasoning by analogy but transference based directly on a pairing of my body here with that body there is to designate the point where the descriptive and constitutive demands intersect, giving a name to the mixture in which the paradox should be resolved. But what does this "apperceptive transposition", this "analogical apperception", really signify? If the *ego* and the *alter ego* are not coupled from the very beginning, they never will be. For this "coupling" implies that the meaning of all my experience refers back to the meaning of the experience of the other. But if the coupling is not originally part of the constitution of the *ego* for itself, then the *ego*'s experience will not incorporate any reference to that of others. In fact, the most remarkable thing about the fifth *Meditation* is the many descriptions which explode idealism; for example, the concrete images of the coupling, or the discernment of an alien mental life on the basis of the consistency between signs, expressions, gestures and postures which fulfil the anticipation of another's lived experience, or the role of imagination in analogical apperception: I could be there if I could project myself . . .

In spite of these admirable descriptions, what remains enigmatic is how the *alter ego* can be both transcendent and an intentional modification of my monadic life: "Thanks to the constitution of its meaning, the other appears necessarily in my primordial 'world', as an *intentional modification* of my self which is objectivated in the first instance . . . In other words, *another monad* is constituted, by appresentation, in mine" (*Hua* I 144; *CM* 115). It is this enigma, this paradox, indeed this latent conflict between two projects – a project of describing transcendence and a project of constituting in immanence – that the recourse to *Auslegung* may be able to resolve.

So let us go back to the point where the fourth *Cartesian Meditation* defines the entire phenomenological enterprise in terms of *Auslegung*. Paragraph 41, which closes the fourth *Meditation*, expressly defines transcendental idealism as "the 'phenomenological self-explication' that went on in my ego" (*Hua* I 117; *CM* 84). The "style" of the interpretation is characterised by the "infinite work" involved in unfolding the horizons of present experiences. Phenomenology is a meditation "indefinitely *pursued*", because reflection is overwhelmed by the *potential* meanings of one's own lived experience. The same theme reappears at the end of the fifth *Meditation*. Paragraph 59 is entitled "Ontological explication and its place within constitutional transcendental phenomenology as a whole". What Husserl calls "ontological explication" consists in unfolding the layers of meaning (nature, animality, psychism, culture, personality), which together form the "world as constituted meaning". Explication is thus mid-way between a philosophy of construction and a philosophy of description. Against Hegelianism and its sequels, against all "metaphysical construction", Husserl maintains that phenomenology does not "create" but only "finds" (*Hua* II 168). This is the hyper-empirical side of phenomenology; explication is an explication of experience: "phenomenological explication does nothing – and this could not be over-emphasised – but explicate the meaning which the world has for us all, prior to any philosophy, and which is obviously conferred upon it by our experience. This meaning can be uncovered (*enthüllt*) by philosophy but never altered (*geändert*) by it; and in each present experience it is surrounded – for essential reasons and not as a result of our weakness – by horizons in need of clarification (*Klärung*)" (*Hua* I 177; *CM* 151). However, in thus linking explication to the clarification of horizons, phenomenology seeks to go beyond a static description of experience, a mere geography of the layers of meaning. The processes of transferring from the self towards the other, then towards objective nature and finally towards history, realise a progressive constitution – indeed ultimately a "universal genesis" – of what we naively experience as the "life-world".

It is this "intentional explication" which encompasses the two demands that appeared to be in conflict throughout the fifth *Meditation*: on the one hand, respect for the alterity of others; on the other hand, anchoring this experience of transcendence in primordial experience. For *Auslegung* does nothing more than unfold the surplus of meaning which, in my experience, indicates the place for the other.

A less dichotomous reading of the fifth *Meditation* as a whole thus becomes possible. *Auslegung* is already at work in the reduction to the sphere of belonging.

For the latter is not a given from which I could progress towards another given, which would be the other. Experience reduced to one's lived body is the result of an abstraction from everything which is "foreign"; by this abstractive reduction, says Husserl, I "bring to light my animate organism, reduced to my sphere of belonging" (*Hua* I 128; *CM* 97). This *Herausstellung* [bringing out] signifies, it seems to me, that the primordial remains always the limit of a "questioning back"; thanks to this *Rückfrage*, reflection glimpses, in the thickness of experience and through the successive layers of constitution, what Husserl calls a "primal instituting" – an *Urstiftung* (*Hua* I 141; *CM* 111) – to which these layers refer. The primordial is thus the intentional limit of such a reference. So there is no need to search, under the title of "sphere of belonging", for some sort of brute experience which would be preserved at the heart of my experience of culture, but rather for an antecedent which is never given in itself. Hence, inspite of its intuitive kernel, this experience remains an interpretation. "*My* own too is discovered by explication and gets its original meaning by virtue thereof" (*Hua* I 132; *CM* 102). What is one's own is revealed only as "explicated experience" (*Hua* I 132; *CM* 102). Even better, it could be said that what is one's own and what is foreign are polarly constituted in the *same interpretation*.

Thus it is as *Auslegung* that the other is constituted both in me and as other. It is characteristic of experience in general, says paragraph 46, that it becomes a determined object only in "interpreting itself by itself; it is thus realised only as pure explication" (*Hua* I 131; *CM* 101). All determination is explication: "This own-essential content is only generally and horizonally anticipated beforehand; it then becomes constituted originaliter – with the sense: internal, own-essential feature (specifically, part or property) – by explication" (*Hua* I 132; *CM* 101).

The paradox of a constitution which would be both constitution "in me" and constitution of "another" takes on a completely new significance if it is clarified by the role of explication. The other is included, not in my existence as given, but in the latter in so far as it is characterised by an "open and infinite horizon" (*Hua* I 132; *CM* 102), a potentiality of meaning which I cannot master in a glance. I can indeed say, therefore, that the experience of others merely "develops" my own identical being, but what it develops was already more than myself, since what I call here my own identical being is a potentiality of meaning which exceeds the gaze of reflection. The possibility of going beyond myself towards the other is inscribed in this horizonal structure which calls for "explication", which calls, in the words of Husserl himself, for an "explication of the horizons of my own being" (*Hua* I 132; *CM* 102).

Husserl perceived the coincidence of intuition and explication, although he failed to draw all its consequences. All phenomenology is an explication of evidence and an evidence of explication. An evidence which is explicated, an explication which unfolds evidence: such is the phenomenological experience. It is in this sense that phenomenology can be realised only as hermeneutics.

But the truth of this proposition can be grasped only if, at the same time, the hermeneutical critique of Husserlian idealism is fully accepted. The second part of this essay thus refers back to the first: phenomenology and hermeneutics presuppose one another only if the idealism of Husserlian phenomenology succumbs to the critique of hermeneutics.

Notes

1 This essay reflects the changes of method implied by my own evolution, from an eidetic phenomenology in *Freedom and Nature* (1950), to *Freud and Philosophy* (1965) and *The Conflict of Interpretations* (1969).

2 The "Nachwort" first appeared in the *Jahrbuch für Philosophie und phänomenologische Forschung* (1930); it was subsequently published in *Husserliana* v, edited by H. L. van Breda (The Hague: Martinus Nijhoff, 1952; hereafter cited in the text as *Hua* v), pp. 138–62.

3 The word "verliert" reappears three times: *Hua* v 145.

4 Martin Heidegger, *Sein und Zeit* (Tübingen: Max Niemeyer, 1927; hereafter cited in the text as *SZ*), p. 149 [English translation: *Being and Time*, translated by John Macquarrie and Edward Robinson (Oxford: Basil Blackwell, 1978; hereafter cited in the text as *BT*), p. 189].

5 Hans-Georg Gadamer, *Wahrheit und Methode* (Tübingen: J. C. B. Mohr, 1960; hereafter cited in the text as *WM*), pp. 250ff. [English translation: *Truth and Method* (London: Sheed and Ward, 1975; hereafter cited in the text as *TM*), pp. 235ff.].

6 See "Hermeneutics and the critique of ideology", P. Ricoeur, *Hermeneutics and the Human Sciences*, ed. and trans. John B. Thompson (Cambridge: Cambridge University Press, 1981), pp. 63–100.

7 Martin Heidegger, "Hegels Begriff der Erfahrung" in *Holzwege* (Frankfurt: Vittoria Klostermann, 1950) [English translation: *Hegel's Concept of Experience* (New York: Harper and Row, 1970)].

8 Jean-Paul Sartre, "Une idée fondamentale de la phénoménologie de Husserl: l'intention-nalité" in *Situations 1* (Paris: Gallimard, 1947) [English translation: "Intentionality: a fundamental idea of Husserl's phenomenology", translated by Joseph P. Fell, *Journal of the British Society for Phenomenology*, 1, no. 2 (1970), pp. 4–5]. Reprinted in this volume.

9 Edmund Husserl, *Logische Untersuchungen* II (Tübingen: Max Niemeyer, 1900; here-after cited in the text as *LU* II), pp. 61ff. [English translation: *Logical Investigations* I, translated by J. N. Findlay (London: Routledge and Kegan Paul, 1970; hereafter cited in the text as *LI* I), pp. 299ff.].

10 Edmund Husserl, *Cartesianische Meditationen* in *Husserliana*, I, edited by S. Strasser (The Hague: Martinus Nijhoff, 1950; hereafter cited in the text as *Hua* I), p. 30 [English translation: *Cartesian Meditations: An Introduction to Phenomenology*, translated by Dorion Cairns (The Hague: Martinus Nijhoff, 1960; hereafter cited in the text as *CM*), p. 99].

NAME INDEX

Page numbers in **bold** indicate sections specifically attributed to the named person

SUBJECT INDEX

prejudice); and judgement 211, 263, 283–4; as object presented 277, 283–4, 437, 453, 531, 549, 552; objective 33, 125, 165, 166, 170–2, 211, 496; personal 210–11; as relation 276, 277, 283

unconcealment (*aletheia*) 254
unconscious 46, 209, 225, 315, 391–2, 549, 564; *see also* psychoanalysis
understanding (*Verstand, Verstehen*): as anticipatory *see* as fore-meaning and fore-structures of; of Dasein *see* Dasein; faculty of 8, 151; as fore-meaning 315–16, 326–7, 328–9, 336, 576, 584, 586; fore-structures of 314–15, 317, 328–9, 583–4; in hermeneutics 311–12, 326–37, 582; and misunderstanding 316, 331–2; in phenomenology 8, 19, 193–4, 311–12, 326–37; as productive 330–1; universality of 336–7, 583–4
unity 46, 66, 84, 90, 95–8, 114, 125, 126, 144, 154, 207, 214, 328, 561; *see also* body, consciousness, ego, object and person
universality: of being *see* being; of evidence *see* evidence; of human life 349, 352, 356; of understanding *see* understanding; of world *see* world; *see also* essence, ideal and meaning
universals 55, 69, 450, 595; *see also* ideal
univocal ideal 595–6
univocity *see* meaning
unpredictability 372–3
un-readiness-to-hand *see* Dasein
use-object *see* Dasein, and equipment
utilitarianism 369–70

value: aesthetic 126, 140; ethical 6, 16, 126, 200, 474, 582; of other *see* other; practical 140; of reflection *see* reflection; *see also* things as value-laden
valuing 147, 261–2
verification 165–7, 184, 271; *see also* evidence, intuition and truth
vision *see* perception and sensations
visual field 80, 110
violence 367–9, 486, 517, 570, 585
vocation 173
volition 148, 240–1, 419–20, 575

war 519
wholes and parts: of acts 82, 95–8, 140; of objects perceived 80, 114–16, 140, 142, 216, 269–70, 438–9; in understanding 326–7; *see also* parts
will 11, 240–1, 402–3, 419–20, 431, 530, 575, 590

woman: and authority 473, 480, 488, 496, 502–3; body of 467–70, 475–6, 480, 487–8, 500–1; and child 469, 473, 479, 483, 494, 503, 505; destiny of 471, 478–9, 490, 499, 500; and economics 469, 479–84, 506; and history 480–4, 488–9; horizon of 490, 491–2, 505; immanence of 490, 495, 501–2; and maternity 468, 469, 473, 474, 480, 483–4; as object or other 470, 477–9, 484, 498; as passive 487, 489, 490, 492, 494, 495; and revolt 483, 492, 493, 494, 496; sexuality of *see* sexuality; situation of 470, 473, 483, 484, 486–506; transcendence of 478–9, 501, 506; world of 486, 487, 488, 491–2, 501
word and thing 98
word-meaning 67–8, 71, 87, 97–8, 135, 139, 189, 360, 516, 518, 521–5, 556, 559–60, 576, 584, 593–4
work 364–6, 371, 481, 483, 491, 504, 506; *see also* labour
world: and absolute consciousness 386, 404–5; actuality of 47, 88, 94, 128–30, 152, 156, 157, 167–70, 171; being-in-the-world *see* Dasein; of body 428, 431, 432, 433, 434; as centre 454–5; as constituted *see* as idea and as meant; as contemporaneous with ego 386, 404–5; as cultural 155; destruction of 581; as environment 289, 290, 291, 298 (*see also* as surrounding); of evidence as original 167–72; of experience 2, 29, 128, 152, 154–8, 161–3, 166, 383–4; homelessness in 346–50, 360; homely 346–7, 370; as horizon 15, 154–6, 161, 164, 169, 459, 587; as idea 170, 210, 211, 349, 396–7; of individual 201, 205, 206–7, 209–11, 289; as intersubjective 163, 171, 294, 597; as life-world (*Lebenswelt*) 3, 62, 152, 153, 154–5, 157, 163–72, 587, 592–3, 598; as meant 16, 130, 151, 158, 170, 534, 598; and mind 5, 529; as nature 128–9, 288, 290, 294–5, 367; of person *see* of individual; as pregiven 3, 62, 152, 154–6, 161, 163–7, 172, 437, 439, 581; prescientific 151, 155–6, 158, 164–8, 444–5; as realm of objects 289, 295, 439, 587; scientific 156, 165–71, 439, 444, 454–5; singular 211–12, 439–40; spatial 15, 47, 290–1; and subject *see* subject; as surrounding (*Umwelt*) 5, 15, 151–2, 156, 212, 397; temporal 47, 94, 122, 128–9, 152; universality of 165; of woman *see* woman
writing *see* différance and language

X-pole *see* noema

zig-zag approach 74; *see also* play as back and forth process